# Converging
# Media

# Converging Media

**SIXTH EDITION**

A New Introduction to
Mass Communication

## John V. Pavlik
RUTGERS UNIVERSITY

## Shawn McIntosh
MASSACHUSETTS COLLEGE OF LIBERAL ARTS

New York    Oxford
OXFORD UNIVERSITY PRESS

Oxford University Press is a department of the University of Oxford.
It furthers the University's objective of excellence in research, scholarship, and
education by publishing worldwide. Oxford is a registered trade mark of Oxford
University Press in the UK and certain other countries.

Published in the United States of America by Oxford University Press

198 Madison Avenue, New York, NY 10016, United States of America.

For titles covered by Section 112 of the US Higher Education Opportunity
Act, please visit www.oup.com/us/he for the latest information about
pricing and alternate formats.

**Library of Congress Cataloging-in-Publication Data**
Names: Pavlik, John V. (John Vernon), author. | McIntosh, Shawn, author.
Title: Converging media : a new introduction to mass communication / John V.
    Pavlik, Shawn McIntosh.
Description: Sixth edition. | New York : Oxford University Press, [2018]
Identifiers: LCCN 2017034858 | ISBN 9780190646653 (print text)
Subjects: LCSH: Mass media. | Digital media. | Internet.
Classification: LCC P90 .P355 2018 | DDC 302.23—dc23 LC record available at
https://lccn.loc.gov/2017034858

Printing number: 9 8 7 6 5 4 3 2
Printed by Webcom in Canada.

To my wife, Jackie,
and my daughters,
Tristan and Orianna

**—J.V.P.**


To my parents,
Dennis and Kathie

**—S.M.**

# BRIEF CONTENTS

# CONTENTS

**PART TWO**    MASS-COMMUNICATION FORMATS

## 3  Print Media: Books, Newspapers, and Magazines   59

**Features**

INTERNATIONAL PERSPECTIVES: **CAN THE INTERNET SAVE ENDANGERED LANGUAGES?   160**

MEDIA PIONEERS: **HIRONOBU SAKAGUCHI   172**

CONVERGENCE CULTURE: **VIDEO GAME VIEWS OLD AND NEW   177**

ETHICS IN MEDIA: **IS PLAYING VIDEO GAMES BAD FOR YOU?   182**

**PART THREE** | MEDIA PERSPECTIVES

## 7  The Impact of Social Media    187

**Features**

INTERNATIONAL PERSPECTIVES: **SOCIAL NETWORKS OF INFLUENTIAL LANGUAGES    197**

MEDIA PIONEERS: **JACK DORSEY    202**

CONVERGENCE CULTURE: **ARE WE REALLY SEPARATED BY SIX DEGREES?    207**

ETHICS IN MEDIA: **CYBERBULLYING: NEW TWISTS ON AN OLD PROBLEM    215**

## 8  Journalism: From Information to Participation    221

---

**PART FOUR**    MEDIA AND SOCIETY

**11 Media Ethics    293**

**Communication Law and Regulation in the Digital Age    321**

 **Media Theory and Research    353**

## 14 Mass Communication and Politics in the Digital Age 385

## 15 Global Media in the Digital Age   407

### Features

*Converging Media* provides extensive content on the twelve core values and competencies of the Accrediting Council on Education in Journalism and Mass Communications (ACEJMC). As a nationally elected member of the ACEJMC from 2004 to 2007, John V. Pavlik recognized that the ACEJMC-based learning goals provide a useful benchmark for assessing student learning. By covering the twelve core values and competencies, this text provides a strong foundation for students to become well-rounded journalists and experts in mass communication.

| ACEJMC LEARNING GOALS | HOW *CONVERGING MEDIA* SUPPORTS |
| --- | --- |
| **1. FREEDOM OF SPEECH:** Understand and apply the principles and laws of freedom of speech and press for the country in which the institution that invites ACEJMC is located, as well as receive instruction in and understand the range of systems of freedom of expression around the world, including the rights to dissent, to monitor and criticize power, and to assemble and petition for redress of grievances. | • Regulation of journalism and mass communication in the digital age including libel and censorship (p. 328)<br>• Fairness (p. 327)<br>• The public's right to know (p. 322)<br>• Media systems around the world (p. 344) |
| **2. HISTORY:** Demonstrate an understanding of the history and role of professionals and institutions in shaping communications. | • Origins of photography, movies, television, and video games (p. 122–125)<br>• History of journalism (p. 223)<br>• History of advertising (p. 272)<br>• History of public relations (p. 258)<br>• History of media law and the regulation of electronic media (p. 332)<br>• Early research on media effects (p. 359)<br>• History of recorded music and radio (p. 95)<br>• History of print media (books, newspapers, magazines) (p. 62)<br>• History of the Internet (p. 164) |
| **3. GENDER, RACE, AND SEXUALITY:** Demonstrate an understanding of gender, race ethnicity, sexual orientation, and, as appropriate, other forms of diversity in domestic society in relation to mass communications. | • Effects of media and advertising on women and men (p. 75)<br>• Role of women in the history of magazines (p. 84)<br>• Diversity in the newsroom (p. 247)<br>• Minority newspapers (p. 247) |
| **4. GLOBAL SOCIETY:** Demonstrate an understanding of the diversity of peoples and cultures and of the significance and impact of mass communications in a global society. | • Relationships among various global and local media sources (p. 419)<br>• Cultural and socioeconomic impact of global media (p. 414)<br>• "International Perspectives" boxes throughout (example, p. 415)<br>• International theories of the press (p. 409)<br>• Media in a global society appears as a theme in several chapters |
| **5. THEORY:** Understand concepts and apply theories in the use and presentation of images and information. | • Photography, movies, and television (p. 122–129)<br>• Grammar of media (p. 40)<br>• Information overload in the digital age (p. 53)<br>• Major media theories and research (p. 354) |

| ACEJMC LEARNING GOALS | HOW *CONVERGING MEDIA* SUPPORTS |
|---|---|
| **6. ETHICS:** Demonstrate an understanding of professional ethical principles and work ethically in pursuit of truth, accuracy, fairness, and diversity. | • "Ethics in Media" boxes throughout (example, (p. 393)<br>• Chapter on media ethics, including accuracy and the pursuit of truth (p. 293)<br>• Chapter on communication law and regulation in the digital age (p. 321)<br>• Fairness and diversity (p. 247) |
| **7. CRITICAL AND CREATIVE THINKING:** Think critically, creatively, and independently. | • "Convergence Culture" boxes throughout (example, p. 177)<br>• "Media Matters" at the end of most chapters (example, p. 218)<br>• Discussion Questions throughout (example, p. 34)<br>• Critical-Thinking Questions in selected image captions (example, p. 61)<br>• Foundations for critically examining media presented early in the text (example, p. 4) |
| **8. RESEARCH:** Conduct research and evaluate information by methods appropriate to the communications professions in which they work. | • Chapter on media theory teaches students to evaluate research methods and findings (p. 353) |
| **9. WRITING ABILITY:** Write correctly and clearly in forms and styles appropriate for the communications professions, audiences, and purposes they serve. | • Appropriate writing style for particular media and for the communities and purposes that media professionals serve (p. 7)<br>• Importance of clear and accurate writing in news creation (p. 83) |
| **10. EVALUATION OF WORK:** Critically evaluate their own work and that of others for accuracy and fairness, clarity, appropriate style, and grammatical correctness. | • "Ethics in Media" feature "What is 'Fake News,' Exactly?" provides a self-reflective case study (p. 245) |
| **11. NUMERICAL AND STATISTICAL CONCEPTS:** Apply basic numerical and statistical concepts. | • Data for students to analyze about newspaper circulation and readership and advertising impact (p. 71)<br>• Pricing structure of the recording industry (p. 101)<br>• Figures and tables throughout apply numerical and statistical concepts (example, p. 69) |
| **12. TECHNOLOGY:** Apply tools and technologies appropriate for the communications professions in which they work. | • Social media (p. 187)<br>• Interactive media (p. 157)<br>• Role of mobile media, such as the iPad, in delivering video (p. 162)<br>• Mobile media and digital books (p. 65)<br>• Impact of touchscreens on human–computer interface (p. 163)<br>• Use of digital technology in journalism (p. 241)<br>• Impact of digital technology and mobile media on advertising (p. 282) |

# Features

### MEDIA PIONEERS

### TIMELINES

### TABLES

## FIGURES

# Preface

Disruption is a one-word description for the state of contemporary journalism and mass communication (JMC). Changing economics, technology, and political forces are just some of the complex factors reshaping the contours of JMC. As online, mobile technologies become increasingly ubiquitous and social networks have come to dominate much of the communication landscape, the financial foundation for mainstream media has shifted in dramatic fashion. Advertising has declined in most media companies and flowed to platforms such as Facebook, Google, YouTube, and Twitter. Consumers access media through their smartphones and other networked devices. They participate in the journalism and mass communication process by posting their own photos, video, and other content online and sharing the online posts they encounter.

Political winds have swept over the JMC landscape as well, ushering in debates about so-called fake news, media ethics, and the role of journalism in democracy. Globalization has become far more than a buzzword, as citizens consider the ramifications of an increasingly international media mix. Online subscription-based media entertainment such as the video services of companies like Netflix have found high levels of interest among millennials and others interested in on-demand media content.

Advances in technology are delivering new media content formats such as augmented reality and virtual reality. While the platforms for such content are still somewhat specialized and expensive, they in many ways may represent the future of journalism and mass communication: interactive, multisensory, and immersive.

Privacy may be little more than a memory in an age when ubiquitous high-definition cameras, big data analytics, and social media are generating massive databases encompassing nearly every man, woman, and child around the globe. "Most of us have fully identified, high-definition frontal photos of ourselves online," says Alessandro Acquisti, associate professor of information technology and public policy at Carnegie Mellon University (in a *60 Minutes* interview with Lesley Stahl, 2013). On Facebook alone, users have posted billions of photos of themselves, their friends, and their relatives. Facebook continues to refine its facial-recognition technology, which will make tagging friends easier but which will also help others track you.

The existence of such vast repositories of data, valuable for security and commercial potential (such as individually targeted advertising), raises concerns for civil liberties, including freedom of speech and the right to privacy. An even bigger question is who has the right to own and control this information, especially with the telecommunications companies and Internet giants contributing to the NSA's surveillance programs.

Meanwhile, the transformation of media into digital form and the convergence of media formats and industries have continued unabated. Research indicates that we now spend more time using digital devices than we do with any other medium, including television. Digital content is more likely to be viewed on a tablet or a smartphone than it is on a laptop or a desktop computer. Digital distribution is now the dominant format for music, television, and radio, whether delivered terrestrially, by satellite, or via the Internet. Thanks to tablets and e-readers, ebooks have seen a dramatic surge in popularity. Newspapers and magazines, which have experienced significant declines in print circulation, are nonetheless seeing growth in tablet, smartphone, and online distribution. Digital movies, television, and video-game distribution is now mainstream, with companies such as Netflix and Amazon producing and streaming their own original and highly acclaimed television shows. Tablets and other mobile devices are blurring the lines between Internet, movies, and television while allowing technology companies like Google, Apple, and Amazon to challenge traditional media distributors.

Our engagement with media has also changed, becoming more active as mass and interpersonal communications converge. Any person can broadcast his or her opinion on Twitter or via other social media, and increasingly people do so while consuming traditional media, such as television. They post comments and engage in conversation about popular shows. Interactive media, including video games, constitute an increasingly popular form of entertainment.

Convergence also operates on a global scale today. The globalization of media industries and distribution has produced a cultural convergence that, at best, enables diverse local viewpoints to be heard and, at worst, smothers local culture in a homogeneous, commercialized and Westernized culture. Yet the impact of other viewpoints is beginning to shape the content of new Hollywood blockbusters and other forms of Western media.

Rarely have there been such differences in media usage between the digital natives and those who grew up in a pre-Internet era of mass communication. One group may enjoy reading a printed newspaper over breakfast; the other group may get their news on a tablet—if they get any news at all. One group may have impressive collections of CDs and DVDs; the other group may have their music and movie collections in the digital, online "cloud" and accessible from any location or on their portable devices. The older group may worry how increased product placement may affect the type of shows that are produced; the younger group may wonder what product placement is and why it matters. One group may believe that it is nobody's business what their relationship status is; the other group may publicly post that and much more personal information on social-networking sites.

Interestingly, this media divide is often represented in the college classroom, where college students are the digital natives and their professors are generally from an older mass-media tradition. Yet the two parties converge, just like the media discussed in this book, to form a greater understanding of where media have been, where they are today, and where they are going.

One way to look at the state of mass communication today is that convergence is bringing us the kinds of tools that audiences have long wanted with their media—the ability to have greater control over what they watch, read, or listen to and the ability to share their stories and their lives with others. But with that greater control also comes greater responsibility and a greater need for us to understand how our media work and how they may affect our society and political systems. A double-edged sword cuts both ways, but which way it cuts depends largely on who is wielding it.

## *Converging Media,* Sixth Edition: An Updated Introduction to Mass Communication

Change is a constant in the mass-communication industry, and in recent years this transformation has rocketed forward with surprising speed. Students are changing. The field is changing. The world is changing. Yet these changes go largely unnoticed in most textbooks. An introductory textbook should provide a foundation of knowledge for students learning a new field. But when the foundation sits on a bed of shifting sand, the introduction needs to be revised continually.

*Converging Media: A New Introduction to Mass Communication* embraces these developments as well as the impact of JMC on society. This book also explores the evolving career pathways for those interested in a professional future in any of the associated fields.

The sixth edition of *Converging Media* follows the class-tested formula of the previous edition by offering:

- **A Fresh Perspective.** Through the lens of convergence, our book shows how different aspects of media are parts of a whole and how they influence each other. Digital media are not relegated to special features or an isolated chapter; they are integrated throughout every chapter. This reflects better the world as students live in it and prepares them to understand the changes that are taking place. This organization invites students and professors to engage in timely discussions of media within a larger framework of understanding traditional mass-communication topics.

- **Comprehensive Coverage of Traditional Media.** In order to understand the present, we have to study the past. We cover the development and historical influences of print and electronic media and the issues these media face today. The communication professions of journalism, advertising, and public relations are viewed from historical, societal, and career perspectives, giving students insights into how they interact and influence each other.

- **Unique Coverage of Social Media.** As the first introductory mass-communication textbook to devote a chapter to this emerging area, we place social media within a larger media and sociocultural context. Today's popular social media tools are given a historical context and are connected thematically to older online communication tools. Social media are such an integral part of the media mix for so many people, and often used uncritically, that they must be covered in an introductory course, not introduced in an upper-division media and technology course.

- **Cutting-Edge Examples.** We have chosen examples that are diverse, interesting, and up to date. We have written *Converging Media* with students always in mind—understanding the changing world they live in today. Taken from popular media that are familiar and relevant to undergraduates, the examples illustrate how the landscape of media has evolved—and is still evolving.

- **Cultural Context.** Mass communication, media technologies, and convergence take place firmly within a sociocultural milieu that simultaneously affects and is affected by these forces. Understanding this cultural context is vital for a complete grasp of convergence and today's media environment. The authors emphasize the cultural influences and implications of media technologies while explaining how they work and how they were developed.

- **Emphasis on Ethics.** The book has a chapter devoted entirely to ethics (Chapter 11) and continues to thread ethics-related discussions throughout other chapters, as appropriate (see Ethics in Media boxes). Students should learn that ethical considerations are tightly linked to a full understanding of mass communication and media. Ethics can also help guide us in the complex and often-confusing world of converging media, giving a basis for sound and humane decisions on media use and production and new technologies and the way they affect people.

- **International Perspectives.** A chapter on today's global media environment (Chapter 15) provides a broad perspective on media in various countries and the social, economic, and cultural effects of media globalization overseas and domestically. The remaining chapters also highlight international perspectives in feature boxes and in the text itself. Through comparisons and contrasts, students obtain an appreciation for different media systems throughout the world and how they work.

## Features for Students

We have kept features limited and focused on a few key areas that will help bring out interesting and relevant aspects of the content discussed in the book.

- **Convergence Culture** boxes showcase how media impact our social, political, and popular culture in sometimes dramatic ways. New or updated examples are provided in every chapter in this edition and speak to current social, political, and cultural issues in recent news.
- **Media Pioneers** boxes examine the careers of visionaries and leaders in the world of media both historically and in the contemporary scene. They feature individuals past and present who have made or are making media history (e.g., Doris E. Fleischman). Subjects represent a diversity of past and present, media vocations, and cultural and ethnic backgrounds. This feature now appears in every chapter and three are new to this edition and several are updated.
- **Ethics in Media** boxes, appearing in select chapters, discuss timely issues related to ethical practices and issues in mass media. Six are new to this edition and the others are updated.
- **International Perspectives** boxes take a global perspective on chapter topics, showcasing how the use of media and technology and media industries are similar to or different from the U.S. context and why that is so. Two are new to this edition.
- **Timelines,** appearing in select chapters, provide a history, or even prehistory, of different media, such as newspapers, television, and social-networking site launches, giving the context for their development.
- **Media Matters** measure students' knowledge of traditional and digital media and encourage critical thinking about media-related topics.
- **Chapter Opening Vignettes** have been updated for currency, and ten have been completely revised and are new to this edition.
- **Discussion Questions** are now located throughout each chapter.
- **Critical Thinking Questions** accompany many photo captions, asking students to engage deeply with the image and topic it represents and providing useful topics for lively class discussions or brief assignments.
- **Further Reading** assignments round out each chapter.

## Changes to the Sixth Edition

This sixth edition has undergone several changes to keep pace with the rapidly evolving world of media. Most artwork has been updated or replaced throughout all chapters.

- **Coverage of New Issues.** Throughout the text, we have updated and expanded coverage of critical topics, including the convergence of interpersonal communication and mass communication through social networking media, gamification, augmented reality and virtual reality, cybersecurity, and mobile media. Noteworthy chapter-specific changes include:

### Chapter 1

○ New chapter opening on the hack of Netflix's *Orange Is the New Black* and what it means for online security for media companies

○ Updated Media Pioneers box on Oprah Winfrey and how she spans traditional and online media worlds

○ New Convergence Culture feature box on PewDiePie and the role of YouTube stars

○ New Ethics in Media feature box on whether people who have Macs pay more because of online targeting

○ New International Perspectives box feature ("A 'Comedy' of Cultural Convergence") discusses the controversial international response to Sony's *The Interview*

### Chapter 2

○ New chapter opening discussing fake news, the importance of recognizing the truth, and discerning credible sources

○ Updated framing of political issues in media

○ Updated discussion of media grammar

○ New Ethics in Media feature ("When Media Report Rape Allegations") describes the way the media responded to Brock Turner, the Stanford rapist

○ Updated discussion of media entrepreneurship

○ Updated Convergence Culture box ("Evaluating Online Information") on recognizing hoaxes and media on the web

○ New discussion of media echo chambers

### Chapter 3

○ Updated industry statistics for books, ebooks, audiobooks, newspapers, magazines, and online subscriptions

○ Updated discussion of book censorship around the world

○ Discussion of the Trump bump in newspaper subscriptions, especially digital, at leading national news media

○ New discussion concerning the rise of 360-degree video reporting

### Chapter 4

○ Updated music and radio industry statistics

○ Updated Media Pioneers box featuring Amanda Palmer

○ Updated state of music and audio promotion and distribution

- Updates on streaming music industry, including expanded discussion on popular platforms like Spotify
- Updates on radio industry, including ownership and revenue shifts

## Chapter 5

- New chapter opening on the latest research regarding the psychological and health effects resulting from binge-watching
- Updated industry statistics for film and television
- Updated information on photography, including a new International Perspectives feature on Breaking Silence, Smita Sharma's international project that tries to break the stigma of sexual violence through photos
- New Convergence Culture feature on 4K television ("Home Theater—Really, This Time) and other technology advances in film and TV
- Updates on changes in revenues and ownership among major visual media companies

## Chapter 6

- New chapter opening about professional video gamers and their six-figure salaries
- A new Virtual Reality section that places focus more on virtual reality rather than augmented reality
- New Media Pioneers feature box on Hironobu Sakaguchi, one of the pioneers of video games and creator of *Final Fantasy*
- Ethics in Media feature box ("Is Playing Video Games Bad for You?") on the latest research that examines the benefits and drawbacks to playing video games
- Updated information on the video-game industry, including console developments and anticipated games
- New International Perspectives box ("Can the Internet Save Endangered Languages?") describing the prevalence of languages and dead languages, and the Internet's ability to preserve and spread said languages, such as the Native American Ojibwe
- New Convergence Culture box ("Video Game Views Old and New") describes new features of *Minecraft* and the experience of playing it using Samsung's immersive Oculus Rift

## Chapter 7

- Updated opening vignette regarding violence via Facebook Live, and its social and legal repercussions
- Rise of social networks like Snapchat, Instagram, and its parent Facebook, including its effect on humans as social beings and critical thinking
- Updates in Social Media Timeline
- Role of entrepreneurship in social media, especially through Facebook

## Chapter 8

○ New chapter opening on the worldwide collaborative journalism project that published the Panama Papers

○ New Ethics in Media feature box on fake news and how it relates specifically to journalists' roles and work ("What Is 'Fake News,' Exactly?")

○ Updated information on the state of the news industry across mediums

○ New Convergence Culture box ("Digital News Organizations Come into Their Own") describing the rise in popularity of digital organizations and their credibility, but also the ways in which online versus print articles can change

○ Updated information on new business models being tried by various groups, and the implications for journalism as it is under attack in the United States and elsewhere

○ New section on constructive journalism

## Chapter 9

○ New chapter that focuses solely on public relations, rather than combining public relations and advertising

○ Expanded coverage of public relations firms, roles, and trends

○ Updated and expanded coverage of the role of rhetoric and strategic communications in public relations, including the rhetorical triangle, the elaboration likelihood model, and the top five independent PR firms

## Chapter 10

○ New, standalone chapter that focuses solely on advertising

○ New chapter opening on the Cure for Wellness "fake news" advertising campaign that backfired on a movie studio

○ Expanded coverage of the advertising industry, trends, and issues in advertising

○ New and revised material regarding content marking and other new advertising types being done online, including a new Convergence Culture feature ("Content Marketing: Blurring the Line Between Journalism and Advertising?")

○ New ethics feature box ("Does Marketing Affect What Drugs We Take?") on direct-to-consumer (DTC) advertising for pharmaceuticals and its practical and ethical implications

○ New section on in-game advertising

## Chapter 11

○ Updated opening vignette on the ethics of the *Rolling Stone* rape case and its court ruling

○ New International Perspectives feature on International Women's Day and the impact of social media ("Global Action: Uniting Women Worldwide Through Social Networks")

- New Ethics in Media feature ("Dialogical Ethics in Action"), discussing Kendall Jenner and the failed Pepsi commercial she starred in
- New discussion of sexual harassment issues at Fox News, including the Bill O'Reilly situation
- New discussion of cyberbullying
- New discussion of First Lady Melania Trump and her mistakes using Twitter
- Updates on media careers and role of ethics

## Chapter 12

- New chapter opening considering media and the Trump executive order banning immigrants from predominantly Muslim nations and refugees
- New Ethics in Media feature ("Does the Punishment Fit the Crime?") on Terry Bollea's (Hulk Hogan's) lawsuit against Gawker, which ultimately forced the website to shut down
- Updates on Convergence Culture box feature ("The Great Network Neutrality Debate") regarding the FCC and FTC and media rulings
- Updates on International Perspectives box feature ("The Rise and Fall of Russian Media") describing Vladimir Putin's alleged treatment of journalists

## Chapter 13

- Updated opening vignette regarding Electronic Arts' promotion of violent video games after the shooting attack at Pulse, a gay nightclub
- Updated discussion of research on media effects
- New discussion of the Professor Watchlist and targeting of liberal professors in Convergence Culture feature ("How Free Is Academic Freedom?")
- New Media Pioneer feature on virtual reality content developer Nonny de la Peña
- Newly included discussion of media theories in "Theories of Communication" section
- New Ethics in Media feature ("Advertising's Effects on the Sexes") describing positive body campaigns by companies like Dove

## Chapter 14

- New chapter opening on Trump's "enemy of the people" statement about the press and its echoes to dictatorial regimes
- Updated information on media and politics in the 2016 presidential election
- New and updated material on the role of social media in the presidential election, including campaign spending
- New Convergence Culture feature on the role of super PACs and their coverage and involvement with the media ("Super PACs and Media")
- New Ethics in Media feature ("Can Imagery Lead to Action?") evaluating the ethical choices made by Kathy Griffin and others whose images and words touched a nerve with the public
- New material on major media incidents early in Trump's presidency

**Chapter 15**

  ○ Updated opening vignette discussion of the media and ISIS

  ○ New Ethics in Media feature regarding role of media humor and satire in international context, including *Charlie Hebdo* ("Humor and Ethics: The Role of Satire and Religion")

  ○ Updated Convergence Culture feature regarding *The Guardian* ("Breaking News on a Global Scale")

- **Emphasis on Careers in Media.** In addition to the Media Pioneers features, which present the contributions and career foundations of innovators and leaders who have shaped and continue to shape the world of media, a **Media Careers** section appears at the end of each chapter (with the exception of Chapter 1). This section discusses traditional and emerging career paths in the industry as related to the topic of each chapter.

- **Discussion Questions.** Formerly located at the end of each chapter, discussion questions have been integrated throughout the chapters at the end of relevant sections in order to strengthen critical thinking.

- **Further Reading.** The sixth edition includes on average three to four new sources per chapter.

## How the Book Is Organized

*Converging Media* has the comprehensive mission of explaining not only the world of digital media and social media but also the basics of communication theory, ethics, and traditional mass-communication forms, while also assisting in the development of media literacy skills. It does this using a class-tested, multipart structure.

### PART 1: THE CHANGING MEDIA LANDSCAPE

**Chapter 1** explains the multifaceted nature of convergence (and disputes over its definition) to see how the nature of mass communication is changing. **Chapter 2** discusses media literacy, which helps meet students' need for solid critical-thinking skills in the twenty-first century's complex and fast-changing digital-media environment, including notions of fake news. Providing an early foundation in media literacy ensures that students will bring a critical perspective to the remainder of the book.

### PART 2: MASS-COMMUNICATION FORMATS

**Chapter 3** begins the exploration of traditional media with a discussion of the print industry and the digital dynamics to which it is now subject. **Chapter 4** explores sound—namely, the recording industry and radio. The recording industry has of course been at the forefront of changes that digital media have brought to their industry through sharing of music files, and radio is increasingly facing questions about its role as people come to expect music on demand and there are more options for bands to promote their music, such as in video games and on television shows. **Chapter 5** looks at visual media—photography, movies, and television—and examines how each of these developed and influenced the ways that we see media. Photography is often ignored in books such as this but is an important aspect of the development of our media usage. Technological advances in photography not only led directly to motion pictures but contributed to the increased importance we place on visual media today. **Chapter 6** explores how interactivity and user interface have played fundamental roles in the development of the Internet and video games. The chapter also discusses gamification as well as the promise and perils of virtual and augmented reality.

## PART 3: MEDIA PERSPECTIVES

**Chapters 7**, **8**, **9**, and **10** examine the way that digital and social media are changing traditional communication professions. **Chapter 7** provides an overview of social media, which is allowing the public to talk back to media producers and companies. Users of social media can also band together and create entirely new projects outside the traditional media professions. Journalism, the subject of **Chapter 8**, is probably the field most threatened by the digital democratization of news reporting, but recent developments such as the collaboration on publishing the Panama Papers show that perhaps new models of journalism may be successful. Public relations is now its own chapter, **Chapter 9**, which allows a deeper dive into persuasion and the practice of public relations. Advertising is also now its own chapter, **Chapter 10**, and likewise has allowed for greater depth into advertising on its own and the challenges it faces with more fragmented audiences and greater media choice than in the past.

## PART 4: MEDIA AND SOCIETY

Part 4 shows the broader social effects of developments related to media. Media ethics receives a full treatment in **Chapter 11**, with an in-depth discussion of the ethical issues each profession faces. We explore the unique dilemmas raised by digital technologies, including the threats to privacy. **Chapter 12** explores legal and regulatory aspects of media, especially as related to the First Amendment. For students interested in gaining a deeper understanding of media or who are considering a career in academia, **Chapter 13** introduces some major media theories and presents different types of research, examining the strengths and weaknesses of each. **Chapter 14** thoroughly examines politics and communication, an area that in introductory books is often confined to U.S. election coverage. Although the 2016 U.S. presidential election and first several months of Trump's presidency are discussed, international politics and media are not ignored. **Chapter 15**, on global media, introduces the notions of the public sphere and public opinion and looks at the media's role in democratic and nondemocratic countries throughout the world. The globalization of media technology, industry, and content highlights international issues, including the digital divide, cultural imperialism, and cybersecurity.

# Acknowledgments

Creating a book such as this is very much a collaborative effort, and the authors have benefited greatly from the advice and wisdom not only of the reviewers, but of those who adopted the first, second, third, fourth, and fifth editions of the book. These adopters sometimes had to work hard to persuade colleagues and departments that *Converging Media* was the text to use to introduce students to mass communication. We can only hope that the argument is easier to make with this sixth edition as we witness a growing number of books about media convergence in the market.

We would also like to thank the adopters who wrote to us over the years asking when a revised edition would be published and who offered encouraging words about the usefulness of the book when there were still plenty of professors who were not convinced that a new approach to teaching mass communication was needed or who thought that only minor tweaks to curricula would do the trick.

John Pavlik truly appreciates the love and support of his family, especially his wife, Jackie, and his daughters, Orianna and Tristan. Shawn McIntosh is similarly grateful for the love and support of his wife, Naren, and his son, Altan, who is growing up in this evolving media world and whose questions about media old and new always help Shawn see media in new lights.

We want especially to thank the editors at Oxford University Press with whom we worked: Toni Magyar, our editor; Katlin Kocher, editorial assistant; Braylee Cross, marketing manager; and Katerina Hull-Fossas, marketing assistant. They immediately understood and shared our vision of what this textbook should and could be to introductory mass-communication courses. Their insights and advice helped this book surpass our expectations. We also wish to thank Dr. Mary Ann McHugh, whose extensive editing and creative contributions have streamlined and updated much of the text. We are grateful for the fine job of Oxford's production group: production manager, Lisa Grzan; production editor, Marianne Paul; and art director, Michele Laseau. The copyeditor, Mary Anne Shahidi, also helped clarify and simplify and made great improvements throughout the book.

And last but certainly not least, we wish to thank the following reviewers for the detailed and insightful feedback on various parts of the book and instructor resources.

## SIXTH EDITION REVIEWERS

Anthony J. Miceli, *Gannon University*

Scott Brown, *California State University, Northridge*

Steven Keeler, *Cayuga Community College (SUNY)*

Bridgett P. Robertson, *Virginia State University*

Richard T. Craig, *George Mason University*

Courtney C. Bosworth, *Radford University*

Bonnie Newman Davis, *NCA&T State University*

Kimetris Baltrip, *Kansas State University*

Robert Mejia, *State University of New York, Brockport*

Karen McDevitt, *Wayne State University*

Beth Olson, *University of Houston*

Suda Ishida, *Hamline University*

Claire Rhodes, *Florida State College at Jacksonville*

Jennifer Marshall, *California Lutheran University*

Benjamin Lohman, *Orange Coast College*

Jeff Boone, *Angelo State University*

Thom Gencarelli, *Manhattan College*

## FIFTH EDITION REVIEWERS

Amelia H. Arsenault, *Georgia State University*

James Brancato, *Cedar Crest College*

Scott Brown, *California State University, Northridge*

Jennifer Fogel, *State University of New York–Oswego*

Shari Hoppin, *Troy University*

Jenn Mackay, *Virginia Tech*

David Magolis, *Bloomsburg University of Pennsylvania*

Andrea McDonnell, *Emmanuel College*

Andrew Nelson, *Loyola University New Orleans*

Stephen Swanson, *McLennan Community College*

## FOURTH EDITION REVIEWERS

Joseph Abisaid, *Monmouth College*

Nathan Atkinson, *Georgia State University*

Jeff Boone, *Angelo State University*

Pennie Boyett, *Tarrant County College–Southeast*

Allison Butler, *University of Massachusetts–Amherst*

Elizabeth B. Christian, *University of New Haven*

Sara Drabik, *Northern Kentucky University*

Mara Einstein, *Queens College*

Jason Genovese, *Bloomsburg University of Pennsylvania*

Aimee Gillette, *Howard Community College*

Meredith Guthrie, *University of Pittsburgh*

Jeffrey B. Hendrick, *Jacksonville State University*

Mark Hungerford, *University of New Hampshire*

George Johnson, *James Madison University*

Hume Johnson, *Roger Williams University*

Tom Kelleher, *University of Hawaii–Manoa*

Vincent Kiernan, *Georgetown University*

Daekyung Kim, *James Madison University*

Derek Lackaff, *Elon University*

Ryan Lange, *Alvernia University*

David Magolis, *Bloomsburg University of Pennsylvania*

Rick Marks, *College of Southern Nevada*

Joy A. McDonald, *Hampton University*

Meaghan Meachem, *Lyndon State College*

Wendy Nelson, *Palomar College*

Pamela O'Brien, *Bowie State University*

Andrea Otanez, *Everett Community College*

Eun-A Park, *University of New Haven*

Richard D. Pineda, *University of Texas–El Paso*

Hilary Russo, *St. John's University*

Jessie M. Quintero Johnson, *University of Massachusetts–Boston*

CarrieLynn D. Reinhard, *Dominican University*

Karen A. Ritzenhoff, *Central Connecticut State University*

Kevin Tankersley, *Baylor University*

Anita J. Turpin, *Roanoke College*

Tammy R. Vigil, *Boston University*

Justin Walden, *Pennsylvania State University*

Jamie Ward, *University of Michigan–Dearborn*

Matt Weidman, *Widener University–Exton*

Ronald A. Yaros, *University of Maryland–College Park*

## THIRD EDITION REVIEWERS

Lonny J. Avi Brooks, *California State University, East Bay*

Ovril Patricia Cambridge, *Ohio University*

Skye Dent, *Fayetteville State University*

Marie Dick, *St. Cloud State University*

Paul Glover, *Henderson State University*

Chandler Harriss, *Alfred University*

Myleea D. Hill, *Arkansas State University*

Hans Ibold, *Indiana University*

Daekyung Kim, *Idaho State University*

Viktoria Kreher, *Southern Illinois University, Carbondale*

Carole McNall, *St. Bonaventure University*

Robert M. Ogles, *Purdue University*

Ted Satterfield, *Northwestern Oklahoma State University*

Lauren Reichart Smith, *Auburn University*

Elyse Warford, *Georgia State University*

Scott Winter, *University of Nebraska–Lincoln*

## SECOND EDITION REVIEWERS

Charles Apple, *University of Michigan–Flint*

Charlyne Berens, *University of Nebraska–Lincoln*

William R. Bettler, *Hanover College*

Joseph S. Clark, *Florida State University*

David Cundy, *Iona College*

James Ettema, *Northwestern University*

Michael Robert Evans, *Indiana University*

Thom Gencarelli, *Manhattan College*

Roger George, *Bellevue College*

Donald G. Godfrey, *Arizona State University*

David Gore, *Eastern Michigan University*

Margot Hardenbergh, *Fordham University*

Chandler Harriss, *Alfred University*

Karima A. Haynes, *Bowie State University*

Jeffrey B. Hedrick, *Jacksonville State University*

Tamara Henry, *American University*

Patricia Holmes, *University of Louisiana–Lafayette*

Seok Kang, *University of Texas–San Antonio*

Greg Lisby, *Georgia State University*

John Madormo, *North Central College*

Charles Marsh, *University of Kansas*

Stephen J. McNeill, *Kennesaw State University*

Olivia Miller, *University of Memphis*

James E. Mueller, *University of North Texas*

Robert M. Ogles, *Purdue University*

Selene Phillips, *University of Louisville*

Marshel D. Rossow, *Minnesota State University–Mankato*

Ted Satterfield, *Northwestern Oklahoma State University*

Randall K. Scott, *University of Montevallo*

Brad Schultz, *University of Mississippi*

Arthur L. Terry, *Bethel University*

Mina Tsay, *University of Kentucky*

## FIRST EDITION REVIEWERS

Robert Bellamy, *Duquesne University*

Gerald Boyer, *Maryville University*

Mark Braun, *Gustavus Adolphus College*

Margaret Cassidy, *Adelphi University*

Steven Chappell, *Truman State University*

Joseph Chuk, *Kutztown University*

Vic Costello, *Gardner-Webb University*

David Gordon, *University of Wisconsin–Eau Claire*

Charlotte Kwok Glaser, *College of Notre Dame*

Colin Gromatzky, *New Mexico State University*

Steven Keeler, *Cayuga College*

Yasue Kuwahara, *Northern Kentucky University*

Dianne Lamb, *George Southern University*

Mitchell Land, *University of North Texas*

Jeremy Harris Lipschultz, *University of Nebraska–Omaha*

Arthur Lizie, *Bridgewater State College*

John Lule, *Lehigh University*

Thomas McPhail, *University of Missouri*

Anthony Olorunnisola, *Pennsylvania State University*

Kathleen Olson, *Lehigh University*

Ronald Roat, *University of Southern Indiana*

Marshel D. Rossow, *Minnesota State University–Mankato*

Andris Straumanis, *University of Wisconsin–Eau Claire*

L. Lee Thomas, *Doane College*

Max Utsler, *University of Kansas*

# About the Authors

**John V. Pavlik** is a professor in the Department of Journalism and Media Studies at the School of Communication and Information, Rutgers, the State University of New Jersey. He is also faculty associate at the Columbia Institute for Tele-Information. Having published widely on the impact of new technology on journalism, media, and society, Pavlik has also authored more than a dozen computer software packages for education in journalism and mass communication. He is co-developer of the situated documentary, a new type of digital storytelling using mobile augmented reality. He is former associate dean for research at Northwestern University in Qatar and a former senior fellow at the San Diego Supercomputer Center. He was the inaugural Fulbright Distinguished Chair in Media Studies in 2008 at the Academy of Fine Arts, Vienna, Austria. He received his PhD and MA in mass communication from the University of Minnesota and is a 1978 graduate of the School of Journalism and Mass Communication at the University of Wisconsin at Madison.

**Shawn McIntosh** is an assistant professor of digital journalism and communication at the Massachusetts College of Liberal Arts, where he teaches courses in news writing, data visualization, publication design, literary journalism, and is the adviser to the student newspaper *The Beacon*. Formerly, he was a lecturer in strategic communication at Columbia University's School of Professional Studies, where he taught graduate courses in theories of persuasion, communication ethics, and digital media. McIntosh was an editor and freelance writer for ten years for various newspapers and magazines in the United Kingdom, the United States, and Japan. He was also co-site manager and senior producer at Fathom, an online educational website consortium of leading academic institutions, museums, and research organizations in the United States and England. His research interests include social media; media, power, and democracy; and collaborative journalism. He received a BS in microbiology from the University of Idaho and an MS in journalism from the Graduate School of Journalism at Columbia University.

# Converging
# Media

# Mass Communication and Its Digital Transformation

Many Netflix subscribers eagerly await the release of the newest season of its most popular, award-winning series *Orange Is the New Black*, about prisoners in a minimum-security women's prison in Connecticut. Based loosely on Piper Kerman's 2010 memoir *Orange Is the New Black: My Year in a Women's Prison,* the TV comedy-drama covers the lives and back stories of the various inmates while it critiques larger social issues such as the consequences of privatizing prisons, guard and prisoner relations, and the difficulties ex-convicts face in reintegrating into society.

Netflix itself became a crime victim when hackers intercepted ten episodes of season 5. Netflix refused to pay a ransom, so hackers released the episodes more than a month before the planned June 9, 2017, release date.

The hacker or hackers, which go by the name darkoverlord, claim to have episodes from other networks, such as Fox, ABC, and National Geographic. The material seems to have been stolen from Larsen Studios, a production facility, in 2016.

Streaming services like Netflix have become increasingly popular, challenging traditional television networks and cable services and their advertising-based business models with a subscription business model that can be watched via the Internet. Some may consider it poetic justice that an industry disruptor like Netflix is, in turn, being disrupted by an illegal activity like hacking, but the example shows just how much convergence has blurred the lines between traditional media, the Internet, and social media.

Furthermore, the hack does raise issues of Internet security as it reminds us of how interconnected we are and how even one weak link in our online network can affect a much greater number of people and companies. Although Netflix executives no doubt hope that darkoverlord may one day be wearing an orange prison jumpsuit, the chances of finding the hacker or hackers and bringing them to justice is slim, especially if they are overseas.

## LEARNING OBJECTIVES

>> Define convergence.

>> Discuss the main types of convergence and their implications for communication.

>> Explain the eight major changes taking place in communication today because of convergence.

>> Define mass communication.

>> Describe the basic theories of mass communication.

>> Identify the basic components and functions of the mass-communication process.

The media of mass communication have long played a fundamental role in people's lives. The media inform, educate, persuade, entertain, and even—or perhaps especially—sell. Media can provide personal companionship and public scrutiny. They can shape perception on matters great and small. They can function in countless and increasing ways as extensions of one's self, and play a fundamental role in shaping our identities.

We will examine the nature of mass communication and how it is changing in the digital and social media age when people are connected globally by electronic networks. Specific technological advances are producing widespread societal, cultural, and economic changes as media producers and consumers face a new world of media symbols, processes, and effects.

Few communications technologies better encapsulate the fundamental aspects of convergence than two seemingly very different devices: the telephone and the television. We will first look briefly at the history and evolution of the telephone as a communications device because it touches on almost every important issue that we are dealing with today regarding the Internet and digital media. Furthermore, the phone continues to be at the heart of some of the most innovative changes taking place in how we communicate with each other and how we interact with the world and with media. At the end of the chapter, we will take a brief look at television, how it continues to be at the forefront of convergence, and how it is changing our relationship with the media.

> **DISCUSSION QUESTIONS:** Keep a diary for a day of the media you consume (and create). Note the sources of your news, the types of online communication you use with friends and family, and the frequency of your phone use (talking and texting). What did you learn from the diary?

## Telephony: Case Study in Convergence

Although nowadays we may take the portability of our cell phones for granted, this mobility has important repercussions for many activities. First, we are no longer tied to a specific place when making or answering a phone call. The question "Where are you now?" when calling a friend's landline need not be asked—your friend is obviously at home; otherwise, he would not have answered the phone.

By being able to communicate anywhere and anytime, you are able to coordinate with others with greater spontaneity than in the past. Prior to widespread use of cell phones, if you had a sudden change of plans (or change of heart) regarding a meeting with someone, you had very limited ways to let the person know you would not show up. Coordinating meeting times and places among several people in a group took much more effort and did not allow for last-minute changes. Also, consider how much more we use a phone we carry, as opposed to when you had to travel to the location of the phone (e.g., home, a phone booth). This makes us more likely to call or text to share information on the spot—sometimes to the annoyance of those around us as we communicate with distant others and ignore people nearby.

Our familiarity with the phone belies its revolutionary character from a communications standpoint. Before the phone, people could not talk directly to others whom they could not physically see. In an emergency, the only way to inform the proper authorities was to physically go where they were and let them know. The phone played a major role in changing our patterns of communication with each other and thereby changing social relations. But it was the telegraph, created more than thirty years before the telephone, that first revolutionized our speed of communication.

The telegraph was the first means of electronic communication, using a series of taps on a keypad that represented dots and dashes to spell out words. These signals were transmitted over telegraph wires connecting one location to another. Telegraph operators were specially trained to code and decode messages, and the result was a thriving new industry that grew during the mid- to late nineteenth century. This innovative form of instantaneous communication led to entirely new kinds of business enterprises, including personal messaging services and "newswire" services such as Reuters and the Associated Press.

As the telephone network spread, telephone lines started to clutter the landscape.

Telephones adopted the principles discovered with telegraphy but allowed voice to be transmitted. Although Alexander Graham Bell is the inventor of record for the telephone in 1876, others were also working on how to transmit voice electronically through wires; and there is some evidence that Bell's invention may have borrowed liberally from existing, similar patents. Still, after years of lawsuits, it was Bell who won out. This parallels the many suits and countersuits seen today as companies claim patent infringement on Internet or software inventions and technologies (e.g., Nokia and Apple's 2016 suits against each other regarding infringing patents).[1]

Regardless of who can claim credit for inventing the telephone, it was easier for the general public to use than the telegraph. Even so, it was not immediately thought of as an interpersonal communication device, largely because it was expensive and difficult to connect every single household to the telephone network. This parallels the "last mile" issue in twenty-first-century broadband, or high-speed, Internet connections coming directly into homes and touches on the importance of networks in our communication environment. It also highlights how seemingly obvious uses for new communications technologies become apparent only much later. How they may be used or adopted is very much an open question that relies not only on the technology alone but on a range of economic, social, and cultural issues at the time.

Despite the dramatic changes it would bring to communications, the phone was initially either ignored or thought of as simply a novelty. With subsequent technological improvements that made it easier to hear and to increase the number of voices that could be carried on a single wire, the telephone became more widely accepted. The ring of the telephone was a death knell for most telegraph companies, just as later media technologies rendered earlier technologies obsolete and changed entire industries in the process.

Initially, especially in Europe, the telephone acted as a kind of early radio. Wealthy patrons paid a fee to listen to music performances that were sent along the wires, and some public venues would pipe in sermons or performances for their patrons.[2] For several years in Budapest, Hungary, Telefon Hírmondó delivered news over the telephone, with subscribers dialing in at certain times to listen to someone reading the news of the day. A similar service was also tried in 1911 in Newark, New Jersey, but lasted for only a few months before closing.

Delivering news over telephone wires is not something new with the Internet, and it also shows a public desire for information and entertainment "on demand," much like we get our media through online streaming services. What was still missing at that time was an economic model that could support a business such as telephone newspapers. This issue is commonly dealt with today by media companies that need to see a return on investments before they are willing to experiment with new ways of doing business.

The decision whether to make the telephone a government-run agency or a private enterprise was an important crossroad, and the choices made in Europe (government) differed from those made in the United States (private enterprise). Even into the twenty-first century, these choices have had profound repercussions for the actual and perceived development, use, and control of the Internet. And it continues to be the case that new technologies often inherit the baggage of political or social decisions made much earlier.

Leaving the early development of American telephone systems to private enterprise resulted in many incompatibilities among competing systems. Local telephone companies sold their own telephones, which would often not work with other telephone systems. The issue of compatibility between systems is still seen today in the form of competing computer operating systems, gaming systems, Internet browsers, and other electronic devices, including ebooks and tablet computers.

During the formative years of the telephone industry, the U.S. government sought to eliminate such incompatibilities in the phone network by granting one company, AT&T, a monopoly on the telephone system. This, too, had important repercussions for later developments in telecommunications. Just as the monopoly telegraph company, Western Union, had done in the late 1800s when it became apparent the telephone was a threat to its business, AT&T in the 1960s and 1970s tried to hamper the development of a new kind of network that would potentially hurt its business. The network needed to develop the Internet was not compatible with the AT&T system. Even though AT&T realized the new network was more efficient, the telephone company feared losing dominance and initially refused to adopt it.

Government regulation or private enterprise, monopoly powers, and business interests at the expense of the public interest are issues still very much with us today. How much we pay for services, how services are bundled and how they set up payment plans, and a variety of other business decisions are influenced by the laws and regulations that have been created, often as a result of industry lobbying efforts.

Just as economic factors may influence how we use the telephone, such as what types of data plans we have, social and cultural factors play an equally important role in determining whether a technology is adopted. Initially, people do not know how to act or interact with a new technology. Consider the classic story of the farmer, for example, who in the early days of the telephone went to town to place an order for supplies. The store clerk told him to place his order directly with the company over the phone, so the farmer dutifully wrote out his order, rolled it up carefully, and then jammed the rolled note into one of the holes of the phone handset and waited.

If this seems too silly to be true, recall your own reactions when you have to use an unfamiliar TV remote control. The variety of functions seen in phones today stretches its very definition compared to even twenty years ago. Young people today in much of the world would consider a phone that does not take pictures or play video games or provide an address book a dinosaur. In short, the phone continues to evolve as a multifunctional communications device. The smartphone connects us to our friends and to the world of information and entertainment through the

Internet via almost one billion mobile applications (apps). It provides a nearly seamless interface between interpersonal and mass communication, as we access via a favorite app a review of a restaurant and then subsequently snap a photo of our meal to share via Instagram. We might even wirelessly post our own review on the spot, after which it can be seen by potentially millions of people worldwide.

All these aspects of the development and use of the phone—ranging from the technical, legal, and regulatory to the economic, social, and cultural—touch on the notion of media convergence. But as we will see, convergence is a debated concept and has multiple layers of meaning. As we explore this phenomenon, we will unpack its many layers and reveal how they encompass some of the most dramatic transformations taking place in communications today.

Today's cell phones typically have a variety of functions that have nothing to do with the traditional functions of the phone.

# Three Types of Convergence

**Convergence** is known broadly as the coming together of computing, telecommunications, and media in a digital environment. It is important to study and understand convergence because what might first seem like wholly technological or media issues profoundly influence our economic, social, and cultural lives as well.

There is some disagreement among scholars over a single definition of convergence, an indication of the far-reaching consequences of the changes taking place in mass communication today. Indeed, many transformative forces for which we have still to develop adequate descriptions are in play, changes whose effects are also uncertain. For now, the term "convergence" seems to come closest to encompassing many of these forces. Some argue that convergence has already occurred, and in many respects you could say that is true. But we believe that convergence is an ongoing and dynamic phenomenon that continues to shape the world of traditional media.

We can look at three main categories of convergence as in Figure 1-1 as ways to frame our understanding of the changes taking place today in the media industries: technological convergence, economic convergence, and cultural convergence. As you will see, these three categories actually overlap in many respects.

**convergence**

The coming together of computing, telecommunications, and media in a digital environment.

## TECHNOLOGICAL CONVERGENCE

Perhaps the most easily visible aspect of convergence is the rise of digital media and online communication networks. Technological convergence refers to specific types of media, such as print, audio, and video, all converging into a digital media form. Such types of convergence are easily apparent in news organizations—for example, where today's journalists often need to be able to tell stories using text, audio, video, and even interactive media.

Digital media often change the very nature of their traditional counterparts and affect how we use and perceive them. For example, although you can look at an ebook on a Kindle as simply digital print, the fact is that a Kindle ebook alters the reading experience. One obvious way is that because of its storage capacity, you can easily carry many books in one device. Furthermore, you can change the text size to make reading more comfortable, look up words, annotate and index sections, and even purchase new books on the spot through a wireless Internet connection.

FIGURE 1-1  Three Types of Convergence and Their Influence on Media

Technological Convergence

Media content changes
Media type changes
Media use changes
Media distribution changes
Media audience changes
Media profession changes

Cultural Convergence

Attitude/value changes

Media organization changes

Economic Convergence

Precisely because users can alter the look and size of the text they are reading, the notion of page numbers also becomes meaningless on a Kindle—much to the chagrin of students who realize they need to cite quotations taken from a book. You can even share your highlighted passages with others, making book reading a collaborative experience, much like it was in the early days of books when reading was generally done aloud.

Most of these activities, such as looking up an unfamiliar word in a dictionary, already occur with printed books. The significant difference, however, is that a single device now allows for all these actions, eliminating the need to carry a separate dictionary or permanently mark a book. Activities that used to be separate or cumbersome are now easier and folded into the media experience. Not simply a matter of convenience, these changes fundamentally alter how we interact with our media. We may be far more likely to look up a word on a Kindle than if we had to walk to the shelf to get the dictionary, for example. The music, television, and film industries, which we will look at in later chapters, provide other examples of how our media use changes thanks in large part to changes in technology.

This form of convergence, although highly relevant for today's communications professionals, is not the only way to think of convergence. The changes that come from new technologies also affect business models and established industries, which often see the upstarts as threats to their dominance. These fears can be valid, as sometimes these new companies become larger and more powerful than established ones. Google, founded in 1998, is a case in point. Started as a search engine, today it generates much of its revenue from advertising due to its popularity as a search tool. Even so, in August 2015 Google itself announced that it would change its company name to Alphabet, with Google simply being one part of a corporation. Today you can see Google expanding into the field of self-driving cars, for example, and in many other areas not directly related to media or online searches.

Ebook readers such as the Kindle and the Nook have transformed the reading habits of people around the world, not to mention the book industry. **CRITICAL THINKING QUESTIONS:** How do you think ebooks are influencing the notion of books and reading? Are ebooks better or more useful than traditional books? Which would you rather read, and why?

## ECONOMIC CONVERGENCE

Economic convergence refers to the merging of Internet or telecommunications companies with traditional media companies, such as Comcast with NBC Universal. Traditional media companies have grown fewer and much larger in the past fifty years through mergers and acquisitions, a process we define as **consolidation**, not convergence. Economic convergence occurs when formerly independent media enterprises further the success of one another because they fall under the same corporate umbrella. Entertainment companies may own news stations; large corporations traditionally outside of the media business, such as GE, may purchase media companies like NBC. This can result in conflicts of interest when corporate parents don't want some aspects of their businesses covered in the news or when a news outlet gives prominent coverage to a movie produced by a studio also owned by the corporate parent.

Economic convergence also has important repercussions for the nature of the media, telecommunications, and computing industries. A telecommunications company that also owns a media company can speed the transmission of its own content and slow the content from competing companies, thus influencing customers to watch more of its own material. It could also control the type of content its customers see by blocking material from certain websites.

The Internet is not causing this type of behavior: There are numerous historical examples of media owners censoring content or blocking public access. But what makes this issue more significant and prominent is the combination

**consolidation**

A process whereby traditional media companies have grown fewer and much larger in the past fifty years through mergers and acquisitions.

### MEDIA PIONEERS
# Oprah Winfrey

You may be surprised to learn that Oprah Winfrey, known as "the Queen of All Media" and considered in some rankings to be the most influential black woman in the world, came from very humble beginnings.

Born to a teenage single mother in 1954, Orpah Winfrey lived in poverty during her childhood and claims to have been molested as a child and early teen, resulting in pregnancy at fourteen. Tired of people mispronouncing her name as "Oprah" rather than Orpah, she finally just let it become Oprah.

Oprah started in radio at nineteen, and helped develop a more confessional style of radio and later television talk show that Phil Donahue had pioneered. *The Oprah Winfrey Show*, which was nationally syndicated from 1986 to 2011, was the highest rated show of its kind in television history.

The popularity of *The Oprah Winfrey Show* created something called the "Oprah effect," which referred to her popular book club segment on the show. When she discussed a book on the segment, even obscure titles quickly became bestsellers.

Oprah's power as a media personality and business can be seen in the way she has successfully bridged traditional media and online media. She has launched several magazines, including *O, The Oprah Magazine*, and published a memoir in 2017. She also had a satellite radio contract and continues to appear on television regularly.

Although not necessarily an Internet pioneer in the sense of creating new online business models, products, or apps, her website oprah.com attracts 6 million users a month, complementing and expanding her media empire.

That media empire has propelled her to become North America's only black multibillionaire, and the richest black person in the United States. She has also been generous with her wealth: She was named as one of America's top philanthropists by *Businessweek* in 2004.

of consolidated media giants and ever larger audiences. Despite the explosion of channels and media content, our choices may be narrower than they appear. Consider the increasingly frequent temporary blackouts of channels as cable companies and media conglomerates fight over "carriage rights": agreements to broadcast a company's signal. In 2012 over 20 million DirecTV subscribers were blocked by Viacom (owner of CBS, Comedy Central, and MTV, among many others) as the two companies negotiated fees. In late 2014 and into early 2015, satellite provider DISH Network stopped carrying Fox News and Fox Business channels because of disagreements over licensing charges.

It is difficult to determine a true winner in the court of public opinion, as the agreements tend to lead to higher cable bills for consumers, who are encouraged by the companies to apply public pressure but who seem to have limited clout. However, in a cultural shift, the relationship between the audience or public and media producers is changing, and here we are able to see greater disruption.

## CULTURAL CONVERGENCE

Culture refers to the values, beliefs, and practices shared by a group of people. It may refer to a population at large, such as Americans, or to various subgroups within a larger group who may share certain ethnic, social, or professional traditions and practices, such as Irish Americans, video gamers, or corporate attorneys.

A powerful aspect of cultural convergence occurs through the globalization of media content when, for example, crime procedural dramas like *CSI*, *NCIS*, or *Criminal Minds* are top-ranked shows in several European countries; or when Japanese anime, or animation, finds popularity in the United States. The popularity of such shows across a variety of nations speaks to some aspect they possess that foreign audiences identify with or aspire to. On the downside of cultural convergence, however, a significant concern is the impact of global media on multiculturalism, or the diversity of culture, especially internationally.

But we can also look at cultural convergence from the perspective of how we consume, create, and distribute media content. The shift from an audience that was forced to be largely passive and silent, simply consuming content produced by large-scale media companies to a public that can now produce and share content with others cheaply and easily is one of the major themes of this book and a crucial component of cultural convergence.

Although mass communication will continue, in the sense that media companies and others will continue to produce messages for large audiences, a significant trend involves more personalized and frequent messages tailored to the needs of individuals. Furthermore, what was traditionally considered interpersonal communication, such as email, can also be widely distributed by individuals through online networks, making the dividing line between interpersonal and mass communication increasingly hard to distinguish.

The ability of companies to better target people with personalized advertising and messages by tracking their online activities raises important issues of privacy, consumer rights, and media business economic models. Whether people will become more active in media production and more engaged in civic or political activities than in the past remains open to debate, with some scholars taking an increasingly critical look at how media corporations and

Digital technology has allowed more people to create professional-quality videos and other media content.

## INTERNATIONAL PERSPECTIVES
# A "Comedy" of Cultural Convergence

Given the current tensions between North Korea and the United States, the release of the Seth Rogen comedy *The Interview* in late 2014 and early 2015 almost seems like a comedy in its own right. The movie seemed an unlikely candidate to spark an international incident that became a cause célèbre for free speech, increased fears about cyberwarfare between nations, and led to U.S. sanctions against North Korea, but that is exactly what happened. This curious chain of events also highlights—often unexpectedly—just how much digital media has transformed mass communication.

North Korea was vocal in its displeasure about the planned Christmas Day release of the comedy *The Interview* in which Rogen and James Franco play a pair of celebrity tabloid-show producers chosen by the CIA to assassinate North Korean leader Kim Jong-un.

On November 24, Sony Pictures, distributor of the film, learned that its computer systems had been hacked. In the days that followed, sensitive corporate data—including a string of embarrassing emails between executives, early versions of screenplays, and executive salaries—were leaked to the public. Sony and some cybersecurity experts, including those in the FBI, blamed a North Korean group, while other experts were doubtful.

On December 17, after receiving threats that theaters showing *The Interview* would be blown up, Sony cancelled its theatrical release, an executive decision widely criticized as a blow to free speech. Less than a week later, Sony reversed itself and announced that *the movie* would play in theaters that still supported it and be available to rent on video-on-demand (VOD). Just before New Year's, several cable and satellite companies announced deals with Sony to show *The Interview* for pay-per-view, on iTunes, Xbox Video, YouTube Movies, Google Play, and other on-demand services, long before

the usual three-month window between theatrical release and airing on cable or DVD. Between December 24, 2014, and January 4, 2015, *The Interview* earned $31 million, making it Sony's number 1 online film.[3]

Several ironies make this fiasco worthy of its own comedy feature film. First, it was not government that threatened free speech but corporate interests, ranging from Sony Pictures itself to theater owners who refused to show the movie. Second, the United States issued more sanctions against North Korea in early January, even though cybersecurity experts were still debating who was actually responsible for the hack. Third, it showed that even when confronted with a legacy of artificial constraints from an earlier mass-communications era, convergence will prevail, especially when there are other distribution channels available such as home entertainment systems.

companies, in general, are turning online public participation to their advantage through online tracking and targeted advertising. In one future, there is an engaged public who uses digital media and online networks to further interactivity and democracy prevails; and in another, there are established media conglomerates and technology companies that hijack public interests for their own ends, including stifling political dissent or unpopular opinions. Such tensions and concerns will shape the nature of the Internet and digital media use far into the twenty-first century.

**DISCUSSION QUESTIONS:** Discuss ways in which you have engaged with others through social media or on websites. Do you think this has made you more politically active? Why or why not?

# Implications of Convergence

Whether an Internet-connected world will ultimately and fundamentally improve society is impossible to say; yet, for better and for worse, digital media have changed and will continue to transform the relationship between mass-communication industries and the public. Media organizations face many challenges, but so do media consumers as the nature of our media environment changes. Some general trends can be discerned that will provide a better perspective on how our digital-media use is changing our media world and, by extension, our social and cultural worlds.

Clearly, the changes brought about by convergence have had dramatic implications. Within the larger framework of the three types of convergence, these changes affect eight different areas, recurring themes addressed throughout this book:

1. Media organization
2. Media type
3. Media content
4. Media use
5. Media distribution
6. Media audience
7. Media profession
8. Attitudes and values

## MEDIA ORGANIZATION

In the world that predated convergence, media content was created and published or broadcast on predetermined schedules by centralized media organizations in which a central unit or individual controls content production and distribution as well as marketing and other functions. A newspaper was printed and distributed daily or weekly; a television show appeared at a certain time on a certain day, and audiences often scheduled their social lives around these known schedules. The economics of the media system throughout most of the nineteenth and twentieth centuries heavily favored a mass-production model with centralized control. Only large companies could bear the costs of content creation, production, marketing, and distribution.

Internet-based media can be less centralized, partly because many of the associated costs have been greatly reduced. Of course, movies, television shows, and many other types of mass-produced media still rely on the old production and distribution models; but now new marketing avenues on the Internet make it easier to mass distribute media products, as illustrated by Sony Pictures' *The Interview* example.

Unlike public service media, most media companies throughout the world operate to make a profit. Advertising is one of the main sources of revenue for these organizations, and advertisers today are spending less in traditional media and more online. The gap is beginning to narrow, although many media companies are still not making up the difference with online advertising. This has increased the financial pressure, especially in print media, which, having seen the largest drop in advertising, has led to layoffs, reduced printing and pages of newspapers and magazines, closings, and buyouts of struggling companies.

Concentration of media ownership, or consolidation, was a growing trend even before digital media. Convergence is in some ways fueling media consolidation by leading traditional media giants such as Time Warner to join with a former online colossus such as America Online, giving rise in 2001 to the short-lived AOL Time Warner. In 2010, AOL, long jettisoned from Time Warner, bought one of the most popular blogs on the web, *The Huffington Post*, yet another illustration of how the boundaries between traditional technology companies and media companies have blurred. Furthermore, the much-maligned Time Warner Cable, the second-largest cable company in the United States, was purchased in 2015 by Charter Communications for nearly $80 billion and rebranded as Spectrum.

The trend is clear: Analog and digital media are rapidly being consolidated into the hands of a few very large, very powerful, and very rich owners, an economic structure referred to as an **oligopoly**. These media enterprises are increasingly likely to be part of large, global media organizations publicly owned and accountable to shareholders, whose main interest is the financial bottom line. When traditional telecommunications companies, such as Comcast, join with large media companies, such as NBC Universal, it gives the companies a tremendous centralized control over what access and content are available to media consumers, which is problematic.

Related to changes in media organization and structure are changes in the types of media or ways in which we get our media content. The seemingly insignificant decision to watch a television program on a TV on a specific day and time or on demand on a mobile device actually has significant consequences for media organizations, advertising revenues, and audience analytics, which help determine advertising rates.

**oligopoly**

An economic structure in which a few very large, very powerful, and very rich owners control an industry or collection of related industries.

## MEDIA TYPE

Just what constitutes a television or radio receiver, or TV or radio programming, is in a state of flux. Once, it was simple. Radio programming was what a listener heard on a radio. Today, however, radio stations can transmit their programming via Internet or satellite and listeners can tune in via car radios, computers, or smartphones and may even choose to download content to listen to later. Moreover, these radio station websites can include images, graphics, text, and video. The audience can sometimes even choose how they want to get content, such as watching the video, listening to the podcast, or reading the story.

Media empires have been built on owning certain kinds of media, and complex governmental laws regulate different media industries and media ownership. In the United States, for example, print media enjoy more free-speech protections than the more tightly regulated electronic broadcast media, and cable providers similarly enjoy greater freedom than broadcast networks. This raises the question of how text on the Internet should be treated—does it have the same First Amendment protections as its print counterpart because it is simply words? Or should it be treated as electronic media because it is delivered electronically? And now, as more people watch TV on mobile devices, what are the responsibilities of the Internet provider in all of this, as simply the distributor but not the creator of the content itself? Many of these questions have yet to be settled.

## MEDIA CONTENT

Stories told in a digital, online medium can connect with other types of content and other stories much more easily than in any other medium. This is done primarily through the use of **hyperlinks**, clickable pointers to other online content. Online interactive advertisements encourage visitors to click on the ads and go to the sponsor's website, or play a game, or take a survey. In entertainment programming, hyperlinked content allows a viewer to explore a story in a nonlinear narrative, whose outcome may be determined by the user's choice of links. Advertisers are increasingly demanding results in terms of how many people actually clicked on their ads or performed some other function, rather than simply being satisfied with how many viewed the page on which the ad appears.

On-demand content has become increasingly popular. In the traditional media world, the publisher or broadcaster set the schedule for news, entertainment, and marketing information. Children growing up in an on-demand media world of YouTube, podcasting, digital video recorders (DVRs) and streaming services may not readily understand why the same options don't always exist while listening to the radio or watching a traditional television channel that has no on-demand features. The changes have happened so fast and been so extensive that new terms have been created to highlight the differences between a generation that has grown up with digital technologies and those born in the analog era. **Digital natives** are the postmillennial generation that has grown up with digital and social media, whereas **digital immigrants** are older generations that may also use digital media, but that generally have more trouble adapting in varying degrees to the digital media world.

**Digitization**, the process that makes media computer readable, is transforming both how and when media organizations distribute their content. Delivery no longer occurs solely through traditional channels but also via the Internet, satellites, mobile devices, and a host of other digital technologies. Increasingly, content is available twenty-four hours a day, with news organizations updating news continuously and for a worldwide audience.

Digital technology is similarly transforming the production cycle and process as illustrated by Figure 1-2. In fact, the transformation may be even deeper in terms of media-content production. Whether in Hollywood motion pictures, television shows or news, books, magazines, newspapers, or online, producing media content has rapidly become almost an entirely digital process. Shot with digital cameras and edited on computers, movies can be sent by high-speed Internet to digital movie theaters. Reporters working for news operations capture their raw material with digital devices as well, writing, producing, and editing their stories digitally. Even book authors typically compose on a computer, with digital words remaining the norm throughout the production process, being read on e-readers, smartphones, or tablets.

Digital media are challenging our understanding of media content as static or unchangeable. This is especially evident in a **wiki**, a website that can be edited by anyone. Wikis have grown in popularity, revealing the demand among web users for such a function. The wiki owes much of its success to Wikipedia, where the

**hyperlink**

Clickable pointer to other online content.

**digital native**

A term coined in 2001 by author Marc Prensky for a member of a younger generation that has grown up with and is consequently very comfortable using digital media and adapting to rapid technological changes.

**digital immigrant**

An individual who grew up in the analog media era and who generally has more trouble adapting to new digital technologies, despite perhaps a desire to use and understand them.

**digitization**

The process that makes media computer readable.

**wiki**

Website that lets anyone add, edit, or delete pages and content.

**FIGURE 1-2** "Media Iceberg"

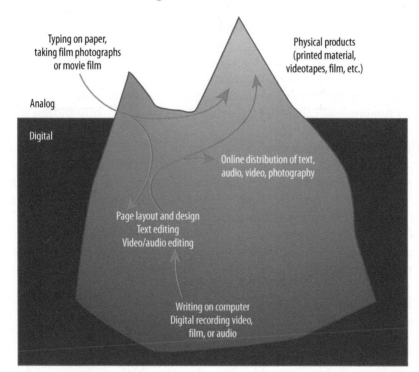

stuffy and authoritative encyclopedia article became a collaborative hybrid of encyclopedia and breaking news updated by users.

Of course, content was never actually unchangeable; it just seemed that way. A book could be reprinted as a new edition, yet for most readers the changes between editions were, practically speaking, impossible to discern. An online book is a much more fluid and dynamic document, with discussion forums on book material incorporated into the contents, ongoing online discussions between the author and readers, and interactions among readers.

Similarly, mash-ups of existing media have become common thanks to digital editing tools for music and video. Any popular item produced from mass media (e.g., advertisements, movie trailers, music videos, political speeches) has the potential of being quickly transformed into a number of user-generated parodies or send-ups, most done simply for the fun of creating something rather than for commercial gain. Consider the many mash-up videos of President Trump "playing" an accordion as he speaks and gestures with his hands. Online discussions and mash-ups exemplify increasing audience interaction and participation, one of many changes in media use.

**DISCUSSION QUESTIONS:** Discuss any media content you have created in the past week or so (posting pictures to social media, forwarding videos or stories, etc.) and what happened with that media. Did you check your uploaded content to see how many likes or shares you received? Who saw the content you posted, and did it reach a wider audience than you thought it would?

## MEDIA USE

The pervasiveness of the media system, expanded exponentially by modern global satellite communications, entails unprecedented access to mass communication. Fewer and fewer places on the globe are truly isolated, even famously remote and physically inaccessible locations. In May 1996, climber and guide Rob Hall was trapped high on Mt. Everest for more than a day after a sudden storm hit. Facing certain death—unable to descend and unable to be rescued—Hall was nonetheless capable of speaking to his pregnant wife in New Zealand by satellite phone.[4]

An always on, always present media environment, which had begun to emerge even before the advent of the Internet, has arrived. This environment has several implications for industries and for consumers, how we use media, and what we expect from them. Media companies have to find content to fill the time, and thus we are seeing more encore performances of hit shows or movies on channels like TNT, showing the same movie two or three times in a row and on multiple nights. Streaming services such as Netflix show popular television series from the past, even creating modern-day revivals such as *Fuller House*, *Twin Peaks* or *Gilmore Girls: A Year in the Life*.

Although the TV is still the first screen or the most used, it is often employed in combination with a tablet or a smartphone, a phenomenon called "the third screen" or "the fourth screen," depending on the relative position of the movie screen in terms of public use. Playing video games or watching videos on smartphones make media even more ubiquitous. Research shows we live in a multiscreen world where the tablet has begun to replace the personal computer or laptop.[5]

Pervasive mass communication means better access to entertainment, information, and news—in theory. It can also mean that media organizations can turn us into super-consumers of media of questionable social or civic value. One might, for example, question the value of viewing a lowbrow reality show on your mobile phone while riding the bus or spending hours at home watching funny cat videos on YouTube.

All the activities mentioned here are predicated on the broad assumption that individuals have ready access to computers, a broadband Internet (wired or Wi-Fi) connection, and the knowledge and skills to use them. Many in advanced, industrialized countries take these as givens, but these digital advantages are far from universal, even within developed countries.

Better Internet access has neither arrived equally to all nor allowed everyone to benefit equally from that access. People in lower socioeconomic groups in industrialized countries have lagged in almost every category of Internet access. The high cost of telecommunication services, including broadband Internet, keeps many from being able to develop the skills and knowledge that can help them participate fully in society.

Although above the worldwide average for Internet speeds, the United States is still far behind dozens of other countries. It has been making gains in high-speed Internet penetration and affordability of available services, as well as Internet speed, however. In the first six months of 2016, the United States achieved average download speeds above 50 Mbps (megabits per second) for the first time ever, a 42 percent increase year-over-year.[6] However, there are still great disparities of broadband access between urban and rural areas, with as many as 39 percent of people in rural populations below the FCC target speeds of 25 Mbps download and 3 Mbps upload speeds.[7] South Korea is widely considered to have the fastest

Internet in the world, although several Scandinavian countries also typically rank highly, along with Asian countries like Japan and Singapore.

## MEDIA DISTRIBUTION

Content is much more fluid, dynamic, and rapidly transmitted around the globe in an online environment. The expansive reach of global media and instantaneous communications is not without its perils, however, for events in distant places can have far-reaching repercussions. False rumors about political or company leaders can demonstrate the power and danger of rapid global communication. For instance, a fake tweet in the spring of 2013 from a hacked Associated Press account claiming President Obama had been injured in an explosion temporarily wiped out $130 billion in the stock market.

Comments to online articles can often be rude and obnoxious rather than polite and helpful to truly foster further understanding and thoughtful discussions. **CRITICAL THINKING QUESTIONS:** Have you ever made rude or demeaning comments on articles or posts online? Have you ever received such comments based on posts or stories you've done? What was your reaction, and how did it make you feel?

The Internet enables audiences around the world to participate in a dialog about global events and issues, bringing individuals separated by thousands of miles and various political and cultural boundaries into direct contact with each other. It is not clear what the net effect of this sea change in communication will be, but it is clear the foundation is potentially being laid for a more connected and engaged global public. Increased connectivity and engagement do not necessarily mean more rational discussion or civilized debate, though, especially as people discover that what they may consider cultural common sense others may consider heresy. Consider the vitriol displayed in many discussion groups, even among people of the same culture but whose opinions differ.

Audiences are increasingly active in their communication with each other and with the creators of mass-communication content, a trend that can decrease corporate power as it increases consumer control. Through **viral marketing**, the online equivalent of word-of-mouth advertising, a popular website, product, or piece of content can rapidly reach millions of online users, all without corporate promotion or advertising dollars. The success of **peer-to-peer (P2P)** file-sharing programs demonstrates how an Internet audience can shift the balance of power from media organizations to consumers, even though those organizations created and provided that content in the first place.

Digital media make it easier than ever for the public to create and distribute media content, whether it is **user-generated content (UGC)** such as an original drawing done via illustration software, an animation or video, or a song sampled and mixed from current hits by famous recording artists. Writing and music have led the way in consumer-created content—especially music, where remixes of previously recorded (and copyrighted) material are common. This is not to say that the average person now has the same ability to produce and create a hit song as a major recording label, for most individuals lack the marketing and promotion resources that a recording label has at its disposal; but the basic capability of producing and distributing at least exists. Media companies have failed to control the channels of media distribution as they once did, and the Internet continues to threaten their business models. This has led to important changes in how consumers view and use content while changing the relationship between media companies and their audiences.

**viral marketing**

Promoting a product, service, or brand online through word of mouth, usually via online discussion groups, chats, and emails.

**peer-to-peer (P2P)**

The basis of file-sharing services, a computer communications model and network whose computers are considered equal peers who can send, store, and receive information equally well.

**user-generated content (UGC)**

Content created by the general public for distribution by digital media.

Creative Commons tries to ensure that content creators retain control of their works and allow it to be used as widely as possible by keeping it in the public domain rather than under copyright restrictions. **CRITICAL THINKING QUESTIONS:** Visit the Creative Commons website and click on the "Find CC-licensed works" link (under the Explore heading). Search for some content of interest, such as "hip hop" via SoundCloud (Music) or ccMixter (Music). Do you think Creative Commons is a good idea, and if so, how are artists supposed to earn money if they do not copyright their material and make it easy for anyone to copy?

**produsers**

Audiences who no longer are simply consumers but also produce content.

Creative Commons, a nonprofit organization, has made a range of "copyleft"—playing on the notion of "copyright"—contracts for content creators that help ensure creative works remain in the public domain. Under the various contracts, creators allow their content to be used by anyone for free but with certain stipulations, such as they must be credited or the content can be used only if it isn't sold. Another common stipulation within the community is that people using the content must allow it to remain free for public use.

## MEDIA AUDIENCE

Traditional mass communication is largely one way, from the sender of a message to the receiver. Relatively large, heterogeneous, and anonymous audiences have relatively few means by which to communicate either with each other on a mass scale or with the creators and publishers. Audiences in the age of convergence can now more easily and quickly communicate with each other and with those who create and publish mass-communication content via social media, email, online forums, and other interactive media. In addition, they can create the content themselves and reach far larger audiences with less expense than was possible with traditional media. They are generally not anonymous because they can be tracked through user names or IP addresses.

Audiences aren't willing to wait for the evening news or the next day's newspaper for developments in a breaking story. They can get their information and entertainment from literally thousands of sources around the world. Audiences are no longer content to sit back and listen in silence to what the media report; they actively seek, relay, and question the most recent information on social media, blogs, instant messaging, and other informal communication channels. There have been cases of employees finding out about looming company layoffs through websites hours before the company officially announced its plans, and military family members learning of the death of a loved one in combat through social media before the military was able to inform the family.

Digital media do not cause people to become active media producers, called "**produsers**" by some media scholars in an attempt to capture how we now use and produce (not just consume) content. Nevertheless, digital media provide people who are so inclined with ready tools to produce media far more cheaply and easily than with analog alternatives. Active audiences have two important implications for media companies: They may compete for the limited time of target audiences, and they may become more critical consumers of mass communication, which is relevant to media literacy, the topic covered in Chapter 2.

As produsers, people learn to become more critical of the media and to raise questions about the quality of the news, information, and entertainment they receive. Interactive media let the public speak to a general audience and directly to traditional media producers, thereby imparting a sense of shared experience, even perhaps community, as people see that others may feel as they do; such as finding a particular advertisement offensive or considering a certain show rather lame. An interactive public is more likely to be an active public, organizing and working together on common problems. Those who have developed trusting relationships through interaction are less likely to perceive themselves as anonymous faces in a crowd or isolated individuals who have no voice.

Risks accompany these changes, however. Actively choosing the media you want to see, hear, or read can narrow the scope of news or entertainment that you

CONVERGENCE CULTURE
# A Star Is Born: PewDiePie and YouTube

Felix Kjellberg (pronounced "shell-berg"), otherwise known as PewDiePie (rhymes with "cutie pie"), is the most subscribed user on YouTube, with over 54 million subscribers as of April 2017 and over 15 billion video views since he started his channel in 2010.

His profanity-laced outbursts and humorous comments as he plays video games have helped propel some indie games to massive popularity in a YouTube version of the Oprah effect.

And although he is nowhere near the size of Oprah's media empire, he did make $15 million in 2016, according to Forbes, thanks in part to his YouTube Red series *Scare PewDiePie* and his book *This Book Loves You*. In 2013, only three years after he started his channel, it was estimated he made $4 million, rising to about $7 million each of the next two years.

PewDiePie's success is an exemplar of an interesting convergence of new media types and genres and old media business models, namely advertising. YouTube gives a percentage of its ad revenue, and with such high viewership numbers PewDiePie can earn six figures on that revenue alone.

What's more, his genre, known as "Let's Play," is relatively simple and easy to produce because it consists entirely of capturing on video a game player as he or she plays a game, commenting along the way. The casual style feels like you are sitting alongside a friend and watching him or her play a game.

People raised on traditional video programming may wonder what is so interesting about watching someone sit and play a video game, but 54 million subscribers apparently think otherwise.

However, the limits of the amateurish, casual media culture that YouTube helps popularize can be seen when someone rises to PewDiePie's stature and gets sponsored by the likes of Disney's Maker Studios, as he did.

In February 2017 the *Wall Street Journal* reported that some of PewDiePie's non-gaming videos contained anti-Semitic remarks and Nazi imagery. Although some other YouTube stars defended PewDiePie's comments as jokes that were taken out of context, Maker Studios nonetheless cut ties with him. PewDiePie later posted a video apologizing for his comments, although he still blamed media coverage for taking his comments out of context.

would otherwise get. The late Michael Dertouzos, former MIT Media Lab director, called the tailoring of news to one's specific interests "The Daily Me." Today it is known also as a filter bubble, and technology often plays a role in tailoring what content we see based on our past online habits. Some scholars worry that this phenomenon could fragment audiences into small groups of like-minded individuals who avoid interacting with other groups and who see and select only news and information that reinforces their beliefs and values. Many have blamed this trend for the polarization of political views in the United States, as seen especially during the last presidential election.

## MEDIA PROFESSION

Obviously, all the changes that convergence has brought to mass communication will also change the way communications professionals do their jobs. Just as digital media absorbed traditional print, video, and audio, divisions between print and electronic journalists, and between advertising and public relations practitioners, will fade. In addition to writing effectively, more newsrooms today expect reporters to use video and audio to tell stories. To better reach and persuade audiences, those in advertising and public relations find themselves increasingly using tools that were previously the sole domain of the other profession.

To take advantage of digital media, new skills have to be learned, and it will be more important than ever not to abandon the fundamental principles and ethics of each profession in the inexorable march toward the digital realm. This is no easy order given how corporate parents can exert pressure to blur the lines between news and entertainment or news and promotion.

Giving the audience a chance to respond to and interact with journalists as well as provide their own news coverage in the form of **citizen journalism** is another important development in journalism today. A mistake in a story can be publicly countered in the discussion section of the story, and then corrected in a revised version. Citizens can provide news content such as raw video or audio, or report on stories of relevance to their locales that big news operations may not deem newsworthy or that may not have the resources to cover.

**citizen journalism**

The gathering and sharing of news and information by public citizens, particularly via mobile and social media, sometimes via traditional media.

## ATTITUDES AND VALUES

Changes in audience interactions and the ability for almost anyone to potentially be a broadcaster have had repercussions for companies. United Airlines suffered a public relations crisis in April 2017 when several passengers on a flight recorded a passenger being forcibly dragged off the plane when he refused to give up his seat. The videos quickly went viral worldwide, sparking others to come forward to share their negative experiences with United.

Because most people on the web do not physically make contact with each other and know one another only through their online interactions and communication, establishing a sense of trust has become crucial. A growing number of reputation systems aid users in this effort, such as votes on Reddit and "karma points" on Slashdot, a popular technology news and discussion website. Managing an online reputation is serious business for companies as well as for individuals. Imagine the potential impact of bad reviews on eBay for someone trying to make a living by selling items on the site. Companies are also vulnerable and can fall prey to disinformation campaigns, which makes monitoring rival blogs and online discussions important.

Reputation and transparency rely on digital relationships founded on trust and respect. Media companies that do not realize this will suffer in the long run. For many, it means a shift in corporate policies or philosophies and a loss of the control they have enjoyed through much of the mass-communications era. Conventional wisdom among some executives is that today employees are more willing to spend company time doing personal things, like shopping online, than they were in the past. But, on the other hand, companies, which also may expect to answer business emails while at home or on vacation, must accept that the blurring of company time and private time is a large-scale trend.

The convergence of digital media has led to confusion over our traditional notions of privacy, both for individuals and for companies. Although privacy laws in a number of cases have clearly been violated, even by traditional standards, often what is acceptable or even legal and what is not is still a source of confusion. A person writing a blog, for instance, may consider it a private journal. So if a potential employer mentions inappropriate postings during a job interview, the candidate may be angered by what she feels is an invasion of her privacy. Similarly, information that always has been public but too cumbersome to retrieve, such as property deeds or police arrests, is now easy to find online. An arrest for a minor incident while in college may still appear online years later with an easy search by name and school, for example, following the person long after the deed has been done.

One component of privacy is alone time, and these moments have become increasingly rare in an age of pervasive media. Maintaining a sense of privacy can be difficult when we are getting barraged with updates from Facebook friends or receiving text messages. Some even argue that digital natives raised on social media have lost the ability to appreciate or even tolerate solitude, once a coveted commodity. Other studies have shown that people who regularly use Facebook are not as happy as those who do not, mostly because we tend to compare what we are doing with what others in our group are doing and feel our activities are not as fun or exciting as what others are doing, a phenomena typically called **FOMO**, or fear of missing out.

Wireless communication between devices, without the need for specific human direction—such as swiping a debit card at a supermarket checkout—makes it easy to establish a profile of a person simply through his electronic transactions over a short period of time. The ability to track consumers with such accuracy, especially on the web and through mobile devices, means that we can personalize our media content; but it also means that companies can create very detailed profiles of us as consumers, even without our express permission, for **behavioral targeting** in their advertising campaigns.

Mass-communication organizations can keep detailed and updated records on their audiences by tracking their paths within their websites through intelligent software agents and programs known as **cookies**. Cookies make it easier for you to visit websites because they "remember" you, so you do not need to log in every time you access the Internet. They also give you personalized content based on your settings and past browsing history. Cookies provide invaluable information for media organizations to better understand an audience's media behaviors, preferences, and habits. Advertisers on websites also add cookies to your computer so they can track your browsing behavior as well. Surveillance is an increasingly powerful tool, as the data collected is sold to other companies and used to estimate advertising rates. However, it raises serious concerns about the erosion of privacy.

So far we have discussed how convergence has been changing the media industries and their business models, the issues communications professionals have faced with the advent of new technologies, the nature of the relationship between media producers and audiences, and legal and ethical matters that have yet to be addressed.

### FOMO

Fear of missing out, or the feeling when we look at friends' Facebook posts that they are doing more exciting things than we are doing and that we are missing important group interactions.

### behavioral targeting

Advertisers tracking individuals' web-browsing behavior to provide ads that closely match the topics of sites visited or searches made.

### cookies

Information that a website puts on a user's local hard drive so that it can recognize when that computer accesses the website again. Cookies also allow for conveniences like password recognition and personalization.

In 2012, the Poughkeepsie (NY) *Journal News* published online an interactive map providing the names and addresses of all registered handgun owners in New York and Rockland counties. Although perfectly legal, the map sparked many debates among people on both sides of the gun rights issue. **CRITICAL THINKING QUESTION:** Is it ethical to make these data so easily and widely available for all? Should media make such personal information available if it helps foster more debate about important topics, regardless of ethical concerns?

## ETHICS IN MEDIA
# Do You Pay More if You Own a Mac?

Web analytics allows people to see much more information about site visitors than traditional media ever could. As an example, even a free service like Google analytics allows you as a site owner to see what page users came from to your site, how long on average they stayed on your site (and even particular pages), what countries they came from, what links they clicked on, what search terms were most commonly used to find your site, what percentage of people viewed your site on mobile devices or computers, and what operating systems they used, such as Apple, PC, or Linux. You can even see what time of day is the most popular for visitors to your site.

This unprecedented level of surveillance has created whole new job categories of professionals based on analyzing and strategizing content around analytics. It has also created more work for communications professionals, as many journalists, for example, now have to track their stories and may adjust their publishing schedule to maximize views—especially if their income depends on how much their stories are shared on social media.

Advertisers demand analytics data in order to better target their advertising, claiming that such data helps them provide more relevant and helpful ads for users (never mind that users may not want ads in the first place).

However, the very same analytics data provided to site owners and advertisers has been used to target different users unequally. In 2012, the *Wall Street Journal* reported that the travel site Orbitz priced hotels differently for PC users compared to Apple users, with Apple users seeing ads for hotel rooms at prices as much as 30 percent more than what PC users saw.

The same principles could be applied to any advertisement, or even website content itself. For example, a Mac user could see an ad for an expensive foreign car, while a PC user may get an ad for a cheaper domestic one. Or a PC user could get a certain restaurant or store discount that a Mac user may not get, or that may not be discounted as much.

Do you think it is ethical for companies to target different audiences with different offers based on the amount of information they can glean from their typical online behavior? What could some of the positive implications be of such targeting? What are some of the negative implications?

---

You have gotten a glimpse of the powerful transformations taking place today in mass communications and the media and will see even more detailed examples in subsequent chapters.

But before we can move forward, we have to take a step back and look at what mass communication itself is and how media scholars theorize it operates. We will then be able to use these foundations to better understand the changes taking place today.

## Mass Communication in the Digital Age

The traditional mass-communication model differs from other forms of communication, such as **interpersonal communication**, which is communication between two or more persons. Interpersonal communication often interacts and intersects with **mass communication**, communication to a large group or groups of people that remain largely unknown to the sender of the message.

### INTERPERSONAL COMMUNICATION

Interpersonal communication is usually interactive, or flowing at least two ways, and tends not to be anonymous. Think of chatting with a friend or a small group.

**interpersonal communication**

Communication between two or more individuals, often in a small group, although it can involve communication between a live speaker and an audience.

**mass communication**

Communication to a large group or groups of people who remain largely unknown to the sender of the message.

Responses are generally immediate, and the speaker or speakers will often adjust their messages based on the responses they receive. Interpersonal communication involves both verbal and nonverbal messages: not just what was said, but how it was said.

These same principles apply to live public speaking, even though this is a one-to-many model, and opportunities for audience feedback will be more limited than in a casual small-group setting. The speaker and the audience can communicate through a variety of nonverbal cues such as facial expressions, physical contact, or body language. If speakers see looks of boredom or audience members yawning, they can adjust their presentation accordingly in an effort to make it more interesting.

Interpersonal communication can also take place through a **medium**, or communication channel, such as the telephone, when texting or talking, or the Internet, when participating in a chat room or on a discussion board, for example. Note how the mediation limits some aspects of interpersonal communication compared to face-to-face interactions. Visual cues are absent either on the telephone or online (unless using a webcam), and meanings can be misconstrued in text messages (even those supplemented with emoticons). The online medium also blurs the line between interpersonal and mass communication, as a private email or text can be forwarded to many other people.

Interpersonal communication takes place between two or more people, is interactive, and can happen face-to-face or through a medium. It can also involve nonverbal cues, such as body language, that can indicate participants' emotions.

**medium**

A communication channel, such as talking on the telephone, instant messaging, or writing back and forth in a chat room.

## MASS COMMUNICATION

Media of mass communication refer to any technological means of communicating between large numbers of people distributed widely over space or time. Ever since Johannes Gutenberg invented the Western world's first mechanical printing press in Germany in 1455, one general model of communication has traditionally characterized mass media, whose central features, as articulated by different theorists, are also outlined in Table 1-1.

According to this framework, media companies create content they believe the audience will want and distribute that content to an audience who has very few ways to provide immediate feedback. This premise has characterized all media of mass communication—books, magazines, newspapers, broadcast television or radio, cable or satellite TV, recorded music, or motion pictures. Digital media, however, have radically changed that model, as we will see throughout this book.

In the traditional mass-communication model, content creators play a fundamental role in society by representing and defining reality (consider the work of journalists or other communication professionals) or by creating fictional works to explain, interpret, or entertain (consider the work of artists, authors, and film auteurs). Authors and artists create stories about issues and events; they write books and articles; they create music or motion pictures; and then they publish, broadcast, or present their creations at set dates or times and in set locations.

Some mass-communications models, such as live television or broadcast radio, are **synchronous media**, which require the audience to be assembled simultaneously for the broadcast, transmission, or event. Others are **asynchronous media**, such as newspapers or magazines, or recorded television or audio programming, for example, which do not require the audience to assemble at any given

**synchronous media**

Media that take place in real time and require the audience to be present during the broadcast or performance, such as live television or radio.

**asynchronous media**

Media that do not require the audience to assemble at a given time, such as printed materials and recorded audio or video.

**TABLE 1-1** Traditional Theories or Models of Analog Media

| THEORY OR MODEL | MAIN FEATURES OR CHARACTERISTICS |
|---|---|
| General Mass Media | 1. Communication flow is largely one-way, from sender or source to receiver or audience.<br>2. Communication is from one or a few to many (i.e., one or a few sources generate and distribute content to large, heterogeneous audiences).<br>3. Communication is anonymous (sources typically do not know their audiences, and audiences do not know the sources, except at a general level).<br>4. Audiences are seen as largely passive recipients of the messages distributed by the media, with little opportunity for feedback and practically no opportunity for immediate feedback or interaction with each other. |
| Shannon and Weaver Transmission Model (see p. 357) | Information source<br>Transmitter<br>Channel<br>Receiver<br>Destination |
| Schramm's Simplified Communication Model (see p. 358) | 1. A source, who encodes<br>2. a message, or signal, which is transmitted (via the media or directly via interpersonal communication) to<br>3. a destination, where the receiver decodes it. |

**time shift**

Recording of an audio or video event for later listening or viewing.

time. With today's digital recording devices, we can easily **time shift** and record a live concert or sporting event so that it can be watched anytime, thereby turning synchronous media into asynchronous media.

## MASS COMMUNICATION AND CONVERGENCE

Digital media and online networks have blurred the line between interpersonal and mass communication. The media companies built on mass-communication models, despite facing many challenges in the digital era, are not disappearing anytime soon, and neither will certain fundamental aspects of mass communication.

What is changing, however, is the interplay between mediated interpersonal communication and mass communication: Interpersonal communication is capable of adopting some characteristics of mass communication, and mass communication is trying to adopt certain characteristics of interpersonal communication in an attempt to remain relevant to audiences. Let's examine some examples.

Email is considered a form of mediated interpersonal communication, yet, as anyone who has had his or her inbox clogged with forwarded jokes from Aunt Gertrude can attest, it can also be broadcast to many recipients, following the one-to-many model typical of mass communication.

**blog**

Short for weblog, a type of website in which a person posts regular journal or diary entries, with the posts arranged chronologically.

Despite their interpersonal tone and scope, some weblogs, or **blogs**, have become very influential among the public or among decision makers, with readership greater than that of many well-established mainstream publications. Blogs may allow immediate feedback or discussion from readers, who often must be registered to post feedback and are therefore not anonymous—thereby weakening two of the linchpins in the definition of mass communication. Yet it is hard to claim that the most popular blogs are not a type of mass communication because of the numbers of audience members reading them and the lack of interaction between the blog author and a respondent.

Twitter also follows a blended mass-communication and mediated interpersonal-communication model, as people broadcast their tweets to thousands or even millions of followers, yet the followers can retweet and interact with each other and their followers in a way that more closely emulates mediated interpersonal communication than it does mass communication.

The fragmented nature of audiences on the web complicates attempts to define a "mass." Some websites have small but dedicated followings, while others have millions of visitors a month, reaching far more people than your typical local newspaper. Yet the local newspaper would traditionally be considered a type of mass communication, unlike an early viral YouTube video such as "Charlie Bit My Finger—Again!," despite over 848 million views ten years after being posted and well over two thousand various remixes and spoofs, including videos of the two brothers several years after the original video.

It is important to remember that much of the interaction and conversation that occurs online does so because of the information and entertainment generated from mass communication. Consider a TV series like *Star Trek*, which ran for only three seasons in the late 1960s but continues to have a thriving fan subculture that consumes—and creates—content about the series and its actors, not to mention the various movies and television-series spin-offs from the original *Star Trek*. Even videos such as "Charlie Bit My Finger," for example, have given rise to a handful of fan clubs on Facebook (including a Mexican one)—but these would generally be much more limited in scope and duration than the fan subculture that has arisen around a series like *Star Trek*. The daily mix of news, information, and entertainment that we consume through mass-communication channels gives us fodder for remixes, blogs, interactions with each other—and reactions to media producers who provide the content.

## Functions of Mass Communication

Defining mass communication was once straightforward. The media were relatively stable and well known. The functions of mass communication in society were also relatively well understood and thoroughly researched. Studies by Harold D. Lasswell, Charles Wright, and others suggest that these functions have tended to fall largely into four broad categories: surveillance, correlation, cultural transmission, and entertainment.[8] These functions can be a useful lens through which to examine various forms of mass communication.

### SURVEILLANCE

In mass communication, **surveillance** refers primarily to the role that journalism plays in providing information about processes, issues, events, and other developments in society. This can include news on the latest military activities, weather alerts, and political scandals. Aspects of advertising and public relations as well as educational communication can also serve surveillance functions.

**surveillance**

Primarily the journalism function of mass communication, which provides information about processes, issues, events, and other developments in society.

Although surveillance is an important function of mass communication, repeated exposure to a story can have negative effects. After you hear about a plane crash, are you more concerned about flying for an upcoming trip?

One weakness in the surveillance function is that an excess of news about disasters, murders, or other unusual events can skew the audience's perception of what is normal in society. Receiving too much information on a particular topic can also promote apathy. Consider how media coverage of shark attacks, for example, can make people believe that there has been an increase in attacks when, in fact, there has not. Excessive coverage of celebrity scandals may seem like trivial examples that lead to audience apathy, but skewed or apathetic responses to coverage of wars or disasters, especially in developing countries, are more significant and problematic.

## CORRELATION

**correlation**

Media interpretation ascribing meaning to issues and events that helps individuals understand their roles within the larger society and culture.

**Correlation** refers to the ways in which media interpret events and issues and ascribe meanings that help individuals understand their roles within the larger society and culture. Journalism, advertising, and public relations all shape public opinion through commentary, criticism, or even targeted marketing campaigns. Polls or surveys allow individuals to learn what others think about an issue and where their views fit within mainstream opinions. People may even shift their views or beliefs subtly to better align themselves with a desirable social group.

By correlating one's views with those of other groups or perceived notions of general public opinion, the media can help maintain social stability, although this function can be taken too far, and the media can thwart social change or block a full range of views from being disseminated to a mass audience. Interpretation can also tend to favor established business or elite interests over disadvantaged or minority groups, increasing the apparent credibility and authority of the dominant culture.

## CULTURAL TRANSMISSION

**Cultural transmission** refers to the transference of the dominant culture, as well as its subcultures, from one generation to the next or to immigrants. This includes socialization, which the media perform by teaching societal rules and depicting standards of behavior. This function is especially important for children but also necessary for recently immigrated adults adjusting to a new culture.

Not all aspects of cultural transmission are viewed favorably. It has been criticized for creating a homogenized culture that promotes mindless consumerism as a means to achieve happiness rather than imparting more humanistic, and ultimately more rewarding, values such as an appreciation of multiculturalism and diversity.

## ENTERTAINMENT

The entertainment function is performed in part by all three of these activities (surveillance, correlation, and cultural transmission) but also involves the generation of content designed specifically and exclusively to entertain. Although some claim that this function helps raise artistic and cultural taste among the general populace, others disagree, arguing that mass media encourage escapism and promote lowbrow entertainment at the expense of high art.

Entertainment can also perpetuate certain stereotypes about various groups, wittingly or unwittingly. These can be especially hard to detect because they are often presented as part and parcel of a story line that makes oversimplified characters seem natural in context. For good and for bad, powerful cultural principles and symbols permeate entertainment, transmitting specific sets of values that can go unquestioned.

> 💬 **cultural transmission**
>
> The process of passing on culturally relevant knowledge, skills, attitudes, and values from person to person or group to group.

Wartime propaganda posters provide windows into how public opinion can be shaped.

**DISCUSSION QUESTIONS:** Consider your own use of social and digital media. What is the source of much of what you discuss with your friends online—does it come from news or politics or primarily entertainment sources such as television, movies, and music? What implications do you think your habits have for notions of the public?

# Television: The Future of Convergence

We started this chapter by looking at the telephone, an example of a communication technology whose role in convergence you may not have considered. We will end by looking briefly at television, particularly at how convergence has shaped television today and how it will affect its future.

We will discuss the invention and development of television in Chapter 5 and focus here on the role convergence has played for this quintessential mass-communication technology. Television's dominance as a mass medium in the latter half of the twentieth century through today means it has been much discussed, debated, and studied. Television has been blamed for everything from a decline in young people reading to a rise in societal violence. Few mass-communications technologies have shown such a striking impact. Despite disagreement about the degree to which television may affect our culture and society, the belief that television has certain detrimental (or beneficial) effects has influenced everything from government regulation to the kinds of commercials and programming we see. The enormous popularity of television makes it a powerful instrument for teaching people culture and social norms—or at least idealized norms.

Television viewing habits changed with the advent of the remote control. Channel-surfing made it easy for people to later name and understand the process of web surfing that occurs on the Internet. Digital video recorders (DVRs) also changed TV viewing habits. The use of **product placement** has grown in response to advertisers' fears that viewers fast-forward through commercials when watching recorded programming. Product placement shows a convergence of normal programming with advertisement content, often not recognized as such.

Over the years, television has been able to adapt to new methods of distributing content. Over-the-air broadcast towers used to be the primary way that people received their television signals; today cable and satellite systems are dominant, with streaming services like Netflix, Hulu, or Amazon Prime quickly ascending in popularity. However, cable television systems are not new. They were first created in 1948 so that viewers in areas where over-the-air signals could not easily reach could get television programming, long before most households had cable systems.

The first transatlantic satellite signal was sent in 1962, when television as a mass medium was still not even fifteen years old.[9] Entertainment, especially movies and sports programming, played a role in encouraging the growth of cable and satellite–cable partnerships in the 1970s. Today, entertainment is a driving force with the growth of streaming services, many of which are increasingly creating original programming to rival that of the big networks and cable companies like HBO.

In 1978, Ted Turner launched WTBS Atlanta as a national **superstation**, a local TV station that reaches a national audience by beaming its programming nationwide via satellite to local cable systems, which then transmit to local subscribers. In 1980, Turner employed the same technological combination to launch the first twenty-four-hour TV news network, the Cable News Network (CNN). Today, many countries use similar systems for their own national broadcasting. In a country like Indonesia, which has hundreds of islands, a cable system between islands is simply not practical. Using satellite to beam programming to local cable operators, who connect viewers in their areas with cable, has proven to be an economical solution.

Television is a major communications industry in its own right. But when it began as a mass medium in the late 1940s, its rapid rise in popularity was seen as a threat by the film industry, which blacklisted actors if they performed on television shows. It took several years for the film industry to realize that television could replace the second- and third-run movie theaters as a source of additional revenues for older films. The specter that the movie industry feared of mass audiences staying home and watching television instead of going out to the movies never materialized; people still went in droves.

Today, the tug-of-war between the movie industry and television for attracting audiences continues, even as some film companies own television channels through the process of consolidation. The latest battles have been taking place in the area of 3D, which used to be seen solely in movie theaters. Not only has 3D viewing technology for movies gotten better, but television screens have rapidly caught up; and now 3D television is also on the market.

**product placement**

A form of advertising in which brand-name goods or services are placed prominently within programming content that is otherwise devoid of advertising, demonstrating the convergence of programming with advertising content.

**superstation**

A local TV station that reaches a national audience by beaming its programming nationwide via satellite to local cable systems.

Perhaps one of the biggest areas of convergence is the melding of the television and the personal computer or mobile device. Television is becoming more interactive, encouraging viewers to do things like vote for their favorite *American Idol* contestants (although still not through the television—they use mobile phones for that). At the same time, a growing number are watching television programming on their PCs, tablets, or smartphones. In the future, it may not matter much whether we think of television as merged with mobile device or mobile device as merged with television; we will simply have a high-definition screen with which we can interact, accessing the web or social media even as we watch our favorite programs.

We see convergence taking place in altered viewing habits, thanks in large part to streaming services. We can watch entire seasons of series, and Netflix-original series are usually released with all episodes available for viewing at once, rather than a weekly scheduled release like broadcast television series. These changes in distribution and availability have led to **binge-watching**, or watching many episodes of a series over several hours.

**binge-watching**

Watching a television series, usually on a streaming service such as Netflix, over several hours at a time.

**DISCUSSION QUESTIONS:** Consider watching the same film on TV, a PC, a tablet, or in a theater. List several ways in which these viewing experiences differ, and identify the relative advantages and disadvantages of each.

## LOOKING BACK AND MOVING FORWARD

This book takes the premise that mass communication as we have known it is fundamentally changing, perhaps to the point where this term is no longer a relevant or accurate description of current communication. Convergence is, broadly speaking, the process where we are seeing these transformations take place on technological, economic, and sociocultural levels. Many of the ramifications of convergence will likely not be realized or fully known for years to come, while others seem to have had immediate and dramatic effects on our media landscape.

What we have today is a fascinating and confusing mixture of mass-communication industries and business models combining with various emerging digital technologies and communications practices that simultaneously threaten and hold great promise for traditional media companies and the communications professions. Issues of consumer privacy, of copyright, and of affordable access to the Internet, among other legal, regulatory, and ethical issues, have yet to be worked out, and the decisions that will be made will have far-reaching consequences for industry, the media, and the general public.

The public may finally have some say in the matter in the new digital media environment. Through communication tools that give the public unprecedented power to share information with each other and to "talk back" to those in power, people are able to connect and organize on any number of issues important to them, affecting policy changes through online and offline means. We have already seen the power of online organizing for various politicians in terms of getting donations and engaging young people to participate in political campaigns. Will the Internet and other digital media flourish and produce a rich montage of diverse voices? Or will the emerging global media system be a homogenous blend of commercial banality where news and entertainment are little more than commodities that sit with equally insipid user-generated content? It is still an open question, but dealing responsibly with issues like these is the moral mandate of mass communication in the digital age. In this book, we hope to give you the tools to do so.

## MEDIA MATTERS  THE NATURE OF "INTERMASS" COMMUNICATION

Even before the Internet era, scholars were asking how mass media and interpersonal communication affected each other.[10] Where is the dividing line between interpersonal and mass communication in your media world? Is the line disappearing?

1. How long have you had a Facebook page?
2. How often do you update or add content to the page, and what prompts you to do so?
3. How would you feel if your professor or a potential employer insisted that you friend them so they can see your page?
4. Are you starting to spend more time on social media sites other than Facebook? Which ones? Why are you changing your usage patterns?

5. Are you typically on the web or social media when you watch TV?
6. Do you often text or chat online with friends while watching the same program?
7. Have you ever uploaded music, videos, or other content to file-sharing sites?

According to World Internet Project research, chances are good that you have participated in many if not most of these activities.[11] This shows that the line between interpersonal and mass communication is a blurry one indeed.

## FURTHER READING

*Revolutions in Communication: Media History from Gutenberg to the Digital Age,* 2nd ed. Bill Kovarik (2015) Bloomsbury Academic.

*The Art of Immersion: How the Digital Generation Is Remaking Hollywood, Madison Avenue, and the Way We Tell Stories.* Frank Rose (2012) W. W. Norton.

*Convergence Culture: Where Old and New Media Collide.* Henry Jenkins (2008) NYU Press.

*The Master Switch: The Rise and Fall of Information Empires.* Tim Wu (2011) Vintage.

*The Coming Convergence: Surprising Ways Diverse Technologies Interact to Shape Our World and Change the Future.* Stanley Schmidt (2008) Prometheus Books.

*Understanding Media Convergence: The State of the Field.* August Grant, Jeffrey Wilkinson (eds.) (2008) Oxford University Press.

*Media Organizations and Convergence: Case Studies of Media Convergence Pioneers* (LEA's Communication Series). Gracie Lawson-Borders (2005) Lawrence Erlbaum Associates.

*Spreadable Media: Creating Value and Meaning in a Networked Culture.* Henry Jenkins, Sam Ford, and Joshua Green (2013) NYU Press.

*The History of the Telephone.* Herbert Casson (2006) Cosimo Classics.

*America Calling: A Social History of the Telephone to 1940.* Claude Fischer (1994) University of California Press.

*The History of Wireless: How Creative Minds Produced Technology for the Masses.* Ira Brodsky (2008) Telescope Books.

*Digital Disconnect: How Capitalism Is Turning the Internet Against Democracy.* Robert W. McChesney (2013) The New Press.

*What Will Be: How the New World of Information Will Change Our Lives.* Michael Dertouzos (1997) HarperEdge.

# Media Literacy in the Digital Age

Fake news became a major issue in the 2016 U.S. presidential campaign and has only grown in its importance and impact since the election. Of course, the notion of fake news is not new: It has been around since at least the nineteenth century. In fact, in 1896 U.S. populist presidential hopeful William Jennings Bryan complained bitterly about the fake news of his day. He said that you simply should not trust the lying media. His words resonant loudly in the twenty-first century.[1]

And it isn't only in the United States that fake news resonates. In countries as far away as China, complaints of fake news have become widespread.[2] In March 2017 the state-run media of the People's Republic of China declared that reports of torture against political opponents were fabrications. One government tweet claimed such accusations were "FAKE NEWS," and another said they were "prejudice-based." An article in the *People's Daily* claimed the criticisms were nothing but "cleverly orchestrated lies."

Knowing what news and information to trust has become a major challenge as political leaders offer "alternative facts" and question virtually every established source of once-recognized reliable sources, from the FBI to CNN.[3] In an era in which no source of information seems sacred, the notion of media literacy has never been more vital. Being able to evaluate news and information quickly, confidently, and judiciously is a skill of critical importance to both the average citizen and the media professional.

News flows via the Internet at breakneck speed and reaches the public in interactive form. Each person must decide what to believe in a blizzard swirling with news and information. Moreover, each citizen can make choices about what information to "like" or "share" online with friends, family, or followers. The impact of such decisions may be far-reaching and might play a key role in a wide variety of areas—from elections to the marketplace.

News and information, whether in digital or analog form, bear certain qualities and characteristics. The grammar of the media can offer important clues about what information is credible, what is of dubious value, what is likely propaganda

**LEARNING OBJECTIVES**

>> Define media literacy.

>> Explain how mediated and nonmediated communication differ.

>> Define the role of semiotics and framing in influencing our understanding of the world and media content.

>> Define media grammar and describe its various aspects in different media.

>> Explain how commercial forces influence media organizations and content.

>> Define media bias and its effects on media content.

>> Use basic media-literacy skills to improve your critical thinking when consuming media content.

meant to deceive, and what is offered as satire and humor in an otherwise sometimes bleak media arena.

Comparing the varying perspectives on fake news across the centuries and the continents raises interesting questions about the role of media in our increasingly global society. Have the media gradually helped change public attitudes about the nature of news and information? As political leaders increasingly decry what they see as fake news, has public trust in any source of information eroded?

Also, a media outlet itself may influence the acceptance of stories as truthful or false. If a piece of news bursts into public view via Twitter instead of a mainstream news source such as the *New York Times*, do you think public reaction will be any different?

We live in a media society. Mass media surround and influence our world in a variety of ways. They entertain us, they inform us, and they sell us everything from household products to political candidates. Although we often tend to study media and mass communications as something separate from our culture, society, and daily lives, the fact is that media are just as real as the "real world."

Media are pervasive in modern life, making it more important than ever to understand how their messages may influence us. We must look critically at all media we encounter: We need to understand how media organizations work as businesses, how they fit into other aspects of society, and how they can influence culture and manipulate public opinion.

In this chapter, we explain some basic principles of media literacy in both nondigital and digital media while teaching you to analyze critically the media messages you encounter.

> **DISCUSSION QUESTIONS:** Compare news articles about the size of the crowd at President Trump's inauguration. Look at how the *Huffington Post* characterized the crowd size.[4] What differences do you see in how the stories were depicted, and what effect do you think such framing had on public opinion about President Trump and his popularity as reflected in the size of the inaugural crowd?

## Education and Media

In school, we learn to read, write, and do arithmetic. We learn about history, other cultures, literature, science, and politics. We learn athletic skills and teamwork; we can even learn about art, mechanics, computer programming, and cooking.

But we also learn much from our daily and extensive interactions with media content—some may even argue that we learn more of practical value from daily exposure to media than to class content during a typical school day. The common component of the four functions of mass communication mentioned in the previous chapter—surveillance, correlation, cultural transmission, and entertainment—is that they essentially educate and inform us.

This raises a significant question: If media are so pervasive in our lives, why aren't we studying them in the same way that we study geography or biology, for example? Why can we take a class in high school on how to dismantle a car engine but not one that teaches us how to deconstruct our modern systems of media and mass communications?

The question highlights two interesting and related issues. First, it shows that education, like media, is not something separate from our lives. We are learning all the time, even when not in a formal academic setting such as a classroom or when doing homework. Second, given that we are learning all the time through our interactions with each other and with media content, we must strive to ensure that what we are learning is accurate and useful. This requires skills to examine where that learning is coming from and how it may be affecting our thought processes.

Educators have recognized a growing need to teach media-literacy skills to school-age children, starting as young as kindergarten or elementary school and continuing to high school graduation. Some countries, such as Canada and Australia, have taken the lead in media-literacy education, while the United States generally lags behind. This is changing, however, and a growing number of states, such as New Jersey, have implemented statewide media-literacy guidelines for K–12 schools.

## What Is Media Literacy?

Being able to read a book, navigate a website or post a tweet, and recognize that a background music change signals a scary part of a movie are all types of media literacy. Some fall under what we would consider the traditional meaning of the term "literacy," and others can be classified as visual literacy or computer literacy. Media literacy encompasses all these skills and many more, and the various approaches to media education differ to some degree on what exactly media-literacy education should entail.

**Media literacy** can be defined as the process of critically analyzing media content by considering its particular presentation, its underlying political or social messages, and its media ownership or regulation that may affect the type of content we receive. Some approaches to media education emphasize media-creation skills as a way to examine our media critically, through either creative media projects or alternative media production such as recreating a popular commercial from a feminist perspective.

Developing media literacy is an ongoing process, not simply a goal. Even though you can never attain perfection, it is always possible to improve your media literacy and thus become a wiser media user. The importance of media in contemporary society makes it imperative that audience members think critically about media content to better control their actions and not be controlled by media messages. Learning new skills in creating media, such as taking courses on graphic design or video production, can help further your media literacy.

Media-literacy scholar W. James Potter talks about building "knowledge structures," ways to visualize developing one's level of knowledge on a given topic or topics.[5] If, for example, you have a basic understanding of the history of the World Wide Web, and someone claims to have been on Facebook since 2001, you can be confident that he or she is incorrect: Facebook was not created until 2004 (and then only for Harvard students).

Still, media literacy entails more than simply remembering historical facts. Media consumers should always question what they see, hear, or otherwise experience when receiving or interacting with mediated communication. Is a news story

💬 **media literacy**
_____

The process of interacting with and critically analyzing media content by considering its particular presentation, its underlying political or social messages, and its ownership or regulation issues that may affect what is presented and in what form.

Learning media-literacy skills has become even more important for students today. At campuses around the nation, professors like Melissa Zimdars at Merrimack College are addressing media literacy issues and skills head-on. When Zimdars started keeping a list of popular but unreliable news sites and then made her list public, she received a lot of attention—some praise and some criticism. Why do you think some readers might be critical of Zimdars's list?

biased? Why is it even news? Does a popular television show or video game encourage gender or racial stereotypes or antisocial behavior? What is an advertiser really trying to sell and to whom? These are just a sample of the kinds of questions critical media consumers should ask.

It is important to develop knowledge not just about the media but also about the larger social, political, and economic forces that influence media content, media production, and communication technologies in general. To that end, we must first step back and consider what a medium is. Then we will look at some of the concerns people have had over the years about the effects that media may or may not have on us.

## What Makes Mediated Communication Different?

An enduring and fundamental concern about the media is that what we see and hear through mediated communication—the signs, symbols, and words from books, cinema, radio television, and various digital platforms including social networking media—can somehow affect us in ways that nonmediated communication does not. This assumption has led to a large body of research on media effects, which we discuss in more detail in Chapter 13.

Some theoretical frameworks offer explanations of how we may make sense of the world through media and how the media messages we receive seem somehow natural.

### SEMIOTICS

**semiotics**

The study of signs and symbols.

**Semiotics**, the study of signs and symbols, goes back in some form to Plato and Aristotle. Contemporary semiotics has been greatly influenced by Ferdinand de Saussure, the father of linguistics, and his notion of signs as having dual properties. These properties are the signifier, or the form; and the signified, or what the form represents (some semioticians propose a third component, an interpretant, between these two). For example, an image of a rose, the signifier, may signify any number of things, or signifieds, depending on the context (see Figure 2-1). An image of a rose on a Valentine's Day card may mean one thing, whereas a rose tattoo with blood-dipped thorns on the arm of a biker may mean something else entirely.

Context plays a major role in the audience's understanding of the signified, even when the signifier remains the same. The power of signs to affect our thinking should not be underestimated. René Magritte's famous painting of a pipe that also says "This is not a pipe" illustrates how we typically take the sign as reality. Most people, when shown his painting and asked what it is, will reply, "A pipe." But Magritte is absolutely correct: His picture of a pipe is not actually a pipe—it is simply a picture of a pipe.

We must also remember that in semiotics, "sign" does not simply refer to visual images but to words as well. Words could be considered a more complex form of sign, for we have to learn that certain sounds carry particular meanings (which are entirely arbitrary). There is no logical reason that the color red is called "red" in English, "rojo" in Spanish, and "aka" in Japanese; all of these are simply linguistic conventions for those particular languages.

Rene Magritte's famous "This is not a pipe" picture reminds us how we mistakenly understand the representation of something as the thing itself.

**FIGURE 2-1** Semiotic Signifier and Signified

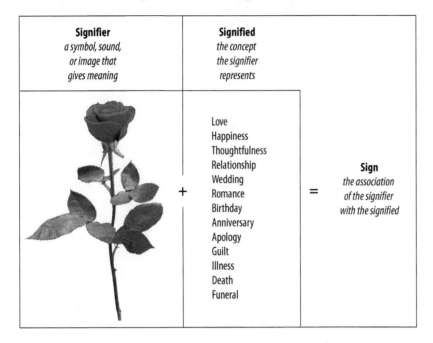

| **Signifier**<br>*a symbol, sound,*<br>*or image that*<br>*gives meaning* | **Signified**<br>*the concept*<br>*the signifier*<br>*represents* | |
|---|---|---|
| | Love<br>Happiness<br>Thoughtfulness<br>Relationship<br>Wedding<br>Romance<br>Birthday<br>Anniversary<br>Apology<br>Guilt<br>Illness<br>Death<br>Funeral | **Sign**<br>*the association*<br>*of the signifier*<br>*with the signified* |

When Gertrude Stein said, "A rose is a rose is a rose," she was highlighting the semiotic principle that we subconsciously associate items, such as a rose, with imagery and emotions. A rose (the signifier) can mean many different things (the signified), depending on the context. Examining this relationship (the sign) deepens our understanding of the ways we generate meaning when we communicate.

Although this point may seem rather obvious, another semiotic insight is not quite so evident. Once we learn what certain sounds mean (or what certain visual images mean), we take what we have learned as natural and accept it largely without question. This fact makes the creation and use of signs extremely powerful because it not only influences our thinking but even directs certain behaviors. Think of what you do without question, for example, whenever you are driving and come to a stop sign.

Similarly, an indexical sign is visual but signifies something else to which it is not actually related except by association. Consider the image of a floppy disk in most software programs that indicates the "save file" function. Most computers in use today do not even have floppy-disk drives, yet we understand what the image has come to represent.

Some scholars argue that semiotics is the heart of communication. Noted semiotician and novelist Umberto Eco, in his book *A Theory of Semiotics*, asserts, "Every act of communication to or between human beings—or any other intelligent biological or mechanical apparatus—presupposes a signification system as its necessary condition." In other words, without a common understanding of what signs mean, whether they are visual or lingual, we would not be able to communicate.

Some knowledge of semiotics is required for a deeper understanding of the processes of communication and the production of meaning among people and in cultures. It is also especially important for advertising professionals who seek insights into how target audiences may receive various ad and branding campaigns.

## FRAMING

🗩 **framing**

The presentation and communication of a message in a particular way that influences our perception of it.

*POLITICS*

*Trump, in Optimistic Address, Asks Congress to End 'Trivial Fights'*

### BREITBART NEWS DAILY: TRUMP'S TRIUMPHANT ADDRESS

*The New York Times* and *Breitbart News* quite differently frame their coverage of President Donald Trump's first address to a Joint Session of Congress on February 28, 2017. The *Times*, a mainstream news source, describes the address in more reserved tones, calling it "optimistic," adding that the president told the members of Congress it is time to end "trivial fights." Meanwhile, *Breitbart*, a conservative news source, describes Trump's speech as "triumphant."

All forms of mass communication, including news, employ **framing**, which works in much the same manner as signs in semiotics. It relies on the notion that we classify, organize, and interpret things into certain schema, or frameworks, to simplify the complex. We have to do this just to get through the day; if we carefully considered and analyzed every message we received, we would never be able to leave the house in the morning. Instead, we take mental shortcuts with much of what we encounter, letting some things go unexamined as we carry on with our lives.

Frames act much like signs and symbols in semiotics: Once accepted, they appear natural and go largely unquestioned. They also shape our perceptions of people, places, issues, and events. Two words—"rights" versus "benefits"—provide a simple example of framing. If an Iraq War veteran is lobbying the government to obtain better health care and services for injuries, demanding veterans' rights has a different connotation than asking for veterans' benefits. The term "benefits" suggests something extra, a privilege perhaps not available to other people and therefore unequal or unfair. Arguing for veterans' rights, on the other hand, suggests something fundamental that is being withheld.

Framing may sound simply like spin, but it is not. We all frame our world, and good communicators know how to frame debates in ways that favor their views and disadvantage those of opponents. A persuasive communicator who wins the framing battle also likely wins that particular debate. Pollster and political communications consultant Frank Luntz helps conservative politicians reframe words to persuade others. See Table 2-1 for examples.

Similarly, George Lakoff, UC Berkeley professor of linguistics and cognitive science, discusses liberal framing, often chastising Democrats for failing to employ persuasive depictions of controversial issues such as health care. See Table 2-2 for examples of liberal reframing. Note how some of these have successfully become the dominant term for the issue, just as some terms have for conservative frames.

Framing is of great consequence in today's world because of the ubiquity of mass-communication media. It is easy to see how this media coverage can shape our perceptions of

Through framing, the media tell us how to think about an issue or topic. For example, one news outlet might frame a story about funding for Planned Parenthood as a matter of women's reproductive rights, while another might frame it in the context of abortion.

**TABLE 2-1** Reframing Political Issues for Conservatives

| NEVER SAY | INSTEAD SAY |
|---|---|
| Tax cuts | Tax relief |
| Inheritance tax | Death tax |
| Undocumented workers/aliens | Illegal immigrants |
| Drilling for oil | Exploring for energy |

Source: Frank Luntz, *Words That Work: It's Not What You Say, It's What People Hear*

**TABLE 2-2** Reframing Political Issues for Liberals

| ISSUE OR CAUSE | DISCUSSED AS |
|---|---|
| Tax subsidies | Corporate welfare (Ralph Nader) |
| Gay marriage | Same-sex marriage |
| Tax increases for the wealthy | Paying a fair share |
| Abortion debate | Pro-choice or women's rights |

the world, especially when "framed" conversations are intensified by the **echo effect**, a phenomenon that occurs when people surround themselves with online voices that echo their own, reinforcing their views and the belief that those opinions are in the majority when, in fact, they may not be. But, as we will see, concerns about media effects are not new.

**echo effect**

A phenomenon that occurs when people surround themselves with online voices that echo their own, reinforcing their views and the belief that those opinions are in the majority when, in fact, they may not be.

## Early Concerns of Media Effects

Over the last century, public concern has arisen about the possible effects of each new medium of mass communication as it has emerged. Questions have been asked about each medium's impact on culture, political processes, children's values and behaviors, and the like. In the 1920s, much of the public became worried about the depiction of sex, violence, and lawlessness in film. In recent years, questions have proliferated about how the Internet and video games may influence us, even perhaps altering how we think.

Such anxieties have a long history. In the 1800s, critics warned that newspapers caused juvenile crime. Moralists believed that the flow of sensational news stories about crime and vice would lead people to imitate such immoral behavior. In 1888, *Punch* magazine attributed Jack the Ripper's crimes committed in Whitechapel, a rough inner-city district of London, to "highly coloured pictorial advertisements."

Alarm about the effects of media on children has even deeper roots. We know that in ancient Greece, philosophers Socrates and Plato worried about the influence of literacy on children. Plato was especially apprehensive about the morally corrupting resonance of poetry, particularly allegorical tales such as Homer's *Battles of the Gods*, which he sought to ban.[6] In 360 BCE, Plato offered this reasoning:

> Children cannot distinguish between what is allegory and what isn't, and opinions formed at that age are usually difficult to eradicate or change; it is therefore of the utmost importance that the first stories they hear shall aim at producing the right moral effect.

> *HE REPUBLIC*

It is hard today to appreciate the profound effect writing once had on society. No longer was a good memory prized as it was in a nonliterate oral culture, because memorization was not needed to store information. The form of storytelling changed with writing because repetitive phrases were no longer needed as memory prompts for storytellers, and the rhythm and cadences of what was written differed from what had been spoken.

Moreover, storytellers could lose control of their words in written form. Someone could take a person's words and twist their meaning, with no chance for an immediate response or perhaps any response at all. In fact, the author of a work had no way of knowing who might read it or when. Greek children sneaking off with a scroll of poetry to read in secret may seem comical; but in a fundamental sense, this is no different from kids today sneaking into an R-rated movie in the multiplex or surreptitiously removing the parental controls on the cable TV service or computer.

Plato's issues with writing as a new medium relate to its particular media grammar, knowledge of which is integral to the development of media literacy.

## Media Grammar

**media grammar**

The underlying rules, structures, and patterns by which a medium presents itself and is used and understood by the audience.

First, a critical consumer of media messages must understand **media grammar**, the underlying rules, structures, and patterns by which a medium presents itself and is used and understood by the audience. Each medium of mass communication presents its messages uniquely. With media familiar through widespread use or exposure, we do not often think about the extent to which media grammar affects our perceptions—what we see and how we see it. In many respects, it becomes background in much the same way that semiotic signs become natural to us. Nevertheless, media grammar can have profound implications for our understanding of media content. We become more aware of it when we encounter a new medium whose rules we do not yet know.

Here, we will look briefly at the main forms of media, the basics of their particular grammar, and their potential effects on our perceptions and expectations.

Even without knowing the language, we can often recognize what kind of foreign newspaper we are viewing simply from the look of the publication. **CRITICAL THINKING QUESTION:** What visual aspects of the newspaper help us identify its type of publication and its type of target audience?

### PRINT MEDIA

Print media, partly due to their long history compared to other types of mass communication, have developed a very sophisticated media grammar. Everything about a printed book—its physical dimensions, the artwork on its jacket, the size and style of the typeface, whether it is hardcover or paperback, whether it contains pictures or not—conveys important messages to the potential buyer beyond the actual content. Within a book itself, several aspects of media grammar have evolved over the years. Spacing between words to aid reading comprehension is an early example, as are page numbering, tables of contents, indexes, and chapter headings. Many of these conventions we now take for granted actually took years to become widely adopted and standard in books.

Newspapers have their own types of media grammar that have also evolved over time and that continue to change. An obvious example is the number of color photos and graphics in newspapers today compared to forty years ago. Because space is limited in a newspaper, more graphics means less room for text. Many media critics and journalists have complained that this packaging of news into relatively short, easy-to-read units accompanied by splashy visuals does readers a disservice by not providing them with the necessary depth of information. Proponents of the trend argue that to compete with television and other visual media for audience attention, newspapers must present news in formats that accommodate readers' busy lifestyles.

Most newspapers are organized into sections, such as sports, business, and local news. Not only do these help organize information so that readers can quickly find stories that interest them, but they also create parameters for what types of stories to expect. Sections also help define where certain advertisers prefer to appear in the paper, showing how media grammar can intersect with commercial interests.

Magazines use sophisticated graphic and design techniques, even more so than newspapers, and feature more long-form writing, often with just one or two articles per page and multipage pieces. Advertising often takes up a full page, and in some magazines it is hard to tell immediately if something is an ad rather than graphics at the beginning of a feature. Magazines combine certain elements of books and newspapers in their media grammar. Because of their length, they usually have a table of contents (many also have an advertiser index) that helps readers rapidly access specific articles. Like newspapers, magazines are often divided into subject-related sections within their topic areas.

Given that the grammar for print media developed over hundreds of years, we have adapted surprisingly quickly to the rise of electronic media, especially audio and, later, video.

## RADIO AND RECORDED MUSIC

Radio and recorded music have their own grammar, one based only on sound. Radio uses a combination of audio techniques to achieve different ends. These include volume changes, multiple audio tracks, **actualities** (i.e., edited audio clips from interviews with people), sound effects, and **voice-overs**, all of which can be used to convey information, capture attention, or evoke a mood or scene.

Recorded music typically conforms to particular stylistic conventions, especially regarding length (less than five minutes a song) and music format. Popular music genres, such as hip-hop, rock, and country, have certain rhythms, lyrical styles, and sounds that make them clearly distinguishable. This underlying media grammar of specific categories or genres makes it easier to market and promote artists. Once again, we see how media grammar can interact with the economic interests of the media. Radio stations brand themselves by the genres they generally play, making it easier for audiences to pick stations that play music they like.

**actualities**

Edited audio clips from interviews with people.

**voice-over**

An unseen announcer or narrator talking while other activity takes place, either on radio or during a television scene.

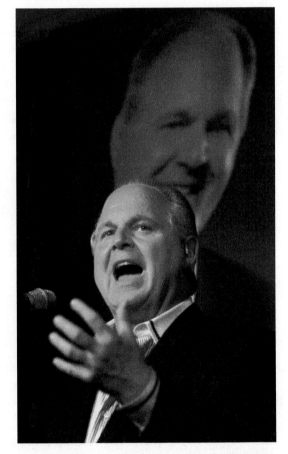

Rush Limbaugh is a conservative commentator, considered the father of today's politically oriented talk show format.

Still, putting music into genres such as this has its drawbacks. Someone with a sound or style that does not readily conform to a well-established genre may find it harder to get airplay because radio stations are reluctant to play something that does not fit nicely into their established formats. An artist may also find it difficult to get a recording contract in the first place, for a recording label will not want to sign someone it believes radios will not want to promote.

Even the apparently chaotic talk radio has a well-defined media grammar. It is one of the few traditional mass-communication formats to include frequent interaction between media producers or hosts and the audience. Despite its highly interactive nature, however, those who call in are obviously in a subordinate position, as they do not control how long they speak and can even be disconnected at any time.

Although radio developed years before television became a mass medium, and some of the earliest television shows were taken directly from popular radio programs, media producers and audiences had already developed a fairly complex visual grammar, thanks in large part to the popularity of movies.

## FILM AND TELEVISION

Film and television have much shorter histories than print, but they have developed an intricate media grammar based on editing, camera angles, lighting, movement, and sound.

In the early history of film, for example, most movies were only a few minutes long and either simply recorded daily activities or essentially filmed short stage plays. Filmmakers started producing more sophisticated story lines for their short films and introduced a technique unique to film at the time—crosscut scenes. By crosscutting different scenes to simulate events happening simultaneously in two different locations (think of the classic scenes of a train heading down the tracks and a woman tied to the tracks by the villain), filmmakers were able to tell much more complex and dramatic stories. Further, increasing the speed between crosscut scenes increased dramatic tension.

With many more such tools at their disposal, today's filmmakers are able to convey a lot of information, all through visual or audio techniques. Think of how we respond to background music and strong shadows in horror movies, or how we understand a dream sequence or flashback, or how we visually distinguish good characters from bad even before the plot or dialog has revealed their true natures.

The media grammar of television fiction employs many of the same techniques seen in movies, although television production budgets are, of course, much smaller than movie budgets. Consider the media grammar of an average sitcom—it is usually shot on a set, with perhaps fewer than half a dozen locations (almost always indoors), and the actors come and go as if on a stage. The camera is usually stationary, although multiple camera angles are used; and punchlines are reinforced by

In what has been dubbed geek-chic TV, *The Big Bang Theory*, the most popular comedy since *Friends*, follows the exploits of another group of friends, most of whom are nerdy scientists. This multi-cam sitcom prompts mirthful responses from its devoted and enormous TV audience with a prominent laugh track. **CRITICAL THINKING QUESTION:** With closed captions instead of volume on, watch an episode of your favorite sitcom that has a laugh track. Do you chuckle as readily without the auditory cues?

a **laugh track**, which in some sitcoms can be timed with almost clockwork precision (even if the line isn't particularly funny).

Other types of television shows—such as game shows, soap operas, talk shows, and news—have their own media grammars. Television news, especially, has borrowed some elements of online media grammar—which had originally borrowed heavily from television for graphical user interfaces such as windows and digital video. Examples include multiple windows on the television screen showing different kinds of information and scrolling news tickers across the bottom of the screen giving updates.

> **DISCUSSION QUESTIONS:** Consider the media grammar of a popular film, focusing especially on how camera angles give the audience cues as to what to think and feel about the characters. Identify as many different camera techniques and their possible meanings as you can and compare with other students' interpretations.

## DIGITAL-MEDIA GRAMMAR

We may be thoroughly familiar and comfortable with the Internet and social media, but many people throughout the world have limited or no contact with the online realm, whose grammar is still developing. The web of 2004 bears little resemblance to the web today, and the web will look even more different ten years from now.

Even with constant changes in the web, certain elements of media grammar have been established. **Hypertext**, for example, is generally either underlined or otherwise set apart typographically or graphically from nonlinked text. More and more web designers are following an unwritten rule to include a website logo in the upper-left corner of the screen linked to the website's home page. Icons in the form of buttons, badges, and other symbols create a visual, interactive language that lets us interact easily with the content and inform others on our social networks what we are reading or doing. Other examples include more or less standardized icons for functions such as printing, opening a document, playing a video, emailing a document, and zooming in or out.

The media grammar of digital media evolves with our communication devices. Today, we think nothing of swiping across the screen on our mobile phone to move to a new window or pinching the screen to zoom out. These kinds of touch-screen interfaces, in turn, affect the design and features of websites, further changing the look and feel of the web.

The digital media grammar has adopted freely from traditional media forms that it has absorbed, but it has also continued to innovate and create new ways for us to interact with the media. For example, the shift from a point-and-click interaction with a mouse to touch-screen swipes and "pinches" to manipulate the content helps make us aware that there is nothing

> **laugh track**
>
> A television sitcom device that generates prerecorded laughter timed to coincide with punchlines of jokes.

> **hypertext**
>
> Text online linked by HTML coding to another web page or website or to a different part of the same web page.

Many websites share certain conventions that users have come to expect, such as a link in the upper-left corner back to the home page. Of increasing importance as well is the grammar of various mobile and social networking media. The compactness of a 140-word tweet, the visual dynamics of a ten-second video on Snapchat, or the social capital of liking someone or something on Facebook all shape our perceptions of reality.

natural about how we use media today. The same principle applies to how the evolution of our current media system operates and how it has evolved, even though we are often so embedded in that system that it is hard to step outside of it and examine it critically.

## Implications of Commercial Media

Even in open and democratic societies with a free press, economic factors and corporate decisions often influence what is and is not covered in the news and what kind of entertainment is created for the general public. Rarely do typical media consumers think of the commercial factors that shape the content they see every

### MEDIA PIONEERS
# Marshall McLuhan

International cultural icon and provocative media prophet Marshall McLuhan is known today less for a prolific body of writing than for a couple of prescient precepts so oft repeated they now border on the cliché. Yet the scholar who coined aphorisms as familiar as "the global village" and "the medium is the message" leaves a colorful pioneering legacy as a public intellectual few academics can claim.

"Academic" was nonetheless a profession the twenty-year-old undergraduate expressly rejected in 1930s Western Canada. As Terence Gordon explains, "He was learning *in spite of his professors* (emphasis in original), but he would become a professor of English in spite of himself."[7] After receiving a BA from the University of Manitoba, McLuhan went on to Cambridge University, where he finished another BA (1936), required to proceed to an MA (1939) and a PhD (1942). Following a period of agnosticism in his youth, McLuhan became a devout Roman Catholic (a conversion his Baptist mother had discouraged); and from 1946 until experiencing a stroke in 1979, he taught at St. Michael's College at the University of Toronto.

With spectacular sales of *Understanding Media: The Extensions of Man* (1964) came pop-culture fame, a degree of mainstream recognition arguably unprecedented for a North American academic. During the cultural revolution of the sixties and seventies, McLuhan counted iconic figures as diverse as then Canadian prime minister Pierre Trudeau and hippie guru Timothy Leary among those he influenced. Marshall advised Pierre on television appearances and allegedly inspired Tim's buzz phrase "turn on, tune in, drop out."[8] "Whatcha doin', Marshall McLuhan?" was a recurring line on *Laugh-In*, a popular TV comedy of the era. In 1969, *Playboy* made a serious attempt to answer such a question in a lengthy interview with McLuhan at home in the Toronto suburbs where he lived with his wife and several children. Woody Allen, in his 1977 tour de force *Annie Hall*, even cast McLuhan as himself in a cameo scene satirizing a pedantic and pretentious media professor.

McLuhan, however, was not simply famous for being famous. A rare visionary, he foresaw in the sixties, long before the Internet, a global village created by the movement from print to electronic media. And one of his most significant and enduring contributions to the yet undefined area of media literacy was a directive to look beyond the superficial content of the message and consider how the intrinsic, various, and complex effects of the medium—another message in itself—affect our perceptions.

In spite of, or perhaps because of, his arresting pronouncements and his celebrity status, the work of the Canadian media theorist has been denounced by some for dilettantism, cryptic rhetoric, and empirically unsubstantiated claims that unabashedly baffle, among other perceived flaws. McLuhan, characterizing his academic inquiries as "probes," remained apparently unfazed by critics, even wryly professing to share some of their confusion: "I don't pretend to understand it. After all, my stuff is very difficult."[9]

day, forces that affect everything from what types of entertainment shows are produced to what kind of news is reported.

These activities happen at the local, national, and international levels. At the local level, reducing the number of reporters at a news organization to save money can result in a noticeable drop in local coverage, such as coverage of area schools. The newspaper company may save money, but the public is poorer for the lessened coverage of local issues. A company that advertises heavily in a local newspaper may gain undue influence in the paper's decision as to whether to publish articles critical of it by threatening to withdraw its advertising. Or a newspaper publisher with other business interests in tourism or real estate, for example, may influence coverage by discouraging or even forbidding reports on certain crimes that may hurt these commercial ventures.

Such manipulation of content is not confined to small-town media outlets. In 1998, HarperCollins, a subsidiary of Rupert Murdoch's News Corporation, cancelled a book by Chris Patten, former British governor of Hong Kong. *East and West* was reportedly highly critical of China's policies, and Murdoch at the time was courting China to accept Murdoch's Star TV satellite and cable programs. Similarly, a few years prior, he removed the BBC from Star TV when Chinese leaders expressed displeasure at the BBC's reports on the killings in Tiananmen Square in June 1989. More recently, accusations swirled about Murdoch's undue influence on the 2013 elections in his native Australia, where he controls 70 percent of the capital city news circulation. The publishing mogul was allegedly using his newspaper headlines and even front pages to promote his candidate and party of choice.[10]

These incidents are not meant to illustrate that Rupert Murdoch is particularly greedy or selfish; similar stories of corporate decisions influencing what we see or do not see can be told about all of the major media corporations and will be covered in more detail throughout the book, especially Chapter 11 on media ethics.

**DISCUSSION QUESTIONS:** Would you be willing to pay an annual television licensing fee if television networks and cable companies promised to show fewer commercials? If so, how much would you be willing to pay? Would you pay more to see no commercials?

## COMMERCIAL-MEDIA DEBATE

Media scholar Robert McChesney has written several books that reveal how corporate media have adversely affected the quality of communications content we receive and how media companies have lobbied the government to further their own corporate interests at the expense of the public interest. He claims that today's corporate media giants actually harm our democracy and political processes in a number of ways. These range from poor news coverage that does not challenge the status quo (especially when it comes to media companies' own business investments) to banal entertainment that dulls our senses and incessant advertising that implies happiness is found through consumerism—although, as we discuss later, most media outlets depend on that very advertising to exist.

According to McChesney, the commercial nature of mass communications underlies all mass media. And all would agree, regardless of political ideology, that

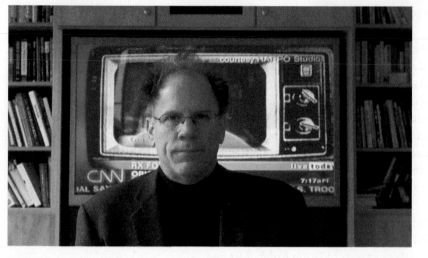

Media scholar Robert McChesney founded Free Press to promote media reform and to weaken the power of corporate media giants.

it takes money to run a media organization. The question becomes one of where the money comes from—the commercial marketplace or public sources of funding.

Arguably, media companies are businesses just like any other; and a business that fails to turn a profit will fail to do right by its private owners or shareholders if it is publicly traded. In recent history, media businesses have been among the most profitable of any industry, with annual profit margins typically around 20 percent.

On the other hand, critics of our corporate media system argue that media companies are not like other companies, that their "products"—the signs and symbols that shape our culture and views of the world through the news and entertainment we consume—influence our thinking and behavior considerably more than other types of products. Therefore, media companies should be publicly funded so that they are not as beholden to the marketplace and the influence of market logic on media content.

Proponents of commercial media identify the profit motive as a key incentive for media companies to produce quality content that people will want to watch or read. The Disney Company, for example, is among the most profitable of major publicly owned media companies in the United States. And it is recognized for its quality entertainment products, including award-winning motion pictures, recorded music, and television (it owns the ABC television network and ESPN, the sports channel on television).

Critics claim, however, that financial pressures can lead media companies, especially publicly traded companies, to focus on the short term with decisions such as cutting costs or laying off staff, actions that may increase near-term profits but decrease the quality of a product such as news coverage. These profits may be immediate but not sustainable.

Critics also assert that consumers actually have fewer media content choices than we believe, thanks in large part to the concentration of media ownership.

**DISCUSSION QUESTIONS:** Imagine a media system that is entirely publicly funded and government run. What problems might arise with such a system, and how might programming be different?

## CONCENTRATION OF MEDIA OWNERSHIP

Economies of scale provide financial incentives for most companies. Strictly speaking, "economy of scale" refers to the decrease in unit manufacturing cost that results from mass production. Media enterprises can reduce costs and increase profit by becoming larger and reaching a larger market with their content. Of course, just getting bigger doesn't necessarily translate into greater economies of scale, but it is the

## INTERNATIONAL PERSPECTIVES
# Mobile Telephony in the Developing World

Despite the prevalence of the Internet and personal computers in the United States and other industrialized countries in Europe, South America, and the Asia-Pacific region, an even stronger competitor to the Internet and PC has emerged in the developing world—the mobile phone.

Mobile telephony can hold several advantages over the Internet in many developing countries. First, poor telecommunications infrastructures in these countries often make landline calls expensive and sporadic at best for those who have phones. Without adequate phone lines, let alone consistent electric power, it is nearly impossible to depend on a PC or regular Internet service. Many of these countries do not have cable television

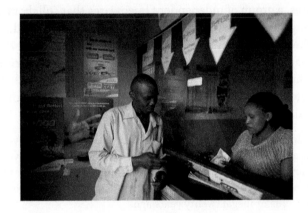

wires, relying instead on satellite transmission of cable content, when allowed by the governments. In countries such as Malaysia, for example, owning a satellite dish is a crime.

Mobile telephones provide an easy and relatively cheap way to communicate, and text messaging allows further mass coordination so that the phone becomes part of a larger, ad hoc, mass-communication system. They also foster a sense of community among phone users. In Nigeria, for example, women generally run the various stalls in the urban market, coordinating prices with sellers in different locations by mobile phone. What's more, recognizing their common interests and grievances, these sellers joined together to try to alleviate some of the greater problems they faced.

Kenya's M-Pesa, a mobile payment system, has become the primary source of remittances by Kenyans in the city to relatives in the countryside. So popular is M-Pesa that its transactions comprise 31 percent of Kenya's gross domestic product (GDP).[11] M-Pesa was launched by mobile telecommunications company Safaricom, which has nineteen million customers in Kenya, fifteen million of whom use M-Pesa.

Africa's vast number of mobile phone users, estimated at seven hundred million, or 70 percent of the African population, and the lack of bank access for many, means that mobile phone payments are a promising growth area.[12] It shows how technology and economics converge to help developing countries leapfrog rich industrialized countries in some areas.

As low-cost smartphones expand their reach in the developing world, and as companies such as Google begin to deliver free, high-speed, wireless Internet service through its "Project Loon" using aerial balloons, mobile Internet becomes another compelling advantage to mobile media.

basic reason behind a fundamental trend in media over the past half-century. Successful media enterprises have acquired, either through purchase or merger, other media enterprises and have thereby grown in size and scope. Newspaper companies have bought other newspaper companies; radio-station groups have bought other radio-station groups. Cross-media enterprises have acquired other media enterprises, sometimes extending internationally as well. The result is a media system that is increasingly large, multifaceted, and global in ownership. These companies compete with other large media enterprises and across international borders.

Some critics have argued that despite the possible economies of scale, media conglomerates and media monopolies (i.e., when only one media organization serves the public or community) have a significant downside. Greater concentration

News Corporation

Despite News Corporation's split into two separate companies in 2013, one focusing on entertainment and the other on publishing, both are still independently in the top tier of media conglomerates based on company value.

**media oligopoly**

A marketplace in which media ownership and diversity are severely limited and the actions of any single media group affect its competitors substantially, including determining the content and price of media products for both consumers and advertisers.

of ownership, or fewer owners owning more media, results in less diversity of media voices and the possible silencing of minority and non-mainstream views—a disservice to the public.

In his book *New Media Monopoly*, Ben H. Bagdikian, one of the most vocal critics of concentrated media ownership, presents evidence that during the 1990s, a small number of the country's largest corporations purchased more public communications power than ever before. In 1983, the biggest media merger to date was a $340 million deal involving the Gannett Company, the newspaper chain that bought Combined Communications Corporation, whose assets included billboards, newspapers, and broadcast stations. In 1996, Disney's acquisition of Capital Cities/ABC cost $19 billion. In 2001, AOL's acquisition of Time Warner dwarfed even this deal at $160 billion.

Although we have not seen deals of this size in the 2000s and 2010s, acquisitions typically continue to occur in the billions of dollars. These include cable provider Comcast's acquisition of NBCUniversal from parent company General Electric for $30 billion in 2009 and completed in 2013; Google's purchase of YouTube in October 2006 for $1.6 billion; and the McClatchy newspaper chain purchase of thirty-two Knight-Ridder newspapers in March 2006 for $4.5 billion.

These large companies, Bagdikian contends, have built a communications cartel within the United States, a group of independent businesses that collaborate to regulate production, pricing, and marketing of goods. This cartel controls industrial products such as gasoline, refrigerators, or clothing. But also at stake are the symbols—the words and images—that define and shape the culture and political agenda of the country. In other words, a cable provider such as Comcast, which in many markets is the sole provider, now also controls the content from its NBCUniversal media properties. Bagdikian writes,

> Aided by the digital revolution and the acquisition of subsidiaries that operate at every step in the mass communications process, from the creation of content to its delivery into the home, the communications cartel has exercised stunning influence over national legislation and government agencies, an influence whose scope and power would have been considered scandalous or illegal twenty years ago.

Bagdikian further notes that 99 percent of the daily newspapers in the United States are the only daily in their cities. Similarly, all but a few of the nation's cable systems are monopolies in their cities. Most of the country's commercial radio stations are part of national ownership groups, and just a half-dozen formats (e.g., all news, rock, hip-hop, adult contemporary, oldies, easy listening) define programming. The major commercial television networks and their local affiliates carry programs of essentially the same type all across the country. Looked at from this perspective, the media do not offer the diversity in content that one would expect, even as the number of TV or radio channels increase.

This system is called a **media oligopoly**, a marketplace in which media ownership and diversity are severely limited and the actions of any single media group affect its competitors substantially, including determining the content and price of media products for both consumers and advertisers.

Nine diversified media giants dominate the media worldwide. Many of these international conglomerates are themselves part of a larger company comprising nonmedia business interests or contain in their financial portfolio significant nonmedia commercial properties and investments. They include a wide range of media or channels of distribution. Note that three of the nine started as computer or technology companies and that Google didn't even exist until late 1998.

Each of these nine companies is responsible for much of what we see, hear, or read in traditional media or interact with on the web. Of course, these are not the only media companies in the world: McChesney identifies a "second tier" of about fifty large media companies operating at the national or international level, each doing more than $1 billion of business a year. Any of these second-tier companies, in and of themselves, can be considered a huge media power with an array of business interests, although their revenues pale in comparison to the big nine.

Concentration of media ownership grew even more intense in 2016 with a series of major media mergers and acquisitions across the United States and worldwide. Among the notable acquisitions are Microsoft's $28 billion acquisition of the social network LinkedIn and the Gannett Company's acquisition of the previously family-owned *Record* newspaper of Bergen County, New Jersey, and other news properties.

Becoming literate about the concentration of media ownership and consolidation of media companies into ever-larger companies does not entail simply learning the inside scoop on who owns what. As Bagdikian, McChesney, and other scholars have indicated, the power that these media wield has serious political, societal, and cultural repercussions. If much of the media we consume comes from a handful of large conglomerates, it raises questions about the role that **media bias**, how information may be skewed toward a particular viewpoint, might play in forming our views of politics, society, and culture.

> **media bias**
>
> A real or perceived viewpoint held by journalists and news organizations that slants news coverage unfairly, contrary to professional journalism's stated goals of balanced coverage and objectivity.

---

**DISCUSSION QUESTIONS:** Consider your level of media diversity by listing the types of shows you watch, material you read, and music you listen to. Trace three different media in this list back to their corporate parents. Classify your tastes into genres, and compare with someone else to assess the diversity of your media consumption.

---

## Media Bias

Both the left and the right claim that the media, especially the news, are biased against them; and both sides can cite various examples in the media, in scholarly studies, and in popular books that supposedly prove their points. If the media make neither side happy, then they must be doing something right, some might say. Still, this rather glib response to an apparent paradox circumvents the very real issue of media bias and how to recognize it.

Professional journalism has a strong culture of what used to be called "objectivity" but is now referred to as "fairness and balance," or the professional duty to cover an issue so that all sides are presented accurately and justly. This also means that professional news reporting should not reveal a journalist's personal views.

We tend to think of the news as objective—a belief supported by its media grammar, particularly the camera angles, lighting, distance between the subject and interviewer, sound, and intercut scenes that all affect our perceptions. The "objective point of view" in television news interviews treats the viewer as an observer. Typically, the camera is kept still, with shots over the shoulder of the journalist interviewing a subject. Prior to the interview, the journalist instructs the subject never to look directly into the camera, a privilege reserved for the news anchor or

Daytime TV shows such as *The Talk* can sometimes bring formerly taboo or controversial social subjects to the public's attention.

field reporter, who often summarizes or concludes her report in this manner that establishes eye contact with the audience. This grammar encourages the viewer to see significant differences between subject and reporter—specifically, the latter's greater authority and objectivity.

Any notion of objectivity or even balance in news coverage has been challenged for a number of reasons. Many question its very possibility. This becomes especially problematic with news stories that feature various groups who may not self-identify the same way they are identified by news organizations. A framing bias could affect a journalist's choice of terms, defining someone as a "terrorist" rather than "rebel," for example. Because most news is about some type of conflict, and because conflicts often involve a disagreement over basic facts or even definitions of terms, news organizations often get caught in semantic battles.

Another criticism of the balanced approach is that in striving for balance, news organizations can simply become stenographers for opposing sides, dutifully reporting what each side says but never providing any context for readers or viewers, thus depriving the audience of relevant information. According to this view, news organizations would serve the public better if they provided more openly partisan commentary and critique on news events, rather than trying to pretend they are above the fray and simply reporting from a fair and balanced perspective.

Finally, some question whether balance, even if it were attainable, is always even a worthy goal. W. Lance Bennett in *News: The Politics of Illusion* argues that giving various positions equal consideration in a debate can confer on them equal legitimacy when this may not be the case, leaving readers and audiences confused about whose views are more credible. (Who knows? After all, both sides had equal airtime.) Many believe, for example, that challenging knowable and empirical realties on purely political grounds only muddies the waters of what should remain a scientific debate.[13]

Media scholars on the left claim that the media are not biased to favor liberals but actually skew toward promoting conservative or at least corporate-friendly ideologies. Eric Alterman, author of *What Liberal Media? The Truth About Bias and the News*, argues that the constant refrain from conservative commentators about the media's liberal bias has made many media outlets present more conservative views than they would have otherwise. When representatives of the political left are enlisted to provide an opposing perspective, they are often much closer to the center than some equally qualified experts who may be more liberal, thus shifting the debate to the political right.

Media scholars also cite many examples of pro-business and pro-government bias in news coverage, regardless of the political party in office. Some were highly critical of the complacency of news organizations during George W. Bush's administration as Republican leaders made their case to invade Iraq, which turned out to have neither weapons of mass destruction, as the administration claimed, nor a role in the Al Qaeda attacks on September 11. They also point to coverage of the financial crisis in 2008 that left fundamental issues leading to the crisis largely unquestioned. If media organizations truly had a liberal bias, they say, then there would have been greater critical reporting on such events and more discussion about reforms, rather than the considerable parroting of political and corporate elites that took place with few proposals for systemic changes.

---

## ETHICS IN MEDIA
# When Media Report Rape Allegations

Mainstream news media report on a wide range of violent crime. But one type gives journalists particular difficulty: reporting on violence against women, especially sexual assault and rape. Illustrative is a 2016 case involving the early release from prison of a man convicted of the sexual assault of an unconscious woman.

After serving just half of his six-month sentence, convicted sex offender Brock Turner was released from prison. The case had generated news headlines nationally and internationally for a number of reasons, including the short sentence he received for the horrific crime, and for his status as a student athlete at a highly respected and major U.S. university. As the *Intercept* noted, a broad spectrum of mainstream U.S. and international news media received heated criticism for their stories about Turner's release. Leading news sources, including the Associated Press, the BBC, CNN, MSNBC, *Sports Illustrated, TIME,* and *USA Today,* referred to Turner in their lead sentences as a "Stanford swimmer." "TIME," the *Intercept* reported, "referred to Turner as a swimmer and didn't note that he had committed a sexual assault until the third line of the story. The magazine called him a 'former Stanford student and star swimmer.'"[14]

The Turner case came at a time of intense national debate about not only sexual assault on college campuses but also how media report on the matter. Coverage sometimes casts doubt on the veracity of the victim's allegations,

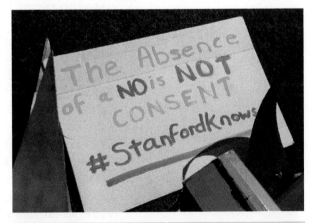

**CRITICAL THINKING QUESTIONS:** Conduct a Google search on the topic of sexual assault or rape and Brock Turner. Read the report of the *Independent,* which examines the complexities of the case and how to accurately report it. Do news reports about sexual assault before the conclusion of a trial unfairly damage the reputation of the victims by questioning their veracity? Or do they unfairly harm the reputation of the accused? Should the media report on allegations that the legal system has not fully vetted?

and often frames the perpetrator in ways that downplay the nature of the crime (e.g., "Stanford swimmer" rather than "convicted sex offender").

Media bias occurs not only in news stories, however. Entertainment media play an important role in propagating stereotypes and demonizing certain behaviors. They can also normalize people and activities too. Popular daytime talk shows featuring formerly taboo subjects, ranging from transgender children to domestic violence, can help make discussion of such issues more acceptable, which can in turn lead to these subjects appearing on television shows or dramas, thus becoming even further embedded in our popular culture landscape.

Similarly, advertising can play a role in propagating certain stereotypes or in promoting cultural norms, which has drawn criticism from some groups. In 2013, a Cheerios ad depicting an interracial couple with their child generated thousands of complaints and negative comments in social media from those who considered the portrayal of a black husband and a white wife offensive. Children, on the other hand, saw nothing wrong with the commercial when asked.[15]

Understanding how media bias may affect our thinking and commonsense assumptions about the world is an important aspect of media literacy. Next, we will discuss how to develop media-literacy skills that improve our critical thinking.

> **DISCUSSION QUESTIONS:** For one day, note how many social media posts you see expressing conservative political views, how many presenting liberal views, and how many dealing with pop culture or entertainment. How might the results influence your views of the world and news?

## Developing Critical Media-Literacy Skills

One assumption underlying criticisms of media bias and media effects is that the public is largely passive and accepts unquestioningly the media it consumes. However, audience research has shown that audiences can be quite active in interpreting and using media. Media-literacy skills help us become more engaged and aware media consumers and producers as we learn to think critically about what we receive and transmit.

We have looked at basic media-literacy skills in the form of understanding media framing and bias, as well as the role of media grammars. More advanced critical media-literacy skills help us question our fundamental assumptions about media and think about it in alternative ways.

Here, we provide a brief guide on how to think critically about media you encounter. These skills can be applied in varying degrees with any media, ranging from advertisements to movies, news, and even video games.

1. **What is the purpose of the media content?** Is the purpose to persuade, inform, or entertain? How might the media be working across these functions, perhaps in hidden ways? For example, an advertisement's main purpose may be to persuade you to buy a product, but it may also entertain and inform while doing so. A news story may be presented as primarily informative, but the nature of the story may also persuade audiences to adopt a new position or confirm their existing assumptions about the world.

2. **Consider the source of the media.** Is the news story coming from a media organization known for its political views on either the left or the right? If the source is not a well-known media company but a blogger,

## CONVERGENCE CULTURE
# Evaluating Online Information

The Internet is full of hoaxes, cranks, scams, and cons. The up-to-the-minute, 24/7 nature of news online and via social media and its low-cost distribution make the Internet an ideal place for misinformation to spread quickly because facts cannot always be quickly verified. Exacerbating the problem is the growing frequency of cyberattacks from around the world. One such cyberattack occurred in October 2016 and caused the disruption of a wide array of online media services including Twitter, Spotify, and Amazon. Beyond retail, Amazon provides web hosting services to many media enterprises, including Netflix, and the cyberattack disrupted users' ability to access video and other content. Numerous other digital media were affected as well: Users experienced significant delays in accessing sites such as CNN, the *Guardian*, *Wired*, HBO, and *People*. The U.S. Department of Homeland Security is reportedly investigating but has yet to identify a party responsible for the global denial-of-service attack. The rise of the Internet of things, or the billions of devices from TV sets to refrigerators to light bulbs connected to the Internet, is expected to make the threat of cyberattack even more acute, as each device gives cybercriminals another point of entry into a network or vulnerability.[16]

But perhaps even more pervasive are fake news stories meant to deceive or mislead. Such fake news can circulate widely and rapidly sometimes with little or no vetting for truthfulness. The importance of not understanding the grammar of social media and failing to recognize fake news became a particularly hot topic of debate during the 2016 U.S. presidential campaign when social media platforms including Facebook were flooded with fake news items such as "Pope Endorses Trump" and shared by millions.

It is essential for the reader to employ critical thinking skills and media literacy to discern whether a story is likely false. In some cases, a fake story might be deliberately false, as in propaganda. In other cases, it might be satire and not meant to deceive. Fake news often has improbably bold headlines or is poorly written. In any case, the astute audience member will check out story with another source and do her or his own fact checking before sharing it with friends or family.

How do you know when you are being fed a line when online?

- Check the "About Us" section of a website to get background information on who runs it. Do the site's operators identify their mission, their principles, and their sponsors, or do they seem evasive and unclear?
- Scan the sites they link to. Most websites link to others who share their views or similar beliefs. Researchers have found that users of social media often live in an online echo chamber, being exposed to the same narrative over and over.[17] This can lead people to repeatedly see and hear the same points of view on a wide range of issues and events, and thereby reinforce their beliefs, even when those beliefs are belied by the facts. Those living inside a media echo chamber rarely see the diversity of viewpoints available in the wider world. As a result, users can often fall prey to false news or conspiracy theories as everyone they are sharing information with online seems to believe those same things.
- Compare the information on the website with similar stories on other websites, both from branded news names and from smaller sites. If a well-known or respected group has made an important and relevant announcement, the organization's website should post that information as well.
- Question the name of the organization that owns the website. Lobbying groups and other organizations trying to push a specific agenda will often adopt names that mask their true goals or cast them in a euphemistic light, or they will create front groups to hide behind. SourceWatch, a project of the Center for Media and Democracy, is one good website for learning more about the names behind the organizations that appear in the news.
- Do not immediately trust information that lacks a date somewhere on the page. Information that may have been accurate when first posted may well be out of date when you visit the site.
- Cautiously consider information you read from discussion groups, chat rooms, blogs, and tweets, even if the person posting claims to be an expert on the subject. Try to confirm the information with another source, and examine the speaker's academic or professional credentials through a quick Google search. As the famous *New Yorker* cartoon of a dog sitting at a computer talking to another dog said, "On the Internet, nobody knows you're a dog." In the Internet age, that dog could be just about anywhere or anyone in the world.

examine the types of organizations the blogger links to for a sense of his or her likely political views. Most websites and blogs link to other sites whose views reflect their own.

3. **Examine framing of media content.** How might the choice of words affect how media consumers perceive the information? How could alternative words possibly change the overall impression of what was written? In news stories, who is interviewed, who is treated as an expert and what organizations do they work for, and how are they framed within the stories? Who is quoted earliest in the story, and who is quoted more often?

4. **What stereotypes are presented?** It takes practice to question stereotypes that appear so frequently they seem natural. One way to challenge your thinking about portrayals of other groups in the media is to consider what you would think if you or your group were portrayed that way. Would you agree with that representation or stereotype? Would you be offended?

5. **Question the media ecosystem.** Identify and question stereotypes as reflected in the media environment or community of channels both online and off (i.e., the media ecosystem). Think about whom the stereotypes help and whom they harm. Is a group or organization profiting in some way from promoting harmful stereotypes, and does the stereotyped group have the same access to media as the dominant group? If not, why not? What kind of media might the stereotyped group produce if it had equal access to media production and distribution?

6. **Make the media.** Learning media production skills beyond writing is invaluable for media literacy as well as for the job market, especially for communications professions. Reconstructing a commercial, a music video, or even a news program from an alternative perspective is an excellent way to challenge your assumptions about the presentation of media and their messages. Thinking about the entrepreneurial possibilities is valuable as well. With the media business in a state of disruption driven by technological, economic, and cultural shifts, innovation is urgently needed, and some of the best ideas have come from journalism and media students.

## MEDIA CAREERS

Careers in the media are in transition as jobs evolve and new occupations emerge. According to Alissa Quart, senior editor at *the Atavist*, one of the most important new media career paths is in the area of social justice. These journalists contribute to media literacy by researching and writing on the often complex topics of criminal justice, income inequality, and race, gender, and class. Reporting on these sensitive matters requires both a good sense of societal concerns and strong critical thinking skills. Leading media organizations such as the *New York Times* have recently hired inequality editors and reporters, and more such positions are in the offing around the nation and the world.

## LOOKING BACK AND MOVING FORWARD

Media literacy is not a goal to reach but an ongoing process; skills can always be improved to become a better mass-media consumer, user, and participant. Media literacy involves thinking critically about the media and questioning how different media organizations may be biased in of their selection of stories, their coverage of stories, and even their choice of whom to quote in interviews or invite to speak in panel discussions.

Entertainment media also have biases and can propagate ethnic and gender stereotypes. We may be unaware of the commercial forces that shape the content, largely because we see the end product and not the processes behind the scenes that created the media product.

Consider how commercial forces may not always have the best interests of the public at heart, even when media companies claim they are serving the public or simply giving people what they want. Digital and social media present both an opportunity and a threat for the media and communication industries.

Longstanding corporations, institutions, and entire industries are being turned upside down by the digital revolution. Businesses built on analog technologies of production and distribution are trying to figure out how to adapt in the digital age. New efficiencies of creating and delivering content in a digital, networked environment are emerging throughout the world. Long-held, highly profitable business models based on analog technology are less viable in a digital marketplace. Changes in our media environment also create a greater need for media literacy, especially in the digital realm.

The problem of dealing with the enormous amounts of information available to us, **information overload**, affects everything from government agencies being able to act rapidly on intelligence they have gathered to workers being able to share relevant knowledge within companies.

**information overload**

The difficulties associated with managing and making sense of the vast amounts of information available to us.

Some say information overload has also affected the quality of students' work and even their basic understanding of how to research and synthesize information to create new ideas. Some college students submit research papers that are simply cut-and-paste pastiches of material taken from different websites—sometimes without even changing original font styles. Even students who realize that this is not actually the correct way to write a paper can have a hard time discerning trustworthy sources of information on the web.

Some people claim that the constant interruptions typically seen in the workplace have hampered productivity and creativity, with tasks taking longer to complete than in the past and workers feeling less able to concentrate for the extended periods required to tackle complex problems. Email is a major culprit in information overload, but the rise of social media has no doubt contributed to today's frequent interruptions.

Nevertheless, the new digital world means new business opportunities. It means opening new markets formerly restricted by political, economic, and geographic boundaries. It means new storytelling formats that bring true interactivity to media. Whether these fresh opportunities will enhance media diversity remains to be seen. The continued concentration of media ownership suggests that the big media companies threatened by the digital shift are starting to regain control of the media environment.

The rise of user-generated content and social media directly challenges traditional media companies who commanded the public's attention throughout most

Critics contend that Apple deliberately deleted songs from users' iPods if they had been downloaded from competitors' services.

of the twentieth century. The ways the public is creating media, often on nonmarket principles and simply for the joy of sharing and interacting with others, belie the notion that the public is as happy with its mainstream media content as media conglomerates would have us believe.

As some people are discovering, profits are not necessarily the end goal in the sale of packaged media products such as bestselling books. Seth Godin, a noted author on Internet advertising and marketing, makes his books freely available for download on the Internet. What would appear to be the fast track to the poorhouse is Godin's successful strategy to get his books in the hands of many influential people, including business leaders and conference organizers, who then invite him (and pay him well) to speak at events and conferences.

Companies sustain their efforts to keep the public satiated with (and paying for) a never-ending stream of media content that maintains the primarily one-way flow of content from media producer to audience. Scholars such as McChesney doubt the Internet will become a transformational communication technology that can improve democracy and better engage citizens. Whether this occurs or not will depend largely on how media literate the public becomes and how well we develop our moral reasoning and ethical thinking to create the kind of society we want to live in, not just have to live in.

## MEDIA MATTERS    TESTING YOUR MEDIA LITERACY

You may consider yourself media literate and technologically savvy because you have grown up surrounded by traditional and digital media. But media literacy entails much more than being able to tweet or recalling all the movies in which your favorite actor has appeared. See what you know and what you can find out to determine some of what media literacy involves.

1. Consider a current popular movie that you have seen. Discuss some of its ethnic, religious, gender, or other stereotypes, and consider why they appear. Do they have any consequences for the groups stereotyped?

2. Working in a small group, describe your favorite genre of music (e.g., hip-hop, rock, country) without using the name of the genre, the titles of any songs, or the names of popular artists. Do not hum or imitate the music style. See who can figure out the genre first. Why do you think it was so hard for you to explain without explicitly naming the genre, the songs, or the artists?

3. What visual elements do you normally associate with television news? Compare your list with that of your classmates, and then discuss how and why you think these visual elements came to define the format called "news."

4. In what ways may an advertiser influence the news, if at all?

5. Do you consider information from a blog or tweet or via a mobile device more or less trustworthy than material found on an organization's website? Why do you think so? How do you decide what information to trust online?

6. Conduct an online search for the top ten movies of the past year, and note what genres they fall into (e.g., action, thriller, romantic comedy). Why do you think some genres seem more popular than others?

7. Would you sign a petition in support of tort reform that limits the amount people can sue companies via frivolous lawsuits? What about a petition against the Corporate Immunity Act, which would prevent litigants from fully recovering the damages inflicted on them by corporate wrongdoing? What is the difference between these two?

**FURTHER READING**

*Media Literacy*, 6th ed. W. James Potter (2012) Sage Publications.

*Approaches to Media Literacy: A Handbook*, 2nd ed. Art Silverblatt, Jane Ferry, Barbara Finan (2009) M. E. Sharpe.

*Digital and Media Literacy: Connecting Culture and Classroom*. Renee Hobbs (2011) Corwin Press.

*The New Media Monopoly*. Ben H. Bagdikian (2004) Beacon Press.

*The Political Economy of Media: Enduring Issues, Emerging Dilemmas*. Robert W. McChesney (2008) Monthly Review Press.

*Digital Disconnect: How Capitalism Is Turning the Internet Against Democracy*. Robert McChesney (2013) The New Press.

*The Problem of the Media: U.S. Communication Politics in the Twenty-First Century*. Robert McChesney (2004) Monthly Review Press.

*Jamming the Media: A Citizen's Guide to Reclaiming the Tools of Communication*. Gareth Branwyn (1997) Chronicle Books.

*Citizen Muckraking: How to Investigate and Right Wrongs in Your Community*. The Center for Public Integrity (2000) Common Courage Media.

*The Conquest of Cool: Business Culture, Counterculture, and the Rise of Hip Consumerism*. Thomas Frank (1997) University of Chicago Press.

*Convergence Culture: Where Old and New Media Collide*. Henry Jenkins (2008) NYU Press.

*New Media, Old Media: A History and Theory Reader*. Wendy Hui Kyong Chun, Thomas Keenan (2007) Taylor & Francis.

*The Filter Bubble: How the New Personalized Web Is Changing What We Read and How We Think*. Eli Pariser (2012) Penguin Books.

*The Wealth of Networks: How Social Production Transforms Markets and Freedom*. Yochai Benkler (2007) Yale University Press.

*Bodies in Code: Interfaces with Digital Media*. Mark Hansen (2007) Routledge.

*News: The Politics of Illusion*. Lance Bennett (2012) Longman.

# Print Media
## BOOKS, NEWSPAPERS, AND MAGAZINES

I n a long-running case, a court found in 2013 that Apple Inc. had conspired to raise the prices of ebooks. As a violation of the Sherman Antitrust Act, this ruling paved the way for lower prices and greater transparency in the ebook marketplace, an increasingly dominant part of the global publishing industry.

Initiated in 2009, a government antitrust suit accused Apple and five major publishers of colluding to set 2010 prices of ebooks so no publisher could undercut Apple. When Amazon's Kindle was practically the sole e-reader, ebooks typically cost $9.99, a price that jumped to $14.99 after the debut of Apple's iPad, which could also perform the same function. The publishers—HarperCollins, Hachette, Macmillan, Penguin, and Simon & Schuster—settled with the government, while Apple continued to fight the suit. In July 2014, however, without admitting wrongdoing, Apple agreed to settle a class-action lawsuit from states and consumers with a payout of up to $400 million, subject to further appeals.[1]

Amazon controls about 67 percent of the ebook market worldwide.[2] An already tense relationship with publishers soured further when Amazon, formerly a retailer of ebooks, entered the publishing business and became a direct competitor. The government suit claims that publishers worked clandestinely with Apple to promote non-Kindle ebooks to break Amazon's near monopoly on ebooks through its Kindle reader.

Ironically, the antitrust suit actually strengthens Amazon's position, replacing a perceived monopoly with an actual one. A commanding position in ebooks allows Amazon to absorb losses on sales as it attracts more Kindle buyers and locks in the market. Yet supporters of the book-publishing industry, including many bookstore owners, are not persuaded that Amazon's monopoly is good in the long run, as competition provides incentive for such a company to continue to innovate and to maintain low prices.

At the heart of the matter here is a classic confrontation between a traditional business model—in this case, book publishing—and a bold new entrepreneurial competitor that wants to encourage reading while adapting to new distribution methods and pricing models.

Print media are arguably facing some of the biggest challenges from digital media, ranging from declines in advertising revenues to changing patterns of reading among the public. Print will continue, however, to play an important role in the media landscape—even when text is read in electronic form.

Representing the beginning of mass communication, print media originated in the typographical era of the Middle Ages. Mass forms of mechanical printing and typography contributed to sweeping social transformation in Europe, including mass literacy and the Renaissance. Adapting to such technological change challenged society—a recurring problem encountered by subsequent ages. In 1962, noted communication theorist Marshall McLuhan claimed the following about electronic media in *The Gutenberg Galaxy*, an observation that applies equally to the digital age: "We are today as far into the electric age as the Elizabethans had advanced into the typographical and mechanical age. And we are experiencing the same confusions and indecisions which they had felt when living simultaneously in two contrasted forms of society and experience."

McLuhan, among others, argues that the medium of the printed word has even changed the way we think. Reading lets us ponder. We can reread and rethink passages of written text, developing responses in ways simply unavailable with the spoken word. If, as scholars claim, the print format promotes critical-thinking skills and refined, logical arguments, it raises questions regarding the effects on our abilities to think logically and critically as we read less and consume more audio or video digital media.

> **DISCUSSION QUESTIONS:** Do the Internet and the digital media age constitute a media revolution as far-reaching as that brought about by the printing press? Identify some societal and technological similarities and differences between now and the mid-1400s to support your argument.

## Functions of Print Media

Print media, in the form of books, newspapers, and magazines, serve many overlapping social functions. Among the most important are cultural transmission from generation to generation, the diffusion of ideas and knowledge, and entertainment.

### TRANSMISSION OF CULTURE

Media, in all their forms, teach us the language, values, and traditions of a culture. Although not the sole means of transmitting culture, books, newspapers, and magazines convey what society considers right or wrong, acceptable or unacceptable. Reading often introduces immigrants and children to societal rules and norms. Ancient religious texts such as the Bible, the Koran, or the Torah have successfully imparted cultural mores and values for centuries.

### DIFFUSION OF IDEAS AND KNOWLEDGE

Education in particular transmits culture, and books are central to lifelong formal and informal education. Textbooks and other works of nonfiction impart everything from philosophical theory to psychological self-help, teaching us not only how to do things but also how to understand and appreciate the arts, literature, history, contemporary society, and the social and natural sciences.

Newspapers and magazines inform us of and interpret the latest events so that we can make sense of the world. Here we read about recent foreign events as well as new discoveries, fashions, and trends. Special-interest magazines feature particular fields or hobbies, knowledge that helps us connect with others who share our interests.

## ENTERTAINMENT

Sometimes we read for specific knowledge; sometimes we read for the sheer joy of it. The printed page can offer escape or diversion, allowing us to travel to exotic places or distant planets where we encounter fantastic creatures and memorable people. Popular books often become the basis for films or cable series, such as *Game of Thrones*. A film version of a favorite novel may disappoint, though, because the locations and characters fail to resemble what we originally imagined.

Comic books and picture books, providing young readers with some of their first adventures in reading, are designed to entertain. Short stories, nonfiction magazine articles, and books can both engage and inform, however. As their literacy skills develop, children advance to early reader books such as *The Cat in the Hat* by Dr. Seuss, chapter books such as *Charlotte's Web* by E. B. White, young-adult (YA) fiction such as *To Kill a Mockingbird* by Harper Lee and the 2015 release of her long-awaited *Go Set a Watchman*, and nonfiction such as *The Diary of a Young Girl* by Anne Frank.

Accessing the thoughts of the ancients through their texts may allow us to find commonalities across centuries. Great literature can elevate our senses and make us feel new emotions as characters come to life. Readers who may not otherwise know or care about our legal system or our military intelligence can, nevertheless, learn much from legal thrillers such as *An Innocent Client* by Scott Pratt in the Joe Dillard series or military action stories such as *Tom Clancy: Support and Defend* by Mark Greaney, who is continuing the popular Jack Ryan series started by author Tom Clancy.

Still, data from the Pew Research Center indicates that total book reading continues to be popular, with nearly three-quarters of Americans (73 percent) reading a book in any format (printed or electronic) in 2016, down slightly from four-fifths (79 percent) in 2011. Meanwhile, ebook reading is growing rapidly, with more than a quarter (28 percent) in 2016 having read an ebook in the past year.[3] This is up from less than a fifth (17 percent) having read an ebook in 2011.[4]

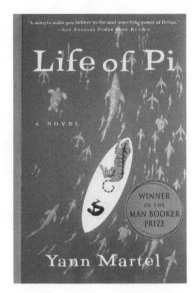

An enduring source of entertainment for young and old alike, some books subsequently become the basis for feature films. **CRITICAL THINKING QUESTIONS:** Think of movies you may have seen after reading the book. Does it make any difference whether the book you read was in print or electronic form? Why was this the case?

## Distinctive Functions of Books

Even before books existed in the form that we know today, compiling comprehensive knowledge in a single document was considered a vital, even sacred, endeavor. Historically, religious texts have shaped beliefs and worldviews so profoundly that wars continue to erupt over conflicting doctrine.

Staged book burnings attest to the social and cultural significance of books throughout history and right up to today. Consider, for example, the Danish man who burned a Koran and posted video of it to Facebook on December 27, 2015. In 2017, he was charged with the crime of blasphemy in Denmark.[5] Some groups

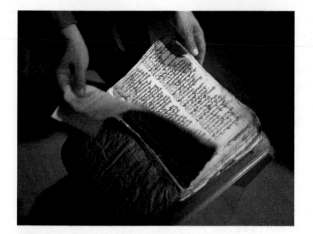

Islamic State militants have sought to purge cities they've invaded in Iraq and Syria of books, antiquities, and other artifacts that do not conform to their extremist interpretations of Islam.

have burned books they believe corrupt children, including those widely considered classics. Texts have been banned for sexual content or political messages critical of the government. Although more common in the early-to-mid-twentieth century, this still occurs, as when Lebanon banned the controversial 2003 novel *The Da Vinci Code*.

Textbooks, although intended primarily to impart objective knowledge, can express values through omission as much as inclusion. Whether high school science textbooks should discuss both evolution and creationism is still a subject of heated debate in the United States. China and Korea censure Japanese history textbooks that either ignore or euphemize Japan's World War II military atrocities. Purported cultural values of books written to entertain can also stir controversy. The *Harry Potter* book series by J. K. Rowling has been criticized for not featuring stronger female characters in central roles and even for promoting witchcraft.

These examples demonstrate the book's enduring cultural relevance and authority in the digital age. Newspapers and magazines neither present the same sense of established knowledge and compiled wisdom nor allow for the unfolding of long or complex stories. The growing popularity of e-readers attests to the important role that books still play in our lives.

## History of Books to Today

Since the Sumerians of 3500 BCE pressed marks into wet clay tablets, creating what some scholars consider the first book form, authors have been recording textual narratives. By 2500 BCE, writers in western Asia were using animal skins as scrolls, a more portable form than clay tablets. The ancient Egyptians wrote the *Book of the Dead* in 1800 BCE on papyrus. Between the first century BCE and the sixth century CE, the **codex**, a manuscript of bound individual pages, began replacing the scroll, establishing the modern book form. Book publishing continued to evolve through innovation and invention: block printing in China by 600 CE; movable copper-alloy type in Korea in 1234 CE; and the Western world's first mechanical printing press in Germany in 1455 CE.

🗨 **codex**

Manuscript book of individually bound pages.

Korean copper-alloy type was the first printing to use metal plates, hundreds of years before Gutenberg's European press.

### MONASTIC SCRIBES

Until the invention of printing, books had to be laboriously copied by hand. In the Middle Ages, specially trained monks, or scribes, copied religious and classical works in monastic writing rooms called scriptoria. Largely dedicated to promoting the ideas of the Christian Church, many books in this era were written in beautiful calligraphy and were richly illustrated.

Early books were published in scroll format and then codexes. Until paper arrived from China via the Middle East in the later Middle Ages, European scribes wrote on parchment or vellum made from treated hides of goats, sheep, or calves. Because copying and illustrating by hand were extremely time-consuming, and creating parchment was expensive, books were generally not widespread before the end of the Middle Ages.

The Gutenberg Bible, like most books of the period, had lavish hand-colored illustrations alongside the printed text.

## JOHANNES GUTENBERG

The Christian Church grew in Europe along with the need for religious texts. In 1455 CE, this need inspired **Johannes Gutenberg** (1400–ca. 1468) to invent printing with lead, using movable type, and pressing oil-based ink on paper with a converted wine press.

Born to an upper-class merchant family in Mainz, Germany, Gutenberg met the silversmith Prokop Waldvogel in Avignon in 1444 who taught the craft of "artificial writing," as early printmaking was called. In 1450, Gutenberg formed a partnership with the wealthy Mainz burgher Johann Fust to complete his own printing invention and to print the famous **Gutenberg Bible**, or "forty-two-line Bible," whose 1455 publication is considered the beginning of mechanical printing.[6]

Despite the advent of new printing technology, the handmade tradition continued. Books were still bound by hand, and illustrators embellished printed pages with drawings and artistic flourishes to match the expectations for handwritten manuscripts. Combining a printing press with existing bookbinding technology enabled mass production at a fraction of the time and cost of an equal number of hand copies. Religious and cultural centers of Europe initially welcomed the printing press with enthusiasm.

## BEGINNINGS OF MASS COMMUNICATION AND MASS LITERACY

Critical to the growth of Renaissance culture, the printing press spread scientific discoveries and religious beliefs—some of which challenged the authority of the Catholic Church. Many books copied by scribes, especially scientific works, were printed in Latin, effectively reducing readership to elites educated in the classics. Printers rapidly discovered that books and broadsheets printed in local common languages (the vernacular) found an eager audience as more common people

**Johannes Gutenberg**

German printer credited with creating the first mechanical printing press in 1455.

**Gutenberg Bible**

Bible printed by Johannes Gutenberg in Europe in 1455, considered one of the first mechanically printed works.

Noah Webster is most famous for his dictionary, but he also published a grammatical textbook used widely throughout much of the nineteenth century.

### dime novel

First paperback form whose cost of 10¢ made it accessible even to the poor.

### mass-market paperback

Inexpensive, softcover books small enough for a back pocket and sold in bookstores, supermarkets, drugstores, and other public places.

Dime novels, relatively affordable paperbacks that first appeared in 1860, made a range of tales accessible to an increasingly literate public.

learned to read. Books had left the quiet monastic scriptoria and entered the bustling commercial world of printmakers and the average person.

Despite this increase in printed materials from the Renaissance onward, literacy was not universal. Most Europeans and Americans remained illiterate until the nineteenth century. In colonial America, education was available largely to the wealthy, who could afford to hire and house private tutors for their children. Textbooks played a crucial role in the increased public education of the early 1800s that helped reduce illiteracy among the general population.

One of the first textbooks in America, the *New England Primer*, published initially circa 1690 by Benjamin Harris, introduced children to the English alphabet, the rudiments of reading, and basic Christian values. In 1783, Noah Webster, known today for *Webster's Dictionary*, wrote *A Grammatical Institute of the English Language*, a response to the popular textbooks imported from England that conveyed English cultural values. Known popularly as the "Blue Back Speller," Webster's textbook provided tutorials on language, religion, morals, and domestic economy. McGuffey Readers, first published in 1836, became standard reading books for schoolchildren throughout the nineteenth century.

Nineteenth-century textbooks, like modern ones, reflect contemporary social mores. Issues such as slavery and racism were not challenged. Today, textbook content on topics such as evolution and the Civil War is debated. To appeal to the widest cross section of society, textbooks tend to avoid controversial subjects, embracing perspectives and knowledge generally agreed on within the dominant group.

## CHEAPER AND SMALLER BOOKS

Successful publishing has always been driven by wider distribution and lower production costs. The printing press and digital books—and all the trends in between—appeared as a result of these forces. Wider distribution of a popular book, usually one that entertains, is one way to make money; lower prices that make the book affordable for many is another. The dime novel and, later, mass-market paperbacks, satisfied both these criteria.

### Dime Novels

Accessible to even the poor, the **dime novel** sold for 10¢, as its name suggests. In 1860, Irwin P. Beadle & Company introduced this first paperback book, which initially featured stories of Indians and nationalistic pioneer tales. Ann S. Stephens wrote the first dime novel, *Malaeska: The Indian Wife of the White Hunter*. Within a year of publication, *Malaeska* had sold more than three hundred thousand copies. By the 1870s, dime novels included melodramatic fiction, adventures, detective stories, romances, and rags-to-riches tales.

### Mass-Market Paperbacks

In 1939, Robert de Graff's company, Pocket Books, introduced **mass-market paperbacks** in the United States, a line of plastic-laminated books adorned with its familiar kangaroo mascot, Gertrude, priced at 25¢ and sized small enough for a back pocket. The paperback revolution stemmed from offering books in places such as drugstores and supermarkets, a mass-distribution network alternative to established bookstores.

The post–World War II baby boomers, who became the students of the 1950s and '60s, were dubbed "the paperback generation." They were raised on Dr. Benjamin

Spock's bestselling paperback *Dr. Spock's Baby and Child Care* and influenced by paperbacks such as J. D. Salinger's *Catcher in the Rye* and Kurt Vonnegut's *Slaughterhouse Five*.

## Print-on-Demand

One interesting development in printing that began in the late 1990s is **print-on-demand (POD)**. High-quality color laser printing and binding machines can print a single book in a few minutes at a fraction of the traditional cost with tiny print runs that can make available and affordable books otherwise difficult or impossible to obtain.

POD enables writers to publish using low-cost printers and sell their paperbacks online or even in some bookstores. The combination of low-cost, digital, and online technologies has released a flood of POD and ebooks published by authors in recent years. In 2013, over 458,000 books were self-published, a 437-percent increase since 2008, with ebook publishing dropping slightly and print books rising 29 percent over the year before.[7] Industry watchers claim that this shows how the self-publishing industry is maturing and how printed books are still very relevant for self-published authors. A growing number of POD publishers, such as Xlibris, Virtual Bookworm, and Lulu Publishing, publish books for as little as $400, not including editing or other potential costs for an author.

In 2002, the Internet Archive (www.archive.org) formed a group dedicated to digitizing and archiving all kinds of media. In its first year, the Internet Bookmobile, a Ford minivan with a computer and a POD printer, toured U.S. cities giving people access to more than twenty thousand public domain books in its digital archive, all available in minutes and at a fraction of bookstore costs. The Internet Archive hoped it might prove a cost-effective option for libraries tasked with pursuing late books and reshelving them.

## Ebooks

Ebooks offer various advantages over printed books, permitting us not only to read text but also to make electronic annotations and bookmarks and to search via an interactive table of contents or by keyword. In the late 1990s, major publishers, preparing for a surge in consumer demand, experimented with the online sale and distribution of ebooks. Despite a slowdown in the growth of self-published ebooks, mainstream publishers are still betting on the growth of the ebook market.

**print-on-demand (POD)**

Publication of single books or tiny print runs based on customer demand using largely automated, nontraditional book-printing methods such as the color laser printer.

Brewster Kahle, Internet Archive founder, has built a vast digital library of more than one million public domain books, all available for free download to any Internet-connected computer or mobile device.

## INTERNATIONAL PERSPECTIVES
# Global Ebook Marketplace

While the American public has been hungry for ebooks since 2008, the digital appetite has been smaller internationally, where only some 20 percent of ebook sales occur. In European countries such as Germany, Spain, France, and Sweden, ebooks accounted for less than 1 percent of total book sales in 2008. By 2014, the European Commission reports the ebook market share in Europe rose to 10 percent.[8] In other parts of the world less economically developed and less literate, including much of Latin America, Asia, and Africa, ebook sales have been virtually nonexistent.

Yet some organizations, such as O'Reilly Media, report that ebooks are poised to take off globally. In Europe, sales of the Amazon Kindle have been rising as e-reader prices decline. In the United Kingdom, the 2010 arrival of the Amazon Kindle unleashed pent-up demand. Within nine months, ebooks were outselling hardcover print. In 2011, Amazon introduced the Kindle to Germany, France, Spain, and Italy. Apple reported in 2010 that sales of its Italian iBooks skyrocketed from 150 to 1,000 copies a day within the first four days on sale.

By 2013, demand had increased with the simultaneous release of most new ebook titles in multiple languages. In addition, geographical licensing restrictions had relaxed while navigating ebook copyright law—a complex dance among authors, agents, publishers, and distributors—had become easier.

Ebook cost has dampened international growth, however. Outside the United States, the average price in 2016 of a newly published ebook was $12–$14, plus taxes, compared to an American sticker price of $7.72. And in the potentially huge market in China, with one-sixth of the world's population, ebooks have been an especially tough sell. Many Chinese read on their phone using "online literature" platforms such as Cloudary where user-generated content dominates. Moreover, digital publishing, like publishing in general, is controlled by the government, which has entered the market cautiously.

Nevertheless, as these various and diverse challenges are met, the global demand for ebooks is expected to rise dramatically, particularly in Japan, South Korea, and China, with sales of nearly a billion total ebooks in 2016 in those three countries.[9] Total revenue for ebook sales worldwide is expected to top $10 billion in 2017, with annual growth of nearly 4 percent.[10]

Yet, printed books have seen a recent increase in sales: Physical books sold at a 3.3 percent higher rate in 2016, the third straight annual increase.[11]

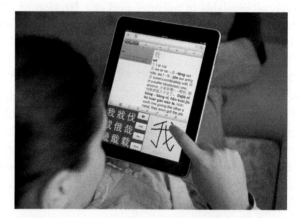

Digital e-readers enable ebooks and other content to be displayed in a variety of languages and alphabets.

The 2007 launch of Amazon's Kindle ebook reader was heralded as the latest technological breakthrough, a potential tipping point toward digital. Older Kindle models, with 4 GB of memory, can store up to thirty-five hundred titles, according to Amazon; whereas the Kindle Fire, with 8 GB, can store seven thousand titles—along with allowing movie viewing, listening to music, and playing games. Penguin Random House, Simon & Schuster, HarperCollins, and other major publishers have embraced ebook readers such as the Kindle, the Sony Reader, and Barnes & Noble's Nook, making many more titles available digitally. Offering free sample chapters and other marketing techniques have promoted growth, as have improvements in hardware, such as screen clarity and greater storage. Popular tablets, including the iPad and Kindle Fire, have also expanded the market, blurring the distinction between an exclusively ebook reader and a multifunctional entertainment device that includes ebook functions.

One of the more intriguing and unique capabilities of ebooks is socially networked reading.  Ebooks are digitally connected to a network, which raises potential privacy concerns but allows interactive capabilities in which readers can not only read the book but discuss it over time and space. Goodreads is an ebook service available to anyone. Readers log onto the site www.goodreads. com, where they can create their own electronic book shelf. Users can search for ebooks, look at friends' ebook lists, request new ebooks, and add ratings to ebooks they have read.

## Current Book-Industry Issues

In 2015, the book-publishing industry's annual worldwide revenue was $113 billion, the largest sector among media entertainment and publishing industries.[12] U.S. net revenues were $29 billion, essentially showing slow growth from 2012.[13] Despite an enormous global market, tremendous consolidation of worldwide industry ownership has impacted the diversity of book titles and perspectives.

At least three significant trends affect book publishing. First, industry mergers and consolidation enable publishers to increase profit margins by reducing operating costs associated with warehousing, marketing, and sales. Increased size also means more leverage with dominant retail giants Barnes & Noble and Amazon.com in negotiations that include obtaining prominent display locations in bookstores and on the web.

Traditional publishing companies, however, increasingly see Amazon as a competitor: partly because of its dominance in the independent publishing and ebook sectors, with 65 percent of the ebook trade, and partly because it insists on setting ebook prices lower than what traditional publishers would like to charge for some titles. Conflicts between publishers and Amazon arose because they could not agree on the percentage of sales that a distributor like Amazon should get; and Amazon's creation of a subscription model for ebooks, Kindle Unlimited, also challenged traditional methods of book sales (and authors' royalties, leading to many complaints among authors).

Second, the book-publishing industry is intertwined with global media and the entertainment industry. Increasingly, profits for the biggest publishers are derived from technology products and services, such as electronic databases and educational testing. Some books are published and subsequently adapted or licensed for film or TV and other entertainment sectors, such as video games.

Third, the emergence of online booksellers, ebooks, and on-demand printing is transforming sales and distribution, growth that renders an uncertain future for traditional brick-and-mortar bookstores and even the power of traditional publishers to set prices. Amazon.com, bn.com, and others are capturing a rising percentage of total book sales, even as they dominate ebook sales. Mega-bookstores such as Borders and warehouse shopping outlets selling discounted books were thought to have the needed economies of scale to compete with online enterprises. Yet in July 2011, Borders, the second biggest bookstore chain in the United States, closed all its stores after filing for bankruptcy several months earlier. Independent bookstores are also suffering. Even large ones like Portland-based Powell's have laid off employees, one of many changes implemented to cope with consumer change.

Based on annual revenue in 2014, Thomson Reuters, after acquiring news giant Reuters and selling its textbook division in 2007, is now second to Pearson, ahead of third-ranked RELX (Reed Elsevier).[14] This is a clear example of the way mergers and digital media are affecting the publishing industry, for Thomson earns the majority of its revenue from electronic databases and not printed books or journals. Thomson Reuters maintains headquarters in New York, but its parent corporation is actually in Canada.

McGraw-Hill Education is the top-ranked U.S. company, ranking ninth in the world in 2014, followed by Scholastic in twelfth place, and Wiley in thirteenth. Only seven of the top fifty-six book publishers worldwide have their parent company headquartered in the United States, although several have joint Canadian/U.S. or European/U.S. ownership.[15] Overseas companies (Bertelsmann, based in Germany, and Pearson, based in England) jointly own familiar publishers such as Random House and Penguin, which merged in 2013.[16]

## Sales and Readership of Books

For more than twenty years, the patterns of book sales have been unsteady. The industry has grown slightly overall, but total revenue has varied by a few percentage points every year, and different categories sell well or poorly depending on the year.

Categories are the most important concept in book sales. Each has different markets and different strategies for reaching their audiences, and each is affected differently by economic and other factors. For example, during the most recent recession, sales of trade books, or books intended for general readership, fell because people had less disposable income. On the other hand, professional, technical, and scholarly books rose as a category, as businesspeople bought books to educate themselves rather than going to more expensive business seminars. Textbooks make up the largest portion of the publishing industry in terms of sales, followed by the category Other Books and Services, which includes religious texts and general reference works

**FIGURE 3-1** Book Publishing Products and Services Segmentation

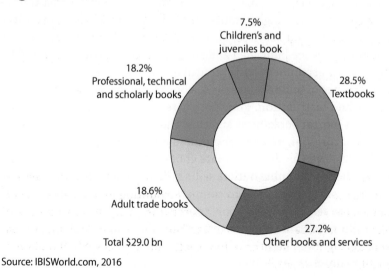

7.5%
Children's and juveniles book

18.2%
Professional, technical and scholarly books

28.5%
Textbooks

18.6%
Adult trade books

27.2%
Other books and services

Total $29.0 bn

Source: IBISWorld.com, 2016

**FIGURE 3-2** Revenue from Ebook Sales, 2009–2016 (in millions of dollars)

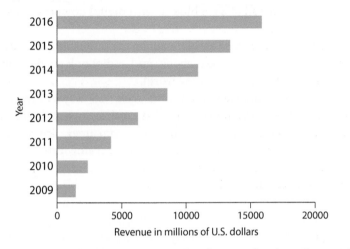

Source: Statista (2016). "Global E-book Revenue." Retrieved April 11, 2017, from https://www.statista.com/statistics/280249/global-e-book-revenue-by-region/

(about 10.6 percent), and other services, including digital publishing and design services for independent authors (16.6 percent). Figure 3-1 shows the different categories used by the book-publishing industry that make up its $29 billion in net revenues in 2014.

As Figure 3-2 shows, a slight downward trend has generally characterized revenue growth in the publishing industry, despite the increase in self-publishing sales (which are not included in these statistics except for any revenues generated by publishers from their various support services to authors). Publishers actively seek potential bestsellers, as a single bestselling title can have dramatic effects on a publisher's revenues for the year. For example, the *Fifty Shades of Grey* trilogy in 2012 contributed to a 75 percent rise in operating revenue for publisher Random House, and a 22.5 percent increase in global revenue.[17]

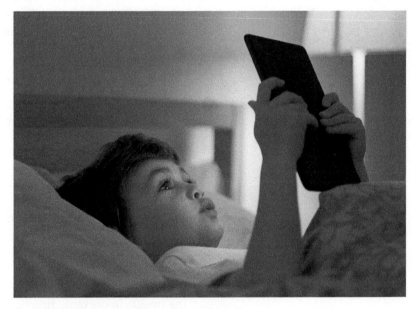

Ebooks have proven especially popular among youth.

## Outlook for Books

The recession hurt the industry, and the growth of digital media has affected few enterprises as greatly as book publishing. Ebooks, accounting for only about 1 percent of total book sales in 2008 and then 22 percent in 2012, surpassed sales of hardcover books early in 2012—and ebooks had been outselling mass-market paperbacks on Amazon eighteen months before that.[18] Ebook sales, $859 million in 2012 exceeded $9.7 billion in 2016.[19]

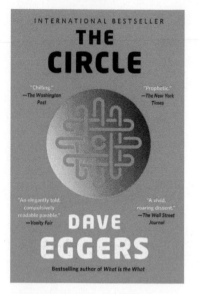

Books like Dave Eggers's *The Circle* have not only proven hugely popular reading among the YA set but have also been adapted to film, this one starring Emma Watson and Tom Hanks in a 2017 release.

Another area of tremendous growth has been audiobooks, both downloaded and physical. In 2015, there were forty-three thousand new audiobooks released, up from thirty-six thousand in 2014, and just twenty thousand in 2013.[20] Industry retail sales are estimated at $2.8 billion, with digital downloads accounting for 62 percent of net sales.[21]

The biggest takeaway from these data about the publishing industry is there is tremendous growth in printed book, ebook, and audiobook production, sales, and consumption in the U.S. and around the world.

Even as ebook sales increase, publishers seek new ways to increase revenue more quickly. One growing avenue of revenue is services such as design and technology support to independent authors. What price consumers are willing to pay for ebooks remains a question, with different publishers trying different pricing structures such as offering older titles at deep discounts, around $2.99, and newer titles around $12.99 or more. In March 2011, HarperCollins Publishing announced that library patrons could check out an ebook only twenty-six times before the library must repurchase it. The disagreements between online sellers such as Amazon and the publishing industry are being closely watched, as the results could have dramatic effects on pricing of ebooks and greatly affect the publishing industry.

Reflecting remarkable media convergence are some series of books authored by women around the world that have captured immense YA readership and have been blockbuster movies or major television series. These include Stephenie Meyer's supernatural *Twilight* series and Suzanne Collins's *Hunger Games* trilogy. Famed for her Harry Potter series, J. K. Rowling has also written an adult novel, *The Casual Vacancy*, which premiered as a BBC TV miniseries in 2015.[22]

**DISCUSSION QUESTIONS:** Consider the "wish list" of books you would like to read over the summer or during break, perhaps. What made you choose those books for your list?

## Distinctive Functions of Newspapers

Portable and inexpensive, newspapers consist largely of words, photos, and graphics printed either daily or weekly on lightweight paper stock. Printing and distribution account for roughly 65 percent of production costs; the actual creation of the news, including reporters' salaries, accounts for only about 35 percent. "News" papers also consist largely of advertising, roughly 60 percent in the typical daily U.S. format.

The most important function of modern newspapers is surveillance—informing the public of important events—yet they also perform correlation and entertainment functions. Opening and section front pages are typically all news, the most significant of which is placed "above the fold," on the top half of the page. As newspapers tend to serve communities defined by geographic, political, cultural, or economic borders, sections are generally organized by geography, including local, national, and international news; and topic, including business, culture, health, science, sports, and technology.

### LOCAL NEWSPAPERS

The vast majority of U.S. newspapers serve local geographic communities (usually city-based but with zoned suburb editions), monitoring their government, law enforcement, business, religion, education, arts, and other institutions. Some news, typically the product of larger news services such as the Associated Press and Reuters, is regional, national, or international. Local papers provide a legal record of the community's public communications, running obituaries and various announcements. Important in the local economic infrastructure, they also carry extensive advertising for community products, services, and businesses. Yet, the volume of advertising dollars being spent in local newspapers has been in steep decline and is gutting the total revenues for the newspaper industry.

## NATIONAL NEWSPAPERS

A few newspapers have emerged as truly national, with readership throughout the country. *The New York Times*, *USA Today*, and *The Wall Street Journal*, for example, each offer their own distinctive brand of news. *The New York Times*, the "paper of record" in the United States, also known as the "Old Gray Lady," offers especially strong coverage of international events and issues. *The Wall Street Journal*, bought by Rupert Murdoch's News Corp. in 2007, is the nation's leading newspaper covering business and finance. Many working in these industries also consider the *Journal* a must-read.

In 1982, newspaper mogul Al Neuharth launched *USA Today*, a strong mix of general-interest news featuring colorful graphics and easy-to-read sections, an overall design inspired by television. Prior to its launch, most newspapers were drab and filled with long columns of text. *USA Today* took ten years to become profitable; but in the meantime, it transformed the look and feel of most newspapers in the United States and many around the world.

Even more significant was its new economic model. Using then-new satellite communication technology, content was sent electronically to printing and distribution centers throughout the country, a

Japan's *Yomiuri Shimbun* has a circulation of more than fourteen million, the largest of any newspaper in the world.

**FIGURE 3-3** Trend Line in Newspaper Circulation in the United States Through 2016

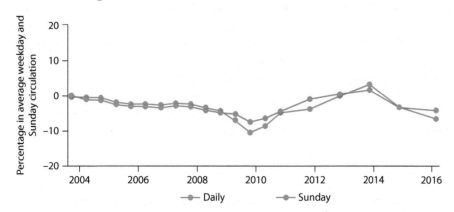

Source: http://www.journalism.org/2016/06/15/newspapers-fact-sheet/

cheaper method that permitted nationwide distribution for a daily paper, subsequently adopted by *The New York Times* and *The Wall Street Journal*.

Despite the relatively large circulation of *The Wall Street Journal* and *USA Today*, their circulation numbers are dwarfed by those of the world's largest dailies in Japan, the *Yomiuri Shimbun* (over ten million), the *Asahi Shimbun* (eight million), and the *Nikkei Keizai Shimbun* (over three million). The coverage of the *Nikkei Keizai Shimbun* resembles that of *The Wall Street Journal*.

About 75 percent of the top one hundred papers are in Asia, including the largest English-language newspaper, the *Times of India* (four million). In the United Kingdom, the three top dailies are all sensationalist tabloids: *The Sun* (two million), the *Daily Mail* (1.8 million), and the *Daily Mirror* (one million). Each of these papers has seen steady declines in their circulation since 2008 when they had circulations of 3.2 million, 2.3 million, and 1.5 million, respectively. Most newspapers are seeing print circulations diminish as readers increasingly go online. Moreover, national newspapers are also struggling to attract advertising dollars. Somewhat offsetting this decline in advertising revenues has been an increasing flow of subscriptions to the digital or online presence of newspapers. *The New York Times* and the *Washington Post*, for example, have both seen dramatic increases in their digital subscriber base since 2015. *The Times* reported an estimated 2.5 million subscribers, mostly digital only, in 2016.[23] Driving much of this growth has been the entrepreneurial efforts of these leading news media to develop new approaches to quality journalism, including producing daily 360-degree video journalism storytelling.

## History of Newspapers to Today

News pamphlets or brochures, precursors to newspapers, were printed in Germany in the 1400s. From the early 1600s, newspapers or news sheets were printed in Germany, Holland, and England. As printers often faced government censors and even imprisonment, few publications had regular schedules. The first English-language newspaper published in what is today the United States was *Publick Occurrences, Both Foreign and Domestick*. Although it was published only once—on September 25, 1690, in Boston—more newspapers followed. The American colonial press took two forms: commercial papers and political papers.

*Publick Occurrences,* although published only once, is considered the first newspaper in colonial America.

### 💬 partisan press

A press, such as colonial newspapers, typically aligned with a particular political party and presenting information to help its cause, with no sense of objectivity or balance in news coverage.

### THE COMMERCIAL PRESS AND THE PARTISAN PRESS

Merchants published the commercial papers. *The Boston Daily Advertiser* and the *Daily Mercantile Advertiser*, for example, reported on ship arrivals, departures, and cargo as well as weather and other items of commercial interest.

After independence and prior to the 1830s, most U.S. newspapers were affiliated with a political party or platform. Political parties sponsored *the Federal Republican and Daily Gazette*, for instance, which featured articles by often anonymous political figures. The **partisan press**, as it was called, did not subscribe to the modern principle of unbiased and impartial coverage and frequently and liberally borrowed news from other newspapers without attributing sources.

## COLONIAL READERSHIP AND FINANCES

A subscription to either a commercial or a political paper cost $8–10 per year or about 6¢ an issue. This was beyond the reach of the average worker, who made just 85¢ a day. Readership was largely limited to those who supported the political position of the paper and to society's well-educated, landowning, and affluent groups. By 1750, most colonists who could read had access to a newspaper, although the elite generally remained the literate class.

## THE GOLDEN AGE OF NEWSPAPERS

In the 1830s, technological developments began to transform newspapers, ushering in a golden age of newspapers in America that lasted until about 1930, when radio began to dominate.

Prior to the 1830s, printing presses, powered by hand (and briefly by horses), could print only two hundred to six hundred one-sided sheets per hour, severely limiting circulation. But in the 1830s, the development of steam-powered presses producing up to four thousand sheets per hour on both sides made mass-scale printing possible.

Seizing the opportunity, publisher **Benjamin Day** launched *The New York Sun* on September 3, 1833. Instead of traditional subscriptions, newsboys in the streets sold the daily newspaper and its sensationalized stories for only 1 cent. The **penny press** truly offered news for the masses, reaching a circulation of eight thousand almost immediately and thirty thousand within three years, enormous success that astounded contemporary publishers. As with Gutenberg's printing press some four centuries earlier, news was no longer only for the political or commercial elite but for everyone.

A new marketing function also emerged with the penny press, which attracted large audiences and, consequently, businesses hoping to reach mass markets. The newspaper price did not cover printing and distribution costs, but the penny press began advertising medicines, entertainment, and jobs as well as items on which the commercial and partisan press frowned, such as theater, lotteries, and abortionists. Advertising became the primary revenue source in the modern business model.

Newspapers proliferated in the golden age, feeding the appetite for news in large eastern cities such as New York, Boston, and Philadelphia. Between 1870 and 1900, the U.S. population doubled, the urban population tripled, and the number of daily newspapers quadrupled. The 1880 U.S. Census counted 11,314 newspapers. Metropolitan newspapers sprouted throughout the nation, helmed by innovators whose names still resonate such as James Gordon Bennett, Horace Greeley, Joseph Pulitzer, William Randolph Hearst, and E. W. Scripps.

**Benjamin Day**

Publisher of *The New York Sun* who originated the penny press in 1833 by offering his paper on the streets for a penny.

**penny press**

Newspapers that sold for a penny, making them accessible to everyone. Supported by advertising rather than subscriptions, they tried to attract as large an audience as possible.

**DISCUSSION QUESTIONS:** Some journalism scholars are calling for newspapers to return to an era of partisan coverage, or to at least abandon the focus on objectivity that newspapers promoted throughout most of the twentieth century. Would you favor this type of coverage? Why or why not?

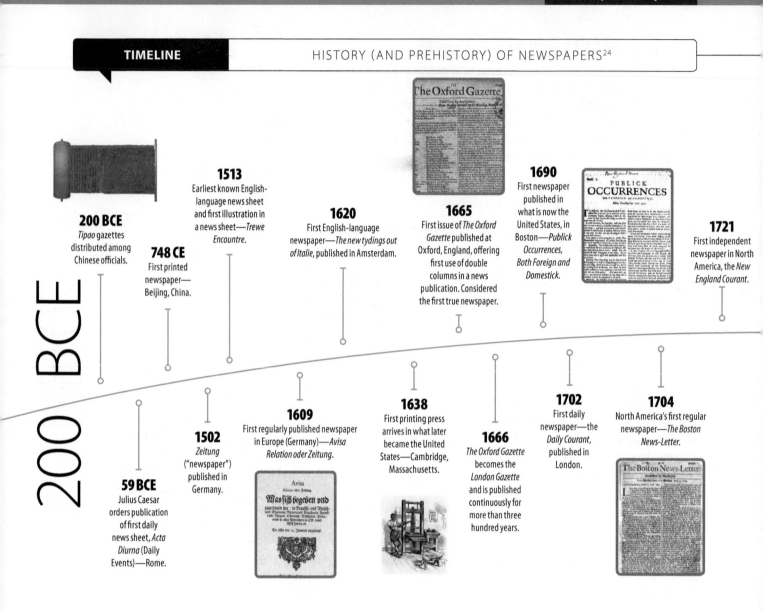

## 200 BCE

**200 BCE**
*Tipao* gazettes distributed among Chinese officials.

**748 CE**
First printed newspaper—Beijing, China.

**1513**
Earliest known English-language news sheet and first illustration in a news sheet—*Trewe Encountre.*

**1620**
First English-language newspaper—*The new tydings out of Italie,* published in Amsterdam.

**1665**
First issue of *The Oxford Gazette* published at Oxford, England, offering first use of double columns in a news publication. Considered the first true newspaper.

**1690**
First newspaper published in what is now the United States, in Boston—*Publick Occurrences, Both Foreign and Domestick.*

**1721**
First independent newspaper in North America, the *New England Courant.*

**59 BCE**
Julius Caesar orders publication of first daily news sheet, *Acta Diurna* (Daily Events)—Rome.

**1502**
*Zeitung* ("newspaper") published in Germany.

**1609**
First regularly published newspaper in Europe (Germany)—*Avisa Relation oder Zeitung.*

**1638**
First printing press arrives in what later became the United States—Cambridge, Massachusetts.

**1666**
*The Oxford Gazette* becomes the *London Gazette* and is published continuously for more than three hundred years.

**1702**
First daily newspaper—the *Daily Courant,* published in London.

**1704**
North America's first regular newspaper—*The Boston News-Letter.*

## Current Newspaper-Industry Issues

After World War II, the urban society that had supported the penny press shifted to a more suburban population that spent considerable time commuting by automobile and relied more on radio, TV, and eventually the Internet. Tired suburban commuters preferred television for both news and entertainment in the evenings, driving afternoon papers into decline. Eventually, one paper or a morning and evening edition supplanted two or more competing dailies.

The **Newspaper Preservation Act of 1970** was intended to preserve diverse editorial opinion in communities where only two competing, or independently owned, daily newspapers exist. The two papers are ostensibly competitors but can sometimes be owned by the same company or work under a **joint operating arrangement (JOA)**, provided for by the Act. A JOA is a legal agreement that permits newspapers in the same market to merge their business operations yet maintain separate editorial operations. Today, nine cities in the United States are served by two or more major daily newspapers operating under a JOA, with eleven cities served by different newspapers under common ownership. Critics argue, however, that JOAs essentially permit monopolies.

**Newspaper Preservation Act of 1970**

Created in 1970 to preserve a diversity of editorial opinion in communities where only two competing, or independently owned, daily newspapers exist.

**joint operating arrangement (JOA)**

Legal agreement permitting newspapers in the same market or city to merge their business operations for economic reasons while maintaining independent editorial operations.

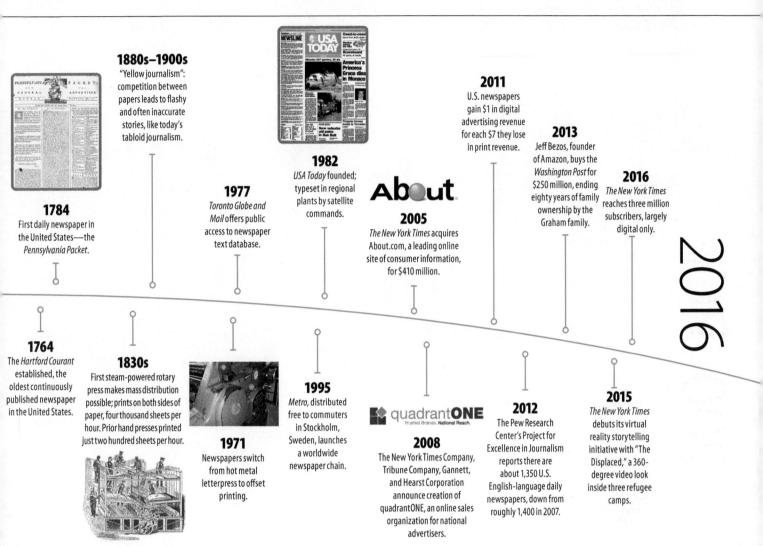

**1880s–1900s**
"Yellow journalism": competition between papers leads to flashy and often inaccurate stories, like today's tabloid journalism.

**1982**
*USA Today* founded; typeset in regional plants by satellite commands.

**2011**
U.S. newspapers gain $1 in digital advertising revenue for each $7 they lose in print revenue.

**2013**
Jeff Bezos, founder of Amazon, buys the *Washington Post* for $250 million, ending eighty years of family ownership by the Graham family.

**2016**
*The New York Times* reaches three million subscribers, largely digital only.

**1784**
First daily newspaper in the United States—the *Pennsylvania Packet*.

**1977**
*Toronto Globe and Mail* offers public access to newspaper text database.

**2005**
*The New York Times* acquires About.com, a leading online site of consumer information, for $410 million.

**2016**

**1764**
The *Hartford Courant* established, the oldest continuously published newspaper in the United States.

**1830s**
First steam-powered rotary press makes mass distribution possible; prints on both sides of paper, four thousand sheets per hour. Prior hand presses printed just two hundred sheets per hour.

**1971**
Newspapers switch from hot metal letterpress to offset printing.

**1995**
*Metro*, distributed free to commuters in Stockholm, Sweden, launches a worldwide newspaper chain.

**2008**
The New York Times Company, Tribune Company, Gannett, and Hearst Corporation announce creation of quadrantONE, an online sales organization for national advertisers.

**2012**
The Pew Research Center's Project for Excellence in Journalism reports there are about 1,350 U.S. English-language daily newspapers, down from roughly 1,400 in 2007.

**2015**
*The New York Times* debuts its virtual reality storytelling initiative with "The Displaced," a 360-degree video look inside three refugee camps.

Modern newspapers are still changing significantly, particularly with regard to the news and advertising content. Even leading newspapers are more likely to pander to popular taste to maintain circulation numbers. Departing from the editorial tradition (established after the penny press days) of selecting newsworthy topics regardless of general appeal, many newspapers are deferring to marketing polls and focus groups when setting standards for content, tone, and layout. To cut costs, many newspapers have closed international news bureaus and even statehouse news bureaus, relying instead on wire service news. Brightly colored photos and graphics like those pioneered in *USA Today* can, if properly executed, actually aid and enhance reading. Done poorly, however, they can trivialize the news and even confuse or mislead.

Newspapers have been experimenting with the electronic delivery of news to consumers since the late 1970s when newspapers such as the *Globe and Mail* (Toronto) allowed public access to their news databases. Yet most early efforts were not very successful in the days before widely available personal computers or Internet access. Reading text on computer screens was also very tiring.

Many newspapers view the Internet as a threat to their business model for subscriptions and advertising. Some have opted to reduce the days per week they print.

Others, such as *the Christian Science Monitor* and the *Seattle Post-Intelligencer*, have eliminated paper format altogether. Most adaptations involve some combination of an expanded online presence and greater interactivity, including user-generated content, which begins to blur the traditional line between reporter and reader.

## NEWSPAPER CHAINS

Another successful business model has relied on the newspaper chain. Traditionally, U.S. newspapers were owned by families, individuals, or political parties generally residing in the communities their newspapers served. In the twentieth century, both in the United States and globally, ownership became increasingly concentrated; and most newspapers today are part of a group ("chains") owned by a privately held or publicly traded company.

The newspaper business has historically been among the most lucrative enterprises, earning double the profit margins of other industry sectors. Profit margins in the 1990s were often in the range of 20 percent of gross revenues. Newspapers became a desirable target for investors. Large newspaper chains have successfully bought up smaller independent local or regional newspapers that faced shrinking audiences and advertising revenue as well as rising costs for newsprint and other necessary resources. Profit margins have narrowed drastically for newspapers, no longer making them investment targets. Some major papers, such as the tabloid *New York Daily News*, lose millions of dollars each year as they search for buyers.

### Benefits of Chains

Chain resources are one of the benefits for smaller, struggling newspapers. This can be especially important in communities where a single advertiser accounts for considerable advertising revenue, a situation that may compromise the rigor of reporting on this company. Chains also offer shared resources for news gathering, especially when covering regional, national, or international stories—much as newspapers have benefited from a working relationship with the Associated Press.

### Problems with Chains

Chains, especially those publicly owned and traded, can pressure local newspapers for higher profits. One common cost-cutting strategy is eliminating reporters and filling the news hole with wire service copy or material from the chain's other papers.

Chain-owned newspapers can weaken the connection between the local media and the local community. As cheaper wire service or chain-produced content squeezes out local reporting, people are forced to look elsewhere for local news. This sets up a spiral of decline—as readership drops, so do advertising profits, forcing more cost cuts either through fewer pages or reduced staff, making the paper even less relevant to readers.

## LEADING NEWSPAPER CHAINS

From the beginning of the twenty-first century, an accelerated pace of chain mergers and sales transformed the business landscape. In 2006, for example, the McClatchy Company, the eighth-largest chain in the United States, paid $4.5 billion to buy Knight Ridder, the second-largest newspaper chain at the time, well known in the industry for its innovative expertise with new technologies. The industry continues to change dramatically with seemingly monthly acquisitions and mergers. In 2015, Apollo Global, a management company, was working toward purchasing Digital

First Media, which only a year before bought up Media News Group; and Gannett was poised to acquire ten of the newspapers currently in the Digital First Media portfolio once the Apollo deal went through. (See Figure 3-4.) In 2016, Gannett purchased *The Record* of Bergen County, NJ, one of the last family-owned newspapers in New Jersey.

## DECLINING NUMBER OF DAILY NEWSPAPERS

Since 1940, the total number of daily newspapers has dropped more than 21 percent, with 1,331 weekday dailies in the United States in 2014. In 2000, the number of morning dailies first exceeded, and has continued to exceed, the number of evening papers. Since 1940, the number of evening papers has decreased 51 percent, whereas the number of morning papers has increased over 100 percent, doubling since 1980 to 862 daily, with 525 afternoon daily papers in 2009. The number of Sunday papers has increased 65 percent since 1940, reaching a high of 917 in 2005 but falling to 923 by 2014.[25]

Citizen journalism is often criticized for failing to meet professional standards. **CRITICAL THINKING QUESTIONS:** In what instances do you think that this criticism is justified? Identify two or three news stories that might have been told very differently or not at all had citizen journalists not documented events. How can you tell if this type of reporting is legitimate or not?

# Sales and Readership of Newspapers

The printing press, newsprint, ink, press operators, delivery trucks and drivers, and maintenance of subscriber databases as well as various other non-news-related production and distribution costs make up roughly two-thirds of the overall cost of publishing a newspaper. That activities other than producing news account for most of the cost presents a considerable opportunity for digital newspapers.

Still, newspapers are having trouble adapting to the digital era. Readership, circulation, and advertising were continuing to diminish even before digital media. Shrinking circulation has made newspapers less appealing to advertisers, who have gone online—although not necessarily to the online newspaper.

One notable difference here is that the online newspaper sites compete directly with the leading national broadcast and cable television news. In fact, with growing calls for converged newsrooms and wider broadband access among the general public, newspaper websites increasingly feature audio, video, and multimedia.

Online newspaper sites also face direct competition on a number of other online fronts such as blogs, news aggregators such as Google News and Reddit, international news outlets such as Al Jazeera, social media, and **citizen journalism**. A field that has exploded with the growth of digital media, citizen journalism broadens the scope of news content, increases the diversity of voices in the public sphere, captures compelling stories as they often unexpectedly unfold in real time, and reveals images that might otherwise have remained hidden. Despite its many benefits, trained journalists often view this particular brand of competition with skepticism for its lack of professional standards, most notably on the dimensions of veracity and objectivity.

## CIRCULATION AND READERSHIP

Newspaper **readership** (number or percentage who read a newspaper) is larger than **circulation** (number of copies sold or distributed) because of "pass-along readership," readers who read the same copy. A growing U.S. population makes

**citizen journalism**

The gathering and sharing of news and information by public citizens, particularly via mobile and social media, sometimes via traditional media.

**readership**

Number or percentage of newspaper readers.

**circulation**

Number of newspaper copies sold or distributed.

it appear that the number of newspaper readers has not decreased greatly. As a percentage, however, diminished readership and time spent reading are evident. Young readers are fewer than those between thirty-five and sixty-five. Yet despite this sharp decline in recent years, statistics indicate that the young are reading news online or on mobile devices in higher numbers than they were, with digital content often published by daily-newspaper parent organizations.

> **DISCUSSION QUESTIONS:** Consider your campus newspaper. How often do you read it, and do you actively seek it out when it is published? How would you get information on the school and events if you did not have the campus paper?

## ADVERTISING

Advertising generates close to two-thirds of U.S. newspaper revenue, with the rest from subscriptions. In other countries such as Japan, subscription prices are higher, and the revenue split is closer to 50–50. Since 2006, advertising revenue has fallen 48 percent, 26 percent in 2009, but only 6.3 percent in 2010. Online ad revenues, which grew quickly before 2008 and then declined slightly between 2008

### CONVERGENCE CULTURE
# Freesheets: Riding the Rails of Newspapers' Future?

It looked like a crazy idea, even back in 1995. At a time when newspapers were already struggling with rising costs and budget crises and just starting to understand the threat of the World Wide Web, Pelle Tornberg launched a free daily newspaper in Stockholm for subway commuters.

Designed to be read in fifteen minutes, the *Metro* was a colorful tabloid, with short articles on a variety of topics. Its target audience was an elusive yet lucrative readership for advertisers—the young, affluent, and urban—precisely the demographic that had largely stopped reading newspapers.

Now there are 210 free newspapers in fifty countries, with a total worldwide circulation of forty million. The *Metro* chain of freesheets has expanded throughout Europe, Latin America, and Asia and into New York, Boston, and Philadelphia. They are now in a hundred cities in twenty countries and publish in eighteen languages.[26]

Free newspapers remain the fastest-growing segment of newspapers worldwide, although growth has slowed in some key markets. *The New York Metro* and its competitor, *am NewYork*, have been struggling to attain the kind of popularity seen in Europe. Even there, however, freesheets have had to close down in some cities.

Freesheets have shown themselves to be sustainable and popular, although environmentalists still protest this proliferation of printed paper, their concerns

about trees compounded by those about recycling that, they argue, uses harmful chemicals. The worldwide *Metro* chain claims to be the largest newspaper in the world. As tablet use rises, however, freesheet readers may transfer to paid-circulation newspapers; and the question remains whether reading freesheets will instill a lifetime habit of reading newspapers online or offline. The impact of electronic paper, or paper-thin flexible displays, now seen in Samsung's flexible OLED phone, may prove even more transformative.

and 2010, still fell far short of making up for the lost print ad revenues. Figure 3-5 shows that while print ad revenues have declined by more than half since 2003, online ad revenues have more than doubled—even though online ad revenues are still less than 18 percent that of print ad revenues.

As Figure 3-6 shows, advertising in all three main categories for newspapers—retail, national, and classifieds—has been down sharply since 2005. Sites such as Craigslist and eBay and services such as Groupon have siphoned away classified ads, down 75 percent since 2005, traditionally a large portion of newspaper advertising revenue. Job recruitment has fallen the greatest: Newspapers received revenues from recruitment classifieds of $8.7 billion in 2000 but only $760 million in 2011 and revenues have continued to decline in the years since.

Publishers generally believe that online advertising could continue to grow but will likely not be enough to support publications as print advertising did. Consequently, they are still exploring revenue options, especially the digital paywall, in which readers must pay after receiving a certain number of stories for free. Although this seems to be working for big-name newspapers such as *The New York Times*, smaller newspapers that compete with hyperlocal citizen journalism sites for local readers' attention may have less success with this option.

**FIGURE 3-5** Print Versus Online Ad Revenue (2011–2015)

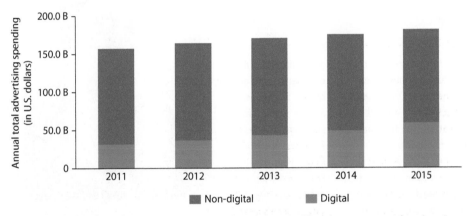

Source: Pew Research Center (http://www.journalism.org/2016/06/15/digital-news-revenue-fact-sheet/)

**FIGURE 3-6** Newspaper Print Ad Revenue Declines

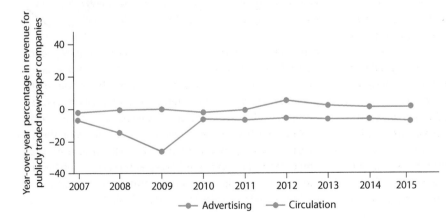

Source: Pew Research Center (http://www.journalism.org/2016/06/15/newspapers-fact-sheet/)

# Outlook for Newspapers

"The rumors of my death have been greatly exaggerated," once quipped Mark Twain, after reading his own obituary in a local newspaper. Can the same be said for newspapers?

We consider six major trends in light of this question. First, more newspaper executives are outsiders, with little appreciation or understanding of the industry's unique aspects. Second, digital subscription models progress slowly. Willingness to pay for digital subscriptions is often promoted through bundling with other incentives, such as receiving a Sunday paper or offering some stories for free. Third, understanding and measuring audiences have become increasingly critical in an online world where social media have made clicks or page views less relevant than they were only a few years ago. Fourth, local coverage is increasingly important (although staff reductions have made it harder to provide), some of which occurs on citizen journalism sites or with bloggers. Still, this coverage is typically not nearly as extensive as that of professional reporters covering local beats. Fifth, smaller but more numerous revenue streams need to be developed as alternatives

## MEDIA PIONEERS
# Ruben Salazar

On August 29, 1970, while riots stemming from a Chicano civil rights march raged in the chaotic streets, tear gas launched by a Los Angeles County sheriff flooded the Silver Dollar Cafe and sent its occupants rushing out the back door—all except one unable to react, having been killed instantly by the direct impact of the tear-gas projectile. The victim was forty-two-year-old Ruben Salazar, a name unfamiliar to many Americans but a man who would soon become a martyr to many Chicanos. No charges were filed after a formal inquest, yet lingering questions about the circumstances of his death continue to enhance the Salazar mystique.

In a distinguished career cut tragically short, the most prominent Latino journalist of his day interviewed Robert F. Kennedy, Richard Nixon, Dwight D. Eisenhower, and César Chávez, among other luminaries. Salazar, whose children were raised to speak only English at his Anglo wife's request, did not set out to become an activist, much less an icon in the burgeoning Chicano movement. A *Man in the Middle*, the apt title of a 2014 PBS documentary, Ruben was born to a conservative family of immigrants from Juarez and grew up in El Paso, where he majored in journalism at the University of Texas while working as a reporter and editor for the college newspaper.

Still, his early reporting revealed signs of the muckraking for which he would later be known. One of his first articles for the *El Paso Herald*, for example, described the notorious local jail, whose deplorable conditions he had experienced firsthand

after feigning public drunkenness to get arrested. Subsequently, Salazar worked for the *Los Angeles Times* as a foreign correspondent in Viet Nam and in the Dominican Republic and as bureau chief in Mexico City. Salazar's later domestic reporting and columns exposed the many social injustices that Mexican Americans confronted in Los Angeles, such as inferior political representation, education, employment, and housing—a mission he also pursued as news director of KMEX, a Los Angeles Spanish-language TV station.[27]

A stamp issued by the U.S. Postal Service in 2008 commemorates this activist journalist's pioneering achievements. Ruben Salazar, in an era that had yet to appreciate or even invoke the value of diversity, embodied it in his relentless and principled pursuit of the complexities of professional and personal truths. An independent observer, a critical thinker, and a man of the people, he offered this metaphor on the dual cultural identity that informed his work: "The international bridge that connected Juarez and El Paso symbolized the division of my life. No matter which way I crossed this bridge, I could not leave either side behind."[28]

to traditional advertising and subscription-based models. Sixth, after the government bailout of the U.S. auto industry, advertising increased across all media channels. Relaxed restrictions on political advertising also greatly helped newspapers and other media.

Today's 24/7 news cycles mean newspapers must constantly update content. Other changes to meet audience needs may include interpreting or analyzing news events and more interactive multimedia; but these efforts could bring them into direct competition with news magazines, both print and digital, and make concepts like a weekly or even a daily newspaper obsolete.

## Distinctive Functions of Magazines

Three factors clearly distinguish magazines from newspapers. First, magazines typically feature longer treatment of topics. Magazines gained popularity in the 1800s with serial novels, released one chapter at a time over many issues, or excellent short stories. Charles Dickens, author of *A Tale of Two Cities*, *A Christmas Carol*, and *Oliver Twist*, published many of his classics first as serials. Edgar Allan Poe also published most of his stories first in magazines. The circulation of *Lady's and Gentleman's Magazine* jumped from five thousand to twenty-five thousand the year Poe started writing for it, publishing *Murders in the Rue Morgue*, considered the first modern detective story, in the April 1841 issue. Many contemporary writers introduce their books with chapters or other excerpts in print or online magazines, or they create books from a series of magazine articles. Samuel Huntington's influential *The Clash of Civilizations* began as a 1993 magazine article.

Second, magazines are published at regular but less frequent intervals, most typically monthly, although weeklies and quarterlies are also common. Thus, this less time-sensitive writing tends to be more in-depth, analytical, interpretative, and creative.

Third, magazines have typically been published on higher-quality paper stock intended to be kept considerably longer than dailies. This paper is usually eight and a half by eleven inches. Certain magazine publishers, however, have reduced their size by a quarter or half inch, saving money on printing costs while maintaining advertising and subscription fees. Other magazines, such as *Rolling Stone* and *ESPN Magazine*, print on larger stock that stands out on crowded shelves.

A magazine tends to have a defined audience, without which attracting advertisers may pose a problem. (*LOOK* and *LIFE*, two general-interest magazines of the mid-twentieth century, are notable exceptions.) Magazines serve several important functions for their respective audiences and society, especially surveillance, correlation, entertainment, and marketing. Surveillance, the most basic function, is ordered by subject matter rather than geographic area. (Travel or regional-interest magazines are notable exceptions.) Most magazines cover specific topics such as science, health, or sports; some treat highly specialized topics

Because of their highly visual nature, magazines are well suited for the tablet format.

such as doll collecting, harness racing, or scuba diving. Other magazines, such as *People* and *Entertainment Weekly*, aim largely or exclusively to entertain.

Many magazines have national, regional, or even international readership and distribution. The longer news stories found in major publications, such as *the Economist* and *TIME*, can provide greater detail than newspaper articles. Higher-quality magazine paper can support exceptional photography and illustrations well suited to covering fashion, nature, entertainment, and science.

Almost all magazines serve a vital marketing function for a broad cross section of goods and services. Readers often spend more time perusing ads than reading content, especially with fashion magazines such as *Vogue*, *Glamour*, and *GQ*. These feature not only the latest designer news but also the hottest ads. Most magazines have developed tablet editions, sometimes adding audio and video content. Specific audiences are increasingly targeted by iPad magazines, such as *Cosmopolitan for Latinas* and *Uptown*, aimed at African Americans.

> **DISCUSSION QUESTIONS:** Identify and describe the magazines you typically read, why you read them, and how you read them (print, digital, or some combination of both).

## History of Magazines to Today

The early histories of magazines and newspapers are interwoven. Their technological, business (i.e., advertising), and journalistic/entertainment functions overlapped, and both helped spur the development of modern mass media. Not until 1731 did the first English-language periodical use "magazine" in its title: *The Gentleman's Magazine*, published in London. Benjamin Franklin published *Poor Richard's Almanack* in 1732, a predecessor of the modern magazine. In 1741 in Philadelphia, the first magazine was published in North America, the *American Magazine, or a Monthly View of the Political State of the British Colonies*. In 1811, the first newsweekly magazine, *Niles' Weekly Register*, was published.

In the nineteenth century, magazines helped a young America define itself and reach a nationwide audience. Newspapers were primarily metropolitan or local, while some magazines spoke to a national audience. Magazines such as *Harper's Weekly* also took the lead in developing sports journalism in the 1800s, reporting on, for example, the Schuylkill regatta in September 1876. Frank Leslie founded a variety of periodicals in this era, including one of the first influential newsweeklies, *Frank Leslie's Illustrated Newspaper*, launched in 1855. In 1871, he hired Miriam Florence Folline as editor of *Frank Leslie's Lady's Journal*. Frank's business went bankrupt in 1877; but after he died, in 1880, Miriam, whom he had married in 1874, took it over and skillfully restored its financial health. One of the wealthiest and most powerful women in journalism, she bequeathed some $2 million to the cause of women's suffrage.

In 1888, *National Geographic*, founded by the National Geographic Society, debuted, and it introduced color plates in 1906. Time Inc., founded by Henry Luce, bought humor and general-interest *Life* magazine in 1936 and made it into a weekly newsmagazine with a large format and excellent photography that produced many iconic images of the mid-twentieth century. Weekly publication ceased in 1972 due to dwindling circulation, but different iterations followed: a themed news magazine; a monthly news magazine; a Sunday newspaper supplement; and finally, in 2009, a website featuring many of its famous images. Focusing on its cable and film interests, Time Warner announced in 2013 it would spin off Time Inc. into a

In the later nineteenth century, national magazines helped the growing United States establish a common sense of identity and culture.

separate, publicly owned company. It currently owns several magazines, including *TIME*, *Sports Illustrated*, and *Fortune*.

Just as the efforts of nineteenth-century newspaper publishers laid the foundation for posterity, so did the influential work of a number of important magazine journalists from the late nineteenth and early twentieth centuries. Among the most important were the **muckrakers**, dubbed so by a disapproving President Theodore Roosevelt because they pioneered investigative reporting of corrupt practices in government and business. "Muck" was the polite term for the manure, mud, and straw mixture found in stables. Notable muckrakers included Ida Minerva Tarbell, Joseph Lincoln Steffens, and Upton Sinclair (author of *The Jungle*). Lengthy investigations meant muckrakers often reported for magazines rather than newspapers. Muckraking investigative journalism served as a foundation for much of the long-form, investigative reporting seen today in a variety of leading news media, particularly quality public service digital initiatives such as *ProPublica*.

**muckrakers**

Journalists, particularly magazine journalists, who conduct investigative reporting on major corporations and government; they were dubbed muckrakers in the early twentieth century for the "muck" they uncovered.

## Current Magazine-Industry Issues

In the 1940s and 1950s, television quickly drew national advertisers seeking large audiences. Consequently, general-interest magazines such as *LIFE* and *LOOK* saw their business base dissolve.

Magazine publishers, who had to adapt to survive, stopped publishing general-interest magazines in favor of specialized magazines on almost every conceivable topic, a move that attracted advertisers who wished to target specific audiences. Nearly eighteen thousand specialized magazines are now available in print, online, and on mobile devices.

Entrepreneur John H. Johnson recognized the unmet media needs of African Americans, founding *Ebony* magazine in 1945. His hometown high school in Arkansas City, Arkansas, was "whites only," so Johnson's family moved to Chicago, where he got his formal high school education. His mother funded his business by pawning her household furniture and giving her son $500 to start *Ebony*, which now has a circulation of more than 1.2 million. Johnson became a leading cross-media owner in the United States, with a book publishing company, a nationally syndicated television program, and two radio stations.[29] One of the first African Americans to appear on the Forbes 400 List, Johnson had an estate valued at $500 million on his death.

Magazines specialize in several major topic areas. In fact, Bacon's annual directory of magazines lists 225 market classifications. Ten of the most important, at least in terms of circulation, are news, fashion, women (with at least three major subgroups: middle-aged and older women, women under thirty-five, and teenage girls), families (especially aimed at parents of children under age twelve), sports (with some general interest but many specialized by sport), ethnic, medical/health, political, farm (*Farm Journal* alone has a circulation of 815,000), and lifestyles (type of home, region, cooking, etc.).

## Sales and Readership of Magazines

Contemporary magazines, like all media, are increasingly subject to ownership consolidation and media concentration. The magazine industry did not suffer the same steep drops in circulation and advertising seen with newspapers during the recession. Nevertheless, it did suffer; and the recession claimed some notable victims, such as *U.S. News & World Report*, which stopped publishing in 2010 and went entirely online except for its college- and hospital-ranking issues. *Newsweek* also changed dramatically between 2007 and 2010, cutting staff and revising format to accommodate a revenue decline of 38 percent. Eventually, the Washington Post Company sold *Newsweek* to Tina Brown's *The Daily Beast*; and on January 4, 2013, it became a digital-only publication. In August 2013, it was sold to IBT Media.

Despite established magazines going to online-only editions, hundreds of new magazine titles are published every year. Most do not survive more than two years. The leading circulation magazines reflect general trends. Even the top print magazines, which target specific audiences and cover specialized subjects in depth and with quality, are not immune. Those with the largest circulation appeal to large and growing audience segments, such as aging baby boomers who are more likely to read a print format than younger people. However, young people are also proving to be avid magazine readers (although often in digital-only form), with 90 percent of college students saying they had read a magazine in the last month.[30]

Table 3-1 compares the top ten paid-circulation magazines in the United States in 2016.[31] The positions of both *AARP The Magazine* and *AARP Bulletin*, publications

## TABLE 3-1 Top Ten U.S. Paid-Circulation Magazines*

| RANK | PUBLICATION | CIRCULATION |
|:---:|---|:---:|
| 1 | AARP® | 23,144,225 |
| 2 | AARP Bulletin | 22,700,945 |
| 3 | Costco Connection | 8,740,785 |
| 4 | Better Homes and Gardens | 7,645,364 |
| 5 | gameinformer | 6,353,075 |
| 6 | AAA Living | 4,898,168 |
| 7 | GOOD HOUSEKEEPING | 4,315,026 |
| 8 | FamilyCircle | 4,056,156 |
| 9 | People | 3,418,555 |
| 10 | Woman's Day | 3,275,962 |

*Data as of June 30, 2016
Source: Alliance for Audited Media, 2016

of the American Association of Retired Persons, reflect the fact that America's population is aging. In 1972, most of the magazines were either women's or general interest with subscriptions. In 2016, the top two magazines, sent as AARP membership perks, have circulations far greater than the rest.

After years of slow but steady declines, the magazine industry is finally starting to see some growth, thanks to increased advertising and readership in digital editions, a trend the industry predicts will continue. This prediction is supported by specific magazine data in Table 3-2 that shows digital magazine sales, both subscriptions and single copies, are growing and, in many cases, vastly exceed newsstand sales.

## TABLE 3-2 Digital Issues a Significant Portion of Magazine Sales

*Average digital issue circulation for subscription and single copy sales*

| | 2011 | | 2012 | | 2013 | | 2014 | |
| --- | --- | --- | --- | --- | --- | --- | --- | --- |
| | SUBS | NEWSSTAND | SUBS | NEWSSTAND | SUBS | NEWSSTAND | SUBS | NEWSSTAND |
| The Atlantic | 2,360 | 592 | 6,122 | 661 | 9,788 | 468 | 10,266 | 713 |
| The Week | N/A | N/A | 2,602 | 42 | 2,626 | 161 | 3,327 | 28 |
| The New Yorker | 27,372 | 1,953 | 51,157 | 799 | 73,802 | 8,837 | 80,153 | 9,956 |
| The Economist | 5,321 | 85 | 5,944 | 181 | 8,674 | 145 | 7,351 | 69 |
| TIME | N/A | N/A | N/A | N/A | 44,938 | 5,259 | 49,191 | 16,001 |
| The Nation | 9,205 | 58 | 14,720 | 129 | 25,928 | 121 | 27,941 | 63 |
| National Review | 5,918 | 4,012 | 14,764 | 459 | 11,561 | 163 | 10,338 | 113 |
| Fortune | N/A | N/A | N/A | N/A | 9,107 | 4,821 | 11,666 | 9,105 |
| The New Republic | N/A | N/A | 3,374 | 110 | 6,788 | 170 | 7,992 | 118 |
| Rolling Stone | 15,190 | 519 | 19,976 | 674 | 24,121 | 2,349 | 28,913 | 23,506 |
| Vanity Fair | 11,171 | 7,132 | 43,351 | 3,604 | 60,820 | 18,018 | 62,746 | 17,530 |
| New York Magazine | 786 | 304 | 2,848 | 296 | 5,200 | 6,939 | 19,463 | 26,112 |
| Bloomberg Business Week | 18,334 | 171 | 36,911 | 53 | 37,423 | 727 | 54,004 | 2,725 |
| Wired | 17,629 | 10,076 | 73,066 | 3,423 | 86,178 | 16,843 | 75,369 | 20,870 |

Source: Alliance for Audited Media, AAM Audits and Publisher Statements. "News Use Across Social Media Platforms." (Pew Research Center, Washington, DC, April 2015. Retrieved April 11, 2017, from http://www.journalism.org/2015/04/29/news-magazines-fact-sheet/)
Note: *National Review, Bloomberg* and *New York Magazine* twelve-month audits come out in June. 2011 data for *Bloomberg Business Week, National Review,* and *New York Magazine* are from the six-month publisher's statements ending in December 2011. 2012 data for *The New Republic* are for three months ending December 2012; before 2012, *The New Republic* was not audited by AAM. *Newsweek* hasn't been audited since August 2013 and did not report digital replica copies for any of the years before. *Forbes* does not break out digital issues in AAM's statements.

# Outlook for Magazines

The rise in popularity of tablets and other portable devices with relatively large screens and high resolution has helped increase reading activity, including longer-form content, compared to the laptop or PC era. Paragraph Shorts, an iPad app launched in 2013, features short stories from publications around the world such as *The Paris Review*, *The New Yorker*, and *The Guardian*; and notables such as Ira Glass of PRI's (Public Radio International) *This American Life* narrate audio stories.

Although long-form narratives typically seen in magazines such as *the New Yorker* and the *Atlantic Monthly* must compete with a range of other content, including video or audio content, there appears to be a market for these types of stories, even if in primarily digital form.

Full-color pages and high-quality glossy paper make print magazines both expensive to produce and environmentally unfriendly, even with recycled paper and vegetable inks. Visually enticing and readable magazine pages may also be their saving grace, though, as tablets improve and more magazines go digital. For now, high-quality print is still more readable than text on a similarly sized tablet screen, although the differences are rapidly narrowing, and digital offers multimedia and interactivity. Magazine ads, print or digital, can be works of graphic art, and the portability and relatively low cost of a magazine do not make consumers feel like they are making a major investment.

Certain magazines can also serve an important social function. Publicly reading *The New Yorker* imparts a very different impression of the reader than *Popular Hot Rodding* or *Guns & Ammo*. In fact, magazines considered prestigious can operate as subtle social markers simply by being displayed on the coffee table in the home or office, even if the magazine is never actually read.

It seems the public is willing to pay for an online subscription to a magazine perceived as the voice of authority in a specialized area. *Consumer Reports Online*, one of the few subscription success stories in the online-magazine world, has over three million subscribers who can access archived articles and reviews.[32] Enhancing this product is the Consumer Reports Mobile iPad app that allows subscribers to consult an authoritative source while out shopping.

The type of magazine content we see today may not change much, but the way in which we see it will. Despite several pressures, magazines continue to maintain some important advantages over newspapers as relevant print-based products. In the long term, however, print magazines will likely lose their relative importance, whereas better tablet screens, such as Apple's iPad high-resolution retina display, give magazines a new lease on life and a digital home.

## MEDIA CAREERS

The title of book editor seems self-explanatory, but these professionals do much more than just edit (although they do that, too). Book editors are responsible for reading unpublished manuscripts submitted by authors and determining which ones may be most successful on the market. A book editor who successfully finds and shepherds a bestseller or two through the publishing process is well on the way to an impressive career in the book publishing industry.

Although one may imagine a successful book editor working in a global publishing house such as HarperCollins and hobnobbing with famous authors, thousands of smaller publishing companies, including academic and textbook publishers, offer rewarding careers (if not quite the same fame and glory). Editors can become knowledgeable about specialized academic areas, working with leading scholars in their fields to help them publish their books.

Good writing and editing skills are needed, of course, as well as a keen eye for detail and an understanding of the changing trends in the market. Liberal arts graduates, by training and interest, often make good editors, as they can draw from their knowledge on a range of subject matter while employing their critical thinking and writing skills. An increasingly essential skill is the entrepreneurial spirit and innovative leadership that the media professional brings to her or his work. Identifying opportunities for new experimentation, especially where it may intersect with social networking and the traditionally print-based media, is a quality that can enhance career opportunities in books, ebooks, newspapers, magazines, and other areas of publishing in the twenty-first century.

## LOOKING BACK AND MOVING FORWARD

In a media-saturated world of eye-catching multimedia and flashy graphics, gray, quiet, dull print seems like it will be less appealing to many. Indeed, some studies indicate a worrisome decline in reading among adults, especially young people. If print has improved our ability to think logically and rationally, that raises questions about how today's digital media may be affecting our thinking, adversely or otherwise. However, even with the proliferation of new media options, reading remains an important activity—some may say it could become even more important, especially if media literacy and critical-thinking skills decline.

From an economic perspective, media industries that have relied on printing on paper are facing grave challenges, not because the content has become irrelevant but because the packaging has changed. Just as scrolls eventually gave way to books and the form of writing also evolved, printed books are beginning to yield to digital formats that may produce equally revolutionary transformations.

Similarly, newspapers and magazines are facing drastic adjustments. There is nothing sacred or magical about the form of the modern newspaper (although for people who grew up reading newspapers, it may seem so); and if papers are to survive, they may need to go digital—as some major newspapers are doing. This change is not simply one of form: It will alter the nature of the newspaper and likely even the nature of news itself because it allows print to converge with audio, video, and multimedia. Whether this reduces the importance of the written word or how it alters it in our minds remains to be seen.

Print published on paper will never disappear entirely, of course; sailboats did not disappear with the rise of steamships, nor did horseback riding with the invention of railroads and cars. But the changes that will inevitably occur will transform our society and culture. And the records that will be kept—most likely in written form, albeit stored digitally—will give future historians a rearview mirror that will reveal far more about us than we realize today. Entrepreneurship may prove to be the hallmark of successful media innovation in publishing whether in print or online.

---

## MEDIA MATTERS　　PRINT MEDIA

1. Do you prefer to read your textbooks in ebook format? Other than cost, do you notice any difference in how you read texts online compared to in print?

2. Where did you buy your latest book or ebook that was not a textbook?

3. What is the oldest book you own?

4. When was the last time you read a printed newspaper?

5. Compare the print version of your favorite newspaper with its digital version. Which format do you prefer, and why?

6. What do you feel are the greatest challenges facing print media in a digital age?

7. Do you subscribe to any magazines? Which ones? Do you prefer to read them on a tablet?

8. If you subscribe to a magazine, print or digital, describe how you typically read it. For example, do you read some sections first and jump around, or do you read it cover to cover? Do you read it over a month or soon after getting it? Are your reading patterns different in the print edition versus the digital? Why or why not?

9. What do you think the magazines you read regularly say about you as a consumer?

10. How do you think the major societal functions of books, magazines, and newspapers may change in the age of digital media?

---

## FURTHER READING

*A History of Reading*. Alberto Manguel (1997) Penguin.

*An Introduction to Book History*. David Finkelstein, Alastair McCreely (2005) Routledge.

*The Book: A Global History*. Michael Suarez, H. R. Woudhuysen (2014) Oxford University Press.

*Books: A Living History*. Martyn Lyons (2011) J. Paul Getty Museum.

*Preserving the Press: How Daily Newspapers Mobilized to Keep Their Readers*. Leo Bogart (1991) Columbia University Press.

*-30-: The Collapse of the Great American Newspaper*. Charles M. Madigan (ed.) (2007) Ivan R. Dee.

*The Vanishing Newspaper: Saving Journalism in the Information Age*. Philip Meyer (2004) University of Missouri Press.

*The Death and Life of American Journalism: The Media Revolution That Will Begin the World Again*. Robert McChesney, John Nichols (2010) Nation Books.

*The Magazine from Cover to Cover*. Sammye Johnson, Patricia Prijatel (2006) Oxford University Press.

*Magazines: A Complete Guide to the Industry*. David Sumner, Shirrel Rhoades (2006) Peter Lang.

*Out of Print: Newspapers, Journalism and the Business of News in the Digital Age*. George Brock (2013) Kogan Page Limited.

*Pulp Culture: The Art of Fiction Magazines.* Frank M. Robinson, Lawrence Davidson (2007) Collectors Press.

*Newspaper Online vs. Print Ad Revenue: The 10% Problem.* Scott Karp (2007) Publishing 2.0.

*The Curse of the Mogul: What's Wrong with the World's Leading Media Companies.* Jonathan A. Knee, Bruce Greenwald, Ava Seave (2009) Portfolio.

*Just My Type: A Book About Fonts.* Simon Garfield (2011) Gotham Books.

# Audio Media
## MUSIC RECORDINGS, RADIO

Taylor Swift is an award-winning musical artist whose popularity around the United States and the world has made her one of the most successful artists of the twenty-first century and kept her at the top of the Billboard charts. She is also at the center of the continuing revolution in the distribution and sales of recorded music. Swift stunned the music industry on November 3, 2014, when she pulled her entire music catalog from the online streaming music service Spotify.[1]

Swift has never endorsed free music and explained her logic in frank and plain terms: "Music is art, and art is important and rare. Important, rare things are valuable. Valuable things should be paid for." Some anticipated that Swift's album *1989*, released in 2014, saw a boost in sales as a result of fans not being able to hear it on Spotify. One anonymous music industry source attributes high sales to other factors, however: "There are reasons why you can sell 1 million units, but it's got nothing to do with not providing that album to Spotify."

Whatever the causes, predictions for the album's success, both critical and commercial, proved accurate. Not only did her fifth studio album receive industry acclaim, it topped iTunes sales charts in over 95 countries on its release and went on to sell some 9 million albums worldwide as of December 31, 2015. It became the highest-selling release since 2002 and the top-selling album of 2014 in the United States. It also made Swift the first artist in music history to have three albums sell 1 million or more copies in the first week. In 2015, Swift, twenty-five, became the youngest person to make Forbes's list of the world's most powerful women, ranked at number 64.

In February 2015, Swift received the International Federation of the Phonographic Industry (IFPI) Award, recognizing her as the most popular recording artist worldwide in 2014. Across all music formats including physical sales, downloads, and streaming, she led Billboard charts that featured artists such as Katy Perry, Beyoncé, Eric Church, Sam Smith, Ed Sheeran, Coldplay, and One Direction. Swift has managed to thrive in an industry where sales have long been in decline, and 2014 in general was no exception to the downward trend.[2]

While Swift topped the list of musical moneymakers in 2016, with $170 million in earnings, second on the list was One Direction with $110 million in earnings (http://www.forbes.com/sites/zackomalleygreenburg/2016/11/30/the-worlds-highest-paid-musicians-of-2016/#778ffb40f411). Next is Adele with $80 million, who is one of the few leading musicians who still makes the majority of her earnings from recorded music sales. Fourth is Madonna with $76 million, and fifth, Rihanna, with $75 million.

Regardless of form or format, listening to music remains a national pastime, second only to time spent watching television. People get their music via various media—on the radio through online, broadcast, cable, or satellite transmission, or on demand through personal mobile devices such as an MP3 player or smartphone. Music is often playing in the background as people go about their daily activities or engage with other media, such as video games or books. Couples often have "their" song that seems to speak meaningfully to their particular relationship (despite the fact that it was written for mass appeal), and many a teen has played air guitar in front of the mirror while dreaming of rock stardom.

Music is an essential element of movies and television, an audio cue to what to expect or feel in particular scenes. The low-pitched, menacing music in *Jaws* (1975) whenever the shark was going to strike heightened tension as viewers feared for its next victim. The theme became so famous that other movies reprised it as parody, and daily conversation is often similarly peppered with the musical "dun, dun, dun, dun . . ." to suggest imminent trouble.

> **DISCUSSION QUESTIONS:** Is recorded music more important for teenagers than, say, people in their forties? Explain your answer.

## The Recording Industry

Similar to other media-entertainment enterprises, a few very large firms (often subsidiaries of even larger media corporations) control the music industry. Because record labels do not profit from music that lacks strong mass-market appeal, styles tend to fit well-established genres, even to the point of being formulaic and homogeneous. This situation is improving, however, as online music distribution makes more diverse artists available to fans.

## Distinctive Functions of the Recording Industry

Appealing to just about everyone, young and old alike, recorded music serves a variety of functions, primarily **entertainment** and **cultural transmission**. Education is an important form of cultural transmission. Children, especially, listen to recorded music, sometimes the same songs over and over, learning vocabulary, musical rhythms, and the pleasure of dancing. Musical tastes help people define themselves as members of a particular social group. Music can transmit culture both verbally and visually as fans adopt new expressions and emulate new styles that cross ethnic and socioeconomic boundaries.

Some argue that such cultural transmission has a potential dark side, however, a debate that intensified after the 1981 launch of MTV, whose twenty-four-hour format required scores of videos to fill airtime. Suddenly, how band members looked became as important as how they sounded. Hair bands became popular in the 1980s, groups such as Mötley Crüe, whose manes, makeup, and tight pants all played well on TV. New music channels found a home on cable in the 1990s, including channels devoted to diverse and specific genres such as heavy metal or country.

**entertainment**

Providing or being provided with amusement or enjoyment.

**cultural transmission**

The process of passing on culturally relevant knowledge, skills, attitudes, and values from person to person or group to group.

Artists may combine controversial lyrics with provocative video that critics argue send young, impressionable viewers socially unacceptable messages that may desensitize them to violence against women, for example, or promote Satanism. Research indicates that between 40 and 75 percent of music videos do contain sexual imagery, although it is generally mild and nongraphic. Sexism remains strong, however. Women are much more likely to be scantily clad, sexually objectified, and dominated by men.[3] With the rise of YouTube and other online video services, an even broader array of potentially objectionable content is available on demand.

Although MTV, YouTube, or other sources of music video may not always represent the finest work of this commercial, profit-driven enterprise intended to entertain, the recording industry also produces music that rises to the level of true art. Whether the genre is jazz, opera, pop, or hip-hop, countless studio recordings have earned critical praise for their enduring cultural impact.

> **DISCUSSION QUESTIONS:** In what ways have MTV and the music video, whether online or via television, influenced the recording-arts industry and popular music?

## History of Recorded Music

The recording arts developed in the 1870s, becoming the first medium of mass communication not based on print. They predated mass-media cinema at the turn of the century; and radio, invented in the 1890s, did not develop as a mass medium until the 1920s. In 1877, Thomas Edison patented his first "talking machine," the **phonograph**, using a tinfoil cylinder to record telephone messages. Edison held a monopoly in the recording industry for nine years until telephone pioneer Alexander Graham Bell and inventor Charles Tainter invented an improved audio-recording device, the **graphophone**, which used beeswax rather than tinfoil.

The Columbia Phonograph Company soon entered the picture with its own technology, selling recordings on wax cylinders that could be played on coin-operated machines. The Victor Talking Machine Company also launched the **gramophone**. Developed by inventor Emile Berliner, it used a flat disc rather than a cylinder to record sound.

Few dramatic changes occurred in music-recording technology over the first one hundred years. Even the mid-1950s creation of grooved vinyl long-play (LP) albums at 33 rpm (revolutions per minute), allowing playing times of forty to forty-five minutes rather than the two and a half minutes of the shellac 78 rpm albums, simply improved existing production processes and sound quality rather than revolutionizing them.

Electromagnetic tapes such as eight-track tapes, and later cassettes, created in 1965, actually provided poorer sound quality than LPs, but consumers were willing to trade audio quality for portability. Compact discs, developed in 1980, were the first conveyor of digitally recorded songs and the first real technological breakthrough in the recording arts since Edison's time. Not only can digital technology improve the sound quality of older recordings by removing unwanted noise such as pops and hisses, but it also allows for easy creation of "duets" by live and dead singers, such as the song "Unforgettable" by Nat King Cole and his daughter Natalie.

**phonograph**

First patented by Thomas Edison in 1877 as a "talking machine," it used a tinfoil cylinder to record voices from telephone conversations.

**graphophone**

An improvement on Thomas Edison's phonograph in recording audio, it used beeswax to record sound rather than tinfoil. Developed by Alexander Graham Bell and inventor Charles Tainter.

**gramophone**

Developed by inventor Emile Berliner, it used a flat disc rather than a cylinder to record sound.

It was a technological challenge to record sound on devices that would be easy for the public to use.

## FROM TIN PAN ALLEY TO HOLLYWOOD

The history of recorded music involves both technology and artistry, physical changes in the material recording as well as cultural changes in the genre of music likely to be recorded. In the early days, much of the popular music in America was created in New York's historic Tin Pan Alley, an area in Manhattan on West Twenty-Eighth Street between Broadway and Sixth Avenue, where music publishers had located close to theaters and vaudeville houses. Before record players became widespread, sheet music of songs heard in these venues was played at home. Existing for seventy years until roughly 1950, when radio and television became more important music promoters, Tin Pan Alley eventually became a generic reference to the music-publishing business that hired composers and lyricists on a permanent basis to write popular songs.

From George and Ira Gershwin to Cole Porter, many great composers were associated with the early days of Tin Pan Alley. Perhaps the artist most synonymous with the time is Irving Berlin, who achieved stardom in 1911 when his song "Alexander's Ragtime Band" became an international hit. He went on to pen such classics as "Blue Skies," "God Bless America," "White Christmas," and "There's No Business Like Show Business."

As Hollywood developed and motion pictures with sound emerged in the late 1920s and early 1930s, a recording industry also emerged in Los Angeles. The growth of musical recording and radio in the first half of the twentieth century enabled musicians and fans to hear many musical forms. A diverse array of black, Latino, Native American, Asian, and white artists created songs with audience crossover appeal that laid the foundation for much of popular music today, including rap and other formats.

## ROOTS OF ROCK AND ROLL

The roots of rock and roll lie in a blend of musical forms, including blues vocalizations; gospel musical structures; urban rhythm and blues (R&B) instrumentals; and white western and "hillbilly" strains, or rockabilly. In the late 1940s and early 1950s, a combination of country artists, such as Hank Williams and Tennessee Ernie Ford, and R&B artists, such as T-Bone Walker, Fats Domino, B. B. King, Ruth Brown, and Muddy Waters, helped shape the character of early rock and roll.

The dog Nipper "listening to his master's voice" is a widely recognized symbol of what started as the Victor Talking Machine Company.

From 1954 to 1959, rock and roll took off. Bill Haley and His Comets (western swing crossover), Ray Charles (gospel/R&B), Elvis Presley (rockabilly), Chuck Berry (R&B), Buddy Holly (rockabilly), and Ritchie Valens (Chicano rock) led the way. Popular rock vocal groups included the Platters, the Penguins, and Dion and the Belmonts as well as teen idols such as Frankie Avalon and Brenda Lee. Although much of the music owed its original inspiration to black artists, most of the commercially successful rock stars of the day were white.

This changed when Detroit's Berry Gordy Jr. started Motown Record Company in Motor City, Detroit, his hometown and a city with a historically large black population. Gordy was yet another black musician who had barely profited from his successful songwriting. With $700 borrowed

Irving Berlin was a noted composer of many of the twentieth century's most popular songs.

R&B performers Diana Ross & the Supremes were the most commercially successful Motown act and one of the most popular American vocal groups of all time, boasting twelve number 1 pop singles on the Billboard Hot 100.

from his sister and a makeshift studio in the basement, Gordy signed a kid off the street named Smokey Robinson and his backup singers, the Miracles, and started producing their music. The group quickly released a string of hits, and other successes followed when Gordy signed Diana Ross & the Supremes, Marvin Gaye, Stevie Wonder, the Jackson Five (with Michael Jackson), and many more talented black artists. By 1983, Motown was the largest black-owned company in the United States, with annual revenues of $104 million. Some thirty years after founding Motown, Gordy sold it to MCA Records in 1988.

In the 1960s, rock evolved to include Motown, as well as soul, "girl groups," surf rock, and folk. In addition to wielding musical influence, certain popular musicians also had great social and cultural impact, influencing trends and tastes, clothing and hairstyles. Folk artists such as Bob Dylan wrote songs that became anthems for social movements and shaped public opinion about the war in Vietnam, the environment, and civil rights. Reflecting his broad social influence and consummate artistry, in 1997, Dylan was nominated for a Nobel Prize in Literature.

The Who, who announced their 1982 tour would be their last, has continued to sell out arenas all over the world, with their 2014/2015 tour commemorating their 50th anniversary as a band. Founded in 1962, the Rolling Stones rock band (not shown) performed its first concert in Cuba in 2016.

## REDEFINING ROCK

"The British invasion" redefined rock in the mid- to late 1960s, with breakout groups such as the Beatles, the Rolling Stones, and the Who heightening its energy and popularity. Experimentation with drugs increased among youth in general and rock musicians in particular. Some new music strains emerged in rock, including

Rapper and entrepreneur Jay Z became the biggest artist to launch an album with an app, giving him the best opening-week sales of his career. In an unprecedented deal, Samsung purchased one million copies of *Magna Carta Holy Grail* for customers to download for free. This digital distribution method generated a new revenue stream along with a new set of problems, including piracy, server overload, and intrusive requests to access information on users' phones.

psychedelic, jazz, and early heavy metal forms. Today, a number of these early bands and artists, some of whom are even in their seventies, are still touring, much to the delight of legions of old and new fans alike, willing to pay top dollar for the experience. These living—and still performing—legends include groups who prematurely announced farewell tours decades ago.

In the 1970s, music moved from being socially conscious and experimental to highly produced and flamboyant. Glam rock bands flaunted dramatic makeup on stage, and sometimes off, as KISS did for many years. Disco appeared for a brief time in the mid-1970s, when punk also started, the latter being a response to the perceived overcommercialization of popular music. The 1980s saw the rise of heavy metal music, while pop bands such as Culture Club and Wham! sang blithely of love and infatuation. Rap left the urban streets for the mainstream in the late 1980s and early 1990s; while Seattle bands such as Nirvana, Soundgarden, and Alice in Chains developed a dark sound dubbed alternative or progressive rock.

Musical genres continue to transform and splinter as they wax and wane in popularity. Even older genres, such as swing, sometimes enjoy a short resurgence. Mainstream country music has come to sound more like country rock, for example, and some songs appear as crossover hits on both pop and country charts.

## The Recording Industry Today

On the corporate side of recording, a handful of companies controlled the industry by 1909. Geoffrey P. Hull notes that although these companies experienced major changes, a three-way corporate oligarchy dominated the music industry until the 1950s, when a variety of notable industry-wide changes set in. These included greater competition due to the growth of rock and roll and diverse new recording labels such as Motown.

Like other media companies, record labels have been consolidating. In 1998, there were six **major labels**, and in 2004 only five, including Bertelsmann Music Group (BMG) and EMI. In 2008, Sony Music absorbed BMG; and in 2012, Universal Music Group acquired EMI. Now once again, three companies have oligarchical control, each a subsidiary of a larger media empire: Universal Music Group (UMG), Sony Music Entertainment, and Warner Music Group (see Table 4-1). UMG alone controls more than 29 percent of the worldwide market for recorded music. **Independent labels**—ranging from small local companies producing and distributing the music of only one or two artists to large labels such as Disney—have the majority of music titles, estimated at about 66 percent by SoundScan and the Recording Industry Association of America (RIAA), yet only about 20 percent of the sales.

Similar to book publishing, the vast majority of releases sell fewer than 5,000 copies per year, with only a handful of recordings, numbering in the hundreds, selling more than 250,000 a year. Yet these few, largely releases by major labels, account for over half the total sales volume. How do they manage to produce so many of the big hits? Some say they reap the rewards of producing and marketing the

**major labels**

Universal Music Group, Sony Music Entertainment, and Warner Music Group—the three biggest recording-arts companies, which control much of the music industry partly through their powerful distribution channels and ability to market music to mass audiences.

**independent labels**

Small companies that produce and distribute records. Not part of the three major-label corporations, they include those producing only one or two albums a year as well as larger independents such as Disney.

**TABLE 4-1** The Major Record Labels and Their Main Subsidiary Labels

UNIVERSAL MUSIC GROUP

warner | music | group

SONY MUSIC

## MEDIA PIONEERS
# Amanda Palmer

When alternative rocker Amanda Palmer took a hiatus from the punk-cabaret duo the Dresden Dolls and decided to make her first solo album her way, she turned her back on her record label and turned instead, with open heart and empty hands, to her fans. The request? A relatively modest $100,000 to be raised on Kickstarter, one of several digital crowdfunding platforms employed by a growing number of artists. The response? An overwhelming $1.2 million—contributions from nearly twenty-five thousand of the faithful, generated in a matter of weeks in 2012.

Depending on the amount of their pledge, fans would receive recordings in various formats or related artwork perhaps. And the most financially committed, many of whom met through Twitter or Facebook to pool together the requisite $5,000, could enjoy a private concert and house party with Amanda herself.[4]

Reactions to Palmer tend toward the extreme: a vibrant visionary to fans, an entitled egotist to critics. Regardless, her provocative and unapologetic resume in the art of asking, the title of a recent TED talk that she elaborated into a book, remains pioneering and eclectic. After graduating from Wesleyan College, she spent five years as a busker in Boston's Harvard Square, a living statue called the Eight-Foot Bride. Appreciative passersby would drop money in her hat, an activity that Palmer likens to fan funding of digitally recorded music through services like Kickstarter. In both cases, audiences need to step forward and provide direct support for artists they value.

Not surprisingly, given her philosophy and business model, Palmer is vocal about the "magic" of Twitter, which, as she observed in her TED talk, allowed her to "ask instantly for anything anywhere"—a couch to sleep on, a piano to practice on, a home-cooked meal to savor backstage. And she waxed similarly effusive about the Internet in general as a means of connecting intimately and sharing freely: "Celebrity is about a lot of people loving you from a distance, but the Internet and the content that we're freely able to share on it are taking us back. It's about a

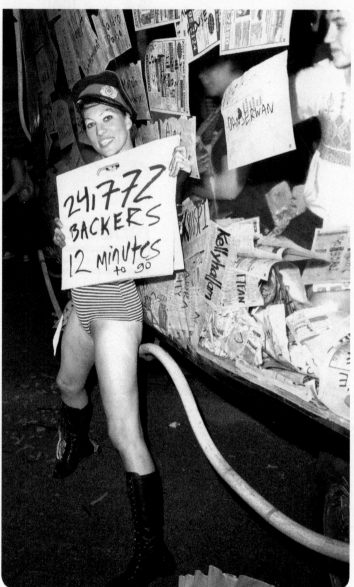

few people loving you up close and about those people being enough."[5]

In 2015 Palmer launched a new crowdfunding initiative on an alternative platform, Patreon. This campaign pledged to give any supporter who provided $1 would gain access to a patron-only feed, and those who gave at least $3 would get downloadable music content.[6]

best music from the best artists. Others say even marginal music from the major labels will dominate sales because of superior marketing.

Nevertheless, revenues have declined steeply since 2001, the beginning of the digital piracy era. In 2000, worldwide recorded music revenues were $36.9 billion. By 2015, global music sales were just $14 billion (including synch revenues, payment for use of a song in another soundtrack, such as a commercial or TV show), down more than 55 percent, according to the IFPI, a London-based organization that represents the interests of the recording industry worldwide. The industry has struggled to stem the flood of free versions or mash-ups of songs found on file-sharing services, and the RIAA and IFPI claim that file-sharing services encouraging illegal downloads are to blame for the decline in sales. Other observers say the picture is more complex than that.

Yet, the worst years may be behind, as 2016 saw a 3 percent uptick in total recorded music industry revenues, back to $15 billion worldwide. Notably, nearly half, or 45 percent of the total, are digital revenues, up to $6.7 billion, almost double the volume from 2009. [7] Consumers are increasingly willing to buy songs online via iTunes and other services, according to IFPI. However, the purchase of entire digital albums continues to decline. [8]

More encouraging news for the music industry is the fact that global revenues from streaming and subscription services increased 45 percent in 2015, reaching $2.9 billion for the first time. As CD sales drop, major retail chains such as Best Buy and Walmart, where 65 percent of all CD sales occur, give them less floor display space. Consumers' increasing use of mobile devices, especially Internet-connected smartphones, is driving the use of online music services. The waters are further muddied by exclusive distribution deals with major chains like Walmart. In 2008, AC/DC's *Black Ice*, sold exclusively at Walmart, was the fifth-highest-selling album of the year. Although sales of independent releases have also grown dramatically with the Internet and digital distribution, they continue to be low relative to most major labels, whose marketing resources and business model give them the competitive edge.

---

**DISCUSSION QUESTIONS:** How many songs in your music library have you downloaded for free? How much would you have spent if you'd purchased each song for 99¢? How many downloaded songs from new artists persuaded you to purchase that artist's CD or to buy digital song or album downloads? Do you prefer to use streaming services to access and listen to music?

---

## Recording-Industry Business Model

Throughout much of the twentieth century, the basic business model in the recorded-music industry involved creation, promotion, and distribution. These three main activities have not changed fundamentally, although some of their components have been altered in the digital age.

### CREATION

Acting as gatekeepers, the major record labels sign talent and subsequently support these artists in the creation and recording of music. Because of their financial investment in the process, they have historically reaped the greatest financial rewards, with most artists receiving royalties of only around 10 percent of gross, or overall, sales.

Being signed to a major label does not mean that a struggling band has finally made it: Most releases sell fewer than 5,000 copies annually; only a handful sell more than 250,000. Of these sales numbers, 10 percent, about $2 per album sold, is not much income for a band.[9] For every Adele selling millions of albums, there are thousands of artists who sell only a few thousand indie or major-label albums and who never get airplay.[10]

## PROMOTION

Promoting artists and their music is crucial to commercial success. Artists perform in concerts, for which additional royalties are received; but music gains exposure largely through radio, television, film, and, increasingly, video games, commercials, and mobile phone ringtones. In the past three decades, music videos have also been important. Yet, the big promotional vehicle for music in the twenty-first century is social media, where artists or their labels can offer their music online or where fans can share the latest music news or talk about their favorite songs and artists.

Major labels get considerably more airtime than indies on radio, a primary promotional vehicle. Record labels traditionally provide radio and television programmers with free copies of recorded music and music videos in exchange for airtime on their stations and channels. Unscrupulous programmers or disc jockeys in major markets have sometimes received cash, gifts, or other secret payments—**payola**—in return for increased airplay. Payola was very big in the 1950s until the Federal Trade Commission (FTC) ruled it unfairly stifled competition from smaller labels with fewer financial resources.

Payola, or "pay for play," reduces diversity on the air and is punishable today with fines or even imprisonment. Record labels have circumvented such restrictions, enforced by the Federal Communications Commission, by having artists give radio interviews in exchange for promotion, holding special events in certain markets, and giving away tickets or backstage passes in conjunction with the radio station.

### 💬 payola

Cash or gifts given to radio disc jockeys by record labels in exchange for greater airplay of the label's artists or most recent songs. After several scandals in the 1950s, the practice is now illegal.

## DISTRIBUTION

Although recording formats have varied, the method of distribution has evolved more slowly, but change is afoot. Record labels make copies from a master version and send the albums, tapes, or CDs to local retail outlets for sale to consumers. Online stores such as Amazon act much like their physical counterparts. Unfettered, however, by concerns about store display space, they can stock more CDs than retail stores, including CDs that are less popular. Still, by 2017 an increasing portion of the music distribution was online, either in the form of downloadable songs from online stores such as Apple's iTunes or via streaming services such as Amazon Music, Apple Music, Google Play, Pandora, Slacker, Spotify, and Tidal. Many are predicting the decline of downloadable files as well, eventually to be fully replaced by streaming services. iTunes music sales peaked in 2012 at $3.9 billion; they are expected to be just $600 million in 2019. In 2016, Americans listened to 431 billion songs via streaming music services.[11]

**Long tail** marketing and distribution allow businesses to succeed by selling a greater variety of items but fewer of each.

### 💬 long tail

The principle that selling a few of many types of items can be as or more profitable than selling many copies of a few items, a practice that works especially well for online sellers such as Amazon and Netflix.

Another aspect of digital media and the Internet has been changing distribution much more radically. Consumers no longer have to buy a physical product. They simply download songs either through a subscription service or à la carte. Not only can the general public easily copy and distribute music, they can also create flawless copies with no loss in sound quality. Using widely available software, they can personalize content with mash-ups of multiple songs. These developments are affecting industry business models for music distribution profoundly.

**DISCUSSION QUESTIONS:** Think of two songs from two different genres that you particularly like. Now imagine making a mash-up creatively combining elements of both songs. What commercial potential might your new mash-up have, if any?

## PRICING STRUCTURE

The pricing structure for recorded music is, of course, key in determining income for the label, the artist, and others in the distribution chain. In the 1970s, when vinyl LPs were the standard, list price (the consumer price) was about $6 (about $26 in 2012 dollars). In the 1980s, the compact disc was introduced, and CDs as a percentage of album sales gradually increased from just 22 percent in 1988 to 91 percent in 2001. List prices for CDs were about $19 in the early 1980s (about $39 in 2012 dollars), with wholesale prices about $12. Online album prices are somewhat lower, with typical prices for albums sold on iTunes at about $10 and even less on Amazon.

Music lovers around the world are using software like MiniMash to mix their own tunes from two or more songs by other artists.

Over time, as production volume increased, production cost decreased; consequently, wholesale prices fell to about $10, with list prices at about $15 or often less with promotional discounts. Today, manufacturing costs for record labels are about $1 per CD, with artist and producer royalties about $2 per album (roughly 10–20 percent of the list price) and distributor charges about $1.50. Marketing costs (roughly 50¢) tend to be quite low because radio stations and music television provide most of the promotion for free. Thus, a label typically has a gross profit of $5 per CD sold. This admittedly simplified model still serves to illustrate how immensely the industry profits.

# Outlook for the Recording Industry

In 2015, Nielsen SoundScan and Billboard announced that music sales had decreased more than 10 percent between 2013 and 2014, continuing a steady decline since the early 2000s.[12] This pattern has only accelerated in 2016 and 2017. Most artists now generate the largest share of their revenues from touring and online streaming services. Once thought obsolete, vinyl sales saw a slight uptick in 2014, but they make up only 3.5 percent of total recorded music sales. Revenue growth from streaming services is sustainable, some good news that suggests digital media, the bane of the music industry, may also be a boon.

## DIGITAL RIGHTS MANAGEMENT AND ILLEGAL FILE SHARING

Critics argue that the music industry and major record labels have only themselves to blame for the general decline in music sales. Rather than embracing early on the potential of digital technologies and the Internet for generating new kinds of revenue streams, they resisted change in a number of ways that proved futile.

### digital rights management (DRM)

Technologies that let copyright owners control the level of access or use allowed for a copyrighted work, such as limiting the number of times a song can be copied.

Security of copyrighted material remains a prime concern for record labels. Their past initiatives in **digital rights management (DRM)**, such as limiting digital copies of purchased music, have been viewed as heavy-handed. Most DRM efforts with physical media like CDs have also proved unsuccessful because security codes have been quickly hacked. By 2009, none of the major record labels used DRM on their CDs, claiming the associated costs exceeded the gains.

DRM is far more common with online music, although not all online sellers use it. For downloaded music, DRM restricts either the types of devices that can play the downloaded song or the length of time the song can be played, or it limits access in some other way, such as requiring an ongoing subscription, as with TIDAL. Generally, music services offering DRM versions of songs online have lower price points than non-DRM songs, which do not restrict formats or copying files between devices.

Since 2001, the recording industry has sued various file-sharing services and Internet service providers (ISPs), successfully shutting down and eventually bankrupting music file-sharing pioneer Napster. The RIAA even sued several thousand individuals for sharing files. Bad publicity ultimately made this practice untenable, though, and at the end of 2008, it opted to pressure the ISPs to cut off those users from the Internet rather than sue them individually.

Many ISPs have blocked access to file-sharing services because of the threat of lawsuits and the heavy load such sharing imposes, slowing down the networks even for users not sharing files. Universities, with their fast Internet connections and music-loving young masses, have been prime targets of the RIAA, which has pushed for special ethics education for new students to discourage the illegal file sharing of copyrighted works.

The recording industry has also been more aggressive in pursuing file-sharing services themselves. In late 2010, a four-year RIAA court case concluded with a federal judge shutting down popular file-sharing service LimeWire, with fifty million users monthly, after which BearShare, another file-sharing service, saw a sharp rise in users. As soon as one service closes, people apparently just seek out other existing or new services. Some proposed legislation, such as requiring digital security devices, supports industry efforts. Manufacturers, however, are resisting such directives, as are groups such as the Electronic Frontier Foundation (EFF), an advocate for citizen or consumer rights.

## Electronic Frontier Foundation

The EFF is a not-for-profit organization that focuses on issues of privacy and developments in communications technologies.

### NEW BUSINESS MODELS EMERGING

The music industry needs to develop new ways to sell music that match consumer interests and patterns of media use. To that end, two main business models seem to be emerging: downloads and subscription services.

Downloading music is hardly a recent activity. Not until the advent of Apple's iTunes in 2003, however, did the music industry finally succeed in getting consumers to pay for their downloads. Many in the recording industry, artists included, worried that à la carte song downloads would mean the death of the album, concerns that have proven to be largely valid. In the United States in 2013, there were 1.26 billion sales of individual songs online, seven times the volume of online album sales, which totaled just 118 million, according to data from Nielsen SoundScan. Added content such as behind-the-scenes

Giving consumers more choice in how they get their music has been a difficult adjustment for the major record labels.

footage, exclusive interviews, and games makes downloading an entire album appealing, but not sufficiently so for many consumers to justify the higher price of entire collections of songs. Although small compared to song and album downloads, downloaded ringtones demonstrate how songs may be popular in a variety of formats, including those that normally would never have been considered mass media.

Subscription services, having grown remarkably in recent years, offer great potential for new types of revenue streams. Many subscriptions operate on a **freemium** model: Some content is free, but a monthly subscription is required to take advantage of all the site has to offer. Different versions of the freemium model are currently being tested, such as advertising-supported content for the free service but no ads for the premium service. Other ways to distinguish the paid tier from the free tier include access to special content or songs that can be downloaded to other devices.

In North America, recent growth has made Slacker Radio and Pandora two of the biggest music-streaming and subscription services. Pandora has more than eighty-two million active listeners as of February 2017, up from twenty-five million in 2008, and claims 4.39 million paying subscribers.

Sweden-based Spotify, launched in 2008, has become the world's most popular digital music service with one hundred million listeners. It has forty million paying subscribers. Spotify's subscribers listen to seventeen billion hours of music in total annually, with more than half (52 percent) of the music heard via users' smartphones. Spotify has paid out $5 billion in rights to labels, publishers, and collecting societies representing artists.[13] Spotify became available in the United States in July 2011, expanding the field of music-subscription competitors. The company's revenues topped $2 billion in 2015.

Apple entered the field in 2013 with its own streaming music service, Apple Music, attracting seventeen million listeners in 2016. As the names and functions of these services suggest, the lines have blurred between Internet radio and online music subscription services, making it hard to identify exactly where radio ends and downloading or streaming songs begins.

The recording industry is looking at working directly with ISPs, some of which offer their own branded music-subscription services to customers. They are also considering partnerships with mobile operators that will facilitate getting songs and music content from mobile devices.

> **DISCUSSION QUESTIONS:** What advice would you offer a record-label executive for creating a successful business model in the digital age?

## 🗨 freemium

Subscriptions that provide some content for free but require a monthly subscription to take advantage of all the site has to offer.

Drake's "One Dance" was the number 1 streamed song worldwide in 2016.

Streaming music service Spotify in 2016 had forty million paying subscribers worldwide who streamed more than eight billion hours of music.

## What Is Broadcasting?

The term "broadcasting" originally referred to the practice of planting seeds by casting them broadly in a field rather than depositing them one at a time. In the early days of broadcasting as we have come to know it, wireless communications, initially only radio, provided point-to-point communication where telegraph lines were impractical or unreliable. Its main purpose was ship-to-ship or ship-to-shore communications for quick emergency transmissions. Subsequently, radio technology was developed to broadcast wireless messages widely to multiple locations. Dozens of years later, television allowed for the broadcasting of moving pictures as well as audio via wireless technology.

**broadcast**

Originally a reference to casting seeds widely in a field that was subsequently applied to the fledgling electronic medium of radio and later television.

Early radios were often built to fit in with other living room furniture.

**amplitude modulation (AM)**

Radio carrier signal modified by variations in wave amplitude.

**frequency modulation (FM)**

Radio carrier signal modified by variations in wave length/frequency.

**Broadcast** technology works essentially the same way in both radio and television. A transmitter sends messages over a part of the electromagnetic spectrum to a receiver or antenna that translates the message to the radio or TV. The receiving device then decodes the audio or visual electromagnetic waves so that they can be heard or seen.

## Radio

Radio, the most widely available medium of mass communication around the world, is also the second-most heavily used medium in the United States (after TV): People listen to radio, on average, over 2.5 hours per day, although different types of research suggest disparate findings. For example, compared to observational studies, self-reports of radio usage tend to underreport radio listening greatly, likely because radio is often playing in the background while people do other things, even while they consume other media such as reading a book or going online.

At least 99 percent of all U.S. households have at least one radio receiver, similar to most industrialized countries. Even developing nations have relatively high radio penetration. Radio is less expensive to produce, transmit, and receive than television; radio receivers are highly portable—even wearable—and radio doesn't require literacy to understand. There are basically three types of radio broadcasting: **amplitude modulation (AM)**, **frequency modulation (FM)**, and satellite. Yet satellite radio, like so-called Internet radio, employs an entirely different method of delivering audio programming than traditional AM and FM radio. Both are "broadcast" in the sense that they reach mass audiences, but satellite's delivery makes it more akin to airplane audio programming than true broadcasting. Low-powered radio, often in the FM format, also varies from the general terrestrial broadcast formats. Less expensive to transmit, it has enabled many highly localized community radio stations to operate around the United States and internationally.

## Distinctive Functions of Radio

Around the world, radio is a medium of news and entertainment. The low cost of both radio receivers and broadcasting has made it a particularly important and ubiquitous medium of mass communication in the developing world. Even in remote rural areas, it disseminates important information, such as agricultural instructions for easy, cheap, and rapid farming. Radio is also used globally as an emergency broadcast system for events such as severe storms, natural disasters, and military conflict, largely because of its portability and flexible power source. Radio receivers can operate easily for long periods on battery power alone.

In industrialized societies, radio has a broad array of functions, perhaps more diverse than any other of the traditional analog media. Talk radio provides information, debate, and even limited audience interactivity with listeners who call in. News programming offers breaking news as well as traffic and weather reports, school closings, and more. The broadcasting of recorded music for entertainment, the mainstay of commercial radio, benefits the public, artists, and the recording industry.

## ETHICS IN MEDIA
# Mashed-Up and Mixed-Up Musical Ethics

In 1977, legendary artist Marvin Gaye produced a sensational hit called "Got to Give It Up," a song that has remained familiar and popular over the years.

Four decades later, recording artist Robin Thicke produced the contemporary hit "Blurred Lines," which critics contend is little more than a digital rip-off of Gaye's masterpiece.[14] The aptly named "Blurred Lines" illustrates the challenges of ethics in media in the digital age. Thicke's song entered the musical charts in the summer of 2013 and quickly rose to the top of national and global markets, where it stayed for six weeks, selling more than six million copies and helping catapult Thicke to international fame.

Marvin Gaye died in 1984, tragically shot by his father in an apparent argument. His family now claims that Thicke essentially took the melody from Gaye's original hit and remixed it into the melody of "Blurred Lines."[15] Thicke has since admitted that he was high on drugs and alcohol when the new song was coproduced with international musical sensation Pharrell Williams and "T.I." Clifford Harris Jr. Thicke claims he cannot remember cowriting the hit and does not believe he would even have been capable of contributing to its creation. He also admits lying to the media at the time of the song's release about his part in writing the song.

Thicke and his musical partners also filed suit, defending their claim to having created "Blurred Lines" without stealing from Gaye's previous hit. They acknowledge a resemblance between the tunes, but claim the contemporary hit is tribute to Gaye, not theft. In March 2015, a jury disagreed, awarding the Marvin Gaye estate $7.3 million of the $25 million they sought in damages.

See if you agree with this view that the 2013 hit is a largely derivative mash-up of Gaye's classic song. Log onto YouTube, Vimeo, or another online music service and search for both songs. Listen to "Blurred Lines" and "Got to Give It Up" and compare the melodies and the beat of each song. What is your conclusion? Does Thicke owe more than an apology to the Gaye family?

# History of Radio

Radio boasts a remarkable history. Technically, economically, and programmatically, it has changed considerably since its early development, and it continues to evolve in the digital age. The following discussion reviews the development of radio from its early days in the late nineteenth century to the early twenty-first century.

### Heinrich Hertz

Physicist who demonstrated the existence of radio waves in 1885, setting the stage for the development of modern wireless communications. The measurement unit of electromagnetic frequencies was named for Hertz.

Guglielmo Marconi invented radio telegraphy, or the wireless telegraph, in 1899.

### Granville T. Woods

Inventor of railway telegraphy in 1887, a type of wireless communication that allowed moving trains to communicate with each other and with stations, greatly reducing the number of railway collisions.

### Guglielmo Marconi

Italian inventor and creator of radio telegraphy, or wireless transmission, in 1899.

### Lee de Forest

Considered the father of radio broadcasting because of his invention that permitted reliable voice transmissions for both point-to-point communication and broadcasting.

## WIRELESS TELEGRAPHY

Many inventors and scientists around the world were experimenting with radio technology around the same time. In 1884, German **Heinrich Hertz** began working with electromagnetic waves, and in 1885, he demonstrated the existence of radio waves. The measurement unit of electromagnetic frequencies was named for Hertz, whose work set the stage for the development of modern wireless communications, both fixed and mobile, a portion of which Americans have come to know as radio.

Another scientist experimenting with radio technology was African American **Granville T. Woods**, who in 1887 invented railway telegraphy that allowed messages to be sent between moving trains and a railroad stPation. This invention decreased railway collisions and alerted engineers to obstructions ahead on tracks.[16]

In 1899, Italian **Guglielmo Marconi** invented radio telegraphy. What he dubbed "the wireless," as it came to be called in much of the English-speaking world, made real-time audio transmission possible. Although transmitted in the form of Morse code dots and dashes without a wired connection, it might be deemed the first real radio transmission.

Kentucky farmer Nathan B. Stubblefield, called by some the *real* inventor of radio, created and demonstrated in 1892 a wireless communications device that could even transmit voice and music over a short distance, about five hundred feet. Stubblefield made his invention available to the Wireless Telephone Company, which proved to be a fraud. Because he never patented his device, he failed to reap the commercial rewards, dying tragically of starvation in 1928, alone and penniless on the dirt floor of a shack.[17]

## EXPLORING RADIO'S EARLY POTENTIAL

The U.S. Department of Agriculture (USDA), recognizing radio's potential, financed Canadian Reginald A. Fessenden's early research for gathering reports and distributing them broadly. In 1901, Fessenden obtained a U.S. patent for his new radio transmitter with a high-speed electrical alternator that produced "continuous waves." His design is the basis for today's AM radio. In 1912, the USDA started transmitting weather reports by radio in telegraphic code.

## VOICE TRANSMISSION

In 1906, Swedish-born inventor Ernst Alexanderson was among the first to build a high-frequency, continuous-wave machine capable of broadcasting the human voice and other sounds. An early radio station broadcast featuring a person's voice and a violin solo used his invention.

Although Italian Marconi and Canadian Fessenden did much of the early inventing work, American **Lee de Forest** developed a unique voice transmitter that proved reliable for both point-to-point radio communication and broadcasting; and by 1907, de Forest's company was supplying the U.S. Navy's Great White Fleet with arc radiotelephones for its pioneering around-the-world voyage. This feat helped establish de Forest as the father of radio, although, in reality, radio had at least three men who could claim that title.

## RADIO BEFORE, DURING, AND AFTER WWI

Despite its evident practical uses, radio required improved technology to become a mass medium. With considerable financial support and direction from the U.S. military, research on the vacuum tube helped produce a reliable radio transmitter and receiver by about 1915. Using the perfected vacuum tube radio transmitter, de Forest's "Highbridge Station" 2XG introduced nightly broadcasts, a so-called wireless newspaper for amateur radio operators.

All this activity ceased when the United States entered World War I in April 1917. At this point, the U.S. government either took over or completely shut down all radio stations. For the duration of the war, private citizens could not legally own or operate a radio transmitter or receiver without special permission. The military continued to conduct research on radio technology and lifted radio restrictions when the war ended in late 1918. Regular commercial radio broadcasts began in

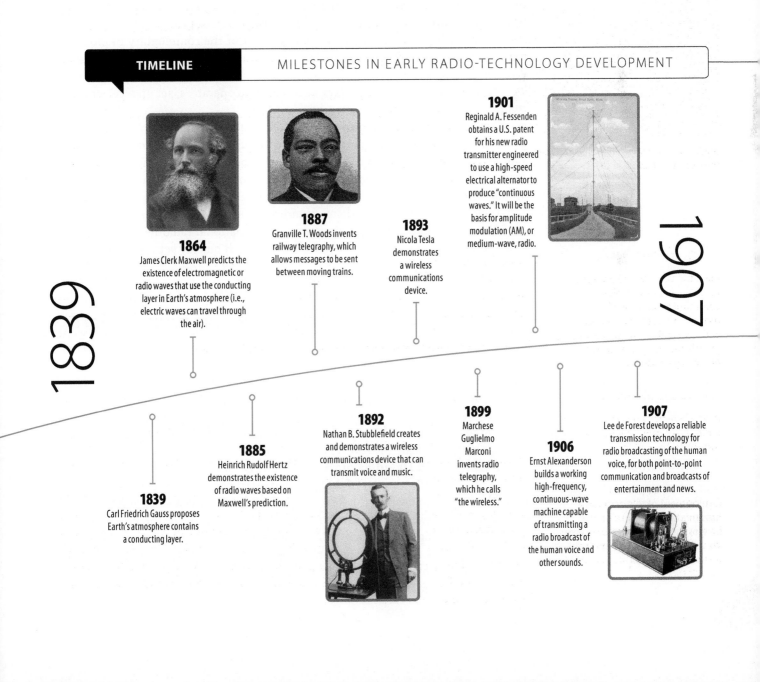

**TIMELINE** — MILESTONES IN EARLY RADIO-TECHNOLOGY DEVELOPMENT

**1839**

**1864**
James Clerk Maxwell predicts the existence of electromagnetic or radio waves that use the conducting layer in Earth's atmosphere (i.e., electric waves can travel through the air).

**1887**
Granville T. Woods invents railway telegraphy, which allows messages to be sent between moving trains.

**1893**
Nicola Tesla demonstrates a wireless communications device.

**1901**
Reginald A. Fessenden obtains a U.S. patent for his new radio transmitter engineered to use a high-speed electrical alternator to produce "continuous waves." It will be the basis for amplitude modulation (AM), or medium-wave, radio.

**1907**

**1839**
Carl Friedrich Gauss proposes Earth's atmosphere contains a conducting layer.

**1885**
Heinrich Rudolf Hertz demonstrates the existence of radio waves based on Maxwell's prediction.

**1892**
Nathan B. Stubblefield creates and demonstrates a wireless communications device that can transmit voice and music.

**1899**
Marchese Guglielmo Marconi invents radio telegraphy, which he calls "the wireless."

**1906**
Ernst Alexanderson builds a working high-frequency, continuous-wave machine capable of transmitting a radio broadcast of the human voice and other sounds.

**1907**
Lee de Forest develops a reliable transmission technology for radio broadcasting of the human voice, for both point-to-point communication and broadcasts of entertainment and news.

1920 when AM station KDKA of Pittsburgh, Pennsylvania, reported results of the Harding–Cox presidential election.

## WIDESPREAD PUBLIC ADOPTION OF RADIO

In the United States in the early 1920s, roughly six thousand amateur radio stations and forty-six hundred commercial stations run for profit had licenses. There were also some amateur enthusiasts who could be likened to computer geeks in the early days of personal computers and the Internet; but for most of the public, radio was still a novelty with limited application.

However, a sporting event on July 2, 1921, would help establish radio as a major medium of mass communication. People across the country were keenly interested in the heavyweight boxing title fight between champion Jack Dempsey and challenger Georges Carpentier. Radio networks did not yet exist, so only one station, a temporary long-wave station, WJY, broadcast the bout live, with technical support from the Radio Corporation of America (RCA), which, as a radio receiver manufacturer, wanted every American household to have a radio set (or two).

Broadcast organizers telegraphed a transcript of the commentary to pioneering station KDKA in Pittsburgh. It then broadcast the fight with a slight delay. With relatively few personal radio receivers, most listeners gathered in halls where local organizers, including volunteer amateur radio operators, set up receivers and charged admission to offset costs.

The evident breakthrough and promise of the new communications technology generated much media commentary, helping propel radio to mass-communication status. A broadcasting boom began after the Dempsey–Carpentier fight, with hundreds of radio stations springing up across the country, similar to the proliferation of web servers in the mid- to late 1990s. Radio receivers were selling as fast as RCA and others could manufacture them. American Telephone and Telegraph Company (AT&T) began implementing programming for a national radio network in 1922 with flagship station WEAF in New York City, which quickly set the standard for the entire industry.

## FM RADIO, EDWIN HOWARD ARMSTRONG, AND DAVID SARNOFF

**Edwin Howard Armstrong**

Columbia University engineering professor who invented FM radio transmission.

**David Sarnoff**

Head of RCA, he promoted the development of television as a mass medium yet blocked the development of FM radio for years because RCA produced and sold AM radio receivers.

In 1934, an important innovation in radio transmission technology occurred when Columbia University engineering professor **Edwin Howard Armstrong** (1890–1954) invented FM radio (and later, stereo FM radio) with his colleague John Bose. Armstrong completed his first field test on June 9, 1934, sending an organ recital via both AM and FM from an RCA tower on top of the Empire State Building to the home of a trusted old friend on Long Island. The FM organ came through loud and clear. The AM version had much more static.

Armstrong and **David Sarnoff** (1891–1971), head of RCA, had started out as friends, who both recognized the great potential of radio broadcasting, but FM radio threatened to destroy the RCA empire built on the mass sales of AM radios, or "radio music boxes." Once Sarnoff realized the magnitude of the invention, he blocked Armstrong by ordering RCA engineers to ask for more tests, lobbying federal regulators to deny Armstrong a license to test his invention, and even trying to obtain his patent. Armstrong responded as best he could, filing suit against RCA and many other radio companies infringing on the Armstrong FM radio patent.

Tragically, in 1954, Armstrong, who had never enjoyed commercial success in his life, committed suicide after long-running legal battles left him virtually penniless and his marriage broke up. Ironically, his many lawsuits were settled shortly after his death, leaving a fortune to his widow and the Armstrong Foundation. The story of Armstrong's invention and Sarnoff's machinations to protect the RCA business model mirrors some Internet developments in which legal wrangling or threatened business interests have prevented better technologies from prevailing.

For most of the first half of the twentieth century, AM radio listenership far exceeded FM. In the late 1970s, this shifted, and today FM listenership and stations are in the vast majority. FM radio ascended for a number of reasons, among them the inclusion of an FM dial in most car radios, changes in programming, and regulatory changes, combined with the fact that FM has less static.

Edwin Howard Armstrong, inventor of FM radio, spent much of the latter part of his life battling companies that tried to squash FM radio because it threatened business models based on AM radio.

## CREATING A VIABLE BUSINESS MODEL FOR RADIO

Just as with the Internet, the question of how to make radio broadcasting a viable business would prove complex and controversial. Experiments with commercial sponsorship through the mid-1920s drew outspoken criticism of advertising on public airwaves. The controversy was exemplified in the May 1924 issue of *Radio Broadcast* magazine, which sponsored a contest awarding $500 for the best essay on "Who Is to Pay for Broadcasting—and How?"

Eventually, a confluence of commercial interests, government decisions (sometimes influenced by commercial interests), and lack of coordination among advocates of publicly supported broadcasting made privately owned stations with on-air advertising the standard business model that continues to this day. Consequently, the engine that drives profits is audience size, especially among key demographic groups attractive to advertisers.

## THE RISE OF RADIO NETWORKS

During the 1920s, the first commercial broadcasting networks were formed, initially as radio networks—affiliated radio stations in multiple cities all broadcasting a common core set of programming—and later as national television networks. Prior to the passage of the **Radio Act of 1927** and the creation of the **Federal Radio Commission (FRC)**, the predecessor to the **Federal Communications Commission (FCC)**, broadcasting was lively but haphazard. Numerous competing stations on the same or nearby frequencies often caused reception interference. Few regulations regarding transmitter power meant stronger signals could drown out weaker local transmitters. The FRC revoked thousands of radio broadcast licenses and instituted a system that favored fewer high-power stations over smaller but more numerous local low-power stations. This policy benefited large commercial companies over educational, religious, and small private broadcasters.

The National Broadcasting Company (NBC) was founded in 1926 when Sarnoff of RCA purchased New York station WEAF (now WNBC) from AT&T for $1 million. That same year, NBC bought WJZ (licensed to Newark, New Jersey, but transmitting in New York) from Westinghouse and thus created the first network.

CBS (Columbia Broadcasting Station) became the second network, first as the United Independent Broadcasters in 1927; and then, after going on the air with a partner, the Columbia Phonograph and Records Company; and finally becoming the Columbia Broadcasting System. In 1928, cigar maker Sam Paley bought CBS

### Radio Act of 1927

An act of Congress that created the Federal Radio Commission, intended to regulate the largely chaotic airwaves and based on the principle that companies had a civic duty to use airwaves, a limited public good, responsibly.

### Federal Radio Commission (FRC)

Formed by the Radio Act of 1927, the commission, the precursor to the FCC, created a policy that favored fewer high-power radio broadcasting stations rather than more numerous low-power stations.

### Federal Communications Commission (FCC)

Established in 1934, the principal communications regulatory body at the federal level in the United States.

## CONVERGENCE CULTURE
# NPR and PRI: America's Public Radio Networks

National Public Radio (NPR) debuted on April 19, 1971, with live coverage of the Senate Vietnam hearings; and a month later, it broadcast *All Things Considered*. A not-for-profit membership organization, NPR produces and distributes news, cultural, and informational programs, linking the nation's noncommercial radio stations into a national network. It broadcasts about one hundred hours of original programming each week, heard on more than nine hundred public radio stations nationwide by an audience of twenty-five million.[18] NPR.org reaches about nineteen million visitors a month on its various digital platforms.

Public Radio International (PRI), established in 1983, produces and distributes additional public radio programming, such as *Marketplace* and Garrison Keillor's *A Prairie Home Companion*, to some nine hundred affiliate stations in the United States, Puerto Rico, and Guam and via SiriusXM satellite radio. PRI's international programs include *The World*, produced in collaboration with the BBC World Service and WGBH Radio Boston.[19]

Public radio distinguishes itself from commercial radio in a number of ways, including more extensive, impartial, and original audio news, especially long-form audio reporting as heard on *Morning Edition* and *All Things Considered*. NPR also offers extensive programming in classical and folk music, jazz, and opera, featuring a variety of live transmissions of the performing arts from theaters and concert halls. Evening programs include those that introduce listeners to classical music as well as to international musicians and unique musical styles.

for $400,000, installing his son William as head and moving network headquarters from Philadelphia to New York. Under William's longtime leadership, and later under that of his corporate heir, Frank Stanton, CBS maintained the number 1 position, describing itself as the Tiffany Network—although it was also called Black Rock, a reference in part to the black marble façade of its midtown Manhattan headquarters.

By 1935, fifty-eight of sixty-two stations nationwide were part of either the NBC or the CBS network. Not until the 1940s did ABC, a third commercial network, emerge.

## CONSOLIDATION IN RADIO STATION OWNERSHIP

Throughout most of the twentieth century, radio ownership in the United States was relatively diverse. This was partly a result of federal laws preventing any one person or organization from owning more than twenty FM stations and twenty AM stations nationwide. Regulatory changes in 1992 and the passage of the Telecommunications Act in 1996 resulted in new FCC rules that eliminated such restrictions, although an owner must still be a U.S. citizen. Former FCC duopoly rules prohibited sole ownership, operation, or control of more than two AM and two FM stations in the largest markets. The combined audience share of the co-owned stations was also limited to 25 percent, with even further restrictions for smaller markets. Now the FCC permits a single entity to own substantially more in the same service market.

This shift in regulatory policy produced a trend in the 1990s and early twenty-first century toward increasing consolidation. Since the passage of the act, more than 4,400 radio stations have changed ownership, and the radio industry has become more of an oligopoly. For most of the first fifty years of radio broadcasting, radio was a small business; and owners, even if affiliated with a national network, were longtime residents of their station's town. Although this is still the case in many smaller towns, most stations in big cities have become part of a larger corporate entity.

Increasingly, groups now control eight or more stations in a single market, and the most powerful media groups own most of the large, highly profitable stations. Some support consolidation for a number of reasons, including increased efficiency; more economical, centralized production; larger budgets that permit greater programming experimentation and development; and better management. But critics argue that remote group ownership typically means less sensitivity to local concerns.

In the past few years, however, certain radio groups have been deconsolidating and selling some of their vast holdings. iHeartMedia, formerly named Clear Channel, sold almost half of its 1,200 radio stations and all of its fifty-one television stations after 2007, partly because of its intent to become a privately held company and partly because of FCC regulations. Despite these sales, iHeartMedia's stations and markets exceed those of the total number of the next three radio groups combined, although the 2017 merger of CBS Radio and Entercom creates a new group of 244 radio stations with revenues of $1.7 billion, second only to iHeartMedia.[20] In 2008, Cumulus Media, the second-largest radio group in 2011 in number of AM and FM stations owned, also went private. Although the move away from consolidation may seem like a good thing for the industry, the shift from publicly traded companies to privately held firms may also mean more business decisions based purely on the bottom line without consideration of the public role of radio stations.

---

**DISCUSSION QUESTIONS:** Two major movements have shaped the development of radio: the shift early on from small, independent stations to large-scale, powerful commercial stations and the later shift from terrestrial radio stations to online personal radio stations. Identify some consequences of these changes, and explain which you personally consider most important.

---

# The Radio Industry Today

Declining American radio revenues every year since 2006 have shown a reversal, with a 5.4 percent rebound in 2010 and another 1.2 percent increase in 2011 to $14.1 billion, according to BIA/Kelsey, a group that tracks and advises the radio industry. Revenues have increased even more substantially in recent years, with PwC reporting revenues of $21.8 billion in 2016 for the U.S. radio industry.[21] In addition, online radio revenues are also growing, and BIA/Kelsey expects them to be nearly $1 billion by 2018. The turnaround was, in part, due to a rise in digital revenues, which industry experts believe will continue to grow in the coming years. Today, there are approximately ten thousand commercial and twenty-five hundred noncommercial radio stations in the United States, the latter group including NPR affiliates and college, community, and religious stations.

All U.S. stations are assigned call letters designating the station and their geographic location east or west of the Mississippi River. Stations east of the Mississippi have W as their first call letter, and stations to the west, K, although some exceptions exist for call letters assigned before boundaries were determined, such as KDKA in Pittsburgh. Under an international agreement issued at the London International Radiotelegraphic Conference in 1912, different countries were awarded different letters. The United States received KDA through KZZ.

# Radio Station Programming

Radio grew in its early years to become a dominant medium of mass communication. Large audiences assembled to listen to individual programs during much of the first half of the twentieth century. But the rise of television in the years following World War II provided serious competition, a new media landscape to which radio, like magazines, adapted by specializing.

This specialization takes a number of forms, including program formats, the time of day for certain formats, and especially audience demographics. In radio, a day is broken up into different time segments called "dayparts." The 6 a.m. to 10 a.m. **daypart**, for example, is when most people listen to the radio as they get ready for work or school or during their commute. Accordingly, the programming emphasizes frequent news, traffic, and weather reports as well as some of the more outspoken talk radio shows such as *Imus in the Morning*.

Radio stations are organized by programming into dozens of formats that draw varied audiences.[22] Contemporary-hit radio, for example, attracts a much different audience than the country format—by far the most popular in the United States, with 2,115 stations, as Table 4-2 shows. The fastest-growing format is Spanish language.

To reduce operating costs, more and more stations are relying on computerized automated systems that use remote DJs and set music. DJs ostensibly chattering and choosing songs in a local studio may never have even visited the city from where they are ostensibly broadcasting. Automated programming can cause problems during times of emergency. In 2002, for example, a train carrying ammonia derailed in Minot, North Dakota. Emergency services were in disarray, and power was out in many places. Yet, as there was no actual staff at the six Clear Channel radio stations (out of nine stations in the city), regular programming was not preempted with evacuation or safety information for concerned residents.

> **daypart**
>
> A segment of time radio and television program planners use to determine their primary audience during that time of day or night.

---

**DISCUSSION QUESTIONS:** List the techniques your favorite radio station uses to distinguish its music format and the station itself. Consider things such as sound effects, promos, and DJ style. Now find a station of a similar genre elsewhere in the country (via the Internet). Listen to it, and identify similarities and differences.

---

# Outlook for the Radio Industry

Industry experts remain cautiously optimistic and predict slight growth in the future, thanks in part to an expected increase in digital revenues that, although large, will remain a fraction of overall revenues. Terrestrial radio stations will continue to exist and promote music, despite the rising popularity of music subscription services and downloadable music. Sales of stations to the top radio groups have been relatively steady in recent years, and further consolidation will likely continue. Radio groups are also buying music subscription services, such as iHeartMedia's 2011 acquisition of Thumbplay, which was not even a year old.

Slacker, Pandora, Spotify, and the like often promote their services as personal radio stations. Users can create and save their own playlists in "My Stations" or "Channels," names meant to evoke radio, whether on the desktop, mobile, or wearable device. Their on-demand nature, which actually makes them more like

TABLE 4-2 Most Popular Radio Programming Genres

| Genre | NUMBER OF STATIONS (United States) |
|---|---|
| Country | 2,115 |
| News/Talk/Information | 1,364 |
| Spanish | 859 |
| Classic Hits | 855 |
| Sports | 779 |
| Adult Contemporary | 605 |
| CHR Top 40 | 579 |
| Classic Rock | 488 |
| Oldies | 379 |
| Religion | 317 |
| Rock | 302 |

Source: "Leading Radio Formats in the United States as of June 2016, by Number of Stations," Statista, accessed January 7, 2016, https://www.statista.com/statistics/252230/top-radio-formats-in-the-us-by-number-of-stations/

personalized audio programming than what has traditionally been considered radio, highlights the blurring of online music subscription services, downloadable audio, and traditional radio.

Podcasting and satellite radio are also affecting our perceptions of what constitutes radio. Most radio stations have websites where they promote their shows, provide extra content as podcasts, and let users listen live to shows. Proponents hype satellite as the future of radio while skeptics dismiss it as having an unsustainable business model.

## PODCASTING

Increasing in popularity from 2004, podcasts are not identical to other downloaded or streaming formats. Although they are downloaded in one respect, the technology that interfaces with the user's computer differs from that of a direct file download. Podcasts are often episodic or belong to a series of related content, such as a news program or an investigative report. They are also easy to get and download, much like RSS (Rich Site Summary) feeds do with blogs, sending subscribers new content automatically.

Podcasts permit more flexible content delivery. Listening at the actual time of a certain report is no longer required, nor is visiting a website to download an audio file. Users can simply subscribe to receive podcasts and listen at their convenience on their computer or mobile device. Podcasts have proved popular not only for talk-based radio, such as NPR features, but also for sports and music. Several companies in recent years have begun specializing in podcasting farm news—information on weather, commodity prices, and other news of agricultural interest—that harkens back to radio's earliest days. Easy and inexpensive to produce, podcasts could allow local radio news to be heard once again in communities where distant radio conglomerates now own stations.

Among the most popular podcasts to date is *Serial*, which debuted in 2014.[23] Produced by the creators of the public radio program *This American Life*, *Serial* offers a series of episodes that examine via in-depth reporting a true story told in audio narrative form. The first series, which reexamined the 1999 murder of a Maryland teen, generated a following of more than forty million people.[24] *Serial* continued its success with a second season focused on the case of Sgt. Bowe Bergdahl, a soldier held captive by the Taliban in Afghanistan for five years and now awaiting sentencing for having deserted his Army post.

The creators of *Serial* and *This American Life* collaborated to produce *S-Town*, a podcast also focused on true crime. *S-Town* made podcasting history with ten million downloads in four days.

## SATELLITE RADIO

More akin to audio programming than to traditional broadcast radio, satellite radio uses digital signals broadcast from a satellite, beaming the same programming across a much wider territory than its terrestrial cousin. With up to seventy channels of CD-quality music in a variety of formats, and dozens of third-party news, sports, talk, and old-time radio programs (most of them commercial free as a subscription-based service), satellite radio has won a loyal audience of twenty-four million subscribers in the United States. And as with cable television, its subscription system imposes fewer content restrictions.

Sirius Satellite Radio, which started out as CD Radio in the early 1990s, launched its satellites in 2000 and began broadcasting in 2002. When XM Satellite Radio launched soon after, the two companies competed vigorously in offering exclusive access to various sports channels, hosted music channels, and noted talk-radio hosts. In 2004, shock jock Howard Stern signed an exclusive five-year, $500 million contract with Sirius. Some media observers claimed this was a game changer that greatly enhanced the status of satellite radio. Others saw it as reminiscent of the wasteful spending of the dot-com boom of the late 1990s and argued that Stern would essentially disappear from the public eye (or ear) because of the smaller satellite radio audience.

Artist Ed Sheeran's third album *Divide* has had one billion views on YouTube.

## INTERNATIONAL PERSPECTIVES
# Trusting in the Power of the Airwaves

Radio has proven to be a very important information source in developing countries, where spotty electricity service, inhibitory government regulations, low levels of education, and scant incomes have kept most people from a television, let alone a computer and Internet connection. Radios, however, are nearly ubiquitous, thanks in part to their portability, low cost, and ability to run on batteries or solar power or by hand cranks. Because radio does not require literacy, it has proven especially valuable in communicating with poor, often rural populations—such as in Southeast Asia, Latin America, and Africa—as a means of development and distribution of innovations such as new agricultural techniques or health advances.

UNESCO, the United Nations Education, Scientific and Cultural Organization, reports that 95 percent of the world's population has access to radio, about double the percentage that has Internet access.[25] UNESCO states that radio plays an especially important role in the developing world because of its ubiquitous presence, low cost, and reliability.

The implications of radio's capabilities are important for nongovernmental organizations (NGOs) and others working in the developing world, for they highlight how important it is for those from developed nations not to take for granted certain cultural assumptions about media and how they are used. For example, an award-winning print advertising campaign about disease prevention in the United States or Europe may not be understood or even seen by wide swaths of the population in a developing country, whereas a radio message could reach many more people who will perceive it as a reliable source of information.

Kenyan women listening to the radio.

In mid-2008, Sirius completed its acquisition of former competitor XM Satellite Radio and became Sirius XM Radio. The company almost filed for bankruptcy in early 2009—as large debts came due—but Liberty Media, owner of DirecTV, rescued it at the last minute, acquiring 40 percent ownership in the process. Sirius XM Radio continues its technological innovation, improving receivers and providing mobile phone apps, for example.

## MEDIA CAREERS

Career paths in radio and the recording industry are among the most rapidly changing and unsettled in the media industry. Perhaps the most exciting opportunities involve entrepreneurial approaches. These career paths emphasize both digital savvy as well as a sense of innovation in how to produce popular audio-format programming that can appeal to an increasingly mobile and international marketplace. Listeners typically discover new music on the radio, often online; but the vast majority in the important demographic of young listeners ages 12–24 use YouTube to watch videos and keep up to date with the latest hits.[26]

A few serious fans may turn their passion for music into a career as a DJ at a radio station or nightclub. Disc jockeys who work at special events such as weddings or fundraisers need to be familiar with various types of music. Others may specialize in a particular genre. Regardless, DJs need to be sensitive to the musical tastes of their particular audience because their success depends on the ability to develop a loyal following of radio listeners or club hoppers. Sometimes disc jockeys transition to careers in the record industry, although for most, spinning remains only a part-time gig.

Those with an entrepreneurial spirit may have an especially strong outlook for success in the arena of digital audio. With the growth of new interactive audio technologies such as the Amazon Echo with the Alexa digital assistant, the potential for innovative approaches to how users interact in the digital audio world are wide open.

## LOOKING BACK AND MOVING FORWARD

Radio is still an evolving medium, with many forms of delivery including traditional terrestrial broadcasting, online distribution, and satellite transmission via Sirius XM Radio. Future radio delivery may not lie in the heavens, but it will undoubtedly be grounded in certain consumer behaviors and desires readily apparent across all media, especially with music.

Although transmission and hardware will continue to change, radio itself—or, more accurately, the delivery of audio content to a mass audience—seems destined to remain an important form of mass communication. This is largely because radio, almost alone among mass media, allows people to engage easily in other activities while listening. No matter how advanced or portable media technology becomes, we cannot watch TV or read a book or newspaper while driving safely, for example. The shift to an on-demand and participatory media environment will become more significant. Satellite radio has signaled this shift, along with the various music subscription services or personal radio stations.

Services such as Pandora, Slacker, and Spotify may well represent the future of radio: a highly personalized system that not only responds to your musical tastes but uses special algorithms and collaborative filtering to suggest new artists who play similar styles of music. These changes may so drastically alter how radio stations think of their programming that the term "radio" may technically become obsolete or come to mean something very different.

Business models or ways of creating, promoting, and distributing music are still in transition. Although advances in technology improved both the sound quality and portability of recorded music, basic business policies endured. Innovative musicians are using digital crowdfunding to underwrite their own musical enterprises, circumventing the traditional record labels.

There are two main schools of thought about the state of the music industry today, which also apply to other entertainment media such as television and film. One camp claims that the music industry has only itself to blame for not adapting earlier to the digital repercussions for established business models. Rather than initiating bullying lawsuits, record labels should focus on developing alternative revenue streams, some of which already have growing sales such as digital downloads of à la carte songs, music subscription services, and ringtone sales.

The second school of thought explains diminished sales as the consequence of file sharing, viewed as theft, pure and simple. So although the interest in music remains as strong as ever, new revenue sources are still far from making up for losses of recent years, a drop-off that the industry blames on illegal practices that hurt not only corporations but also artists who rely on royalties to survive.

**MEDIA MATTERS**    THE REVOLUTION WILL NOT BE TELEVISED; IT WILL BE MASHED UP

1. Have you ever bought a vinyl LP?

2. Have you ever bought a song online?

3. What media device do you typically use to listen to music?

4. (T/F) Revenue from digital music (mostly downloads and subscriptions) surpassed CD revenue for the first time in 2012.

5. Where is the dividing line between radio stations that have call letters starting with K and those starting with W?

6. What is the most popular music format for radio stations?

7. Why is radio called "the wireless" in other English-speaking countries?

8. (T/F) Satellite radio does not have the same restrictions regarding content as broadcast radio stations.

9. Do you pay to subscribe to one or more music subscription services such as Pandora, Slacker, or Spotify?

10. How much would you be willing to pay per month to listen to commercial-free radio?

**ANSWERS: 4.** True. **5.** Mississippi River. **6.** Country music. **7.** Because it was perceived as a wireless form of telegraphy. **8.** True.

## FURTHER READING

*All You Need to Know About the Music Business*, 8th ed. Donald Passman (2012) Hal Leonard Corp.

*The Business of Music*, 10th ed. William Krasilovsky, Sidney Shemel, John Gross, Jonathan Feinstein (2007) Billboard Books.

*The Future of Music: Manifesto for the Digital Music Revolution*. David Kusek, Gerd Leonhard (2008) Berklee Press.

*Appetite for Self-Destruction: The Spectacular Crash of the Record Industry in the Digital Age*. Steve Knopper (2009) Free Press.

*The Listener's Voice: Early Radio and the American Public*. Elena Razlogova (2011) University of Pennsylvania Press.

*Empire of the Air: The Men Who Made Radio*. Tom Lewis (1993) Harper Perennial Library.

*Hello, Everybody! The Dawn of American Radio*. Anthony Rudel (2008) Houghton Mifflin Harcourt.

*Sound Business: Newspapers, Radio, and the Politics of New Media*. Michael Stamm (2011) University of Pennsylvania Press.

*Censorship: The Threat to Silence Talk Radio*. Brian Jennings, Sean Hannity (2009) Threshold Editions.

*Something in the Air: Radio, Rock, and the Revolution That Shaped a Generation*. Marc Fisher (2007) Random House.

*Right of the Dial: The Rise of Clear Channel and the Fall of Commercial Radio*. Alex Foege (2009) Faber and Faber.

*World Radio TV Handbook 2013: The Directory of Global Broadcasting*. WRTH editors (January 15, 2013) WRTH.

*Radio Content in the Digital Age: The Evolution of a Sound Medium*. Angeliki Gazi, Guy Starkey, Stanislaw Jedrzejewski (2011) Intellect/University of Chicago Press.

*Masterful Stories: Lessons from Golden Age Radio*. John V. Pavlik (2017) Routledge.

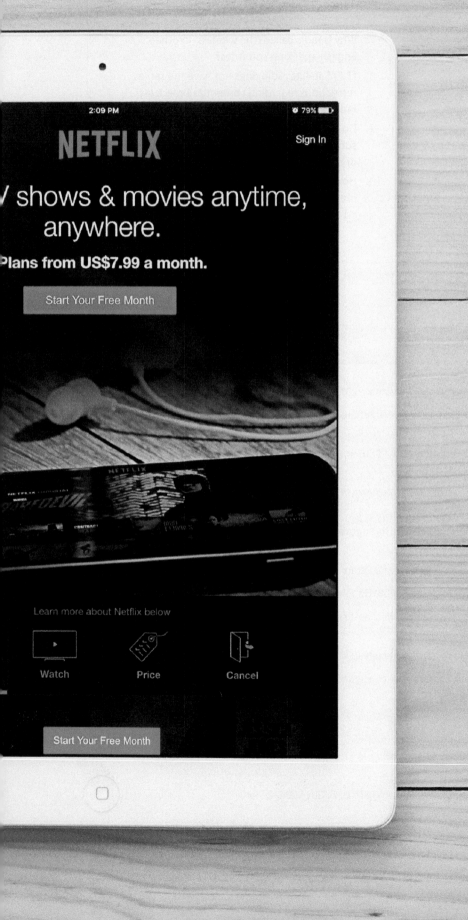

NETFLIX

Sign In

V shows & movies anytime,
anywhere.

Plans from US$7.99 a month.

Start Your Free Month

Learn more about Netflix below

Watch     Price     Cancel

Start Your Free Month

# Visual Media
## PHOTOGRAPHY, MOVIES, AND TELEVISION

The image of the couch potato has long been a popular trope in the media—someone sitting on a couch, staring blankly at the TV screen, surrounded by unhealthy snacks and soda.

But lately new concerns have arisen among some experts and psychologists because of the rise in new forms of watching TV, namely binge-watching. Binge-watching is not necessarily new, nor is it necessarily a result of streaming television services such as Netflix. Network stations have long promoted marathon weekends of popular series, which is essentially advocating for binge-watching.

What has experts concerned, however, is how much more binge-watching is taking place than in years past. A March 2016 study by Deloitte found that 70 percent of U.S. consumers binge-watch TV, averaging five episodes per sitting.[1] Millennials aged fourteen to twenty-five watch more streaming shows than they do traditional TV.

Because 56 percent of people who binge-watch prefer to do it alone, it is considered antisocial activity. Connections have also been made between binge-watching and loneliness and depression, as well as lack of self-control. Other negative health effects have also been associated with binge-watching, such as obesity. However, there still have not been enough studies to determine if binge-watching is causing some of these effects, or if it is the other way around—in other words, if people who are more lonely or depressed are more likely to binge-watch.

Still other experts believe that the alarms about binge-watching are misguided and are simply the latest anxiety about a new type of media behavior that we have heard before, especially as video gaming became more popular and we heard similar warnings about the bad effects of video games. Later studies on video games showed that they also have some positive effects.

It is still too early to tell on which side binge-watching will fall, as studies large enough to determine effects are still being conducted. All we can do is wait . . . and watch.

**cord-cutters**

Those who have switched from cable or other connections to Internet-delivered TV.

**cord-nevers**

Those who have known only mobile or wireless Internet-delivered TV.

**surveillance**

Primarily the journalism function of mass communication, which provides information about processes, issues, events, and other developments in society.

**cultural transmission**

The process of passing on culturally relevant knowledge, skills, attitudes, and values from person to person or group to group.

Despite President Trump's claims about his inauguration having the highest attendance ever, photographic evidence clearly shows there were fewer people than at President Obama's first inauguration.

**camera obscura**

A dark box or room with a small hole that allows an inverted image of an outside scene to be shown on the opposite inner wall.

**Louis Daguerre**

Inventor of the daguerreotype, an early type of photography.

Photographs, television, and movies shape our world, with journalism, entertainment, and art highlighting the importance of the visual in our lives. The photographic lens has long defined the linear narrative of visual storytelling, and recent changes with digitization allow visual media to render and create realities even more vividly. The past hundred years of filmmaking still provide the foundation for digital videographers as they explore more portable equipment and more sophisticated editing tools and effects.

Changes resulting from online consumption of video, film, and television are not yet fully understood, but already for many the Internet is a more significant source of imagery than is television. Sources of video content online include the popular YouTube and many similar video-sharing sites. **Cord-cutters** are increasingly common among those who once relied on a cable or other connection to get their TV, whereas **cord-nevers** are those who have known only mobile or wireless Internet-delivered TV.

# Photography

Long important to mass communications, still images, or photographs, continue to perform two main functions: **surveillance** and **cultural transmission**. Photos and other images can verify factual claims. Whereas words might provide the narrative, photos confirm its truth, whether it involves a purported plane crash, an extramarital affair, or a mass grave in a war-torn country. Despite the possibility of being digitally doctored, photographs are still one of the surest ways to support facts. They transmit culture by what they show, how they show it, and which emotions they stir. At a glance, a photograph can tell a story or convey information quickly while engaging and entertaining the audience.

**DISCUSSION QUESTIONS:** Have digital film and television made photography less relevant? Why or why not? How do you explain the popularity of the "selfie"?

## HISTORY OF PHOTOGRAPHY

The principles involved in creating photographs had been around hundreds of years before photography was invented. The earliest recorded use of a **camera obscura**—a dark box or room with a small hole that allows an inverted image of an outside scene to be shown on the opposite inner wall—is in the writings of Leonardo da Vinci, who explains how a camera obscura can aid drawing scenery, moving a sheet of paper around until the scene comes into sharp focus for tracing.

The other important element, understanding how light can affect certain chemicals, was also known for hundreds of years. Although some scientists could produce photographs with various light-sensitive chemicals, they had no way to make the images permanent. In June 1827, Joseph Niépce (1765–1833), using an asphalt-like material that hardened after exposure to light, created a picture, although it was unclear and required eight hours of exposure.[2]

After the death of Niépce, his partner, Frenchman **Louis Daguerre** (1787–1851), unveiled in January 1839 the **daguerreotype**, a method of creating a positive image on a metal plate, which reduced exposure time to thirty minutes or so.[3] Advances occurred over the next 150 years in exposure time, image quality, and color photography. As cameras became more portable and user-friendly, their popularity increased with the general public. And the Internet and wireless communications made it possible to share photos instantly with friends, family, or the entire world through social media.

In the early days, when specialized knowledge was still required, **Mathew B. Brady** (1822–1896) was highly acclaimed for his Civil War photos and portraits of famous people, many of whom are best known to us today through his work. Historians have criticized Brady for sometimes arranging his subjects, including battlefield corpses, for dramatic photocomposition purposes, a practice considered unethical in modern journalism. Nevertheless, Brady and other photographers helped the public see the conflict in the Civil War through the lens of the press, the first war documented by means of photography.

Early photography was not limited to journalism. Notably, Eadweard Muybridge (1830–1904) used it for scientific documentation. His famous photo series was the first to document how a horse runs. Such applications help us see things that the human eye alone cannot. Today, scientific images of the heavens and of the microscopic alike captivate us. Some are even considered visual art.

**daguerreotype**

Photograph created by exposing a positive image on a metal plate.

**Mathew B. Brady**

Nineteenth-century photographer acclaimed for his Civil War images and portraits of famous people.

The powerful images of Civil War dead are provocative even today, although Mathew Brady sometimes moved corpses for certain photographs, a practice considered unethical today.

## PHOTOGRAPHIC INDUSTRY TODAY

The photography industry, like the more prominent film and television industries, has experienced great change. Consider the impact of digital cameras. Only ten years after film sales peaked in 1999, Kodak announced it would stop making Kodachrome color film. Despite efforts to capitalize on the shift to digital by selling digital cameras and photo printers, Kodak continued to lose money and declared bankruptcy in January 2012. Fujifilm, headquartered in Tokyo and the world's largest photographic company, has also seen business diminish, but it integrated digital technology more effectively into its business model and has a range of popular digital cameras as well as inkjet and laser photo paper.

Today, professional photographers have more powerful cameras than ever before, and digital cameras and even smartphone cameras allow anyone to take professional-quality pictures without manual camera adjustments.

# Movies

Still images were to mass media of the mid-nineteenth century what motion pictures were to the twentieth. At the end of the nineteenth century, activity could be recorded for the first time. More important for the movie industry, technology could not only re-create reality but also *create* it.

*Rolling Stone* magazine received heavy criticism over this cover photo of Dzhokhar Tsarnaev, convicted and sentenced to death for setting bombs that killed three people and injured scores more at the 2013 Boston Marathon. **CRITICAL THINKING QUESTIONS:** Do aspects of the photograph seem to glamorize Tsarnaev? If so, which ones? Would another photograph, from a different angle or with a different expression, provoke the same reaction? Do you think people would react differently to a photo of Tsarnaev on the cover of *TIME Magazine*?

### INTERNATIONAL PERSPECTIVES
## Breaking the Silence Around Molestation

It is often said that a picture is a worth a thousand words, but photojournalist and documentary photographer Smita Sharma is showing how powerful images can also help break the silence around sexual violence in India.

India's National Crime Reports Bureau estimates that at least 92 women are raped daily, most by family members or people known to the survivor. In 2013, there were over thirty-three thousand reported cases of rape. True numbers are likely much higher: Many local police do not bother to investigate rape cases because they consider it normal.

Sharma's cousin, Kamalika Das, was molested by a classmate when she was thirteen years old. Despite severe criticism and rejection from school authorities, Das fought for justice for four years, until she took her own life at the age of seventeen.

The culture of shame and silence that revictimizes rape survivors is rampant in India, making it extremely hard for women to report incidents, let alone be sure they achieve justice. Sharma, herself a survivor of molestation when she was eighteen, decided to use photography to give women a voice.

Sharma has traveled through several Indian states, visiting cities, towns, and remote villages, taking photos of sexual assault survivors for a photo project called Not My Shame. She is getting funding partly through Kickstarter and is also working with other organizations that assist sexual assault survivors.

Through her photo project, Sharma hopes that she can help break the culture of shame and ostracization around sexual assault that is so common in India.

---

**TIMELINE**   DEVELOPMENT OF PHOTOGRAPHY

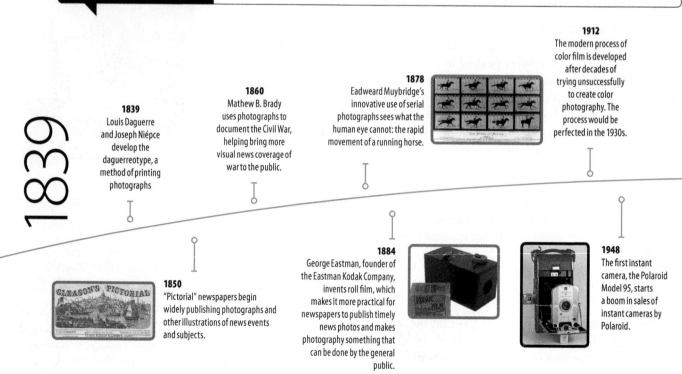

# 1839

**1839**
Louis Daguerre and Joseph Niépce develop the daguerreotype, a method of printing photographs

**1850**
"Pictorial" newspapers begin widely publishing photographs and other illustrations of news events and subjects.

**1860**
Mathew B. Brady uses photographs to document the Civil War, helping bring more visual news coverage of war to the public.

**1884**
George Eastman, founder of the Eastman Kodak Company, invents roll film, which makes it more practical for newspapers to publish timely news photos and makes photography something that can be done by the general public.

**1878**
Eadweard Muybridge's innovative use of serial photographs sees what the human eye cannot: the rapid movement of a running horse.

**1912**
The modern process of color film is developed after decades of trying unsuccessfully to create color photography. The process would be perfected in the 1930s.

**1948**
The first instant camera, the Polaroid Model 95, starts a boom in sales of instant cameras by Polaroid.

The primary function of motion pictures is to entertain, with millions enjoying the sweeping epics, slapstick comedies, romance, action, and adventure of feature-length films. However, as with much entertainment, cultural transmission is also important. Many fans and critics alike consider cinema a serious visual art form comparable to painting, sculpture, or architecture, with a history of important social influence. Still, most commercially produced motion pictures in the United States are intended to make money, only occasionally rising to the level of serious art.

Some cable television channels are devoted almost exclusively to films—such as the Independent Film Channel, Turner Classic Movies, and American Movie Classics—in addition to the frequent (and repeated) showing of movies on commercial and cable channels such as TNT. Cable channels like Home Box Office and Showtime started out showing only films, but have since expanded to include many award-winning original television series. This means films remain part of the entertainment landscape long after leaving theaters. Yet, despite competition from other media, predictions that movie theaters would close as people stayed home watching television have proved unfounded.

## History of the Movie Industry

In 1891, **Thomas Alva Edison** (1847–1931) created the Kinetoscope, a "peep show" precursor to the motion picture viewer. Yet Edison's failure to patent this technology permitted two French brothers, Louis Lumière (1864–1948) and Auguste Lumière (1862–1954), to patent a more portable camera, film-processing unit, and projector in 1895, a suitcase-sized single device that allowed shooting in the morning and footage that could be processed in the afternoon and projected

### Thomas Alva Edison

His inventions included the electric light, the phonograph, and the Kinetoscope. Edison's lab in Menlo Park, New Jersey, had over sixty scientists and produced as many as four hundred patent applications a year.

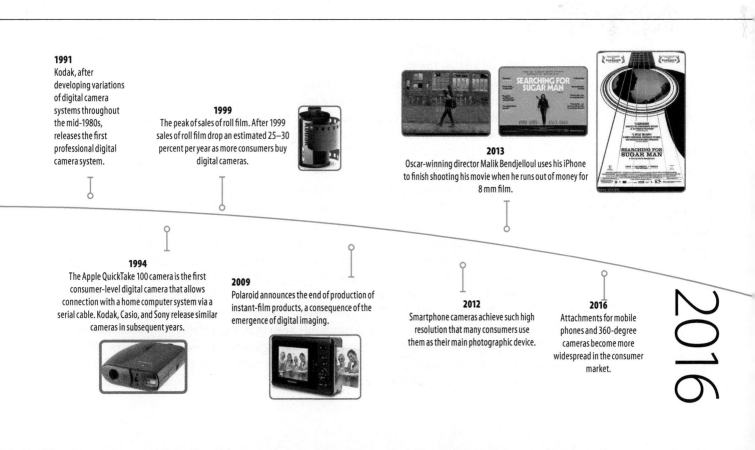

**1991**
Kodak, after developing variations of digital camera systems throughout the mid-1980s, releases the first professional digital camera system.

**1999**
The peak of sales of roll film. After 1999 sales of roll film drop an estimated 25–30 percent per year as more consumers buy digital cameras.

**2013**
Oscar-winning director Malik Bendjelloul uses his iPhone to finish shooting his movie when he runs out of money for 8 mm film.

**1994**
The Apple QuickTake 100 camera is the first consumer-level digital camera that allows connection with a home computer system via a serial cable. Kodak, Casio, and Sony release similar cameras in subsequent years.

**2009**
Polaroid announces the end of production of instant-film products, a consequence of the emergence of digital imaging.

**2012**
Smartphone cameras achieve such high resolution that many consumers use them as their main photographic device.

**2016**
Attachments for mobile phones and 360-degree cameras become more widespread in the consumer market.

2016

for an audience in the evening. On December 28, 1895, the Lumières debuted their process to a paying audience at the Grand Café in Paris, showing a series of ten 15- to 60-second glimpses of real scenes recorded outdoors. Soon the rage all over France, the Cinématographe was clearly based on Edison's machine but could show motion pictures to many simultaneously.[4]

Failing to recognize their invention's potential, the Lumières reproduced daily life rather than telling a story. Louis felt that the novelty of viewing moving images on a screen that could be seen by walking outside would eventually wear off. This mindset differed from that of other film pioneers, such as Edison and Georges Méliès, who saw that film could change reality as well as replicate it.

## SILENT ERA: NEW MEDIUM, NEW TECHNOLOGIES, NEW STORYTELLING

Adding sound to film was not technologically feasible in the beginning. Silent films could more easily cross language barriers than their "talkie" descendants because their few words, usually presented as text on the screen, could easily be translated into the local language.

Early film storytelling was limited and short (a few minutes). Nevertheless, filmmakers around the world soon had Cinématographes and experimented with new ways of visual storytelling, many of which are still used today and taken for granted in movies.[5]

### Méliès and Griffith

Unlike the Lumières, Frenchman Georges Méliès (1861–1938) used the medium to conjure and create illusions. He was the first to make objects suddenly appear, disappear, or change. Among the most memorable was his celluloid transformation of a carriage into a hearse. Méliès pioneered innovative special effects, including the first double exposure (*La Caverne maudite*, 1898), the first split-screen shot (*Un Homme de tête*, 1898), and the first dissolve (*Cendrillon*, 1899).

Méliès notwithstanding, many silent films were little more than novelties. But by the 1910s, the medium began to evolve into an important storytelling vehicle. *Birth of a Nation*, American D. W. Griffith's 1915 controversial classic, was the first major full-length film to introduce many innovative cinematic techniques such as crosscutting (parallel editing) to portray battle scenes. He often depicted the action in one set of shots moving from right to left while another moved left to right.

### Murnau, Flaherty, and Eisenstein

Innovation in filming, lighting, editing, and storytelling continued throughout the silent era. In 1922, German director F. W. Murnau (1888–1931) created *Nosferatu*, an unforgettable adaptation of Bram Stoker's Dracula tale that helped develop the language of film. Also in 1922, American Robert Flaherty (1884–1951) directed *Nanook of the North*, the first great documentary film. This depiction of the life of an Eskimo whaler is still shown in college anthropology courses. Flaherty edited the film in New York after living among the Eskimos for six months while filming.

Russian filmmaker Sergei Eisenstein (1898–1948) pioneered fast cuts between scenes, similar to the editing commonly seen in music videos. Until then, most filmmakers kept the camera stationary, confining scenes to the picture frame. In 1925, he released *Battleship Potemkin*, a silent depiction of the 1905 revolt in Odessa by Russian sailors. A famous editing sequence, "The Odessa Steps," intercuts shots of

## The Photojournalist's Dilemma: Immersion in Conflict

Vice News has emerged since its launch in December of 2013 as a pioneering enterprise in reporting the news without the traditional filter of mainstream media. Vice News reporters have used wearable technologies such as Google Glass and Livestream to deliver video news in real time from around the world to audiences everywhere. Editors at Vice News subscribe to a model of journalism called the "immersionist" school. Many in the news industry and academy view these methods as the antithesis of traditional news reporting by diving deeply into stories and not attempting to provide coverage of a wide array of topics.

In 2014, Vice News used Google Glass to transmit via the Internet real-time video reports via Livestream for hours on end. Reporters using Google Glass delivered largely unfiltered footage of protests in Istanbul, Turkey; Montreal, Canada; and Ferguson, Missouri.[6] Providing narrative audio to accompany this raw coverage, these video streams gave viewers extraordinary depth of reporting on breaking news.

Critics, however, contend that such unfiltered reporting may fail to provide the critical perspective needed to put events into meaningful context. Reporters, critics claim, need to maintain a certain level of healthy skepticism to avoid being manipulated by organizers of events.

Video journalists and photojournalists sometimes struggle with critical questions such as these, and a core part of the answers deals with journalism ethics. The Society of Professional Journalists code of ethics states that a reporter's first responsibility is to the truth, a difficult objective to achieve when covering conflict. This is especially true in war, where, as Phillip Knightly observes, truth is the first casualty. Does a photo or a video tell the truth? Can they do so, even with an appropriate caption or narration? What about the rights of the subject of the photo or video?

Perhaps just as important are the ethical consequences of trauma for the reporter witnessing such atrocities.[7] In the theater of war, photojournalists and their news organizations have an ethical mandate not only to report the truth but to recognize and try to minimize harmful health consequences. Post-traumatic stress syndrome (PTSD) can manifest itself in the form of nightmares, flashbacks, and judgment errors. PTSD occurs in more than a quarter (28.6 percent) of war correspondents, about the same rate as among combat veterans and higher than among police officers.

trapped townspeople with shots of czarist troops firing on the crowd, an emotionally charged scene imitated in homage in several films including Brian De Palma's (1987) *The Untouchables*.

**DISCUSSION QUESTIONS:** Camera-equipped drones are rapidly emerging as important tools for motion-picture storytellers, with the BBC in 2014 using a camera-equipped drone to create a documentary and other videographers using this innovative technology. How might video from drones change the ways filmmakers tell stories?

## SOUND AND COLOR

Although technology had to some degree revolutionized movies, sound and color were needed to fully recreate what people saw and heard. By the turn of the nineteenth century, several alternative but complex and cumbersome methods of producing color motion pictures had been developed, such as hand tinting or hand coloring scenes. Around 1920, a system used a beam splitter with a prism to divide

Breaking with the contemporary norm, *The Artist* in 2011 was both in black and white and silent. It won five Oscars, including Best Picture.

light entering the lens, capturing the different colors on alternating frames. This produced the first successful feature-length color films in the 1920s.

Technicolor Motion Picture Corporation, founded in 1922, became the standard for color motion pictures for the next three decades. Among the earliest Technicolor films were *The Black Pirate* with Douglas Fairbanks in 1925 and *Gone with the Wind* and *The Wizard of Oz* in 1939. Not until the 1950s did color films, captured without prisms, beam splitters, or alternating frames, become more common.

Sound was easier. Even the earliest silent movies were not wholly silent. Live pianists, actors, and even entire orchestras added sound during showings. Actors sometimes accompanied showings, talking about their roles and answering

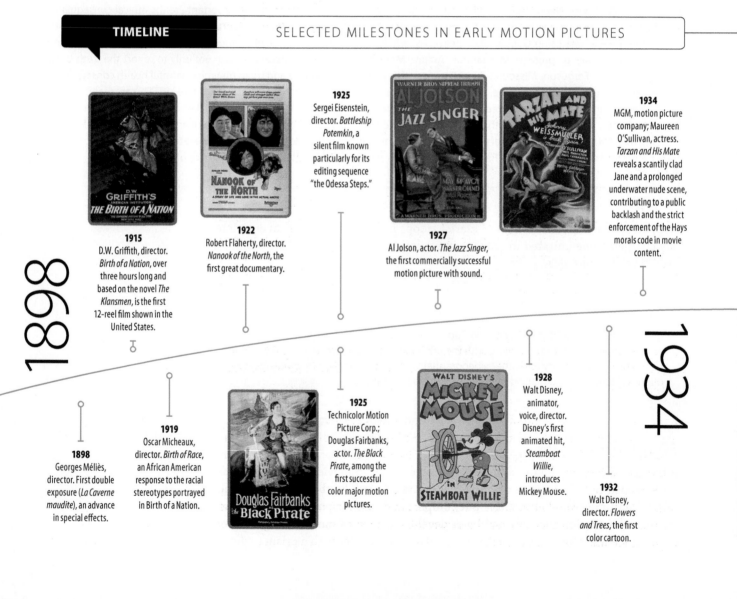

**TIMELINE**    SELECTED MILESTONES IN EARLY MOTION PICTURES

**1898**

**1915**
D.W. Griffith, director. *Birth of a Nation*, over three hours long and based on the novel *The Klansmen*, is the first 12-reel film shown in the United States.

**1922**
Robert Flaherty, director. *Nanook of the North*, the first great documentary.

**1925**
Sergei Eisenstein, director. *Battleship Potemkin*, a silent film known particularly for its editing sequence "the Odessa Steps."

**1927**
Al Jolson, actor. *The Jazz Singer*, the first commercially successful motion picture with sound.

**1934**
MGM, motion picture company; Maureen O'Sullivan, actress. *Tarzan and His Mate* reveals a scantily clad Jane and a prolonged underwater nude scene, contributing to a public backlash and the strict enforcement of the Hays morals code in movie content.

**1898**
Georges Méliès, director. First double exposure (*La Caverne maudite*), an advance in special effects.

**1919**
Oscar Micheaux, director. *Birth of Race*, an African American response to the racial stereotypes portrayed in Birth of a Nation.

**1925**
Technicolor Motion Picture Corp.; Douglas Fairbanks, actor. *The Black Pirate*, among the first successful color major motion pictures.

**1928**
Walt Disney, animator, voice, director. Disney's first animated hit, *Steamboat Willie*, introduces Mickey Mouse.

**1932**
Walt Disney, director. *Flowers and Trees*, the first color cartoon.

**1934**

audience questions before or afterward. In 1896, a paying audience saw the first sound film short in Berlin.

In 1927, Al Jolson starred in *The Jazz Singer*. This first commercially successful "talkie" was not a sound movie by contemporary standards. It contained little dialog but had subtitles and recorded music played back, a technology soon replaced by the superior sound-on-film systems (i.e., an optical soundtrack). In 1925, the first motion picture to synchronize sound was produced, more as a technical experiment than as a commercial endeavor.

By 1929, recording and playing back sound synchronously with the image had become more practicable. Very few silent films were made after this time, with the notable exceptions of those by Charlie Chaplin in the 1930s and *The Artist*, a 2011 French film shot in black and white that won three Academy Awards including Best Picture.

Some silent-era stars could not adapt to the talkie era either because of heavy foreign accents or unappealing voices. Screenwriting and filming changed dramatically, as stories were written for the spoken word rather than visual effect. Slapstick comedy was out, and witty one-liners and jokes were in. Because of cumbersome microphones, cameras also became more stationary; and experimentation with moving cameras, innovative editing, and interesting camera angles became less common. Although there were winners and losers with the development of sound, the industry itself was unfazed by technological change. In the words of Al Jolson, "You ain't heard nothin' yet."

## HOLLYWOOD MOVIE MOGULS

The U.S. motion picture industry began on the eastern seaboard, especially New York City, the center of entertainment, with its Broadway and vaudeville theaters. Thomas Edison's laboratories were also nearby, in New Jersey. Soon after, the powerful movie moguls of the early 1900s created Hollywood, where better weather permitted year-round film production. Actors, producers, and directors relocated, and a split developed between theater (and, later, television) in New York and film in Hollywood. Most television shows are now filmed in Hollywood studios as well, where the U.S. movie industry is securely based. A number of regional centers for movie production also exist, including those in Toronto and Vancouver, Canada. Let's consider some Hollywood movie moguls active in the first half of the twentieth century.

### Warner Brothers

Born in Poland (except for Jack), the Warner brothers, Albert (1884–1976), Harry (1881–1958), Jack (1892–1978), and Sam (1887–1927), founded a movie studio in 1923 that left a lasting mark on the industry. In 1903, Harry hocked his family's delivery horse to buy a used Edison Kinetoscope projector with which the brothers created a traveling movie show in Ohio and Pennsylvania. In 1905, they opened a small theater, and then moved into film production and distribution. They launched "Warner Features" in St. Louis, Missouri, and then Warner Brothers Studio in California.

Sam Warner's "canned vaudeville" propelled the studio to a leadership position. In 1927, *The Jazz Singer* launched the new era of motion pictures with sound, the first of many classics during the powerful studio system, including *Captain Blood* (1935) and *Casablanca* (1942).

## Walt Disney

Walt Disney was a pioneer in animation and entertainment and a talented animator in his own right.

Born in Chicago, Walter Elias Disney (1901–1965) expressed an early interest in drawing and enrolled in the Kansas City Art Institute in 1915. With $40 in his pocket, Walt left Missouri in August 1923 for Los Angeles, where his older brother Roy lived. Combining their meager resources and borrowing $500, the brothers set up shop in their uncle's garage and soon began making animated films.

In 1928, their first hit, *Steamboat Willie*, introduced Mickey Mouse, who talked and sang, featuring Walt's own voice but very little of his own skillful animation. Thus, a star was born that made Disney a household name. In 1937, Disney's first full-length feature animation, *Snow White and the Seven Dwarfs*, broke all box office records. In the next five years, Disney also produced *Pinocchio*, *Fantasia*, *Dumbo*, and *Bambi*. During World War II, most of the Disney facilities produced special government work, including propaganda films for the armed services. Walt opened Disneyland in Los Angeles in 1955 and Walt Disney World in Orlando in 1971.

Always on the technological cutting edge, Disney introduced Technicolor with the 1932 animation *Flowers and Trees*. Part of the Silly Symphonies series, this first color cartoon won Disney his first Oscar. Also a pioneer in television, he produced his first programs in 1954, including the popular *Mickey Mouse Club*, and was among the first to offer color programming with *Walt Disney's Wonderful World of Color* in 1961. Disney won forty-seven Academy Awards, more than anyone else, and seven Emmys.

## Samuel Goldwyn

Born in Warsaw, Poland, Schmuel Gelbfisz (ca. 1879–1974) died Samuel Goldwyn in Los Angeles, having emigrated from England in 1899. He produced *The Squaw Man* in 1914, directed by Cecil B. DeMille, and his production company became the foundation for Paramount Pictures, eventually built by Adolph Zukor. In 1916, he joined forces with the Selwyn brothers and cofounded the Goldwyn Pictures Corporation.

In 1924, his company merged with Louis B. Mayer and Metro Pictures to become Metro-Goldwyn-Mayer. Although his "Leo the Lion" trademark endured, Goldwyn was ousted, and he created an independent film company, which produced such classics as *Wuthering Heights* (1939), *The Pride of the Yankees* (1942), *The Best Years of Our Lives* (1946), *Guys and Dolls* (1955), and *Porgy and Bess* (1959).

## Marcus Loew

Marcus Loew (1870–1927) ran a nickelodeon theater in the earliest days of movies, expanding his holdings over the next several years to create Loew's, a movie chain of luxurious theaters, and getting involved in making movies as well. In the 1920s, he merged his Metro Pictures, Samuel Goldwyn's Goldwyn Picture Corporation, and Mayer Pictures, creating Metro-Goldwyn-Mayer (MGM) Pictures. Unlike the other moguls, he preferred New York, his birthplace, and did not move to Hollywood.

## Louis B. Mayer

In 1907, Louis Burt Mayer (1885–1957), perhaps the most famous and feared movie mogul, renovated a rundown movie theater in Boston that he parlayed into the largest chain in New England. In 1917, he funded Louis B. Mayer Pictures with great profits from his showing of *Birth of a Nation*. He became vice president of MGM in the 1920s and is credited with creating the Hollywood studio star system. In 1927, Mayer teamed with Douglas Fairbanks Sr. to form the Academy of Motion Picture Arts and Sciences.

**DISCUSSION QUESTIONS:** Could a group of new digital filmmakers revolutionize the industry and dominate movie production and distribution like the early Hollywood movie moguls? Why or why not?

## Hollywood Star System

For the first several years of the film industry, actors' and actresses' names did not even appear in the movie credits. Then shrewd studio heads cultivated fan interest, creating personas for popular stars, complete with false histories to market them better, a practice that continues today to some degree. Paramount Pictures (1912), Columbia Pictures (1920), Metro-Goldwyn-Mayer (1924), Warner Brothers (1923), and 20th Century Fox (1935) all held long-term contracts with star directors and actors.

During this era, stars were unable to seek their own contracts for individual films but could be loaned to another studio, often in exchange for other stars. They were also expected to be highly productive, sometimes starring in five or six films a year. Warner Brothers' Humphrey Bogart starred in forty films between 1934 and 1943. *Casablanca* was just one of four he made in 1943. Many films of this era, including *Casablanca*, were not great works of cinematic art but popular entertainment for studio profit.

People often saw these films for the stars they had come to know and for the characters they often represented. Gary Cooper, star of *Mr. Deeds Goes to Town* (1936) and *Meet John Doe* (1941), was known as a tall, awkward, humble man of integrity—the quintessential American, the strong, silent type. Jimmy Stewart played the same kind of person, immortalized in Frank Capra's holiday classic *It's a Wonderful Life* (1945).

*Citizen Kane* has been hailed as one of the greatest films of all time.

The studio star system and long-term actor contracts ended in the late 1940s with the confluence of several forces. First, in 1948, the U.S. Supreme Court divested studios of their theater empires because of monopolistic practices revealed in *United States v. Paramount Pictures*. **Independent films**, those produced outside the major studios, could then be shown in theaters and became financially viable. Independent producers were also able to rent large studios on a per-project basis and benefit from their extensive distribution networks while the studios welcomed the additional income. Studios productions still had an advantage, however. Booking their films in blocks made it cheaper for a theater to show several popular studio films than to take a chance on a single independent film.

Second, the rise of television reduced theater audiences, especially for second- or third-run films. Although studio heads once threatened to blacklist any actor who moved to television, this ban was soon lifted as big names such as Bob Hope and Lucille Ball gave the new medium star power. Conversely, actors like Clint Eastwood who became popular on TV transitioned successfully to film. Today, many actors move from popular shows such as *Saturday Night Live* or situation comedies to movies, and many movie stars can be seen on original cable or streaming movies or series.

**independent films**

Films made by production companies separate from the main Hollywood studios.

## THE DIRECTOR AS AUTEUR

Following WWII, French film critic André Bazin introduced the notion of the filmmaker as author, or **auteur**. Although some early filmmakers, such as D. W. Griffith and Sergei Eisenstein, could be seen as auteurs, in the intervening years filmmaking in the United States became a more collaborative, corporate enterprise—a trend promoted by Hollywood's studio system.

The 1950s French New Wave directors were probably the most influential auteurs. Important directors included Jean-Luc Godard (*Breathless*, 1959), Louis Malle (*Zazie dans le métro*, 1960), and François Truffaut (*The 400 Blows*, 1959). These directors used technologies and camera techniques that were innovative for their day, such as the now-common handheld cameras and freeze frames.

One of the most influential international film auteurs was Japanese director Akira Kurosawa, some of whose early films were remade by others as westerns. *Seven Samurai* (1954) became *The Magnificent Seven* (1960) starring Yul Brynner and Steve McQueen; and in 1964, Sergio Leone remade *Yojimbo* (1961) as *A Fistful of Dollars*, starring Clint Eastwood. Two characters in the classic *The Hidden Fortress* (1958) are said to be the models on which director George Lucas, a great admirer of Kurosawa and Japanese cinema, based C-3PO and R2-D2 in *Star Wars* (1977). Kurosawa also borrowed from the West for *Throne of Blood* (1957) and *Ran* (1985), based on Shakespeare's *Macbeth* and *King Lear*, respectively.

Important American filmmakers have also contributed to the auteur movement. Among them are Blake Edwards, who directed *Days of Wine and Roses* (1962), and Stanley Kubrick, who directed *2001: A Space Odyssey* (1968), *Dr. Strangelove* (1964), *Full Metal Jacket* (1987), and *Eyes Wide Shut* (1999). Other notable contemporary American film auteurs are Martin Scorsese, whose films include *Taxi Driver* (1976), *The King of Comedy* (1983), and *The Age of Innocence* (1993); David Lynch, who made *Eraserhead* (1977), *Blue Velvet* (1986), and *Wild at Heart* (1990); and Spike Lee, who often makes movies that deal with race relations or controversial issues (*Do the Right Thing*, 1988), depictions of historical people and events (*Miracle at St. Anna*, 2008), and documentaries (*When the Levees Broke: A Requiem in Four Acts*, 2006). Quentin Tarantino has a unique cinematic and storytelling style, sometimes criticized for being too violent, as seen in films such as *Reservoir Dogs* (1992), *Pulp Fiction* (1994), *Inglorious Basterds* (2009), and *The Hateful Eight* (2014).

## TECHNOLOGICAL INFLUENCES ON MOVIE GENRES

Modern cinema comprises a variety of types, or **genres**. One basic distinction is between nonfiction, or documentaries, and fiction, by far the dominant type. Rarely shown in American multiplex cinemas, documentaries, if released theatrically at all, are shown in mostly urban art-house theaters to limited audiences. Notable exceptions have been the documentaries of Michael Moore, who created *Bowling for Columbine* (2002), *Fahrenheit 9/11* (2004), and *Sicko* (2007), all of which had theatrical releases. Documentaries have proved to be increasingly popular on streaming services, providing new venues for audiences.

Jean-Luc Godard was one of the important directors of the French New Wave.

**auteur**

Director as storyteller, or author, of a film.

**genres**

Topical categories.

Among the most familiar and popular genres of fiction film are action/adventure, comedy, romance, science fiction, suspense, historical, horror, western, fantasy, musical, biography, and drama. In many cases, there are subgenres, such as crime drama, and some films cut across two or more genres, such as romantic comedy.

Technology has always influenced filmmaking and film genres from the days when short reels allowed films of only five minutes or less, which hampered the creation of complex stories, to the development of synchronized sound, which made the cameras stationary and changed movies from action- to speaking-oriented styles.

Today, digital technologies allow filmmakers to design and populate entire realistic worlds. George Lucas, of *Star Wars* fame, was at the forefront of spectacular computer-generated special effects, although critics charge these were sometimes at the expense of storytelling and character development. Digital technology has allowed for more realistic animation, and studios such as Pixar are using the less labor-intensive new technology to produce animated feature films—although it is still questionable how much money is saved after the costs for high-end computer systems to generate special effects are factored in. James Cameron's *Avatar* (2009), which he waited for more than ten years to make until the technology could match his vision of the film, cost over $300 million. As the first film to gross over $2 billion worldwide, the heavy investment more than paid off. Such was not the case for the effects-heavy *Green Lantern* (2011), which cost $200 million to make and may have topped out at only $260 million in worldwide ticket sales.

New technologies also affect which movies are popular. High-tech gadgetry in our daily lives and today's fast-paced media environment have parallels in many recent science fiction and technology-oriented movies. Slower-paced, character-driven movies based on historical events appeal less to younger audiences. Plots can also be interpreted differently because of changes in technology. A suspense movie made in the 1980s in which tension is created by the main character's difficulties in finding a public telephone would likely make young viewers today wonder why the character doesn't simply use his cell phone or borrow someone else's.

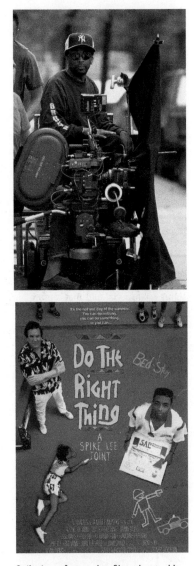

Spike Lee often makes films that tackle controversial or sensitive topics related to race, discrimination, and society.

**DISCUSSION QUESTIONS:** Technological limitations kept film reels short, so only a few minutes of footage could be shown at a time. In what ways could current technological limitations hamper our ability to tell stories through the Internet? How could storytelling be enriched?

## OTHER ENTERTAINMENT SOURCES FOR MOVIES

Movies have always relied heavily on other media as sources for stories. Some of the earliest films were nothing more than filmed stage plays, including Shakespearean dramas. Others were based on popular novels or stories, as are many movies today.

Successful original movies would sometimes inspire a TV series, such as *M\*A\*S\*H* (1970), itself based on a novel; the subsequent television series of the same name ran from 1972 to 1983. Although it still occasionally occurs, such as with *Terminator: The Sarah Connor Chronicles*, today movies are equally likely to derive their inspiration from popular TV series, video games, cartoons, and even the web.

Actors wear special suits that capture body motion against the backdrop of green screens, which allow for any scenes to be shown as a backdrop. These computer-generated image (CGI) effects create amazing special effects. **CRITICAL THINKING QUESTIONS:** Do you think documentary films should be allowed to use special effects or CGI to enhance their storytelling or narrative power? Why or why not?

*Assassin's Creed* (2016) was yet another movie based on a popular video game that underperformed at the box office and was generally panned by audiences.

Although *The Amazing Spider-Man* (2012) and *The Dark Knight* (2008) were hugely successful, many movies created from TV, comics, or video games have been less so. The past several years have seen a spate of movies based on popular television sitcoms, cartoons, and especially comic book characters: the Fantastic Four, Iron Man, Thor, Captain America, the Incredible Hulk, and several Batman releases. The venerable Superman even made a return appearance in *Man of Steel* (2013) and an exit of sorts in *Suicide Squad* (2016).

*Undercover Brother* (2002), a parody of blaxploitation films of the 1970s, was one of the first movies derived from an animated web series on a site called Urban Entertainment. A bidding war started among studios for the movie rights—showing how studios are mining the web for story ideas. The web also allows studios to gauge public interest through viral marketing efforts.

Studios have tried to cash in on the popularity of some video games and characters such as *Super Mario Bros.*, *Tomb Raider*, and *Resident Evil*. *Super Mario Brothers* (1993) did poorly at the box office, but *Lara Croft: Tomb Raider* (2001), although critically panned, did well enough to spawn a sequel in 2003 and a prequel, *Tomb Raider* (2018), based on a 2013 video game of the same name.

## DVDS AND STREAMING

Lower production costs for videotape created new opportunities for filmmakers who would not otherwise make feature films. Yet the movie industry strongly resisted the introduction of consumer videocassette recorder models in the 1970s, even suing VCR manufacturer Sony for encouraging illegal copying, copyright infringement that they claimed would ruin the movie business. This, of course, did not happen; and in fact, video (and now DVD) sales and rentals are double the revenue of box office receipts.

Two changes radically altered the video market. First was the move from videotapes to DVDs, which provide more portability, better video and audio quality, and extra features unmatched on videotapes. Digital video also allowed low-budget directors to shoot professional-quality footage at a fraction of actual film cost. Editing and other postproduction work can also be done on computers or dedicated editing workstations. In only a few years, videotapes were replaced by DVDs, which in turn were replaced by the Blu-ray format, which offered even better sound, picture quality, and storage.

Even Blu-ray discs may seem obsolete because of the changes in how people rent or buy videos. Netflix, created in 1997, has transformed the video rental business by letting consumers use their broadband connection to stream movies and other video content on demand. The established video-rental model had involved going to a store, choosing a movie, and returning it within twenty-four or forty-eight hours to avoid late fees. DVD-rental kiosks, such as Redbox, have also made DVD rentals easier and more convenient; but by 2014, the DVD rental business itself had become obsolete.

Without expensive store rentals and other overhead costs, Netflix can maintain a larger, more diverse inventory. By March 2017, Netflix had almost 99 million subscribers worldwide paying about $10 a month for unlimited viewing of streaming movies and other video content.[8] Blockbuster, king of video rentals in the 1990s, filed for bankruptcy in 2010 and now seems like a distant memory. Netflix has also seen a radical shift in its subscribers, with DVD-only subscribers declining from 11.2 million in 2011 to 4.1 million in 2016, a small fraction of their total subscriber numbers.

Many industry experts believe that DVDs will eventually go the way of videotapes because of the popularity of subscription streaming services like Netflix, Amazon Prime, and Hulu Plus. These services forgo any physical product, as consumers simply stream movies to their devices and watch them.

The trend can be seen clearly when looking at DVD sales and rentals versus streaming revenues in 2016. DVD sales and rentals still accounted for most of the revenues, $12 billion, but dropped 7 percent compared to the year before; whereas subscription streaming revenues rose to $6.2 billion, a rise of 23 percent.[9] Revenue from subscription streaming services overtook DVD sales for the first time in the United Kingdom in 2016.

Much of the movie industry is not happy with the trend toward subscription streaming services, partly because they fear digital piracy and partly because profit margins are much higher on DVD and Blu-ray sales than digital streaming. Nevertheless, the trends are clear and the movie industry is currently trying to find ways to increase revenues in a world where streaming services are ever more popular. One idea is to shorten the window between theatrical release and streaming or DVD release, perhaps with a service that charges subscription prices as high as $50 but that allow subscribers to see movies as soon as two weeks after a theatrical release.

Netflix and other subscription streaming services have rapidly been increasing their production of original shows and series, some of which are earning film and TV awards and critical acclaim.

## Movie Industry Today

Today's motion picture industry contrasts significantly with the vertically integrated entertainment companies that owned not only the means of production but also the distribution system (i.e., the movie theaters). The Supreme Court's antitrust decision of 1948 forced studios to sell their theaters, and today much more power rests with the artists making the films, especially directors and high-paid actors and actresses.

The major studios have adapted to changing conditions and still frequently decide which movies to make and promote. Given the high costs, including several million dollars spent in marketing and specialized technical knowledge, movie production still requires large organizations like the movie studios to bring everything together.

Like other media industries, major studios are part of much larger media conglomerates. (See Table 5-1.) The major studios make movies under a variety of subsidiary production companies, some of which are quite large in their own right. Although lacking vertical integration, they still benefit from sister companies. For example, a Paramount picture may appear on CBS News (both owned by Viacom), or a Pixar picture on ABC News (both owned by Disney), or a 20th Century Fox picture on Fox News (both owned by 21st Century Fox).

A motion picture costs on average over $70 million, although movies often top $100 million, especially with special effects or big Hollywood stars. Marketing costs can add another $30 million to $50 million. Production, the largest single expense category, is usually about 25 percent of the total budget, including set construction, filming on location, film copies for distribution, and crew salaries. Almost all workers, from actors to screenwriters to cinematographers to carpenters, belong to unions that have standard salary rates and rules.

A filmmaker typically approaches a movie studio with a script, which may be original but is often adapted by a screenwriter from a novel or real-life story. A studio will often demand changes, sometimes major revisions, before agreeing

**TABLE 5-1** Ownership Among Major and Subsidiary Film Studios

| MAJOR MEDIA COMPANY | MAJOR FILM STUDIO | SUBSIDIARY FILM STUDIO |
|---|---|---|

### MEDIA PIONEERS
# Kathleen Kennedy

With a career spanning more than three decades as producer of more than sixty major films distinguished by over one hundred twenty Academy Award nominations, Kathleen Kennedy advanced through the celluloid ceiling with digital force. As Sally Field told the CinemaCon crowd in April 2013 when presenting Kennedy with the Pioneer of the Year Award, "In an industry that is not and has not been female friendly, . . . Kathy has beaten those odds the only way a woman can—by being so much better than most everyone else."[10]

This is high praise—wholly supported by an extensive, diverse, and distinguished filmography that includes *Raiders of the Lost Ark* (1981), *E.T. the Extra-Terrestrial* (1982), *The Color Purple* (1985), *Back to the Future* (1985), *Who Framed Roger Rabbit* (1988), *Jurassic Park* (1993), *Schindler's List* (1993),

*Twister* (1996), *The Sixth Sense* (1999), *Persepolis* (2007), *The Diving Bell and the Butterfly* (2007), *The Curious Case of Benjamin Button* (2008), *The Adventures of Tintin* (2011), *War Horse* (2011), *Lincoln* (2012), and *Star Wars: Episode VII—The Force Awakens* (2015). As of 2014, Kennedy's films had grossed over $11 billion worldwide.[11]

One of Hollywood's most successful producers, male or female, Kennedy still flies under the radar with remarkable grace and characteristic modesty. She attributes her success in part to luck and good timing; others point to her astute judgment, formidable work ethic, empathy with cast and crew, and diplomacy when liaising between directors and studios.

Kathleen grew up in Redding, California, and graduated from San Diego State University with a BA in film. Her identical twin, Connie, is an executive producer at Profile Studios, a virtual production company for film and games that specializes in interactive storytelling. Her younger sister, Dana, is also a media professional, an Emmy-winning broadcast journalist, former news anchor, and talk show host.

Kennedy became Steven Spielberg's assistant on *Raiders of the Lost Ark*, after which she, her husband Frank Marshall, and Spielberg formed Amblin Entertainment in 1982. Ten years later, Kennedy and Marshall created their own production company. In 2012, George Lucas, with whom she had also collaborated over the years, selected her to become president of Lucasfilm. Kennedy is also a member of the Board of Governors and Board of Trustees of the Academy of Motion Pictures Arts and Sciences (AMPAS).

Having closely observed and embraced dramatic technological change in her stellar career, she maintains that the essence of great film—great storytelling—remains the same while the tool chest has expanded. "We've talked a great deal about the role that filmmaking technology has played in creating the Star Wars saga," says Kennedy. "We're incredibly excited to find ways to combine state-of-the-art visual effects with the practical approaches that were instrumental in making the original films so iconic; we plan to use everything in the toolbox to continue the Star Wars story."[12]

to bankroll and distribute a movie. Creative differences may arise that can kill projects before they start or force filmmakers to seek support from other major or independent studios. The movie *Rain Man* (1988), starring Tom Cruise and Dustin Hoffman, was almost never made because studio executives demanded an action-packed chase scene involving Hoffman's autistic character.

Once a project has finally been approved and the actors' contracts and schedules agreed on, shooting can begin. This can take several weeks or even months, depending on schedules and other issues. After shooting, the filmmaker is still looking at several more months of postproduction work and editing hours and hours of footage into movie length. This, too, can produce creative differences, as studio executives may demand a happier or otherwise different ending based on early audience feedback. Deleting or even reshooting or shooting entirely new scenes may be required. The Ridley Scott classic *Blade Runner* (1982) is one of the most famous cases in which the studio required a reworking of the director's ending to make it more upbeat. Of course, several versions were later released, including a "director's cut" that more closely adhered to Scott's vision. Musical scores, dubbing, and voice-overs are also added during postproduction.

**DISCUSSION QUESTIONS:** Discuss new ways movie theaters might be able to use their large screens and space to show digital film not only from big-name moviemakers but from local artists as well. How might this affect the local movie theater and its role in the community?

Oscar-nominated 9/11 picture *Zero Dark Thirty* stirred up controversy for Sony Pictures when victims' families complained that the movie's producers had not obtained their permission to use audio recordings, although in the public domain, of actual victims of the World Trade Center disaster. **CRITICAL THINKING QUESTIONS:** Although these voice recordings are in the public domain, do you think it is ethical for a commercial movie to use them without obtaining permission of the families of the victims or paying them royalties? Why or why not?

## Marketing and Distribution for Movies

Marketing and distribution, often key to a movie's success, are quite expensive. A movie that debuts in one thousand theaters nationwide, however well attended, simply will not earn as much as one that fills half the seats in over three thousand theaters. Major studios can still distribute a movie more widely than independent film companies can. The Internet, however, has proven a valuable means of distribution due to its low cost and its potential to build audiences over time and space. A growing number of websites provide an extensive selection of independent and short films online.

The main channel for marketing movies is TV advertising. Heavy advertising occurs two weeks before release because it is nearly impossible for a movie to become popular after poor attendance following release. Much research, effort, and expense go into creating appealing movie trailers and packaging to reach the right target audience. Although studios advertise in other outlets, such as newspapers, radio, and billboards, almost 60 percent of spending is on network- and cable-television advertising. For some movies, such as *Paranormal Activity*, the web and word-of-mouth are important, but these and social media are still a small but growing part in the overall marketing mix.

Movies have a regular pattern of exhibition "windows," places where they are shown that help increase revenues. When studios were at their strongest, they could control theatrical releases at what were deemed "first-run" theaters and then, after appeal faded there, second-run theaters. Movie studios determined which theaters were first-run and second-run and had agreements that assured theaters of exclusive showing privileges within a certain geographic area for a certain amount of time.

The usual exhibition windows for movies start with domestic theatrical release, then proceed to international release, video-on-demand (VOD), pay cable channels (HBO, Showtime, etc.), network or cable TV, and then syndicated TV. Each window has a specified time, and the windows generally do not overlap. Some of these windows are starting to change, or may change in the near future because of the rising popularity of subscription streaming services.

Another example of change is how some blockbusters have been released simultaneously worldwide. Successful movies may get released to video earlier than usual to take advantage of theatrical residual popularity; or, if deemed not worthy of theatrical release, they get the "straight to video" label and head directly to DVD or on-demand distribution. VOD will probably be first after theatrical release, even though today it often appears simultaneously with the video release.[13]

## Movie-Industry Business Model

A seemingly simple business model—get as many people as possible to pay to watch a movie—becomes more complicated when considering the varied ways to watch movies today other than in the theater and how important box office popularity is to attracting viewers in later exhibition windows. Increasing the complexity are the other means by which studios can generate revenue, including licensing deals, product placement, and promotional tie-ins.

The independent film *Napoleon Dynamite* (2004), for example, cost $400,000 and grossed $46 million worldwide. Because movies are so expensive to make and market, however, most lose money. High cost and high risk mean Hollywood studios seek safety in blockbusters, with their usual spate of sequels and generally formulaic stories and characters.

Audiences have been declining steadily over the past several years even as U.S. box office revenues have continued to rise, thanks to increasing ticket prices of about 5 percent a year and 3-D movies, which can charge about $3 more than non-3-D.[14] In 2016, gross U.S. box office revenues were at an all-time high, $11.38 billion, an increase of 2.2 percent over the previous year, even though 2016's overall audience of $1.31 billion was down substantially from 2002's record $1.6 billion (with box office receipts less than $10 billion), and slightly down from 2015's $1.32 billion tickets sold.[15]

U.S. box office revenues are not nearly as important from a financial standpoint as they used to be because international sales account for a larger proportion than they once did. DVD rentals and sales are usually the biggest money generator for movies, long since surpassing box office revenues, although they too are declining as revenues from subscription streaming services are increasing.

Licensing deals can also generate revenue. With popular movies such as the *Toy Story* series, the studio receives royalties for licensing the rights to make toys, blankets, pajamas, and other goods based on the characters. Yet more caution has been exercised in recent years because these deals turn out poorly if a movie does not succeed at the box office. Promotional tie-ins, such as those with fast-food chains, can generate revenue as they generate interest in the movie. **Product placement**, using or showing real-life products in a movie, can also create revenue, although the overall amount is small compared to box office sales or DVD rentals and purchases.

💬 **product placement**

A form of advertising in which brand-name goods or services are placed prominently within movie content that is otherwise devoid of advertising, demonstrating the convergence of programming with advertising content.

Despite competition from a number of other forms of entertainment, movies continue to be highly popular. *Star Wars: Rogue One* was the highest earner domestically in 2016, grossing over $532 million.

# Outlook for the Movie Industry

Digitization has had profound effects on the movie industry, some of which are already being seen in the industry itself and in theaters. Amazing special effects using digital technology can far surpass previous efforts. As computer power increases, computer-artist and programmer skills improve, rendering surfaces like snow, skin, and fur more realistically.

Movie studios have long been promoting 3-D movies as the Next Big Thing, but this time several noted directors are also cheerleaders, including Steven Spielberg, Peter Jackson, and James Cameron, all of whom have released 3-D movies. Some proponents even claim that 3-D will revolutionize cinema in the same way that sound revolutionized the early film era.

Many mainstream movies are now released both in conventional format and in 3-D. In 2014, blockbuster 3-D films such as *The Hobbit: The Battle of the Five Armies* and *Guardians of the Galaxy* offered high-quality immersive viewing experiences. With increasingly lucrative ticket prices, it's not surprising that moviemakers are turning increasingly to 3-D.

Movies in 3-D format still require special glasses. Viewing quality, however, has improved dramatically in recent years, and these movies have become so important that writers now adapt scripts to incorporate 3-D effects. "You build sequences differently when you know things have to pop out and jump at you," says Kieran Mulroney, a script writer for Warner Bros.' *Sherlock Holmes* sequel, as reported in the *Los Angeles Times*.[16]

Movie studios also save through digital-film distribution. It costs up to $2,000 to produce, duplicate, and ship one forty-pound celluloid film print to a movie theater, and most studios ship prints to about four thousand theaters nationwide if they hope for a blockbuster. That means $6 million just in distribution costs for a major film.[17] A digital film, on the other hand, is simply sent over satellite or through broadband to a movie theater. In addition, endless perfect copies can be made, just as with other digital media, eliminating the need to receive even more prints when film breaks or its quality declines after repeated showings.

One obstacle to the movie industry's adoption of digital distribution, despite potential savings, was concerns over piracy. The studios watched the music industry's battles with file-swapping services such as Napster in the early 2000s and torrent streaming services like BitTorrent and realized that they are prime targets for similar practices. Nevertheless, the year 2013 seemingly marked the end of celluloid-film

*The Croods*, a DreamWorks animation released in 2013, was created from 250 billion pixels, making it one of the highest-resolution movies ever.

distribution to theaters in major markets.[18] Some industry experts estimate that digital distribution saves movie studios $600–800 million per year. By 2015, more than 99 percent of theaters in the United States received movies digitally via satellite.[19]

Now that the movie industry has adopted digital technology at all levels of production, the moviegoer will likely see great improvement in picture quality (including 3D) and sound as well as movie availability. More independent films could be shown in major theaters because the theaters and studios will not be banking on the same large audiences to break even because production and distribution costs will be lower.

## Television

According to the Kaiser Family Foundation, children between eight and eighteen spend more time (6.5 hours a day on average) in front of some kind of screen—TV, computer, cell phone—than engaged in any other activity except sleeping. And

CONVERGENCE CULTURE
# Home Theater—Really, This Time

TV makers have long promoted home theater systems that promise visual experiences that are supposed to rival those of the movie theater. However, for the most part over the years, buyers of expensive home theater systems and high-definition TVs have been disappointed, not least because the popcorn at home never seems as good as at the movie theater.

But 4K resolution promises to change that. The standard refers to the resolution of the number of pixels horizontally, 3,840 (nearly 4,000), and a vertical resolution of 2,180. By comparison, HD, or high-definition, has a resolution of 1,080.

Although the 4K standard has been around since the early 2000s, it has started to gain traction in the consumer market only since about 2014, as 4K television prices dropped sharply. Another factor hampering the popularity of 4k is the limited availability of programs shot in 4K. By 2025, it is estimated that more than half of U.S. households will have 4K-capable TVs.

Early adopters of 4K will be able to experience theater-quality images (if shot and distributed as 4K-compatible) because that has been the standard for digital cinema for several years now. Bring on the tub of popcorn.

With mobile devices, a viewer can use the Internet from anywhere in the world to place shift on her or his television viewing.

💬 **time shift**

Recording of an audio or video event for later listening or viewing.

💬 **place shift**

Viewing video from anywhere using the Internet to access content.

💬 **cathode-ray tube (CRT)**

Device in older televisions and computers using electron beams to transmit images to the screen.

more time is devoted to television than to any other medium. The average viewer today who lives to be seventy-five will have spent eleven years watching TV.

Many critics think television is mindless entertainment that does nothing for social skills and physical fitness. Others point to quality content, educational television, news, and cultural programming. Today's interactive television can even get the couch potato off the couch and physically active. With the increase in original series and shows created by subscription streaming services like Amazon Prime and Netflix, not to mention the many quality shows from subscription cable, many are claiming that we are entering a new golden age of television programming.

Terrestrial TV, or over-the-air broadcast TV, had traditionally been the norm, but today more than two-thirds of homes get TV via cable or satellite. Moreover, most households watch DVDs or VOD via television. Consumer recording devices for television were an important development, allowing the audience to **time shift**—that is, watch a program anytime after the original broadcast rather than be held hostage by a broadcaster's scheduling.

Time shifting helped tilt the balance of power toward the audience in choosing media content—a trend that will continue as TV has switched to a digital format. As with radio, digital media complicates the very definition of television, especially as TVs take on more interactive programming and TV programs are viewed on computers, tablets, and smartphones. Mobile devices allow time shifting and let viewers **place shift**—that is, stream video via the Internet.

The widespread use and content range of television help it serve its entertainment, surveillance, correlation, and cultural transmission functions. More U.S. households have televisions than telephones—about 97 percent have at least one TV—and it is the most influential mass-communication medium. More Americans get their news from television than from any other source, making its surveillance function preeminent. More Americans get their entertainment from television than from any other mass medium as well. Entertainment programming plays an important role in the cultural transmission of new trends and social norms.

Television became a mass medium providing a common set of experiences much faster than film, music, and radio. It displaced radio, which had supplanted national magazines. Although more channels and audience fragmentation may reduce this effect, television continues to shape people's attitudes on a variety of social and cultural issues.

# History of Television

Most TV sets and computer displays traditionally used a **cathode-ray tube (CRT)**, conceived in 1859 by German mathematician and physicist Julius Plücker. British chemist William Crookes built the first functional CRT in 1878. In 1873, British telegrapher Louis May discovered that selenium bars exposed to light conduct electricity. Some consider this the basis of photoconductivity, a critical foundation for the electronic transmission of visual and audio information. In 1881, British inventor Shelford Bidwell transmitted silhouettes using selenium in his "scanning phototelegraph," an electrical method that contributed to the development of modern television.

### SEEING THE LIGHT: THE FIRST TELEVISION SYSTEMS

In 1884, German inventor Paul Nipkow developed a concept for mechanical television that used a rotating disk. In 1923, Scottish inventor John Logie Baird created

Baird Television, the first mechanically scanned television device to profit from sending pictures through the air. Some consider Baird's thirty-line TV the first high-definition TV for its many more lines of resolution and finer visual detail.

In 1927, Philo T. Farnsworth transmitted the image of a dollar sign across his San Francisco apartment using his scanning-beam and synchronization-pulse technologies. This was the first electronic wireless transmission of an image, the initial step toward electronic television. His first "broadcast" transmitted images from a Jack Dempsey/Gene Tunney fight and scenes of Mary Pickford combing her hair (from *The Taming of the Shrew*).

Philo T. Farnsworth transmitted the first wireless electronic image, the first step toward electronic television.

## MODERN TELEVISION TAKES SHAPE

Much better image resolution was needed for television to be adopted by the public. The CRT screen, with its greater number of scanned lines, afforded a better picture. In 1939, David Sarnoff demonstrated 441-line TV technology at the New York World's Fair that drew national and international attention. That same year, the National Broadcasting Company (NBC) began regularly scheduled broadcasts to only four hundred sets in the New York area. Development of television was interrupted by the beginning of World War II. There were just seven thousand receiving sets and only nine stations in the United States in early 1946. By 1949, ninety-eight stations existed in fifty-eight markets. In 1950, 3.88 million households had television, 9 percent of the total population of 43 million.

By 1948, there were four commercial television networks: NBC, CBS, ABC, and DuMont (this last network failed in 1955). By the end of 1955, TV households numbered 30.7 million, 64.5 percent of U.S. households; and U.S. advertisers were spending more than $300 million on TV time. By 1960, 45.7 million U.S. households (87.1 percent) had at least one television set.

Color television broadcasting debuted in 1951 with a live CBS telecast from Grand Central Station in New York. Unfortunately, only twenty-five receivers could accommodate the technology, while the 12 million existing black-and-white sets displayed a blank screen. In 1953, color broadcasting launched in the United States when the FCC approved a modified version of an RCA system compatible with existing screens. Color television was only the next step in the ceaseless effort to present sharper and better pictures.

## PROGRAMMING AND GENRE INFLUENCES

Much early TV programming came directly from radio, where talented actors and comedians such as Jack Benny adapted their routines for television. The influence of stage and film also lent much to early television. Dramas sponsored by Hallmark began in 1948, migrating among CBS, NBC, and ABC for over sixty years before running on Hallmark's own channel. Westerns from both radio and film were particularly popular, and although Hollywood studios initially resisted, bringing film to television provided yet another revenue source.

Considerable original programming occurred in the forms of hosted children's shows, variety shows, situation comedies, sports, and news talk shows. From this diversity emerged a more formal organizational division of programming: entertainment, sports, and news.

*The Ed Sullivan Show* helped establish the variety show format and introduced many new artists to the American public.

The 1950s, often referred to as the golden age of television, featured many critically acclaimed commercial successes. An entire postwar generation grew up with the children's show *Howdy Doody*; the first filmed TV sitcom, *I Love Lucy*; Jackie Gleason's *The Honeymooners*; Rod Serling's *Twilight Zone*; and *The Tonight Show*, among many others. *The Ed Sullivan Show*, debuting in 1948 as *Toast of the Town*, established the variety format and often attracted half of all viewing households. In 1964, 73 million viewers nationwide tuned in to see the Beatles on that show.

## Pushing the Programming Envelope

By the 1970s, significant program developments were afoot. Standard one-dimensional genres were infused with more complex, realistic characters and story lines. In 1977, ABC launched its twenty-six-hour miniseries *Roots*, based on the novel by Alex Haley.

The Public Broadcasting Service (PBS) began broadcasting in 1970, inheriting programs from National Educational Television, a noncommercial network founded in 1954. Most famous among these was *Sesame Street*, arguably the most influential TV program for children, which has run continuously since 1969. From 2016, first-run episodes appeared on cable pay subscription service HBO. Operating as a not-for-profit corporation owned by member stations, PBS has often been the home for commercially unviable programming in the arts and sciences, consistently winning more television awards for high quality than commercial television and cable networks combined.

*Monday Night Football*, started in 1970, became a cultural mainstay and led to more sporting events broadcast outside of the traditional weekend slot, producing greater revenue opportunities for sports franchises. Some sports, such as basketball, even changed their rules to promote a faster-paced and more exciting game.

*All in the Family*, the highest-rated program of the 1970s, introduced controversy into the situation comedy genre with its bigoted character Archie Bunker. Its success encouraged others to explore many contemporary social and civil rights issues, although many more simply repackaged popular genres such as police dramas, mysteries, and science fiction.

In 1980, producer Stephen Bochco introduced a new genre of gritty police drama on NBC. *Hill Street Blues* featured several prominent characters, all with various story lines, and a realistic, often-chaotic quality that added dramatic elements of a soap opera. He continued to develop the genre in the 1990s with ABC's popular *NYPD Blue*.

## Cable Comes of Age

Music Television (MTV) debuted in 1981 as a cable channel with its first music video aptly titled "Video Killed the Radio Star." The title proved prophetic. Having dramatically changed music promotion, MTV continued to introduce innovative, although not always culture-enhancing, programs such as *The Real World*, *Jackass*, *The Osbournes*, and MTV's most-viewed series ever, *Jersey Shore*. MTV exemplified a sea change in television programming—from the networks' one-size-fits-all strategy to a fragmented and specialized approach on cable or satellite channels devoted exclusively to travel, sports, and even specific sports such as golf or soccer, movie classics, television classics, cartoons, science, science fiction, home improvement, crime, animals, law, and history.

MTV, or Music Television, became such a part of youth culture after it debuted that teens who were once labeled "Generation X" were also called the "MTV Generation."

Several cable channels began to develop their own dramatic programming, occasionally attracting more viewers than many network shows. *Game of Thrones* toward the end of its fourth season displaced *The Sopranos* in June 2014 as HBO's most-watched series, with an average gross viewership across all platforms of 18.4 million. HBO had been making original feature films, but original, critically acclaimed series such as *The Sopranos*, *Sex and the City*, *Boardwalk Empire*, *Westworld*, and *Game of Thrones* have made the major networks finally take notice of cable. Reflecting the growing Latin American population in the United States, in the 1980s the Reliance Capital Group launched the Spanish-language network Telemundo Group. Cable and satellite television companies support channels that target ethnic groups while also offering access to some international and foreign-language programming. Today, usually for an additional monthly fee, many subscribers can get cable channels in Russian, Chinese, Japanese, Hindi, Tagalog, and Arabic, among other languages.

Critics of network television programming say the networks have only themselves to blame for large-scale defections to cable channels, in particular a risk-averse corporate culture that encourages copying popular programming rather than innovating. Cable TV programming can be more innovative and edgy because it is unfettered by FCC content restrictions on network profanity or partial nudity. Another factor that works against networks is their need to attract as large an audience as possible to charge higher rates for commercials, something that subscriber-based channels such as HBO do not have to consider.

## Filling the Days

A staple of early television was the soap opera, so named because, first on radio and then on television, its principal sponsors advertised household products aimed at the daytime serial's primary audience, homemakers. Indeed, Proctor & Gamble produced both soap and soap operas, notably *Guiding Light*, the longest-running TV soap at nearly sixteen thousand episodes between 1952 and 2009; *As the World Turns* (1956–2010); and *Another World* (1964–1999). One by one, the soaps have died as more women entered the workforce and audiences shrank. Soaps have lost a quarter of their audience since the 1980s. No new English-language soaps have been introduced since the 1990s.

Many fans wax nostalgic over the loss of favorite soaps, which set important new standards for daytime television by discussing topics like abortion and illegitimate pregnancy. Soap operas also introduced some of today's biggest movie and television stars, including Morgan Freeman, Kelsey Grammer, Tommy Lee Jones, James Franco, Amanda Seyfried, and Brad Pitt.

Not all are gone. *Days of Our Lives* and *General Hospital* remain daytime fare. Full-length episodes of *Guiding Light* are still available at CBS's website. Telenovelas, Spanish-language soaps with passionate and sometimes violent tales, are still popular on Spanish-language TV, although they typically run only for a few months or years by design. Exceedingly popular in commercial television's first full decade was the game or quiz show, a format that had been successful in radio as well. By the end of the 1958 TV season, there were twenty-two network quiz shows, one of every five shows. As it happened, many were rigged; and after a public scandal and subsequent congressional investigation involving the popular *Twenty-One*, new rules emerged for regulating game shows.

An even cheaper format, the talk show, has largely replaced daytime game shows. *Dr. Phil*, *Jerry Springer*, *Rachael Ray*, and *The View*, for example, have

Born in Colombia, Sofia Vergara stars in one of the most popular shows on American television, *Modern Family*, and is the highest paid actor on television.

assumed much of the role that soaps used to play in bringing controversial issues to the public arena.

### Filling the Nights

The popularity of the prime-time game show was revived when ABC's *Who Wants to Be a Millionaire* became a ratings leader after its debut in 1999. Like *Survivor* and *Big Brother*, it was a copy of a European show, reversing a long trend of European television's emulating successful American game shows. Although its success was relatively short lived, lasting only three years, the show helped spawn a number of other prime-time game shows. Despite the rapid rise and fall of some of these, others that air before prime time have enjoyed greater longevity, such as *Jeopardy!* and *Wheel of Fortune*.

Prime-time network programming is now dominated by dramatic series, reality shows, and situation comedies, with occasional made-for-TV movies or broadcasts of popular movies that have already appeared in theaters. The latter have become less important, however, as many viewers now choose to see uncut movies without commercial interruptions on DVD, cable, satellite, or streaming online.

### Sports

Some of the biggest television events involve sports. The Super Bowl, for example, annually draws one of U.S. television's largest audiences. Every four years, the World Cup soccer tournament draws large worldwide television audiences. Television commentator Les Brown explains how sports constitute a near-perfect program form for television, "at once topical and entertaining, performed live and suspensefully without a script, peopled with heroes and villains, full of action and human interest and laced with pageantry and ritual."[20]

Sports provide an ongoing venue for technical experimentation. Instant replay debuted in the 1963 Army–Navy football game, and slow motion replay came shortly thereafter. Not only do these now-standard techniques enhance viewing, they have become tools to assist officiating in certain sports, although not without occasional controversy. The rise in popularity of poker-tournament shows has been attributed in part to miniature cameras that allow viewers to see what hands players are holding as they place their bets.

Although sports events still populate the major networks, Disney's ESPN has become the

Soccer is one of the most widely watched sports worldwide.

dominant sports channel, drawing an industry-high $6 billion in annual subscriber fees. Yet it faces growing competition, including Al Jazeera's two twenty-four-hour sports channels (focused on soccer) and Rupert Murdoch's Fox Sports, a twenty-four-hour sports channel featuring NASCAR races, major league baseball and football games, soccer, and more.

Media play a role in determining what types of sports get promoted (and thus which ones become lucrative corporate sponsorships). The popularity of extreme sports and types of fighting besides boxing, such as mixed martial arts, has risen. Generally, slow-paced or highly individualistic sports fare worse than faster-paced events or exciting team sports. One notable exception is golf, likely due to its upscale demographic attractive to advertisers.

Professional wrestling blends sports and entertainment. World Wrestling Entertainment (WWE) combines the physical showmanship that has long defined professional wrestling with ample doses of sexuality and character-driven story lines—complete with crooked bad guys who cheat popular wrestlers of their rightful titles.

## Reality Shows

It may be surprising to learn that reality shows have roots in the earliest days of television. Game shows like *Truth or Consequences*, whose contestants performed wacky stunts for prizes, or Alan Funt's *Candid Camera*, a classic prank show, were very popular in the 1950s and 1960s. In the 1980s, shows like *COPS* and *America's Funniest Home Videos* (*AFV*) debuted, and they continue to air today. *AFV* is a precursor to the kind of **user-generated content (UGC)** often uploaded to YouTube or other video websites.

Reality shows became much more popular beginning in 2000 after *Big Brother* and *Survivor* were both hits in the United States. *American Idol*—which can trace its lineage (including home audience voting by phone) directly back to popular talent-search shows of the 1940s, such as *Arthur Godfrey's Talent Scouts*—remained a top-rated show and launched singing careers for several of its finalists and winners until it ended in April 2016.

Reality shows are a versatile genre. Home improvement channels have capitalized on the format with shows like *House Hunters* and *Fixer Upper*, and lifestyle channels have had success with shows such as *Extreme Makeover*, *The Biggest Loser*, and *Dating Naked*. Practically any situation, real or fantasized, can be adapted to this format, and viewers enjoy watching both "regular" people and celebrities in various challenging situations.

Reality television is profitable for television networks because production costs are much lower than those of scripted programs with actors, sets, and writers paid union wages. The format has proven popular in Europe and Asia, making licensing deals appealing. In addition, many reality shows generate

**user-generated content (UGC)**

Content created by the general public for distribution by digital media.

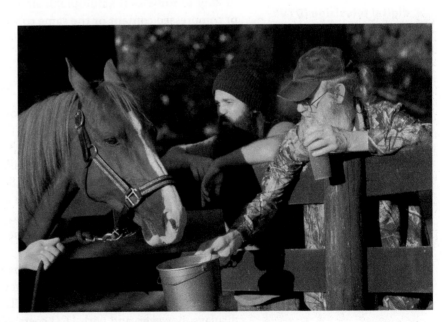

Reality shows remain very popular despite the fact many do not truly capture any "reality" with which most viewers would be familiar.

extra money through product placement. Watch an episode of *The Biggest Loser* and count how many times brand-name products are mentioned.

Despite their name, few of these shows actually capture "reality." Through postproduction editing techniques and loose direction regarding how to act or what to say, the shows present a contrived narrative that may bear little resemblance to the participants' experiences at the time. Although reality shows have made some people celebrities, they also routinely subject participants to public ridicule on social media.

> **DISCUSSION QUESTIONS:** How many reality shows do you watch? Categorize them according to their genres, such as documentary style, reality legal programming, reality competition, social experiment, and hoaxes. Do you think certain genres have more redeeming social or educational value than others, or are there good and bad to be found within each category?

## DIGITAL TELEVISION: PREPARING THE WAY FOR CONVERGENCE

The video and audio of the electronic television's display terminal have evolved since its early years. Long before the digital revolution in 1973, NHK (Japan Broadcasting Corporation) began research on analog **high-definition television (HDTV)**, demonstrating Hi-Vision in 1981, which had much higher resolution, sharper color, a wider aspect ratio, and superior audio. In 1990, an American company, General Instrument Corporation, proposed all **digital television (DTV)**, which became the global standard for next-generation TV. Note that HDTV can be digital, and digital TV can be HDTV, but the two were not always synonymous.

Since June 2009, all television broadcast signals in the United States were switched to digital. DTV enables the convergence of computing, television, and telecommunications that makes new storytelling techniques possible as well as linking to **multicast** (multiplex), simultaneously transmitting multiple channels of compressed content or the same content but at different times. DTV is another step toward converging TVs and PCs or other digital devices (e.g., tablets).

## THE RISE OF FLAT-PANEL DISPLAYS

Large-screen, flat-panel, high-definition displays have changed the television-viewing experience. They bring near-theater-quality sound, color, and picture clarity to living rooms, sometimes in 3-D and all while saving space. Two main types of flat-panel displays have gradually overtaken CRT television: liquid crystal displays (LCDs) and plasma displays. Seen in digital alarm clocks, laptops, and tablet computers, LCD screens also use much less power than the traditional CRT display. At the end of 2007, LCD outsold CRT sets worldwide for the first time. In 2008, they became the majority of sets sold, at just over 50 percent, and their sales continue to grow.

Plasma displays, created around the same time as the early LCD screens, appeared to have a number of advantages over LCDs in terms of picture quality, viewing angle, and screen size. With LCDs now nearly matching the size of plasma displays, however, and with LCD costs generally lower, plasma screens, as well as projection TV, have become less popular for large-screen, HDTV viewing.

### high-definition television (HDTV)

Modern television technology that produces a much higher resolution image, sharper color, a wider aspect ratio, and superior audio. Ultra-high definition is next-generation TV with even higher resolution video; 4K TVs can display video at 4,000 lines of resolution, compared to the 420 lines of standard definition TV.

### digital television (DTV)

Television system in which all information broadcast by cable or through the air is in digital, or computer-readable, form.

### multicast

Simultaneous transmission of multiple channels of compressed content or the same content but at different times.

# Television Distribution

Screen-image quality matters little if there is no way to mass distribute content—thus the early importance of television networks, derived directly from the existing national radio networks. Television programming is distributed in four ways: broadcasting, cable, direct-to-home satellite, and over the Internet. Many millennials have consumed much of their TV over the Internet rather than through the other three forms, while older audiences are more likely to have used the other forms to receive programming.

## BROADCAST TV

Broadcasting (terrestrial wireless) is the traditional means of over-the-air TV distribution for networks, affiliates, and local stations. ABC, CBS, and NBC were all originally radio networks; and Fox, launched in 1986, became the fourth national network, owned by News Corp. The broadcasting networks dominated television viewing until the 1980s when cable and satellite TV made program and audience fragmentation inevitable. Today, about 15 percent of U.S. households receive terrestrial signals on their primary TV set, but broadcast programs are also carried on cable and satellite TV. In fact, the three traditional commercial networks still have a cumulative monthly audience reach of 65 percent.[21]

Former First Lady Michelle Obama's appearance on the 2013 Academy Awards television broadcast was digitally altered by Iran's semiofficial news agency Fars to cover her chest and shoulders, conforming with Iranian restrictions on images of the female body in media. **CRITICAL THINKING QUESTIONS:** Do you agree with Fars's decision to alter the former First Lady's appearance digitally to conform with local conservative religious views? Why or why not?

## CABLE TV

Many think cable TV was invented in the 1980s. But the first systems, **community antenna television (CATV)**, were built non-commercially in Mahoney City, Pennsylvania, and Astoria, Oregon, in 1948. In these communities, over-the-air reception was poor or nonexistent due to hilly terrain or distance. A nationwide cable system did not begin expanding rapidly until the 1970s, when local cable systems grew from about two thousand in 1970 to more than four thousand in 1980.

In the 1980s, the government began deregulating the industry, permitting companies to buy cable television systems nationwide. Early cable giant Tele-Communications, Inc. (TCI), now a subsidiary of AT&T Broadband, took advantage of deregulation, spending $3 billion for 150 cable companies across the United States. By the end of the decade, 50 percent of U.S. households were wired for cable TV.

💬 **community antenna television (CATV)**

Cable television developed in 1948 so communities in hilly or remote terrain could still access television broadcasts.

## SATELLITE TV

Direct broadcast satellite (DBS) emerged in the United States in the 1990s as a serious competitor of traditional terrestrial broadcast and cable television. Although already a viable commercial television alternative in Europe, sustained efforts to launch DBS in the United States had failed until the 1994 launch of DirecTV.

Prior to that, most direct-to-home satellite systems required expensive, large, three-meter dishes. DirecTV and other 1990s DBS entrants introduced inexpensive, compact, eighteen-inch dishes that could be installed without professional help and whose subscription price rivals that of cable. With its 20 million subscribers, DirecTV ranks second only to cable multiple system operator (MSO) Comcast in terms of subscribers, while rival Dish Network, with 14 million subscribers, ranks third.

## Television Industry Today

Television station ownership has continued to consolidate since the passage of the 1996 Telecommunications Act. The 35 percent rule now permits groups to own stations that nationwide reach up to 35 percent of television households and to own two stations in major markets.

There are more than ten thousand local cable systems and two satellite distributors, yet consolidation in the video-distribution industry has resulted in relatively few companies—roughly six hundred MSOs—controlling cable television and satellite TV for more than 90 percent of American subscribers. As Table 5-2 shows, the

**TABLE 5-2** Top Multichannel Video-Programming Distributors in the United States, 2016

| CABLE/SATELLITE MSO | NUMBER OF SUBSCRIBERS |
|---|---|
| Comcast | 22,508,000 |
| DIRECTV | 21,012,000 |
| Charter COMMUNICATIONS | 17,236,000 |
| dish | 12,491,000 |
| verizon FiOS | 4,694,000 |
| at&t U-verse | 4,281,000 |
| Altice | 3,469,000 |
| Sling TV (Internet-delivered) | 1,180,000 |
| Frontier | 1,125,000 |

Source: Leichtman Research Group, Inc., accessed May 1, 2017, http://www.leichtmanresearch.com/press/031617release.html

top multichannel video-programming distributors have nearly three-quarters of all cable TV subscribers.

However, a larger trend is accelerating as more homes get broadband access. In 2016, SNL Kagan reported that 13 percent, or roughly one out of every six U.S. households, had broadband but not cable TV subscription. During 2016, over four hundred thousand households stopped subscribing to cable TV packages from the biggest cable systems. Experts attribute the growing ranks of cord-cutters to the expensive TV packages offered by cable companies that consist of many channels subscribers pay for but do not watch. As a result, some cable companies are offering "skinny bundles" that include limited numbers of channels. Even so, consumers still cannot pick channels à la carte and pay for individual, non-premium channels, and often the skinny bundles still come with extra costs and fees.

## CABLE SYSTEM STRUCTURE

The typical cable system features a tree-and-branch architecture. A headend, or main office, is the center, with fiber or coaxial cable trunk lines, feeder lines, and drops to end users. The 1990s move from analog to digital technology entailed upgrades costing most cable companies millions or billions of dollars not only to improve and expand channel capacity but to add interactive features, such as two-way capacity (e.g., for program ordering), cable modems, and set-top box converters for high-speed Internet.

Although most cable companies advertise modest price hikes of 3 or 4 percent a year, mostly to cover increases in licensing costs from broadcast and cable content providers, *Consumer Reports* says that in truth most price increases are much higher because companies add on various fees that does not appear in their advertising.

## SATELLITE VERSUS CABLE

DBS offers more than three hundred digital programming channels, compared to nearly two hundred for cable. Satellite subscriptions are usually cheaper than cable, even basic cable, but installation costs are involved with satellite dishes and other equipment.

The greatest DBS problem is its lack of a full local array, important for local news, weather, and other programming. Despite great channel capacity, it cannot carry every local station, only those in the largest markets, which require subscribers to pay a fee.

Cable companies have been strongly criticized for increasing monthly subscription costs and providing poor customer service. Most areas have only a single cable provider, although this is changing in some urban or heavily populated areas. Cable companies are introducing more services—such as VOD, DVRs, and video gaming—to compete with satellite and the Internet.

# Television-Industry Business Model

Business models vary with television-signal delivery. Traditionally, terrestrial broadcasting networks relied primarily on selling advertising, one-minute or thirty-second ads, adding up to between sixteen and twenty-two minutes of an hour-long program.

Advertising revenues generated network profits and subsidized the development of new shows. They also created a culture among networks very similar to that in Hollywood—a risk-averse mindset that sought hit television shows to attract the

*NCIS* became the world's most popular TV drama in 2013 as it entered its twelfth season. It also boasts two spin-offs featuring stories set in Los Angeles and New Orleans. **CRITICAL THINKING QUESTIONS:** What accounts for the international appeal of *NCIS*? Identify a number of popular series with spin-offs. Do you think the spin-offs proved as popular as the originals? Why or why not might this be the case?

largest audiences, which meant more lucrative commercial spots. This promoted a copycat trend as other networks scrambled to emulate hit shows the next season.

The importance of tracking audiences led to the Nielsen ratings, a way to measure how many people in various markets were watching a particular show. As Nielsen ratings became the yardstick of success, small drops in viewership could have profound consequences, such as moving shows to different days or time slots or canceling them completely.

Founded in the 1920s by Arthur Nielsen for radio-audience measurement, the system relies primarily on two means of data collection. First is the diary of self-reported TV-watching behaviors. Second is the set meter, a digital device that automatically collects viewership data from TV sets. Set meter data are combined with viewing data collected by individual "people" meters as well. In 2013, Nielsen announced it would begin collecting data about viewership from DVRs. Ratings are calculated by dividing households viewing a program by the total number of TV households. So a rating of 25 would mean one-quarter of all TV households (estimated by Nielsen at 116.3 million in 2014) watched a particular program. Nielsen reports ratings by demographic group as well, collecting its most detailed and comprehensive data four times a year during "sweeps." Nielsen data show a continuing trend of declining viewership of live TV, with the average American watching 4 hours and 32 minutes of live TV each day, 12 percent less than in 2013.

Cable's fragmentation of audiences made the Nielsen ratings a less accurate measure. Even hit cable shows usually have smaller audiences than low-rated network shows. Like satellite, cable services are typically offered in tiers, varying program packages at varying rates. The main cable services are basic, premier channel, and per program, either pay-per-view or VOD. The FCC requires basic service, the minimum level, to include all local over-the-air television broadcast signals and all public, educational, or government-access channels. Basic cable channels air commercials even as they charge a monthly subscription fee. Smaller audiences mean lower advertising rates, however.

Premium cable subscribers get commercial-free content in various bundles, including HBO, Cinemax, and Showtime as well as specialized and foreign-language channels. Additional monthly fees can range anywhere from $4.99 to $16.99 a month. Pay-per-view services include fights or other sporting events, usually for around $50, while the increasingly popular VOD costs anywhere from $2.99 to $16.99 to download a movie. Some services offer free on-demand content along with paid programming. VOD services will continue to grow, especially as networks, cable, and satellite compete with online television services and streaming services like Netflix.

An alternative to advertising and subscription-based models is public broadcasting. In the United States, PBS, a private, not-for-profit corporation owned by member stations, depends on a combination of annual federal appropriations, corporate sponsorships, and private viewer contributions, the latter two making up the vast majority of its funds. Different yet is the British Broadcasting Corporation (BBC). Started in the United Kingdom in 1936, it receives an annual fee collected by the government as a broadcasting tax levied on all TV and radio receivers.

**DISCUSSION QUESTIONS:** If you had to restrict your viewing to only one of the following for a month—network television, premium cable, or video on demand—which would it be and why?

# Outlook for the Television Industry

The switch to an entirely digital television signal in the United States in 2009 freed up some areas of bandwidth used by analog while allowing broadcasters and cable operators to offer new products, including VOD and other interactive services. More significantly, it signaled another step toward an exclusively digital media world.

Although cable and satellite operators have had to adjust to digitization changes, network television has arguably been most affected, as audiences are drawn to other viewing options such as edgier or more innovative cable shows. And as audiences shrink, so do advertising revenues.

Networks are experimenting with online viewing, such as with Hulu.com, founded in 2007. Co-owned by NBCUniversal, News Corp., and Providence Equity Partners, Hulu was easily able to expand content from subsidiary companies Fox, NBC, Sony Pictures Television, Warner Brothers Television, and others. The networks have also made a notable effort to have online streaming video of a distinctly superior quality to the videos found on YouTube, usually using a subscription model.

In 2015, HBO Now launched Internet streaming of its original programming and movies in an exclusive partnership with Apple, a convergence of media and technology that should appeal to a generation of cord-cutters and cord-nevers. The streaming service costs $14.99 a month, and its April debut coincided with a new season of *Game of Thrones*, HBO's most popular series.

## MEDIA CAREERS

Entertainment is serious business at home and abroad, a dynamic field in a state of constant growth. The U.S. entertainment industry generates billions of dollars, revenue accrued in domestic and international markets. Rewarding careers in the visual arts of photography, film, and television are too numerous to list. Identifying the specific path that you would most like to pursue is an important first step.

The most high-profile positions, for the few who attain stardom, are in acting; but actors would be nowhere without talent behind the scenes in the major professions of casting (both locations and people), art, camera and lighting, costuming and makeup, special effects, production, directing, and writing. Numerous career options exist within each of these categories.

Media jobs in the television and movie industry also include creative opportunities for reporters and publicists. These positions require both skill in multimedia production as well as an understanding of social media and a strategic appreciation of the changing nature of TV and film in the increasingly interactive, mobile, and on-demand global marketplace. Jobs in the field are extremely competitive, however, and one must be willing to start working in small markets initially, possibly for years, before being able to move to larger markets or even media hubs like New York City or Los Angeles.

## LOOKING BACK AND MOVING FORWARD

Deregulation and the passage of the Telecommunications Act of 1996 paved the way for mergers and consolidation in the cable industry in recent years. Cable TV now offers consumers bundled packages of telephone, cable television, and Internet service. Verizon, traditionally a telecommunications company, has begun offering more regions in the United States direct-to-home fiber-optic lines, FiOS, a service whose popularity has contributed in part to the decline in cable subscribers. Other telecommunications companies, and even Google, have also been starting to offer fiber options for consumers in some cities.

More people are joining the cord-cutters and cord-nevers, turning away from cable and other traditional pay TV services and toward broadband Internet services, wired and wireless, to access and watch VOD, live and interactively. If consumers use a cable provider for their telephone service, which rules apply—cable TV regulations or phone regulations? Why should an email sent over telephone wires be treated differently, from a legal perspective, from an email sent via cable? This goes to the heart of the so-called network neutrality debate roiling broadband policymakers.

From both a production and a distribution point of view, digital has presented a challenge to industries stretching back to the nineteenth century. Consumers have been increasingly empowered as both creators and distributors of their own movies and photographs. Reduced prices and their convergence with the Internet via mobile devices such as the tablet and the smartphone have made digital cameras ubiquitous.

Increasingly, TV viewers are holding another digital screen, such as a tablet or a smartphone. Multiscreen viewing, a trend likely to increase, was evident with Super Bowl XLIX. More than two-thirds of viewers were also using a handheld device and sending 24 million tweets, often interacting via social media with friends or family.

This century will continue to reshape the visual storytelling of photographs, television, and motion pictures in an increasingly public and participatory environment of social media and interactive technology. These changes in media production and consumption also present various problems, however, including the impact of such transformations on privacy and cultural transmission.

## MEDIA MATTERS

1. Find a photograph that you feel is particularly powerful and discuss what it is about the photo that makes it so.

2. Have you ever owned a camera, digital or otherwise, or have you used only your phone as a camera?

3. How do you think your media consumption influences your social life, such as what friends you tend to hang out with, when and where you meet, and what you talk about? Does your identity reflect your media consumption, or does your media consumption affect your identity?

4. Why did some of the earliest film pioneers, such as the Lumière brothers, believe film to be a novelty that would be a short-lived fad?

5. Keep a diary for a week of the television shows you watch, how long you watch them, and how (TV, computer, VOD, a mobile device, etc.). What patterns do you see, and what implications do they have, if any, for your media consumption?

6. Are you a multiscreen viewer? It what ways does this media habit detract from and enhance the viewing experience?

## FURTHER READING

*American Photography: A Century of Images*. Vicki Goldberg, Robert Silberman (1999) Chronicle Books.

*Film Art: An Introduction*, 8th ed. David Bordwell, Kristin Thompson (2008) McGraw-Hill Higher Education.

*Hollywood! A Celebration*. David Thomson (2001) DK.

*The Film Snob's Dictionary: An Essential Lexicon of Filmological Knowledge*. David Kamp, Lawrence Levi (2006) Broadway Books.

*Film: A Critical Introduction*, 2nd ed. Maria Pramaggiore, Tom Wallis (2007) Allyn & Bacon.

*The Film Encyclopedia: The Complete Guide to Film and the Film Industry*, 6th ed. Ephraim Katz (2008) Collins.

*The Business of Television*. Howard Blumenthal, Oliver Goodenough (2006) Billboard Books.

*The Columbia History of American Television*. Gary Edgerton (2009) Columbia University Press.

*Dangerous Lives: War and the Men and Women Who Report It*. Anthony Feinstein (2003) Thomas Allen.

*The Inventor and the Tycoon: A Gilded Age Murder and the Birth of Moving Pictures*. Edward Ball (2013) Doubleday.

*Rebel Without a Crew, or How a 23-Year-Old Filmmaker with $7,000 Became a Hollywood Player*. Richard Rodriguez (1996) Plume.

*Movies: Discovering Careers*. Facts on File (2012) Ferguson.

*The Digital Filmmaker's Handbook*, 5th ed. Sonya Schenk, Ben Long (2014) Cengage Learning.

# Interactive Media
## THE INTERNET, VIDEO GAMES, AND VIRTUAL REALITY

The parental refrain familiar to most video gamers, "Stop wasting your time—it's not like you're going to be able to make a living doing that," has lost some of its credibility when taking into account the incomes of the top ten professional video gamers.

In their various careers, these young men, mostly from South Korea and the United States, with a couple from Europe, earn between just over $400,000 to about $2.2 million.

If playing video games as a career seems like a dream job to you, keep in mind that it is not all fun and games. Just as with any competitive profession, the name of the game is practice, practice, practice. For example, the members of Team Liquid, a professional League of Legends team, typically practice for fifty hours a week (most full-time jobs expect you to work forty hours a week), not including the time they spend on their own simply playing the games. Korean teams are known to practice even more, upward of seventy to eighty hours a week.

Prospective pro gamers can join various professional gaming organizations online, such as Major League Gaming and National Electronic Sports League; they fill out a profile that indicates their gaming profiles and what games they play. Depending on the organization and how it is organized, players compete in various teams and can work their way up the ranks.

They also compete in tournaments; many of the largest tournaments not only have corporate sponsors but also offer prize money for winning teams in the high five figures or even low six figures.

Professional gamers earn much of their income from sponsorships, just like many top athletes, and the quality and amount of sponsorships, in turn, depend on how many viewers a gamer attracts on his or her social media channels or live streams.

Just how far video gaming has come from the arcade halls of the 1980s to the geeky pastime of home consoles and personal computers shows the integration and evolution of interactive media into our lives.

## LEARNING OBJECTIVES

>> Define the elements of interactivity.

>> Explain the importance of interactivity in terms of modern media.

>> Describe the historical development of user interfaces, the Internet, and the World Wide Web.

>> Explain how digital distribution empowers audiences to act as distributors themselves.

>> Describe why user interface is important to mass communication.

>> Explain how emerging trends will affect user interface and the way we use media.

>> Discuss relevant similarities between today's video-game industry and that of older media.

>> Explain what augmented reality is and how it can be used by media and other companies.

>> Identify some of the ethical issues related to interactive media.

Digital media transformed mass communication by allowing audience members to interact with content, media producers, and each other. Interactivity has had sweeping implications for all aspects of media and communication.

In the past, audiences were largely recipients of news, advertisements, and entertainment from media producers. Newspapers, magazines, and books had limited distribution and a restricted amount of news or information. Likewise, radio and television stations covered only specific geographic areas (as local stations still do). Although cable and satellite expanded the reach of television, viewers still had few opportunities to interact. A publisher or broadcaster sent media content to a large audience that could do little to influence the experience, short of not watching or reading at all.

Today, the audience can choose not only the type of content and media source but, in many cases, how, where, and when to engage with it. People can use their smartphones anytime, anywhere: They stream a TV show, read an ebook, or listen to a podcast or audiobook. Rather than trying to decipher unclear lyrics by listening over and over to a song, people can go to any number of song-lyrics sites and learn the actual words. Furthermore, audiences can easily distribute content to each other through email, blogs, Facebook, Twitter, and other social media. Interactivity has produced dramatic changes in the public's relationship with media. Its power to engage and involve users also raises new ethical issues, which we explore in this chapter.

In this chapter, we will focus on two main arenas where interactivity is most readily apparent: the **user interface (UI)**, which enabled the development of the Internet itself and the burgeoning video-game industry, and the emerging fields of augmented and virtual reality, which promise to further change our media usage.

**user interface (UI)**

Junction between a medium and the people who use it.

## Interactivity Defined

**Interactivity**, a crucial aspect of digital media, has been defined in many ways. According to media and Internet scholar Sheizaf Rafaeli, it is "the condition of communication in which simultaneous and continuous exchanges occur."[1] In other words, interaction involves two or more parties communicating through an ongoing give and take of messages.

For our purposes, we will define interactivity as having the following elements:

**interactivity**

For digital-media purposes, interactivity consists of three main elements: (1) it is a dialog that occurs between a human and a computer program, (2) the dialog occurs simultaneously or nearly so, and (3) the audience has some measure of control over what media content it sees and in what order.

1. It is a dialog that occurs between a human and a computer program (this includes emails, online chats or texts, and discussion groups; at either end of the communication flow, a human interacts with a computer program— the Internet is simply the channel).

2. The dialog affects the nature or type of feedback or content received, changing as the dialog continues.

3. The audience has some measure of control over media content and the order in which it is seen (e.g., getting personalized or localized information, magnifying an image, clicking on a hyperlink).

These three components include almost all the activities that characterize our interaction with digital media and distinguish it from our interaction with traditional media. Some may consider changing television channels interactive, but the viewer is unable to engage in dialog with the television and cannot alter the nature of a program on a particular channel. The level of interactivity involved in changing channels with a remote is simply not the same as that which characterizes Internet use.

In a dialog, both parties adjust their messages in response to feedback, thus changing the nature of subsequent messages. Consider a simple example: You are eager to share a funny story with a friend, but observing that he looks depressed, you ask what is wrong rather than launching into your narrative. The feedback you received altered your message. If you had sent a letter instead, the story would have been conveyed as originally intended regardless of his state of mind.

The same thing happens in an interactive media environment, not only between users but between computer programs and users. Someone reading a news story may click on a hyperlink for an unfamiliar name, taking that reader to another website that describes the person, which in turn may lead to other interesting links. This essentially changes the story for that particular user, who may have a very different sense of it than someone who read the same story but did not click on those links.

Similarly, two people may have very different impressions of the same story after typing in their zip codes to get personalized or localized information or after viewing a multimedia slide show of the story as opposed simply to reading text or listening to it on the radio. Traditional media devices do not permit switching, such as moving from a printed newspaper story to audio.

**DISCUSSION QUESTIONS:** Consider the differences between immediate interactivity, such as pushing a button or discussing on IM, and delayed interactivity, such as email or a discussion board post. How does the change in time affect conversations and relations?

## Interactive Media Versus Mass Media

Interactive media can present information in a way that encourages users to learn and explore. Online quizzes, surveys, and games appear in many places on the web, ranging from news sites to interactive advertising, although many such items could be considered gimmicks. A far more important aspect of interactive media is how it changes the media experience for users. The dialogic nature of interactive media can personalize our relationship with content and make it more relevant and compelling. We engage not only with media but also with others through social media, online chat, instant messaging, emails, and discussion forums—interactivity that may further increase content relevance.

Interactive media also change our concepts of narrative and what makes a story. The control typically enjoyed by producers in traditional media could well be a thing of the past in an interactive media environment. Users on varied narrative routes may wind up in different places because choices made during the story or in video role-playing games may determine the ending. A growing number of interactive documentaries illustrate the significance of storytelling via varied narrative routes. Among the best examples are the award-winning *Hollow: The Story of a Dying County in West Virginia*;[2] *Fort McMoney: An Interactive Game Based on An Oil Boomtown*;[3] *Le Mystere de Grimouville: A Mystery in a French Community* (requires French);[4] *One Shared House*; and *Inside Disaster Haiti*.[5]

Interaction is important for media companies in other ways. Companies can see how many people visited, how long they stayed, who commented on a particular story, and where they went next, along with much other information about users and the devices they used to access the site. This knowledge can influence editorial

A Web-based documentary like *One Shared House* allows visitors to explore different narrative arcs and learn more about the practice of co-living, or unrelated people living together through necessity. **CRITICAL THINKING QUESTIONS:** In what ways do interactive narratives empower the audience? What kinds of challenges do journalists face when creating this kind of interactive narrative?

content as publishers seek larger audiences. A type of story that gets more page views may tempt publishers to produce more such pieces, just as it is tempting to write article headlines that lean toward **clickbait**, or overhyped headlines that seem exciting but that may actually not really represent what the article is about.

The ability to interact with the media and point out errors or biases has embarrassed some news organizations, as readers happily post to the sites and share on social media. Although newspapers have long published corrections, lag time, space limitations, and editorial control over what receives an official correction have limited usefulness. In an online, interactive environment, readers can see comments and corrections from users along with the story.

The ability to learn what others may be saying about a particular news story or type of media content greatly democratizes our information environment. It helps us understand others as a community, albeit perhaps a specialized or temporary

**clickbait**

Articles and headlines written in an exciting or dramatic way in order to get users to click to read the article, when, in fact, the article may not deliver on the promise of the headline.

---

## INTERNATIONAL PERSPECTIVES
# Can the Internet Save Endangered Languages?

Every fourteen days a language dies.

We are used to hearing about endangered and extinct species, so it may seem strange to hear those terms used for languages as well. However, just like species, languages do become endangered and even extinct, a trend that has been growing as major languages like Chinese, English, and Spanish gain prominence as more and more people use the Internet.

UNESCO projects that by the end of this century, more than half of the seven thousand languages spoken today will become extinct. Over half the languages spoken today have fewer than ten thousand speakers, and a quarter will have fewer than one thousand native speakers. According to linguists, a language is considered endangered or "dying" if there are only a few adult native speakers and children are not learning it as a native language, such as speaking it in the home. A language is considered extinct if it is no longer spoken at all as a native language, with any speakers having learned the language through formal education.

The loss of different languages is not confined to remote regions in distant parts of the world. It is happening everywhere—from the United Kingdom (Cornish and Scottish Gaelic) to Bolivia (Aymara) to the United States (Tongva and Ojibwe).

Even as the Internet has played a role in destroying minority languages—and some would argue language in general—it is also playing a major role in trying to revive and preserve them.

Facebook is available in over seventy languages, and users can suggest new languages for Facebook to add. Twitter is available in over forty languages. Wikipedia also features numerous language editions, primarily relying on volunteers to add entries and provide content in that language so it becomes a useful resource.

Others are using the Internet to provide lessons in indigenous languages and to bring speakers and learners together in face-to-face classes, while also using the Internet to digitally preserve native sounds, pronunciations, literature, and other cultural artifacts.

The Native American language Ojibwe is a classic example of an endangered language. Although it has eight thousand to ten thousand speakers, many of them are over seventy years old, with few children learning Ojibwe as a native language. The creators and contributors of Ojibwe.net use social media and the Internet as a way to attract young people to the language and to connect with important aspects of their cultural heritage.

According to Anna Luisa Daigneault of the Living Tongues Institute of Endangered Languages, "Having endangered languages on the Internet has a really strong impact on the youth because it shows that their language is still relevant today. When people use their language it shows that they're proud of speaking . . . it."[6]

one. Yet it also threatens the traditional balance of power between media organizations and the audience. But before we address these issues, let's take a look at the feature that enables interactivity—the user interface.

# Historical Development of User Interfaces

So familiar a feature is the user interface (UI), the junction between a medium and a user, that we rarely give it a second thought and tend to forget that we had to learn everyday practices like clicking a mouse or saving a document. Computers, because of their relative complexity, have more UI issues than traditional media, such as books.

Digital media have enabled a more active audience, one familiar with word processing, browsers, email, and so forth. The interface has helped shape these uses while empowering users, functions critical to the future of mass communication. Media content is essentially wasted if users cannot find a given website and access the desired information. The user interface should be intuitive and natural yet appropriate to the medium and customizable in content.

> **DISCUSSION QUESTIONS:** Give the address of a familiar website to a partner, and without looking at the screen, instruct the partner to complete certain tasks on the site. How difficult is it to explain the user interface or certain functions when you cannot look at the site and do it yourself? Why do you think this is so?

## TELEVISION INTERFACES

Before the development of the computer, we did not generally employ the term "user interface." This is because traditional analog media were not designed to be interactive, and the equivalent of the user interface was generally unchanging. Turning a dial or pushing a button to receive content was an easy task to master. The development of the electronic user interface has both technological and social dimensions, getting people accustomed to using new technologies in a mass-communication context. Had the public not been familiar with television, it might not have been as ready to adapt to the Internet and computers.

Technological improvements in computer monitors, often now called displays, once they became the standard interface with computers, have largely been driven by the desire for more of the qualities that we have come to expect from television screens, such as color, a screen of certain dimensions, and crisp images. Although computer makers originally borrowed from television in creating monitors, television has returned the favor in borrowing from the online world of screen windows, scrolling text or tickers, and multiple items on various topics on a single screen, not to mention interactive touchscreens.

The TV remote control is not only one of the most important transformational technologies in television but also often the source of friction between the sexes and among family members. The first TV remote control was introduced in 1950.[7] Zenith introduced the Lazy Bones, a remote control connected by a wire to your TV set. In 1955, Zenith introduced the Flash-Matic, the first wireless TV remote, which used a flashlight to change channels. The following year, Zenith's Space Command used ultrasound to change channels but also had the unintended

Remote controls have grown increasingly complex as we have gained more functions and channels on our television sets.

consequence of disturbing household pets. Most modern TV remote controls use infrared technology.

The remote control altered viewing habits, as viewers could now easily toggle back and forth between channels, or channel surf, avoid commercials or uninteresting segments in programs, or simply watch multiple sports events.[8] Frequently changing channels could be considered a simple form of **multitasking**. Remote controls changed our media behavior in subtle yet important ways, preparing us for **human–computer interactions**.

## INTUITIVE INTERFACES

Because computers and humans use different languages, some kind of interface, or "translator," is needed to allow communication between the two. The ideal, intuitive interface can be figured out quickly and easily; it should seem natural on first use.

In the earliest days of computing, the user interface was anything but simple. Usually, only the inventor or a highly trained specialist could operate a computer, interact with it, or access information contained within it. Data were entered on punchcards, often requiring hundreds of cards to represent even a simple piece of information, such as a series of numbers or names. The output of a computer analysis was typically printed on paper, which might take many minutes or even hours with a slow dot-matrix printer. If computers were to be more useful, they needed not only to become more powerful but also to develop a better interface for both the input and output of information. Even today, improvements and refinements continue to be made in the intuitive interfaces discussed next.

### Keyboards

The first typewriters, developed in the 1870s to make writing faster, had keyboards arranged alphabetically, but it turned out this was a poor design because some keys were used more often than others and, if typed too quickly, would jam together. Christopher Latham Sholes developed the QWERTY keyboard (after the first row of letters in the upper-left-hand corner of the keyboard) in which the most frequently typed keys (such as "a" and "t") are spread far apart, slowing down the user and thus discouraging jamming.

Jamming became a nonissue with the invention of electric typewriters, but the QWERTY legacy endured, which explains why August Dvorak's keyboard, created in the 1930s and designed for maximum typing efficiency, was never adopted. His keyboard allows users to type more than three thousand words with minimal reaching. The standard QWERTY keyboard can be reprogrammed to the Dvorak layout easily with free software, but most people have never even heard of it.

### Computer Mouse

In 1968, Douglas C. Engelbart invented the computer mouse, made of wood and used with a companion keyboard. His inspiration was a now-classic article in the July 1945 edition of the *Atlantic Monthly* by Vannevar Bush titled "As We May Think." It discussed how the computer could be a desktop tool. Engelbart's mouse enabled the easy manipulation of computer data by pointing and clicking as desired. Although a major development in the evolution of the intuitive interface, the computer mouse may also become an artifact of computer history with the rise of touch-sensitive screens on computers and mobile devices.

**multitasking**

In a computer environment, doing several activities at once with a variety of programs, such as simultaneous word processing, spreadsheet, and database work while conducting real-time chat through an instant-messenger service.

**human–computer interaction**

Any interaction between humans and computers, either through devices such as keyboards, mice, and touchscreens or through voice recognition.

The Dvorak keyboard is much more efficient for typing than the standard QWERTY keyboard, greatly increasing typing speed and accuracy.

## Touchscreens

In 1974, the Control Data Corporation (CDC) introduced PLATO (Programmed Logic for Automated Teaching Operations), the first computer system to have a touch-sensitive video display terminal.[9] Before tablet computers and smartphones, ATMs were the most common example of touch-sensitive screens. Despite greatly facilitating human–computer interaction, touch-sensitive interfaces have certain drawbacks: the need to be within reach of the screen, which means large screen sizes would bother our eyes; and extremely small screen sizes, such as on smartphones, that limit interaction, just as with keyboards. The latter problem was resolved to a large extent with tablets that provide tactile feedback during typing.

## Natural Input Methods

The first computer that could accept natural handwriting with an electronic stylus was sold in 1979, although it could not translate into computer-readable text until almost twenty years later. Among the most natural or intuitive user interfaces, as well as the most elusive, are computer voice recognition and speech synthesis. A hallmark of science fiction for generations, they are gradually becoming integral to the computing and mobile phone environment. For example, users can now get audio responses to questions they ask of intelligent personal assistants such as Siri, Google Assistant, and Cortana. Speech recognition is not without its weaknesses as well. Imagine, for example, the cacophony in a library or classroom if everyone input information or notes in their computers via voice recognition software.

## GRAPHICAL USER INTERFACES

Three developments helped make desktop computers capable of full multimedia: first, the development of greater computing power and increased storage capacity; second, the addition of audio and video; and third, the creation of a graphical user interface. The foundation for the modern **graphical user interface (GUI,** pronounced GOO-ey) was created, like many other computer innovations, at Xerox Palo Alto Research Center (PARC). Debuting in 1974, Xerox's Alto, a computer with a graphical user interface navigated with a mouse, never caught on with the public. However, Steve Jobs of Apple was inspired when he saw it demonstrated and used it for the early Apple Macintosh computers, which revolutionized human–computer interaction.

**graphical user interface (GUI)**

Computer interface that shows graphical representations of file structures, files, and applications in the form of folders, icons, and windows.

Fashion meets function in the Apple Watch from Apple, but the learning curve for navigating the small, new interface raises unique UI issues.

The graphical user interface for personal computers and, later, the web, enabled digital media to compete vigorously with traditional mass media. Educating and entertaining in ways unimaginable with analog, it not only changed how the audience accessed and utilized information, potentially transforming passive media consumers into active media users, it also changed how media organizations created, produced, and presented stories. Businesses seeking to reach the growing number of consumers online resulted in the commercialization of the World Wide Web, whose history is inextricable from that of the graphical user interface to which we now turn.

## Historical Development of the Internet and the World Wide Web

Expensive computers often large enough to take up entire rooms in the organizations or institutions that owned them originally ran machine-specific languages and programs. They could not communicate with one another prior to the creation of the Internet, whose foundations were laid in 1969 when the Defense Advanced Research Projects Agency (DARPA) launched the Advanced Research Projects Agency Network (ARPANET). The first national computer network connected many universities around the country for advanced, high-speed computing applications and research. Still, computers could not yet transmit information easily via the network because there was no "common language" or protocol, a set of rules that facilitate communication between parties who normally speak different languages.

The next important development was email, which "kind of announced itself," said Ray Tomlinson, the computer engineer who invented it in 1971. The *Guinness Book of World Records* claims the first email message he sent was QWERTYUIOP—the

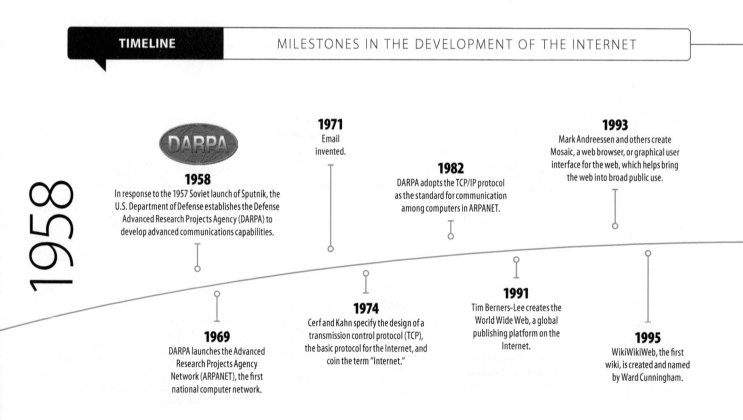

**TIMELINE**    MILESTONES IN THE DEVELOPMENT OF THE INTERNET

1958

**1958**
In response to the 1957 Soviet launch of Sputnik, the U.S. Department of Defense establishes the Defense Advanced Research Projects Agency (DARPA) to develop advanced communications capabilities.

**1969**
DARPA launches the Advanced Research Projects Agency Network (ARPANET), the first national computer network.

**1971**
Email invented.

**1974**
Cerf and Kahn specify the design of a transmission control protocol (TCP), the basic protocol for the Internet, and coin the term "Internet."

**1982**
DARPA adopts the TCP/IP protocol as the standard for communication among computers in ARPANET.

**1991**
Tim Berners-Lee creates the World Wide Web, a global publishing platform on the Internet.

**1993**
Mark Andreessen and others create Mosaic, a web browser, or graphical user interface for the web, which helps bring the web into broad public use.

**1995**
WikiWikiWeb, the first wiki, is created and named by Ward Cunningham.

keys on the third row of the keyboard. And, according to Tomlinson, the symbol @ ("at") was the obvious choice for the symbol to separate the names of individuals from their machines: "As it turns out, @ is the only preposition on the keyboard. I just looked at it and it was there. I didn't even try any others."[10]

Electronic mail was a significant advance, but clearly something more robust was needed, a simplified, common language in which computers could speak to each other and by which they could send and receive large amounts of data.

## INTERNET PROTOCOL

In 1974, Vinton Cerf and Robert Kahn introduced the term "Internet" and specified the design of a **Transmission Control Protocol (TCP)** as part of its main protocol. Jonathan Postel, as a graduate student at UCLA, outlined along with Cerf certain key principles of today's Internet protocols (IPs).

Although the exact date when the Internet officially started is difficult to pin down, in 1982, the U.S. Defense Department adopted TCP/IP as the basis for the ARPANET, requiring universities that wanted to remain in the network to follow suit. Moreover, at this time, researchers began defining an "internet" (lowercase *i*) as a connected set of networks using TCP/IP, and the "Internet" (uppercase *I*) as a set of connected TCP/IP internets.[11]

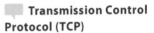 **Transmission Control Protocol (TCP)**

A part of the main protocol for the Internet that allows computers to easily communicate with each other over a network.

## WORLD WIDE WEB

For its first decade, Internet activity required knowledge of a variety of arcane commands and terminology, and its principal users were academic and government researchers. In 1991, Tim Berners-Lee, a British researcher at CERN, a physics

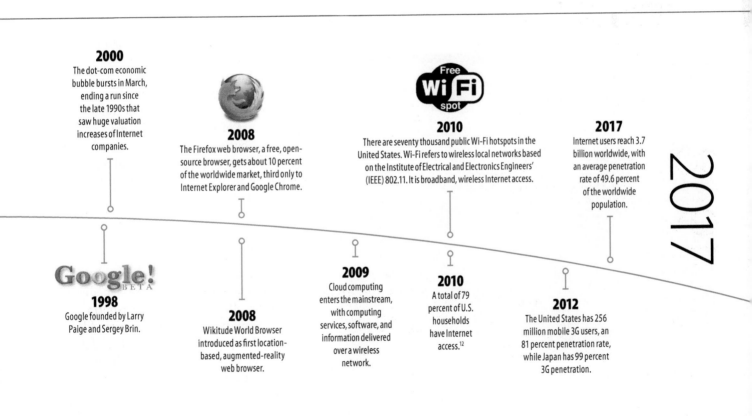

**2000**
The dot-com economic bubble bursts in March, ending a run since the late 1990s that saw huge valuation increases of Internet companies.

**2008**
The Firefox web browser, a free, open-source browser, gets about 10 percent of the worldwide market, third only to Internet Explorer and Google Chrome.

**2010**
There are seventy thousand public Wi-Fi hotspots in the United States. Wi-Fi refers to wireless local networks based on the Institute of Electrical and Electronics Engineers' (IEEE) 802.11. It is broadband, wireless Internet access.

**2017**
Internet users reach 3.7 billion worldwide, with an average penetration rate of 49.6 percent of the worldwide population.

**1998**
Google founded by Larry Paige and Sergey Brin.

**2008**
Wikitude World Browser introduced as first location-based, augmented-reality web browser.

**2009**
Cloud computing enters the mainstream, with computing services, software, and information delivered over a wireless network.

**2010**
A total of 79 percent of U.S. households have Internet access.[12]

**2012**
The United States has 256 million mobile 3G users, an 81 percent penetration rate, while Japan has 99 percent 3G penetration.

2017

laboratory in Switzerland, invented the World Wide Web (WWW), altering the Internet's limited, specialized nature and opening it up to a much wider group of users. Berners-Lee created **Hypertext Transfer Protocol (HTTP)** that enabled users to connect to other web pages or sites whose content is displayed and formatted with **Hypertext Markup Language (HTML)**.

As a global electronic-publishing medium accessed through the Internet, the World Wide Web fostered the most fundamental shift in human communication since the printing press five centuries earlier. It enabled inexpensive many-to-many communication over distance and time while making computer use easier for many nontechnical people. The next development would further lower the barrier and increase Internet access for the masses.

### Hypertext Transfer Protocol (HTTP)

A protocol that enables the standardized transfer of text, audio, and video files, as well as email, from one address to another.

### Hypertext Markup Language (HTML)

A coding format that describes how information should look on the web.

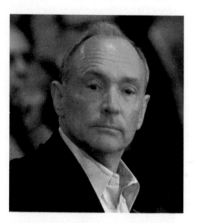

Tim Berners-Lee created the World Wide Web to make it easier for people to find information online.

## GRAPHICAL WEB BROWSERS

The creation of graphical web browsers helped even nontechnical people navigate the Internet. Formerly, most information online was text based. A graphical web browser brings multimedia, such as images or icons and other visual tools, to the web interface, making it more user-friendly. In 1993, Marc Andreessen, then at the National Center for Supercomputing Applications (NCSA) at the University of Illinois at Champaign–Urbana, created a graphical user interface called Mosaic. Although GUI browsers Viola and Erwise were also created in 1992, by the end of 1993, Mosaic had become the best-known web browser.

In 1996, Microsoft created Internet Explorer (IE) to compete with Netscape (formerly Mosaic and then called Netscape Navigator). Because Microsoft offered Internet Explorer for free and eventually bundled it with the Windows operating system, IE became the dominant browser in only four years, with 75 percent usage, compared to Netscape's 25 percent. By 1999, at its peak, IE had 99 percent of the browser market. AOL bought Netscape that year and announced in 2007 that Netscape would be discontinued.

Firefox, an open-source browser created by the Mozilla Foundation and launched in late 2004, presented the first serious competition for Internet Explorer. By early 2015, without advertising or marketing, Firefox had captured about 10 percent of the browser market, most of it from IE. Google's browser Chrome, debuting in late 2008, now has the biggest browser market share at 44.5 percent, followed by Safari at 25.4 percent and all versions of IE at 15.5 percent.[13]

## BROADBAND

A crucial element for online communication to reach its full potential as a mass medium is **bandwidth**. This coaxial or fiber-optic cable of varying capacity is perhaps more readily understood metaphorically as a pipe that delivers data (rather than water) to your home. Tapping the large data pipe, or "fat pipe," allows

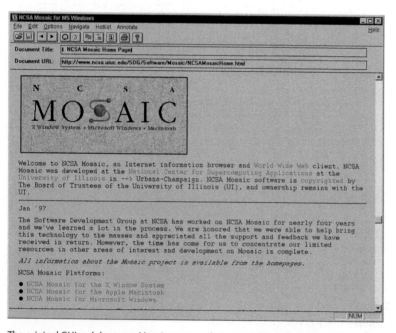

The original GUI web browser, Mosaic, was revolutionary when released in 1993.

data to flow directly at high speeds; through thin pipes, data arrives at a trickle, no matter how fast the personal computer.[14]

Without high-speed, or **broadband**, connections, most people cannot receive audio or video in real time or of the same quality as television or radio. Broadband Internet behavior differs considerably from dial-up connection activity. Broadband users are more likely to produce and distribute media content, and their online expenditures are more than double.

Broadband connections also allow us to receive vast amounts of verbal and visual information from a variety of global sources that increase our knowledge as they broaden our cultural horizons. The inability to access the same information as others can become a serious disadvantage in terms of education or career possibilities. In the United States, broadband telecommunications costs can be high, which means that those at the lower end of the socioeconomic scale spend proportionately more for what many see today as a basic necessity.

## DISTRIBUTION DYNAMICS

Even for people who may not be interested in creating original media content or who have no computer programming skills, today's broadband speeds and extensive networks accelerate the distribution of content. Consider, for example, a photograph from a local online newspaper. A user can easily copy the picture to his or her local drive, separate from the article it accompanies (it is also easy for the user to manipulate the photo, but for our discussion here, that is not important). She or he could then share the digital photo via Facebook or Twitter with, say, two hundred people.

Assume that only half of those two hundred people send it to two hundred other people. Within two "generations," over twenty thousand people could see the photo, all within a matter of minutes after it was originally sent and at virtually no cost to the senders. Distribution no longer depends on sending content from a central location to a passive audience. Rather than accessing media content from central servers, users can keep it on personal computers with large hard drives for storage and make it available to others on the Internet. Many localized distribution points have replaced a few centralized distribution points, creating the basis for **peer-to-peer (P2P)** applications, such as popular music-sharing services.

> **DISCUSSION QUESTIONS:** See how the Internet can track you. Do a search on Amazon for a product that you would never purchase; then over the following days track what types of ads you see on different websites. How long does it take for the ads to revert back to topics that are actually more relevant to you?

Decentralization of distribution means a loss of control for media companies because a single company cannot dictate what every single computer or mobile device among the public may or may not distribute. This translates into potential lost revenues because copies are made and shared among millions of Internet users without any payment to the copyright holders. This is precisely what happened with music online. The music industry's concerns stemmed from the fact that each member of the public who uses file-sharing applications becomes a potential distributor of content merely by having certain files others would like to download. No one has to send anything.

**bandwidth**

The carrying capacity and speed of telecommunication networks that determine how much information can be sent and how fast it can travel over the networks.

**broadband**

A network connection that enables a large amount of bandwidth to be transmitted, which allows for more information to be sent in a shorter period of time.

Mobile broadband Internet access gives Americans high-speed connectivity anywhere, anytime.

**peer-to-peer (P2P)**

The basis of file-sharing services, a computer communications model and network whose computers are considered equal peers who can send, store, and receive information equally well.

## FIGURE 6-1 Client/Server and Peer-to-Peer Networks

A client/server network relies on a server to provide content to people on the network, and content on a P2P network exists on various individual computers and is shared among them.

File-sharing services using P2P networks started making the news in late 1999 primarily because of the rapid rise in popularity of Napster, a program created by eighteen-year-old Northeastern University student Shawn Fanning. Napster let Internet users easily share MP3 files, a compression format for digital music. College campus networks slowed as millions of students downloaded and shared music, and the music industry discovered just how active audiences could be when empowered by digital distribution.

Napster's centralized servers made it an easy target to shut down through legal action. But other file-sharing services that do not rely on centralized servers have been nearly impossible to bring to court, partly because they are based overseas or frequently move their server locations.

Streaming files can also be shared on a P2P network in various ways without a centralized server. **Swarming** with BitTorrent, perhaps the most popular file-sharing protocol on the Internet today, allows users who would otherwise have to pay high server and bandwidth costs to distribute large video and music files easily. Its general operating principle encourages sharing dynamics: The more content a user shares, the more content that user can access. Internet TV services such as Joost used similar swarming techniques to share streaming video files. Many of the file-sharing services created in the early 2000s, such as Kazaa, Limewire, and BearShare, around the time when BitTorrent appeared, have since disappeared.

P2P networks serve other purposes as well, from distributing computing projects to creating an information network impossible to censor or shut down. Should a central company server go down, the content will likely remain available. As long as someone with the material is online, it can be downloaded. This ready availability demonstrates an interesting intersection between technological convergence and cultural convergence, as more people become accustomed to sharing files with one another.

Today file sharing services like Dropbox, Microsoft's OneDrive, and Google Drive make it easy for people to work on collaborative projects and share documents that are stored "in the cloud," or on remote servers. Although not purely P2P services in the way BitTorrent is, they share certain characteristics in terms of letting people store and easily access and share remote documents.

### swarming

The process used by some P2P systems in which multiple downloads of the same file are temporarily coordinated to accelerate the downloading process.

# Video Games

Of the numerous interactive ways to use the Internet, which is the most popular? Recently, video games and social media have surpassed email in measures of Internet activity, although it is worth noting that more messages are still sent via email than through the U.S. Postal Service, and email marketing remains a cost-effective form of advertising for many companies. Online video gaming has exploded thanks to the graphical user interface, which revolutionized, if not wholly created, the industry. Advances in graphic capabilities helped video games grow from a computer-geek pastime to a huge business on par with, if not surpassing, other forms of entertainment media.

Played on computers or other electronic devices with graphic capabilities, video games—whose content is often borrowed freely from movies, television shows, and other areas of pop culture—demonstrate convergence in action. In turn, some popular games, such as *Lara Croft: Tomb Raider* and *Resident Evil*, have spawned movies. And **machinima**, a whole new genre created by video-game enthusiasts, takes cross-fertilization even further with 3-D animated movies modeled after video-game scenarios and characters.

Many game-related websites have active discussion groups in which fans of a particular game help each other with questions; complain about aspects of the game; compose cheat codes; provide hints for finding special bonus treasure; and even create **mods**, modifications to games. This ardent dedication, the envy of many other media companies, may court other dangers, however, such as addictive behavior.

Video sales have eclipsed U.S. domestic movie box office receipts since 2001. Increasingly, we see commercials for upcoming games that look like movie trailers, and the anticipation among gamers for certain releases exceeds that of movie blockbusters. Technology, in the form of the video-game consoles, and content, in the form of popular game titles, have been closely intertwined as the industry, games, and technology continue to evolve with the rise of social and mobile gaming.

**machinima**

A combination of *machine* and *cinema* that uses 3-D animation techniques and characters from popular video games to make movies.

**mods**

Short for "modifications," user-created code changes that alter how video games are played or look.

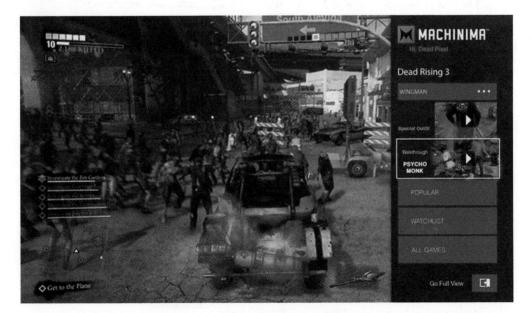

The Machinima app on Xbox One represents a new generation of video games that feature cinema-quality video production.

# Historical Development of Video Games

For a relatively new medium and industry, video games have seen many transformations in the past nearly fifty years. Companies have come and gone while certain titles, such as *Pac-Man* and *Super Mario Bros.*, became part of popular culture. Whole new ways of playing games have developed at the cutting edge of user interface and human–computer interactions.

Dating the birth of video games is difficult. In the 1950s, computers programmed to play checkers and chess, for example, could be found in university laboratories or government agencies but were far beyond what any average consumer could ever afford or use. Here, we consider only some of the major developments in popular video games.

**TIMELINE** MILESTONES IN THE DEVELOPMENT OF VIDEO GAMES

**1962**
The first computer-based video game, *Spacewar!*, is created by MIT student Steve Russell.

**1972**
The Magnavox Odyssey, the first home video-game console, is launched.

**1979**
Milton Bradley's Microvision is the first handheld game console, grossing $8 million in its first year of release. Limited games, small screen, and lack of industry support led to its downfall in 1981.[15]

**1983**
Nintendo releases the Famicom in Japan, released as the Nintendo Entertainment System (NES) in the United States two years later, starting the third generation of video-game consoles.

**1988**
Sega Genesis is released, starting the fourth generation of video-game consoles.

**1994**
Sony releases the PlayStation, a console that uses discs instead of cartridges, the fifth generation of video-game consoles.

**1962**

**1972**
The arcade version of *Pong* is created and quickly becomes popular.

**1977**
Atari releases the Atari 2600, the most successful video-game console of its time, starting the second generation of video-game consoles.

**1980**
Pac-Man is developed by Namco and designed by Toru Iwantani; it will become one of the most influential video games of all time.

**1985**
Nintendo releases *Super Mario Bros.*, which sells ten million copies by the end of the year and becomes the game that defined "platforming." Until 2008, it was the overall bestselling video game.[16]

**1989**
Nintendo releases Game Boy, the first handheld video-game player since the ill-fated Microvision, selling 110 million units worldwide.

**1999**
Sega releases the Dreamcast, a console that pioneered online gaming and began the sixth generation of consoles.

In 1972, Atari released the arcade version of *Pong* (a home version was released in 1975), and Magnavox released the sports-related home video game *Odyssey*, which could be played on the television. Coin-operated arcade games and home video games with consoles and controllers competed for players in the early days.

Arcade games initially had the advantage. The first generation of video-game consoles was simply the games themselves; if a customer wanted to buy a different game, then that person had to buy a different console. The golden age of video arcade games spanned the early 1980s to the early 1990s, fading once console games became as powerful as arcade games and consoles provided the same games with the same quality. Consequently, there are fewer video arcades today. Those that do exist emphasize immersive simulation games, such as racing cars, space

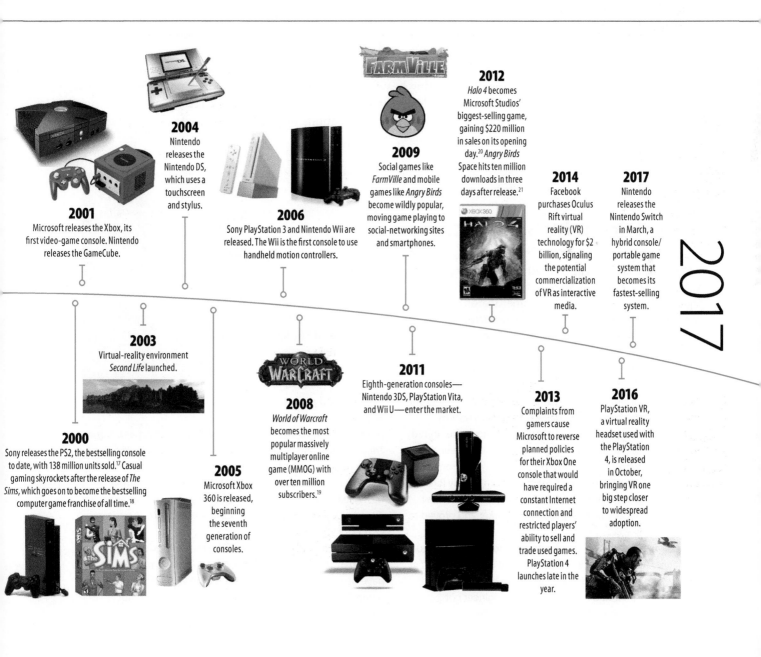

**2012**
*Halo 4* becomes Microsoft Studios' biggest-selling game, gaining $220 million in sales on its opening day.[20] *Angry Birds Space* hits ten million downloads in three days after release.[21]

**2004**
Nintendo releases the Nintendo DS, which uses a touchscreen and stylus.

**2009**
Social games like *FarmVille* and mobile games like *Angry Birds* become wildly popular, moving game playing to social-networking sites and smartphones.

**2014**
Facebook purchases Oculus Rift virtual reality (VR) technology for $2 billion, signaling the potential commercialization of VR as interactive media.

**2017**
Nintendo releases the Nintendo Switch in March, a hybrid console/portable game system that becomes its fastest-selling system.

**2001**
Microsoft releases the Xbox, its first video-game console. Nintendo releases the GameCube.

**2006**
Sony PlayStation 3 and Nintendo Wii are released. The Wii is the first console to use handheld motion controllers.

**2003**
Virtual-reality environment *Second Life* launched.

**2011**
Eighth-generation consoles—Nintendo 3DS, PlayStation Vita, and Wii U—enter the market.

**2008**
*World of Warcraft* becomes the most popular massively multiplayer online game (MMOG) with over ten million subscribers.[19]

**2013**
Complaints from gamers cause Microsoft to reverse planned policies for their Xbox One console that would have required a constant Internet connection and restricted players' ability to sell and trade used games. PlayStation 4 launches late in the year.

**2016**
PlayStation VR, a virtual reality headset used with the PlayStation 4, is released in October, bringing VR one big step closer to widespread adoption.

**2000**
Sony releases the PS2, the bestselling console to date, with 138 million units sold.[17] Casual gaming skyrockets after the release of *The Sims*, which goes on to become the bestselling computer game franchise of all time.[18]

**2005**
Microsoft Xbox 360 is released, beginning the seventh generation of consoles.

2017

Early gamers still fondly remember the iconic Atari 2600 VCS, the first game console that let players change game cartridges.

battles, and first-person shooters. Even these may lose their appeal, however, as VR headsets enter mainstream use.

The second generation was developed in 1977 with Atari's release of the first cartridge-based video-game console, the Atari 2600 VCS, which allowed users to play different games by switching cartridges. Games such as *Space Invaders*, *Combat*, and *Breakout* became very popular and helped make the Atari the dominant console until the early 1980s when toymaker Mattel released a different system, starting one of the first console wars, which still occur today.

In 1985, Japanese playing-card company Nintendo released its Famicom (a shortening of "Family Computer") console in the United States as the Nintendo Entertainment System (NES). An 8-bit console, it ushered in the third generation of more powerful consoles, with better graphics and more processor power. Popular games such as *Super Mario Bros.* and the *Legend of Zelda* made NES the bestselling console in video-game history. In 1989, Nintendo released Game Boy (GB), a hugely popular mobile player.

The 1990s and 2000s saw console makers Nintendo, Sega, Sony, and later, Microsoft competing heavily as they developed increasingly powerful gaming systems and struck deals with game-developer companies for exclusive title rights. The fourth, fifth, and sixth generations of game consoles were largely delineated

## MEDIA PIONEERS
# Hironobu Sakaguchi

Game developer Hironobu Sakaguchi had wanted to create a role-playing game (RPG) for some time when working at Square, but the company refused, worried that an RPG game would not sell well. Finally, after seeing the success of RPG *Dragonquest* in Japan, the company agreed to let Sakaguchi make his game.

He convinced three other colleagues to join his development team, which eventually grew to seven total, and they created the first of what would become one of the most enduring and iconic franchises in video game history: *Final Fantasy*.

Released in Japan in 1987 for Nintendo, and in the United States in 1990, the fantasy RPG game follows the adventures of four Light Warriors who must rescue their world from evil forces. Borrowing from game dynamics of other early RPGs, such as *Dungeons & Dragons*, *Final Fantasy* introduced new game elements as well to the Japanese market and proved to be a huge hit.

Sakaguchi and his team went on to produce nearly annual *Final Fantasy* sequels, including the lauded *Final Fantasy VII* in 1997, which some consider the best video game of all time.

Sakaguchi intended to be an electrical engineer but dropped out of university and became a part-time employee of Square. His first two years at Square were not promising, as he failed to create any hit games and wondered if he had made the right career choice.

However, *Final Fantasy* changed all that, and his various roles as producer or supervisor for such PlayStation classics as *Chrono Trigger* (1995) and *Paradise Eve* (1998) helped ensure his place in the pantheon of influential game developers.

After leaving Square in 2004 and founding his company Mistwalker, Sakaguchi developed *Blue Dragon* (2006) and *The Lost Odyssey* (2007) for Xbox360, as well as *The Last Story* (2011) for Wii.

Sakaguchi said in 2016 that if the technology was as advanced in 1987 as it is today then *Final Fantasy* may never have been made. "I might not even think about making games," he said. "It would look too intimidating. It is not something I could make on my own."[22]

by either the shift from cartridges to disc-based consoles or the ever-increasing console power from 8- to 16- to 32-bit systems.

Sony's PlayStation, launched in 1995, used CDs rather than cartridges, making games cheaper. More powerful consoles also allowed for 3-D graphics. PlayStation 2 (PS2), launched in 2000, could function as a DVD player as well and became the most popular console of its time.

In 2001, Microsoft released Xbox, the company's first console. Although sales lagged behind Sony's and Nintendo's consoles, one of the most popular game titles, *Halo: Combat Evolved*, was available only on the Xbox. Mobile gaming systems continued to evolve as well, with the Nintendo DS and PlayStation Portable released in 2004 and 2005, respectively.

In late 2005, Microsoft released the first of the so-called seventh-generation game consoles, the Xbox 360, which had an even more powerful processor. In late 2006, however, Nintendo leapfrogged ahead again and released the Wii, a seventh-generation console that included handheld motion controllers. Wildly popular for the 2006 holiday season, it quickly sold out in stores. It wasn't until late 2010 that Microsoft released its own motion-sensing input device for the Xbox 360, Kinect, which used the player's body motion as a "controller" and followed certain voice commands.

The motion sensors in the Wii and Kinect have radically changed how players interact with games. No longer do players simply sit and press buttons with their thumbs (although many still do). Rather, game players can run in place, exercise, dance, do yoga, and even fight as the video game captures their motions in real time.

The next generation of consoles, such as Xbox One, PS4, and Wii U, have added or improved on capabilities such as voice commands and face recognition.

In another dramatic change, more gaming systems are shifting to online-only modes, forgoing discs. Online services like Steam, Xbox Live, and UPlay allow gamers to play their games from any console or computer, and they facilitate easy downloading of updates and even player mods. These services require a broadband connection, however, and Xbox One's attempt to move their services entirely online drew complaints about restricting players' use of games.

Eighth-generation video-game consoles give users an immersive and interactive experience.

> **DISCUSSION QUESTIONS:** Discuss a video game you loved to play as a child or young teenager. Why did you like it so much? Why did you finally stop playing it? What feelings do you have when you come across the game, in either its original or a revised form? How do you think issues in this chapter regarding user interface and the nature of the video-game industry may have influenced your impressions of the game?

## Types of Video Games

There are as many video games as there are genres, which many games freely mix and match. As Table 6-1 shows, some of the most popular genres are sports, action, racing, role playing, simulation, and shooter. Genres help set parameters on content and game-play dynamics.

Table 6-1 shows other points of interest. First is the prevalence of tried-and-true titles, especially Nintendo's Mario franchise. Note also the general dominance of Nintendo, claiming the top fourteen titles and seventeen of the top twenty. Many Wii games are also on the list.

**TABLE 6-1** Bestselling Video Games (to 2017)

| RANK | GAME | | YEAR | SALES |
|---|---|---|---|---|
| 1 | Nintendo: Wii Sports | | 2006 | $82.5M |
| 2 | Nintendo: Super Mario Bros. | | 1985 | $40.2M |
| 3 | Nintendo: MarioKart Wii | | 2006 | $35.6M |
| 4 | Nintendo: Wii Sports Resort | | 2006 | $32.8M |
| 5 | Nintendo Game Boy: Pokémon Red/Blue | | 1996 | $31.4M |
| 6 | Nintendo Game Boy: Tetris | | 1999 | $30.3M |
| 7 | Nintendo DS: Super Mario Bros. | | 2006 | $29.8M |
| 8 | Nintendo: Wii Play | | 2006 | $28.9M |
| 9 | Nintendo: Super Mario Bros. | | 2009 | $28.4M |
| 10 | Nintendo: Duck Hunt | | 1984 | $28.3M |
| 11 | Nintendo DS: Nintendogs | | 2005 | $24.7M |

| RANK | GAME | | YEAR | SALES |
|------|------|---|------|-------|
| 12 | Nintendo DS: MarioKartDS | | 2005 | $23.2M |
| 13 | Pokemon: Gold/Pokemon Silver | | 1999 | $23.1M |
| 14 | Nintendo: Wii Fit | | 2007 | $22.7M |
| 15 | XBOX360: Kinect Adventures! | | 2010 | $21.9M |
| 16 | Nintendo: Wii Fit Plus | | 2009 | $21.8M |
| 17 | PlayStation 3: Grand Theft Auto V | | 2013 | $21.2M |
| 18 | PlayStation 2: Grand Theft Auto San Andreas | | 2004 | $20.8M |
| 19 | Super Nintendo: Super Mario World | | 1990 | $20.6M |
| 20 | Nintendo DS: Brain Age | | 2005 | $20.1M |

Source: VGChartz Game Database, http://www.vgchartz.com/gamedb/

Computer users continue to engage in massively multiplayer online games (MMOGs), such as *ARK: Survival Evolved,* and massively multiplayer online role-playing games (MMORPGs), such as Activision Blizzard's *World of Warcraft*. In this kind of game, players create characters and participate in online quests or missions. They work with other players in real time using chats and text messaging to join teams, fight with or against one another, and gain treasure or experience through battling monsters. Console video-game makers see this area as one with great potential and have been moving to establish their own MMOGs. Examples of this with first-person shooters are multiplayer versions of games like *Call of Duty* and *Far Cry 3* in which players can either work together in teams or simply participate in free-for-all online combat.

Most MMOGs and MMORPGs use either a subscription model or some variation of a freemium model in which people can play for free but have limited access to the game world or to character development. Many games have also developed in-game economies in which more advanced players can sell or barter items. Some people use real money to buy virtual items that will help them in the games. In China, some enterprises pay people to play and acquire items that can then be sold on auction sites.

> **DISCUSSION QUESTIONS:** Discuss which types of video games you enjoy and their genre or genres. What makes those games fun for you? Which is your favorite, and why? Do you enjoy online games or those played on mobile devices?

## Video-Game Industry

Video games sold strongly in the 2000s. Sales did not dip until the recession in 2008. In 2017, global video-game sales grew 10 percent, or nearly $10 billion, over the same period last year. Worldwide, mobile gaming continued to increase to $38 billion, while the PC market was $33 billion. Console games accounted for $6 billion.[23]

For much of the history of the development of video games, many small, independent video-game publishers coexisted with Japanese giants like Nintendo, Sega, and Konami. From the late 1990s and especially in the past several years, there has been rapid consolidation among video-game publishers throughout the world, much as in book publishing and the recording industry previously. Large video-game publishers may develop their own games internally, but often they either contract game development to studios or buy the developer companies outright and run them as subsidiaries.

Today, except for the odd hit, such as *Minecraft* from independent developer Mojang, most games come from subsidiaries of a handful of larger game-publisher companies, some of which themselves may be subsidiaries of global media companies. The largest gaming company by revenue is Japan's Nintendo. Activision Blizzard, formed by a merger in 2008 of popular game publisher and developer Activision and Vivendi Games (itself a part of NBCUniversal), is the second largest. Some of the company's popular titles in the separate Activision and Blizzard divisions include the *Warcraft* series, *Call of Duty*, the *Tony Hawk* franchise, and *Skylanders Giants*.

Electronic Arts (EA), founded in 1982, is one of the oldest and largest video-game publishers and developers, third after Nintendo and Activision Blizzard. EA's well-known titles include many popular sports titles, such as the *Madden NFL* and the *FIFA* series, along with popular action and combat series such as *Crysis* and *Mass Effect*.

Ubisoft, based in France, is Europe's largest independent game-development company and the third largest in the United States. Its popular titles include the *Assassin's Creed* series, the *Far Cry* series, and the *Tom Clancy* series of games. ZeniMax Media, a U.S. company, has acquired several well-known smaller developers in recent years including Bethesda Softworks, maker of the popular fantasy role-playing *Elder Scrolls* titles.

In recent years, social and mobile games have grown rapidly. In 2009, Zynga launched *FarmVille* on Facebook. Playable on a browser or a mobile device, it had sixty-nine million users within a year—a tremendous growth rate when compared to storied game franchises like the online *World of Warcraft*, which has 7.4 million subscribers. **Social games** can coexist easily on popular sites like Facebook and

🗨 **social games**

Online or mobile games that are played in real time with others or that encourage simultaneous group playing.

## CONVERGENCE CULTURE
# Video Game Views Old and New

Former college journalism student Palmer Luckey has emerged as a digital media trailblazer at the ripe old age of twenty. Taking his idea for a virtual reality headset to the crowdfunding website Kickstarter in 2012, Luckey quickly amassed some $2 million in funding, enabling him to create a working prototype. That captured the attention of another wunderkind, Mark Zuckerberg, founder of social media giant Facebook, who then acquired Luckey's virtual reality enterprise, Oculus Rift, investing $42 billion in the start-up.[24] Moving rapidly toward the consumer media marketplace, Oculus Rift signals the arrival of fully immersive and interactive media.

Although it did not achieve the same start-up acclaim as Oculus Rift, there was another unusual hit in 2014: the latest version of the game *Minecraft*. Created in 2009 for the PC, the game's simple and blocky graphics belie the complexity of the game, as players can literally interact with every element in the game world.

If *Minecraft* resembles video games from the 1980s and early 1990s visually, its sales figures reflect the popularity of video games today. *Minecraft* has sold more than ten million copies for the PC and more than fifty-four million across all platforms.[25] And like today's social games, *Minecraft* has multiplayer options that allow people to compete against each other. A comparison of the seemingly disparate *Minecraft*

and Oculus Rift reveals one thing in common—YouTube. Gamers across all platforms record and share their play online to create helpful video reviews and tutorials for others. They, too, discuss user-created modifications—mods—to the game.

Fans have also created scene-by-scene video presentations of their experience playing *Minecraft* using the Oculus Rift. Wearing this headset, gamers can play *Minecraft* within a completely immersive environment. Characters are rendered and edited just like in video or film. These YouTube mods have impressive viewing numbers approaching a million or more.

A *Minecraft* movie is apparently in the offing, and a wide variety of *Minecraft*-themed video parodies can be found on YouTube, ranging from Katy Perry to Coldplay, when they aren't being shut down for copyright infringement claims by the artists or their producers. This illustrates cross-fertilization between old and interactive media and some of the problems that accompany the hybridization.

encourage players to recruit new participants from their network of friends.

The huge number of players for games like *FarmVille* meant an attractive audience for advertisers, generating a revenue stream that enabled Zynga to keep the game free, even as some social game developers moved to advertising-free models because they were generating more revenues from in-game purchases. The information on user behavior that Zynga collects is also a potential gold mine for marketers. Advertisers could use this in combination with other demographic or behavioral data to create highly targeted ads. With the popularity of social games, advertisers are once again considering ways to get their ads in front of people during the games.

Recent research has indicated that a family can bond by gaming together while improving communication among family members. **CRITICAL THINKING QUESTIONS:** Have you ever played a board game with your family? A video game? Why or why not might this be the case? Which video games do you think your family might enjoy most as a group activity?

## Trends in Video Games

Some experts initially thought that the video-game market would be limited to males in their teens or younger. Yet research has shown that when the first young people who grew up with home-console video games in the 1980s and 1990s reached their twenties and thirties, they kept playing; and females were playing in greater numbers. The growth in tablet computers has increased the popularity of social and mobile gaming.

Today, game publishers tend to release games on multiple platforms. Previously, each console had specific games exclusively, leading to tough decisions for consumers regarding which console to buy. The statement "Content rules" applies especially to video games, for a handful of popular titles and series make up a large portion of the revenues. As industry consolidation continues and game-development costs rise—with budgets sometimes in the millions of dollars—companies will tend to stick with tried-and-true "blockbuster" series. But online and mobile gaming have seen significant growth as mobile devices and Internet-connected consoles are used to play against live opponents around the world. This may reduce the number of new or innovative genres or games in traditional arenas as game publishers try to revive popular titles from earlier years.

Those outside the industry see potential for other settings, such as education. **Serious games**, or applied games, educate players about history or politics, for example, while they entertain. Video games are increasingly used in settings to help train or educate people, providing simulations that other media simply cannot. Emergency workers and city planners may practice their skills in simulated real-world situations and see the results of certain decisions. Video games have helped some in nursing homes stay mentally sharp and get mild exercise with a Wii, for example.[26]

**serious games**

Games created to be fun and educational that use game dynamics to instruct players on topics.

The U.S. Army used video-game training for officers deployed in Iraq, putting them in tense situations requiring quick decisions.

# Gamification

**Gamification**, in general terms, is the use of game-like mechanics and thinking in a nongame setting, earning points or rewards, for example, for responding to a survey or writing a product review. Such techniques are not new to the Internet: Consider how you earn points when using some credit cards or how Boy Scouts earn merit badges. Online media provide many opportunities for gamification, including encouraging social competition or community recognition of achievements.

Whereas the term "gamification" itself was coined in 2010, its principles emerged earlier as ways of better engaging people in mundane tasks. Because we often compete with each other and like to be rewarded, recognized, and generally admired, a growing number of sites have integrated various tools to encourage us to do exactly that. I may earn a badge for answering questions from other users on a site. Some badges may be harder to obtain than others, encouraging me to write more reviews or edit more articles. Displaying my badges to others in the community may encourage others to want more. Sites may encourage voting, which creates competition among ideas or proposals and interaction among users.

Such techniques have promoted the growth of many popular sites. The location-based social-networking site Foursquare uses badges and titles to encourage frequent check-ins, increasing the site's usefulness for everyone as more people participate.

Gamification techniques can be seen in many fields, including marketing, customer service, and education. Sites like Khan Academy and the language-learning site Duolingo employ gamification to enhance learner engagement. Duolingo users learn parts of a foreign language in modules that unlock other modules and earn digital gold coins as they complete lessons. Gamification has critics, however, who claim that it fosters unnecessary competition, discourages collaboration, and creates a false sense of satisfaction in earning badges for relatively trivial actions.

> **gamification**
>
> The use of game-like mechanics in nongame settings, such as earning points, badges, or rewards for performing certain actions.

Badges are typically used in gamification to help give users incentives to participate in a site or perform certain actions.

# Virtual Reality

**virtual reality**

The replacement of the real world with a digitized, virtual one, a mainstay of science fiction stories hyped in the late twentieth century.

**augmented reality**

Digital overlays of information on a screen that correspond to what is being looked at in the real world through the screen.

**Virtual reality** replaces the real world with a digitized, virtual one, a mainstay of science fiction stories hyped in the late twentieth century. VR headsets entering the mass market, even if they are still pricey, signal the beginning of making those sci-fi visions a (virtual) reality.

Video games and, to a lesser extent, scientific or educational uses, are driving the adoption of virtual reality among the public, and as the price of headsets and television screens that can handle the high-resolution images drops, more people will be using VR headsets.

Although VR headset manufacturers such as Oculus, HTC, and Google had not released sales numbers for their headsets, it has not stopped some industry experts from predicting that VR revenues would be $7 billion in 2017, rising to $75 billion by 2021, with location-based VR such as in malls and theaters being a major source of revenue in the immediate future.[27] Similar to VR, **augmented reality** overlays digitized information onto what we see in the real world, adding information that would not otherwise be visible to us or including additional information about what we are viewing.

Thanks to television sports, we are already familiar with augmented reality. Sports scores, player stats, the yellow first-down line in football, and other extra information shown throughout games can all be considered limited versions of augmented reality. True augmented reality overlays information onto real-world, context-specific scenarios personalized to each user.

For example, a person with an augmented-reality head-worn display could be looking at the ruins of an ancient Greek amphitheater. The display could overlay any number of visuals, such as what it would have actually looked like in its day. Augmented reality could be useful for tourism in other ways, providing visual cues for public transit or pop-up restaurant reviews.

This idea is not new. In the late 1960s, computer scientist Ivan Sutherland created the first head-worn computer display, with limited graphics and computing power. Since the 1970s, researcher Steve Mann has been experimenting with various head-worn, augmented reality displays. Columbia University professor Steven Feiner, a pioneer in augmented reality, has been creating various augmented-reality prototypes since the early 1990s.

Augmented reality appears most frequently online for advertising and on consumer product websites. The augmented dressing room on a site like Tobi.com allows shoppers to upload pictures and "try on" a variety of dresses overlaid on the photo. You can vote yes or no or even forward the picture to friends. Taking augmented reality one step further is Bodymetrics, a company that installs a dressing booth in department stores that scans the body and then shows your "virtual self" in 3-D with different types of clothes, eliminating the need to actually try on each outfit.

First available to testers in 2012, Google Glass more closely approaches the vision of Mann and Feiner for augmented reality—and highlighted the unforeseen problems with new technologies. It lets people access a variety of information regarding what they are observing. A user could ask for sushi restaurants in the area and receive visual cues about restaurants around the corner or blocks down the street. Or a person could access historical photos to see what the neighborhood looked like one hundred years ago.

However, a user can also record a conversation with someone, or access information about the person he is talking to while speaking to the person, which many feel is an invasion of privacy.

Being able to secretly record what is being seen had managers at several Las Vegas casinos nervous, and they announced they would not allow people wearing them into the casinos. The glasses also invited judgments about the "cool" versus "geek" factor. A popular Tumblr blog, *White Men Wearing Google Glass*, pokes fun at the Silicon Valley tech types wearing the glasses. Such representations hurt sales, and in January 2015 Google announced the end of the public phase of Glass development, although it said it would continue to develop wearables as an internal research program.

Samsung is one of many companies around the world that have introduced augmented reality head-worn displays to access the Internet through immersive media.

> **DISCUSSION QUESTIONS:** Some contend that secretly recording conversations or activities, even when the acts recorded occur in a public space, is a violation of privacy. State and defend your position on the matter.

# Ethics of Interactive Media

The power of interactive media to engage and involve consumers of media content raises many ethical issues. Some of these are amplified issues that we encounter with traditional media; others are largely new. Some touch on age-old concerns regarding free speech, the role of advertising in society, and trust.

Interactivity requires faith in others because users must trust those they deal with on the web. Face-to-face communication includes cues and mannerisms that help us establish trust with others, but online we rely on words and the results of our interactions.

Consider what would happen if you were in a chat room discussion with a number of members over the course of several days, greatly enjoying the discussions and the feeling that you have met some interesting, like-minded individuals. Then imagine your sense of betrayal if you learned that one or more of the participants was actually a computer program that gave context-specific responses to human posts. Your trust in that chat room—and perhaps all chat rooms where you did not know the individual participants personally—would likely be broken.

Trust between people is similarly relevant because we expect (or hope) that others will respect our views even if they disagree with them and that they will debate in civilized ways. Most people know how disruptive an obnoxious poster can be to a discussion group, spouting incendiary views simply to draw a reaction. **Trolling** degrades the quality of the discussion and wastes time.

Complaints about advertising's influence have also intensified in an interactive environment. At the forefront of this are video games for children created by companies, such as toy manufacturers, that feature their products prominently in the games. Because of the high level of engagement in video games, critics worry that unaware young users are absorbing hidden commercial messages.

**trolling**

Posting deliberately obnoxious or disruptive messages to discussion groups or other online forums simply to get a reaction from the participants.

## ETHICS IN MEDIA
# Is Playing Video Games Bad for You?

Some psychologists claim video-game addiction is on the rise. People have collapsed and died after playing video games for days without eating or sleeping. In South Korea, after returning home from a twelve-hour gaming session at an Internet cafe where they played a virtual-life game similar to *Second Life,* a couple found their three-year-old daughter dead. Twenty-six-year-old Xu Yan died in 2007 in Jinzhou, China, after reportedly playing online games continuously for two weeks during the Chinese lunar New Year holiday.[28]

The social aspects of massively multiplayer online role-playing games (MMORPGs) have been blamed for teen suicides, such as the thirteen-year-old Chinese teen in 2004 who, after playing *World of Warcraft* for thirty-six hours straight, left a suicide note that he wanted to be with his heroes in the game. Others have taken online betrayals or thefts of virtual magic weapons or equipment seriously enough to kill themselves or physically hurt others. Children have become violent when not allowed to play games, and children and adults have skipped school or work to play.

Researchers still do not entirely understand the nature of video-game addiction, although they assume it stimulates the same dopamine receptors that affect other types of psychological addictions such as gambling. Game designers carefully engineer games to best stimulate these receptors.

Research from 2009 conducted by the Centre for Addiction and Mental Health in Toronto, Ontario, on nine thousand students from grades 7 to 12, shows that about one in ten school-age children spends seven or more hours a day in front of a computer screen. An even greater portion of children this age report having a video-game addiction problem. With the growth of mobile gaming on smartphones and tablet devices, screen time has only increased, as has the likelihood of addiction.

Mental health experts say signs of addiction include the following:

- Inability to stop the activity or playing much longer than anticipated
- Neglect of family and friends
- Lying to employers and family about activities
- Problems with school or job
- Carpal tunnel syndrome
- Dry eyes
- Failure to attend to personal hygiene
- Sleep disturbances or changes in sleep patterns

Psychologists believe that online games are addictive in part because they give people who feel like they do not fit into regular society a chance to interact easily with others and to redefine themselves. Other studies have shown that video games, especially character-driven games that encourage a range of activities and exploration, can help people experiment with new identities and new ways of seeing themselves, which in turn can help them in real-life social situations. A 2014 study shows that video-game play can actually influence the physical development of the brain.[29]

Two 2011 studies from Colorado State University report the potentially positive effects of the popular multiplayer online game *World of Warcraft.* These studies find that players can get involved in the game to the extent that they block out their external environment. Researcher Jeffrey Snodgrass reports such "absorptive experiences" can be positive and provide mental health benefits.[30]

Violence in video games is also a major concern to certain groups claiming that the game interactivity influences children more than simply passively watching violence on television. This is one reason the Entertainment Software Rating Board (ESRB) was created for video games and mobile apps. Similar to the movie-rating system, it ranges from EC (early childhood) to A (adult only). Ratings correspond to levels and realism of violence, sexual content, and strong language.

**Behavioral targeting** also raises ethical issues. A website tracks your browsing or search behavior and then delivers relevant advertisements. After looking at travel sites, you may get ads for deals on your Facebook page or see travel ads appearing on other sites for several days afterward.

**behavioral targeting**

Advertisers tracking individuals' web-browsing behavior to provide ads that closely match the topics of sites visited or searches made.

**DISCUSSION QUESTIONS:** Identify some instances in which you have encountered trolling. Is trolling more likely to occur on certain sites? What has been your response to such behavior? Explain your reaction.

## MEDIA CAREERS

Careers in interactive media represent a growing opportunity, especially for anyone with an entrepreneurial spirit. Most notably, innovators with a new idea for an interactive media enterprise, such as a new app or a video game, may develop an idea for a digital media prototype and then perhaps solicit funding on a crowdfunding website. Another possibility in interactive media is as a player. Professional video-game playing is on the rise, and an increasing number of colleges even offer scholarships to students who show potential and skill at video-game play. With the growth of augmented and virtual reality, a new career pathway has also emerged for students interested in creating content for those platforms, especially with VR cinema companies such as Jaunt.

Jobs also exist for those who write creatively, particularly in the genres of fantasy and sci-fi. Screenwriting and storyboarding skills are also an asset. Game developers come up with a concept; writers develop compelling settings, plots, characters, and dialog that bring their concept, an imaginary world, to life. Writers need not be programmers, but they need to be familiar with the latest in video technology and passionate about gaming. Competition is fierce not only for players but also for candidates in this job market, which makes networking an even more important activity for those hoping to break into the industry. Because of the high demand among prospective employees, salaries tend to be lower than comparable programming or design jobs in other industries, such as working for social media firms.

## LOOKING BACK AND MOVING FORWARD

With the convergence of computing, telecommunications, and media, technological changes can affect media and mass communication powerfully. Increased computer-processing power created better opportunities for a graphical user interface that made computers much more accessible to the average person, which expanded audiences online. Advances in technology will likely further alter our interaction with computers in unforeseeable ways, yet some general patterns in the following broad categories are evident: easier accessibility, more immersive media environments, and seamless or fluid interfaces. The video-game industry is leading the way in these fields because the very success of games depends on how enjoyable and playable they are.

Like traditional media, the video-game industry has consolidated. As with Hollywood movie studios, companies show a strong propensity for producing "blockbuster" game titles. The video-game industry now rivals Hollywood in terms of total revenue, with $99.6 billion earned globally in 2016.[31] Video-game industry revenues make it a likely candidate to become the largest media segment of all. Wireless handheld devices such as mobile phones and tablet computers are now commonplace. They raise important user-interface questions for content on small screens, such as how people can input information naturally yet privately. Geography and location matter because most devices have GPS receivers. From a user-interface perspective, this means that maps will become increasingly important as graphics-layered information on screen. Map-based GUIs can provide everything from information on the nearest restaurant, including reviews, to local points of cultural or historical interest.

Accessing media content will be increasingly easy, but accessing the content one wants when and where one wants it may be harder than ever unless sound principles in user-interface design are applied to search-and-find functions.

A variety of forms of immersive media are emerging and expanding in the online environment. These include 3-D visualizations, virtual reality, 360-degree photography and video, and augmented reality. Immersive media environments can provide experiences unlike those encountered in traditional media or even in the typical digital-media environment, providing new opportunities—and new challenges—for user interfaces.

Interfaces that change to suit our informational and entertainment needs will gradually replace largely static web pages. We will not necessarily have to "go to" a website to get information; rather, we may have some version of the web on a wearable computer and interact with the screen through voice commands or even eye movements. Wearable computers capable of recording do raise privacy issues, among other ethical and social concerns.

It is important to remember that the online environment with which we are familiar is not simply one in which we receive a variety of media content in different forms, although that continues to be a large part of it. It also includes various ways to communicate directly with media producers, other audience members, and one's social network. Our user interface helps us receive the kind of information and entertainment we want and easily communicate and interact with others. Interactivity is one of digital media's central and distinguishing features.

## FURTHER READING

*Understanding Media: The Extensions of Man*, reprint ed. Marshall McLuhan, Lewis Lapham (1994) MIT Press.

*Bias of Communication*, reprint ed. Harold Innis (1991) University of Toronto Press.

*A History of Modern Computing*. Paul E. Ceruzzi (1999) MIT Press.

*Interface Culture: How New Technology Transforms the Ways We Create and Communicate*. Steven Johnson (1999) Basic Books.

*The Rise of the Image, the Fall of the Word*. Mitchell Stephens (1998) Oxford University Press.

*About Face 3: The Essentials of Interaction Design*. Alan Cooper, Robert Reimann, David Cronin (2007) Wiley.

*Designing with the Mind in Mind: Simple Guide to Understanding User Interface Design Rules*. Jeff Johnson (2010) Morgan Kaufman.

*Don't Make Me Think, Revisited: A Common Sense Approach to Web Usability*, 3rd ed. Steve Krug (2014) New Riders.

*The Ultimate History of Video Games: From* Pong *to* Pokémon—*The Story Behind the Craze That Touched Our Lives and Changed the World*. Steven Kent (2001) Three Rivers Press.

*The Video Games Guide: 1,000+ Arcade, Console and Computer Games, 1962–2012*, 2nd ed. Matt Fox (2013) McFarland.

*Reality Is Broken: Why Games Make Us Better and How They Can Change the World*. Jane McGonigal (2011) Penguin.

*1001 Video Games You Must Play Before You Die*. Tony Mott (ed.) (2010) Universe.

*Replay: The History of Video Games*. Tristan Donovan (2010) Yellow Ant.

*The Google Story: Inside the Hottest Business, Media, and Technology Success of Our Time*. David Vise, Mark Malseed (2006) Delta.

*Planet Google: One Company's Audacious Plan to Organize Everything We Know*. Randall Stross (2008) Free Press.

*Click: What Millions of People Are Doing Online and Why It Matters*. Bill Tancer (2008) Hyperion.

*Augmented Reality: Theory and Practice*. Dieter Schmalstieg, Tobias Hollerer (2014) Addison-Wesley.

*The Innovators: How a Group of Hackers, Geniuses, and Geeks Created the Digital Revolution*. Walter Isaacson (2014) Simon & Schuster.

*Glow Kids: How Screen Addiction Is Hijacking Our Kids—and How to Break the Trance*. Nicholas Kardaras (2016) St. Martin's Press.

# The Impact of Social Media

**LEARNING OBJECTIVES**

>> Define social media.

>> Explain the differences between social media and traditional media.

>> Identify the different types of social media.

>> Explain the historical development of social media within a larger mass-communications context.

>> Assess how audiences are changing from consumers to "produsers."

>> Discuss the potential negative effects of social media use.

Justine Sacco, a thirty-year-old senior director of corporate communications at IAC, tweeted several jokes about travel on her way from New York City to visit family in South Africa. At Heathrow Airport in London, she wrote "Going to Africa. Hope I don't get AIDS. Just kidding. I'm white!" None of her 170 Twitter followers responded; and she got on the plane, blissfully unaware of how that tweet would change her life.

Eleven hours later, upon landing in Cape Town, she learned from a friend's text that @justinesacco had become the number 1 trending topic on Twitter—and not because of her sense of humor. The editor at Valleywag (essentially a gossip blog) was forwarded her tweet by someone, retweeted it to his fifteen thousand followers, and posted it on the Valleywag site. From that, a public backlash and shaming of Sacco began.[1]

Within weeks, she lost her job at IAC while being continually hounded by the media and receiving death threats online, even after she issued a written apology that attempted to clarify she was not racist and had simply been trying to offer social commentary about the bubble of white privilege.

Sacco's case follows a pattern similar to that of others whose various transgressions have provoked public shaming through social media—name-calling, death threats, and invasions of privacy, sometimes followed by termination of their employment.

In January 2017, four young adults in Chicago brutally attacked and tortured a special needs man. What riveted the nation and even much of the world, however, was the fact that the four, two men and two women, used Facebook's real-time capacity to livestream video of their assault. Within days, the four had been apprehended by Chicago police and charged with kidnapping and aggravated assault.

It is unclear whether the capacity to livestream the attack is what triggered the heinous behavior or whether it was simply a horrible act of violence caught on video. Was the livestreaming a form of social capital? Should Facebook be held responsible for the livestreaming of violence? These are just some of the questions roiling the digital media industry and society. Something to keep in mind is the adage "Don't shoot the messenger simply because you don't like the message." Yet, the fact that the four African American perpetrators are heard in the livestream making statements such as "F*ck white people" (the victim was white) adds fuel to the fire, adding a racial overcast to the debate.[2]

Just as the rapid speed of communication among the public on social media has intensified the ability to apprehend criminal suspects or to publicly shame people—even for minor transgressions—the same dynamics can be a force that accelerates good works and enhances positive feelings. Consider the Michigan mother who created a "Happy Birthday Colin" Facebook page asking people to send her eleven-year-old son birthday greetings. The page quickly went viral, generating over ten thousand messages, cards, and letters for Colin, who has a condition similar to Asperger's that makes it difficult for him to make friends. *Good Morning America* decided to enhance his special day—as icing on the cake, so to speak—by hosting a surprise birthday bash in Times Square that featured the Rutgers marching band and a subsequent trip to Disney World.[3]

The tools and capabilities of social media have existed since the earliest days of the Internet, but not until the past few years has their potential been realized by businesses, including media companies. Many of the changes have been driven from the ground up rather than by traditional media companies, a fact that empowers social media and often threatens traditional business models. Social media have altered roles and working practices in journalism, public relations, and advertising.

The rise of social media has also brought some ugly social issues to the fore. The potential harm and perhaps prevalence of such negative behaviors as bullying have increased because of social media, with dozens of cases reported just in the past few years of young people committing suicide because of cyberbullying. Of course, racism and bullying did not originate with social media. However, because they make such bad behavior more public, social media do raise new issues and can make the behavior seem more common.

## Defining Social Media

Social media continues to be defined and redefined by scholars, professionals, and the press. Finding a description on which everyone agrees is difficult, partly because the tools for social media change with advances in technologies, and popular sites or trends touted as the Next Big Thing seem to lose popularity almost as quickly as they enter the limelight. Nevertheless, we can examine the elements underlying some commonly used definitions and then apply these to the realm of mass communication.

According to John Jantsch, author of *The Duct Tape Marketing* blog, social media can be defined as "the use of technology combined with social interaction to create or co-create value."[4] He keeps the definition concise because his readers are busy marketing professionals. PR professional and social media expert Brian Solis defines social media as "a shift in how people discover, read, and share news and information and content. It's a fusion of sociology and technology, transforming monologue (one to many) into dialog (many to many)."[5] In other words, social media represent a convergence of mass communication and interpersonal communication. Anvil Media, a search-engine marketing firm, provides a definition derived from sociology: "An umbrella term that defines the various activities that integrate technology, social interaction, and the construction of words and pictures. This interaction, and the manner in which information is presented, depends on the varied perspectives and 'building' of shared meaning, as people share their stories, and understandings."[6]

These definitions all mention the intersection of technology, social interaction, and information sharing, seemingly simple elements that will continue to transform many aspects of mass communication. Before looking at them in more detail and exploring how they are changing mass communication and media industries, we will examine how social media differ from traditional media.

## DIALOGIC COMMMUNICATION

Traditional media use a broadcast, or monologic, model of one-to-many communication, whereas social media employ a more dialogic model of many-to-many communication. Of course, this does not mean that mass-media audiences prior to the Internet never spoke with one another—there were fan clubs, letters to the editor, and a variety of ways to interact. The flow of communication, however, favored the broadcaster sending a message to many people simultaneously, with audience members having limited means to share their thoughts with each other on a mass scale.

Consider how a viewer in the 1970s might have been able to share his reactions to the previous night's episode of a popular yet controversial situation comedy like *All in the Family*. If he watched with friends or family, he could of course comment during or after the show. He might also discuss the program at the office the next day. If, however, a viewer felt particularly strongly about a racist remark made by the character Archie Bunker and felt that others should know how offensive the remark was, options to communicate these feelings to a broad audience were limited, expensive, and generally did not generate dialog.

He could write a letter of complaint to the network or the FCC, with no guarantee that he would hear from either. He could write a letter to the editor of the local newspaper; but even if published, it would reach a limited audience of only the paper's readers (and specifically those who read the letters to the editor that day). He could purchase an advertisement in the newspaper, which might get more attention than a letter to the editor, but that would be expensive, or the paper might choose not to accept such an ad. Or he could create a flyer, make photocopies, and hand them out or mail them to people, which would be both expensive and time-consuming.

If the viewer was persistent (or persuasive) enough or if he attracted enough supporters and perhaps held a demonstration or march, his crusade might get picked up as a news story in the local paper or television, thus perhaps attracting more people to his cause. Although at first glance this would seem to be a kind of many-to-many form of communication, consider the mechanisms by which it occurred—his message was communicated primarily through mass-media channels. Furthermore, it is unlikely that he would have had the resources—time, money, or media attention—to carry out a campaign like this in the first place.

Now let's look at what a viewer would do circa 2017. Let us say that a racist comment made by Peter, the father, on the animated Fox show *Family Guy* offends a viewer. Her first public complaint is likely not a letter to the FCC or the Fox network but a tweet from her Twitter account, perhaps even with a hashtag that helps others easily find tweets on the topic. Or perhaps she weighs in on the discussion board of the show's website. Or maybe she goes to any number of other discussion groups or fan sites devoted to *Family Guy* and comments there.

Today audiences are able to express their displeasure with shows through a range of social media outlets, including showing excerpts of the shows themselves.

Clay Shirky, a writer, consultant, and NYU professor, examines the social and economic effects of Internet technologies.

Perhaps she finds within a couple of days that someone who shares her views has created a mash-up video of such stereotypes found on various prime-time shows or in the news. The video is uploaded to YouTube, where it is viewed hundreds of thousands of times within a couple of weeks. It may appear on a news aggregator site such as Reddit, getting even more views and generating further discussions among YouTube viewers both for and against the position conveyed in the video. Or she may create an online petition on a site such as Change.org, asking people to boycott the show or write letters of complaint to the network. If the video is viewed enough times or talked about enough, or the petition gets enough signatures, then mainstream news organizations may cover the story, amplifying public interest and discussion even more.

What is notable in this latter example is that, except with the original source material, traditional mass-media organizations are not involved (until perhaps later in the process), yet far more members of the public may be affected in a very short time than would have been the case in the 1970s—or even the 1990s. More importantly, our viewer may never even consider writing a letter to the editor of the local newspaper or to the FCC. A complete media ecosystem can be created and sustained through social interaction using tools that social media provide. Mainstream media may still play a role, of course, but they do not have to be involved as in the past.

This follows what new-media scholar and NYU professor Clay Shirky calls a "publish, then filter" model.[7] Traditional media industries such as news are based on a "filter, then publish" model of information. From a vast universe of possible information, specialists or professionals (editors, music producers, etc.) select their content, making decisions based partly on the limitations of their medium, such as time limits in TV news or space limits in print media.

This material—the news in a newspaper or the bands promoted by a major record label or MTV—is then distributed to the general public. The public is likely completely unaware of all the other possible types of information it could have received. Media business models have been built on this way of controlling and disseminating information, and even entire professions have made this model an essential part of their professional identities. An example is journalism, commonly described as necessary for a healthy democracy because of its role in informing the public and monitoring the government. Journalists function as gatekeepers, professionals with special access to the halls of power and unique skills and training that presumably give them the ability to decide what information should be disseminated to the public.

Yet, as seen in the "publish, then filter" model, prevalent in social media, many of these professional assumptions are being challenged, as are the business models. If the public can connect directly with the vast universe of information out there and find what is relevant through a combination of social networks, ratings systems, and online discussions, then what functions do organizations that restrict the flow of information to the public serve?

This is not to say that traditional mass media are no longer important or powerful. The media serve an important **agenda-setting** function in that they provide us with much of the material that we talk about, even if they do not necessarily tell us what to think. The media also tend to amplify events through their coverage because they generally have larger audiences than the majority of social media sites, even though traditional media audiences continue to fragment. In addition, much of what is talked about on social media derives from entertainment or news content created and distributed by traditional media organizations.

**agenda setting**

Media's role in deciding which topics to cover and consequently which topics the public deems important and worthy of discussion.

**DISCUSSION QUESTIONS:** Consider the traditional "filter, then publish" model and the "publish, then filter" model. What do you think are some of the biggest weaknesses of each type? Can you think of certain types of media that may be better suited to one type over the other? Why?

## SOCIAL PRODUCTION

Another fundamental difference with traditional media is the collaborative aspect of social media that threatens established media business models used throughout much of the twentieth century and into this one. Most people cannot afford to start a newspaper or create a radio or television station. Digital media and the Internet greatly reduce costs for creating and distributing media content widely, to the point that they are well within the reach of many.

Collaborative, or participatory, media trace their roots to the **free and open-source software (FOSS)** movement. This type of participatory or social production contrasts sharply with the standard profit-making business models that rely more heavily on proprietary licensing agreements and intellectual property protections to protect products. To understand the difference, think LibreOffice versus Microsoft Office or Wikipedia versus *Encyclopaedia Britannica*. As the name suggests, the FOSS movement wants software to be freely available and the source code open to anyone to make modifications and improvements.

Although not always free in the sense of "no cost," this movement was informed by a strong spirit of keeping the information freely available to anyone and letting everyone share in the benefits. Commonsense theories of human behavior suggested that nobody would work hard on a project only to have others benefit greatly from it. Yet without the collaborative efforts of a good number of computer programmers and engineers committed to sharing information and knowledge freely, the backbone of the Internet would not exist. No company would have spent the resources to create the structure needed, especially when there had been no clear way to profit from it.

The open-source model did indeed work. The Apache web server program, the Linux operating system, and the LibreOffice software suite are all open-source developments that continue to play significant roles in computing today. Some countries have adopted LibreOffice for all government agencies, a mandate that raises the distinct possibility that other institutions will follow suit to diminish compatibility issues.

Computing and media companies operating with mass-communication business models are not sitting idly by, however, while a new and different media ecosystem based on collaboration, interaction, and sharing emerges. Some companies have incorporated open-source software into their own product lines. IBM experienced a larger and swifter increase in revenues than expected after switching to Linux. Oracle simply purchased the MySQL database system, reneging on a promise to keep it truly open

> 💬 **free and open-source software (FOSS) movement**
>
> A movement advocating software to be freely available and the source code open to anyone to make modifications and improvements.

Dear Mr Branson,

**REF: Mumbai to Heathrow 7th December 2008**

I love the Virgin brand, I really do which is why I continue to use it despite a series of unfortunate incidents over the last few years. This latest incident takes the biscuit.

Ironically, by the end of the flight I would have gladly paid over a thousand rupees for a single biscuit following the culinary journey of hell I was subjected to at the hands of your corporation.

Look at this Richard. Just look at it:

I imagine the same questions are racing through your brilliant mind as were racing through mine on that fateful day. What is this? Why have I been given it? What have I done to deserve this? And, which one is the starter, which one is the dessert?

You don't get to a position like yours Richard with anything less than a generous sprinkling of observational power so I KNOW you will have spotted the tomato next to the two yellow shafts of sponge on the left. Yes, it's next to the sponge shaft without the green paste. That's got to be the clue hasn't it. No sane person would serve a dessert with a tomato would they? Well answer me this Richard, what sort of animal would serve a dessert with peas in?

I know it looks like a bhaji but it's in custard Richard, custard. It must be the pudding. Well you'll be fascinated to hear that it wasn't custard. It was a sour gel with a clear oil on top. It's only redeeming feature was that it managed to be so alien to my palette that it took away the taste of the curry emanating from our miscellaneous central cuboid of beige matter. Perhaps the meal on the left might be the desert after all.

Anyway, this is all irrelevant at the moment. I was raised strictly but neatly by my parents and if they knew I had started dessert before the main course, a sponge shaft would be the least of my worries. So let's peel back the tin-foil on the main dish and see what's on offer.

Social media have altered the power dynamic between consumers and producers. Consumers can now force a response from companies when they review or complain about a company's products.

# LibreOffice®

Open-source software, which allows anyone to access its source code and is often free, demonstrates how successful social production can be.

**CRITICAL THINKING QUESTIONS:**
Do you favor open-source software models such as LibreOffice? If you had developed the software yourself and had a proprietary interest in it, would your opinion differ?

### distributed computing

Individual, autonomous computers that work together toward a common goal, typically a large, complex project that requires more computing power than that of any individual computer.

source. Microsoft chose to compete head-to-head with LibreOffice's predecessor OpenOffice, offering libraries and other public institutions free computers—loaded with Microsoft software, of course.

The success of the open-source model also raised the question that if it works for software, then why can't it work for entertainment, journalism, advertising, public relations—or any kind of content and knowledge production? Collaboration on such an unprecedented scale is seen with projects such as Wikipedia in part because of our powerful and cheap computers. Large-scale projects can be broken down into small components, making them easy for people to do and allowing individuals to contribute when and how they choose.

In what is called **distributed computing**, any number of volunteers can assist in a project without inconveniencing themselves because the program works in the background. The free computing power amassed through the various users is much greater than any research project could afford. The website also informs people of progress, thereby engaging the public in a field they might otherwise have ignored. Examples of projects using the power of distributed-computing networks include seeking cures for diseases such as cancer, working on models of global warming, using protein-folding programs to test for new drug combinations, and even searching for extraterrestrial intelligence (SETI).

We see this culture of collaboration and openness in a range of media production today, ranging from crowdsourced news sites to reviews of everything from movies to restaurants to consumer products. Mainstream media companies encourage citizen reporting, letting the public send raw video footage or photographs from breaking news events, which may be aired after being vetted by editors and a show's producers.

We also see a combination of nonmarket principles of collaboration with market forces in crowdfunding sites like Kickstarter (see the Media Pioneers box in Chapter 4). People propose projects or goals and ask the community to donate money to their cause. If the financial goals are met within the allotted time, then the project is funded. Its creators often inform the funder community of progress and sometimes give them samples of the finished project, such as a video or CD.

This gradual change in our online culture, in the ways we freely help each other or simply use our computers to advance the general common good, demonstrates how technological and economic factors have altered our assumptions about people acting selfishly or not helping others.

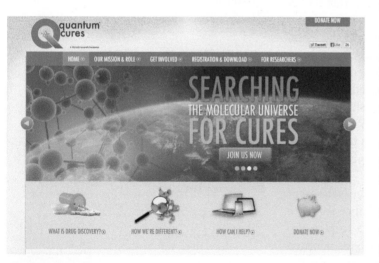

Distributed computing combines the excess computing power of many computers to perform operations that not even supercomputers could perform alone.

**DISCUSSION QUESTIONS:** Have you ever made a decision to see a movie, buy music or a book, or go to a particular restaurant based on user reviews? If so, do you think that you have an ethical obligation to also contribute reviews that could guide others? Why or why not?

# What Is "Social" About Social Media?

Cultural norms may have changed, but media have always had a social component. From the earliest days of print, people read aloud and in groups. In the 1930s and 1940s, families congregated around the radio to listen to their favorite programs; and people came together to listen to music, dance, and socialize. Even television, a medium maligned as passive and isolating, often has important social aspects, as families and friends get together to watch and discuss shows and sporting events. Some of HBO's most popular original series, such as *The Sopranos*, generated what became known as "water-cooler buzz," or discussions among workers about a show the day after it aired, which in turn created more interest among people who hadn't seen the show.

How are social media more "social" than traditional media? This is an important question. If traditional media are no less social than what is being touted as a revolutionary, transformative new kind of media, then it would follow that Web 2.0 and all the talk about it is just the latest hype about new technology.

The Center for Social Media in the School of Communication at American University identifies five fundamental areas in which people's media habits are changing: choice, conversation, curation, creation, and collaboration.[8] These five components provide an excellent framework for understanding social media better.

## CHOICE

The public has far more media choices than in the past and far more options of media styles and genres than ever before. Even so, thinking of the public or audience primarily as passive consumers of media ignores the variety of ways people can interact and find the media content they want. Through search engines, recommendations from friends (often known only from online interactions), RSS feeds, and, of course, traditional media channels, people today are generally more proactive in getting the type of content they want.

Note that "more choice" does not necessarily mean "better quality." Simply because there are many more options does not mean that the quality of content people may find is going to be better. Greater choice, however, does mean that more media types and channels are competing with each other to attract the attention of the audience. This alters the production, promotion, and marketing of media and even what types of content may be created in the first place.

## CONVERSATION

From the earliest days of the Internet, conversation was important, and it continues to be a defining characteristic of social media. Discussion groups, Usenet, email, IM, and Twitter have been or continue to be important tools that enable people to communicate easily with each other on a scale and in ways not possible with traditional media. Companies have had their reputations tarnished or enhanced because of online conversations, unknown artists have become famous through them, and funny or embarrassing moments caught on a video recording have made some people instant (if short-lived) celebrities.

Comcast has learned the hard way about the power of social media. In 2006, a customer posted a video on YouTube of a Comcast technician sleeping in the customer's home while waiting on hold—with Comcast—for over an hour. In 2008, Comcast was ranked at the bottom of the American Customer Satisfaction Index, and hundreds of customers contributed their complaints to the website Comcast-MustDie.com. As part of its efforts to improve customer service, Comcast started monitoring blogs and online conversations and discussing customer concerns directly in the online forums. Many companies follow online discussions about themselves, but Comcast took an extra step in often responding to bloggers and engaging in conversation with them. Today, their actions are considered a prime example of a company improving through listening to its customers.

Many companies have discovered that their brands and corporate images are not what they claim in traditional advertising or public relations efforts but what the customers say they are. The focus on conversation is one other example of the shift from a lecture to a dialog between companies (including media companies) and the public.

## CURATION

With so many options available today, how can people find the kind of media content they like? The traditional gatekeepers of information and knowledge, such as media professionals and librarians, are finding their roles changing in the social media environment. One major change is a shift from a "gatekeeping" model to what Australian media scholar Axel Bruns calls a "gatewatching" model in which people act as their own filters, classifiers, and reviewers.

Classifying content happens through an activity such as **tagging** or creating **folksonomies** of definitions. This helps bring some order to the vast array of content out there, and it helps in searches. An important difference in tagging is that people are not waiting to hear from an authority on how to classify terms, such as a librarian would do—they are doing it themselves. Sites such as Instagram, Flickr, Facebook, and YouTube have all encouraged tagging among users, which makes the content more searchable and helps users recognize relations among terms they may never have seen before.

News aggregation site Reddit is an example of how curatorial activities can enhance a site's relevance for everyone. Users vote either positively or negatively on stories that have been submitted, and stories with the highest percentage of positive votes get pushed to the front page. This creates a natural hierarchy of content, where typically material deemed most relevant or interesting to the Reddit community becomes more visible to other users of the site, even if they do not vote on stories themselves.

The online environment lends itself to a curatorial mode of contributing to the social media space. It is fairly easy to tag something with terms, or to write a one-paragraph review of a book or movie, or to write a few lines about a product recently purchased. It is also much easier to find, and publicize, fault with something. Online reviews have become increasingly important in consumers' decisions on items ranging from household goods to media products.

**tagging**

Using searchable keywords to define a piece of information, file, image, or other type of digital media in a nonhierarchical system.

**folksonomies**

Collection of tags created by users that provide metadata (data about data) regarding information.

Reddit users participate by voting for or against stories, pushing the most popular content to the front page of the site.

## CREATION

The digital-media tools that facilitate the creation of content have played a major role in the rise of user-generated media content. Cheaper communication technologies allow more people to create media, whether it is the printing press in Renaissance Europe or the high-speed Internet in the twenty-first century. The ability to distribute content cheaply and easily to a mass audience, along with the chance to interact with others, is probably the most crucial aspect of how the Internet is transforming mass communication. Without this ability, the media landscape today would look vastly different. It could even be said that social media as we know them now would not exist.

Simply because the tools are readily available to create media does not, of course, mean that everyone will start producing great works of art. Most people, in fact, will be satisfied consuming media and not creating anything, and there will be far more amateurish or poor-quality content online than high art. Yet even if only a small percentage of the people online create and share content, the pool of media content will be larger than that in the traditional media world because of the sheer numbers of people online.

Creating content is not without its challenges. As noted elsewhere in this book, intellectual property laws are being challenged by a digital culture that sees nothing wrong with borrowing freely from existing media to create something new. Furthermore, many people online have come to expect a variety of media content for free. Rather than encourage creativity, as intellectual property laws were meant to do, more restrictive laws may have the opposite effect by removing creative material from the public domain. Nevertheless, content creators should be compensated for their work.

## COLLABORATION

The willingness to collaborate on a common good for no personal monetary gain is perhaps one of the biggest surprises one encounters when examining social media. It is one thing to spend hours creating an app with the hopes of copyrighting it for licensing or offering it for money, but quite another to do so and provide it to the web community for free use or to provide open access to your project and invite others to work on and improve it.

A number of cases of collaboration extend from the online realm to offline, especially in organizing people around politics or social movements. In fact, the most successful uses of online tools in political campaigns have included ample opportunities for people to socialize in real-world settings as well. This was the lesson exemplified in the 2016 presidential campaign of Bernie Sanders, Democratic senator from Vermont. Perhaps not surprisingly, a study by social media research firm Captiv8 revealed that Trump and Clinton had the most followers (14.1 million and 9.3 million respectively) on social networks such as Twitter, Facebook and Instagram, while Sanders had only about half as many (5.7 million). Although Trump and Clinton had more followers on social media networks, Sanders's followers were substantially more engaged and were significantly more likely to attend campaign rallies and other events in the real world, especially on college campuses.[9] Although Sanders eventually dropped out of the presidential race, his campaign demonstrated the importance of engaging the public during presidential campaigns both on- and offline.

Likewise, organizations such as Sunlight Labs and Code for America have partnered with government agencies and other organizations to host civic hackathons, bringing coders and others together to work jointly on finding solutions to common government problems. One example of this is Boston's Citizens Connect

Civic hackathons, in which coders and others gather over one or two days to work on computing solutions for government or civic issues, have become increasingly popular in recent years in the United States and around the world.

Source: https://www.linkedin.com/pulse/islamabad-civic-hackathon-2016-asim-ghaffar

app, which lets Boston residents easily report various civic issues such as potholes and track the progress of the problems getting fixed.

In some ways, the realization that people need real-world socializing to complement their online socializing harkens back to the earliest days of social media, long before that term was applied. In fact, the need to meet, interact, and discuss was an impetus for the earliest online communities, many of which are precursors to today's social media tools and are still widely used today.

> **DISCUSSION QUESTIONS:** Which of the five ways in which our media habits are changing (choice, creation, curation, conversation, or collaboration) do you think is the most important? Why?

## Types of Social Media

Smartphones and tablets have made it easy for people to keep up with social media or online news at all times.

In 1980, France launched its videotext service—text delivery over the air or by cable for presentation on television screens or other electronic displays—known then as Teletel and later as Minitel. Ahead of its time, Minitel was one of the most successful, early interactive online information services before the web. Minitel worked because the government subsidized it and provided every home with an access device. Its biggest problem turned out to be the emergence of the World Wide web, which quickly outclassed the stand-alone Minitel communication terminals. Despite these drawbacks, there were still 10 million Minitel users in 2009, yet France Telecom finally closed the Minitel service in June 2012.

Many of the tools we now commonly associate with social media were used before social media became an Internet phenomenon. Even the pre-web Minitel had what it called its "blue rooms," adult-oriented chat rooms, the only part of

## INTERNATIONAL PERSPECTIVES
# Social Networks of Influential Languages

Just like people, languages can also be mapped via social networking principles to reveal which networks are the most extensive and most important.

In social networks, a hub is someone or something that has many connections to others, essentially acting as a communications or information focal point. One study on the influence of various languages that appeared in the *Proceedings of the National Academy of Sciences* by researchers at MIT, Harvard, Northeastern University, and Aix-Marseille University looked at three separate communication networks: books, tweets, and Wikipedia articles. They examined the output of all three networks done in various languages and mapped their translations to other languages to determine which tended to be most translated, thus reaching more people.

It is perhaps no surprise that English was a central hub, making it the best language to spread your message to other languages in all three networks, even though it is only the third most common native language, spoken by 5 percent of the global population. A few other languages, such as French, Spanish, Russian, and German, worked as intermediate-level hubs in much the same way as English, except on a smaller scale. This means that even though the actual number of native speakers of some of these languages may be relatively small, books, tweets, and Wikipedia articles tended to get translated to and from these languages at a disproportionately high rate.

Chinese, Hindi, and Arabic—which combined represent the native languages spoken by nearly a quarter of the world's population—all had fewer connections in the networking map, meaning works written in these languages got translated to and from other languages far less than the number of native speakers would otherwise indicate.

What does this mean for native English speakers studying a foreign language? At least in terms of tapping into global conversations and knowledge and spreading a message, it may be better to study a language such as Spanish or German than Chinese or Arabic.

the service that generated a significant revenue stream. The use of modern social media grew significantly with web-related advances that facilitated creating and sharing content. Other differences include the rapid growth of the web audience and the increase in broadband Internet connections that enhance user experience. Wireless Internet capabilities have also expanded access to social media.

Here, we will look specifically at how some social media tools have developed and been used over time. In most cases, people have found ways to subvert the tools to their own ends, making the service less useful for everyone. In response, communities have created social norms and rules of behavior along with punishments for transgressions.

## EMAIL

Email, or electronic mail, was one of the first uses of the Internet and until 2008 was the most popular Internet activity. In 2010, email moved down to third place, following social-networking sites and online gaming.[10] Email can be overlooked as an element of social media, but its ease of use, prevalence, and capacity to send messages to more than one person make it a powerful communication tool.

Although email is an exchange of messages via telecommunication between two people, an individual can easily create a mailing list and send out a single message to multiple people, in a sense broadcasting the message. This capability has caused more than a few red faces, as anyone can attest who has been on a mailing list in which one member made disparaging remarks about another member, thinking the response was going only to an individual and not to the entire list.

Mailing lists differ from discussion boards in that messages posted get sent directly to subscribers' email inboxes rather than to an online location that a member must visit to read the messages. **Listservs** are automated mailing-list administrators that allow for easy subscription, cancellation, and delivery of emails to subscribers. Many organizations use them to keep their customers or supporters informed of the organization's activities or special deals.

The principles that allow for easy creation of mailing lists are also responsible for what many consider the scourge of email—**spam**, unsolicited email advertising. Spam, once rare and considered extremely bad form in the early days of the Internet, is now all too common. Computer programs comb the Internet and find email addresses on websites and social media, "harvesting" them to a central location that a spammer can then use to send messages or sell the list of email addresses to other companies.

A battle continues between spammers and companies creating software to block spam. Automated filtering software often removes much of the spam but may also inadvertently remove desired messages. Spam clogging the Internet and inboxes reflects the downside of being able to share content easily. Lowered costs of distribution on the Internet have helped create online communities and given the public a chance to distribute media content on a par with established media companies, but it has also made it easier for individuals and companies to abuse that distribution system, making it less valuable for all. Legislators are fighting back, however, with increasingly stringent antispam laws that penalize spammers.

The antispam legislation and better spam-blocking software are fighting an uphill battle. In 2010, an estimated 78 percent of all emails sent were spam. Cisco Systems' digital research arm Talos reported in 2016 that 86 percent of the world's email traffic was spam. That totals four hundred unsolicited spam messages per day. About half of those messages consist of sex and dating topics, and nearly 40 percent are on pharmaceutical topics. Because of improved antispam technology, most spam gets blocked before reaching our inboxes. The United States is the number 1 source of sent spam, followed by China, and then Russia, according to Talos

> **listservs**
>
> Automated mailing-list administrators that allow for easy subscription, cancellation, and delivery of emails to subscribers.

> **spam**
>
> Unwanted mass emailing from advertisers.

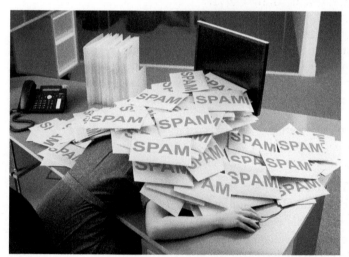

Although spam remains a problem, clogging inboxes and costing companies millions of dollars, antispam technologies and laws have reduced the amount of spam in recent years.

## DISCUSSION BOARDS AND WEB FORUMS

Today, most online discussion boards are on web-based forums that provide a variety of user-friendly tools to create and post discussions. Users can easily follow conversational threads on different topics or search for archived material. The precursor to web forums, **Usenet**, the first file-sharing service, was created in 1979. Members of Usenet posted files to a newsgroup to share with subscribers, group members who could then download and save the files on their computers.

> **Usenet**
>
> One of the earliest discussion forums in use today in which participants discuss topics in categories called newsgroups.

Usenet has decreased in popularity, especially with the rise of the web and the association of the service with pornographers, who used it to send large files. Several Internet service providers (ISPs) either have blocked Usenet servers entirely or allow access only to certain newsgroups within the major categories. Despite its decline in popularity, Usenet presaged many of the principles seen today in social media, including decentralized servers, encouraging communication between users, and enabling users to find others with similar interests in niche categories.

Discussion boards are a vital form of mass communication on the Internet. Their format and asynchronous nature (i.e., not requiring users to be online at the same time) allow for relatively lengthy expositions on topics written whenever convenient for the person sending the message. They also provide value even to members who do not post messages but simply read what others are writing, a practice called **lurking**. Some discussion-board creators encourage newcomers to lurk for a while to become familiar with the tone and type of topics before posting messages of their own.

Because public discussion boards are easily searchable on the web, they provide useful information on a range of specialized topics. People with similar questions can find helpful advice on any number of issues long after the initial discussions take place. One of the earliest online communities, created through discussion groups, is still thriving today. The WELL (Whole Earth 'Lectronic Link) began in 1985 and continues to promote high-quality and interesting discussions among its members, many of whom are noted intellectuals, artists, authors, and creative thinkers. The WELL's policy of requiring real names rather than user names has, according to some, enhanced discussion and fostered a strong sense of community among its members. Now owned by the Salon Media Group, publisher of *Salon* magazine, it charges members $15 a month, one of the few online communities that has successfully charged members simply for discussions.

## CHAT ROOMS

Like discussion groups, chat rooms are usually divided by topic, ranging from highly technical computer issues to pop stars to sex. Chat rooms differ from **instant messaging**, which also takes place in real time, in that instant messaging usually involves an online conversation between two people or a few at most.

Because chat rooms are synchronous, occurring in real time, media organizations can use them to promote special guests online and let the audience "speak" to them, much like a radio station having a musician visit and take listeners' calls.

Chat rooms are not without their own unique communication problems. They can often be chaotic, much like trying to talk to someone across the room at a crowded, noisy party. It can be difficult to tell who is being addressed, although some chat rooms have general rules and guidelines posted for proper behavior. Although messages may be sent in real time, the fact that they must be typed inevitably slows down the give-and-take that occurs during spoken conversations. Some chatters can monopolize the conversation as well or repeatedly post the same message, a practice called **scrolling**, which quickly draws the ire of other chatters in the room.

The video instant messaging service Snapchat, launched in 2011, has become very popular, with an estimated 10 billion videos viewed each day, according to Snapchat.[11] The unique characteristic of Snapchat is the automatic deletion of photos and videos after recipient viewing.

**lurking**

Only reading what others write in online discussion boards but not contributing to the discussions.

**instant messaging**

Often abbreviated IM, a form of real-time communication through text typed over a computer network.

**scrolling**

Simply repeating the same message in a chat room, which quickly draws the ire of other participants.

## BLOGS AND MICROBLOGS

💬 **blog**

Short for weblog, a type of website in which a person posts regular journal or diary entries, with the posts arranged chronologically.

**Blogs,** or weblogs, are an individual's web pages of short, frequently updated postings arranged chronologically, much like a series of diary entries or journal pages. Blogs can contain thoughts, links to sites of interest, rants, or whatever the blogger wants to write about. The earliest blogs go back to 1994, although technological limitations made it more cumbersome to update posts then.

The role that technology plays in social media is clearly evident with the rise of blogs. Not until 1999 did blogs start becoming more popular, largely due to new software tools that made blogging easier and did not require knowledge of HTML code or programming. Blogger.com, created in 1999 and bought by Google in 2003, is one such tool that makes creating, posting, and sharing a blog easy even for non-technical people. WordPress is another very popular blogging platform that offers free blog hosting.

Some blogs, such as *BoingBoing* and the *Huff-Post*, have readerships in the millions and an influential agenda-setting function much like mainstream media. When a blog becomes popular and attracts many readers, responding to most of the comments or discussions becomes impossible for the blogger. In this way, blogs tend to develop the characteristics of traditional broadcasting or publishing models of information or news.

David Karp founded the popular microblog site Tumblr, which has surpassed WordPress in popularity and was purchased by Yahoo in 2013.

News organizations were slow to adopt blogs as part of their media offerings, seeing them as a threat or something that might detract from their credibility. In 2002, Steve Olafson, a longtime journalist for the *Houston Chronicle*, was fired for having a pseudonymous blog in which he criticized local politicians. Today, many big news organizations operate blogs and expect their reporters or columnists to blog regularly.

Although the blog's element of authenticity is vital to conversation or true dialog, its raw, honest, and unfiltered quality often becomes problematic in the business world. Excessively polished blogs or those that simply repeat public relations platitudes are unlikely to generate respect or develop a following. Adopting a more natural, conversational tone with the public and responding to their comments have been difficult for companies accustomed to carefully controlling their public messages.

Blogs have also moved from their text roots to include video, audio, and multimedia, an example of how users are creating content by mixing and matching different media types to make something new. Blogs also play an important curatorial role, as some become popular because the blogger finds the best and most compelling ideas and makes relevant comments about that content, which helps the blog's readers find information of interest to them and to understand it within a larger context.

As their name suggests, microblogs work much the same way as blogs, but the format and technology encourage shorter posts and content. Today, perhaps the most popular microblog is Twitter, which allows only 140 characters to be sent at a time, or tweeted. Launched in July 2006, Twitter has 302 million active users with 500 million tweets sent per day.[12] Many people have started using

Twitter as a kind of curatorial news service, following people who tend to find new or interesting stories.

Some studies have shown that only about 10 percent of Twitter users contribute over 90 percent of the content.[13] That a relatively small percentage of people contribute a disproportionate amount of content is important to remember when considering how media-usage habits are changing. Just because the audience can now create and distribute content easily does not mean everyone will—the vast majority of people seem perfectly happy as consumers of media content.

Tumblr, another popular microblogging service, allows for easy uploads of text and multimedia content. Founded in 2007, the name derives from "tumblelogs," the original term used for microblogs before the latter name became more widely used. In May 2013, Yahoo bought Tumblr for $1.1 billion; in April 2017, Tumblr hosted over 341.8 million blogs and over 148.1 billion posts, surpassing popular blogging platform WordPress.[14]

Chinese microblogging site Sina Weibo ("weibo" means microblog in Chinese), founded in 2009, has been likened to a Chinese version of Twitter, even though it functions more like a Twitter/Facebook hybrid. Although still popular, with over 500 million users, it has suffered because of competition from free messaging and voicemail service WeChat, launched in 2011, which quickly gained nearly 300 million users and continues to rise in popularity.[15] By 2016, WeChat had grown to 846 million users.[16] Notably, the Chinese government blocks virtually all Western social media, thereby making the use of Chinese social networks the most easily accessible option for Chinese citizens.

Many of the most popular social-networking sites in the United States and around the world offer microblogging services as well, although these are often called something like "status updates." Regardless of the name used, updating friends in your social network while out and about is essentially a type of microblogging.

## WIKIS

Wikis have become more widely known, thanks to the phenomenal success of Wikipedia, the collaborative encyclopedia created entirely by volunteers that quickly came to rival the scope and accuracy of established encyclopedias. Like most of today's social media tools, the roots of wikis go back much further. A **wiki**, which means "quick" or "speedy" in Hawaiian, is essentially a web page that anyone can edit. In 1994, Ward Cunningham created the first wiki, WikiWikiWeb, designed for easy sharing of information among computer programmers. He took his wiki public in 1995 and asked developers to improve on it.

In 2001, Wikipedia used a version of a wiki system for its new encyclopedia that encouraged anyone to contribute and edit. This was a drastic change from traditional encyclopedias, the epitome of the gatekeeper media model of authoritative, unidirectional communication to a silent and passive audience.

Today, a variety of wikis are used for different purposes, especially in education. Corporate wikis encourage knowledge sharing among groups, especially when offices are far apart. One important aspect of wikis is the ability to see the editing history of any particular page and to revert to an earlier version if needed. This function keeps an automatic archive of editing changes identifiable by users. In combination with discussion or talk pages associated with each article, it provides a ready way for participants to discuss and debate points.

💬 **wiki**

Website that lets anyone add, edit, or delete pages and content.

WIKIPEDIA
The Free Encyclopedia

Wikipedia is an excellent example of what can be created online by many people collaborating for free.

## MEDIA PIONEERS
# Jack Dorsey

A century and a half after Samuel Morse's initial telegraph transmission—"What hath God wrought?"—Twitter and its thirty-year-old creator, Jack Dorsey, would tweet "just setting up my twttr" and "inviting coworkers." And thus a radical one-to-many communication medium was launched that would crisscross the globe in ways the one-to-one telegraph system never could, yet in a similarly concise textual form. Almost as fast as you could tweet "The Next Big Thing," Twitter was it. Social media quickly embraced downsized expression of 140 characters or less, immediate and entertaining status updates from close friends and distant celebrities, as well as more serious broadcasts from journalists, politicians, activists, and even revolutionaries.

Elegantly simplified responses to complex problems characterize Dorsey's pioneering achievements. When, for example, an artisan friend lost a $2,000 sale because his small business could not justify the costs associated with credit card transactions, Dorsey conceived of and created a tiny card swipe reader that could plug into an iPhone or iPad, instantly making any small operation capable of meeting the costs of handling such sales. This concept and device formed the basis for Square, his foray into the world of seamless retail transactions.

Dorsey, described by one colleague as "a first-rate strategist, a first-rate designer, and a first-rate technologist"[17] and by another as "a technologist with the soul of an artist,"[18] is a dynamic entrepreneur with a holistic concern for his staff and for society. Operating in downtown San Francisco, he has led coworkers on excursions through the city during the day. Not merely a stroll by places of interest, these Friday outings became a commitment to cleaner streets, a project announced in this tweet from Jack: "Tomorrow morning at 11a

Pacific we're going out & picking up trash for 30 minutes. Join us (equipment provided): 5th & Natoma. #cleanstreets."[19]

Dorsey's efforts to make our public communication more democratic, our business transactions more efficient, and our world cleaner will no doubt extend beyond his enterprises with Twitter and Square. In 2013, he joined the board of directors for the Walt Disney Company, and he has also expressed a desire to be mayor of New York City someday.

In 2016, then-presidential candidate Donald Trump captured much attention for his aggressive use of Twitter as a principal means of communication with voters and just about everyone else online or off (mainstream news media often reported stories about Mr. Trump's late-night tweets). Since taking office, President Trump has continued to use Twitter as an unfiltered means to reach the public, and some would suggest even make policy, in 140 characters.

What would seem like a major weakness of wikis—the freedom for anyone to change any content on a page at any time—has actually turned out to be their strength. Low barriers to creating content or adding special expertise make participation easy. Although not without its share of trolls, people who purposely vandalize Wikipedia entries by inserting false or nonsensical information, the Wikipedia community has shown a remarkable ability to police the vast and growing content on the site. Wikipedia has been able to avoid major disruptions of vandals, thanks partly to technology but mostly to the norms and rules the Wikipedia community has created over time, an example par excellence of how collaborative work and social media transform media audiences and operate on principles different from those of traditional media economic models.

Nevertheless, Wikipedia has had growth pains. In August 2009, it announced the need for more restrictive editing rules and page "lock" or "protect" to prevent further editing, a move away from its original freewheeling days. Even earlier, Wikipedia had blocked any changes from ISPs originating from either house of Congress because politicians' aides were continually changing politicians' entries to make them look better, breaking the Wikipedia community norm of neutral point of view (NPOV).

## SOCIAL-NETWORKING SITES

The various social-networking sites have become perhaps the most visible face of social media. What distinguishes these sites from other types of social media is that in some manner they show users connections in their social network.[20] The ability to visualize and share one's social network while allowing others to tap into that map by contacting other people in the network has become an incredibly powerful tool.

Although today Facebook or LinkedIn seems to get all the attention, the first social-networking sites were actually created several years before, and some are still around. Classmates.com, founded in 1995, and SixDegrees, starting in 1997 and closing in 2001, are two early examples of social-networking sites. Classmates.com, as its name suggests, focuses primarily on putting people back in touch with friends from school, work, and the military.

Reconnecting with old friends or creating friendships has proven to be a powerful force for establishing social-networking sites. Friendster, launched in 2002, was the first social-networking site with features similar to those of Facebook and LinkedIn. With the rise of MySpace and, later, Facebook, the popularity of Friendster rapidly waned in the United States but remained strong in Asia. Relaunched as a social-gaming website under new ownership in 2011, Friendster is still popular in some Southeast Asian countries.

The case of MySpace shows just how chaotic the business of social-networking sites can be and how easily companies can lose the trust of users when not considering their audience. Launched in 2003, MySpace became the most popular social-networking site in 2006, only to lose that position in 2008 to Facebook. In 2005, News Corp. purchased MySpace and its parent company, Intermix Media, for $580 million. In June 2011, News Corp. sold MySpace for $35 million—a fraction of its original value—to Justin Timberlake and Specific Media, an advertising network. In mid-June 2013, MySpace launched a new version of the site, deleting, without warning, all the material users had posted on the old version of MySpace. This raised a huge outcry among users, many of whom had lost years of messages with past loved ones, blog entries, and games that they had purchased on the site.

Forbes ranked the cofounder, chairman, and CEO of Facebook number 6 on their 2016 list of billionaires. Mark Zuckerberg's net worth at that time was $44.6 billion.

In late 2003, Facebook began as a project within Harvard University called Face-mash, a version of the website Hot or Not. It launched as a social-networking site under its current name but available only to Harvard students in early 2004. A few months later, it opened to other Ivy League schools and then expanded to include all college students. The next year, it accepted high school students and then companies; and in 2006, it opened to anyone thirteen or older, rapidly overtaking MySpace as the most popular social-networking site thanks to these expansions. By March 2015, Facebook claimed to have 1.44 billion active monthly users worldwide, which makes it the largest social-networking site in the world.

Facebook's rapid rise in popularity led to frequent media reports of potential buyouts from larger media companies, such as Microsoft. Despite these reports, Facebook launched its initial public offering (IPO) in May 2012, the largest in Internet history, valued at its peak at $104 billion.

Although Facebook remains the most popular social-networking site, two different reports in 2014 caused some alarm at Facebook and among investors.

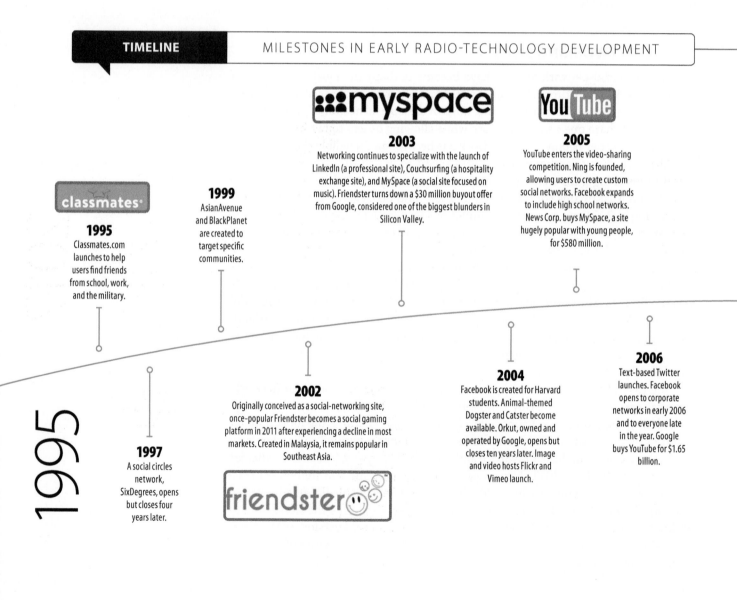

**TIMELINE**    MILESTONES IN EARLY RADIO-TECHNOLOGY DEVELOPMENT

**1995**
Classmates.com launches to help users find friends from school, work, and the military.

**1997**
A social circles network, SixDegrees, opens but closes four years later.

**1999**
AsianAvenue and BlackPlanet are created to target specific communities.

**2002**
Originally conceived as a social-networking site, once-popular Friendster becomes a social gaming platform in 2011 after experiencing a decline in most markets. Created in Malaysia, it remains popular in Southeast Asia.

**2003**
Networking continues to specialize with the launch of LinkedIn (a professional site), Couchsurfing (a hospitality exchange site), and MySpace (a social site focused on music). Friendster turns down a $30 million buyout offer from Google, considered one of the biggest blunders in Silicon Valley.

**2004**
Facebook is created for Harvard students. Animal-themed Dogster and Catster become available. Orkut, owned and operated by Google, opens but closes ten years later. Image and video hosts Flickr and Vimeo launch.

**2005**
YouTube enters the video-sharing competition. Ning is founded, allowing users to create custom social networks. Facebook expands to include high school networks. News Corp. buys MySpace, a site hugely popular with young people, for $580 million.

**2006**
Text-based Twitter launches. Facebook opens to corporate networks in early 2006 and to everyone late in the year. Google buys YouTube for $1.65 billion.

Both reports stated that fewer teens were using Facebook than in previous years, down to 88 percent in 2014 from 95 percent in 2012.[21] Most companies would not worry about such a small dip, especially with so many users, but some wonder if the decline could be the beginning of a long-term trend in which the coveted teen market moves elsewhere for their social-networking needs.

The launch of Google+ in June 2011 was Google's effort to compete with Facebook. Despite Google's dominance as a search engine and its growing number of online services, Google+ remains far behind in terms of active users, with only about 9 percent of Google+'s 2.2 billion profiles having posted anything on Google+, according to one analyst.[22]

Many other social-networking sites have sprung up since 2003, some focusing on professional interests, such as LinkedIn; topic interests, such as Dogster; media or image sharing, such as Pinterest, Flickr, and Instagram; and location-based interests, such as Foursquare and Loopt. Launched in late 2014 with ninety people on its network, Ello, whose manifesto promises never to sell advertising or user

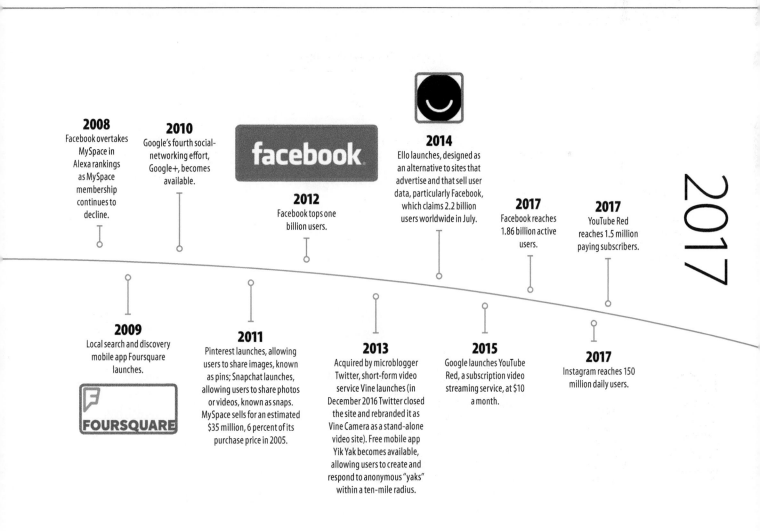

**2008**
Facebook overtakes MySpace in Alexa rankings as MySpace membership continues to decline.

**2010**
Google's fourth social-networking effort, Google+, becomes available.

**2012**
Facebook tops one billion users.

**2014**
Ello launches, designed as an alternative to sites that advertise and that sell user data, particularly Facebook, which claims 2.2 billion users worldwide in July.

**2017**
Facebook reaches 1.86 billion active users.

**2017**
YouTube Red reaches 1.5 million paying subscribers.

2017

**2009**
Local search and discovery mobile app Foursquare launches.

**2011**
Pinterest launches, allowing users to share images, known as pins; Snapchat launches, allowing users to share photos or videos, known as snaps. MySpace sells for an estimated $35 million, 6 percent of its purchase price in 2005.

**2013**
Acquired by microblogger Twitter, short-form video service Vine launches (in December 2016 Twitter closed the site and rebranded it as Vine Camera as a stand-alone video site). Free mobile app Yik Yak becomes available, allowing users to create and respond to anonymous "yaks" within a ten-mile radius.

**2015**
Google launches YouTube Red, a subscription video streaming service, at $10 a month.

**2017**
Instagram reaches 150 million daily users.

data, claimed less than a year later to have millions of followers. Some have described Ello as the anti-Facebook, a moniker supported by the defection of many members of the LGBT community from FB to Ello due to safety concerns about Facebook's requirement for real names on user profiles.

In addition to seeking out social news about friends on these networking sites, many seek out local and world news about events and issues. According to a 2016 Pew study, 62 percent of the general population gets news, most commonly about entertainment, from social media, especially Facebook. Two-thirds of Facebook users get news via the social network, while almost six in ten Twitter users (59 percent) get news via the network. Seventy percent of Reddit users get news from the site, yet this translates to only 2 percent of the general population. (See Figure 7-1.) Users are less likely, though, to follow current events as they unfold on Facebook, unlike Twitter, where many turn for breaking news.

## TABLE 7-1 Most Popular Social-Networking Sites*

| RANK | SITE | UNIQUE VISITORS |
|---|---|---|
| 1 | facebook | 1,100,000,000 |
| 2 | YouTube | 1,000,000,000 |
| 3 | Twitter | 310,000,000 |
| 4 | LinkedIn | 255,000,000 |
| 5 | Pinterest | 250,000,000 |
| 6 | Google+ | 120,000,000 |
| 7 | tumblr. | 110,000,000 |
| 8 | Instagram | 100,000,000 |
| 9 | Reddit | 85,000,000 |
| 10 | VK | 80,000,000 |

Source: http://www.ebizmba.com/articles/social-networking-websites
*As of December 31, 2016

## CONVERGENCE CULTURE
# Are We Really Separated by Six Degrees?

We've all met someone with whom we realized we share a coincidental mutual friend or a similar experience, such as attending the same school or belonging to the same fraternity or sorority. For scientists who study social networks, these amazing coincidences are precisely what make social networks important.

The number and type of our social connections can greatly affect our opportunities in life. If we have a robust social network of people who likewise have robust social networks (not identical to ours), then we are better able reach people in those other networks through our friends. For example, if I want a publisher to consider my novel, knowing an editor at the publishing house who can recommend the manuscript may help it get serious attention.

A popular pop-culture theory claims that everybody in the world is connected by no more than six degrees, or six links in a network. The number of connections or links between you and the U.S. president is theoretically no more than six. The notion that everyone in the world is separated by no more than six degrees gained public attention through a "small world" experiment conducted by psychologist Stanley Milgram in the 1950s. Milgram sent copies of letters to people in the Midwest and asked them to send the letter to the person they thought would most likely be able to forward it to a certain lawyer living in Boston. Out of the forty-two letters that reached the lawyer's home, the average number of links was nearly six, although the range was quite large.

Although Milgram never used the term "**six degrees of separation**," it was popularized in a 1984 play of the same name that also referenced his experiment. The notion became even more widespread with "Six Degrees of Kevin Bacon," a game that calculates the degrees of separation of various actors from Kevin Bacon. This can easily be done through the Oracle of Kevin Bacon website, which uses the Internet Movie Database as its source.

Surprisingly, even long-dead actors are connected with Kevin Bacon or with famous people who are not professional actors but who have appeared in documentaries or movies. This makes sense if you consider the actors gathered on a movie set as a **small world**, a social network of tight connections, people who get to know one another while filming and then get to know a large number of other actors, who then go on to make other movies with different actors.

Although finding an actor or actress separated from Bacon by more than even five degrees is difficult, he is actually not the most connected Hollywood actor. Both John Carradine and Robert Mitchum had far more connections than Bacon. If you know someone listed in the Internet Movie Database, then you can see that person's Bacon number and simply add one more (your link to that person) to see how closely connected you are to Kevin Bacon.

Political news is especially prevalent on social networks, with more than nine in ten Americans (91 percent) in 2016 getting news each week about the presidential campaign via social media.

Pew also found that reading news on these sites does not necessarily promote sharing opinions about what was read. A 2014 Pew survey on social media and the spiral of silence, for example, discovered that people were less willing to discuss the NSA-Snowden story on the public forum of social media than in person. If, however, Facebook users felt their followers or online community agreed with their position, they were about twice as likely to join a FB discussion group on the topic.

 **six degrees of separation**

Notion that everyone in the world is separated from all other individuals by at most six additional nodes in a social network.

**small world**

Tight-knit social network with many strong ties.

### FIGURE 7-1 Social Media as a Pathway to News

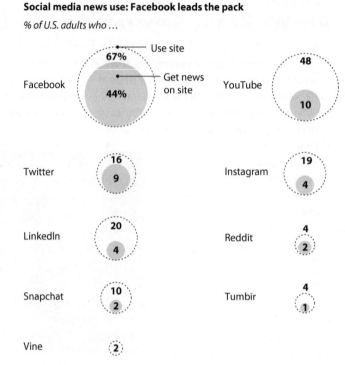

**Social media news use: Facebook leads the pack**

*% of U.S. adults who …*

Use site — Facebook 67% — Get news on site, 44%

YouTube 48, 10

Twitter 16, 9

Instagram 19, 4

LinkedIn 20, 4

Reddit 4, 2

Snapchat 10, 2

Tumblr 4, 1

Vine 2

Source: Survey conducted Jan. 12-Feb. 8, 2016.
"News Use Across Social Media Platforms 2016"
Pew Research Center

## Producers and Produsers

Throughout most of the twentieth century, media companies used technology to address audiences as masses. How many viewers a television show could boast determined advertising rates. Magazine and newspaper ads were priced according to their circulation. Records and movies were made according to which ones would likely draw the biggest audiences or sales. It didn't matter if most subscribers to a newspaper did not read the whole paper—in fact, there was no way to measure easily whether they even read it; claiming a certain circulation was enough. It was irrelevant if most of a television show's viewing audience went to the refrigerator during commercials.

All this began to change with the Internet and social media. Now companies could track audience behavior with more detail than ever before, all without installing special tracking devices, asking the audience to fill out forms or keep a diary, or other intrusive measures. They could see what audiences were watching and doing when they interacted with media. Such tracking produced massive amounts of data and raised the problem of how to analyze such large data sets. This growth in **big data** has spawned entirely new businesses to tackle the data, figuring out what is relevant and what is not, and discovering ways to visualize and explain the data so that they can be used.

What media companies saw when looking at the data did not make them happy. Nor did it make advertisers happy. A website could claim 2 million page views a month, but the same technology that let them state that with accuracy also told advertisers that only a fraction of 1 percent of the viewers clicked on their banner ads, and an even tinier portion acted as desired by buying a product from the advertiser's website.

**big data**

A collection of data sets too large for traditional analytic techniques to sort, analyze, and visualize.

Further, the kind of fragmentation of audiences already seen to some extent with the rise of specialized magazines and cable television channels accelerated with the Internet. Businesses that relied on mass audiences were now able to better watch their audiences, but unfortunately, they were watching those audiences shrink.

Although many more media choices for people caused much of the audience fragmentation, at least part of it was also due to the fact that audience members could now talk to each other and create their own media content. Even worse, they could talk back to traditional media producers in a public forum such as the web. That might help some shows become hits, but it also meant that negative sentiment from the public could keep potential viewers away.

If audiences were active, then advertisers wanted to see the audience actually do something useful for them, like buying their products or at least visiting their websites or registering to get email newsletters. New technologies enabled companies to track and record all these kinds of activities, but they also created a need for new kinds of measurement metrics that could capture the dynamics of audience interaction more accurately.

As discussed in Chapter 1, some of the biggest changes taking place among the three types of convergence have to do with how media are being used differently and the implications for media-company business models that assumed a passive audience. Traditional audiences were seen largely as passive consumers by the mass-media companies that created content to sell to them. The audience might consume media in the form of programs, books, or music, or buy products advertised through various media channels.

Of course, people were not as passive as that relationship would indicate; but until the Internet, and especially social media, the opportunities for people to choose, create, and "talk back" to producers were extremely limited. Now, however, people have the tools to talk back, and many are doing so. What's more, they are not only talking back but simply ignoring the traditional producers and talking to each other and the world at large. Audiences are shifting from simply being consumers of media content to what media scholar Axel Bruns calls **produsers**,[23] although others use the term "prosumers" or just "users." People from all walks of life, from the average citizen to world leaders, use social media to share their messages with friends, family, and everyone who will listen, watch or read, avoiding the need for a traditional media gatekeeper. Oftentimes, the more entrepreneurial the individual, the greater the potential reach and impact. For many, large followings on social networking platforms can translate directly into dollars earned, as many algorithm-driven advertising models automatically seek out the social media figures with the largest number of followers and pay considerable fees to post their ads on those individuals' sites.

This complex relationship dynamic is not easily defined. "Prosumer" still seems to emphasize consumption, almost like a professional consumer or kind of über-consumer. Similarly, "user" does not capture the sense of creation or production, an important element of the social media landscape.

Consumption in one form or another still predominates. Not everyone is (or wants to be) a producer of media content. But to contribute to the larger conversations taking place— to add something, however small, that helps create a greater whole—is easier than ever before. Posting a link to a worthwhile website or blog that others on a discussion board may have never heard of is a form of media production, collaboration, and

**produsers**

Audiences who no longer are simply consumers but also produce content.

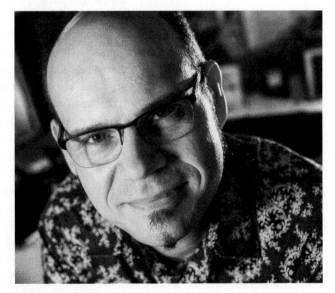

Media scholar Axel Bruns uses the term "produsers" to describe today's audiences as both users and producers of media content.

knowledge sharing that should not be downplayed as nonproductive or unimportant, especially on a large scale.

Furthermore, people do not have to contribute to feel like they are part of a community; it may be enough for many to see that others feel the way they do, connecting them to something larger. We see this sense of activism and community in some of the mass protests that have taken place, especially in countries such as Egypt during the Arab Spring. Social media help people realize there are others—sometimes many others—who share their thoughts and feelings while providing informal media channels to express views publicly and to organize actions. In recent years, social media networks have played a dramatic role in facilitating other social movements, including nationwide engagement in the Black Lives Matter movement, the January 2017 Women's March on Washington, and the April 2017 March for Science.

## REPUTATION, RATINGS, AND TRUST

The change in audiences from consumers to produsers has had a powerful ripple effect, not only on business models but on many social factors. In the traditional-media world, we could rely on certain established brands to give us certain things. *The Wall Street Journal* or *The New York Times* delivered a kind of content that the *National Enquirer* did not, and we learned what to expect.

Today, that has changed. Although the traditional brands still (for the most part) retain their meanings for us, it is more difficult than ever to determine whether to trust information from unknown sources. How do we know that the Amazon review of the book we are considering was not written by someone paid for a glowing assessment or by the author's mother? How do we know that a Wikipedia entry about a prominent figure was not posted by some avid fan, highlighting only positive information and ignoring past scandals? How do we know that the blog about childhood diabetes is not the work of a pharmaceutical company trying to promote its drug?

These and other issues are all extremely important in today's media world; hence the importance of critical thinking and media literacy. Issues of trust and reputation become vital in figuring out what information we can believe. Ratings systems that rank the usefulness of a review or comment help us make that decision. But the question also arises whether the raters are trustworthy or not. This is where social networks can be useful, for we generally trust friends or people we have let into our social networks and are more likely to listen to what they say or recommend. This is one reason **word-of-mouth marketing** (or buzz marketing) has become so important for advertisers. Ratings systems as a measure of gauging trust will develop and become more important in our social media landscape, but some thorny ethical and legal questions have arisen as well.

One big legal concern is figuring out who owns user-generated content on social media sites. If someone decides to write a book based on discussions taken from a site such as the WELL, using extended passages of actual discussions, is this a breach of copyright? How should the poster be compensated, if at all? Is permission needed to use the post or an excerpt of it? If so, how much is fair use and how much is an infringement of intellectual property? These are just some of the issues that social media sites will have to wrestle with in the future.

**word-of-mouth marketing**

Marketing that takes place among customers through discussions with one another.

**DISCUSSION QUESTIONS:** What policies should be adopted regarding content on discussion forums? Who owns the content, those who post it or those who host the site—or should it be there for the taking by anyone? Explain your reasoning and identify who should be responsible for content that is libelous or potentially harmful.

## PRIVACY

Norms for privacy are also changing. For many people older than millennials, making so much of one's life public through posting photos, discussing one's thoughts or desires on a blog, or sharing other highly personal information online feels strange. There is a sense that much of that is nobody else's business or that information should be shared only with a select group of people one knows and trusts.

This "living publicly" generally does not seem to bother millennials, yet many feel their privacy has been invaded when they learn that an employer is raising questions about material found on a social-networking site. Most employers today do Google searches of job applicants and examine social-networking profiles if they can, making decisions about who will be called for an interview accordingly. Some potential employers even insist on access to applicants' Facebook profiles. The goofy profile picture of you partying at your college may be hilarious to your friends on Facebook but not so amusing to a potential employer trying to gauge how you may represent the company.

Facebook has landed in hot water frequently over its policies that invade users' privacy or that threaten to do so. In 2016, Facebook revealed that about 81 million of their accounts might be fake, news that apparently caused company stock to drop to new lows. In an effort to address this security issue (and presumably any attendant financial fallout), Facebook later began enforcing its policy of real names for user profiles to promote identity "authenticity," deactivating accounts with names they deemed fake. Unfortunately, this did not make the FB community safer for all its members. To the contrary, this move heightened the dangers for individuals in certain vulnerable or at-risk groups who rely on anonymity for security, most notably the LGBT community and survivors of domestic abuse. Some Native Americans argued this policy has also hurt them, resulting in the deactivation of accounts with real or legal names that did not appear to meet Facebook standards.

A program launched in 2010 called Instant Personalization allows sites such as Yelp, Pandora, and Microsoft Docs to access what Facebook defines as public information (your name, your picture, your gender, your location, your friends, and all your likes) unless you opt out of it. However, even if you do opt out, if a friend has not opted out, then these sites may still access your information through the friend. Pandora uses the information on music likes, for example, to recommend songs to you based on genre similarities. Although some people may like this easy personalization, others see it as an invasion of privacy.

In 2012, Facebook paid a $20 million settlement in a class action lawsuit for using users' likes in their Sponsored Stories features without first getting their permission. The settlement affected 125 million Facebook users. Facebook was also threatened with a lawsuit for putting users' photos in ads without permission. In 2014, Facebook made it easier to change its notoriously confusing privacy settings and made some minor moves toward improving users' privacy.

There are many temptations for companies such as Facebook and Zynga, the maker of FarmVille (which tracked Facebook users even when they left Facebook, before the relationship between Facebook and FarmVille ended), to invade users' privacy by tracking their online behavior. The data collected are immensely valuable to marketers trying to figure out how best to tap certain markets—especially the lucrative eighteen-to-thirty-four demographic. For many companies, the wealth of data on user behavior they can obtain—and sell—is simply too great to resist, even if it is an invasion of privacy. Facebook jealously guards the data it collects on its members, working out deals with advertisers to provide them with the kind of information they want.

The online advertising industry has been promoting a "do not track" option for users, which would let users state they do not want their online interactions tracked by advertisers. However, while the industry claims to promote such a system, they are also attempting to make the option nonbinding and therefore essentially ineffective.

Companies that are bought by other companies or that go out of business have databases of registered users and online activity that could provide very valuable information. When users registered with a site, however, they likely did not consider that their personal data and on-site behavior might at some point end up in the hands of a different company with less stringent privacy policies.

Now that anybody can essentially be a publisher with her or his own website, private individuals can more easily and unwillingly be thrust into the public eye. With the ubiquity of camera phones and small video cameras, revenge porn, in which former partners post nude or sexually explicit photos of their exes, has been a growing problem. Although still not illegal in many states, thirty-five states have either passed laws making revenge porn illegal; and some members of Congress have promised to write a bill to make it illegal nationwide.

What ethical principles should media companies and the general public follow in deciding whether to post or publish material? Companies often have professional codes of conduct or codes of ethics, but no such general code yet exists for the public publishing content. Journalists often cite the public's "right to know" as a guiding principle when weighing ethical issues regarding publishing a story damaging to someone. Yet it is hard to say that the right to know outweighs someone's right to privacy when publishing a nude picture of an ex-girlfriend or when making defamatory claims about someone on a blog. The law tends to protect social-networking sites and websites, not holding them liable for what members post on the sites, which gives the sites little incentive to police their content.

Despite the valid concerns raised about privacy here, we can see that anonymity can be even more damaging in some cases. The Yik Yak app, which allowed people to post and view comments anonymously within a ten-mile radius, caused problems at universities. Students were victimized by vicious comments, and some students used it to share test answers with other sections. In May 2017, the website shut down and the app became defunct.

> **DISCUSSION QUESTIONS:** Consider your own time spent on Facebook. Have you found yourself using it less than you used to? Why? What are you using to stay connected instead of Facebook?

## TRANSPARENCY

Even supposedly tech-savvy companies leading the social media revolution seem regularly to make blunders similar to traditional-media companies regarding the new audience dynamics, as the Facebook Sponsored Stories example shows. Companies creating faux viral videos or fake grassroots blogs, a practice called **astroturfing**, are often punished in the court of public opinion once their machinations are exposed. Sudden shifts in privacy policies, either unannounced or announced inadequately, have produced similar audience backlash.

**astroturfing**

Creating a movement controlled by a large organization or group designed to look like a citizen-founded, grassroots campaign.

Facebook learned this the hard way in early 2009 when a change in their privacy policy, which had been made a few weeks earlier but went unnoticed by the general public, stated that Facebook would own the rights to user-generated content on the site, including posted photos. Publicized by a consumer interest group, the change elicited immediate and immense outrage, including a threat by the Electronic Privacy Information Center (EPIC) to file a complaint with the FTC.

Facebook quickly reversed the policy and created a group of users to discuss future privacy-policy changes—apparently to little avail, given their subsequent privacy problems just a few years later. Other companies should note these actions and reactions, emblematic of the shifting power dynamic between companies and the public. It would have been far better had Facebook created such a group in the first place rather than only after receiving complaints. Further, Facebook's own customers used the very tools that helped make Facebook so popular to organize against the company.

The need for transparency is becoming increasingly important with social media—a fact that individuals and organizations forget or ignore at their peril. Yet transparency often undermines corporate strategy making and planning because companies do not want to reveal secrets to competitors. Even when business strategy is not involved, what seem like harmless jokes sent by email between colleagues can damage reputations and brands if those emails appear on the web.

Fake Twitter accounts can be quite funny, but they have also caused a great deal of confusion when it becomes unclear if an account is fake or not. Phweeters (phony tweeters) have also crossed the lines of good taste when falsely reporting deaths, such as in 2009 when someone faked a journalist's Twitter account and reported the death of Cincinnati Bengals wide receiver Chris Henry twelve hours before he actually died after falling off a truck. Some news organizations picked up the tweet and reported it as news without first checking the validity of the account.

Transparency is starting to be built into some ratings and review systems. Reviewers can state how long they have had a product, for example, which helps readers gauge if the glowing review is about a product just out of the box or one that has been used for a while.

The balancing act between privacy, transparency, and mining the rich databases of compiled data from user interactions will continue to affect social-networking sites. As a struggle about the rights of consumers versus business interests, it raises this question: Who will watch the watchers? As we will see next, that is not the only struggle we face in a social media world.

During the manhunt that followed the Boston Marathon bombings in April 2013, someone created a fake Twitter account for the suspect Dzhokhar Tsarnaev. The account posted threatening messages to the police. It was exposed as fake, but not before being retweeted, picked up by police scanners, and reported on by the media. Such fakes can cause harm by diverting police attention and resources during a crisis.

## Social Media: The Good, the Bad, and the Ugly

Every new medium has its share of detractors, and the complaints over the ages are surprisingly similar. Real or perceived damage to youth ethics, attitudes, and beliefs is one typical complaint, as is how the new media make us dumber. The Internet and social media have not been immune to this, nor have other digital media, such as video games.

## ARE SOCIAL MEDIA MAKING US LESS SOCIAL?

In this book, we have discussed various ways that people have been able to become more involved in media production and collaborate with each other on any number of issues, ranging from traditional politics to social activism. However, a deeper consideration of how we use social media raises questions. Are all your "friends" on Facebook really your friends? How do you differentiate between Facebook "friends" and friends you actually regularly see or talk to? Using the term "friend" to refer to people one has never talked to directly or met face to face stretches the definition of the word and can produce problems.

Consider what happens when friendship becomes romance online. In January 2013, the website Deadspin broke a story that tarnished not only mainstream sports news organizations but the reputation of one of college football's biggest stars. Notre Dame linebacker Manti Te'o was a media darling throughout the 2012 college football season, especially because of his heartbreaking story about his girlfriend getting injured in a car accident and then later dying of cancer.

The only trouble was, there was no girlfriend. It was all an elaborate hoax played on Te'o, although when exactly he learned of the hoax and how long he kept silent about it remain open questions. The mainstream sports news journalists, perhaps to cover their own embarrassment at not doing adequate research, accused him of concocting the story to win sympathy. It seemed to defy belief that someone could claim a person was a girlfriend when their only communication was online.

By expanding our ability to communicate and be social in a virtual world, social media have made developing and maintaining relationships more complex, especially romantic relationships. The issue has entered pop culture, as seen by MTV's show *Catfish*. The show arranges meetings between people in relationships who have communicated only online. A **catfish** is someone who fakes an online profile, usually to get someone else to fall in love with the fake persona.

Scholars have recently asked hard questions about how we actually use social media. For example, a 2011 study looked at how college students defined the term "hooking up" and found no consensus among students as to what it meant, other than it involved some sort of face-to-face, as opposed to exclusively online, encounter.[24] Hooking up could mean everything from simply meeting for drinks or dinner to kissing to intercourse. What's more, the ambiguity of the term was thought to preserve some sense of privacy that helped give women the same kinds of power that men normally enjoy in our society.

In her book *Alone Together: Why We Expect More from Technology and Less from Each Other*, MIT professor Sherry Turkle examines how in many ways technology has separated us from one another. It gives us the illusion of greater connections and communication but actually makes us emotionally lazy and able to disengage from relationships easily. According to Turkle, young people are not the only ones to blame. Parents may send harmful social signals to their children by being physically but not emotionally present as they continually check their mobile phones and respond to texts or messages. In 2012, one company executive, tired of the barrage of emails, banned all internal emails for one week, forcing people either to meet face to face or to phone each other. He noted that he was better able to focus on big projects without the constant, distracting interruption of email.[25]

A Pew Research Center study in 2015 revealed that 57 percent of teens in the United States say they have made a new friend online. The vast majority of teens (88 percent) text their friends at least occasionally. Whether these digital connections ultimately build lasting relationships is a question some scholars have raised including Turkle, and it continues to be a matter of great debate.

**catfish**

Someone who fakes an online profile, usually to encourage another to fall in love with the false persona.

The MTV reality show *Catfish* helps people in online relationships find out if their partner is who he or she claims to be.

## ETHICS IN MEDIA
# Cyberbullying: New Twists on an Old Problem

Bullying is, unfortunately, not a new problem, and it is hard to prove that the rise in popularity of social media has increased its frequency. What these communication tools have done, however, is make bullying more public and reduce bullies' inhibitions by offering anonymity. At the same time, social media have increased public awareness of how widespread bullying actually is and how damaging it can be to a young person's self-esteem.

Hurtful words formerly spoken in a school hallway can now be written down and posted on social networks, encouraging other nasty comments, as this story from a twelve-year-old Colorado girl demonstrates:

I posted a picture of myself on Instagram and people started commenting these awful things like "Eww ur so ugly" "Why don't you go kill urslef everyone would be happier that way" And I KNOW these people . . . they go to my school. I cried for a good 2 hours. But this wasn't the first time this has happened on all my pictures at least 3 people say something like that. I'm never going on Instagram again. I wish I could disappear so I don't have to go to school.[26]

Many stories are similarly heartbreaking. Secrets can be exposed and broadcast to hundreds of peers in an online social network rather than simply whispered to a few close friends. Other types of cyberbullying are more subtle. Sending frequent text messages or making repeated phone calls is a type of harassment every bit as damaging and anxiety producing as more blatant forms of bullying.

Some teens have killed themselves after being bullied on social media. Education experts understand that social media are not causing the bullying, but they are giving teens and others a much wider platform to show the worst sides of human nature as they struggle with forming their identities, building relationships, and learning to communicate in the modern world.

**DISCUSSION QUESTIONS:** Download an app like Checky, which counts how many times you check your phone or tablet a day, and compare your numbers for the past few days with those of your classmates. What, if anything, does this tell you about how much you rely on your phone?

## ARE SOCIAL MEDIA MAKING US DUMBER?

Scholars have looked at the effect of the Internet and social media on our levels of knowledge and ways of thinking. A growing body of evidence suggests that despite the unprecedented breadth and depth of information available on the Internet, today's young people are more ignorant than ever before about subjects such as politics or history. Many seem to feel that they do not need to remember information because they can always find it online.

In the book *The Dumbest Generation*, Emory University English professor Mark Bauerlein chronicles case after case and numerous studies that indicate American teens and young adults today demonstrate a worrisome lack of intellectual curiosity and a dearth of knowledge about the world in general. They spend much of their time on social media, mostly communicating about mundane issues with each other and making sure they keep their circles of friends. They have far more knowledge of pop culture than of politics, and they see nothing wrong with the belief that pop culture is more important than politics. Bauerlein states that less than 30 percent could say what Reconstruction was, and in 2008, when the book came out, less than a quarter could identify Dick Cheney, vice president at the time.

While Bauerlein highlights some bleak findings about social media and political apathy, social media has also driven some recent political participation among young voters. As we will see in Chapter 14, Barack Obama's 2008 and 2012 presidential campaigns used social media to build and coordinate a nationwide volunteer network. Strong support among previously unengaged young people played an instrumental role in Obama's victories.

A more significant concern is whether heavy Internet and social media use are physically rewiring our brains and making us think differently. A 2007 UCLA study that examined the cognitive differences between heavy and light multitaskers found that heavy multitaskers—those who typically had multiple web browser tabs open, who frequently checked status updates, and who posted updates themselves—performed more poorly on memory and task tests than the light multitaskers.

Exploring these instances further, subsequent studies supported the early evidence that social media use makes it harder for people to concentrate on longer or more complex tasks and that social media users tend to get distracted more easily by trivial matters and not understand or remember more important material. The "always-on" nature of social media and mobile devices creates anxiety when away from social media and a need to always "be present" by commenting to others when connected.

A 2014 study titled "The Invisible Addiction: Cellphone Activities and Addiction Among Male and Female College Students" found that college women reported spending an average of ten hours a day on their cell phones, while college men spend an average of seven and a half hours a day. The most frequent activity is texting, taking nearly 95 minutes a day, followed by emailing at 49 minutes a day and checking Facebook at 39 minutes a day.

The public has a world of information at its fingertips through the Internet, yet ironically, people often squander their greater communicative power on pop culture trivia and an incessant need to keep in contact with others. The discovery of information online does not necessarily equate with the acquisition of knowledge, and in fact, we may express less interest in actual learning because we feel that we can always just look something up.

People who have difficulty focusing their attention and who lack interest in politics may have difficulty acting as informed citizens of a democracy. A perpetually distracted public is easily led—and misled—because people lose the ability to think critically and question (or even recognize) abuses of power.

The fact that we may not always use social media wisely does not mean that social media themselves are bad. They can be used to learn more about the world or to improve one's skills, such as with online training and free or low-cost online courses. They can help us socialize, organize, create, and collaborate in ways never before seen, just as they can isolate and alienate if used to excess or inappropriately.

Growing research shows that heavy social media users are less able to concentrate and tend to get distracted by trivial issues. Yet social media also connect people with the wider world and can enhance self-esteem.

## MEDIA CAREERS

With the rise in popularity of social media, companies of all kinds—not just media companies—have realized they too need to be where their customers are. Although companies often continue to see social media as simply another media channel, savvy organizations understand that social media bring their own ways of speaking and acting that differ from traditional media channels in which companies essentially controlled their messages to a largely silent (and presumably passive) audience.

Two new job titles have been created that did not exist several years ago, and the level of confusion as to what each does is emblematic of the ever-changing and chaotic world that is social media. Social media managers are responsible for the brand on social media; they join in social media conversations, respond to comments, create content, and generally act as the brand itself. They are also involved in strategizing and planning through various social media for the brand, whose performance they also analyze.

Community managers, on the other hand, are responsible for advocating for the brand on social media, trying to reach people who are not familiar with it. A community manager develops a persona as an individual, not as the brand itself, and promotes the brand through social media conversations. Much of a community manager's time is spent simply participating in conversations online about the brand and monitoring blogs or other social media sites where the brand is being discussed. Both job types are well suited to graduates in English and communications, given the emphasis on communicating to others in a natural and conversational way.

## LOOKING BACK AND MOVING FORWARD

Like much of new media, social media actually have firm roots and influences in many aspects of old media, although in this case the term "old" refers more to the earliest days of PCs and the Internet than to radio, TV, or print media. Even so, the changes that social media have brought in a relatively short time have enduring implications for culture, business, and society that researchers are only beginning to explore.

One of the biggest changes, discussed throughout this book, is the difference in the relationship between media producers and consumers. Even without the large marketing and promotion budgets of major media companies, average people have been able to create content that has been seen, heard, or read by millions or even tens of millions of people worldwide.

Thanks to social-networking sites, the networks formed through online communication have become ever more visible and empowering. Numerous projects have demonstrated what can be accomplished when many work willingly together, efforts that can benefit even greater numbers of people. Wikipedia is one such project.

Perhaps even more significant over the long term, however, is how social media have encouraged people to create and share knowledge structures, not just knowledge. Sometimes-heated discussions in forums expose participants to different viewpoints and attitudes. People in collaborative projects must come to some sort of understanding or agreement, thus modifying what is written to satisfy everyone. Although such exposure may not change our beliefs, it may broaden our perspective and make us more willing to accept other positions.

Curation, such as tagging information or reviewing products or media content, also allows us to share knowledge structures or ways of looking at the world.

Providing information about information can reflect worldviews just as accurately as direct comments on a discussion board. A user who tags a photo of fighting in Syria as "genocide" may suddenly see connections to other photos with the same tag and learn of past incidents elsewhere.

Following the actions of many users who are collaborating without even knowing it by using automated systems can yield amazing results. One example is Google flu trends, which uses aggregated data of search terms in the popular search engine to predict flu outbreaks up to two weeks earlier than traditional methods.

Of course, the social media tools available are only as good as the way they are used. Arguably, a community of sorts exists around even frivolous sites, but its value to all but a few may be questionable. Simply because we now have the tools does not mean we will always use them productively or efficiently.

Media companies are struggling to adapt to the world of social media, with mixed success. Companies not willing to give up control of their messages are having more difficulty than those receptive to engaging in the conversational chaos that is social media. Of bigger concern to companies, though, is how to earn revenues from all this incessant chatter, conversations often based on content the companies have spent money to create.

There are no easy answers to this question. Popular social-networking sites are sitting on a gold mine of user data gleaned simply from the interactions and behaviors of active users, data that advertisers are quite willing to pay for to better target consumers. However, the high degree of surveillance we have today does raise important questions about user rights and privacy. Some industries may find it easier to adapt to or to shape the social media landscape in ways that benefit them, while others may be facing a future in which their profession or industry as currently practiced is barely recognizable in ten or twenty years. Essential to any career involving social media will be heightened critical thinking skills. Critical thinking will help the savvy media professional or amateur to discern the truth from the fake, the deceptive from the authentic, and will ensure the most robust and responsible social networking media environment. An explosion of apparently fake news on Facebook and other social media networks during the 2016 U.S. presidential campaign raised new questions about the impact of such false information. How and whether to label or filter fake news, some of which is important satire and some of which is designed as propaganda and meant to deceive, is an important topic as well.

## MEDIA MATTERS    HOW CONNECTED ARE YOU?

1. Estimate how much time per day you spend on social media, via mobile phone, computer, or tablet. Which device do you typically use for social media? Do you use social media more or less often than your friends?

2. What is the longest time you have gone without access to social media? How did you feel when you were not connected? Did your patterns of social media use change afterward?

3. Some researchers have claimed that social media use has made us more isolated, not more social. Do you agree or disagree with this assertion? Defend your argument.

4. When considering a movie, TV series, or book, would you be more persuaded by a review from *The New York Times*, Rotten Tomatoes, your school paper, or a Facebook friend with whom you have interacted only casually once or twice? What factors would influence your decision?

## FURTHER READING

*Social Media: A Critical Introduction.* Christian Fuchs (2013) Sage.

*Socialnomics: How Social Media Transforms the Way We Live and Do Business,* 2nd ed. Erik Qualman (2013) Wiley.

*Wikinomics: How Mass Collaboration Changes Everything.* Don Tapscott, Anthony Williams (2008) Portfolio.

*The Wealth of Networks: How Social Production Transforms Markets and Freedom.* Yochai Benkler (2006) Yale University Press.

*Infotopia: How Many Minds Produce Knowledge.* Cass Sunstein (2006) Oxford University Press.

*Here Comes Everybody: The Power of Organizing Without Organizations.* Clay Shirky (2008) Penguin Press.

*Cognitive Surplus: How Technology Makes Consumers into Collaborators.* Clay Shirky (2011) Penguin Press.

*How Open Is the Future? Economic, Social & Cultural Scenarios Inspired by Free & Open-Source Software.* Marleen Wynants, Jan Cornelis (eds.) (2005) VUB Brussels University Press.

*The Wisdom of Crowds.* James Surowiecki (2005) Anchor Press.

*Perspectives on Free and Open-Source Software.* Joseph Feller, Brian Fitzgerald, Scott Hissam, Karim Lakhani (eds.) (2007) MIT Press.

*The Wikipedia Revolution: How a Bunch of Nobodies Created the World's Greatest Encyclopedia.* Andrew Lih (2009) Hyperion.

*Wiki Government: How Technology Can Make Government Better, Democracy Stronger, and Citizens More Powerful.* Beth Simone Noveck (2010) Brookings Institution Press.

*The Future of Ideas: The Fate of the Commons in a Connected World.* Lawrence Lessig (2001) Random House.

*Remix: Making Art and Commerce Thrive in the Hybrid Economy.* Lawrence Lessig (2008) Penguin Press.

*Blogs, Wikipedia, Second Life, and Beyond: From Production to Produsage.* Axel Bruns (2008) Peter Lang.

*Big Data: A Revolution That Will Transform How We Live, Work, and Think.* Viktor Mayer-Schonberger, Kenneth Cukier (2013) Eamon Dolan/Houghton Mifflin.

*Audience Evolution: New Technologies and the Transformation of Media Audiences.* Philip M. Napoli (2010) Columbia University Press.

*Groundswell: Winning in a World Transformed by Social Technologies.* Charlene Li, Josh Bernoff (2008) Harvard Business School Press.

*Tribes: We Need You to Lead Us.* Seth Godin (2008) Portfolio.

*Six Degrees: The Science of a Connected Age.* Duncan Watts (2004) W. W. Norton.

*Cyber Bullying: Protecting Teens and Adults from Online Bullies.* Samuel McQuade III, James Colt, Nancy Meyer (2009) Praeger.

*To Save Everything, Click Here: The Folly of Technological Solutionism.* Evgeny Morozov (2014) Public Affairs.

*Alone Together: Why We Expect More from Technology and Less from Each Other.* Sherry Turkle (2012) Basic Books.

*The Dumbest Generation: How the Digital Age Stupefies Young Americans and Jeopardizes Our Future (Or, Don't Trust Anyone Under 30).* Mark Bauerlein (2009) Tarcher.

*The Shallows: What the Internet Is Doing to Our Brains.* Nicholas Carr (2011) W. W. Norton.

*Produsing Theory in a Digital World: The Intersection of Audiences and Production in Contemporary Theory.* Rebecca Ann Lind (ed.) (2015) Peter Lang.

# Journalism
## FROM INFORMATION TO PARTICIPATION

n 2015, *Süddeutsche Zeitung* (SZ), one of Germany's leading newspapers, received from an anonymous source leaked internal documents from the Panamanian law firm Mossack Fonseca, the fourth largest offshore law firm in the world.

The 11.5 million documents—more by orders of magnitude than the combined totals of several noted leaks before then—would take years before any single organization could go through them all. SZ decided to work with the International Consortium of Investigative Journalists (ICIJ), who in turn gathered over four hundred journalists in one hundred media organizations from eighty countries to collaborate on analyzing and sorting the documents.

The task was incredibly complex, for a number of reasons. First, the documents had to be converted into searchable formats so they could be easily sorted and found. Second, it took a lot of coordinating journalists among different countries, languages, and journalistic traditions. Third, the investigation had to be carried out in complete secrecy so as to not tip off the people and organizations that appeared in the documents.

Nevertheless, it all came together and the participating news organizations released their news stories worldwide in early April 2016. The 4,700 stories that came out over the following weeks and months led to political resignations, $110 million recovered from organizations, and 6,520 ongoing investigations of people and organizations in various countries over possible tax evasion.[1]

Revelations in the documents from over forty years of records of Mossack Fonseca showed a complex web of interconnections between politicians and corporate elites who have avoided taxes through various shell companies. Although not necessarily illegal, their actions did reveal the hypocrisy of some politicians who have campaigned for tax reforms while avoiding taxes themselves.

In April 2017, the Panama Papers won the Pulitzer Prize for explanatory reporting, one of journalism's highest awards.[2] But perhaps more important for the long-term future of journalism, it showed that new collaborative models could be used in which journalists and news organizations pooled their resources and worked together to uncover complex and important stories.

## LEARNING OBJECTIVES

>> Describe journalism and its role in mass communication and society.

>> Outline important historical developments in journalism that affect how it is practiced today.

>> Discuss journalism today, including different types, and the effects of convergence.

>> Outline legal and ethical issues in the practice of journalism, particularly ethical issues in the digital world.

>> Explain some aspects of the business of journalism and how they affect the practice of journalism.

>> Examine how convergence is affecting business models and careers in journalism.

News organizations walk a thin line between providing a vital public service and thriving, or even surviving, as a business. Serving the public good does not preclude pandering to baser tastes for financial gain, and news organizations that are run as commercial enterprises have been accused of becoming too cozy with powerful business and political interests. Some believe the purpose of journalism is to "comfort the afflicted and afflict the comfortable." How well it is fulfilling these roles as public advocate and watchdog remains a topic of debate on print editorial pages, online discussion boards, and call-in talk shows. This should be viewed as a sign not of the profession's inherent failure but, rather, of its enduring importance in the digital age, where it is not enough simply to inform. Journalism today also needs to encourage public participation, as attested to by the rise of citizen journalism and hyperlocal news.

In addition to mobilizing the public, news is integral to three of the four main functions of mass communication: **surveillance**, **correlation**, and **cultural transmission**. To a lesser extent, journalism also serves the entertainment function. And because news consumption or participation is not a civic duty, many will engage only if it is an enjoyable leisure activity.

## What Is News?

"Man Bites Dog," an oft-cited headline in introductory journalism classes, suggests that news becomes news when it is extraordinary. Reporting does indeed embrace the unexpected. But most news is largely predictable a day, a week, a month, or sometimes years in advance. Consider the types of news stories about any annual event, such as advice on holiday shopping or what the stars will be wearing to this year's Oscars—a glance at news archives will likely uncover a very similar story the previous year and the year before that. Stories that affect the public interest also clearly constitute news: fires, accidents, recent discoveries, and corporate or political corruption, for example, such as in the case of the Panama Papers. Several issues arise when examining the nature of news.

First is the frequent complaint that news dwells too much on the negative—crime, accidents, wrongdoing, and so forth. Although positive news, such as human-interest stories or new business openings, may also be criticized as public relations pieces that do not adequately address significant concerns, negative pieces may send a distorted message that things are worse than they actually are. A focus on events rather than trends amplifies this problem. Although the overall annual crime rate may be falling, coverage of particular crimes, especially sensational ones, will still be pervasive. Trends are not as readily accommodated by the narrative structure of journalism that tends to rely on people, what they did or had done to them, and the consequences. Trends involve data, which journalism has not historically presented effectively, although this has improved with the growth of data-driven reporting and effective graphics, supplemented by individual cases to illustrate a trend.

Critical media consumers understand that diverse people and particular forces, notably advertising and public relations, influence and manufacture the news. It doesn't just happen. Historian and Pulitzer Prize–winning author Daniel Boorstin describes what he calls **pseudo-events**, events staged to attract media attention and influence news coverage, such as press conferences, marches, and rallies. Story selection depends on various factors, including other events that day, the type of news organization, and even the political views of the owner in some cases.

### surveillance

Primarily the journalism function of mass communication, which provides information about processes, issues, events, and other developments in society.

### correlation

Media interpretation ascribing meaning to issues and events that helps individuals understand their roles within the larger society and culture.

### cultural transmission

The process of passing on culturally relevant knowledge, skills, attitudes, and values from person to person or group to group.

### pseudo-events

Events staged specifically to attract media attention, particularly the news.

On a **soft news day**, when editors consider the day's events not especially newsworthy, they will air programming or include human-interest stories. A flood in a distant country killing hundreds may appear on a "World News Brief" page on a slow news day but be omitted if there is important local news. How do editors decide that a popular local high school athlete killed in a traffic accident is more significant than five hundred killed overseas? They try to determine what is of most interest to their readership. Journalists have an **agenda-setting** function, meaning their news choices influence what the public will deem important and discuss.

Despite its strong public service mission, journalism is nevertheless subject to economic realities. Without significant audiences and substantial advertising revenues, most newspapers and newsmagazines, whether print or digital, would cease to exist, as would television and radio news programs. Most newspapers and magazines actually have more space devoted to advertising than to news. The Internet has challenged many of journalism's traditional business models, and falling advertising revenues for traditional media outlets have still not been outweighed by the gain in Internet advertising, leading to searches for new journalism business models.

Let's examine the history of journalism as both a profession and a business, particularly how technological change has driven innovation.

On slow news days, editors are more likely to include features or photos that have little true news value.

**soft news day**

A day on which not much has happened that is newsworthy, entailing the addition of features with less real news value, such as human-interest stories.

**agenda setting**

Media's role in deciding which topics to cover and consequently which topics the public deems important and worthy of discussion.

> **DISCUSSION QUESTIONS:** Think about the predictability of much news. What stories or story topics (e.g., elections, holidays, a follow-up to a story that broke yesterday) are cyclical or predictable in some fashion? Look at today's news and see how many stories you can find that fall into this category. Are there more or fewer than likely occurred out of enterprise or investigative reporting or as a result of some unpredictable occurrence (e.g., a natural disaster)?

## The Historical Development of Journalism

The history of journalism has been synonymous with print, with the **penny press** and mass distribution of newspapers in the early nineteenth century producing a sea change in its theory and practice. To fill pages, editors—who had previously relied largely on "news" proffered by citizens or gathered by a small staff (as well as liberally copying from other newspapers, often without crediting the sources)— now had to hire reporters who actively pursued stories.

Articles were also typically organized chronologically, regardless of the relative importance of the information, and the opinions of editors or publishers (often the same person) mixed freely with other editorial content. No thought was given to presenting all sides of an issue fairly. With the penny press's need to attract as many readers as possible, however, publishers decided to concentrate more on sensational crimes and events than on their personal opinions. And to maintain objectivity or at least the appearance of such, editors began publishing their points of view exclusively on the "editorial" page, a tradition the Western press maintains

**penny press**

Newspapers that sold for a penny, making them accessible to everyone. Supported by advertising rather than subscriptions, they tried to attract as large an audience as possible.

Newsboys helped mass distribute penny papers by selling them throughout cities.

### James Gordon Bennett

Founder of the *New York Herald* in 1835. He initiated features found in modern newspapers including a financial page, editorial commentary, and public-affairs reporting.

### objectivity

Journalistic principle that says reporting should be impartial and free of bias. Because of the difficulties involved in complete objectivity, this principle has largely been replaced by the concepts of fairness and balance.

### Associated Press (AP)

Founded in 1848 as a not-for-profit members' cooperative by a group of six New York newspaper publishers to share the costs of gathering news by telegraph. Today, some fifteen hundred newspapers and five thousand television and radio stations are members.

today to guide public opinion on important matters, such as candidates for office. **James Gordon Bennett**, who founded the *New York Herald* in 1835, introduced, in addition to editorial commentary, a financial page and public-affairs reporting, more staples of modern journalism.

Also important to the development of modern journalism were minority newspapers. Among the earliest was *El Misisipí*, the first Spanish-language newspaper in the United States and first published in 1808 in New Orleans;[3] followed by the first Native American newspaper, the *Cherokee Phoenix* (1828), and the first African American daily, the *New Orleans Daily Creole* (1856). Frederick Douglass, an American statesman, abolitionist, and former slave, was also a journalist who published an antislavery paper, the *North Star*. These minority voices introduced the value of diversity to journalism while promoting more nuanced and balanced alternative perspectives.

## NEWS VALUES AND THE ASSOCIATED PRESS

News continued to evolve, shaped by the democratization of politics, the expansion of the market economy, and the growing impact of an entrepreneurial middle class. One reason news became more impartial—a core value in journalism known as **objectivity**—was the emergence of the news wire service in the 1840s. In 1846, publishers of six New York newspapers organized the **Associated Press (AP)**, in large part to take advantage of the telegraph, a high-speed communications medium too expensive for any single newspaper to afford. Gathering news for half a dozen papers with varying political viewpoints meant AP reports had to be politically neutral; and by the dawn of the twentieth century, these dispatches were virtually free of editorial comment.

Still based in New York, the AP provides textual, audio, and video news, photos, and graphics for its not-for-profit members' cooperative, including fifteen hundred newspapers and five thousand radio and television news operations. Members provide much of the AP content, which in turn any member can use. It employs thirty-two hundred people (two-thirds of whom work as journalists) in over 280 locations worldwide.[4]

The AP maintains the highest standards in journalism, having received fifty Pulitzer Prizes, including thirty for photos. As its website states, "More than 30 AP journalists have given their lives in this pursuit of the news. 'I go with Custer and will be at the death,' AP reporter Mark Kellogg wrote before Custer's final stand against the Sioux. And so he was."[5]

In addition to objectivity, the AP embodies at least four other core journalistic values. Foremost among these is a commitment to *truth* and *accuracy* in reporting. Quotations should be kept in context and reported accurately. Corrections that improve public understanding should be published when errors are detected. AP reporters, like all professional journalists, are committed to the *integrity* of the news. They do not plagiarize, or copy, work. They avoid conflicts of interest. Business reporters, for instance, must divulge their financial interest in a company and abstain from reporting on it. Much of this involves a commitment to the value of *ethics*, the moral basis for news. The AP tries to shield the identity of victims of sexual assault. AP reporters do not misrepresent themselves to get a story. They do not pay sources for an interview or a photo, a standard that certain tabloid and television news operations reject. Source attribution is also an AP ethical mandate. Anonymous sources, who erode credibility, can be used only when the material is information and not opinion or speculation and is vital to the news report; the information is not available except under the conditions of anonymity imposed by the source; and the source is reliable and in a position to have accurate information.[6]

> **DISCUSSION QUESTIONS:** Find an AP article on a major event or significant person and compare its treatment of the topic to that of another news organization (make sure the other article is not sourced from the AP, which is often the case). What similarities and differences did you observe? Did the AP demonstrate a greater commitment to its core values?

## PULITZER AND HEARST: THE CIRCULATION WARS, SENSATIONALISM, AND STANDARDS

Although objective reporting soon became the AP norm, not until well into the twentieth century did most newspapers adopt this model. Throughout the last half of the nineteenth century and the early twentieth century, **sensational journalism**, news that exaggerated or featured lurid details and depictions of crimes or other events, dominated content. Two of the greatest newspaper titans of this era were **Joseph Pulitzer**, publisher of the *New York World*, the *St. Louis Post-Dispatch*, and other papers, and **William Randolph Hearst**, publisher of the *San Francisco Examiner* and the *New York Journal*.

### Joseph Pulitzer

Born in 1847 in Budapest, Hungary, Joseph Pulitzer immigrated to the United States in 1864, serving in the Union army during the Civil War. After moving to St. Louis in 1868, he became a reporter for a German-language paper. Pulitzer purchased the bankrupt *St. Louis Dispatch* in 1878, later merging it with the *Evening Post* to create the *St. Louis Post-Dispatch*. In 1883, he bought the *New York Post* and then the *New York World*.

Embroiled with fellow newspaper mogul Hearst in the circulation wars of the 1890s, Pulitzer used abundant illustrations, a racy style, and colorful headlines to promote the *New York World*. He wanted a focus on city news, compelling stories—humorous, odd, romantic, or thrilling—and accurate writing with attention to detail. By the early 1890s, the *World*'s circulation had risen to three hundred thousand by mixing sensational photographs with good, solid reporting, "crusades" against corrupt politicians, and articles supporting increased taxes and civil service reform, for example.

Color comics in the Sunday papers were another of Pulitzer's most successful innovations. Although not the first newspaper cartoon, *The Yellow Kid*, a comic strip drawn as busy, single-panel illustrations, contributed much to the format many today take for granted.[7] Featuring brash and vulgar antics on the backstreets of the fictional Hogan's Alley, *The Yellow Kid* was in some ways a late-nineteenth-century precursor to the crude kids of *South Park*. *The Yellow Kid* quickly became a central figure in the circulation battles when Hearst lured creator and cartoonist Richard Felton Outcault away from the *World*. Referring to the Kid's famous yellow shirt, critics coined the term **yellow journalism** to describe the sensational style of the Pulitzer and Hearst newspapers.

Joseph Pulitzer was a Hungarian immigrant who founded a newspaper empire in St. Louis and New York.

## MEDIA PIONEERS
# Mary Ann Shadd Cary and Ida B. Wells

Mary Ann Shadd Cary

During the 1800s, as immigration increased and minorities began to identify as groups with shared interests and concerns, various minority or ethnic newspapers appeared in the United States. These papers served the needs of niche audiences, including Native Americans, African Americans, Jews, and immigrants whose native language was not English.

Among the most notable minority newspapers of the day was the *Provincial Freeman*. Founder, writer, and editor Mary Ann Shadd Cary observed in her paper that "self-reliance is the fine road to independence," a principle that her life strikingly exemplified. Shadd Cary was the first African American woman to edit a weekly newspaper and to publish in North America. She was also the first woman publisher in Canada. In addition, she was a teacher and a lawyer, only the second African American woman to earn a law degree.

Born a free black in 1823 in Wilmington, Delaware, Mary, the eldest of thirteen children, fled with her family to Windsor, Canada, after the Fugitive Slave Act, threatening the freedom of free northern blacks and escaped slaves, was passed in the

United States in 1850. In response to a vigorous campaign to deter runaway slaves from escaping to Canada, Mary wrote a forty-four-page pamphlet, "Notes of Canada West," outlining the opportunities for blacks in Canada.

Building on the success of this widely read publication, Mary established the *Provincial Freeman*, a weekly newspaper targeting blacks, especially fugitive slaves. She reported on a variety of important topics, among them lies being spread in the United States that African Americans in Canada were starving. Shadd Cary's father had worked for an abolitionist newspaper called the *Liberator*; after her husband's death in 1860, Shadd Cary returned to America, where she taught and wrote for the newspapers *National Era* and *The People's Advocate*.

Ida B. Wells was another important African American female journalist in the nineteenth century. Born a slave in 1862, six months before the signing of the Emancipation Proclamation, Wells spent her adult life fighting racism, especially the lynching of African Americans. She wrote for the religious weekly *The Living Way* and for various African American newspapers, including *Free Speech and Headlight*. She was elected secretary of the Afro-American Press Association in 1889.

Ida B. Wells

After the four-month Spanish-American War in 1898, Pulitzer abandoned the sensational style that had helped build his brand, developing instead a vision of journalistic excellence outlined in a 1904 article for the *North American Review*.[8] Investigative stories that ran in his papers were instrumental in the passage of antitrust legislation and regulation of the insurance industry. This emphasis on public service journalism and accurate reporting remains a cornerstone of the annual Pulitzer Prizes, which he bequeathed along with an endowment to the Columbia University Graduate School of Journalism after his death in 1911.

### William Randolph Hearst

William Randolph Hearst, the son of a self-made multimillionaire miner and rancher in northern California, studied at Harvard; and at the age of twenty-three, in 1887, became proprietor of his first newspaper, the *San Francisco Examiner*, payment his father had received for a gambling debt. In 1895, the younger Hearst acquired the *New York Morning Journal*; he debuted the *Evening Journal* a year later, enticing away many of Pulitzer's best reporters and editors with higher pay while increasing his chain nationwide to include the *Boston American* and *Chicago Examiner*, as well as *Cosmopolitan* and *Harper's Bazaar*.

William Randolph Hearst's newspapers often had sensational coverage that helped give rise to the term "yellow journalism."

Circulation increased tremendously as the paper attracted readers with colorful banner headlines, splashy photography, and, some say, fabricated news. Hearst was often criticized for his sensational tactics, later immortalized in the now-defunct *News of the World*, a print tabloid newspaper, and in Orson Welles's cinematic masterpiece *Citizen Kane*. Historian Ernest L. Meyer characterizes his work as inflammatory:

> Mr. Hearst in his long and not laudable career has inflamed Americans against Spaniards, Americans against Japanese, Americans against Filipinos, Americans against Russians, and in the pursuit of his incendiary campaign he has printed downright lies, forged documents, faked atrocity stories, inflammatory editorials, sensational cartoons and photographs and other devices by which he abetted his jingoistic ends.[9]

Nevertheless, Hearst's 1933 editorial guidelines articulate news standards that resonate today: "Make the news thorough. Print all the news. Condense it if necessary. Frequently it is better when intelligently condensed. But get it in." In 1945, six years before his death at age eighty-five, he established the Hearst Foundation, which today provides important support for journalism education and other concerns, including health and culture. His ornate 130-room mansion, San Simeon, nicknamed Hearst Castle, was built in the 1920s and still stands as a California landmark.

## THE RISE OF ELECTRONIC JOURNALISM

Newspapers began to suffer in the 1920s with the ascent of radio, which, supported entirely by advertising, offered news more quickly and for "free." And when television began broadcasting news in the late 1940s and early 1950s, newspapers' waning star was eclipsed. News was and still is an important part of how television fulfills its federal mandate to serve the public interest.

Television network news divisions in New York produced many of the early news programs. In 1947, NBC debuted *Meet the Press*, a made-for-TV news

Edward R. Murrow was a noted radio and television journalist in the earliest days of television.

conference where journalists queried various newsmakers, often government officials. Until his untimely death in 2008, Tim Russert had been the longest-serving host of what has become the longest-running series on network TV. In the 1950s, NBC introduced the first early-morning network news show. Host Dave Garroway and chimpanzee sidekick J. Fred Muggs offered a decidedly entertaining approach that the *Today* show still maintains.

### Murrow and News in TV's Golden Age

Setting the standard for television news during its golden age in the late 1940s and the 1950s was distinguished journalist **Edward R. Murrow**, who first achieved fame with dramatic radio news broadcasts from London during World War II. Murrow produced the popular television programs *See It Now* and *Person to Person* at CBS News.

Murrow's comments on television at the Radio-Television News Directors Association (RTNDA) meeting in 1958 ring equally true today for the Internet: "This instrument can teach, it can illuminate, and, yes, it can inspire. But it can do so only to the extent that humans are determined to use it to those ends. Otherwise it is nothing but wires and lights in a box." In *TV Guide* the same year, he offered another caveat: "Television in the main is being used to distract, delude, amuse, and insulate us."

### Changes in Television News

Interesting visuals on which television news relies can often dictate the selection and sequence of stories in a newscast. Perhaps because of its visual nature, television news has always catered to our entertainment needs, evident as far back as the early days of *Today*. Moreover, time constraints of less than thirty minutes or an hour to cover local, national, and international news, business news, sports, and weather constrict feature length.

The introduction of video cameras transformed television news. **Electronic news-gathering (ENG) equipment** allowed journalists in the field to capture and send videotaped news by satellite to the network, where it could be edited and broadcast much more quickly than film. This process has influenced the nature of video storytelling. The late CBS news veteran Bud Benjamin called it "NTV," the video-journalism equivalent of "MTV," with rapid-paced cuts and strong entertainment values.

The rise of twenty-four-hour news channels means a much larger **news hole** to fill and consequently much lower standards for what stations deem newsworthy. Coverage of events that would not otherwise reach a television audience is not necessarily a bad thing, but often this material simply promotes or entertains. The prurient entertainment quality of much TV news was particularly evident in the weeks of almost nonstop coverage of the 2013 Jodi Arias trial, for example, a lurid case in which a woman charged with first-degree murder of her boyfriend testified on the stand about their often-bizarre sexual exploits.

## Foundations of Journalism

Professional, mainstream journalism is still practiced largely conventionally. Reporters cover events and write stories, and editors select what stories to assign and whether they appear, depending on the available pages for print news, which in

**Edward R. Murrow**

A radio and, later, television journalist and announcer who set the standard for journalistic excellence during TV's golden age.

**electronic news-gathering (ENG) equipment**

Tools such as video cameras and satellite dishes that allow journalists to gather and broadcast news much more quickly.

**news hole**

Amount of total space available after advertisement space has been blocked out, typically in newspapers.

Al Arabiya is a television news network funded by Saudi Arabia in part to counter the growing influence of Al Jazeera, the news network started in neighboring Qatar several years earlier.

turn depends on advertising revenue. Even digital-first news media (in which news is reported first in digital format before going to traditional channels) are constrained by screen size and audience attention spans. Digital technology does not change the fact that reporters need to visit places and interview people. Nor does digital technology replace an experienced editor's judgment about what makes a good story and how it should be edited.

To understand which aspects of journalism have already changed and which will likely change more with convergence, we must first consider some of the foundations of journalism.

## THE HUTCHINS COMMISSION AND *A FREE AND RESPONSIBLE PRESS*

In 1947, what became known as the Hutchins Commission published a landmark 133-page report on the American press, *A Free and Responsible Press*. Written by Robert Maynard Hutchins and a dozen other leading intellectuals, this report

Advertorials are designed and written to look like news content but are in fact paid advertisements.

of the Commission on Freedom of the Press argued that the public has a right to information that affects it and that the press has a responsibility, even a moral duty, to present that information because of their constitutionally guaranteed freedom. The commission indicated that the government, the public, and the press could all take steps to improve the functioning of a healthy press. These included government recognition of the same constitutional guarantees for all media, not just print.

The commission recommended that agencies of mass communication finance new, experimental activities in their fields and that members of the press engage in rigorous reciprocal criticism. The commission called on the public to create academic-professional centers for advanced communications study, research, and publication. Among the first such centers was the Media Studies Center, founded by the Freedom Forum in 1984, nearly forty years after the report. The commission also encouraged schools to exploit the total resources of their universities to ensure that their students obtain the broadest and most liberal training. Finally, the commission proposed the establishment of an independent agency to appraise and report annually on press performance. A National Press Council failed, however, although a similar idea has had marginal success in some states.

## SEPARATION OF EDITORIAL AND BUSINESS OPERATIONS

Dubbed the "separation of church and state" in newsroom parlance, this basic principle entails that news coverage not be influenced by business decisions or advertisers, a separation intended to be reflected in page layout that clearly distinguishes between advertising and editorial content. At *The New York Times* headquarters, business and editorial staff even take separate elevators to their offices to avoid potential contact.

Yet many media critics complain that this separation has eroded in recent years as publishers and large media corporations increasingly let commercial concerns influence editorial content. A blatant example was when the owner of the *Los Angeles Times* demanded a special "news" section on the Staples Center, without explicitly informing staff that Staples both sponsored and approved the content. A more insidious example involves management layoffs that hamper original local reporting and force the paper to rely on cheaper but perhaps less relevant wire service news.

## FAIRNESS AND BALANCE IN NEWS COVERAGE

**Fairness** and **balance** in news coverage have increasingly replaced objectivity, a goal that has been questioned in recent years. Critics argue that reporter bias cannot be avoided, and to claim objectivity in a given situation simply masks partiality. Even if the reporter has no strong personal opinion when writing a story, subsequent editing and placement in a newspaper or news broadcast can still

**fairness**

News reporting on all relevant sides of an issue that allows representatives of those various sides the same coverage.

**balance**

Presenting sides equally and reporting on a broad range of news events.

reflect bias. Unintended biases can also inform an editor's choice of assignments and a reporter's choice of sources.

"Fairness" and "balance" mean equal and just consideration of all sides of a topic. This does not mean equal space, however. Support for a fringe candidate from a small group of fifty people, however vocal, would not receive the same amount of coverage as a popular candidate from a major political party. A journalist must consider factors such as contextual importance and source validity or authority.

> **DISCUSSION QUESTIONS:** Look at the front page of your favorite newspaper app or website and assess the placement of stories and photos. What reasons might account for such placement? How would moving a story onto the front page or from the front to another page change your impression of its importance?

## FRAMING THE NEWS

Traditional news media often decide how they will **frame** a story before the reporting is completed and sometimes before it has even begun. Forcing facts to fit a preconceived frame is one of the biggest threats to fairness and balance. Yet this tendency cannot be wholly avoided, partly because it makes writing a news story easier and faster and partly because it helps us make sense of the world. Journalists, who often believe their work simply reflects reality, may not even aware be aware of their frame.

This can create problems, especially when treating more ambiguous and complicated situations that tend to defy simple framing. Consider, for example, the media's tendency to demonize, reducing complex events and people to "good" and "bad" and reporting accordingly. Depending on one's loyalties, a "terrorist attack" could also be described as "armed resistance."

**frame**

Structure or angle given a news story that influences reader understanding covering the event.

> **DISCUSSION QUESTIONS:** Discuss a current event in the news and how it is framed. How does this framing affect the way the topic is being covered? Suggest frames that may allow for more balanced, complete coverage.

## EXPERT SOURCES

Another problematic issue related to framing is the use of expert sources to enhance story credibility, sources that by and large are white and male. A September 2012 study found that particularly underrepresented are Latinos, a population that has more than doubled in the United States since 1990, comprising approximately 17 percent of the total population. Yet expert Latino voices are almost never heard in American English-language news media. In 2006, only 2 percent of the U.S. experts who appeared on PBS *NewsHour* were Latino, and Attorney General Alberto Gonzalez himself constituted 30 percent of those appearances. A 2014 investigation by Columbia University's Center for the Study of Ethnicity and Race revealed network TV to be even worse, with less than 1 percent of all stories on the nightly news programs highlighting Latinos.[10]

## INTERNATIONAL PERSPECTIVES
# Covering Islam

Framing in the news occurs everywhere, but it is arguably most prevalent in coverage of international news. In the 1980s, when Japanese companies were buying American companies, the American media often depicted the trend in warlike terms such as "invasion." This was echoed in recent years as China gained economic might and has wanted to buy American companies, such as Smithfield Foods, America's biggest pork producer; yet similar language is not seen when a Canadian or British company buys an American company.

Due partly to the terrorist attacks on September 11, 2001, Islam has largely been framed in the U.S. media as a monolithic religion advocating violence and repression of human rights, argues scholar Edward Said in his book *Covering Islam*.

Said says that the inaccurate depictions of Islam are created by a complex web of media that rely on

self-proclaimed "Islamic experts" who pontificate on the Middle East and who often equate fundamentalism with Islam, even though Judaism and Christianity face similar fundamentalist movements.

The depictions feed into a nationalistic "us-versus-them" mentality that is similar to the anti-Communist fervor during the Cold War. Not only do these inaccurate portrayals hurt our ability to see Muslims on equal or humanistic terms, they provide a cover for repressive regimes that use Islam as an excuse for unequal policies.

Framing, in other words, paints over a complex reality and, more importantly, shapes our reactions and beliefs to the new reality that it creates. This in turn can affect how we interact with the groups that have been framed and can perpetuate negative stereotypes and discrimination.

"Individuals of either sex, any age, and all races can be heard from on the network news, as long as they are not wielding power or offering expertise. The networks' 'golden rolodexes' of expert consultants are badly in need of updating," observes Andrew Tyndall, who directed a study called *Who Speaks for America? Sex, Age and Race on the Network News*.[11]

## From Event to Public Eye: How News Is Created

News is regularly required to fill the scheduled evening TV broadcast, the morning paper, the weekly newsmagazine, or the website. Like an accordion, news can expand or contract with the day's events, but only to a limited degree. And whether anything of import occurs today, networks will still air at least a thirty-minute newscast (twenty-two minutes, after subtracting for commercials). Sometimes, during a major breaking news event—such as the September 11, 2001, World Trade Center and Pentagon attacks—they expand to an hour or even to continuous coverage.

In the past thirty years, hard news has yielded to lighter fare. In 1980, one of three front-page news stories dealt with government or public affairs, including international events, compared to just one in five today. In 1980, only one in fifty front-page daily newspaper stories featured celebrities, popular entertainment, and related subjects. Today, it's one in fourteen, not including the various teasers and blurbs promoting other parts of the paper. Television news is following print trends, with shorter stories and reduced coverage of politics and government. Forty percent of local TV "news" is now weather, sports, and traffic reporting.

This dramatic and inexorable shift has occurred for a number of reasons. One is an increasingly competitive environment in which newspapers vie with electronic entertainment media for audiences. Also important are changing ownership structure and business models. The resulting staff cutbacks in the past two decades have been substantial and wrought other changes, including the closure of foreign bureaus. News media are struggling to reinvent themselves in an online, digital age. Although TV is still the number 1 news source for most Americans, Pew Research found that as of 2013, nearly half of Americans turn daily to digital news sources, especially via smartphones and tablets.[12]

Regardless of news format, news techniques of gathering, reporting, and presenting information to the public, although refined over the years, have changed surprisingly little. Certain variations exist among print, broadcast, and online journalism; but the basics, which we look at now, remain largely the same.

Sometimes during protests or demonstrations, people act up when they see TV news cameras.

## GATHERING THE NEWS

The AP publishes for members a daily listing of upcoming events, such as important court cases, demonstrations, and press conferences. Most journalists or their assignment editors refer to the AP daybook at night for the next day's story ideas, and the daybook remains a good predictor of the next day's news. Some media critics claim that much news is actually manufactured by media organizations aided and abetted by public relations news releases or video news releases (VNRs) and that press conferences, awards ceremonies, and the like are staged solely to attract public and press attention.

Although news about pseudo-events or based on publicity releases may well be "manufactured," the fact is that journalists must rely heavily on certain sources to stay informed. Reporters also develop sources when covering a **beat**, an area originally structured by geography, much like a police officer's, but now largely defined by subject, such as education, city hall, the state capital, or science. Beats facilitate the cultivation of valuable sources and access to newsworthy developments. Small hyperlocal news sites, which cannot afford specialized reporters, often have general-assignment reporters who cover a range of topics.

**beat**

Reporter's specialized area of coverage based on geography or subject. Common beats in large or medium-sized newspapers include education, crime, and state politics.

Moreover, the media spotlight tends to create more news. A big story such as a natural disaster or a U.S. presidential election resonates through the entire system. Yet even an unusual movie advertising campaign, for example, may trigger more stories about the campaign and its impact on the film's success, which in turn generate more publicity, making the movie more popular and more newsworthy. Some news filters up through the media network. A story in a local paper may be covered by a regional television station where a reporter for a national publication sees it and brings it to the national stage.

## PRODUCING THE NEWS

Once a story has been assigned or selected and the raw material gathered, the reporter has to make sense out of all the interviews, background facts, video, and so forth, shaping these into a compelling story. Yet few journalists have the luxury of putting a story aside for a week to ponder word choice or polish prose. And if the story is breaking news, the reporter will have even less time.

In meetings usually several hours before deadline, newspaper editors decide which stories are most important and where they will be placed in print or online; these spaces are blocked out (advertising space has been blocked out first), an arrangement subject to change in the event of breaking news.

Editors look for logical weaknesses, errors, and gaps in stories, often asking reporters to get more information. Fact checkers research stories for accuracy and sometimes have to replace TKs (meaning "to come") with information they have sought out. Copyeditors correct writing and in-house style errors. In larger

---

## CONVERGENCE CULTURE
# Digital News Organizations Come into Their Own

Social and digital media continue to transform the world of journalism as an increasingly prominent vehicle for quality news and information. In 2010, ProPublica was the first not-for-profit online news operation awarded a Pulitzer Prize.[13] In April 2012, *The Huffington Post* became the first commercial news website and blog to win.[14] Founded by Arianna Huffington, Kenneth Lerer, Andrew Breitbart, and Jonah Peretti, *The Huffington Post* launched on May 9, 2005, as a fully digital, U.S.-based, for-profit operation. It provides original news, online commentary, and aggregated content from other sites on a wide spectrum of subjects including politics, business, entertainment, lifestyle, culture, and comedy.

*The Huffington Post* received a Pulitzer for national reporting for an original series on wounded veterans. In "Beyond the Battlefield,"[15] experienced war correspondent David Wood explores "the challenges that severely wounded veterans of Iraq and Afghanistan face after they return home, as well as what those struggles mean for those close to them." Debuting online, the ten-part series was subsequently expanded and republished for Kindle and iBook.

*The Huffington Post* has evolved and matured since its introduction as largely an alternative to conservative online news such as the *Drudge Report*. In February 2011, AOL acquired the site for $315 million,[16] and founder Arianna Huffington became editor-in-chief of the Huffington Post Media Group. *The Huffington Post* effectively integrates social media both for reporting and for engaging citizens in an online news community. Every story encourages readers to follow and participate on Facebook, Twitter, Google+, and more.

Upon the death of Venezuelan president Hugo Chavez in 2013, the lead story on HuffPost featured a one-inch-tall headline in bold red—"He's Dead"—evoking sensationalist papers of a century ago. Yet the story also exhibited distinctly modern, digital features. A "scroll-over" of Venezuelan President Hugo Chavez's picture below the banner headline provided a "quick read," a paragraph summary of highlights. Clicking on the photo or text below accessed the entire story, with multimedia and interactivity options. Readers could see the total number of social media shares to Facebook, Twitter, Google+, and email as well as thousands of comments on HuffPost Social News. Comments were polarized: for example, "Chavez will live forever in the hearts and minds of his people. The boorish comments of the great unwashed will not survive the night," and "It is about time this man died, too bad it was not at the end of a rope. And the only thing he cared about was himself."[17] Within a few hours, a new blue headline appeared, "Life After Hugo," linking to a story speculating on the future of Venezuela. Clearly, the digital era offers journalists new opportunities both to react to a developing story and to engage with their audience. Along with opportunities come new challenges.

news organizations, headline and caption writers create apt headlines and photo captions to fit the space allotted. In smaller news outlets, a journalist may wear a number of these hats.

Design and page-layout artists create digital versions of copyedited articles in a page-layout program such as Adobe InDesign or online via WordPress. Proofreaders check for errors; after an editor approves an issue, it is sent to the printer, formerly as negative photographs of page hard copies but now entirely as digital pages received electronically.

TV camera crews and reporters usually return to the station to edit footage shot on location and to add voice-overs and graphics. Because time is so critical, news segments are rehearsed and edited down to the second. Breaking or international news is reported live from location, often broadcasting via satellite. Advances in mobile, digital technology have made it increasingly practical to do nonlinear video editing from the field and then transmit a completed video package or story wirelessly, even high-resolution, broadcast-quality material.

Digital video technology has reduced the requirements for shooting broadcast-quality video to a single cameraperson and a reporter, but producing a television news package still involves more technically than writing a print story. Many print news operations now have converged newsrooms.

At a TV station, the producer and reporter decide what to edit and how the story will be put together, usually working with video editors or other technicians who carry out their instructions. Some news anchors also have a role in editorial decisions, whereas others simply deliver the news.

## DISTRIBUTING THE NEWS

The goal of both print and electronic news distribution is the same: to attract as large an audience as possible, which means a higher advertising rate and more income for the media organization. To that end, newspapers and magazines use colorful or dramatic photos on their front pages or covers, often featuring what the editors have decided is the most enticing story. Some magazines may send press releases about particularly noteworthy stories that will appear in the next issue, with the hope that other media outlets will report on these and generate more sales. Particular stories can be syndicated and appear in other print-media outlets.

Print media are distributed through subscriptions and newsstand sales. Subscribers are more valuable to media organizations because they represent a stable revenue base and provide mailing lists that can be sold or rented to other organizations. Material costs for print media, ranging from paper to ink to delivery trucks, can be quite high.

Television stations have short teasers during commercial breaks throughout the evening, usually a provocative question such as "Could the food you are eating be dangerous? Find out at eleven." To keep people watching, stories that served as bait typically appear later in the program, as does the weather. Networks transmit national news shows to affiliate stations, sometimes with time slots available for additional local news content. They also send video feeds of international and national news coverage.

Whether produced originally for print or broadcast, most news is also packaged for digital distribution direct to the consumer. Most news organizations, even those with traditional news products, are committed to digital-first publication to get their stories out to the public quickly before the competition does. Moreover, most if not all news media today engage audiences via social networking. Through

*The New York Times*, along with some other major newspapers, has seen subscriptions rise dramatically.

a combination of Twitter, Facebook, YouTube, and other social media, they share news stories and invite readers to share, expanding their audience and the digital dialog on news. Editors who complain about news aggregators such as Google using their material for free still benefit from the increased online traffic.

## Types of Journalism

Much serious questioning of journalism took place during the widespread challenging of societal norms in the 1960s. Leading reporters such as James "Scottie" Reston of *The New York Times* and Paul Anderson of the *St. Louis Post-Dispatch*, perceiving the limits of objective news reportage, developed **interpretive reporting** that attempted to situate the facts of a story in a broader context. Although critics argue that this approach represents life's complexities no better than does objective reporting, interpretive reporting opened the door to a variety of new styles, including New Journalism, literary journalism, and advocacy journalism.

New Journalism developed in the 1960s and 1970s during a period of great social, political, and economic upheaval in the United States that included both the Vietnam War and the Watergate scandal. Reporters striving to capture the spirit of these complex times and explore current social issues, such as the drug culture, often used literary techniques such as point of view, description of characters' emotions, and first-person narrative. Truman Capote, Tom Wolfe, and Norman Mailer were three prominent authors associated with New Journalism, a style that critics charged blurred the line between fact and fiction.

The roots of literary journalism go back to muckraking, although this modern form does not always tackle social problems with the same fervor. Literary journalism stays closer to true, observable narrative, and its pace may be slow, with frequent, lengthy digressions. Because of standard article length and topic, literary journalism generally does not deal with breaking news, although such events may inspire subsequent stories. John McPhee employs immersive reporting, solid research, and excellent writing to create literary journalism. Other practitioners include Joan Didion, James Fallows, and Robert Kaplan, all of whom write on a range of issues, including foreign affairs and politics.

Another descendent of the muckrakers, one that maintains its critique of society and commitment to political and social reform, is advocacy journalism. Prominent practitioners include Gloria Steinem (founder of the magazine *Ms.* and a leader of the women's movement), Pete Hamill (one-time editor of the *Daily News* in New York), and Nicholas von Hoffman. Much of early environmental journalism was advocacy journalism.

### ALTERNATIVE JOURNALISM

Alternative journalism, or, as it was often called, radical journalism, departed considerably from the traditions of objective reporting. Its roots go farther back to radical and socialist U.K. newspapers published in the nineteenth century to express workers' united voice and shared sense of injustice. Some radical papers had large circulations in their heyday, comparable to popular traditional papers. But because advertisers wanted neither to attract the working-class market nor to be associated with radical political movements, these papers struggled to stay afloat or ended up toning down their political rhetoric.

💬 **interpretive reporting**

Reporting that places the facts of a story in a broader context by relying on the reporter's knowledge and experience.

As an outlet for stories not seen elsewhere, alternative journalism often purposely defied professional conventions, in both tone and topic, much as New Journalism did decades later. Despite alternative journalism's fringe status throughout most of the twentieth century, some of its material would make its way into the mainstream. Magazines such as *Mother Jones*, *The Progressive*, and *The Nation* straddle the gap between radical and conventional. And alternative urban weeklies with edgy, contrarian coverage often geared to a younger audience, such as *Westword* and the *San Diego Reader*, exemplify the genre, although circulations of alt-weeklies has generally been dropping and several noted papers such as the *Village Voice* or the *Boston Phoenix* have either been sold or ceased publication.

Alternative journalism was given a new lease on life in 1999 during the World Trade Organization protests in Seattle when an ad hoc group of protesters, who felt the mainstream press was misreporting or underreporting, created their own independent media movement. Indymedia quickly spread worldwide with the growth of the Internet. Although most Indymedia groups remain small, their decentralized structure and open publishing systems facilitate the contribution of stories by people who may not otherwise get involved in journalism. Indymedia NYC publishes a monthly professional-quality newspaper, the *Indypendent*, along with maintaining a robust website.

The *Village Voice*, an iconic alt-weekly based out of New York City, announced it would stop its weekly print edition in August 2017 and be only online after seeing a drop in circulation, budget cuts, and staff layoffs over several years.

**DISCUSSION QUESTIONS:** Describe the potential pitfalls of one of the alternative journalism types and how these may be avoided or overcome—if possible.

## PUBLIC JOURNALISM

Public journalism, or civic journalism, developed in the early 1990s in response to dissatisfaction with media treatment of social and political issues and concern about the apathy and cynicism among the general public this coverage possibly fostered—including an increasing distrust of journalists. Originating with long-time and respected professionals, public journalism takes a less radical approach than alternative journalism that expands the watchdog role of the press while engaging the citizenry more actively in news creation and discussion. Public journalism strives for more nuanced reporting that avoids framing stories in terms of conflict and extremes.

Various newspapers experimenting with public journalism have reported a higher level of readership trust in the press as well as some signs of increased civic participation and awareness of social and political issues. Some critics argue these efforts are insufficient to break down the barrier between professional journalists and public audiences; others claim they represent little more than boosterism, or advocacy. Partly because of this criticism from peers as well as citizens, public journalism has waned in recent years. Later studies in communities with papers that followed public-journalism principles noted no significant increase in political awareness or public participation.

In the digital world, however, public journalism has thrived in the form of Pro-Publica, the first digital-only, not-for-profit news organization to win a Pulitzer Prize. Known for its investigative reporting and enterprise journalism, ProPublica has produced extensive interactive and multimedia public service coverage of critical topics like the impact of Hurricane Katrina on doctors at a hospital cut off by

With the 2003 U.S. invasion of Iraq, the U.S. military introduced a new approach to managing journalists in the theater of war by requiring all 775 reporters and photographers to be embedded, meaning attached to military units. **CRITICAL THINKING QUESTIONS:** How does the practice of embedding journalists affect the quality of news reporting? Does being embedded help or hinder journalists' pursuit of the truth?

floodwaters. ProPublica has also partnered with more than ninety news organizations, including *The New York Times*, *USA Today*, and Salon.com, to extend its reach and capabilities. It also features an ongoing collection of watchdog reporting titled, in homage to the past, MuckReads. In addition, ProPublica provides interactive tutorials on digital reporting techniques, such as using Google Docs as a news-gathering tool.

Debates on public journalism have also been an entree to further discussion of the challenges professionals face in the early twenty-first century with the rise of citizen journalism.

## CITIZEN JOURNALISM

The Internet and social media have accelerated the growth of citizen journalism, a broad field encompassing everything from blogging to Slashdot to more formal ventures that emulate professional journalism in important aspects, such as OhmyNews, Patch, Meporter, Examiner, and Wikinews. Some scholars even include consumer product-review sites as a form of citizen journalism.

Unlike advocacy or alternative journalism, citizen journalism is usually not associated with an explicitly political or radical agenda, and its driving force has been citizens rather than professional journalists, as in public journalism. Consequently, mainstream journalism has been more willing to welcome these efforts, even if cautiously. Many news organizations, CNN's iReport, for example, have tried to cultivate their audiences as sources of raw news footage. Other news organizations, notably newspapers, have adopted a more integrated and thorough approach in which citizen-journalists post news and stories on a stand-alone website or mobile app, perhaps partially cobranded with the newspaper, which publishes the best stories in a weekly edition. Still other organizations have conducted training sessions for citizen-journalists, teaching them interviewing, reporting, and writing skills.

Mainstream critics claim that citizens are being used as unpaid reporters to fill holes in local news coverage resulting from staff cutbacks. AOL's Patch, for example, employed a model in which thousands of unpaid citizen reporters covered more than one thousand communities across the United States under the direction of hundreds of professional AOL editors. Although Patch's business model proved unsustainable, there are still many Patch sites that publish highly localized stories online.

The track records of original citizen-journalism sites vary. OhmyNews, a South Korea–based site that operates much like a traditional news organization with paid editors and a hierarchical editing structure, has had mixed success. Although very popular and financially strong in South Korea, the English-language website version lost money and had to shut down, as did the Japanese OhmyNews. In 2005, citizen-journalism advocate Dan Gillmor launched Bayosphere to cover the San Francisco Bay Area, but seven difficult months later he largely abandoned the project for practical and economic reasons.

Wikinews is a citizen-journalism site that users can edit, as they can with Wikipedia.

Citizen-journalism sites all emphasize participant conversation and interaction. As gatekeeping becomes gatewatching, and the line between the professional practitioner and the audience blurs, the journalist's privileged position as arbiter of the news is undermined. The role of citizen journalism during the Arab Spring of 2011 illustrates the potential impact of such reporting. Videos uploaded to YouTube and reports provided via mobile social media proved pivotal in quickly getting out to the world firsthand eyewitness accounts from Tahrir Square and elsewhere, a kind of **crowdsourcing** of news that is becoming increasingly common for both large-scale breaking news stories, in which the public provides raw footage and information from multiple perspectives, and for stories that have lots of data or information to parse through.

> **crowdsourcing**
>
> Using raw data gathered from the public and citizen-journalists to help create a news report.

Despite the great potential to increase citizen engagement on local, national, and international levels, citizen journalism lacks a standard business model to promote sustainability and support paid reporters and editors. In recent years, there have been several attempts to create nonprofit business models, funded in part by philanthropic organizations and subscriptions or memberships. Some news organizations such as the Texas Tribune have found success with these kinds of models, and others continue to experiment as they accommodate the new reality of diminished advertising revenues and a public that so far still seems reluctant to pay for news online.

Citizen journalism, despite its pitfalls, signals a shift toward more interactive citizen participation in the news-gathering and reporting process. As NYU journalism professor Jay Rosen observes, "Journalism should be a conversation, not a lecture."

**DISCUSSION QUESTIONS:** Go to a citizen-journalism site such as Wikinews and compare its news coverage with that of mainstream news sites. How are they similar, and how are they different?

## CONSTRUCTIVE JOURNALISM

With its roots in principles of civic journalism, constructive journalism is a growing type of journalism that was started in Scandinavia in the late 2000s. The principles behind constructive journalism, which is also sometimes called solutions journalism, acknowledge that typical negative, event-driven coverage in the news tends to disincentivize the public from active civic engagement. To counter this, constructive journalism attempts to frame stories within larger contexts that offer potential solutions to problems as a way to empower readers.

Several news organizations in Denmark, Sweden, and the Netherlands have participated in constructive journalism projects; HuffPo started one such project in 2011; and *The Washington Post* began a section titled "The Optimist" under constructive journalism auspices. It is still too early to tell whether constructive journalism will have a long-term impact on journalistic practices or if it will be considered a relatively short-term fad, but its growth and interest among some professionals and academics demonstrate how news organizations in the twenty-first century are trying to navigate the digital world.

## AN INTERNATIONAL PERSPECTIVE

There is nothing sacred about the inverted-pyramid structure of news stories or the emphasis on fairness and balance. Most Americans do not realize that journalism can be practiced in various ways because any experience they might have with foreign news is likely limited to the English-language BBC, whose treatment resembles American coverage.

An examination of news styles, from Europe to Asia and the Middle East, reveals a remarkable diversity in the writing, editing, and even selection of news. Reporters' opinions and feelings may be more prevalent or obvious in ostensibly factual news accounts. Since the Arab Spring, for instance, the volume of news sources from the Middle East has expanded. Some new voices present a narrative of sympathy for Arab suffering and popular rage against U.S.-backed Arab governments and their leaders, such as the ousted Hosni Mubarak in Egypt.

In many countries, journalists still face censorship or licensing restrictions that naturally shape the kind of news produced. Journalists in many monarchies, from Norway to Jordan, for instance, are prohibited from publishing anything that might be deemed critical of the royal family. Dubbed "lèse majesté," derived from the Latin "laesa majestas," meaning "injured majesty" in Latin, these laws often carry stiff penalties for infringements, including prison sentences and harsh fines. In such environments, journalists may act more like government stenographers, simply recording meetings and events that the state deems important to publicize, with a state-approved editorial voice.

For instance, a Muscat, Oman, court in 2012 sentenced four bloggers to jail for allegedly insulting the Sultan. Such penalties can have a chilling effect on journalism, even in a hot desert climate. As seen in early 2015 in Paris, objections to press coverage can even take the form of violent assaults on journalists. On January 7, 2015, Muslim extremists attacked a Paris publication, *Charlie Hebdo* (or Charlie Weekly), known for its satirical coverage of Islam, killing at least a dozen persons. Such terrorist attacks pose a threat to free and independent journalism everywhere.

"Je suis Charlie" ("I am Charlie") became a motto for freedom of speech and the press in the wake of the Charlie Hebdo massacre. **CRITICAL THINKING QUESTIONS:** How did religious leaders of different faiths respond to this particular massacre and to the general practice of religious satire? Do you agree or disagree with their positions and beliefs?

## Journalism in the Digital World

Mainstream news organizations have not always been quick to adopt new digital resources. Busy work schedules and corporate reluctance to subsidize professional training and development have contributed to this resistance. Clearly, journalists recognize the value of the Internet. And mobile devices, especially the multifunction smartphone, soon became a second vital device in the digital reporter's toolkit. Some organizations are experimenting with far more radical digital innovation. Pew reports that as of 2013, "a growing list of media outlets, such as *Forbes* magazine, use technology by a company called Narrative Science to produce content by way of algorithm [computer], no human reporting [writing] necessary."[18]

At present, however, journalists confront a more pressing threat than the computer algorithm. The increased power of human audience members to communicate with journalists and with one another in a public forum, whether as citizen-journalists or simply as participants on a blog, is undermining the journalist's traditional role of authority and gatekeeper. Now online readers can point out, quite publicly, when a journalist errs. And although some news sites such as NPR have blocked discussions because of offensive user comments, many organizations have found that if they do not provide a discussion forum, readers will simply go elsewhere to discuss stories.

As Table 8-1 illustrates, four of the top ten global news sites in May 2017 were based on print publications and three on television news networks or partnerships. Three originated online: *Google News* and *Yahoo! News* are essentially news aggregators, publishing stories composed by other outlets. *The Huffington Post* has developed acclaimed original reporting. The large online audience for news, although a good thing, presents challenges for the news industry in the form of increased competition and decreased advertising revenues.

Digital platforms such as tablets and smartphones are also breathing new life into long-form journalism and nonfiction storytelling. *The Atavist* app featured original text and multimedia nonfiction as well as award-winning magazine or book-length material from a variety of sources but was discontinued in 2015. Partners publishing via *the Atavist* included *The Wall Street Journal*; *The Paris Review*; and TED (Technology, Entertainment and Design), a not-for-profit organization that shares provocative ideas. In one such TED story, the nonfiction tale *The Sinking of the Bounty*, Matthew Shaer investigates the tragic sinking of the ship used in the 1962 movie *Mutiny on the Bounty*.

**TABLE 8-1** Top Global News Sites (May 2017)

| RANK | TITLE | UNIQUE VISITORS |
|------|-------|-----------------|
| 1 | YAHOO! NEWS | 175,000,000 |
| 2 | Google news | 150,000,000 |
| 3 | THE HUFFINGTON POST | 110,000,000 |
| 4 | CNN | 95,000,000 |
| 5 | The New York Times | 70,000,000 |
| 6 | FOX NEWS.com | 65,000,000 |
| 7 | NBC NEWS | 63,000,000 |
| 8 | Mail Online | 53,000,000 |
| 9 | The Washington Post | 47,000,000 |
| 10 | theguardian | 42,000,000 |

Source: eBizMBA, http://www.ebizmba.com/articles/news-websites

Advances in technology that have threatened traditional business models continue to change the role of digital news in overall patterns of media use. We can observe certain trends, however, that help us predict the future of online journalism in public news consumption.

## NONTRADITIONAL SOURCES

There are two types of nontraditional news sources: traditional outlets not typically viewed by the public and nonjournalism sites such as blogs and discussion groups. Reading an Indian newspaper online or viewing an Al Arabiya newscast to see how it covers a story exemplifies the former. The growth of the Internet and mobile media has made it substantially easier for the public to access these alternative news voices. Even looking at U.K. media coverage of international issues can often be a valuable and educational experience for Americans, especially English-only speakers, who often receive a fairly narrow range of international news. A high degree of media literacy is especially helpful when assessing news sources and potential biases of alternative media.

Social movements and activism inform the perspectives of certain Native American newspapers. *Akwesasne Notes* originated in 1968 partially in protest against a government-mandated toll on a bridge the Mohawks used to travel from one part of their reservationto another. The production of news in the United States in other languages, particularly Spanish, continues to flourish as the U.S. population becomes more diverse. American Spanish-language TV and online news media generally subscribe to the values and practices of mainstream English-language journalism but feature much greater international coverage.

Some news sources, such as *The Daily Show* and *Last Week Tonight with John Oliver* feature satire, typically of politics or of mainstream news media. Although the creators and hosts of these kinds of programs do not call themselves journalists, their viewers often admit getting much of their daily "news" from these enormously popular shows. Viewers, often young and highly educated, appreciate the less mainstream, commercial, and parochial mindset that characterizes these programs.

Nontraditional digital news sources increasingly view themselves as content providers unfettered by traditional publishers and gatekeepers. NBA.com, for example, publishes extensive news accompanied by video clips. Why would viewers go to CNN or ESPN when they can go straight to the source? Tweeting allows users to write and control their own personal narratives. Subscribing to an influential person's Twitter account or blog can also point people to news that they would otherwise not discover. Celebrity (or presidential) tweets often become news stories themselves.

As personal control over one's own narrative increases, however, professional objectivity and critical evaluation tend to decrease. You are unlikely to find, for example, an exposé on NBA.com about the league's financial wrongdoing. Still, NBA.com will meet the needs of people who do not care about such news and simply want basketball scores and information on the latest trades.

## ONLINE USER HABITS

Online media use differs from traditional use in a number of ways. First, users are generally more active, visiting multiple websites for information. In addition, most prefer to skim material rather than read at length. Shorter attention spans mean greater competition to attract attention to a particular news story. Stories often feature less text and more interactive graphics or multimedia. Whereas top news sites might attract large numbers of viewers, these viewers don't stay for long. Viewers spend on average only eighteen minutes a month, about half a minute a day, on

*Yahoo! News*, for instance. NYTimes.com is a site considered especially "sticky" because paid subscriptions are generally required, and the quality of journalism is high. However, its visitors stay an average of only nineteen minutes a month, the equivalent of spending only thirty-five seconds a day with a paper for which you pay a daily newspaper subscription. USAToday.com keeps visitors an average of only nine minutes a month, twenty seconds a day. The stickiest site, CNN Digital Network, keeps its visitors thirty-five minutes a month, about a minute a day. Overall, these numbers suggest that the digital news experience may lack depth.

Readers accustomed to receiving regular news alerts via text and social media may visit a website or news app only when an alert pops up. This pattern fuels a 24/7 news cycle, forcing newspapers to publish frequent updates to keep up with the competition and capture at least a moment of a frenzied multitasker's attention. Digital tracking of developments throughout the day allows broadcasters to plan accordingly for evening newscasts that offer both fresh material to viewers who are already familiar with a story and sufficient background for those who are not.

Users who want not only essential facts but also context eagerly follow links accompanying stories to related stories or other websites. Story mentions and links on popular websites can end up generating massive volume that crashes a smaller news site's web server—the **Slashdot effect**, named for a frequent occurrence on this very popular technology news site. From a business standpoint, though, media organizations want visitors to remain on their site. This raises the question of what hyperlinks to provide and how to provide them so that users are encouraged to linger or to explore and return.

### Slashdot effect

When a smaller news site's web server crashes because of increased traffic after its mention on popular websites, named for a frequent occurrence on the very popular technology news site Slashdot.org.

## PERSONALIZATION

The Internet allows users to personalize content, ranging from news on local weather to favorite sports teams to stock portfolios. Personalization, an engaging feature unique to online or mobile media, is transforming the way journalists write or produce stories. For example, a standard version of a story can be enhanced with database information on a user's online behavior, location, or stated interests.

Personalization is not without its downside, however. Personalized versions of the news may omit other important information without even identifying such omissions or changes. Highly personalized "Daily Me" news digests may also narrow people's range of interests to such an extent that they have difficulty talking about other topics.

Mash-ups like this one signal an emerging form of media content blended from multiple images.

## CONTEXTUALIZATION

Users able to access a reporter's raw material will still want someone to provide necessary context and interpretation. They prefer not to read an entire political speech or government report, for instance, to determine what, if anything, is important. Although users, for example, may be able to find an interactive map indicating the frequency and type of crime in their neighborhood within the past year, most crime-mapping sites do not provide any context. Users will not learn from mapping sites whether crime rates are increasing or decreasing or what happened to people charged with those crimes. Ideally, a site could provide all this information, along with links to past news stories on specific crimes and other relevant information.

Mash-ups that combine geographic data overlaid with editorial content are becoming increasingly popular and easy to create. The real estate site Zillow, for example, lets users see house locations, estimated values, asking prices, and final selling prices.

## CONVERGENCE

Increasingly, video, audio, and interactive graphics supplement and enhance online text; similarly, text can enrich primarily video stories by providing greater depth and context and different access to information. Truly interactive multimedia experiences that allow the user to stop or replay segments at will, skip familiar information, and learn background information as needed clearly distinguish online journalism from print predecessors.

Technology has changed not only how news is produced and presented but how it is gathered. Digital and video cameras have made photography and videography much easier for journalists, so much so that a single reporter can easily video-record interviews or events for a multimedia news story. Voice of America radio journalists, having been trained in digital-video shooting and editing, can enhance their online stories with video. Other news organizations, such as the BBC, are training many of their journalists in video techniques. Convergence requires journalists to be competent, if not necessarily expert, with the range of tools in the digital toolkit.

### ETHICS IN MEDIA
# What Is "Fake News," Exactly?

The term "fake news" arose during the 2016 U.S. presidential election when it was discovered that individuals and groups were creating fictitious stories and feeding them into social media streams like Facebook, where users widely shared the stories, unaware of—or unconcerned with—their veracity.

One of the more egregious fake news stories—that Hillary Clinton was running a child prostitution ring out of a Washington, D.C., pizza parlor—led one man to drive to the parlor with a gun to stop it. The man was arrested after discharging the gun in the restaurant, and it was revealed that no such ring existed.

However, even long after the election, President Trump continues to mention "fake news" when he refers to the news media, especially when he rails against negative coverage of him or his policies.

Although the sources and causes of the term vary in these two examples, they both share an underlying, corrosive effect on public trust in the media that in the long term could be very problematic.

In the former case, with actual fake stories that may confirm certain readers' biases against people or parties, we see the effect when someone attempts to take matters into their own hands. In the latter case, Trump's spiteful dismissals of any information that does not conform to what he wants undermine the public's trust in the information it gets from the news media, which is already at historic lows in measures of trust by the public. This makes it easy for people to ignore news that does not conform to their

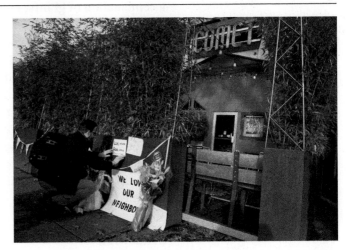

preconceived notions and discourages them from critically examining information.

Combating fake news in its various usages is a complex challenge. Facebook and sites like Google have taken steps to filter out fake news stories, or let users flag certain stories, so even if they are passed along, they carry a label that they are likely fake. Some say these steps are still not far enough, however.

Addressing the challenge of not allowing stories to be called "fake news" simply because one does not agree with them is much tougher. It will likely take work among journalists, educators, and librarians to better educate the public on how to read and think critically and to learn to better understand source material when consuming news and information.

# The Business of Journalism

The early years of the twenty-first century have been challenging for the media, particularly news organizations. Companies that predicted new business opportunities in convergence, such as the former AOL Time Warner or Bertelsmann, invested greatly in developing media services that never made a profit. Those that adopted a more cautious approach see even fewer reasons to invest in new media technologies. Nevertheless, even executives who have been burned say that they simply moved too quickly and that change will inevitably occur.

Advertising revenues have steadily declined for the past several years, profoundly so in print media; and, although growing, online advertising still comprises only a fraction of overall revenues. In 2008, the American Society of News Editors (ASNE) found that the newspaper industry had suffered its largest drop in thirty years, with a 4.4 percent workforce decrease from 2007. Jobs continue to be cut, although more recently at a reduced rate as some online-only and traditional publications have started hiring more people. Still, there are only about half as many journalists working today as there were in 1990.

The spread of the digital metered paywall as introduced by *The New York Times* in March 2011 signals a likely direction for the twenty-first-century business model, and there seems to be slow acceptance of paying for online content, at least for the most well-known papers. Some of the new news organizations such as ProPublica and the Texas Tribune adopt nonprofit models, in which they are funded by a combination of grants, member contributions, and subscriptions. Whether this model will work for smaller, regional publications remains to be seen.

Not only are layoffs common, but entire news bureaus are closing down. In 2000, Cox newspapers had thirty correspondents in Washington, D.C., to cover George W. Bush's presidential inauguration. In 2009, it closed its Washington bureau. Some news organizations have taken what are considered even more drastic steps. In 2009, the respected *Christian Science Monitor* and the 146-year-old *Seattle Post-Intelligencer*, a Hearst paper, opted for digital rather than print editions. A growing number of newspapers have reduced their print publication schedule to three times a week, publishing only digital news the remainder of the week. These trends will continue with newspapers, especially as tablet computers become more popular.

## SALARIES

Salaries for journalism professionals vary with the medium (television is the highest paid, print media the lowest, digital in between); location or market (the larger the market, the higher the pay); position (ownership, higher management, or celebrity status correlates positively with pay); experience; and a variety of other factors, including gender (men are generally paid more than women, as unfair as that may be). Because salaries and overall compensation vary so widely—from $15,000 a year to many millions of dollars—crude averages are relatively meaningless.

In general, network television offers the highest salaries for midlevel producers. National magazines and newspapers pay fairly well, whereas papers in mid- and small-sized markets pay poorly relative to similar-level jobs in public relations, for example. Internet media salaries are good, and stock option plans made a few journalists instant millionaires when the companies went public. Many more, however, missed that gravy train in the dot-com bust.

**FIGURE 8-1** Salary Range for Journalists by Experience

Less than a year    $18,000–$37,000

1–4 years    $20,000–$50,000

5–9 years    $23,000–$69,000

10–19 years    $28,000–$83,000

20 years and above    $35,000–$120,000

Source: Payscale.com

## DIVERSITY IN THE NEWSROOM

American newsrooms have been slow to change. In 1950, African American journalist Marvel Cooke (1903–2000) was hired as a reporter and feature writer for the *New York Daily Compass*. She was the only woman and the only black person on the paper's staff and among the first blacks to work for any white-owned daily newspaper.

The ASNE regularly conducts a survey on employment in U.S. daily newspapers. The numbers of minority and women hires have fallen short of mirroring the percentages found in the general population and fall shorter still when it comes to management. Because of layoffs and hiring freezes throughout the newspaper industry in recent years, the percentage of minority employees has actually risen slightly, to just over 13 percent. Industry watchers worry that the persistent dominance of white males in newsrooms skews news coverage toward material that appeals to them, content that does not reflect the communities of readers or viewers accurately. A 2012 *Extra!* study found that on the opinion pages of *The New York Times*, *The Washington Post*, and *The Wall Street Journal*, Latinos had less than 2 percent of the bylines. None of these papers even had a Latino staff columnist. In more than a year of political book reviews on C-SPAN or *The New York Times Book Review*, not one of the 432 authors, reviewers, or interviewers was Latino.[19]

Bob Butler, reporter at KCBS radio, was president of the National Association of Black Journalists, 2013–2015.

## MEDIA CAREERS

The employment outlook for journalists in the digital age is generally not good, largely a reflection of larger trends regarding the state of the overall economy and related budget and staff cutbacks. After a decade of strong employment and business growth, the twenty-first century got off to a troubled start that hit media and technology companies especially hard. Recently, there have been weakly positive signs, especially among some digital-only news organizations such as *BuzzFeed* and *Vox* that have been hiring.

Still, these are exciting times for journalists, especially those with an entrepreneurial and innovative spirit. Online and mobile journalism, still in their infancy, will play an increasingly prominent role, and possibilities remain for journalists in traditional print, radio, and television if they are willing to adopt new methods and approaches utilizing the digital tools available. Even in traditional newsrooms, journalists now need a wide variety of digital skills and a solid understanding of online and mobile media's unique characteristics. Today's journalists must be as comfortable telling a story through an interactive, multimedia graphic as they are through a traditional text narrative. They may not need the same depth of technical knowledge as programmers or web designers, but they need to be able to converse intelligently with them as stories are produced. In addition to strong writing and storytelling skills, contemporary journalists will benefit from knowing how to use spreadsheets, statistics, databases, code, algorithms, and social media to craft stories from complex raw information, such as Twitter feeds on breaking news events. People who show skills in one or more of these areas are much more marketable than those who know only how to write stories, for example.

No specific college major is necessarily best for journalists, although most have degrees in the humanities or social sciences or journalism itself. A double major in journalism and some other subject area of interest is a great advantage for journalists specializing in those fields. But regardless of undergraduate major, a focus on writing, editing, and storytelling is crucial for a successful career. Students working at a college newspaper or digital news operation have the opportunity to experience this profession firsthand and publish stories, accumulating valuable clips or reels that news organizations will expect job candidates to supply.

What is needed to be a good journalist is a high degree of curiosity, a willingness to engage with the world and with other people, and a passion for storytelling. Journalism is one of the professions in which almost every day one can encounter something completely different, making it an exciting career choice.

## LOOKING BACK AND MOVING FORWARD

Today's 24/7 news cycle and recent budget and staff cuts mean less time to polish the final product and increased dependence on other sources to provide news. Yet despite its various perceived weaknesses and evident challenges, news remains the bedrock of journalism in its mission not only to inform the public of significant events but also to provide important context that helps people better understand these events.

The Internet and digital media are transforming journalism, change that the profession initially resisted rather than embraced. Consequently, many news organizations, especially newspapers, have only recently begun trying to figure out ways to live in the digital world. As advertisers go elsewhere to find audiences, news media are left scrambling to stay afloat and adjust to new realities. Foremost among these is a shift toward audience participation, now considered crucial to the practice of journalism and key to a truly healthy democracy.

Despite all this turmoil, the employment picture for journalism graduates has brightened. Rapid industry change has created new jobs for candidates with "the right stuff" for the convergent newsroom, where professionals no longer declare themselves to be a either a print journalist or a broadcast journalist. The former may be expected to shoot or record multimedia with a digital-video camera or audio recorder. Similarly, the latter are being asked to write text stories to accompany video. The convergent journalist, although not an expert in every type of media, is comfortable with various technologies and with social media.

Although increasingly important, technical expertise alone does not guarantee a successful career. Internalizing and practicing the values of journalism, especially a commitment to truth, accuracy, and fairness, are still paramount. Quality writing and compelling storytelling, especially if enriched with multimedia content, are also essential. Whereas knowing how to use certain multimedia tools, such as basic image editing, is required, knowing which digital tool to use and when is even more important.

Journalism has always been fundamentally concerned with knowledge creation and management. Good reporters have extensive files of sources and contacts they can turn to when they need to know something quickly, and they have developed a sense for discerning good information from bad. In the world of convergent journalism, this ability becomes even more important. With the proliferation of potential sources for information, the public needs to hear trusted editorial voices that can identify and interpret who and what is reliable and significant and why. More than any other media professionals, journalists are equipped to serve this function, perhaps in closer collaboration with citizen-journalists or in new storytelling formats that invite audience participation.

## FURTHER READING

*The Elements of Journalism: What Newspeople Should Know and the Public Should Expect*, 3rd ed. Bill Kovach, Tom Rosenstiel (2014) Three Rivers Press.

*Slow News*. Peter Laufer (2011) Sironi Editore.

*News About News: American Journalism in Peril*. Leonard Downie Jr., Robert G. Kaiser (2002) Knopf.

*Breaking the News: How the Media Undermine American Democracy*. James Fallows (1997) Vintage.

*Custodians of Conscience*. Theodore Lewis Glasser (1998) Columbia University Press.

*Why Democracies Need an Unlovable Press*. Michael Schudson (2008) Polity.

*The Vanishing Newspaper: Saving Journalism in the Information Age*. Philip Meyer (2004) University of Missouri Press.

*The Death and Life of American Journalism: The Media Revolution That Will Begin the World Again*. Robert McChesney, John Nichols (2011) Nation Books.

*The Principles of Multimedia Journalism: Packaging Digital News*. Richard Koci Hernandez, Jeremy Rue (2015) Routledge.

*Feature and Narrative Storytelling for Multimedia Journalists*. Duy Linh Tu (2015) Focal Press.

*Out on the Wire: The Storytelling Secrets of the New Masters of Radio*. Jessica Abel (2015) Broadway Books.

*We the Media: Grassroots Journalism by the People, for the People*. Dan Gillmor (2006) O'Reilly Media.

*Signal: Understanding What Matters in a World of Noise*. Stephen Few (2015) Analytics Press.

*Losing the News: The Future of the News That Feeds Democracy*. Alex Jones (2011) Oxford University Press.

*Page One: Inside the New York Times and the Future of Journalism*. David Folkenflik (2011) Public Affairs.

*Literary Journalism*. Norm Sims, Mark Kramer (1995) Ballantine Books.

*Tell Me No Lies: Investigative Journalism That Changed the World*. John Pilger (2005) Thunder's Mouth Press.

*The News Sorority: Diane Sawyer, Katie Couric, Christiane Amanpour—and the (Ongoing, Imperfect, Complicated) Triumph of Women in TV News*. Sheila Weller (2014) Penguin Press.

*Fake News in Real Context*. Paul Levinson (2017) Connected Editions, Incorporated.

*Weaponized Lies: How to Think Critically in the Post-Truth Era*. Daniel Levitin (2017) Dutton.

# Public Relations
## BUILDING RELATIONSHIPS WITH STRATEGIC COMMUNICATIONS

Positioning a company, product, or person is a challenging core activity in public relations (PR); and when facing a crisis, the challenge becomes vastly more complex. Untoward events that swiftly sully a carefully cultivated image test the mettle of even the most seasoned and accomplished PR professionals. For high-profile figures, whose every move is scrutinized by fans and critics alike, damage control can prove especially problematic. And when the documented missteps of a politician, actor, or athlete surface in the media and go viral, as is so often the case in our digital age, a crisis can quickly escalate into a disaster whose effective management may offer the only hope for salvaging reputations and careers.

Enter—or, rather, exit—Ray Rice, from an Atlantic City elevator, dragging his apparently unconscious fiancée, Janelle Palmer, by her shoulders. Naturally, a witness recorded the horrific incident, and naturally, TMZ, a media outlet that traffics in Hollywood scandal and gossip, broke the news, complete with damning footage. As NFL training camps started in the summer of 2014, when conversation on sports and social media typically turns to early predictions about winners and losers, the spotlight shone brightly instead on the disgraced running back for the Baltimore Ravens and the disgraceful NFL reaction to a shocking video that provided seemingly incontrovertible evidence of abuse.

The initial NFL response appeared woefully insufficient, an assessment supported by a subsequent recording released in September (again by TMZ). The NFL commissioner claimed to have no prior knowledge of this second video that showed Rice knocking his fiancée unconscious in the elevator, and the leading rusher for the Ravens, who had initially only been suspended, was promptly fired.[1]

It was too little, too late, for most. The reputation of professional sports has long suffered for failing to satisfactorily address acts of domestic violence committed by its players. And the handling of the Ray Rice situation was no exception. The management of this crisis did not succeed in improving relations with a skeptical and outraged public, leaving the NFL with a metaphorical black eye.

### LEARNING OBJECTIVES

>> Describe the overview of strategic communications.

>> Explain the theoretical foundations of public relations.

>> Describe the purpose and form of public relations.

>> Outline the history and structure of the public relations industry.

>> Identify various new types of PR strategies with digital media.

>> Examine the impact of digital technologies on public relations.

Antidomestic-violence activists felt compelled to take matters into their own hands, featuring a physical black eye to a powerful effect on social media in an effort to pressure NFL advertisers. Cover Girl had launched a "Get Your Game Face On" campaign portraying female fans sporting jerseys and makeup in the various team colors. A digitally doctored Ravens image dramatically transformed the model's look and the ad's message. Beneath the purple eye shadow appeared a huge reddish black eye, an image that quickly became a meme, often with the hashtag #Goodellmustgo.[2]

Cover Girl did not withdraw its NFL sponsorship, nor did NFL commissioner Roger Goodell resign. Nevertheless, this digital grassroots movement succeeded in increasing public awareness and meaningful dialog about domestic abuse.

Many diverse forces shape mass-communication media. Among the most important are advertising and public relations (PR), types of strategic communications linked by an emphasis on persuasion as well as a big-picture view informed by research. In this chapter, we examine strategic communications in general and the nature and history of public relations specifically, looking at how the PR industry is adapting to the age of social media and convergence.

PR has become increasingly important for all types of organizations and for famous individuals. Historically, many organizations have sought to influence media content and thus public opinion. Positive media coverage can increase knowledge of a company while enhancing its image and credibility. Contemporary public relations uses social media to engage the public or stakeholders in timely and interactive discourse in ways that were not possible in the mass-communication era.

> **📃 earned media**
>
> Favorable publicity—such as a news conference, an event, or a press release—prompted by a public relations source rather than advertising; the opposite of paid media, such as advertising or product placements.

Unlike advertisements, public relations material is not purchased content but rather **earned media**. A staged event or press release may become the basis of a news story. Awards ceremonies or news conferences, for example, suggest article ideas to journalists. Public relations professionals grant exclusive interviews with their clients and generate favorable publicity for clients, ensuring that any potentially damaging information is framed in the least harmful way. During crisis communications situations, such as the disastrous 2010 BP oil spill in the Gulf of Mexico, PR people work to mitigate negative press coverage.

News conferences or other scheduled PR announcements intended to attract favorable publicity are examples of earned media.

Most news media depend on the PR function of corporate, government, or not-for-profit organizations for information in various forms such as scheduled announcements, research studies or reports, corporate financial statements, interviews with executives and employees, and so forth. One measure of the effectiveness of PR is how many news outlets publish or air material based on what the organization has produced.

## Strategic Communications

Central to a range of fields, including advertising, PR, and internal or corporate communications, strategic communications aim to persuade an audience to think or behave as the communicator wishes. Part of what makes this task challenging is knowing which media channel will be most effective for delivering a particular message to a particular audience. Some companies, for example, have been heavily criticized in the media for delivering notices of layoffs via emails rather than face to face—or even worse, employees hearing about layoffs in the media before they are informed by management.

Research on persuasion has identified various types of appeals, ranging from presenting scientific evidence to celebrity endorsement to attractive colors in the company logo. Perhaps the most important factor in successful persuasion is the audience, or, more accurately, knowing and understanding the audience, what they think and feel, their likes and dislikes, and many other factors about them. A large direct-email campaign, for example, does little good if your audience communicates primarily through text messaging or Facebook. Of course, audiences are evolving. Digital, networked media increasingly enable the public to be active participants in a dialog rather than merely passive receivers of messages from large organizations.

Strategic communications attempt to persuade target audiences to act in a certain way. Perhaps you want them to change their behavior by quitting smoking or eating more healthfully. Or maybe you want them to donate to a cause, email their senator, vote for a political candidate, buy your product (or buy more of your product), or maybe just "Like" you on Facebook. What kind of message will most likely persuade people to take the desired action? Will a personalized message be most effective, or will an advertising campaign on TV or online be the best way to reach and convince them? How should the message be crafted, and what tone should it convey? Can it be done in such a way that encourages people to send the message to others in their social network?

These concerns apply equally to an executive proposing company expansion to the board of directors as to a company launching a new product or a not-for-profit seeking more volunteers or donors. In the next two chapters, we will focus on advertising and PR and leave internal corporate communications aside, but the principles are largely the same in terms of the need to know your audience and what will best influence them.

## PERSUASIVE COMMUNICATIONS

The most effective campaigns use persuasive techniques that encourage audiences to agree with the persuader's point in an apparently natural or commonsense way. Audience members may have started out thinking one thing before being exposed to the message, but afterward think differently, often feeling like they came to the conclusion themselves. Unlike coercion, in which people are forced to change because of a real or perceived threat, persuasion often involves people freely persuading themselves. We may think of persuasive communications as a modern phenomenon that developed along with the rise of mass communications. Its roots go back, however, to at least the time of the Greek philosophers and their study of **rhetoric**, the art of persuasion.

Rhetoric was one of the three classical areas of learning that any educated person should know, along with logic and grammar. The three pillars of rhetoric, audience, author, and text, as Figure 9-1 shows, are still useful concepts in crafting persuasive messages today. The text in this case does not necessarily mean a written text (although it can), but essentially any medium used to convey a message. In this sense, a "text" can be a movie, a podcast, a graphic image, or even the desk

**rhetoric**

One of the ancient arts of discourse that focuses on the art of persuasion.

FIGURE 9-1 The Rhetorical Triangle

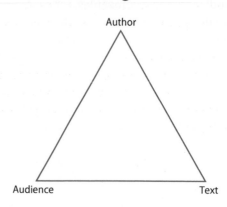

arrangement in a classroom. The author is the creator of the "text," while the audience is the recipient of the text.

> **DISCUSSION QUESTIONS:** Consider the layout of your classroom and positioning of students and the professor. What does this "text" say about each of your roles? About the assumed power structure? About the dissemination and reception of knowledge? In what ways does the classroom text persuade you, subtly and perhaps not so subtly?

Despite strong objections by the likes of Socrates, Plato, and Aristotle, who valued truth, the Sophists, a group of Greek philosophers focused entirely on rhetoric, taught whomever could pay them and saw the truth as largely unimportant, something even perhaps in the eye of the beholder—a surprisingly relativistic, "post-truth era" perspective. For Sophists, the most important aspect of an argument was whether it was persuasive. Despite his criticisms of rhetoric, Aristotle carefully analyzed it and his *On Rhetoric* remains a classic in the field. He discusses three modes of persuasion that still resonate today: logos, ethos, and pathos.

Logos, or an appeal to reason, emphasizes techniques that present careful factual arguments, using supporting evidence from credible sources to make one's case persuasive. Ethos, or appeal to ethics, focuses on techniques that show the speaker's credibility to the audience in order to make the speaker a trusted source of information. Pathos, or appeal to the heart, emphasizes emotional techniques to lower the audience's barriers to persuasion, drawing on emotions like sympathy or patriotism to persuade.

These modes are not mutually exclusive, of course, and skilled orators use these in most effective combinations to persuade their audiences. You can listen to any major political speech and see each of these techniques being used in varying ways.

Although many have argued that facts are more important than persuasion, one only has to look at recent political events to see that facts alone sometimes are not enough to change peoples' minds. Rhetoric remains a foundation of politics, business, and life. In an age when more people than ever can speak publicly, the ability to persuade and make your voice heard above other voices becomes even more vital.

At least two dozen major modern scientific theories of persuasive communication and audience decision making help explain or provide models of persuasion that guide the media campaigns of advertising and public relations. Most such theories include certain assumptions about how our thoughts and emotions affect our behavior. These can be broadly categorized as follows:

1. People's behavior and actions are somehow linked to their cognitions about the world, which generally include attitudes, beliefs, and values, as well as their general knowledge and social influences.

2. How people process information about the world (thinking deeply about issues or only looking at superficial cues) affects what messages they find most persuasive.

3. A persuader's credibility, authority, and attractiveness all can contribute to successful persuasion, although which is most effective depends on the type of message and audience.

A very popular theory about how persuasion works is known as the **elaboration likelihood model (ELM)**. In ELM, it is assumed that we process information, much like a computer, in one of two main ways, depending on a variety of factors, including our level of interest in the persuasive message, our general knowledge of the topic, among other factors.

One route is called central processing, in which we thoroughly examine all aspects of a persuasive message and carefully consider our options before deciding. The other route is known as peripheral processing, in which we do not devote a lot of mental energy to the persuasive message and let ourselves be guided by heuristic cues. Figure 9-2 shows how the ELM works.

Examples of heuristic cues are what we typically see in advertising with celebrity endorsements of products. Just because a movie star is driving a car does not mean the car is the best choice for us, and it has absolutely nothing to do with how the car runs, its safety record or gas mileage, and so on. A central processor would consider all the facts about a potential car before deciding whether to buy it or not, while a heuristic processor may base at least part of his decision on a heuristic cue like the color of the car.

One theory of note takes a different viewpoint than ELM. The **theory of cognitive dissonance** claims that we act first and then rationalize or create reasons for our behavior afterward to make our actions consistent with self-perceived notions of who we are. This theory helps explain a range of otherwise puzzling behaviors, such as why freshmen subject themselves to humiliating hazing rituals to join a fraternity or sorority to which they become intensely loyal.

## THE ROLE OF MEDIA IN PERSUASION

Because people can experience only so many things directly, media are the obvious means by which the public becomes aware of a product or an issue. Getting an advertisement on national television seen by millions simultaneously may have

**elaboration likelihood model (ELM)**

A theory of persuasion that says we process persuasive messages either through a central route or a peripheral route, depending on a range of factors.

**theory of cognitive dissonance**

Theory of persuasion that states we act first and then rationalize our behavior afterward to make our actions consistent with self-perceived notions of who we are.

FIGURE 9-2 The Elaboration Likelihood Model (ELM)

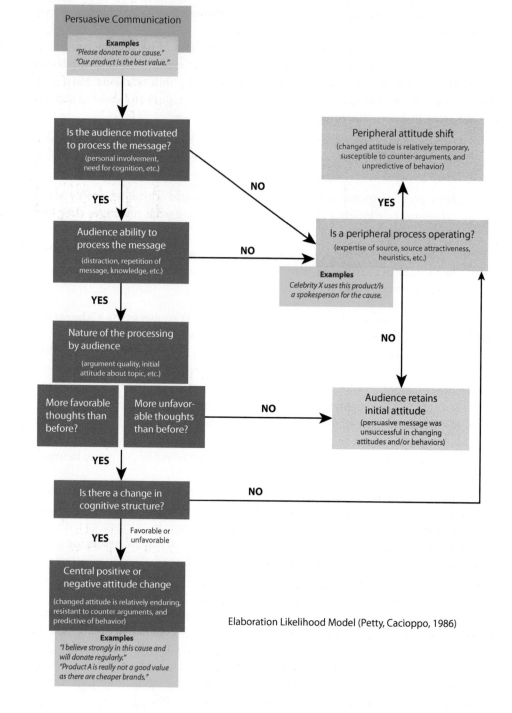

Elaboration Likelihood Model (Petty, Cacioppo, 1986)

a certain effect, but mere awareness is not enough. Too often, marketers assume that once people know about their merchandise or cause, they will want to buy it or participate. This is not the case. Awareness is only the first—and in many ways, the easiest—step in the process of persuasion.

Still, the media often have their own kind of credibility. An appearance on national television may confer on someone an air of authority as an expert, which may lead to further invitations to speak at other events or on other shows. You are more likely to watch a YouTube video recommended by a trusted friend than from someone you do not know. Similarly, research has shown that people are more likely to believe a news story they learned about from a friend than from a media organization. So effective are the media in creating and establishing fame that many celebrities are now known simply for being celebrities and not for being singers, actors, or another kind of talented performer.

Although the **direct effects model** of media influence has been largely disproved, we still believe that media can influence the public in certain ways. From this assumption, it follows that media-based communications campaigns can be strategically designed to produce the attitude and behavior shifts that persuaders desire.

Jade Goody used her fame as a reality TV star in the United Kingdom to publicize the need for women to test for cervical cancer, from which she eventually died.

**DISCUSSION QUESTIONS:** If you are a member of a fraternity or sorority, consider your initiation ritual. Did the ceremony or ritual make you feel more loyal to the group or less loyal? Why do you think that is so? If you live in a dorm or off campus, what are your thoughts on initiation ceremonies or rituals for the Greek system?

**direct effects model**

Model of mass communication that claims media have direct and measurable effects on audiences, such as encouraging them to buy products or to become violent.

## Public Relations

Public relations firms straddle the worlds of companies wishing to enhance their reputations or persuade the public of some message and of media organizations that can widely distribute company messages and publicity. Unlike advertisers, however, public relations agencies do not pay media companies to place content. Rather, these professionals attempt to persuade important gatekeepers, such as editors, journalists, or influential bloggers, that information about their client is sufficiently newsworthy to be published or broadcast.

Another main task of public relations is reputation management, which involves making sure that clients are always seen in the most advantageous light by the public. This raises an interesting question about what exactly "reputation" is, as a company may define its reputation one way while the public may have a very different opinion, especially if there has been a recent scandal about the company. The concept of "reputation" connects directly to the rhetorical triangle, in which the author (PR firm) attempts to create a text (an overall image of a company) through messages to the audience, or public, some of whom might have formed their own opinions about the company based on their interactions—and might have shared their views through social media.

Public relations firms are ideally positioned to understand some of the new interactive dynamics in today's world of social media. Increasingly, these firms, while seeking to mitigate negative news and promote positive information, help companies navigate social media and provide guidance on policies such as having a Facebook page, creating a YouTube channel, and talking with consumers on fan pages or Twitter. Some have dubbed this new, more interactive public relations PR 2.0.

To many journalists, PR is a necessary evil. To others, it's just plain evil. Nevertheless, journalists rely heavily on the information PR firms provide for stories. Public relations is a vital part of the three-way relationship among the media, organizations, and the public (which includes employees, consumers, shareholders, activists [who might oppose certain corporate policies], and regulators). Edward L. Bernays, the late father of modern public relations, used to say that propaganda was better than "impropaganda." The same might be said of public relations. It all depends on how it's done.

> **DISCUSSION QUESTIONS:** Consider the concept of reputation for companies. How would you define reputation, and how do you think it could be measured and given some sort of monetary value? Are there similarities between the concept of reputation for humans and for companies?

## THE HISTORICAL DEVELOPMENT OF PUBLIC RELATIONS

Modern public relations has evolved rapidly and in unique ways, informed by the rise of mass communications and technological advances. Some say PR is the world's second-oldest profession. But it was not recognized as a separate activity until the early twentieth century when a number of publishing activities began to be categorized discretely as either journalism or public relations. Thomas Paine's influential pro-Revolution pamphlets in the 1770s, such as *Common Sense*, and the sympathetic newspaper pieces on the Boston Massacre, for example, would be considered public relations or even propaganda by today's standards rather than journalism.

The first stage of public relations occurred during the nineteenth and early twentieth centuries. Getting publicity in the press (or other media) for a client was a central practice in the age of **press agentry**. As newspapers developed into a form of mass communication, publicity as part of a news story meant increased exposure for a product or a company without needing to pay for an advertisement. Press agentry flourished as practiced by Phineas Taylor "P. T." Barnum, who entered the world of promotion, press manipulation, and show business in the 1830s, creating the famous American circus in 1870. A great showman, Barnum used various techniques to communicate with the public. His staged events, publicity stunts to attract attention, were particularly successful.

Although the term "public relations" had not yet been coined, former journalist Ivy Ledbetter Lee was perhaps its first true modern practitioner. (Muckraking journalist Upton Sinclair, author of *The Jungle*, called Lee "Poison Ivy.") A master of managing the press, Lee once observed, "Crowds are led by symbols and phrases." Many of his innovations became staples of modern public relations practice, including press conferences and newsreels, known today as video news releases (VNRs), video footage provided by PR firms for television stations to use in their news broadcasts.

One of Lee's most visible clients was John D. Rockefeller Sr., the founder of the Standard Oil Trust and the world's first billionaire, who managed his companies and employees ruthlessly, even by the standards of the day. After Rockefeller had the Colorado state militia put down a miners' strike, resulting in dozens of

💬 **press agentry**

Getting media attention for a client, often by creating outrageous stunts to attract journalists.

deaths, Lee produced reports stating that an overturned stove had started a house fire that killed dozens of women and children. Lee was also behind the photographs and newsreels of Rockefeller handing out dimes to poor children wherever he went. So legendary was his ability to manipulate the media that in the early 1930s, the Nazis hired Lee to present a more favorable face for the "New Germany" in the United States.[3]

Press agentry was known for special events and publicity stunts. In 1928, debutantes were invited to march in the Easter Parade in New York City holding their "torches of freedom"—that is, lit cigarettes. This performance was intended to attract media attention and build support for women smoking in public at a time when society frowned on it. The American Tobacco Company, manufacturer of Lucky Strike cigarettes, sponsored the event, created by a man many consider the founder of modern public relations, Edward L. Bernays.

Edward L. Bernays managed some of the earliest and most famous PR campaigns of the twentieth century. He trained during World War I as a member of the Foreign Press Bureau of the U.S. Committee on Public Information (CPI), essentially the propaganda arm of the U.S. government. Bernays often dined with his famous uncle, Sigmund Freud, whose theories he mastered and whose first English-language translations he produced. After the war, Bernays applied the principles of both Freudian psychology and social science, a then-budding field, to the strategic influence and shaping of public opinion. His book *The Engineering of*

General Tom Thumb achieved widespread fame as a performer with master showman P. T. Barnum.

---

## MEDIA PIONEERS
# Doris E. Fleischman

Much has been written about Edward L. Bernays, celebrated as the father of public relations in eulogies upon his death at the age of 103 in 1995. Much less, however, has been published about his wife, Doris E. Fleischman, despite her status as an equal partner in their storied PR firm, whose clients included President Calvin Coolidge, Procter & Gamble, General Electric, the U.S. War Department, the American Tobacco Company, and Sigmund Freud, Bernays's uncle. Although integral to their joint enterprise, her role was played largely behind the scenes, while her husband remained the face and principal name of the business, the man who worked in person with their clients, even on campaigns she had developed or press releases and speeches she had ghostwritten.

Whereas many of her pioneering PR achievements went unnoticed at the time, her earlier feminist activities did not, some even garnering widespread newspaper headlines. She and her husband were members of the Lucy Stone League, a civil rights organization founded in 1921 dedicated to promoting the legal use of a woman's maiden name, a radical initiative for the time. In September 1922, the newlyweds checked into their hotel as Bernays *and* Fleischman, a first for the Waldorf Astoria register.[4] Three years later, she became the first married woman ever issued a U.S. passport in her birth name.

Young Doris seemed poised to accomplish great things in an era that did not always encourage greatness from

women in the public sphere. She received a BA (1913) from Barnard College, where she won varsity letters in softball, basketball, and tennis while a member of Theta Sigma Phi, the national sorority of women in communications. She subsequently worked at the *New York Tribune* as a reporter and an editor for the women's pages and the Sunday edition. Among her more notable assignments were an interview with Theodore Roosevelt and—another first for a woman—covering a prizefight, albeit accompanied by her father, who feared for her safety. Her writings frequently considered the challenges women of her day faced in their domestic and professional lives, a balancing act also suggested by the title of her memoir, *A Wife Is Many Women*.

Her essay "Notes of a Retiring Feminist" implies that these tensions, acute for many early feminists, were never fully resolved: "Mrs. stands to the right of me, and Miss stands to the left. Me is a ghost ego nowhere in the middle." For pragmatic reasons later in life, Fleischman, weary of having to explain herself, increasingly adopted the use of Bernays.

*Consent,* a collection of essays by him and associates on the theory and practice of public relations, became a classic.

Arthur W. Page was the vice president of public relations for AT&T from 1927 to 1946, the first PR person on the board of a major public corporation. He also served on many boards of charities and other organizations. Page helped create ethical guidelines for public relations with his Page Principles, such as "Tell the truth," "Prove it with action," and "Listen to the customer." Today, the Arthur W. Page Society continues his work through various educational programs, networking events, forums for PR executives, and sponsored PR research initiatives.

## TRENDS IN THE DEVELOPMENT OF PUBLIC RELATIONS

One continuing trend as public relations has developed as a profession is establishing a dialog with the public, no longer considered a mute and passive mass audience. In the earliest forms of PR during much of the nineteenth century, communication was largely asymmetric, from the public relations agent through the media to the audience. Audience feedback was not sought. In the early twentieth century, a limited symmetric model of communications was espoused, with the public providing feedback on the efficacy of a campaign. Although this appeared superficially to be dialog, PR representatives still controlled the flow of communications.

> **two-way symmetric model**
>
> Model of public relations that emphasizes the profession as a system of managing relationships among organizations, individuals, and their many publics.

Many of the principles espoused by Page and since adopted by most firms belong to a **two-way symmetric model** of public relations, articulated by pioneering PR educator James E. Grunig. This model emphasizes public relations as a system of managing relationships among organizations and individuals and their many publics, internal and external. Mass communication and social media are key, and building mutual understanding and good relationships is emphasized as much as influencing public opinion.

Research shows that organizational excellence (as defined in terms of accomplishing both short- and long-term objectives) can be achieved with a two-way symmetric model that incorporates the public relations function into senior management and organizational decision making. The two-way symmetric model formally and informally assesses the attitudes, knowledge, behaviors, and intentions of various publics or stakeholders, and it also places a premium on the ethical practice of public relations.

One of the best examples remains Johnson & Johnson's handling of the infamous Tylenol tampering case in 1982, when seven people died of cyanide poisoning from tainted Extra-Strength Tylenol capsules. After the first reported poisoning in the Chicago, Illinois, area, Johnson & Johnson took immediate steps to prevent further tragedy while maintaining clear and open lines of communication with both the media and the public. Along with its parent, McNeil Consumer Products Company, it offered a $100,000 reward for information leading to the arrest and conviction of the tamperer, established a hotline, and opened regional poison-control centers to dispense information and assistance.

After a nationwide recall of all Extra-Strength Tylenol capsules, at a cost of some $100 million to remove and destroy all thirty-one million bottles, in January 1983, the capsules were successfully reintroduced with a triple-sealed, tamper-resistant packaging warning. Johnson & Johnson and McNeil Consumer Products Co. were cleared of any legal liability, although in 1991, they provided the victims' families with an undisclosed settlement, estimated to be as much as $50 million.

Despite the tragedy, Tylenol sales recovered. Journalists often criticize companies in crisis for hiding information from the press and the public, but Johnson &

Johnson was praised for its open and immediate responses. "The public relations people were knowledgeable and available when the media needed to talk to them," said John O'Brien of the *Chicago Tribune*. "They didn't try to sugar-coat anything."

Citizens have been empowered to engage in two-way or multidirectional communication with organizations and their stakeholders, and social media such as Twitter, Facebook, and the blogosphere have nurtured a more organic form of participatory public relations. Launched in 2000, the American Legacy Foundation's national "Truth" campaign engages the public in an antismoking dialog with edgy mass media messages and social media such as Facebook, Twitter, and YouTube.[5] One study found that smoking rates among teens in Florida dropped significantly as a result of the Truth campaign, with only 6.6 percent of Florida teens reporting smoking in the previous thirty days as compared to the national average of 14.4 percent.[6]

> **DISCUSSION QUESTIONS:** If you were running a PR firm, would you accept a company that makes harmful products, such as tobacco, as a client? What about a political group known for its extreme views? Explain your decisions.

## PR AND MEDIA RELATIONS

Although public relations professionals engage in a wide range of activities, they typically devote most of their time engaging with media professionals, including journalists, producers, and others responsible for content. Developing and maintaining these working relationships increase the possibility of obtaining fair or positive coverage of their organizations. When a negative story does occur, the PR professional should be able to communicate clearly and responsibly with media personnel, and several important tools in the PR toolbox aid in the pursuit of desired media coverage.

### Pseudo-Events

One of the most enduring legacies from the early days of modern public relations is the pseudo-event, manufactured by individuals or organizations to capture the attention of the media and consequently the public. Press conferences, protests, parades, and even award ceremonies are all pseudo-events, arguably forms of media manipulation on which the media have become dependent. In fact, as much as 75 percent of news content in even the nation's best newspapers, such as *The Washington Post*, is in some way influenced by pseudo-events. Only occasionally is a story generated through pure enterprise or original reporting without public relations influence.[7]

### Distributing News to the Media in the Digital Age

An important development in media relations is the distribution of corporate or other organizational news, information, and data (whether statistical or multimedia, including audio and video) through news releases or press releases. Formerly typed stories sent through the mail, these are now primarily emailed or posted directly to the web.

Given that influential bloggers and others using social media may be as important as professional journalists in terms of reaching audiences, a press release at times is not even needed. Rather, a well-placed **pitch**, a request to review a client's

"The Donald" first announced that he might run for president in 1988, a possibility he tantalized the press with again in the 2000, 2004, 2008, and 2012 election cycles. "The only one who can make America truly great again" (his words), he finally made it official in 2016, and even his earlier pseudo-events succeeded in making national and international headlines.

💬 **pitch**

Request to review a client's new product or do a story about the client or the product.

## CONVERGENCE CULTURE
# HARD LANDING

The first half of 2017 was not a good period for many U.S. airlines, with a variety of embarrassing incidents having to do with passengers and either airline personnel or airport security.

Perhaps the most notorious, and the incident that seemed to start it all off, was video of an Asian-American passenger being dragged out of his seat and down the aisle by airline security for refusing to give up his seat to another passenger.

The scuffle, captured on numerous mobile phones by fellow passengers, quickly became an Internet sensation—and a major public relations crisis for United Airlines, which just a few years earlier had suffered a setback with the popular "United Breaks Guitars" YouTube video.

But the video of Dr. David Dao being dragged off the plane had no cute music accompaniment, only his tortured cries and screams as security pulled him down the aisle.

United had overbooked the flight, a common practice among airlines, and needed to make space for four crew members. But nobody volunteered, so they randomly chose four passengers to deplane in exchange for an $800 voucher. Dao was one of the people chosen, but he refused to give up his seat because he was heading home to Kentucky after vacationing with his wife, also a doctor.

The issue occurred amidst a time of long-term belt-tightening and reduced services in the airline industry as a whole, and was quickly followed in the news by others complaining of related mistreatment by the airlines and airline employees.

For a competitive industry like the airline business, the image of a customer being dragged off a plane to open a seat for a crew member is not something that engenders goodwill among the public. This incident serves as a reminder of the adage that in today's world "every company is a media company"—even when it doesn't really want to be.

new product, may be enough to get people writing about it and then get mainstream media attention.

### Finding Sources Online

Similar to classified advertising, expert-source clearinghouses that have enhanced the media–PR relationship over the years continue to thrive on the web, which allows highly efficient targeting of communications and searching. *The Yearbook of Experts, Authorities & Spokespersons* is now available online, greatly facilitating, especially when on deadline, such identifications. Perhaps the largest of these clearinghouses is ProfNet, an online service that connects more than fourteen thousand news and information officers at colleges and universities, businesses, research centers, medical centers, not-for-profits, and public relations agencies with journalists and bloggers around the world.

## PR FIRMS AND THE PR INDUSTRY

Press kits have transitioned from analog to digital multimedia, enabling journalists, bloggers, and other content creators to tell stories interactively.

Like other American industries, the business of public relations is tied to the general economy. Financial difficulties have caused companies to cut back on advertising and PR, even though this is arguably when they most need such services. In public relations, revenues are based on a combination of sources: primarily fees for consulting and services; income from specialized communications services such as research, interactive communications, and employee communications; and markups for production services and other media materials. Despite difficult economic situations at times, most organizations realize the need for good public relations, seeing the value in it especially when there may be bad news to deliver.

In the 1990s, public relations firms consolidated, but acquisition slowed considerably in the early years of the twenty-first century. Most acquisitions still occurred internationally among European holding companies such as Incepta Group, Havas, Publicis Groupe, and Cordiant. Omnicom is the one major U.S. communications firm that acquired several technology firms for its subsidiary Fleishman-Hillard.

Although most organizations of any size maintain their own internal PR units, many hire firms to aid their efforts with more specialized services. Media relations during campaigns or crises can be extremely complex, requiring extensive experience with local, national, and global media. PR firms are organized into three main areas:

1. *Core practice areas*: stakeholder relationships the client needs managed, including marketing communications or consumer relations; investor relations; public, not-for-profit, and governmental affairs; corporate and employee communications; political communications; and community relations

2. *Services*: activities the firm provides for clients, including media relations, research, interactive or online communications, writing, lobbying, fundraising, and crisis management

3. *Industries*: business sectors within which the clients operate, including utilities, technology, retail, manufacturing, health care, financial services, and consumer products

Many firms specialize in one or more core practice areas, services, or industries. This enables them to focus resources yet achieve sufficient expertise to serve clients operating on a national or global scale. Most of the larger PR firms offer integrated communication programs (sometimes called integrated marketing communications), a comprehensive set of communication management services, including both public relations and advertising activities.

Table 9-1 provides data on the top five independent U.S. public relations firms according to total worldwide revenues for 2017. Some of the PR firms that are part of the larger agencies include WPP's Hill & Knowlton (approximately $384

**TABLE 9-1** Top Five Independent Public Relations Firms

| FIRM | HEADQUARTERS | NUMBER OF EMPLOYEES | 2016 NET FEES | % CHANGE FROM 2015 |
|---|---|---|---|---|
| Edelman | New York, NY | 5,903 | $874,968,000 | +2.4 |
| W2O Group | San Francisco, CA | 472 | $122,715,000 | +33.0 |
| APCO | Washington, DC | 672 | $120,622,100 | +1.0 |
| Finn Partners | New York, NY | 485 | $76,706,000 | +7.3 |
| ICR | New York, NY | 158 | 55,663,450 | -1.0 |

Source: O'Dwyer's PR Firms Database, 2017, accessed May 29, 2017, http://www.odwyerpr.com/pr_firm_rankings/independents.htm. Used with permission of Jack O'Dwyer, Publisher, O'Dwyer Co.

million) and Omnicom Group's Fleishman Hillard (approximately $605 million), Ketchum (approximately $505 million), and Porter Novelli (approximately $126 million).[8] These PR agencies are all bigger than any of the independent PR firms except for Edelman. Founded in 1952 by former journalist Daniel Edelman, his firm, now run by his son Richard, has nearly six thousand employees in sixty-five cities.

## Changing Trends in PR

Clearly, the professional divisions between advertising and PR are blurring. In the analog age, PR practitioners, unconcerned with brand strategy or other aspects of advertising, dealt primarily with media relations. But today, PR and advertising professionals have to know what the other is doing to maximize the effectiveness of campaigns.

**Integrated communications** involve determining the best ways to manage a brand's image across media channels while learning what the public is saying about the brand through blogs, websites, and other social media, called *social media listening*. Advertising agencies are acknowledging what public relations professionals have long known—a company cannot send a message without considering

> 💬 **integrated communications**
>
> All channels of communication about a company or brand working together to create a cohesive message.

---

### ETHICS IN MEDIA
# Fooling Most of the People Most of the Time . . . Digitally

Online shoppers increasingly rely on customer reviews on websites such as Amazon, Yelp, and TripAdvisor for information about new books, hotels, restaurants, and much more. But how trustworthy are these sources of information? Increasing evidence suggests that many people writing these reviews are in fact paid $5 to $10 to write favorable appraisals by the companies and products being evaluated.[9] Following are two reviews from a Cornell study designed to help ferret out fabricated reviews from honest ones. One is genuine, the other fake. Can you tell which is which?

1. I have stayed at many hotels traveling for both business and pleasure, and I can honestly say that The James is tops. The service at the hotel is first class. The rooms are modern and very comfortable. The location is perfect, within walking distance to all of the great sights and restaurants. Highly recommend to both business travelers and couples.

2. My husband and I stayed at the James Chicago Hotel for our anniversary. This place is fantastic! We knew as soon as we arrived we made the right choice! The rooms

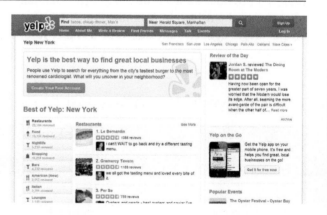

are BEAUTIFUL and the staff very attentive and wonderful!! The area of the hotel is great, since I love to shop—I couldn't ask for more!! We will definitely be back to Chicago and we will for sure be back to the James Chicago.[10]

Don't feel bad if you couldn't tell the real review from the fake one; neither could most people in the study. (Review #2 is the phony one.)

audience response and what it may mean for a company's reputation. Similarly, public relations professionals are understanding that a company or brand exists within a network of relationships and that thinking on a larger, strategic level can help them integrate their messages better to various stakeholders.

Companies are learning—sometimes the hard way—that the online public demands more transparency. Attempts at deception in any manner will likely elicit a strong backlash that will hurt the brand or company. More equitable, symmetrical dialog is occurring as companies learn to talk with their clients or publics through forums, blogs, and social media, a shift from "controlling the message" to "guiding the conversation."

**FIGURE 9-3** Salaries for Corporate PR Specialists by Experience

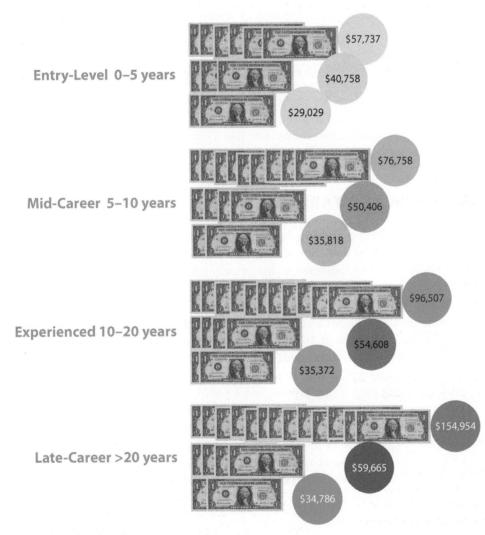

Entry-Level 0–5 years
$57,737
$40,758
$29,029

Mid-Career 5–10 years
$76,758
$50,406
$35,818

Experienced 10–20 years
$96,507
$54,608
$35,372

Late-Career >20 years
$154,954
$59,665
$34,786

## MEDIA CAREERS

A wide variety of interesting and increasingly overlapping jobs exist in PR. The trends in media production and consumption tend to favor strategic communications over fields like journalism (which has seen drastic cuts throughout the industry), and the salaries are generally better than in journalism.

Young people often find rewarding careers in a number of areas in PR, ranging from the creative side to account management to audience research. Larger firms allow greater scope for changing career tracks and industry clients.

Social media are creating new job opportunities in PR firms as well as in large companies with internal marketing or PR departments. Keeping track of what is being said about a company and reaching influential members of the audience through social media are increasingly vital. More importantly, knowing what tool to use when—such as why a company or client should use (or not use) a particular social media tool like Instagram or Twitter—is a skill companies are actively seeking.

The not-for-profit sector should not be ignored when considering a job in public relations. Although salaries are generally lower than in corporations, not-for-profit foundations, charities, and research institutes need the skills of strategic communications just as much as for-profit companies, if not more so. The not-for-profit sector is often particularly focused on issues of social responsibility and benefit, although most corporate PR efforts maintain a commitment in this regard as well, especially those practicing symmetrical public relations.

## LOOKING BACK AND MOVING FORWARD

Underlying advertising and PR, both forms of strategic communications, is the desire to persuade an audience to change an attitude or belief or to take some action. Persuasive communication, historically called rhetoric, has long played a role in human affairs, and today dozens of theories attempt to explain how persuasion works.

Social media will continue to greatly affect strategic-communications professionals, who must keep in mind that transparency and engagement with their audiences will enhance their credibility. Monitoring online conversations about companies—and, more importantly, joining those conversations when appropriate—has become an imperative for public relations professionals.

One thing is increasingly clear: The democratization of media and the capacity for more people than ever before to create and distribute messages make it in some ways harder than ever to be heard. Knowing how to speak clearly above the digital din, how to persuade, how to craft powerful messages, and how to understand audiences are all requisite skills in today's public relations.

## FURTHER READING

*The Skinny on the Art of Persuasion: How to Move Minds*. Jim Randel (2010) Rand Media.

*Thank You for Arguing: What Aristotle, Lincoln, and Homer Simpson Can Teach Us About the Art of Persuasion*. Jay Heinrichs (2007) Three Rivers Press.

*Persuasion: Theory and Research*, 3rd ed. Daniel O'Keefe (2015) Sage.

*Influence: Science and Practice,* 5th ed. Robert Cialdini (2008) Allyn & Bacon.

*Persuasion: Social Influence and Compliance Gaining,* 5th ed. Robert H. Gass & John S. Seiter (2013) Routledge.

*The Conquest of Cool: Business Culture, Counterculture, and the Rise of Hip Consumerism.* Thomas Frank (1998) University of Chicago Press.

*PR! A Social History of Spin.* Stuart Ewen (1996) Basic Books.

*The Father of Spin: Edward L. Bernays and the Birth of Public Relations.* Larry Tye (2002) Holt.

*Spin Sucks: Communication and Reputation Management in the Digital Age.* Gini Dietrich (2014) Que.

*Pitch Perfect: How to Say It Right the First Time, Every Time.* Bill McGowan (2014) HarperBusiness.

*The Media Training Bible: 101 Things You Absolutely, Positively Need to Know Before Your Next Interview.* Brad Phillips (2012) Speakgood Press.

*The Art of Social Media: Power Tips for Power Users.* Guy Kawasaki, Peg Fitzpatrick (2014) Portfolio.

*Social Media: Usage and Impact.* Hana S. Noor Al-Deen, John Allen Hendricks (eds.) (2012) Lexington Books.

*Social Media: Dominating Strategies for Social Media Marketing with Twitter, Facebook, YouTube, LinkedIn and Instagram.* Michael Richards (2015) CreateSpace Independent Publishing Platform.

# Advertising
## THE POWER OF PERSUASION

"BOMBSHELL: Trump and Putin Spotted at Swiss Resort Prior to Election"
"LEAKED: Lady Gaga Halftime Performance to Feature Muslim Tribute"
These were just two of the fake news headlines that went viral in early 2017 amidst a politically turbulent and uncertain time in the United States as Donald Trump took office. Like many fake news stories, they had the look and feel of articles from legitimate news sites with names like the *Salt Lake City Guardian*, the *Houston Dispatch*, and the *NY Morning Post*. The only problem is these news organizations do not exist. Nevertheless, some partisan sites picked up the stories, helping them spread further on social media.

What made these and other fake news stories stand out in a political season of plenty of fake news was that they turned out to be promotions for the thriller *A Cure for Wellness*, a movie about a "fake" cure that actually makes people sicker.

The articles included advertisements promoting the movie and other promotional materials in stories about things like abortion that related to the movie. Twentieth Century Fox and Regency Enterprises even created a fake health website, healthandwellness.co, along with a fake bottled water company, to help promote the film.[1]

When BuzzFeed reported on the promotional campaign, the backlash was swift and harsh, denouncing Fox and Regency for contributing further to the distrust and skepticism many citizens feel toward the media. At first, Regency tried to defend the advertising campaign, saying that it showed parallels to the film's theme regarding fake information, but the media was having none of it. Fox and Regency took down the sites within a couple days and apologized for the campaign.

Neither their misguided fake news campaign nor the outrage over it could resuscitate *A Cure for Wellness,* however. It received mostly negative reviews and brought in a sickly $4.3 million during its opening weekend and a total of $26 million worldwide, far below its $40 million production cost.[2]

**LEARNING OBJECTIVES**

>> Explain the theoretical foundations of advertising.

>> Describe the purpose and form of advertising.

>> Outline the history and structure of the advertising industry.

>> Identify various new types of advertising strategies with digital media.

>> Examine the impact of digital technologies on advertising.

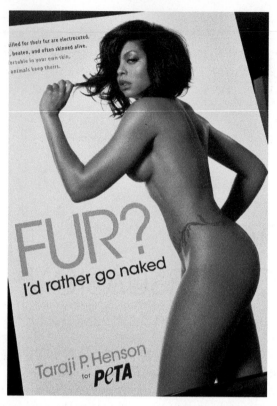

Advertisers carefully consider a range of factors to make ads as persuasive as possible.

The widespread exposure and repetition of television advertisements have made it so many children remember advertising jingles and catchphrases better than basic facts about U.S. government or history.

The U.S. television industry holds its annual TV upfronts in May, when the industry pitches upcoming new shows to advertisers.

Advertising has traditionally been the method by which companies or stores reach a mass audience, utilizing the distribution system newspapers or electronic media outlets have created.

In a digital, networked world, however, almost anyone can distribute information cheaply. It would seem that companies could now eliminate advertising costs by contacting audiences directly. Although true to some extent, especially with the rise in social media, the practice is less prevalent than one would think. One reason is that people generally do not like getting messages from companies, especially through social media, which is often seen as a social and non-commercial space (even though it is not). Another reason is that companies may have expertise in their fields, but they do not always understand how best to persuade their target audiences or how best to produce media content, or have the resources to be able to plan and create sophisticated advertising campaigns. The expertise of strategic-communications professionals is often needed to reach audiences with powerful, persuasive messages and to create an enduring brand or company image.

Advertising, the most ubiquitous form of media content, is paid for by a for-profit or not-for-profit organization, a political campaign, or a wealthy individual. Advertisements provide much of the basic financial revenue that pays for the creation and delivery of media content, whether in print, on broadcast radio or television, on billboards, online, or via mobile devices. Two-thirds of most newspapers and magazines are filled with advertisements (not including ad inserts). Even though most television programming time is devoted to content rather than commercials, consider the number of times the audience sees the same commercial during the course of a program, what advertising media planners call "frequency of exposure." Studies have shown that children tend to remember commercial jingles and catchphrases better than basic facts about U.S. government or history.[3]

Like PR, advertising relies on principles and theories of persuasive communications and the media to have its desired effects in changing behaviors. Although we typically think of advertising as trying to sell us products, it is also used to sell political candidates, ideas, and behavior changes (e.g., cause marketing campaigns to prevent crime or health communications campaigns targeting risky behaviors).

> **DISCUSSION QUESTIONS:** Do you think your behavior has been affected by advertising in any way? If so, how? For example, have you seen a sign for a fast food restaurant and then the jingle enters your head? Did you suddenly decide you were hungry and stop there to eat? How might advertising have affected those decisions? How might advertising have affected your choice of which university or college to attend?

# Advertising

**Advertising** is an ancient form of human communication, with advertisements in papyrus being found in ancient Egyptian, Greek, and Roman ruins. Even earlier, China used audio advertising, with bamboo flute players playing tunes to advertise certain shops. This shows how thousands of years ago people understood the power of a catchy tune that helps us identify the tune with the product being advertised.

Print and electronic media in the latter nineteenth and twentieth centuries that developed their businesses around this advertising model are in the business of selling mass audiences to advertisers. From an advertiser's perspective, the media exist primarily as the means to gather an audience. Communications professionals, while recognizing some truth in this view, would counter that media content must still be interesting, useful, or entertaining to attract an audience.

> **DISCUSSION QUESTIONS:** Some communications professionals say that content is king—that if you do not have good content, then audiences will not read the publication or view the show. State whether you agree with this view, and, if so, how do you explain the plethora of bad shows and entire channels such as Home Shopping Network devoted solely to advertising products? If content is not important, then why do advertisers need media organizations in the first place?

Media organizations determine how much they can charge advertisers for space in their print or digital publication or airtime on their station based on the number of audience members reached or delivered to the advertiser. In broadcasting, this number is the **rating**. In print and online media, it is the **CPM**, or **cost per thousand** audience members. The online model is still evolving, however; and CPM may include the cost per thousand page views or unique visitors to a site, a web page, or a mobile app. In **performance-based advertising**, also used online, advertisers pay only for results, such as actual click-throughs to the advertiser's site, rather than total page views. One of the largest areas of online advertising has become **search-engine marketing**, discussed in more detail later.

Advertising rates vary according to the size and quality of the target audience. In radio, for example, the most expensive time to purchase advertising is "a.m. and p.m. drive time" when audiences are at their peak as drivers commute to and from work. An advertiser for a youth-oriented product may choose to show its

**advertising**

An ancient form of human communication designed to inform or persuade members of the public about some product or service.

**rating**

Used in broadcast media to explain the number of households that watched a particular show.

**cost per thousand (CPM)**

Standard unit for measuring advertising rates for publications based on circulation.

**performance-based advertising**

Any form of online ad buying in which an advertiser pays for results rather than for the size of the publisher's audience or the CPM.

**search-engine marketing**

Paying for certain keywords to show up high in rankings in a search engine, such as Google or Bing.

commercial on prime-time MTV rather than a late-night network slot because, although smaller, the audience is a better fit for their product. A media outlet whose audience is upscale and has disposable income would generally be more appealing to an advertiser than an audience without much spending power.

## THE HISTORICAL DEVELOPMENT OF ADVERTISING

In its earliest form, advertising was conducted as face-to-face, word-of-mouth communication in which buyers and sellers negotiated and bartered for goods and services. However, it quickly became apparent that sellers could not always rely on face-to-face communication to sell the most goods, so in places like ancient Egypt, papyrus advertisements were posted in common, public areas. This practice continued in ancient Greece and Rome, where posted advertisements helped people connect on everything from lost-and-found to new services being offered. The printing press gave rise in the fifteenth century to advertising in mass-communication settings, usually in the form of posters, flyers, or broadsheets. Broadsheet advertisements were a popular technique to attract people to immigrate to the New World. Colonists in the eighteenth and nineteenth centuries could obtain all kinds of information, from where to buy groceries and patent medicines to when a ship was sailing.

By the mid-1800s, ads had become a mainstay for U.S. firms marketing products and services, designed to stand out more prominently from surrounding editorial content. Individuals also advertised their unique products and services, including illegal items such as contraceptives and abortions. One notable case was New York's Madame Restell, who performed abortions and offered contraceptives based on well-known folk remedies for forty years without any medical training. Dubbed "The Wickedest Woman in New York" by the popular press and even tourist guides, she nevertheless used advertisements in the *New York Herald* to try to defend her business and the assistance she gave women who had nowhere else to turn.[4]

Throughout the nineteenth and into the early twentieth centuries there were no standards in advertising, and medicine advertisers often made extravagant and untrue claims about a product's curative powers. Although some newspapers initially refused paid advertising, partly because of the seedy reputation of some advertisers hawking questionable products or services, all eventually accepted ads because it was the only way to lower their prices and subsidize greater numbers of copies in order to reach a much wider audience.

The early twentieth century saw the number of mass-produced and packaged goods expand, which created a greater need for companies to distinguish their products from one another. The automobile industry also began in the early twentieth century, and today it is the largest advertiser, followed by retail, business, and consumer services. Advertising for cigarettes and other tobacco products grew during the twentieth century as well, but not without criticism. In 1919, the magazine *Printer's Ink* warned against "an insidious campaign to create women smokers" in reaction to the portrayal of women smoking in cigarette ads.

### Advertising Agencies

Early advertisers bought newspaper space and targeted local audiences primarily. Not until the 1860s did ads appear in nationally distributed monthly magazines. Among the most successful early sellers of newspaper advertising space was Volney B. Palmer, who bought space in newspapers at a discounted rate and then sold that space to individual advertisers at a higher rate. At first, advertisers still had to create their own ads, but this later changed as agencies started creating ads for clients. Palmer created both the first advertising agency in 1841 and the

MEDIA PIONEERS

## MEDIA PIONEERS
# Madam C. J. Walker

Born on a Louisiana cotton plantation in 1867 to former slaves, Sara Breedlove became the first female African American self-made millionaire in the United States. At the time of her death in 1919, she was also the richest African American woman. She made her fortune creating and effectively promoting her own line of beauty and hair products for black women through her company, the Madam C. J. Walker Manufacturing Company, using the name by which she was known.

Walker's ads were distinctive and effective for several reasons, including their sensitive and attractive portrayals of black women, with Walker herself often serving as the model. At the time, most other ads targeting black women used whites to sell the products or featured unfavorable, stereotypical depictions of African Americans. Walker's ads encouraged sales of the product lines and invited readers to apply to be a local company representative, much like Avon today.

Madam Walker was not just a pioneer of advertising but also a champion of social causes. After the East St. Louis Race Riot of 1917, which resulted in the deaths of an estimated two hundred blacks, Walker joined in a national effort to pass legislation making lynching a federal crime. Walker was also a philanthropist and an inspiration to others, especially women. In one of her many lectures, she once said, "I want to say to every woman present, don't sit down and wait for the opportunities to come . . . you have to get up and make them."

---

long-standing business model for the industry, providing his advertising clients with circulation data and copies of the ads in addition to deducting an **ad-agency commission** from the advertising publication fee as compensation for his efforts.

When the penny press lowered the cost of purchasing a newspaper to a penny from six cents, advertising had to make up for the lost subscription revenues, and the advertising business grew quickly. By the 1860s, there were more than twenty advertising agencies in New York City. When N. W. Ayer & Son, founded in 1869, bought Palmer's firm, the trend toward consolidation began. Ayer built on Palmer's basic media-billing model, which charged clients a fee for placing ads in newspapers and magazines, and he established a standardized ad-agency commission: 15 percent of the total media billings. This agency also set the standard for creative services, with some of the most famous ad slogans of the twentieth century including

**ad-agency commission**

A percentage amount of the cost of an advertisement taken by the advertising agency that helped create and sell the ad.

the De Beers tagline "A diamond is forever"; AT&T's "Reach out and touch someone"; and Camel cigarettes' "I'd walk a mile for a Camel." In 2002, parent group Bcom3 reluctantly retired the venerable Ayer name.

The new electronic media in the twentieth century drew heavily on the resources of the advertising industry, which used radio and television effectively to promote a wide variety of products and services throughout the United States and internationally. Television quickly surpassed print media as the main vehicle for reaching a national advertising market. Online advertising is today the fastest-growing segment, second in volume only to combined cable and broadcast TV advertising. In 2013, for the first time ever, online advertising surpassed broadcast TV advertising. Mobile advertising and video continue to be large and show strong growth.

## Commercial Television

Because three of the four early TV networks were affiliated with radio networks, questions arose: not about whether to support television through advertising, as had been the case originally with radio, but about the best way to do it. Commercials quickly became a mainstay on television. The year 1948 established an early high-water mark for advertising, with 933 sponsors buying TV time. Considering the relatively small number of television sets sold at the time, this indicates how eager advertisers were to reach mass audiences in the new medium.

*Variety* reported in 1957 that during a typical week, viewers saw 420 commercials totaling five hours, eight minutes. In the early days of television, the names of advertisers, who often sponsored whole shows, were included as part of the title, such as *Texaco Star Theater*. The not-for-profit Television Bureau of Advertising, founded in 1953, responded to the emergence of television as the leading medium for advertising with a variety of tools and resources.

One of the most talented advertising professionals in the audiovisual realm was Tony Schwartz, who died in 2008 and whose career spanned most of the twentieth century. A master of implied messages, he became famous for "The Daisy Spot," a 1964 advertisement considered among the most powerful political ads ever aired.[5] It cleverly suggested that Republican presidential candidate Barry Goldwater would likely get the United States embroiled in a nuclear war.

Commercial developments continued to reshape the TV landscape. In the 1960s, ABC extended the station break between programs from thirty to forty seconds to increase profits, and other networks soon followed suit. Within a few years, standard commercial lengths reached one minute. By 1971, networks increased profits further by cutting the length from sixty seconds to thirty without reducing rates a corresponding 50 percent. Networks began the practice of advertising "piggybacking," running messages for two related products from one company in the same one-minute commercial. In 1969, New York's WOR-TV became the first station to air an **infomercial**, a thirty- or sixty-minute program of exclusively commercial content.

Also in 1969, the U.S. Supreme Court applied the **Fairness Doctrine** to cigarette advertising, giving antismoking groups equal airtime to reply to tobacco commercials. In 1970, a congressional ban on radio and TV cigarette advertising took effect, costing the broadcast business roughly $220 million in revenues (approximately $1.4 billion in 2017 dollars). The hard-liquor industry voluntarily banned TV advertising for sixty years, and initial attempts in the early 2000s to advertise hard liquor drew heated criticism. Despite public disapproval, advertising continued; and today, such commercials, often targeting an audience in their twenties or early thirties, can frequently be seen during prime time.

**infomercial**

Also called "paid programming," a thirty- or sixty-minute television show that advertises a product and that usually involves a celebrity spokesperson and customer testimonials.

**Fairness Doctrine**

Adopted by the FCC in 1949, it required broadcasters to seek out and present all sides of a controversial issue they were covering. It was discarded by the FCC in 1987.

Tony Schwartz created "The Daisy Spot," a TV commercial that aired only once as a paid spot but is considered by many the most influential commercial of all time.

## ETHICS IN MEDIA
# DOES MARKETING AFFECT WHAT DRUGS WE TAKE?

The United States is one of only three countries in the world—New Zealand and Brazil being the others—where pharmaceutical and medical device companies can advertise their drugs or devices to consumers through the mass media, known as direct-to-consumer (DTC) marketing.

DTC marketing is heavily regulated by the Food and Drug Administration (FDA), which is why prescription drug commercials include a long list of quickly spoken potential side effects.

DTC marketing is also controversial. Proponents say that it encourages consumers to learn more about various drugs on the market and to have informative conversations with their doctors about them or conditions they may have. Critics—including the American Medical Association, which called for a ban on DTC marketing in 2015—state that it encourages overprescribing certain drugs (because patients ask for them) and purchasing more expensive drugs. Some critics also argue that it helps promote a culture in which natural body changes, such as baldness, are being defined as "problems" or "illnesses" that need medical "cures."

Some research has shown that drugs that were advertised did have much higher prescription rates than non-advertised drugs, and other research shows a clear correlation between increased growth in spending on drug research and spending on marketing drugs.

The pharmaceutical industry is not the only one that has faced restrictions with marketing to consumers. Between 1908 and 1977, lawyers in the U.S. could not advertise in the media, as the American Bar Association believed it made lawyers look unprofessional. It took a Supreme Court case in 1977, *Bates v. State Bar of Arizona*, for the ban to be overturned.

The ethics of advertising various drugs in mass media brings into sharp focus the nexus of the role that media plays in our lives and how it can persuade. Although on the one hand consumers may be more informed about drugs on the market, on the other they also may not be considering the long-term consequences of taking these drugs, or may not even realize how they are being influenced in hidden ways.

## Internet

Although today we are accustomed to a range of advertisements on the web, the Internet began as a resolutely non-commercial space, created with taxpayers' money by engineers and computer scientists motivated more by its potential for expanding communication and knowledge than by profit. The first email marketing message, commonly called **spam**, after the processed meat (whose inspiration was a Monty Python sketch that uses the term), was sent on May 3, 1978, by DEC, a now-defunct computer maker to all of four hundred people on ARPANET, the precursor to the Internet. In 1994, immigration lawyers Canter and Siegel sent an email advertisement to over six thousand on Usenet. Prompting harsh backlash from the online community, this event is now widely held to be the start of the commercialization of the Internet, although seemingly quaint in comparison to the billions of spam messages sent worldwide today.

The first advertisements on the web appeared on *Hotwired* in 1994, the online version of *Wired* magazine. *Hotwired* offered space on the website to fourteen advertisers in the form of the now-familiar **banner ad**. However, because online connection speeds were slow in 1994, the ads could not be large graphics: They remained fairly small, with HTML text primarily. Today, increased bandwidth allows for multimedia ads, and advertisers are considering new types of advertising, including increased use of video, to further attract the consumer's attention.

## THE RISE OF BRANDING

**Branding**, a process intertwined with the growth of advertising, creates in the consumer's mind a clear identity for a particular company's product or trademark. Derived from the Old Norse word "brandr," branding means literally "to burn" and came to mean burning a mark or brand into a product.[6] Branding via advertising developed in the 1890s and early 1900s as companies sought to distinguish their products in an increasingly cluttered and competitive marketplace. With little differentiation among similar products in terms of what they provided or the ingredients they contained, the only way to appear different was to present a memorable brand, or identity, to consumers.

To establish a brand's uniqueness, a catchy slogan and distinctive visual identity are created and then advertised across multiple media, with frequent exposure to the desired audience segment or target group. Among the first to do this successfully was Campbell's Soup, which featured the artwork of Grace Weidersein in 1904 depicting the "Campbell's Kids," images that appear in its advertising to this day. Another highly successful campaign was launched in 1970 to promote Coca-Cola, whose "I'd Like to Teach the World to Sing" commercial became an instant hit. The popular song even sold a million records. Pepsi tried to re-create some of that magic in 2017 with a politically oriented ad that showed Kendall Jenner giving a can of Pepsi to a police officer during a protest. However, the ad was instantly attacked on social media for trivializing the Black Lives Matter movement and quickly pulled from the airwaves.

Brands are especially powerful tools to help distinguish among very similar competitors. Although Pepsi has traditionally lagged behind Coke in sales, in the 1970s, Pepsi's double-blind taste test (neither the tester nor the person running the test knew which was Coke or Pepsi) found, surprisingly, that more people preferred the taste of Pepsi over Coke if they did not know the brands. The subsequent advertising campaign touting this finding increased Pepsi's sales while Coke's sales declined.

**spam**

Unwanted mass emailing from advertisers.

**banner ad**

Original form of advertising on the web, it appears across the top of a website.

**branding**

Process of creating in the consumer's mind a clear identity for a particular company's product, logo, or trademark.

This prompted Coke in 1985 to introduce a new, sweeter formula—New Coke—which was soundly rejected by loyal Coke drinkers. Within three months, the company reintroduced and rebranded original Coke as Coca-Cola Classic, deciding to call the new formula Coke II. Ironically, after the reintroduction of the original Coke, sales outpaced both the new formula and Pepsi. By the mid-1980s, Coke II was sold only in the United States and Canada; and by 2002, it was discontinued entirely. The whole episode is considered a cautionary tale for marketers about branding and about fierce consumer loyalties that may not be apparent from typical market research.

Some products highlight their name to enhance brand recognition, whereas others are easily identified simply by their logo

So hugely successful are some advertising campaigns that their brand names become synonymous with the product itself. Many consumers consider "Kleenex" (introduced in 1924) simply the generic name for facial tissue and "Xerox" generic for photocopy, when in fact they are both company names. This can be both good and bad for the advertiser. Consumers with extremely high brand-name awareness who go shopping for a particular product whose name has come to represent generic alternatives may actually end up buying another brand.

Brands are almost always trademarked. Companies can sue for trademark infringement, claiming that the copycat brand is stealing business by confusing consumers and perhaps hurting the company's reputation with inferior products. Companies may protect their brands zealously, such as when Coca-Cola forced a small café in a remote town in Yunnan Province, China, to change its name from Coca-Cola Café. Companies also attempt to associate themselves with a more famous brand by using a similar logo, colors, or name, such as the cheap electronics maker Coby, whose font is similar to Sony's, and the Northeast-based, urban fast-food chain Kennedy Fried Chicken, with its red and white signage.

In 2017, the music festival Coachella sued the clothing retailer Urban Outfitters for trademark infringement, saying that Urban Outfitters offered lines of clothing using the Coachella name and competing against similar products offered by Coachella.

Protecting a brand is not only about enforcing intellectual property. As much as 70 percent of a company's value may be in its brand rather than in its physical property, such as factories and products. Table 10-1 shows the estimated brand valuation of some major companies. Note that Apple and Google have far bigger brand valuations than third-place Coca-Cola, with Google's brand valuation nearly double that of Coca-Cola's. Companies rise and fall in brand valuation: IBM dropped from fourth to sixth place in brand value since 2014's report. Although in fifteenth place, Facebook showed a remarkable 48 percent growth in brand valuation in 2016, while Amazon, ranked eighth, had 33 percent growth. "Buying the brand" can be a strong incentive in company mergers, and is often worth billions of dollars.

Branding is important to individuals as well, says personal-branding guru Dan Schawbel, author of *Me 2.0: Build a Powerful Brand to Achieve Career Success*. According to Schawbel and dozens of leading technology thinkers he has interviewed, creating a strong personal brand will help define and differentiate the new employee from the competition. Brands will become even more important in the digital age, especially in media industries.

Celebrities fiercely guard their brands, likenesses, and even their names from infringement by others. In 2008, Curtis Jackson—aka 50 Cent—sued Taco Bell for using his stage name, a registered trademark, to promote its value menu. In 2014, an Indiana corporation that owns the likeness rights and other intellectual property related to the James Dean estate sued Twitter for allowing a user to create the account @JamesDean without their permission. *Keeping Up with the Kardashians* sisters Kendall and Kylie have filed to protect "Kendall and Kylie," as well as "Kendall & Kylie."

**TABLE 10-1** Top Six U.S. Companies by Brand Valuations

| COMPANY | 2016 BRAND VALUE ($ MILLION) | CHANGE IN BRAND VALUATION OVER 2015 (%) |
|---|---|---|
| *(Apple)* | 178,119 | 5 |
| Google | 133,252 | 11 |
| Coca-Cola | 73,102 | –7 |
| Microsoft | 72,795 | 8 |
| Toyota | 53,580 | 9 |
| IBM | 52,500 | –19 |

Source: "Interbrand's Best Global Brands, 2016," *Interbrand*, 2016, accessed June 1, 2017, http://www.bestglobalbrands.com/2016/ranking/

**DISCUSSION QUESTIONS:** Consider both a familiar and an unfamiliar industry or category (e.g., cars, entertainment companies, airlines, hotels). Name three brands within each category. How did you become familiar with the brand, through direct use or only through advertising? Did advertising influence your decision to first use that brand?

## SELLING PRODUCTS, SELLING IDEAS

**social marketing**

Advertising and marketing techniques that persuade people to change bad or destructive behaviors or adopt good behaviors.

**public information campaign**

Media program funded by the government and designed to achieve some social goal.

**fear appeal**

Advertising technique that attempts to persuade the audience by scaring them, such as antismoking ads that show disfigured former smokers.

Advertising techniques such as branding can sell more than products or services; they can sell images, ideas, political candidates, or lifestyles. **Social marketing** applies the lessons learned from years of advertising activities and theories of persuasive communications to encourage the public to transform behaviors positively through **public information campaigns**.

Efforts to change attitudes can be an uphill battle, however. First, behaviors that social marketers seek to change, such as drinking or smoking, often involve powerful physical addictions or psychological perceptions (teens may think it's cool to drink or smoke). Second, determining which advertising channels and types of messages will be most effective for the targeted group can be difficult. Third, ethical questions sometimes arise when it comes to which group is deciding what exactly constitutes a "pro-social" message and why other groups may not be targeted. Finally, assessing the success of a social-marketing campaign is problematic, for its effects will generally not be immediately seen, and larger sociocultural forces may influence how the target audience interprets the message or may or may not change its behavior. For example, an antismoking public information campaign may have some effect on people's willingness to smoke, but if taxes on tobacco are also raised, then it becomes difficult to determine which led to a decrease in smoking.

Some social-marketing campaigns will use **fear appeals** to shock people into changing behavior. Television ads, for example, feature smokers who have had surgery for throat or mouth cancer or show graphic images of automobile accidents caused by drunk driving. Fear appeals can be tricky, however. Graphic images may offend some while not being effective for young people who think, "That will never happen to me."

CONVERGENCE CULTURE

## CONVERGENCE CULTURE
# Content Marketing: Blurring the Line Between Journalism and Advertising?

Advertisers have found with the rise of the Internet and social media that people are paying less and less attention to traditional marketing tactics. It has always been relatively easy for us to run to the kitchen during commercial breaks on television, and now it is even easier, metaphorically speaking, to do that with online ads.

Advertisers continue to play a cat-and-mouse game with technology as ad blockers and other techniques arise that let online users avoid advertising. Just as a new technology is unveiled to reach consumers in new ways, someone develops a way to avoid it.

Content marketing seems to promise a way around this dilemma, giving audiences what they want in terms of interesting content online while at the same time letting advertisers get their message to the public in sometimes subtle ways, such as content marketing.

According to the Content Marketing Institute, content marketing is defined as "a strategic marketing approach focused on creating and distributing valuable, relevant, and consistent content to attract and retain a clearly defined audience—and, ultimately, to drive profitable consumer interaction."[7]

Content marketing proponents emphasize the role of interesting and valuable content online as a way to drive users to a site. Many journalists are ideal content creators, as they have good storytelling skills, know how to do research, and create visually appealing graphics to go along with interactive stories. Given the dismal state of the news business in recent years, it may seem like a panacea for people who want to continue writing for a living.

However, critics of content marketing say that it may further erode trust in online content when users read something that turns out to be from an advertiser, who has a definite

message or point of view, even when it appears to be coming from a journalistic source. There are still no firm ethical guidelines for content marketing beyond such bland general statements to "be truthful" and "maintain responsibility and integrity."[8]

In general, content marketers do pay lip service at least to clearly marking when content has been sponsored by a company, although there have been cases, such as in the *Atlantic Monthly*, when a sponsored content article on the Church of Scientology created an uproar among its readers.

Even if content marketing content is written in a journalistic, fair, and balanced way, it raises a larger question about what types of stories will typically be covered by sponsoring companies. Will they be interested in supporting journalistic work that may cast them or their practices in a bad light? Will they sponsor content that has nothing to do with their business interests or marketing efforts? These and other questions have yet to be answered as content marketing evolves.

---

An effective social-marketing campaign for the National Crime Prevention Council used the tagline "Take a bite out of crime" and featured a cartoon dog, McGruff, dressed as a detective. A series of **public service announcements (PSAs)** covering a range of crime-related issues were widely aired on different media channels. Various surveys indicated widespread awareness of the campaign and its anticrime points by adults and children, accompanied by a rise in crime-prevention measures like special locks on doors and windows and security lights.

Today, a digital McGruff offers advice on an interactive website featuring online safety games and videos about how to use the Internet safely, and an app to help

**public service announcement (PSA)**

Advertising-like message from an organization with a worthy purpose that ostensibly benefits the public and for which the media donate time or space.

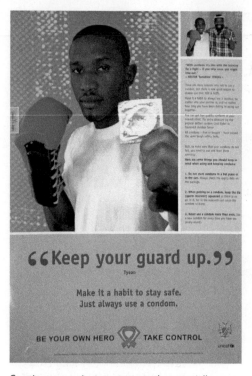

**"Keep your guard up."**
Tyson

Make it a habit to stay safe.
Just always use a condom.

BE YOUR OWN HERO    TAKE CONTROL

Creating persuasive messages can be especially difficult in countries with low literacy rates.

parents safeguard their children's Internet activity, including social media filters. Ironically, the actor who played McGruff the Crime Dog evidently did not learn much from his character. In 2014, he was sentenced to sixteen years in federal prison for drug and weapons charges. Nevertheless, the uncorrupted animated version of the crime-fighting canine, who celebrated his thirty-seventh birthday in 2017, lives on online.

Social-marketing campaigns play an important role in educating people in developed and developing countries about a range of issues to prevent disease and to raise the general standard of living, including safe sex and proper sanitizing techniques to ensure clean water and untainted food. Because of high illiteracy rates and limited access to mass media in some regions, such campaigns must use visual symbols in powerful yet easily understood ways.

## ADVERTISING CHANNELS

Advertising takes a variety of media formats or channels, including some important types that we may not normally consider mass communications. Each channel has certain characteristics that influence how advertising is implemented and how its effects are measured. The type of product or service being advertised helps determine which audience to target, and certain channels are more effective at reaching certain types of audiences. Here we will look at some of the traditional advertising channels, all of which are still in use, after which we will consider how online and digital advertising are changing these.

### Print Media

In newspapers and magazines, commercial messages come in either of two forms: **classified advertising** or **display advertising**. Classifieds appear together in a special section posted by individuals and organizations to sell specific goods or services. Because customers pay by the word or pay a rate up to a certain word limit, messages are usually short and use abbreviations. Despite their small individual size, their large numbers in most papers used to comprise a significant portion of advertising revenue. Most newspapers now put their classifieds online to compete with other online classifieds, auction sites, and discount sites such as Craigslist, eBay, Groupon, and Living Social—sites that have largely decimated the classified advertising revenues of most newspapers.

Display ads are much larger, anywhere from one-eighth of a page to a full page or occasionally foldouts with multiple pages. They often contain images or other graphic elements that help them stand out. Costs vary by size, color, and location (back-cover placement is usually the most expensive). Publishing companies create a **rate card** of the various costs, which may be negotiated by those who advertise multiple times in a highly competitive market. An **advertorial**, a display ad created to look like an actual article in the publication, usually has tiny print on the top or the bottom of the page that says "paid advertisement."

### Electronic Media

Despite decreased commercial time and fragmented audiences, advertising costs in electronic media, which can command larger audiences than print, are generally high compared to those for print media. Even large-circulation magazines of over

**classified advertising**

Advertising traditionally found in print media, especially newspapers but also in some magazines and now increasingly online, that consists of messages posted by individuals and organizations to sell specific goods or services.

**display advertising**

Advertising in print media that usually consists of illustrations or images and text that can occupy a small section of a page, a full page, or multiple pages.

**rate card**

List of advertising rates by size, placement, and other characteristics, such as whether ads are black and white or full color. Frequency discounts are also usually offered, and the listed rates are usually negotiable, especially for large advertisers.

a million readers reach a relatively small audience by network-television standards. Radio or television commercials, "spots," typically run for thirty seconds. Infomercials are paid programming in which a product is demonstrated and promoted for purchase, often with endorsements from a celebrity or satisfied consumers, who are typically paid or otherwise compensated. Pleased "customers" are often professional actors.

**Subliminal advertising**, a subject of controversy for some time, supposedly flashes messages or images briefly to produce an unconscious effect on the viewer. Despite no firm proof that subliminal advertising has any effect at all, it is illegal, and no advertisers have ever admitted to its use.

Another way advertisers attract attention is through **product placement**—products displayed or used by characters in television programs or movies. Product placement has become more important since the arrival of the digital video recorder (DVR), which allows viewers to skip commercials. Critics argue that most viewers do not notice that a product is being advertised, while proponents say this is exactly what makes it an effective technique. Perhaps the most famous case of successful product placement occurred with the blockbuster movie *E.T.* After M&M's refused to allow its famous candy product to be E.T.'s snack of choice, filmmakers opted for Reese's Pieces, a new candy whose sales shot up as the film became a global hit.

> **DISCUSSION QUESTIONS:** In the first report about subliminal advertising, a drive-in movie owner in New Jersey claimed that after flashing subliminal images of soft drinks and popcorn during a movie, sales increased. What other factors might explain the increase in sales?

### Outdoor

**Outdoor advertising** on billboards, taxis, buses, and bus stops, among other places, bombards the public. Store signs are among the oldest forms of public advertising, although their reach is limited to passersby. Even brand-name clothing effectively makes the wearer a walking advertisement—paid for by the consumer who purchased the clothing! Increasingly, municipalities are allowing corporate sponsorship of public vehicles and spaces to help shore up government budgets. Low-power video monitors with advertisements accompanied by news content appear in new public spaces, such as above cash registers and in elevators.

Interactive floor-based displays in airports or malls react to activities like footsteps, creating interesting games that people can play and others can watch—all the while engaging with an advertisement. Interactive outdoor advertising will continue to grow as technology such as face recognition is incorporated into street-level billboards, enabling the real-time display of messages customized to each passing pedestrian.

### Direct Mail

Direct mail marketing, commonly called "junk mail" by recipients, advertises everything from lower insurance rates to credit card offers to pleas to donate to various charities or subscribe to magazines. Some companies make it appear that you have been specially selected

**advertorial**

Display advertisement created to look like an article within the publication, although most publications have the words "advertisement" or "paid advertisement" in tiny print somewhere nearby.

**subliminal advertising**

Persuasive messages, such as an image or word flashed almost imperceptibly on a screen, that supposedly have unconscious effects on the audience.

**product placement**

A form of advertising in which brand-name goods or services are placed prominently within programming or movie content that is otherwise devoid of advertising, demonstrating the convergence of programming with advertising content.

**outdoor advertising**

Billboards and other forms of public advertising, such as on buses or taxis.

Product placement has become a more widely used advertising technique since the arrival of the DVR, which allows viewers to skip commercials.

The Federal Trade Commission allows puffery in advertising, exaggerated advertising claims that "reasonable" audiences would not likely perceive as facts.

or won a lottery and need to send in the material ASAP to claim your prize.

Many organizations rent their subscriber lists on a per-thousand basis; the more detailed the demographic data, the higher the cost. These lists become effective tools in the hands of advertisers who send targeted messages. List owners often seed them with false names to ensure that list renters are using the list only one time. Some savvy citizens use similar techniques to determine who is selling their name. Subsequent mailings in your pet's name, for example, could help identify the culprit.

Telemarketing involves phoning people at home, typically intrusive and annoying calls that many actively screen with voicemail or caller ID. These sales pitches are highly scripted, complete with prepared responses to a range of anticipated answers. The Telephone Consumer Protection Act of 1991 lays out strict guidelines on the times telemarketers may call and requires companies to remove people from call lists if they request it. There is a national "Do Not Call" registry that serves the same purpose. Exemptions include charities, political groups, debt collectors, and surveys.

## ADVERTISING IN A DIGITAL WORLD

Traditionally, 70 percent or more of commercial-media revenues come from advertising, an economic foundation being transformed by digital technology. Advertisers have a greater capacity to track consumers and identify the most effective advertisements, making their data extremely valuable. They are also discovering that many traditional advertising techniques do not work well on the web. Changes in technology and in online user behavior complicate the picture further.

### Cookies

**cookie**

Information that a website puts on a user's local hard drive so that it can recognize when that computer accesses the website again. Cookies also allow for conveniences like password recognition and personalization.

Web experiences, compared to experiences with other media, can be personalized for the user, a key aspect for both advertisers and media-content companies. Almost all websites leave a **cookie**, a small text file loaded onto a computer that identifies specific users who visit a site and where they go afterward. Cookies and web analytics are able to tell what page someone came from before arriving at a page with an ad and how long the person spent on that page. They can "remember" visitors who return and can determine their computer operating system, their web browser and, often, their approximate location.

Cookies not inserted by the content provider are called third-party cookies, like those advertisers place in ads. These cookies can both track and customize advertising messages as well as engage in "cookie pricing." Travel sites, for instance, will sometimes nudge up ticket prices if a pattern of browsing behavior reveals a traveler highly motivated to get a particular route.

Cookies may be outliving their tracking usefulness as new technologies that better track users have become more widespread. Still, some of the "old" digital media methods remain remarkably effective.

### Email Marketing

Until the rise of social media sites such as Facebook and Twitter, email was the most used application on the Internet; and despite spam, it continues to be an incredibly powerful tool for advertising. Like direct mail, email can reach highly targeted audiences who, better yet, have the choice to **opt in** to receive emails, showing their willingness to hear from certain companies.

Email also has the advantage of being cheap to produce and send, especially if the message is text only, without any design or graphics. Free email advertisements are also lucrative for the companies that offer this service, such as Yahoo Mail, Hotmail, and Gmail. Google uses software that scans each email sent via Gmail, analyzes the text, and inserts ads it deems most relevant to the topic.

## Banner Ads

In the early days of the web, most online advertising tended to follow the traditional advertising formats—particularly the display-ad model commonly found in print. Banner advertising, online ads spanning the top of a page like a banner, could be clicked on to visit the advertiser's website. Today, there are a variety of shapes and sizes of banner ads, including tower ads that take advantage of the tendency for users to scroll down. Such ads may also contain interactive quizzes, video, or other animation.

Studies tracking consumers online, however, indicate that banner ads have a very low **click-through rate (CTR)**, meaning a low percentage of users—in this case, an average of 0.06 percent—actually click on them. These disappointing numbers caused advertisers to doubt their effectiveness and seemed to stall the budding online ad industry.

## Pop-Ups and Video

Initially viewed as the salvation for online advertising, pop-ups can be **interstitial ads** or **superstitial ads**. Interstitial ads have proven unpopular because users must close the ad browser window to see the website they originally wanted. To get around this, some ads take up most of a page rather than the whole screen, with a small "x" somewhere in a corner to let users close the ad. Perceived as less obtrusive, superstitial ads have become more widespread. These ads crawl across a screen or appear in a corner and can be created with a variety of multimedia programs and effects.

Ads in videos have grown quickly in recent years. It became clear that online users did not want to watch a standard thirty-second commercial before a short video, so online videos tend to be ten or fifteen seconds at most and sometimes give users the option to click off the ad after only five seconds. Sites such as YouTube have tried overlays at the bottom of screens, like those that promote upcoming shows on network television, and these have also made their way to mobile apps.

## Classifieds and Auction Sites

Online classifieds have been able to take a large chunk of newspaper revenue because they offer several advantages. First, there is little or no need to squeeze text to fit within some predefined word and cost limit. Second, geographic limitations are no longer an issue as long as what is being advertised can be shipped or mailed. This vastly increases the potential audience. Craigslist and other online classifieds websites have been immensely successful for many traditional businesses as well as for small entrepreneurs, who can generate national or international business online with very little overhead or infrastructure cost.

Auction sites have also become popular for many of the same reasons, starting with eBay, founded in 1995. Seller rating and review systems, easy online payment methods, and a high volume of sellers and buyers have created a thriving marketplace, especially useful for small businesses or those working from home. Many unusual items have come up for sale on eBay, including the case of a British man

---

**opt in**

When consumers choose to receive mailings or marketing material, usually by checking a box on a website when registering for the site.

**click-through rate (CTR)**

Rate at which people click on an online advertisement to access more information.

**interstitial ad**

Online advertisement that opens in a new window from the one the user was in.

**superstitial ad**

Online advertisement that covers part of the existing screen or moves over part of it without opening a new window.

Graphiq, formerly FindTheBest, is a privately held research company that uses artificial intelligence to contextualize and create data-driven infographics.

who in 2008 put his entire life—worldly possessions, job, and even friends—up for sale after a bitter divorce. The winning bid was about $380,000, considerably short of what he was asking.[9]

### Search-Engine Ads

Advertising with popular search-engine sites such as Google, Bing, and Yahoo has become one of the most important vehicles for advertisers in recent years. The two main methods of search-engine advertising—search-engine optimization (SEO) and search-engine marketing (SEM)—are unpaid and paid forms of advertising, respectively, yet their goal is the same: to appear as the first entry in a search-engine search.

SEO techniques involve website design, keywords, and links. SEM advertisers either pay a search-engine company for a sponsored link, usually clearly labeled as such (with a colored panel or the words "sponsored links"), or buy keywords sold at auction, paying the search-engine company a set amount every time its site is clicked on when that search term is used. These search engines and other digital media utilize algorithms or computer programs to aid in rapidly targeting ads, tracking consumer online behavior, and more, although a human assistant often makes the process more nuanced.[10]

### Mobile Advertising

The dramatic growth of mobile media since 2000 has altered the advertising landscape fundamentally, with mobile now being the main driver of global ad spend growth, according to ZenithOptimedia. The volume of text messaging, especially among the young, exceeds that of voice calls. As smartphone use proliferates—it is estimated that by 2020 there will be 5.5 billion smartphone users worldwide, 70 percent of the global population—mobile has emerged as a powerful new advertising channel. Facebook has been especially successful at inserting mobile ads between entries on newsfeeds that get users' attention without annoying them.[11] Google announced in mid-2015 that it had changed its search-engine algorithms so that mobile-friendly websites would show up higher in the rankings.

Five trends characterize the mobile advertising marketplace. First, the geolocation capability of mobile technology increasingly enables advertisers to customize messages to the consumer's location. Second, mcommerce, or mobile commerce, is growing rapidly and targeting consumers with real-time messages updated to reflect their current mobile purchases. Consumers out shopping, for instance, use their mobile device to aid in comparative shopping and even price bargaining. Third, real-time mobile billing (RTB) is facilitating a new advertising pricing system optimized by mobile demand. Fourth, as mobile broadband access rises, video ads gain traction even on mobile devices. Fifth, ads tied to in-app downloads such as mobile games have increased greatly, with consumers seemingly willing to accept ads for free apps.

### In-Game Advertising

In-game advertising (IGA) has been growing rapidly, both in dollars spent by advertisers and in the volume of ads themselves. IGA, advertising that occurs inside either online or stand-alone video games for desktop or mobile devices, is distinct from advergaming, games produced only to advertise a product.

IGA can be static or dynamic. A static ad is typically shown as a display in the background, much like an in-game billboard. For example, an Adidas billboard appears in *FIFA International Soccer*. It might also appear during a pause in game play while a game is loading. If static IGA is integrated deeply, the player may have to view or interact with the ad to complete the game. Static IGA cannot be changed once a game is produced and distributed.

As the popularity of online games has grown, so has the placement of dynamic IGA. Advertisers can update these ads remotely, inserting newer versions over time. Such IGA can be tied to specific campaigns or marketing offers. President Barack Obama's 2008 campaign inserted dynamic IGA in several Xbox games.

Some companies offer free versions of games with IGA, such as *Age of Conan*, whose embedded enticements lure gamers to purchase the premium version. Mobile games have increased not only the prevalence of IGA but greatly added to game and in-app purchases as well.

Research suggests IGA has mixed value. A 2009 study showed that 80 percent of gamers could correctly recall a product advertised in IGA, and 56 percent viewed advertisers favorably if IGA allowed them to play for free.[12] A 2010 study indicated that only 36 percent of gamers could correctly identify products promoted in IGA in car-racing games.[13] Most gamers dislike IGA that distracts them from game play itself.[14]

## Behavioral Advertising

Behavioral advertising tracks user behavior and then inserts banner ads with similar topics on subsequent websites visited, which is why, after shopping for items on a site like Amazon, you see ads for the same products on websites you visit later. Advertisers claim it offers users more relevant web ads, but many consider this an invasion of privacy.

Although the behavioral advertising industry has outlined various principles and procedures in attempts to self-regulate, consumer groups and the government have found fault with this rapidly expanding area of advertising. Some companies do not stop tracking online users even after they have opted out. Another problem has been the use of Flash cookies that secretly reinsert a cookie even after the user has cleared her computer of all cookies. In the coming years tensions will likely increase between advertisers and government/consumer watchdog groups regarding best practices and consumer safeguards.

## Viral Marketing

Some of the most successful advertising online is unaided by advertising agencies or expensive marketing campaigns. **Viral marketing**, sometimes called buzz marketing, guerrilla marketing, or word-of-mouth (WOM) marketing, promotes a product, service, or brand through natural online channels; people spread a message because they want to, not because they are being paid to. Humorous or strange videos often work best for this; but such videos, whose appeal is often their unpolished, amateurish quality, are not always a good fit for all brands.

Predicting content that will actually go viral is difficult. The ALS Ice Bucket Challenge, in which people challenged three friends to video themselves dumping a bucket of ice water on their heads or donate to the ALS Association, became wildly and unexpectedly popular in the summer of 2014, especially in the United States. According to the ALS Association, it received over $100 million in July alone, and several other ALS organizations also saw large increases in donations during the latter half of the year.

## Native Advertising

One of the largest growth areas in advertising for online publications is native advertising of several different but related types, including sponsored posts on Facebook or Twitter. Basically, native advertising (which includes content marketing) is the online version of the print advertorial. In other words, the editorial staff of the site or a marketer produces advertising content made to appear like actual content within the publication.

💬 **viral marketing**

Promoting a product, service, or brand online through word of mouth, usually via online discussion groups, chats, and emails.

The ALS Ice Bucket Challenge became wildly popular on social media in the late summer of 2014. **CRITICAL THINKING QUESTIONS:** ALS recently managed to raise a significant sum of money through donations, but do you know what ALS stands for or what its symptoms are? Have you followed any progress in research on ALS since then? Do you consider the Ice Bucket Challenge a success?

One type of native advertising is indicated by the small "sponsored by" or "promoted by" tags in pieces that usually have attention-getting headlines about celebrities or odd news events. Many large online publications—including *The New York Times*, *TIME*, *Forbes*, and *The Atlantic*—have adopted some form of native advertising.

**DISCUSSION QUESTIONS:** Consider articles on sites or suggested posts you may have clicked on in Facebook or other social media. How many of these did you recognize as sponsored content, or did you care? What are the dangers of blurring the lines between editorial and advertising content?

## THE ADVERTISING BUSINESS

Worldwide ad spending for 2017 is estimated to increase 7 percent to $583 billion.[15] Figure 10-1 shows how much each medium spends and is forecast to spend on advertising. Television will continue to sit atop the media food chain, with about 37 percent of total ad dollars in 2017, but that will decrease to almost 34 percent by 2018. Meanwhile, mobile will rise from just over 10 percent to 23 percent in the same period. By 2018, mobile and desktop Internet ad spending combined will be greater than television advertising alone, and the two already exceed the combined total of newspaper, magazine, and radio ad spending. Other media channels will see their percentages change as mobile continues to take a larger share of ad spend, which is a serious concern for newspapers and magazines because they have already seen consistently large drops in their ad revenues the past two decades or so.

## ADVERTISING AGENCIES

Advertising agencies perform many important functions, creating and selling advertising while linking various media with the many companies seeking to sell a product or service. The more than five hundred advertising agencies in the United States, which collectively employ more than seventy thousand people, have four main areas of operation:

1. *Creative*: copywriters, creative, and art directors producing advertising content
2. *Client management*: account executives working with clients

**FIGURE 10-1** Share of Global Advertising Expenditure (%)

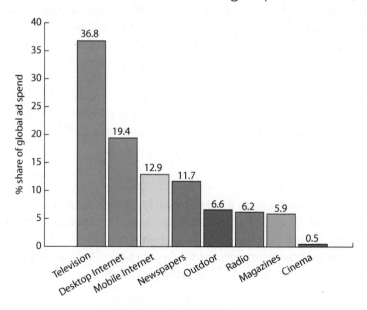

3. *Media buying*: media planners and buyers determining and purchasing media time or space, the area that has traditionally produced agency revenues

4. *Research*: researchers collecting and analyzing media data on consumer characteristics and purchase behaviors

A number of Internet-original firms emerged in the late 1990s. Some have survived as boutique or specialized firms, but many have been bought by larger agencies for their interactive expertise. This follows the trend toward consolidation seen with traditional advertising agencies that still dominate the field. Today, much larger advertising and media-services companies own most of the world's leading advertising agencies, and ninety of the top one hundred firms operate internationally. Most of these firms operate both advertising and public relations enterprises. These full-service companies handle all aspects of the communications business, from campaign planning to creative execution and media buying.

Table 10-2 presents data on the world's five largest advertising and media-services firms, ranked by their revenue in 2016, and some of their biggest advertising and public relations subsidiaries, which are themselves often global operations. In

## INTERNATIONAL PERSPECTIVES
# Hair-Raising Subway Billboard Ad Gets Noticed

Subway commuters in most major cities take the plethora of billboards on walls and platforms for granted, perhaps making a mental note of an upcoming film they'd like to see but, for the most part, ignoring the ads.

To help a billboard ad stand out from the crowd, advertisers have been incorporating interactive technologies to draw greater attention to otherwise static billboards. One notable example occurred in Stockholm, Sweden, where the pharmacy brand Apotek equipped

platform billboards to sense when trains were approaching the platform (for commuters on the platform, the wind coming before the train alerts them to an arrival).

The image on the billboard was a photo of a young woman with a full head of hair. As the train approached and the wind kicked up, the model's hair suddenly started to blow around wildly, seemingly in response to the train. Then the words "Make your hair come alive" and the brand name came on screen. The ad, which can be seen on YouTube, garnered international attention—along with surprise from commuters who suddenly saw a billboard with a moving image.

Later in the year a similar ad appeared on Stockholm's subway platforms, except this time instead, the wind blew a wig off the model, revealing her bald head. This ad for a cancer charity was also a successful attention getter.

Different kinds of interactive billboards can be used to far different effect. A 2013 ad for *The Curse of Chucky* looked much like any other film poster at a bus stop in Brazil until the lights began to flicker and Chucky smashed through the fake glass of the poster box wielding a fake knife. The terrified occupants of the bus stop, however, appeared not to immediately comprehend that they had suddenly become part of an outrageous publicity stunt and were being chased not by the world's most deviant doll but by a small actor made up as Chucky. All the horror, both scripted and apparently genuine, was recorded, of course, and can still be seen on YouTube. As if simply waiting at a bus stop at night isn't creepy enough.

**TABLE 10-2** World's Five Largest Advertising and Media-Services Companies

| AGENCY | MAJOR SUBSIDIARY GROUPS | HEADQUARTERS | WORLDWIDE REVENUES, 2016 ($ BILLION) |
|---|---|---|---|
| WPP | YOUNG & RUBICAM GROUP  Ogilvy  JWT  GREY | London, United Kingdom | 19.4 |
| **Omnicom**Group | DDB°  BBDO  TBWA\  I=I  FLEISHMANHILLARD | Netherlands, operational offices in New York, United States, and Paris, France | 15.4 |
| PUBLICIS GROUPE | Starcom  Starcom MediaVest GROUP  Leo Burnett  SAATCHI & SAATCHI | Paris, France | 9.7 |
| IPG | McCANN  FCB  LOWE | New York, United States | 7.8 |
| dentsu | dentsu DENTSU EAST JAPAN INC.  dentsu DENTSU WEST JAPAN INC.  Dentsu Digital | Tokyo, Japan | 7.3 |

Source: http://www.adbrands.net/agencies_index.htm

2013, Omnicom and Publicis planned to merge to form the world's largest advertising agency, but nearly a year later the deal was abruptly called off. Tokyo-based Dentsu, although a global player in terms of size, is typically not considered one of the "big four" of advertising agencies, as it focuses primarily on Japan, where it dominates the advertising industry with 30 percent of the Japanese market.

## Changing Trends in Advertising

Advertising finds itself as both a major beneficiary of new and emerging technologies and at times its nemesis. On the one hand, advertisers are able to better track and surveille consumers than ever before, but these practices also raise important issues around consumer rights to privacy, who owns the data that is collected, and how that data can be used. On the other hand, the development of tools like ad blockers on web pages makes it harder for advertisers to monetize page views and user engagement.

The ubiquity of advertising has also made consumers more resistant to ads, and when combined with ad-blocking technologies and on-demand viewing behavior, it has become easier than ever for consumers to skip ads online. This has created a kind of cat-and-mouse game between advertisers who want to glean more

**FIGURE 10-2** Salaries for Advertising Account Managers by Experience

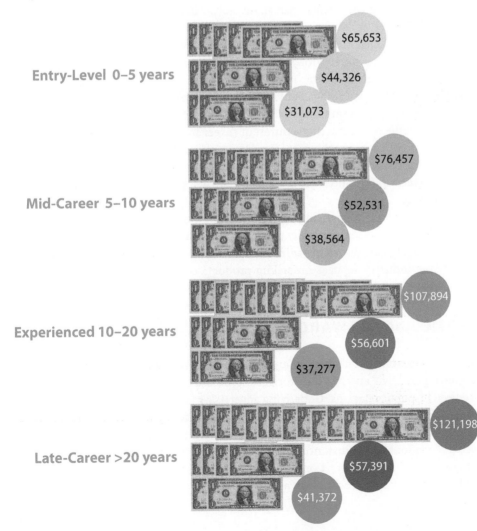

information from consumers and companies that try to help consumers avoid ads, either intentionally or unintentionally.

Advertisers claim that with new technologies and armed with consumer data they can send more highly targeted and relevant ads to consumers. However, this ignores the point that many people say they do not want to receive advertising at all. Given the important role that advertising plays in subsidizing much of the content we see on the web, this cat-and-mouse game will no doubt continue.

Within this context, some trends are clear. With greater powers of surveillance also come new ethical issues around privacy. Whether the advertising industry has the moral rectitude to regulate itself in an ethical manner or will need government regulation remains to be seen. Advertisers also expect more concrete metrics to determine whether their advertising dollars are effective, and this in turn will lead to new advertising payment models built around concepts like click-through rates rather than simply page views or other more hazy traditional criteria. Finally, advertising agencies will become cleverer about how and where ads are delivered, disguising advertising as paid content and other types of content that does not immediately look like traditional advertising.

## MEDIA CAREERS

Advertising can be an exciting career, whether within a large company or at an advertising agency that deals with many corporate clients. There are also many avenues within advertising to attract people, ranging from the creative side to account (client) management to audience research and digital analytics.

In large firms, a person may specialize within a specific industry, such as advertising for high-end fashion houses or for specific retailers, while also allowing flexibility in changing among clients or even industries. Someone working in pharmaceuticals for a few years may switch to telecommunications or consumer packaged goods, effectively starting a different career in a new industry.

Social media are creating new job opportunities in advertising agencies, and especially for those with good digital skills who demonstrate a good understanding of the new technology and tools available, there will be many opportunities to work in advertising.

Although some advertising agencies handle not-for-profit clients or take on social marketing causes, generally there are not as many advertising opportunities in not-for-profits and small organizations as there are in PR. For the most part, the advertising industry focuses on selling products or ideas for companies that can afford to spend money on marketing.

## LOOKING BACK AND MOVING FORWARD

Although news and entertainment are the most popular media content, advertising is the most pervasive, and much editorial content and programming are inspired or influenced by public relations. Underlying advertising is the desire to persuade an audience to change an attitude or belief or to take some action, such as making a purchase.

As public reliance on online and mobile media grows, so does advertising on the web and via mobile, a substantial part of total advertising spending worldwide, surpassing that of newspapers. Consumer research targeting and tracking media behavior has also increased. Technology allows for greater accountability of response rates to advertisements, and advertising agencies have been trying new types of online advertisements that link advertising with ecommerce and mcommerce better.

Advertising revenues support the majority of content we see today. Advertising helps pay journalist salaries and keeps television studios operating. Historically, few people have been willing to pay the full price for the content they get largely for "free," although this is beginning to change as increasing numbers of consumers pay for subscriptions to media or buy content for digital download.

Of course, content has never been truly free. Consumers pay in the form of higher prices for goods, corporate expenses for advertising and marketing being passed on to consumers. Moreover, digital consumers are increasingly and often unwittingly "selling" their personal information online in exchange for "free" digital content. Because such costs are largely hidden from the public, the adoption of subscription-based or pay-per-use models seems less attractive by comparison.

Even in the digital world—and perhaps especially in the digital world—advertising will continue to be a touchpoint for social issues both large and small, raising questions of privacy, surveillance, and values. Advertising will continue to generate demand for goods and services, both creating and reflecting aspects of ourselves as a culture and society.

## FURTHER READING

*Ad Land: A Global History of Advertising*. Mark Tungate (2007) Kogan Page.

*A History of Advertising*. Stephane Pincas, Marc Loiseau (2008) Taschen.

*The Advertising Concept Book*. Pete Barry (2008) Thames & Hudson.

*Advertising, the Uneasy Persuasion: Its Dubious Impact on American Society*. Michael Schudson (1987) Basic Books.

*Guerrilla Advertising: Unconventional Brand Communication*. Gavin Lucas, Michael Dorrian (2006) Laurence King.

*Ogilvy on Advertising*. David Ogilvy (1987) Vintage Books.

*The Conquest of Cool: Business Culture, Counterculture, and the Rise of Hip Consumerism*. Thomas Frank (1998) University of Chicago Press.

*Growth Hacker Marketing: A Primer on the Future of PR, Marketing, and Advertising*. Ryan Holiday (2014) Portfolio.

*Unconscious Branding: How Neuroscience Can Empower (and Inspire) Marketing*. Douglas Van Praet (2014) Palgrave Macmillan Trade.

*The Art of Social Media: Power Tips for Power Users*. Guy Kawasaki, Peg Fitzpatrick (2014) Portfolio.

*Social Media: Usage and Impact*. Hana S. Noor Al-Deen, John Allen Hendricks (eds.) (2012) Lexington Books.

*Social Media: Dominating Strategies for Social Media Marketing with Twitter, Facebook, YouTube, LinkedIn and Instagram*. Michael Richards (2015) CreateSpace Independent Publishing Platform.

*The Daily You: How the New Advertising Industry Is Defining Your Identity and Your Worth*. Joseph Turow (2013) Yale University Press.

*Return on Engagement: Content Strategy and Web Design Techniques for Digital Marketing*, 2nd ed. Tim Frick, Kate Eyler-Werve (2014) Focal Press.

# Media Ethics

Long famous for pop culture pieces and music criticism, *Rolling Stone* has more recently developed a reputation for hard-hitting, investigative reporting, articles such as the provocatively titled "A Rape on Campus: A Brutal Assault and Struggle for Justice at UVA." The nine-thousand-word, in-depth feature, published in November 2014, described the alleged 2012 gang rape of a University of Virginia freshman at a fraternity house party, its subsequent mishandling by the administration, and the pervasive culture of rape on college campuses nationwide.

Author Sabrina Rubin Erdely's story quickly went viral while increasing coveted clicks to RollingStone.com. Three days after the story broke, in response to mounting public outrage, the UVA president suspended all Greek activities and called for an official police investigation.[1] This striking example of news-media agenda setting promoted a national conversation about sexual assault and society's indifference when confronted with what many consider a hidden epidemic of these brutal crimes.

On closer inspection, however, the initially persuasive and compelling exposé began to unravel at the seams as other media professionals advanced critiques that held *Rolling Stone* responsible for a journalistic account that flouted best practices. The essential fabric of the story had been spun from a single thread, relying on one unidentified, uncorroborated source, "Jackie."

At this point, discussion in the public sphere turned swiftly from the subject of sexual assault to the topic of media ethics. More careful reporting, critics argued, would have revealed discrepancies in Jackie's description of events. Yet neither the friends who came to her rescue after the alleged attack nor the alleged attackers were ever interviewed, despite the damning article having quoted them according to Jackie's recollection of what had been said.

*Rolling Stone* announced that their trust in Jackie had been misplaced, a statement that incited even more controversy for its apparent victim blaming. An independent analysis, subsequently conducted at *Rolling Stone's* request, blamed "avoidable" lapses in the fundamentals of reporting, editing, and fact checking.

It also mentioned "the problem of confirmation bias—the tendency of people to be trapped by pre-existing assumptions and to select facts that support their own views while overlooking contradictory ones."[2] In other words, the reporter's search for an emblematic case became at some point the construction of one.

In April 2015, the magazine published the "painful" findings of a team from the Columbia School of Journalism. No one was fired, but the "anatomy of a journalistic failure" was preceded by an official retraction of the original story and an apology to readers, to the Phi Kappa Psi house, to UVA administrators and students, and to rape victims, who might now be more reluctant to step forward.

In November 2016, a jury in a federal court ruled against the reporter of the original story, *Rolling Stone,* and its parent company Wenner Media, despite the article retraction. The jury found them all liable in a multimillion-dollar defamation lawsuit brought by the former associate dean at the University of Virginia, who claimed the article depicted her as the "chief villain" in the story.[3]

Media ethics is not truly a stand-alone subject, for ethical decision-making skills should be part of media professionals' daily practices. Ethical reasoning should be a primary component when considering actions.

To do that, however, requires a solid understanding of ethics and the strengths and weaknesses of various ethical frameworks. This knowledge helps us recognize ethical problems before they arise and deal with them once they do. By focusing on ethics as a separate subject, this chapter gives you the basic tools to make ethical decisions. Anybody working in media should be mindful of how ethics in general and media ethics in particular are integral to our personal and professional lives, and how the decisions of media professionals can have far-reaching consequences for many others.

## Ethics, Morals, and Laws

Technically, ethics is a branch of philosophy that examines moral questions, or questions of right and wrong, and thus is also called moral philosophy. There are many specialties within ethics. One of the main branches attempts to answer moral questions in both theory (moral theory) and practice (applied ethics). Another branch, metaethics, deals with nonmoral questions about morality, such as the nature of moral facts and the meanings of moral statements. In this chapter, we will first look at some moral theories and then examine applied ethics as it relates to mass communication and journalism, advertising, PR, and entertainment in particular.

Although ethics actually refers to the branch of philosophy that examines questions of morality, in common usage, the term "ethics" is often used synonymously with "morals." Morals are what we believe to be right or wrong. The question of why we consider an action such as lying to be wrong is a matter for metaethics and not something we address here. Although it may seem impossible to dictate what is right or wrong for a person in a given situation, ethics provides us with a framework and method for good moral reasoning.

Ethics and laws are not the same. Many of our basic laws are based on moral precepts, but many unethical actions are not illegal. Similarly, many laws are not based on moral precepts (consider traffic parking laws, e.g.). Some laws, such as segregation in the United States or apartheid in South Africa, have been deemed immoral and have eventually been reformed, through civil disobedience and other means, to better reflect what is considered right and good.

# Major Systems of Ethical Reasoning

There is no single underlying and unified ethical system that all people can follow for complete justice and peace. That does not mean, however, we will not benefit from examining the thinking of philosophers, religious leaders, and scholars, and the different ethical systems that have been developed, some over thousands of years. Various classifications of ethical reasoning and moral theories exist, but here we will use a system employed by William Neher and Paul Sandin in their book *Communicating Ethically*. In some ways matching that of noted media ethics scholar Clifford Christians,[4] their classification also diverges to highlight the role of communication in ethics.

Neher and Sandin group the four major systems within the categories of character, duties, consequences, and relationships. We will look at these and also examine the issue of moral relativism.

## CHARACTER, OR VIRTUE ETHICS

Virtue ethics is the oldest of the ethical systems, with roots in some of our earliest religions. The Greeks believed strongly in the notion of virtue and the role of character in living a virtuous life. They aspired to virtues such as courage, modesty, stoicism, and honesty, among other character traits. In virtue ethics, a virtuous character lets you live a virtuous life. Simply acting modest or selfless, when in fact you do not really feel those traits, does not make you virtuous (partly because you are breaking another virtue: honesty).

Many great thinkers have given us lists of virtues, sometimes falling short of meeting their own standards. Benjamin Franklin famously made a list of thirteen virtues and vowed to focus on a different one every week, dutifully logging in a notebook how he fared each day. He soon gave up, though, after realizing he could not practice the virtue of order, or keeping things in their place, only the third virtue on his list.[5] He was also famous for not following his twelfth virtue, chastity. Virtue ethics can give us a framework for the best way to live our lives, but it does not tell us exactly how to do that.

Although virtue ethics may seem old-fashioned, given its long religious and philosophical history, it has become more important in recent years among media ethicists. Its stress on character touches on fundamental aspects of what makes us human, a compelling emphasis absent in some later ethical systems.

There are two virtue-based ethics you are probably familiar with: the Golden Rule and the Golden Mean.

### The Golden Rule

A basic ethical principle in Judeo-Christian belief that dominates most Western societies is often cited as "Do unto others as you would have them do unto you." Another way to express the same idea is "Love thy neighbor as thyself."

This principle could be applied by a journalist when interviewing a grieving relative, for example. By treating the person with respect and dignity and asking themselves how they would want to be treated in the same situation, journalists can perhaps avoid some of the charges of invasion of privacy or tastelessness in coverage often leveled at the media. Some journalists, when interviewed in similar situations, have expressed shock at the realization of how insensitive and intrusive the news media can be during trying times of personal grief.

### The Golden Mean

One of the oldest ethical principles, the Golden Mean, was espoused in different forms by Aristotle and Confucius, each of whom said that finding a balance between two extremes is the most ethical way. This "middle way" may well shift as the extremes shift, of course, and even this principle has to be taken in moderation. Stealing only half, rather than all, the money from a cash register would not be ethical, for example, because stealing is wrong in the first place.

Applying the Golden Mean to news stories would involve trying to find balance and fairness among all sides of an issue. It does not mean automatically giving each side the same amount of coverage or space in the newspaper, however, because the relative importance of the groups must be judged. For example, an extreme fringe group with only a few hundred vocal members should not receive the same amount of coverage on a controversial issue as a long-standing national organization with tens of thousands of members.

According to Aristotle, the process of deciding on a mean is one way we determine what constitutes virtue, and the mean becomes the standard by which ethical acts are judged. This is part of the reason that acts typically deemed wrong, such as stealing, should not be considered one extreme.

### Virtue Ethics in Action

Taking today's much-touted notion of transparency as a virtue, we can see where unethical actions may occur when companies try to hide information or mislead the public. One such case is when the major networks, of which news organizations are a part, fought a proposed regulation that would require television stations to disclose the sources and amounts of political advertising they received. If transparency is a virtue that news organizations demand of other companies, then these networks were acting unethically—if not hypocritically—when trying to keep the information secret. In the end, a kind of golden mean was reached in that only the four major networks and stations in the top markets would have to disclose the information, whereas cable networks and smaller-market stations would not.

> **DISCUSSION QUESTIONS:** Discuss the virtues you think are most admirable in today's world. Why do you think so? How many of those can you honestly say you practice?

## DUTIES

As the name suggests, duty-based ethical systems state that we must follow a prescribed set of rules, or duties, regardless of the outcome. It is our moral obligation to follow these duties, no matter what. Duty theories provide basic principles for moral obligations in life. These may spring from religious beliefs (duties to God), but duties to others and oneself may also be embraced.

Duty-based approaches differ from virtue-based ethical systems in important ways. The virtue-based approach emphasizes the individual's choices within a prescribed framework. In a duty-based approach, individual choice is eliminated in favor of a set of rules that apply equally to everybody.

## The Categorical Imperative

Immanuel Kant was an influential German philosopher in the eighteenth century whose duty-based ethical system stated that actions should be decided on moral laws that would apply to everyone. Kant said that we should create these moral laws only when we have carefully considered if we would want these laws applied to us at all times. He referred to this unconditional moral obligation as a **categorical imperative**. The categorical imperative cannot depend on a personal inclination, goal, or purpose. It encourages one to act for the benefit of others first and not for personal gain. Treating someone with respect, giving to charity to benefit those in need, and lending a hand to help another with a difficult task are examples of actions that reinforce the inherent value of others.

Media organizations can apply Kant's categorical imperative in many ways. Consider, for instance, an advertising firm's decision to turn away clients who sell tobacco or alcohol, or a public relations firm's decision not to accept government clients from nations with poor human rights records. Following categorical imperatives would entail rejecting such clients, no matter how promising the contract.

For news organizations, decisions to publish names of criminal suspects or to cover all serious crimes, for example, would fall under the categorical imperative. In this case, if a newspaper published all names of drivers arrested for drunk driving, it would make no exception for even the mayor or the newspaper publisher.

The strength in duty-based approaches should be clear: Simply by following the rules, you are acting ethically. Nevertheless, obeying certain rules can still complicate many situations. Reporting crime victim names, for instance, seems like a simple policy. But when looking at a stigmatized crime like rape, reporting the victim's name may further harm the victim. Others argue that not treating sexual crimes like other crimes deepens misunderstanding and stigmatization by perpetuating the myth of sexual violence as being somehow intrinsically different from other violent crimes.

**categorical imperative**

In ethical thought, Kant's concept of an unconditional moral obligation that does not depend on an individual's personal inclinations or goals.

Immanuel Kant was an influential eighteenth-century German philosopher who developed the notion of the categorical imperative in ethics.

**DISCUSSION QUESTIONS:** If you believe that telling the truth is always the best course of action, then create a list of cases in which you would lie, ranging from extreme ("I would lie to save my life") to less serious cases ("I would lie not to hurt someone's feelings"). What does this exercise teach about telling the truth as both an ideal and a practical reality?

## Discourse Ethics

German social theorist and scholar Jürgen Habermas, best known for his concept of the "public sphere" (see Chapter 15), has proposed what he calls "discourse ethics" as an ethical framework. Habermas claims that communication is integral to how we understand the world, and when practiced without bias or coercion, it becomes an ethical act brought about through the process of rational interaction, or argument. He proposes several actions for participants in discourse, a formalized discussion in which the ideas of all affected parties are heard and considered on their own merits—rather than outside factors, such as who is more powerful or more persuasive. Discourse ethics prescribes rules but also assumes that justice and equality are most important for a good society.

Principles of discourse ethics could work well when an organization does not agree on the proper course of action. If all affected parties participate in the discussion, they can see other perspectives better, yielding a decision that ideally makes everyone happy. Note that this process is not about finding a compromise simply for the sake of compromise but more about letting people come to a shared and consensual understanding of what is true or correct based on the merits of the argument.

A company promoting a highly unpopular development project may ask a small PR firm to represent them. A discourse-ethics approach to the project could help them decide whether to take on the client. All those in the firm could state their views. They might also solicit opinions from other clients and local citizens whom the project might affect. Bringing in parties normally without a voice would ideally provide new perspectives for all involved and lead to an ethical decision.

### Duties-Based Ethics in Action

The *News of the World*, a 168-year-old U.K. tabloid newspaper with 2.6 million readers, published its last issue on July 10, 2011, with the headline "Thank You and Goodbye." The paper, owned by Rupert Murdoch's News Corp., was at the heart of a shocking scandal involving journalists hacking phones of celebrities, sports stars, politicians, and families of crime victims, all to get material to scoop competing tabloids.

Phone hacking—eavesdropping on private phone calls or messages—is illegal, but a host of ethical issues were also raised by industry experts, the government, and the public regarding whether journalism in the United Kingdom needed further regulation. Further complicating matters, while raising even more legal and ethical concerns, was the revelation that journalists had bribed police officers for information for stories.

In response to public outrage, advertisers promptly pulled their ads from the *News of the World*, which led in part to its sudden closure. Public concern about invasions of privacy, especially by a profession that claims to be the watchdog of government, seriously damaged journalism's reputation. Fierce competition among Britain's tabloids, which specialize in lurid stories, and the drive to sell more papers stifled ethical decision making at the *News of the World*. Adhering to the duties of professional journalists and editors, rather than the scoop mentality of daily tabloids, might have prevented such misconduct.

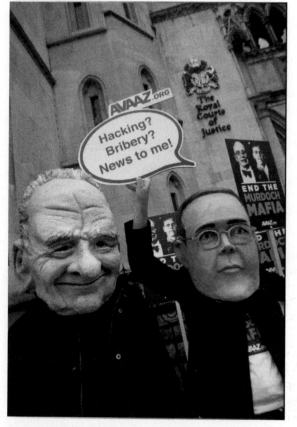

The *News of the World* phone-hacking scandal had massive repercussions in the British press and government.

## CONSEQUENCES

We often consider the likely consequences of our actions as we make ethical decisions. Of course, nobody can predict the future, so exact forecasts may be difficult. Nevertheless, some influential ethical systems look primarily at consequences as ways to judge what is ethically good or not.

## Utilitarianism

Utilitarianism assumes that the most ethical action does the greatest good for the greatest number. A decision or act that severely hurts someone or a small group is still right if it helps many more people.

This may promote a numbers game, thinking of the greatest good strictly in terms of the number of people who benefit. Another way to look at it weighs a small good for a great number of people against a greater good for a small number. Scientific research on animals operates under a utilitarian principle, with many safeguards to minimize potential suffering and harm of test subjects. A small number of animals suffer or are killed to find cures for diseases that may help much larger numbers of people. It may be harder from a utilitarian ethical perspective to justify testing cosmetics on animals than testing animals to find a cure for cancer—a classic case of how both "greatest number" and "greatest good" must be weighed.

Utilitarianism can often be used to justify media coverage of sensitive or painful events for a small number of people because the coverage can help many others. Examples include investigative reports of government wrongdoing in which a few individuals may go to jail or lose their jobs, but society as a whole benefits, or textbook coverage of professionals who have committed ethics violations. **Social marketing** operates under utilitarian principles because it attempts to do the greatest good for the greatest number of people by persuading them to change their behaviors—encouraging them, for example, not to drive drunk, smoke, or binge drink.

**social marketing**

Advertising and marketing techniques that persuade people to change bad or destructive behaviors or adopt good behaviors.

## Social Justice

Egalitarian philosophers believe that what is ethical is whatever brings about the most social justice or fairness for everyone. In this way, the utilitarian belief of "the greatest good" is interpreted as "the most fairness for everyone."

Philosopher John Rawls argued in his 1971 book *A Theory of Justice* that fairness is the fundamental idea behind justice. Yet establishing what is fair in a complex modern society, where certain groups have greater wealth, power, and advantages, is often difficult. To better understand fairness, Rawls advocates that the parties step behind a "veil of ignorance" and give up their usual roles. They must stake out an "original position" on the issue, not knowing what their role may be after it is decided.

By following this procedure, managers in disputes with workers would have to imagine that they may end up part of the labor workforce after the exercise is finished. If so, would they be satisfied with the result proposed by management? From this framework, Rawls says, the parties would be better able to establish fair practices, for they could more clearly see other viewpoints and interests.

Understanding other viewpoints is key to effective media communications. Advertising executives may realize that if they were of a different ethnic group or gender, they might find a proposed advertisement offensive. Newsroom editors may reassess

**DON'T GET PLAYED WHILE BIG TOBACCO GETS PAID**

We're being made to think that hookah and cigarillos are less harmful than cigarettes and the tobacco industry is profiting.

FOLLOW US

Social marketing campaigns to discourage harmful behaviors employ a utilitarian perspective, trying to achieve the greatest good for the greatest number of people.

the workload of reporters after admitting it would be too onerous for them, which may lead to policy changes. Reporters may choose their words more carefully or write the story more thoughtfully if they imagined themselves as the subject of the piece.

Still, such ponderings may seem unrealistic in today's competitive business world. An editor may realize, on a personal level, that the workload of reporters is unfair but may not be able to do anything about it on a professional or organizational level. Asking those in control to step behind a veil of ignorance or follow certain rules of discourse is also asking them to surrender their power and position. And, as with discourse ethics, the dominant group has little incentive to abandon its ability to coerce others.

## Consequence-Based Ethics in Action

Childhood obesity and its accompanying diseases, such as diabetes and high blood pressure, are a growing problem in the United States. The problem is exacerbated in Puerto Rico, where Hispanic cultural norms see a chubby kid as a healthy kid.

As part of an advertising campaign, Subway restaurant let children go grocery shopping while their parents secretly watched on video in another room. The ad showed shocked and horrified parents observing their children fill the shopping carts with junk food. Similar to public service ads in the United States that highlighted the effect of parents' bad shopping habits on children's eating habits, Subway's ads provided a social caution—while also of course reminding viewers that Subway sandwiches are a more healthful option than other fast foods.

A social marketing campaign like Subway's could clearly be seen as using utilitarian principles to promote the greatest good for the greatest number. Even so, it does raise issues of self-interest while downplaying the fact that some of Subway's menu items also are high in calories.

## RELATIONSHIPS, OR DIALOGICAL ETHICS

Neher and Sandin describe dialogical ethics as a process in which ethics are assessed based on each participants' attitudes and behaviors in a communication exchange. In ethical dialogs, the participants are willing to open themselves up and see how the other side views the world and themselves. In dialogical ethics, we do not try to force our own agenda but strive for open and honest dialog that accepts other views without judgment. We do not simply abandon our own views and become uncritical sponges, but we remain open to hearing other views and respecting those we encounter.

Dialog forms the basis of our relations with others. This is especially true with social media because dialog is often the only way we interact with many people online. Further, professions such as advertising and public relations, in which success is measured by how well the audience has been persuaded to buy a product, change a belief, or perform some other action, would seem to be unethical from a dialogical-ethics perspective because they are using people as a means to an end.

These points are valid. Even so, perhaps some of the seemingly unethical issues involving advertising may be mitigated if a dialogical ethical approach is considered.

INTERNATIONAL PERSPECTIVES

# Global Action: Uniting Women Worldwide Through Social Networks

Social-networking sites such as Facebook and Twitter have played important roles in many recent social movements, including International Women's Day, March 8, 2017. From Dublin to Melbourne, millions of protesters marched in support of economic equality and reproductive rights for women. Social media played a pivotal role in the global movement in at least three ways. First, organizers used social networks to motivate and plan the worldwide, one-day event. Second, participants and journalists alike used their mobile devices to photograph and share video of the event. Finally, people around the world continue to engage on social media in their support of the essential rights of women everywhere.

Perhaps not surprisingly, many corporate brands organized social media campaigns to promote the event and capitalize on its marketing energy. Western Union, for instance, produced a video depicting girls from various parts of the world saying "The race is on." The girls then run in hopes of becoming "the first female to run United Nations" or the first to land on the Moon. The video was shared widely on multiple social networks such as YouTube.

In today's world of social media, where audience members communicate regularly with each other, joining the dialog has become increasingly important for companies. A common mistake of organizations as they enter the social media space is trying to control the dialog and squash dissent rather than truly listening to consumers and trying to understand their viewpoints, as dialogical ethics dictates.

## Ethics of Care

The ethics of care challenges many traditional ethical systems and speaks to issues in modern society and communication. This branch of feminist ethics has many variants and has been quite controversial. A number of beliefs characterize feminist thought in general: Women are the equal of men; oppression of women is wrong; categories of male and female and their associated gender roles are socially constructed; the male perspective has dominated throughout history to the detriment of women; and consequently, society has accepted ostensibly male virtues as the standard or highest ideals.

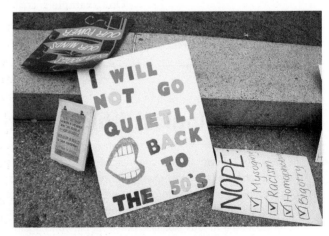

Feminist ethics provide a moral framework that encourages the empowerment of women while protesting discrimination and harassment.

Like dialogical ethics, the ethics of care emphasizes the importance of relationships but places a greater emphasis on improving relationships. In the ethics of care, acting ethically involves caring for oneself and for others within the context of a relationship in real life, not because of abstract principles. It replaces a justice-based ethical system with a caring-based ethical system, the *one caring* and the *cared for*.

Feminist ethics is important in a communication context for a number of different reasons. First, the assumptions that "male" means "normal" has implications for everything from how advertising messages are constructed to who is making the advertisements (and who are simply models within them). Mass communication, in subtle and not-so-subtle ways, helps establish and reinforce the roles of men and women in society. Second, even if women are hardwired differently than men—still a debatable point—promoting caring about others offers a valuable alternative way of conceptualizing communications.

## MORAL RELATIVISM

Moral relativism suggests that none of the ethical systems can be said to be any better than the others and that traditional ethical principles have historically been used primarily to secure the stature of established social groups. The notion of moral relativism derives from anthropological research that recognizes that behaviors deemed wrong in our culture may be considered perfectly normal, even moral, in another culture. This led early researchers to question the basis on which some groups declared their moral codes superior to others.

A weakness of moral relativism is that it leaves no agreed-on rules or principles for discussing ethical issues and reaching conclusions. There is no fundamental component or rulebook for trying to understand the point of view of others, no yardstick of social justice or greatest good, no duties to follow, and no virtues to aspire to that will improve our characters. Each person is out for himself or herself, with no way (or incentive) to communicate and find common ground for understanding.

Moral relativism makes it impossible to justify from an ethical perspective social marketing campaigns that attempt to change others' practices or beliefs. One example is cockfighting, in which roosters with razor blades attached to their

---

ETHICS IN MEDIA
## Dialogical Ethics in Action

In early 2017, Pepsi aired a commercial featuring celebrity Kendall Jenner at a protest event offering a can of the popular beverage to a law enforcement officer, in the hopes of keeping things calm. But instead of fostering goodwill, the ad unleashed a furious backlash on social networks against the international corporation. Citizens widely condemned the commercial as trivializing the Black Lives Matter movement by suggesting that all citizens of color need do to eliminate tensions with police is share a soft drink.

Pepsi quickly pulled the plug on the commercial, but the damage to its reputation will likely last for much longer. Not only have critics identified the exploitive nature of the advertising message, but they have also faulted Pepsi for failing to promote diversity and inclusivity in its commercial message.

feet fight each other to the death and spectators bet on the outcome. It is practiced legally in many countries in Asia and South America (and illegally in the United States and Europe). Using moral relativism, one could not make a valid moral argument that cockfighting proponents are unethical and must be stopped because they see nothing wrong with an event that remains for many a part of their culture.

**DISCUSSION QUESTIONS:** If you had to pick just one ethical system by which to live, what would it be? Why?

## Issues in Ethical Decision Making

One size does not fit all; that is, no theoretical approach will work for all situations, and conflicts between ethical precepts produce ethical dilemmas in life and in media. The ethics of care may often conflict with the categorical imperative. An editor, for instance, may not want to publish anything about his wife's run-in with the law, whereas the newspaper's policy is always to print names of people arrested. Media accounts of their own business practices and mistakes often lack the vigor of their reports on other businesses, a clear violation of the categorical imperative.

The principle of utilitarianism can be used to run roughshod over rights of privacy. Editors often justify intrusive coverage of famous people as "the public's right to know." But what good does such coverage actually serve? Who actually benefits the most from exposing a shocking celebrity scandal? Does the public get important information that somehow makes them better citizens, or has the paper simply sold more newspapers?

A utilitarian argument might also be used to suppress news coverage. A story on the unsafe practices of a local factory could force it to close down and put hundreds of people out of work. In this case, would keeping quiet about the violations serve the greatest good for the greatest number of people?

Media professionals deal with a number of ethical problems on the job, some of which are discussed throughout this book. Because of the nature of work in mass communication, ethical lapses can have far-reaching repercussions, potentially ruining careers, affecting the public's perception and trust of media in general, and in some instances even ending lives.

Corporate decisions made in executive boardrooms far above the typical media professional's level can also have ethical repercussions. Sometimes media professionals may be willing pawns in unethical practices; other times, they simply try to do their jobs as best they can within the dictates of the larger organizational environment.

According to academic Ronald Howard and business consultant Clinton Korver, authors of *Ethics for the Real World: Creating a Personal Code to Guide Decisions in Work and Life*, three disciplines—legal, prudential, and ethical—are important to keep in mind when assessing ethical actions. They claim that we often confuse these concepts when attempting moral reasoning. In other words, we may present our reasoning within an ethical framework, when our reasons are actually prudential or practical, such as improving the company's bottom line.

Howard and Korver offer several easy self-tests to evaluate whether your decision is truly rational or simply a rationalization couched in ethical terms. These include the "other-shoe test" (What would you feel if the shoe were on the other foot?), the "front-page test" (Would you think the same way if what you did was on the front page of *The New York Times*?), the "loved-one test" (How would you feel if the recipient of your action was someone you loved?), the "role-model test" (Would you want your children to model your behavior?), and the "mother's test" (What would your mother think?).

A more systematic method of ethical decision making is called the Potter Box, named after social ethics professor Ralph B. Potter. The Potter Box provides a framework for analyzing a situation, separating facts from opinions, and taking into account those individuals affected by a given ethical issue. Once one has sorted out the facts, defined the situation, and analyzed it, then values and principles (what we are calling ethical frameworks) can be applied and loyalties to different parties can be considered. Figure 11-1 shows how the Potter Box can be used.

Let us use the Potter Box to examine the *Rolling Stone* case from the beginning of this chapter. Imagine that you are an editor at *Rolling Stone* who has received the story by Sabrina Rubin Erdely of the rape at the fraternity. First, you consider the facts of the situation—is the information supported by corroborating evidence? Second, you would consider the values at work, including the professional values of journalism that discourage publishing articles based on unknown sources or conjecture.

Third, you would select the ethical frameworks that could be applied, each of which may recommend a different conclusion. From a consequences-based approach, you may reason that publishing the story helps others by highlighting a much larger problem of sexual assault on college campuses (a rationale Erdely offered even after the *Rolling Stone* apology). A virtues-based approach would argue that *Rolling Stone* ignored truthfulness and veracity—two fundamental principles of journalism—when it published the story. Feminist ethics, although not condoning the shoddy reporting, would emphasize the relationship of the publication with the victim in helping her tell her story (and would—and did—strongly criticize the victim-blaming that *Rolling Stone* engaged in after the story's flaws came to light).

Fourth, as an editor, you would consider your loyalty to *Rolling Stone*, your employer. Would publishing such a titillating and controversial story help sell more copies and enhance your organization's reputation? You may, for example,

**FIGURE 11-1** The Potter Box

reason that it would indeed sell more copies, but without considering the other issues with the story, you may not see beyond sales for the magazine to the harm for individuals and institutions featured in the story—and ultimately for *Rolling Stone* itself.

This later step should help you select among the various responses and rationales that the different frameworks recommend. In the case of *Rolling Stone*, key editorial decision makers were likely not thinking about the underlying ethical and professional principles that should have been considered much earlier in the process.

## Role of Commercialism in Media Ethics

Whether privately held or publicly traded on the stock market, businesses in a capitalist society are expected to make money for their owners. Members of the public invest in companies that are expected to be successful, which means making profits. Media companies are no different from other types of corporations in that regard.

They are, however, uniquely positioned to influence the public compared to other types of companies because of the "product"—media content—they create. Scholars in the Frankfurt School tradition coined the term "**culture industry**" to describe the power of media companies to affect culture. If any other kind of organization, such as a car manufacturer or a cereal maker, wants to influence public opinion, they have to go through the media to do so.

**culture industry**

A term coined by the Frankfurt School to describe how media companies produce or "make" culture in the same way that other companies produce products.

Because of the media's ability to influence and inform the public, some branches of the industry, such as journalism, have special protection under the Constitution; the First Amendment is a case in point. Partly as a result of these protections and partly through historical traditions, media—and journalism in particular—have had a strong public service mission. This may no longer be a mandate when news organizations become divisions of larger entertainment-media corporations with little or no tradition in the unique culture of the newsroom and its commitment to public service.

At the heart of many media-ethics dilemmas are the conflicting goals of informing the public and maximizing corporate profit. These issues can arise in a number of ways. Commercial interests can take precedence over public interests when powerful advertisers cancel or threaten to cancel their advertising in a media outlet. A blatant example could involve toning down or eliminating an unflattering story on a large local advertiser who has threatened to withdraw advertising revenue. More commonly, advertisers may pull their ads when a media organization covers unpopular issues or takes unpopular editorial stands. Examples of this include Southern newspapers that supported the civil rights movement and in doing so lost local

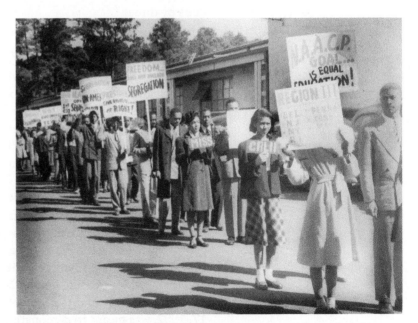

The civil rights movement forced some Southern newspapers to make tough choices when advertisers threatened to pull their ads if the papers appeared to support the movement.

*Real Housewives of Atlanta* was Bravo's first show to get more than two million viewers in the coveted eighteen to forty-nine age range, but has faced criticisms for apparently fabricating portions of their story lines. **CRITICAL THINKING QUESTIONS:** How strictly should "reality TV" stick with real portrayals of people, and is it acceptable for producers to fabricate story lines in order to increase the entertainment value of the shows, even if it portrays some people unfairly in a negative light?

advertisers in the 1950s and 1960s. Although controversial news coverage was not directly about the advertisers, they either disagreed with or did not want to be associated with the newspaper's content for fear of losing business. In 2017, veteran news commentator Bill O'Reilly was fired from his post at Fox News as a consequence of allegations that he had sexually harassed multiple women at the popular news organization. More than fifty advertisers had withdrawn their commercials on the TV news network.

The costs associated with running a modern newsroom have become increasingly problematic ethical concerns. Cutting staff is one of the surest ways to considerably reduce operating costs, but at what expense in terms of news coverage? Fewer staff members means less coverage of certain subjects, such as education and city hall, in favor of more wire-service copy or light features. This practice can provide the public with an incomplete picture of local events and issues. Similarly, investigative reports are often time-consuming and expensive and are less likely to be conducted in a media organization intensely aware of maximizing profits.

Professional training and development also often suffer. Many journalists who want to learn how to use computer-assisted reporting tools or digital media must pay their own way to conferences or workshops and use their personal vacation time to attend. This is despite a push by some news organizations for journalists to become multimedia reporters, doing their stories in print, TV, and audio formats. Production costs are reduced when one journalist is doing the work previously done by three.

## MEDIA TYPES INFLUENCING CONTENT

Various business pressures arise with the various media types. The expense of producing feature-length films, for example, is an important factor for large media companies that want to maximize their profits. A film could have a greater likelihood of getting produced if the media company already owns the rights to the character in the film, for example, and if there is good potential for other media content from within the company, such as music and television shows, to be tied in with the movie to help in marketing.

The individual divisions of a large media company must deal with the demands of the corporate parent to maximize profits. For example, the book-publishing branch may feel pressure to emphasize books from established authors in a popular genre to generate sales, but at the expense of finding new authors or types of books that do not fit established categories.

The need for exciting visual elements has even affected news coverage. *Dateline NBC*'s fifteen-minute segment "Waiting to Explode," which aired November 17, 1992, was meant to demonstrate the danger of the gas tanks exploding in certain models of General Motors' pickup trucks. Yet the production team rigged the trucks to ensure a fiery explosion, and some of the information presented was mis-leading or inaccurate. Only later, through independent investigations and information from sources who were at the initial filming, did the truth behind the segment come out, forcing NBC to issue a public apology and settle the lawsuit that GM had brought against it.[6] In this case, the need to have an exciting visual element likely helped cause the ethical breaches.

On a smaller scale, but no less unethical, was the example of *Today* reporter Michelle Kosinski covering flooding in Wayne, New Jersey, in 2005. She is shown paddling a kayak down a flooded street as she gives her report, only to have two people walk right in front of her, revealing that the water is actually only ankle deep. Despite this, she continues with the report and paddles as if nothing happened.

Not every dramatic photograph on the front page of a newspaper or in television news reports is a breach of media ethics, for newsworthiness is always a consideration for news organizations. It is important to ask, though, whether the decision to include certain elements in visual media was driven more by the need to capture the public's attention than true news value.

## Ethics in Journalism

Because of journalism's unique role in society, its First Amendment protection, and its public service mission, many ethical dilemmas arise in the course of practicing it. Difficult ethical questions play a role in the entire news-gathering and production process. Ethical issues become even more important with the rise of citizen journalism.

Editors must consider whether headlines and captions accurately reflect the important points of a story or simply titillate. Privacy issues play a role when private citizens are thrust by circumstance into the media spotlight. Reporters must consider fairness and balance in their choice of interview subjects. Photo editors and designers must avoid the temptation to alter elements of photos to make them more dramatic. Societal mores and cultural values of the audience must be considered when determining what qualifies as news and how it is reported, although newspapers must also sometimes take highly unpopular stands on issues when acting as the public's conscience.

> **DISCUSSION QUESTIONS:** Do you think that because news organizations receive extra legal protection not enjoyed by most other types of companies that they should also be held to a higher ethical standard? Is this standard more difficult to meet when one journalist is doing work previously done by three? Defend your views.

### PRIVACY RIGHTS VERSUS THE PUBLIC'S RIGHT TO KNOW

Although no actual law states this, the public's "right to know" is often cited as a commonly understood principle when journalists are trying to obtain information that can better inform the public regarding anything from political candidates to corporate wrongdoing to potentially dangerous foods, drugs, or buildings.

Gathering proof of wrongdoing is one of the biggest challenges journalists face. Admissions of guilt are unlikely to come out during an interview—if the subject

Online conversations have raised new issues of privacy and whether messages are public or private, as posts written years ago can be found and reposted by others.

even agrees to one. Journalists are often barred from the very locations they need to visit to gather information. Employees are forbidden by management to speak to journalists or threatened with losing their jobs if they do; police or public officials refuse to see or talk to journalists or are slow in providing requested documentation, even if the documents are public records.

New technology such as miniature microphones and cameras and the old technique of going undercover may seem easy answers to the journalist's dilemma. But the ethics and legality of these tools and actions must be considered. Sometimes these techniques are the only ones that will give access to people engaged in illegal or unethical behavior, such as selling drugs or arms.

Federal law prohibits the media or anyone else from intentionally intercepting, or attempting to intercept, anyone's communication by wire, oral, or electronic means. Citizens have a reasonable expectation of privacy for oral, or spoken, communications, via telephone or over the Internet, for example. State laws vary, however, on whether only one person or both people in a conversation must consent to having it recorded.

Regardless of the legality of intercepting communications, is it ethical? It depends on the circumstances, including whether it is print or broadcast media. The FCC generally prohibits the use of wireless microphones to overhear private conversations unless all parties to the communication have given prior consent. Conversations that occur in a public place, such as a restaurant or bar, however, would not be subject to the same prohibition because people in public places cannot expect the same right to privacy. Broadcast television or radio stations may not record telephone conversations without the consent of all parties, and they must notify the parties prior to broadcasting recorded content. Long-distance calls can be recorded only under limited circumstances, including an announcement made at the beginning of the call indicating it will be recorded or possibly broadcast. Violation of these rules can result in the forfeiture of the station's license, fines, or other penalties.

One area of confusion regarding privacy is whether posting material in a blog or on a social media site like Facebook is public or not. Some claim that it is the same as a public space. An offhand comment in a bar, however, disappears once it is said; but an inflammatory blog post written years ago and later deleted still exists somewhere on the web.

## GOING UNDERCOVER

The legality and ethics of journalists going undercover are also not settled. In many ways, it depends on how ethical or responsible the media professional was in using these techniques. Questions that may be asked in a court of law include the following: Were the media being fair? Does going undercover or using hidden cameras somehow manipulate or distort the situation? Do the undercover techniques help build meaningful information or simply sensationalize the story? If a media professional (or anyone else, for that matter) is convicted of violating the law in going undercover, penalties may include prison terms and fines.

The Internet raises new questions about journalists not announcing their identity. If a journalist participates in a child-pornography online discussion group without revealing her or his identity as a journalist pursuing a story, is it ethical to use others' posts without their permission? Is it ethical to pose as someone other than a journalist to get people to talk as they naturally would in an online forum?

## VICTIMIZING THE VICTIMS

Publicizing details of crimes can contribute to copycat crimes. Journalists must always consider which elements of a story are important and which are simply lurid or titillating. Needlessly mentioning race, gender, or sexual orientation can often be unethical, framing a subject in a way that reinforces social stereotypes and makes crime victims feel like they are being victimized again.

Photographs and video can sometimes tell a story more powerfully than words alone. Yet news value alone does not always justify publicizing dramatic photos or footage. In fact, in cases of human tragedy, sadness, or crime, the repeated presentation of pictures or video can violate personal grief.

Citizen-journalists, often unaware of professional norms or laws, may act unethically or find themselves in legal trouble. In a social media world, the question of who is a journalist and thus who gets special First Amendment protections lacks a clear answer.

Some victims of sexual crimes have been victimized further, not by the mainstream media but by peers who have posted videos or photos of their acts on social media. In 2016, eighteen-year-old Brandy Vela killed herself. She had been a victim of relentless cyberbullying. Brandy's sister Jackie described the posts she received on social media and via text. "They would say really, really mean things like, 'Why are you still here?' They would call her fat and ugly. She was beautiful, absolutely beautiful; the only thing people could find to pick on her was her weight." Brandy's family suspected something was wrong, but did not realize how bad things had become. Brandy had changed her phone number and reported the cyberbullying to the police. But, Jackie explained, the police "couldn't do anything because [the suspects] used an app and it wasn't traceable." The incidence rate of cyberbullying has been increasing as teens too readily use social media to hurt others.[7]

## MISREPRESENTATION AND PLAGIARISM

Instances of journalists distorting or misrepresenting the facts are sadly legion. Janet Cooke, Jayson Blair, and Stephen Glass became textbook examples, an infamous club of journalistic ignominy that highly esteemed and veteran reporter Brian Williams recently joined when he was suspended from his venerable position as NBC anchor amid allegations of misrepresenting events that had occurred while he was covering the Iraq War a decade earlier.

Another problem occurs when journalists misrepresent their relationship to their work, claiming inappropriate authorship of material. The most common type of plagiarism involves copying the work of others without formal attribution. Authors can also plagiarize themselves, however, by reproducing what they have previously published without citing

After admitting he had overstated the risks he faced while covering conflict in the Middle East, Brian Williams was suspended for seven months by NBC in 2015. He is now back doing TV news on MSNBC, the network's cable news channel. **CRITICAL THINKING QUESTIONS:** Was NBC's response appropriate? What does their decision say about their ethical values? What factors do you think may have encouraged Williams to exaggerate the dangers he experienced?

themselves as the source. In 2012, Jonah Lehrer, thirty-one, a noted journalist and science writer, was castigated for self-plagiarism, a sin compounded by an even worse transgression—fabricating quotes from the likes of Bob Dylan. Such revelations torpedoed his rising star, as publishers pulled his books from stores and Lehrer was fired from his job at *The New Yorker* after only two months on the job.[8]

## SOCIETY OF PROFESSIONAL JOURNALISTS CODE OF ETHICS

The Society of Professional Journalists (SPJ) is a large organization of working journalists and student chapters that tries to ensure that journalism is being practiced professionally and ethically as it fulfills its role in society. The SPJ's code of ethics states that journalists should "seek truth and report it" and that "journalists should be honest, fair and courageous in gathering, reporting and interpreting information." These are some of the other principles in the code:

- Test the accuracy of information from all sources and exercise care to avoid inadvertent error. Deliberate distortion is never permissible.
- Diligently seek out subjects of news stories to give them the opportunity to respond to allegations of wrongdoing.
- Identify sources whenever feasible. The public is entitled to as much information as possible on sources' reliability.
- Make certain that headlines, news teasers, and promotional material, photos, video, audio, graphics, sound bites, and quotations do not misrepresent. They should not oversimplify or highlight incidents out of context.
- Never distort the content of news photos or video. Image enhancement for technical clarity is always permissible. Label montages and photo illustrations.
- Avoid misleading reenactments or staged news events. If reenactment is necessary to tell a story, label it.
- Support the open exchange of views, even views journalists find repugnant.
- Avoid undercover or other surreptitious methods of gathering information except when traditional open methods will not yield information vital to the public. Use of such methods should be explained as part of the story.

## Ethical Issues in Advertising

Mass media are a powerful vehicle to influence the public's opinions, even when they are simply trying to inform or educate. It is no wonder, then, that companies spend billions of dollars on advertising each year. Yet numerous ethical issues have been raised involving false and deceptive advertising in the mass media.

Advertising is an important part of how goods and services are marketed in a capitalist economy, and some advertising contains useful product information. Advertising is also the economic engine that drives much of the system of mass communication.

The advertising industry has not been entirely successful at regulating itself. Historically, the government has enacted new laws or regulations after receiving consumer complaints—or sometimes after long campaigns regarding certain advertising practices. The Federal Trade Commission (FTC) and the Food and Drug Administration (FDA) enforce regulations regarding deceptive advertising. Industry self-regulation comes from a variety of trade organizations. One of the main ethical issues, from a mass-communication perspective, is false or deceptive advertising.

## DECEPTIVE ADVERTISING

Deception in advertising is not always illegal because, in some cases, it does not mislead. For instance, real ice cubes would disappear quickly under the photographer's hot lights. Fake ice cubes, on other hand, do not melt, nor do they deceive anyone regarding the taste or look of the beverage. In other cases, however, deceptive claims do mislead the consumer, offering a "going out of business" sale, for example, when the store intends to remain open.

A division of the FTC is assigned responsibility to ferret out deception and can expel such advertising from mass media and even levy fines. The FTC once found a commercial for a toy car misleading, even though it was not false. The toy was filmed in extreme close-up next to the track, making it appear to move rapidly like a blur. After an FTC ruling that children could be deceived by the toy's apparent speed, the ad had to be canceled or modified.

A court ordered Skechers to pay $40 million to customers because it claimed without substantiation that the design of its Shape-ups sneakers would help people lose weight.

## PUFFERY

Nevertheless, the temptation among those selling goods and services, as well as those sponsoring ads, to exaggerate claims is great. **Puffery**, an ethical and legal gray area (sometimes allowed, sometimes not), usually involves an opinion statement about the product. Examples include these familiar advertising slogans:

- "Red bull gives you wings" (Red Bull)
- "Eat fresh" (Subway)
- "For the bold" (Doritos)
- "Now that's better" (Wendy's)

Except for Red Bull, the truth or falsehood of these claims cannot be verified. The FTC permits most puffery, assuming audiences do not perceive these claims as factual. Nobody would actually believe, for example, that wings would grow from drinking Red Bull.

💬 **puffery**

A type of advertising language that makes extravagant and unrealistic claims about a product without saying anything concrete.

> **DISCUSSION QUESTIONS:** Have you ever felt deceived by a product you bought based on seeing it advertised? How did it make you feel, and did you continue to use the product or brand? Why or why not?

## CONFLICTS OF INTEREST IN ADVERTISING

Advertising agencies must be loyal to their clients. It makes little business sense for an agency whose client is a tobacco company to lecture the organization about the harmful effects of smoking. Helping clients sell more product is the advertising agency's professional responsibility, whether they are selling healthy soup or less healthy cigarettes.

Conflicts of interest in advertising can arise in a number of ways. First, employees may find selling harmful products unethical. Some agencies allow employees to choose the organizations they are willing to work with, but making such a choice could ruin a career in other agencies. Second, conflicts of interest occur if an agency works for two competing companies. Even if the teams working for each client are completely separate from each other and based in different cities, confidential information about one client may be divulged to members on the other team. Third, a conflict of interest between loyalty to the client and the actual qualities of the product may arise. An effective advertising campaign can make even a product that lacks the benefits it claims a market leader.

## ADVERTISING CODES OF ETHICS

Various advertising and marketing groups have created codes of ethics for their members. Like all codes of ethics, these are largely unenforceable but act instead as guiding principles and ideals for how the profession or industry wants to present itself to the world.

The American Marketing Association (AMA) lists three ethical norms: Do no harm, foster trust in the marketing system, and embrace ethical values. Many of the values that it gives sound remarkably like virtues, including honesty, responsibility, fairness, respect, transparency, and citizenship. The first code of the American

## CONVERGENCE CULTURE
## Forbidden Fruit

**Ethical consumerism** refers to consumers buying products grown, produced, or manufactured in accordance with their personal ethical standards. Some such ethical concerns include a preference for organic or locally grown produce, fair-trade coffee, and sweatshop-free clothing.

With the rise in popularity of organic foods and fair-trade products, many companies would like their products to seem more environmentally friendly. Although the word "organic" is regulated and may refer to either organic growing practices or the amount of organic ingredients, the word "natural" is not regulated.

Consumers have demonstrated willingness to spend more for products that are good for the environment or produced ethically. For this reason, some companies have engaged in **greenwashing**, inaccurately making products

appear to be environmentally friendly or obtained through fair-trade practices.

A 2013 Oxfam report cited poor labor conditions at Dole fruit banana plantations in the Philippines. It claimed that Dole workers who had tried to join a union were harassed and that pesticides were aerially sprayed on laborers in the fields, among other illegal practices.[9] Dole protested that the report had numerous errors and showed bias against the company in a debate on labeling bananas as fair trade. Nevertheless, Dole agreed to remove its Ethical Choice label from bananas and has committed to ensure workers' rights and improved conditions in its production activities.

Food companies are not the only ones tempted to greenwash. Some energy companies have tried to make their drilling and production activities seem less detrimental. And lobbyists often promote bills that sound environmentally friendly but are not such in practice.

Advertising Federation (AAF) is "Advertising shall tell the truth, and reveal significant facts; the omission of which would mislead the public." Several other points, such as substantiation, comparison, price claims, and testimonials, also address issues of misleading the public.

## Ethics in Public Relations

Public relations people face unique ethical issues compared to journalists, media-entertainment professionals, and advertising people. As with advertising professionals, their loyalties lie with the client; but like journalists, if they present false

### ethical consumerism

A kind of activism in which consumers buy only products that they believe are produced ethically.

### greenwashing

The practice of companies making themselves or their products appear to be organic, environmentally friendly, or supportive of free trade when in fact they are not.

---

## MEDIA PIONEERS
# Kalle Lasn

Activist, author, editor, and documentarian, Kalle Lasn was born in Tallinn, Estonia, in 1942. His family, having fled the advancing Soviet army near the end of WWII, lived in German refugee camps before relocating to Australia. A graduate of the University of Adelaide who studied theoretical and applied mathematics, Lasn wrote war-games computer code for the Australian military. Subsequently, he founded a lucrative market research company in Tokyo that conducted computer-based studies of ad campaigns for global corporations.

Advertising would continue to define his career, although not in the way one might expect given the earlier positions on his resume. World travel and the rebellious spirit of the sixties had a profound and formative influence on young Kalle, particularly the student uprisings in Paris in 1968. In 1970, he moved to Canada, where he turned his talents to filmmaking; and some twenty years later, he established Adbusters with fellow documentarian Bill Smalz.[10]

Based in Vancouver, British Columbia, this nonprofit organization identifies on their website as "a global network of artists, activists, writers, pranksters, students, educators and entrepreneurs who want to advance the new social activist movement of the information age." Their mission involves reclaiming our mental and physical environments through increased media literacy, public education that promotes an aware and engaged citizenry sensitive to the plight of the planet and its people.

Grounded in lefty politics (some might say radically so), the anti-consumerist activism of Adbusters seeks nothing short of a paradigm shift that topples existing power structures while encouraging lifestyles that harmonize ecology and economy.[11] To that end, Lasn relentlessly targets what he views as a major culprit in creating and sustaining the ills of consumer culture—advertising. True to their name, the signature media

of Adbusters are subversive advertisements, or "subvertisements": Joe Camel, the iconic cigarette mascot, revisited as a patient in a cancer ward; or a smiling Tiger Woods, his grin transformed into Nike's logo, the swoosh stripe synonymous with the company he endorses. These spoof ads function as "culture jams" intended to reassign provocative new meaning to familiar media images, satire that conveys political messages about corporate, commercial, and branded products.

Other controversial Adbusters campaigns include Absolute Craze (a spoof on Absolute Vodka), Digital Detox Week, Buy Nothing Day, and Buy Nothing Christmas (whose names speak for themselves), and—most famously—OccupyWallStreet. Conceived on Canada's West Coast and named for Lasn's activist hashtag (#OccupyWallStreet), his brainchild rapidly developed into a global movement protesting social and economic inequality.

or misleading information, their credibility and that of their clients can be lost. In addition, although some public relations practitioners like to claim they are the "conscience of the client," they do not always have access to the corporate channels of power to prevent unethical decisions. Often, they are called in to minimize or negate damage already done.

Some PR firms hire people to attend corporate or government meetings and present testimonials as if they were concerned citizens. They also create faux grassroots campaigns online, **astroturfing campaigns**, designed to present the appearance of citizen support for a company or cause. If people posing at a public forum is unethical, then so too is the online equivalent. Today's 24/7 social-media environment makes damage control difficult, especially when celebrity clients tweet offensive comments. Even when quickly deleted, such posts remain in the public eye, retweeted by the celebrity's many followers. First Lady Melania Trump in 2017, for instance, "liked" a Tweet that suggested she was no fan of her husband, President Trump. She deleted her "like," but it has continued to circulate as others on social media share the post.

> 💬 **astroturfing campaign**
>
> A movement or campaign that looks as though it was created by concerned citizens as a grassroots movement when in fact it was actually created or controlled by an organization with a vested interest in the outcome.

## CONFLICTS OF INTEREST IN PR

Partly because of professional loyalty to their clients, public relations is plagued by many of the same conflicts of interest as advertising. A PR firm may have to manage a crisis communication situation for a disaster caused by a company, even as it sees corporate executives take further PR missteps—such as when BP's CEO at the time, Tony Hayward, said, "I'd like my life back," after their oil spill had claimed eleven lives and devastated the environment in the Gulf.

PR professionals may also have clients who believe that anything they release to the media is newsworthy. Clients may also not like having to adjust to a world where their customers can talk and complain with each other in public forums. Although PR agencies claim to manage relationships with the client's many publics, in truth, many clients do not want an equal relationship with consumers based on dialog and openness. Instead, they want to dictate messages to the public without a response. This dynamic can be difficult for a PR professional who ethically believes in the importance of dialog.

One of the thorniest conflicts of interest occurs when a PR professional is asked to keep material about the client confidential to protect the company's image, such as information about a prescription drug's harmful side effects. Other ethical lapses in PR can have far-reaching consequences, especially when it comes to politics and war.

Hired at a cost of more than half a million dollars by the Kuwaiti government to foster support among the American public and the U.S. Congress, the firm of Hill and Knowlton was widely criticized for clandestine efforts to influence opinion on the Gulf War. They produced and distributed dozens of video news releases (VNRs) to television news operations around the country, aired by many stations without editing and without identifying their source as either the PR firm or the government of Kuwait—propaganda presented as impartial journalism.

Hill and Knowlton also helped organize the "Congressional Human Rights Caucus." In October 1990 at a Capitol Hill hearing, a fifteen-year-old Kuwaiti girl, known only as Nayirah, spoke tearfully: "I volunteered at the al-Addan hospital. While I was there, I saw the Iraqi soldiers come into the hospital with guns, and go into the room where . . . babies were in incubators. They took the babies out of the incubators, took the incubators, and left the babies on the cold floor to die." For months after her testimony, the media and even President George H. W. Bush repeated the Iraqi soldiers' killing of babies as a rationale for U.S. presence in the region.

Later, Nayirah was revealed to be a member of the Kuwaiti royal family whose testimony had been fabricated. A Hill and Knowlton vice president had even coached her on it. Hill and Knowlton was never penalized or formally reprimanded for their campaign, but the CBC (Canadian Broadcasting Corporation) produced an Emmy Award–winning documentary on the subject, *To Sell a War* (1992).

## PUBLIC RELATIONS CODES OF ETHICS

Professional associations such as the Public Relations Society of America (PRSA) and the International Association of Business Communicators (IABC) publish guidelines for ethical public relations practices. According to the PRSA, unethical behavior includes lying by omission, as in failing to release a company's financial information or misrepresenting its performance; deceiving the public by employing people as speakers for public hearings and ostensibly grassroots campaigns; and giving expensive goods or gifts to journalists or politicians to influence their opinion.

On the other hand, their guidelines also state that members must protect the privacy rights of clients and safeguard their confidential information as well as advise appropriate authorities if they discover an employee divulging confidential information. An ethical conflict could easily arise for a PR professional if asked by a company to promote positive news on its financial health rather than report the truth.

Some Native Americans have protested the use of "tribal" clothing by fashion designers and shoppers.

# Ethics in Entertainment

Media professionals in entertainment do not wrestle with the same issues regarding truth and the public as journalists, advertisers, and public relations professionals do. Entertainment is meant to entertain, and the truth may be immaterial in this pursuit. Documentary films or books and movies based on actual events may be judged on their faithfulness to the facts, but straying from the truth does not usually harm their entertainment value. Because of this, entertainment content is not held to the same ethical standards as, say, a newspaper story or an investigative TV report. But ethics do enter into the world of entertainment because of its ability to shape society's beliefs and influence behavior.

## STEREOTYPES IN ENTERTAINMENT

Because entertainment plays such an important part in our lives and is a powerful force for transmitting cultural values, its depiction of stereotypes can be especially hurtful or damaging to groups. At the turn of the twentieth century, minstrel shows were popular in vaudeville, with white actors made up in "blackface" to depict African Americans, often in demeaning or clownish roles. Jewish minstrel shows similarly played on popular stereotypes of the time.

Asians and Asian Americans have faced both positive and negative stereotypes over the years. As many Asians immigrated to the United States in the nineteenth and early

The debate continues: Does violence in entertainment contribute to violence in society?

twentieth centuries, the mass media often depicted them in negative ways. Today, they are often touted as a "model minority" because of their many academic and professional achievements. However, racist stereotypes still appear in the media, such as the controversial 2013 Day Above Ground video "AsianGirlz," removed from YouTube within days due to critical responses in social media. Taylor Swift's 2015 video "Wildest Dreams" also engendered controversy for playing with racial stereotypes, particularly romanticizing colonial Africa.[12]

Some may wonder where the harm lies in good-natured jokes or satiric stereotypes, especially those meant to entertain. Yet underlying stereotypes, often taken for granted, help mold beliefs, especially when the media provide our primary exposure to these groups. Stereotypes of Muslims are a good case in point. According to a 2016 Pew Research Center survey, 49 percent of Americans say at least some Muslims in the United States are anti-American.

Moreover, negative views of Muslims among Americans are even more pronounced depending on one's political affiliation. Almost two-thirds (63 percent) of Republicans say at least half of Muslims in the United States are anti-American.[13] Meanwhile, less than half (41 percent) of Democrats say so. Such perceptions influence in subtle and sometimes not-so-subtle ways how we interact with the groups stereotyped.

> **DISCUSSION QUESTIONS:** Consider a movie or television show that perpetuates stereotypes. Replace that stereotyped group with your own ethnicity or gender and consider how you would feel seeing a member of your group depicted in those situations. How might that make you feel about your group?

This parody poster for the movie *Avengers* portrays the male characters as female characters are usually portrayed, drawing attention to the objectification of women in entertainment media.

## SEX AND VIOLENCE

Depictions of sex and violence have long been staples of entertainment media, and the old adage "sex sells" is even truer for entertainment than for other forms of media. We will look at the legal implications for media and freedom of speech regarding pornography, obscenity, and violence in Chapter 12. Here, we consider the ethical implications of depictions of sex and violence.

At the heart of the issue is the belief that media exposure affects us: Watching too many violent programs can produce violent behavior; people may copy crimes they've seen on television or in movies. Although these media effects will be examined in more detail in Chapter 13, let us assume for now some truth to this claim. If so, then any kind of violent content could be unethical. Within the utilitarian, virtue-based, or another ethical system, would purposely harming others be considered ethical, especially when done simply to profit a company and shareholders?

Another issue arises with sex and violence in the media, even given the fact that most people do not become mass murderers after watching a violent movie. This new issue relates to the earlier points about stereotypes and how they may affect our thinking about certain groups. Consider the double standards about male and female nudity in movies, for example. Rarely do movies show full frontal male nudity, whereas female nudity can be seen much more frequently. Such depictions may give us cues that normalize the treatment of women, but not men, as sex objects.

## MEDIA CAREERS

Relatively few firms have ethics officers (independent PR firm Ruder Finn is a notable exception) whose sole job is helping employees make ethical decisions that affect clients, the public, and even their coworkers. Yet as ethical lapses may have serious repercussions for media companies, even playing a role in closing down the business, as was the case for the *News of the World* newspaper, more companies may be looking to establish ethics officer positions.

Some news organizations have an ombudsman or public editor whose job is to analyze, decide on, and respond to ethical problems that the organization faces when working on various stories. The ombudsman or public editor is usually a well-respected editor or columnist who has spent many years building his or her reputation within journalism.

Most media organizations of any size have legal teams or lawyers who can be consulted when needed, but remember that an organization can act legally even if it is not acting ethically. Do not confuse getting advice on the legality of an action with whether it is ethical or not. And as noted earlier in the chapter, media ethics is not a stand-alone subject. These decision-making skills should inform daily practices for all media professionals, even those whose jobs are not formally dedicated to ethics.

For any media professional, an increasingly important role is that of using social media to promote one's work or organization. In the days before social media, such promotional efforts were often frowned upon, especially in journalism, as an unethical conflict of interest. Yet, in the twenty-first-century's connected world, it has emerged as not only ethically acceptable but a virtual requirement for most media professionals. Using social networks has become a key component of engaging with the audience or the public.

## LOOKING BACK AND MOVING FORWARD

The issue of ethics, although an integral part of our media environment, is too often ignored, misunderstood, or overlooked in the day-to-day hustle of media professionals. Developing moral-reasoning skills takes time and enduring effort. The sheer variety of situations that arise calling for moral reasoning, especially in the media professions, means that there will always be a new challenge ahead. If, however, you can develop good moral-reasoning abilities, you can build on past experiences and results—right and wrong decisions—and apply that knowledge to new situations.

Understanding the various ethical systems and what they deem right can help you find your own moral compass. You do not have to choose an ethical system and stay with it, but you may feel more comfortable regularly drawing from one ethical system over others. Even so, being able to take elements from each one, as the situation calls for, can help you determine the values in conflict and find answers that help ensure ethical decision making.

Some of the later ethical systems, such as the dialogical and ethics-of-care systems, can be especially fruitful in a social media world where conversations online and perceived relationships become more important. Further, the virtues that they espouse in showing respect to others may help mitigate some of the divisiveness and anger that we see today in our political rhetoric and social lives.

## MEDIA MATTERS    HOW MORAL ARE YOU?

Ethical questions can often be difficult because there may not always be a single "right" answer. There are always conflicts between groups and between individuals and society. See if you can come up with ethical solutions to the following scenarios based on real-life incidents:

1. You work in a PR firm whose biggest and most important client is a noted Fortune 500 company. In a meeting with them to discuss future strategy and publishing their annual report, they admit that they have "cooked the books" in some of their divisions to inflate revenues. They say everyone in their industry does it, even as they want promises from everyone at the meeting that they will not divulge that information. What do you do?

2. The TV news crew you are part of is covering an investigative story on a defect in a brand of car. You see other members of the crew wire the car to create a large explosion. Your editor explains that having failed to show the desired results with the first two cars, they are trying to emulate what has been reported to have happened. Do you think this is ethical?

3. While working as a member of the production crew on a reality television series, you befriend one of the cast members. Weeks later, in the editing room, you see the producer piecing together snippets of the hundreds of hours of video and audio to create a loose narrative that puts that cast member in a highly negative light. She has signed a waiver, as is typical, in which she agrees to any depiction of her. Do you think what the producer is doing is ethical?

4. The advertising agency you work for has created an ad campaign for a new soft drink—"The best-tasting orange soda. Ever." You know from the market research and from blind taste tests that the client's soda consistently scored lower than competing brands. Is it ethical to use this phrase in the advertising campaigns?

## FURTHER READING

*Moral Theory: An Introduction*, 2nd ed. Mark Timmons (2012) Rowman & Littlefield.

*Communicating Ethically: Character, Duties, Consequences, and Relationships*. William W. Neher, Paul J. Sandin (2007) Pearson Education.

*Would You Eat Your Cat? Key Ethical Conundrums and What They Tell You About Yourself*. Jeremy Stangroom (2012) W. W. Norton & Company.

*Media Ethics at Work: True Stories from Young Professionals*. Lee Anne Peck, Guy S. Reel (2012) CQ Press.

*The Handbook of Mass Media Ethics*. Lee Wilkins, Clifford G. Christians (eds.) (2009) Routledge.

*Ethics for Public Communication*. Clifford Christians, John Ferre, Mark Fackler (2011) Oxford University Press.

*Living Ethics: Across Media Platforms*. Michael Bugeja (2007) Oxford University Press.

*Lying: Moral Choice in Public and Private Life*. Sissela Bok (1999) Vintage.

*The Cambridge Companion to Virtue Ethics*. Daniel Russell (ed.) (2013) Cambridge University Press.

*Virtue Ethics, Old and New*. Stephen Gardiner (2005) Cornell University Press.

*Moral Understandings: A Feminist Study in Ethics*, 2nd ed. Margaret Urban Walker (2007) Oxford University Press.

*Habermas: A Very Short Introduction*. Gordon Finlayson (2005) Oxford University Press.

*A Theory of Justice: Original Edition*. John Rawls (2005) Belknap Press of Harvard University Press.

*Ethics of Media*. Nick Couldry, Mirca Madianou, Amit Pinchevski (eds.) (2013) Palgrave Macmillan.

*Disconnected: Youth, New Media, and the Ethics Gap*. Carrie James (2014) MIT Press.

*The Ethics of Star Trek*. Judith Barad, Ed Robertson (2001) Harper Perennial.

*Media Ethics Beyond Borders: A Global Perspective*. Stephen J. A. Ward, Herman Wasserman (eds.) (2010) Routledge.

*The Ethics of Star Trek*. Judith Barad, Ed Robertson (2001) Harper Perennial.

*Doing Ethics in Media: Theories and Practical Applications*. Jay Black and Chris Roberts (2011) Routledge.

# Communication Law and Regulation in the Digital Age

P resident Trump has attempted to make good on his campaign promise to ban all Muslims from entering the United States, but as of this writing, he has had his multiple executive orders blocked by federal judges and U.S. appeals courts. It is not clear how this issue will be ultimately resolved, but it raises important questions about constitutional issues, especially regarding the First Amendment, and matters pertaining to individual rights regarding freedom of speech, assembly, and religion.

Myriad organizations, including the American Civil Liberties Union (ACLU), have entered the debate over the state of civil liberties under the Trump administration. Among the actions the ACLU and its affiliates have taken are requests for information under the Freedom of Information Act, which journalists often use to access public records. In this case, the ACLU has sought to learn how the Trump administration directed federal officials with regard to the implementation of the president's executive order regarding the proposed Muslim ban.

> Congress shall make no law respecting an establishment of religion, or prohibiting the free exercise thereof; or abridging the freedom of speech, or of the press; or the right of the people peaceably to assemble, and to petition the government for a redress of grievances.
>
> FIRST AMENDMENT TO THE CONSTITUTION OF THE UNITED STATES

The First Amendment is very much an American invention. Most other countries have no such stipulation in their constitutions, which of course has sometimes resulted in vastly different laws and regulations regarding mass communication and journalism.

Governments decide on policies or overarching objectives that they want to accomplish based on a variety of factors. These factors include the political views of the party in power, the type of government (whether elected by citizens or empowered in some other way), and the general social and cultural norms of the nation. Laws are created and enacted to carry out the government's policies, but which laws are created also depends on the form of government. In democracies, even the party in power may not be able to create laws it wants because of opposition-party actions, or bills may be altered as part of compromises to become laws. Laws, once enacted, are forcibly upheld by the state and carry penalties such as fines or imprisonment if broken. Similar to laws, regulations act as tools to enable policies, but if violated, fines or other less severe sanctions serve as penalties rather than imprisonment.

Although the **First Amendment** guarantees that Congress shall make no law restricting freedom of speech or of the press, interpretations of the courts, elected officials, and legal scholars have permitted some level of regulatory and legal restriction. Some of these laws deal with libel, obscenity, and other media content. Others deal with technical issues related to broadcast-station operation, such as preventing one station from interfering with another's signals; and others pertain to media ownership, intellectual property rights, and fulfilling the requirements of broadcasting licenses. We will look at how these differ and how they relate to media and public policy, primarily in the United States, although other countries will sometimes be examined for comparison.

## The Legal Framework

When printing began in Renaissance Europe, political and religious authorities were quick to recognize the power of publishing to spread not only religious teachings but political edicts as well. Political and religious dissidents, however, found printing presses equally useful in disseminating their views against authority. The tension between government control of the press and the press as a means to be free of political or religious control continues to this day.

The reasons underlying the value of freedom from governmental control were perhaps best articulated by U.S. president Thomas Jefferson, who said, "Information is the currency of democracy." When the first U.S. Congress passed the Bill of Rights in 1789, fewer than three dozen printing presses existed in the country. Despite this small number, the nation's founders recognized the great importance of the press. Jefferson said, "Were it left for me to decide whether we should have a government without newspapers, or newspapers without a government, I should not hesitate a moment to prefer the latter."

The press is a critical watchdog of government and other powerful institutions in society, including business. But as an unofficial "fourth branch" of government, or **fourth estate**, the press must be free from government censorship or control. Although Jefferson referred only to print media, the only form of mass communication during his time, his comments apply equally to electronic mass communication. When we refer to "the press," we include print and electronic media.

In societies where government control over the press, or media, is substantial, as in China or other authoritarian countries where journalists must be licensed to operate, the press cannot criticize the government, its policies, or its representatives. The press usually promotes government positions rather than evaluating them independently. In democratic societies, the press ideally acts as an independent balance of power to government bodies. Yet concentration of ownership and media companies' commercial interests can adversely affect the ability of the press

### First Amendment

Guarantees that Congress shall make no law restricting freedom of speech, press, or religion.

### fourth estate

Another term for the press, or journalism, which acts as a fourth branch of government, one that watches the other branches (executive, legislative, and judicial).

to pursue the public interest impartially. For news organizations, business interests may sometimes outweigh public interests.

Despite the early constitutional admonitions to protect freedom of speech and the press, the government at all levels has frequently tried to infringe on the independence of the press and to censor content. In addition, the government has extended full First Amendment protection only to print media. In *Miami Herald Publishing Co. v. Tornillo* (1974), for instance, the U.S. Supreme Court struck down a Florida statute that required newspapers to give space at no cost to political candidates whose personal or professional character the paper had criticized. Television and radio stations, however, must provide candidates with the opportunity for equal airtime should the station itself editorially endorse or oppose a specific candidate.

Radio, television, cinema, and the Internet have received much less First Amendment protection than print media, and only through extended legal battles have they won a certain degree of freedom. In fact, cinema had no First Amendment protection until the Supreme Court's 1952 *Miracle* decision (*Joseph Burstyn, Inc. v. Wilson*), when the court ruled that the showing of a film could not be prohibited because a censor deemed it sacrilegious.

The historical influences and legal and regulatory decisions on print and electronic media are complex but worth exploring briefly to better understand the restrictions on media content today.

Thomas Jefferson's famous quote about his choice between government and newspapers is often cited to show the important role that journalism plays in a democracy.

## The Foundations of Freedom of Expression

Governments continue to use many means to control media. One heavy-handed method is to jail journalists and editors, not only to silence them but to produce a **chilling effect** on others who may be tempted to write on similar topics.

Yet such tactics can anger the public or damage the government's reputation. More subtle means of control, such as licensing laws for journalists or special taxes on printing equipment, paper, or ink, have been adopted in the past. By controlling the materials needed for printing, governments hoped to be able to control the free flow of information. Government censors, or bodies that examine and approve all printed material, have also been used.

Although different governmental measures persist in various countries, controlling information has become increasingly difficult. This is partly because vastly more information is available and partly because electronic media, including the Internet, have become important information sources alongside print media. Nevertheless, countries like China maintain strict control over electronic media and the Internet. The government blocks certain websites from appearing on searches performed within the country, and companies like Google have agreed to restrictions they would normally not allow, just so they can do business in China. Apple in 2016 agreed to the Chinese government's request that it pull *The New York Times* mobile app for iTunes from the China market.

Our modern concept of freedom of expression has evolved over time, influenced by several major court decisions that dealt with national security issues, libel, or censorship. These cases have dealt primarily with print media, partly because some occurred before electronic media and partly because print media have traditionally received greater First Amendment protections than electronic media.

**chilling effect**

The phenomenon that occurs when journalists or other media producers decide not to publish stories on a topic after a journalist has been punished or jailed for such a story.

## NATIONAL SECURITY

In 1798, the Federalist-controlled U.S. Congress passed the **Alien and Sedition Acts** in response to the possibility of war with France. The acts, which limited freedom of speech, were meant to silence the Jeffersonian Republicans, who supported France. Among other things, the acts prohibited **sedition**, spoken or written criticism of the U.S. government, and imposed penalties of a fine or imprisonment on conviction. Once the threat of war passed, the Sedition Act expired in 1801; but other sedition acts have resurfaced throughout U.S. history, especially during times of war.[1]

Several important legal concepts have developed with court cases that involved issues of national security, one of the main reasons press freedoms are curtailed.

### Clear and Present Danger

The most basic restriction involves speech that meets both of the following conditions: (1) It is intended to incite or produce dangerous activity (as with falsely shouting "Fire!" in a crowded theater), and (2) it is likely to succeed in achieving the purported result. This **clear and present danger** test is subject to criminal-law-enforcement authorities and the judicial system rather than regulatory authorities.

The clear and present danger test emerged from *Schenck v. United States* (1919). In that case, the U.S. Supreme Court unanimously upheld the conviction of Charles T. Schenck for violating the Espionage Act of 1917. Schenck had been distributing handbills urging resistance to U.S. involvement in World War I. He was a Communist but had committed no violent acts. The Court based its decision on the beliefs that the First Amendment is not absolute and that ordinary constitutional rules do not apply in wartime.

### Alien and Sedition Acts

A series of four acts passed by the U.S. Congress in 1798 that, among other things, prohibited sedition, or spoken or written criticism of the U.S. government, and imposed penalties of a fine or imprisonment on conviction. Although they expired in 1801, other sedition acts have been passed periodically, especially during times of war.

### sedition

Speech or action that encourages overthrow of a government or that subverts a nation's constitution or laws.

### clear and present danger

A restriction on speech that meets both of the following conditions: (1) It is intended to incite or produce dangerous activity (as with falsely shouting "Fire!" in a crowded theater), and (2) it is likely to succeed in achieving the purported result.

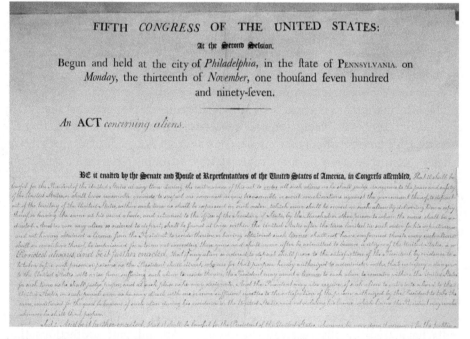

The Alien and Sedition Acts of 1798 were an early example of government attempts to clamp down on dissent and to censor the press.

## Prior Restraint

An important ruling came in the 1931 Supreme Court case *Near v. Minnesota*. Minnesota courts had stopped the publication of an anti-Semitic weekly on the basis that it was a "malicious, scandalous and defamatory" periodical in violation of the state's nuisance law. The Supreme Court reversed the decision, saying that **prior restraint**—the government's preventing or blocking the publication, broadcasting, showing, or otherwise distributing of media content, whether in print, over the air, or in movie theaters—must be used only in cases of serious or grave threats to national security.

In the 1971 case of *New York Times Co. v. United States*, the Supreme Court overturned a lower court ruling that had stopped the *Times* from publishing "The Pentagon Papers," a top-secret Pentagon study of U.S. involvement in the Vietnam War. The government failed to prove that national security interests outweighed a heavy presumption against prior restraint.

In 1979, a district court stopped *The Progressive* magazine (*U.S. v. Progressive*) from publishing "The H-Bomb Secret." The magazine had obtained its information from publicly available documents, and six months later the court injunction was lifted after others published similar material.

Although the courts have ruled that freedom of speech is not absolute, especially during wartime, there is, nonetheless, a strong presumption against permitting the government any form of prior restraint on publication or distribution of speech. The government must clearly demonstrate that publication poses a clear and present threat to national security. This framework seems especially relevant in the aftermath of the September 11, 2001, terrorist attacks on the World Trade Center and the Pentagon.

In 2015, the U.S. Supreme Court ruled the First Amendment applies to social media such as Facebook. In 2014, the Court took up the case involving a man named Anthony Elonis, who posted comments on Facebook threatening his estranged wife and law enforcement.[2] His posts included, "I've got enough explosives to take care of the state police and the sheriff's department"; and "Enough elementary schools in a ten mile radius to initiate the most heinous school shooting ever imagined. And hell hath no fury like a crazy man in a kindergarten class." Convicted of making threats, Elonis has appealed his conviction, claiming his comments were not intended to frighten and were only therapeutic. The Supreme Court overturned the conviction.

In his book *Mass Media Law*, Don Pember describes a **preferred-position balancing theory**. According to this theory, a balance must be struck between speech and other rights, but speech is given a preferred position (especially in print media), and limitations on freedom of speech in print are usually illegal. The government must demonstrate that certain speech threatens national security rather than journalists and media organizations having to prove that it does not.

> 💬 **prior restraint**
>
> When the government prevents or blocks the publication, broadcasting, showing, or distribution of media content, whether in print, over the air, in movie theaters, or online.

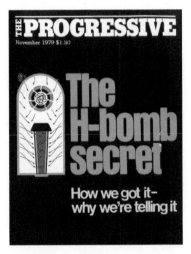

The planned publication by *The Progressive* of instructions for making a hydrogen bomb was a landmark case regarding the government's right of prior restraint.

> 💬 **preferred-position balancing theory**
>
> A legal theory that says that a balance must be struck between speech and other rights, although speech has a preferred position.

**DISCUSSION QUESTIONS:** Do you think the government should have more or less power to exercise prior restraint and block publication or broadcast of material that it feels might hurt national security interests, even from citizens posting to social media sites? Defend your response.

## LIBEL

In the colonial era, the case of John Peter Zenger, a New York printer and journalist, established the relationship between freedom of expression and libel in the United States. Zenger faced a libel suit from the publication of the *New York Weekly Journal*, a political journal. As publisher of the *Journal*, Zenger was responsible for articles that featured scathing attacks on the colonial governor, William Cosby.

Zenger's attorney, Andrew Hamilton, requested that the jury rule on the truth of Zenger's printed statements; and in a surprise ruling in August 1735, Zenger was acquitted of libel. This important precedent established the principle of freedom of the press in early America and departed from the way much of the world considers libel, even today. For example, in England, someone can successfully be sued for libel even if the statements are true and the statements damage a person's reputation.

In the United States, libel is a type of written defamation, such as a false attack on a person's character that damages a person's reputation. **Slander** has historically referred to a similar defamation involving the spoken word. In the twentieth century, libel was extended to broadcasting on television or radio as well as to online communications, even though broadcast media are usually spoken rather than printed.

In the case of *Phipps v. Clark Oil & Ref. Corp.* (1987), the Minnesota court ruled that libel occurs when a publication "tends to injure the plaintiff's reputation and expose the plaintiff to public hatred, contempt, ridicule, or degradation."

### *New York Times Co. v. Sullivan* (1964)

Media historians and legal scholars tend to agree that the most important legal decision to establish a free press in the United States was the 1964 Supreme Court ruling in *New York Times Co. v. Sullivan*.

In 1960, *The New York Times* printed a fundraising advertisement for the civil rights movement that contained minor factual errors. L. B. Sullivan, a Montgomery, Alabama, city police commissioner, said that some of the false statements in the advertisement regarding Montgomery police actions defamed him, even though he was not mentioned by name. A jury agreed and awarded him a half-million dollars. The case eventually went to the Supreme Court, which overturned the lower court ruling.

The Supreme Court ruled that public figures (publicly prominent) and public officials (the makers of public policy) may not sue for libel unless they can prove "actual malice." For non-public figures (private citizens), the standard for libel requires merely that the plaintiff show that a "reasonable person" knew or should have known the defamatory statement was false.

The Court defined actual malice in terms of either (1) the defendant's intent being malicious or (2) the defendant's knowing the statement is false but publishing it anyway. The Court ruled that the common law of defamation violated the guarantee of free speech under the First Amendment and that the citizen's right to criticize government officials is too important to be intolerant of speech

**slander**

A type of defamation that is spoken, as opposed to written (libel), and that damages a person's reputation or otherwise causes harm.

The libel case of Peter Zenger in colonial times was a turning point for what defined "libel" in America.

containing even harmful falsehoods. The ruling has fostered a more robust environment for media to publish criticisms of public figures because they can be found libelous only if they meet the stringent actual-malice test.

## Protecting Journalists Against Libel

Most media organizations have libel insurance to protect journalists. Freelance journalists often do not, though, so the threat of libel can have a chilling effect. This is especially true for online journalists, bloggers, and others who operate on a shoestring budget or who are not widely recognized by media organizations as professional journalists.

Moreover, although there is no prior restraint for libel cases, journalists can be imprisoned for contempt in libel or other cases, such as not divulging the identity of a source or not releasing one's notes.

Five steps can help minimize a journalist's chances of committing libel:

1. Engage in thorough research, including investigating the facts and maintaining good records, establishing and adhering to written criteria in deciding when and what to publish, and using reliable sources.

2. Confirm the identity of the target of your report.

3. Use quotations whenever possible and attribute statements to sources.

4. Report only facts and avoid language that draws conclusions.

5. Avoid bias in reports, and strive for balance (i.e., give the different sides in a debate fair play).

## Shield Laws

**Shield laws** are intended to protect journalists from legal challenges to their freedom to report the news. Journalists have received neither blanket protection from the Supreme Court nor a federal shield law. Yet thirty-four states have enacted laws to protect journalists from having to answer every subpoena.[3] In these states, journalists need not testify or produce materials obtained from confidential sources. Most of the states and territories that lack shield laws provide some court protection for journalists.

In May 2013, the public learned that the Department of Justice had secretly seized the phone records of some Associated Press journalists to discover who had been leaking classified information. In response, President Obama called for a federal shield law, which he had first proposed in 2009.

Without shield laws, legal action might exert a chilling effect on journalists, some suggested, including Reed Hundt, former FCC chairman: "Newsgatherers might be less aggressive and cease to pursue confidential sources or information. Whistle-blowers and other sources could be left without any legal protection from discovery."[4] Under a shield law, the Department of Justice would still likely have obtained the Associated Press phone records, but the journalists involved would have been alerted to this when it occurred rather than after the fact.

Evidence suggests that shield laws have limited effectiveness, based on studies done on the number of subpoenas served to journalists in states with shield laws compared to the number in those without. Opponents of shield laws argue that journalists, given the difficulty inherent in defining this profession, should not be given special protections from answering subpoenas. Others worry that trying to explicitly articulate a definition for journalists could lead to official licensing, which most news organizations strongly oppose as a curtailment of their First Ammendment rights.

**shield law**

A law intended to protect journalists from legal challenges to their freedom to report the news.

## MEDIA PIONEERS
# Anthony Lewis

Most of the media pioneers featured throughout these pages have shaped their fields. Few, however, can claim to have actually *created* the field for which they are known.

The late (2013) *New York Times* journalist and columnist Anthony Lewis could make such a claim. Lewis is widely credited for creating legal journalism, which focuses on covering courts and legal issues. "He brought context to the law," said Ronald K. L. Collins, a University of Washington scholar who compiled a bibliography of Lewis's work. "He had an incredible talent in making the law not only intelligible but also in making it compelling."[5]

Supreme Court judges also admired Lewis's work, with Justice Felix Frankfurter once observing that there weren't two justices sitting on the Court who had more of a grasp of the cases Lewis covered. One of the factors that distinguished Lewis's coverage of court issues was how he brought his own interpretation and opinions into his analysis, going beyond the standard call for objectivity in professional journalism.

Lewis won two Pulitzer Prizes for his coverage of the Supreme Court: in 1955, when he was only twenty-eight, and again in 1963. His published books include *Gideon's Trumpet*, which has been in print since 1964. Another book, *Make No Law*, examined the repercussions of the landmark 1964 case *New York Times v. Sullivan* for libel law in the United States. Despite Lewis's strongly left and liberal views, he did not agree that the press should have a preferred position under the First Amendment. He believed that the First Amendment was meant primarily as a bulwark against government censorship, not as a rationale to give news organizations powers that other groups lacked. Besides writing his column and books, Lewis taught a weekly media-law class at Columbia University's Graduate School of Journalism for twenty-three

years. Through his classes, generations of journalism students experienced his sharp intellect and conversational style that helped bring the law to life.

## CENSORSHIP

**censorship**

The act of prohibiting certain expression or content. Censors usually do not target the whole publication, program, or website but seek to prohibit some part of the content.

**Censorship** refers to the act of prohibiting certain expression or content. It targets specific material within a publication, broadcast, film, or website rather than a work in its entirety. Although rarely permitted in the United States, censorship is routine in countries with authoritarian regimes that prohibit criticism of the government.

The case *Hazelwood School District v. Kuhlmeier* (1988) established that people still in school lack full First Amendment protection. In this case, a school principal was permitted to censor school newspaper articles dealing with pregnancy and divorce. The court found that school-sponsored publications are not a public forum and thus may be subject to censorship to protect the young from harm.

In the United States, censorship is most common in two circumstances: (1) during wartime, when content, especially that being reported from the battlefield, may threaten national security; and (2) with pornographic or obscene content, which can sometimes include graphic violence or detailed accounts of criminal behavior. Citizen groups have long criticized media entertainment companies for portrayals of sex and violence. This has led to fights over censorship and new laws and regulations that have affected the kind of media available to the public, or at least some members of the public.

## The Censorship of Comics

Both governmental and public critics have long scrutinized comics, popular among children and adults. In the McCarthy-era 1950s, psychciatrist Fredric Wertham, published his book, *Seduction of the Innocent*, which contended that violent and sexually graphic comic books caused juvenile delinquency and worse. Wertham's book produced intense pressure from the government and other groups to curtail the graphic sexual and gruesome violent content of comic books, especially horror comics such as *Tales from the Crypt, Haunt of Fear*, and *Vault of Horror*.

According to courts, high school students do not have full First Amendment rights with student publications.

Wertham based his argument on his own observations of juvenile delinquents. He found that many delinquents read a lot of comic books, especially horror comics. He also found that many of these kids were poor readers. Wertham concluded that reading comics, especially horror comics, caused both juvenile delinquency and il-literacy. Although Wertham's reasoning and methodology were flawed, in response to his claims, the U.S. Senate conducted a full-scale investigation in 1954 into the effects of comics on children.

The Senate took no formal legal action against the comics industry. Instead, a consortium called the Association of Comics Magazine Publishers formed the Comics Code Authority (CCA), an industry censorship review board. The CCA read every comic book published and effectively banned sexual content and the most graphic material popular in many horror comics of the day, including torture, sadism, and detailed discussion of criminal acts. A CCA seal of approval appeared on the cover of acceptable comics. The CCA action put many graphic horror comics out of business.

In the 1950s, comic books showing graphic horror and violence were said to cause juvenile delinquency.

The Hays Code, the movie studios' attempt at self-censorship, eventually led to our movie-rating system.

💬 **Hays Code**

A code established in 1930 by the movie industry to censor itself regarding showing nudity or glorifying antisocial acts. Officials for the Hays Office had to approve each film distributed to a mass audience.

💬 **indecent speech**

Language or material that, in context, depicts or describes, in terms patently offensive as measured by contemporary community standards for the broadcast medium, sexual or excretory organs or activities.

## The Hays Code

Some early films, especially prior to 1920, contained considerable nudity or near nudity. Although nudity and sexuality were popular with many filmgoers, some conservative groups were outspoken in their criticism, especially of bare-breasted women or women dressed in revealing clothing. Fearing government censorship, the film industry created the Hays Office, a self-censorship body.

The office produced the **Hays Code** in 1930, outlining many dos and don'ts for the film industry. The Hays Code articulated three general moral principles. First was the intention to prevent production of any motion picture that would "lower the moral standards of those who see it. Hence the sympathy of the audience should never be thrown to the side of crime, wrongdoing, evil or sin." Second, every picture was to present "correct standards of life, subject only to the requirements of drama and entertainment." Third, no picture was to ridicule "natural or human" law.

The code prescribed the proper depiction of content in twelve specific areas, including criminal activity, sex, and religion. By today's standards, many of these prescriptions seem quaint—although well intentioned—and some are offensive, racist, or at least politically incorrect. Still, movies without the Hays Office's stamp of approval might not have received mass distribution by a major studio—a chance most producers were unwilling to take. In the mid-1960s, after a series of Supreme Court cases involving obscenity and a general change in public mores regarding depictions of sexuality, the Hays Code was significantly revised and enforced less stringently. By 1968, the movie-rating system of G, M, R, and X—today modified as G, PG, PG-13, R, NC-17, and X—had replaced the Hays Code. The movie-ratings code has served as a model for industry self-censorship for music, television, and video games.

## Indecent Content

Although not prohibited, **indecent speech** is subject to federal regulation. Broadcasters may not air indecent speech when children are likely to be in the audience, or between 6 a.m. and 10 p.m. This has been called a safe harbor period, and concerned groups sometimes request portrayals of violence or sex to be barred from the time period as well.

Federal law defines indecent speech as "language or material that, in context, depicts or describes, in terms patently offensive as measured by contemporary community standards for the broadcast medium, sexual or excretory organs or activities." Exempted from this definition is profanity that is neither indecent nor obscene. "Damn" is an example of a permitted word. Indecent speech was put to the test in a landmark First Amendment case involving comedian George Carlin.

Carlin recorded before a live California audience a twelve-minute monolog titled "Filthy Words." He opened his routine by contemplating "the words you couldn't say on the public airwaves, the ones you definitely wouldn't say, ever." He then listed those words and repeated them in a variety of contexts. The Supreme Court decision in *Federal Communications Commission v. Pacifica Foundation* (1978) upheld the FCC's power to regulate the airwaves, characterizing the words as indecent but not obscene. The ruling formed the basis for subsequent regulations on indecent speech for broadcasters.

Other entertainers have also pushed the limits of freedom of speech in the electronic media, including comedian Kathy Griffin, who in May 2017 created and posted online a photo of herself holding what appeared to be the severed, bloody head of President Trump. Griffin suggested her intention was political satire, that it was an allusion to the beheadings committed by terrorists such as those of ISIS. Yet, the backlash to her graphic image was swift and powerful. CNN fired Griffin from a position she had held at the cable network for a decade as host of its New Year's Eve show. Griffin apologized for the photo, but it nonetheless established a clear boundary for unacceptable speech in America in 2017.

As part of the **Telecommunications Act of 1996**, the first sweeping federal legislation to rewrite the foundation of communications regulation in the United States since 1934, legislators had sought to curb "indecent" speech online while generally opening up the airwaves to greater innovation. Title V of this effort, the Communications Decency Act, made it illegal to "depict or describe" on the Internet anything considered indecent and made no distinctions between scientific or literary works and pornography. In 1997, however, the U.S. Supreme Court in *Reno v. ACLU* struck down its anti-decency provisions as unconstitutional.

Despite the ruling, some organizations have chosen to self-censor. In 2013, women's groups protested Facebook policy allowing groups, pages, and images that glorified or poked fun at violence against women. Protesters pointed out the contrast with Facebook's long-standing policy of removing photos of breastfeeding mothers from member pages. On Twitter, they shared examples of these violent images from Facebook. Thousands of people sent emails asking major advertisers to abandon Facebook, and protesters claimed to have convinced fifteen brands to do so.[6] After a weeklong campaign, Facebook agreed to improve its standards for detecting and removing such content.

George Carlin's comedy routine "Filthy Words" turned into a landmark case regarding indecent content.

> **DISCUSSION QUESTIONS:** Are FCC standards for indecent speech—that is, what a "contemporary community" considers "patently offensive"—still tenable in online communities? If not, what new standards could be applied? Do you agree that violent images should be censored on Facebook? If so, what kinds of violent images?

## Obscenity

Pornography, or **obscenity**, is deemed unprotected by the First Amendment and is subject to government censorship. In a landmark case, *Miller v. California* (1973), Miller had been convicted in California of mailing unsolicited pornographic brochures. He appealed his conviction on the grounds that it inhibited his right to free speech, but the Court disagreed and outlined three criteria for determining whether content is obscene:

1. An average individual applying contemporary community standards must believe the content, taken as a whole, appeals to prurient interest.

2. The content must show or describe in an offensive manner sexual conduct.

3. The content on the whole must lack serious literary, artistic, political, or scientific value.

Nevertheless, defining obscenity remains difficult, and some would prefer to simply conclude, "I know it when I see it (or hear it)."

### Telecommunications Act of 1996

The first major regulatory overhaul of telecommunications since 1934, designed to open the industry to greater competition by deregulating many aspects of it.

In 2016, under pressure from women's groups, Twitter permanently suspended the account of conservative writer Milo Yiannopoulos after he encouraged his followers to post racist tweets about *Ghostbusters* star Leslie Jones.

### obscenity

One of the forms of speech not protected by the First Amendment and thus subject to censorship. Although an exact definition of the term has been difficult to achieve in various court cases, generally a three-part standard is applied for media content: It must appeal to prurient interests as defined by community standards, it must show sexual conduct in an offensive manner, and it must on the whole lack serious artistic, literary, political, or scientific value.

*Fresh Off the Boat*, the first network show in twenty years to feature an Asian American family, debuted in early 2015 to rave reviews and considerable criticism, stirred by some critics who claim it perpetuates stereotypes. **CRITICAL THINKING QUESTIONS:** Do you agree that comical ethnic depictions such as these do more harm than good? Are cultural stereotypes inherently degrading, and is every cultural group equally vulnerable in this regard? Should negative stereotypes be subject to greater regulatory restrictions?

The digital age has produced unique issues for obscenity cases. One is the ease with which pornography can be distributed across national boundaries. Another is computer-generated pornography that includes realistic images. In April 2002, the Supreme Court struck down provisions in the Child Pornography Prevention Act of 1996, which made it a crime to create, distribute, or possess "virtual" child pornography, or computer-generated images of children in sexual acts (as opposed to images of actual children, which are not protected as free speech). Justice Anthony M. Kennedy wrote for the majority, claiming the act "prohibits speech that records no crime and creates no victims by its production." Although the government argued that real children could be harmed and exploited if a market for virtual child pornography were sustained, Justice Kennedy maintained, "The mere tendency of speech to encourage unlawful acts is not a sufficient reason for banning it."[7]

## Criticism, Ridicule, or Humor

The U.S. Constitution protects stereotypes and other offensive material, as objectionable as they may be. Criticism, ridicule, and jokes about individuals (including government officials), groups, or institutions based on race, religion, gender, national background, or other factors are protected speech, whether in print or electronic media, and may not be regulated by the FCC. In the case of licensed broadcasters, station owners and operators must offer programming that meets the needs of the communities they serve.

The following discussion of the evolution of electronic-communications regulations will highlight the FCC's origin, its role, how regulations differ from those of print media, and how they have influenced today's programming and communication networks.

# Regulating Electronic Media

The origins of U.S. electronic-communications regulations lie in the development of broadcasting in the early part of the twentieth century, starting with radio and later including television. The approach has evolved as a result of changing technical and economic factors.

## EARLY DAYS AND THE RADIO ACT OF 1912 (1911–1926)

The regulation of broadcasting in the United States has included four stages. Prior to 1911, no authority regulated broadcasting, which at the time meant specifically radio transmissions. So little was known about the new medium in its infancy that there was little to regulate. Because radio emerged as a vital technology for ships at sea, especially for making distress calls, the Commerce Department's Bureau of Navigation was put in control of radio and made it a legal requirement in the **Radio Act of 1912** that all large ships maintain radio contact with ships or shore stations. Responsibility for radio regulation rested with the Commerce Department until 1927.

During this period, most radio broadcasters were amateur technology enthusiasts, and obtaining a frequency on which to broadcast was an informal process.

**Radio Act of 1912**

The act assigned frequencies and three- and four-letter codes to radio stations and limited broadcasting to the 360-meter wavelength.

As broadcast historian Mark Goodman points out, "By mailing a postcard to Secretary of Commerce Herbert Hoover, anyone with a radio transmitter, ranging from college students experimenting in science classes to amateur inventors who ordered kits, to newspaper-operated stations, could broadcast on the frequency chosen by Hoover."[8]

By 1926, there were 15,111 amateur radio stations and 536 broadcasting stations in the United States. Despite geographic separation of radio transmitters and various power restrictions on those transmitters, great interference still occurred between the different stations' signals. As radio became what historian Erik Barnouw calls "A Tower of Babel," the need for regulation grew. In the 1920s, much public attention became focused on the new medium of radio and the government's attempts to regulate it.[9]

## INCREASING REGULATION AND THE FEDERAL RADIO COMMISSION (1927–1933)

"The airwaves by 1927 were an open forum for anyone with the expertise and equipment to reach a forum with 25 million listeners," explains Mark Goodman.[10] But the rapid and largely uncontrolled growth of the new medium required a new regulatory structure. The **Radio Act of 1927**, signed into law in February of that year and influenced by railroad regulations, stated that anyone who owned a radio frequency and radio should operate for the "public convenience, interest, or necessity"—even though it didn't define those terms.[11]

The act established the Federal Radio Commission (FRC), with five politically appointed commissioners and a limited staff whose mandate was to sort out the mess in radio. They revoked the vast majority of radio licenses and instituted a new system that favored fewer high-powered stations over many low-powered stations.[12] This change effectively favored radio for big companies over educational institutions, religious organizations, and other groups with small radio stations.

## THE COMMUNICATIONS ACT AND SPECTRUM SCARCITY (1934–1995)

In 1934, Congress enacted the Communications Act, which became the foundation of communications law for the next sixty-two years. The act was based on the premise established in the Radio Act of 1927 that the airwaves were a public good, a limited natural resource that belonged to the people. Licenses were granted to broadcast on the airwaves at no cost, but only to those considered public trustees who were expected to use the airwaves responsibly. Because of the limited nature of the airwaves, the act established regulations based on the notion of "spectrum scarcity," or limited channel capacity. Under this model, news met the public service requirements for radio and television broadcasters.

The Communications Act of 1934 established the Federal Communications Commission (FCC), with five political appointees, including one chair, and a series of bureaus, each assigned responsibility for an area of the growing radio industry. The FCC would eventually assume regulatory responsibility for television, wire, satellite, and cable.

**Radio Act of 1927**

An act of Congress that created the Federal Radio Commission, intended to regulate the largely chaotic airwaves and based on the principle that companies had a civic duty to use airwaves, a limited public good, responsibly.

In radio's earliest days, anyone could create his or her own radio station simply by setting up a tower and transmitter and sending a postcard to the Commerce Department.

## THE TELECOMMUNICATIONS ACT AND THE INTERNET (1996–PRESENT)

The technological transformation of the global communication system, including the Internet, led Congress to enact the Telecommunications Act of 1996, the first major overhaul of the Communications Act of 1934. The convergence of telecommunications, computing, and traditional media in a digital, networked environment required a basic reconstruction of the regulatory framework for the media of mass communication.

The act introduced that new framework. Although it preserved the requirement to serve in the "public interest, convenience, and necessity," the act's new mandate was to foster competition in the communications marketplace. The preamble of the act states that it is intended "to promote competition and reduce regulation in order to secure lower prices and higher quality services for American telecommunications consumers and encourage the rapid deployment of new telecommunications technologies." The digital revolution made the premise of channel scarcity obsolete. The public no longer had only three or four network channels to watch—it now had broadcasting choices ranging from cable or satellite television to, increasingly, Internet-based programming.

The Telecommunications Act of 1996 raises issues that affect not just the structure and regulation of the communications industry but the nature of programming and production. The act promotes direct competition among all telecommunications providers, including terrestrial broadcasters, direct broadcast satellite providers, mobile-communication services, cable providers, what were the regional Bell telephone companies. Further, the act specifically targets violent or sexual programming and interactive services.

Since passage of the act, media ownership has become dramatically more concentrated. Whether this trend will foster competition or create powerful media cartels has been a subject of some debate. The act does not limit the number of television stations a single person or organization may own in the United States, as long as the combined reach is no more than 35 percent of U.S. households. Eli Noam and Robert Freeman point out that these regulatory, economic, and technological trends have resulted in unprecedented programming diversity at the national level and ever-dwindling diversity at the local level.[13]

Because the act eliminates the legal barriers preventing telephone and television companies from competing in the areas of telephone and video services, consumers have seen an increased array of alternative service providers. These include cable companies providing telephone service, for example. Similarly, consumers have seen an increase in the range of both phone and video services, such as VOD, voicemail, and call waiting. Several attempts have been made in recent years to pass further sweeping legislation on issues such as **Network neutrality** (Net neutrality), voice-over IP (VoIP), and other new technologies that either did not exist or were just emerging in 1996.

**Network neutrality**

The principle that broadband networks should be free of restrictions on content, platforms, or equipment and that certain types of content, platforms, or equipment should not get preferential treatment on the network.

## INTERNATIONAL ELECTRONIC MEDIA REGULATION

In many countries, the development of radio as mass communication was an extension of existing government-run telegraph services. Unlike the United States, where commercial forces tended to dominate, in Europe and European colonies, a public service ethos for electronic media was most prevalent. This limited the number of radio or television networks to a few licensed or run directly by the government. The principle of public service led programming to emphasize news, education, and culture rather than pure entertainment.

The European Union in the last twenty years has seen a steady trend toward privatization and less regulation of radio and television. Consequently, European broadcasters have licensed more U.S. programming, making shows like *Baywatch* and *The Simpsons* global hits. While this trend has varied audience programming, it also raises charges of cultural imperialism (discussed in Chapter 15). Local broadcasters may too easily buy American programming rather than support home-grown productions.

The EU's movement toward more liberalization and privatization will likely increase the concentration of media ownership there. Asian countries each have their own regulations and laws; but, with the exception of Japan, India, the Philippines, and South Korea, most Asian countries have more government control over electronic media than the EU or the United States. For example, owning a satellite dish in Malaysia is illegal, and countries like Singapore and Indonesia have strict regulations on content, especially material critical of the government.

## CONVERGENCE CULTURE
# The Great Network Neutrality Debate

Network neutrality, or Net neutrality, is a concept based on an Internet that should not discriminate among the types of content that pass through it. Internet pioneers believed equality and openness to be a foundational premise of the Net, and these qualities have been espoused by other, equally influential Net researchers and innovators.

After the FCC passed certain regulations in 2005, however, the leading cable and phone companies began lobbying Congress to change the laws governing the operation of the Internet. Essentially, these companies sought a tiered system in which content providers would pay according to how much content they sent over the Internet.

Critics of the lobbying efforts claimed that this would destroy the democratic nature of the Internet, making telephone and cable companies Internet gatekeepers with the power to decide what type of content would be sent fast and what type sent slow, and from whom, and even whether some sites or content would be blocked completely. The companies countered that certain content providers using most of the bandwidth should pay more.

The companies also claimed they had no desire to censor the Internet or to control content, but during 2007 and 2008, they did exactly that on several occasions. One case involved a company slowing the speed of content delivery from a rival media company. In another case, AT&T censored part of a comment from Eddie Vedder during a Pearl Jam concert when he criticized President George W. Bush.

In 2012, the entertainment industry encouraged the Stop Online Piracy Act (SOPA) and the Protect IP Act (PIPA), proposals that would allow companies to sue Internet service providers that carried illegal material. A huge uproar among various groups and citizens helped block this legislation, leaving politicians who had created the bills (many of whom had received large donations from the entertainment industry) scrambling to "rework" them.

The debate is a complex one but may soon be resolved as the FCC moves to settle the matter. Former FCC chairman Tom Wheeler had endorsed a proposal by President Obama to reclassify broadband service as a telecommunications, interactive service. This move would have prevented large companies from establishing fast and slow lanes online. Under President Trump, the Net neutrality debate has moved in favor of the telecommunications industry, seeking to relax regulations on the Internet Service Providers (ISPs). The new FCC chairman Ajit Pai has advanced a new position for the commission that would eliminate Net neutrality in favor of the companies that control the Internet backbone, the ISPs such as Verizon, AT&T, and Comcast.

## INTERNATIONAL PERSPECTIVES
# The Rise and Fall of Russian Media

After the demise of the Soviet Union in 1991, great hope arose for a democratic Russia and a free press that would rebuild the country. Russians have enjoyed tremendous growth in available newspapers, magazines, and books as well as an increase in radio and television stations and the type of programming they offer.

Since 2000, however, certain disturbing trends in Russia have sounded the alarm among journalists and media scholars. One is the concentration of media ownership and owner expectations regarding uncritical coverage of themselves and their interests. Although not as overtly as in the era of Soviet media control, the private owners of many media companies nevertheless exert undue influence over editorial content and programming.

Of even greater concern is how dangerous Russia has become for journalists critical of the government. Since Vladimir Putin first became president in 2000, thirty-four Russian journalists have been killed, with only two of the murders solved. As of May 2017, at least three Russian journalists have been killed just this year. These include Yevgeny Khamaganov, who died of unexplained causes, and Dmitry Popkov, who was discovered dead from gunshot wounds.[14]

The term "extremism" has been broadened to include any criticism of the government. As a result,

journalists who criticize the government or its policies face jail time, and the publications they work for can be shut down. Some allege that the evidence is growing and irrefutable that President Putin has ordered the killing of journalists he does not like.[15] In 2014, Putin introduced another expanded press law that classifies interactive media, such as blogs with at least three thousand readers, as mass communication. Blogs are therefore subject to the same restrictive laws governing newspapers and other heavily regulated Russian media, including criminal penalties for libel and fact-checking errors.

# The Federal Communications Commission (FCC)

**The Federal Communications Commission (FCC)**

Established in 1934, the principal communications regulatory body at the federal level in the United States.

The **Federal Communications Commission (FCC)** is the principal communications regulatory body at the federal level in the United States. Some would say the FCC is also a lightning rod for criticism because of its prominent position on the communications regulatory landscape. Oftentimes, regardless of how the commission rules, some group is left unhappy and vocal about its displeasure.

The FCC consists of five commissioners appointed by the president for five-year terms, each of whom must be confirmed by the Senate. The commission must include at least two representatives of each of the major parties to help ensure its nonpartisan nature.

Among its principal duties, the FCC allocates new broadcast radio and television stations and renews the licenses of existing stations, ensuring that each licensee is complying with laws mandated by Congress. The FCC does not license TV or radio networks—such as CBS, NBC, ABC, Fox, CW, and PBS—except when they are owners of stations. Cable TV and satellite channels are available only to subscribers and have fewer rules to abide by than network broadcasters.

## UNIVERSAL SERVICE

An important item for the FCC is the definition of "universal service," a notion central to, but not defined in, the 1934 act. The act, which identifies universal service as "an evolving level of telecommunications services that the commission shall establish periodically under this section," recognizes six key principles:

1. Quality services at reasonable and affordable rates
2. Access to advanced telecommunications and information services throughout the United States
3. Access in rural and high-cost areas
4. Equitable and nondiscriminatory contributions to the preservation and advancement of universal service
5. Specific, predictable, and sufficient federal and state mechanisms to preserve and advance universal service
6. Access to advanced telecommunications services in elementary and secondary schools and classrooms, health care providers, and libraries

Debates arise from this evolving concept of universal service. One could imagine that it should include fully interoperable high-bandwidth, two-way communication services in homes because during much of the twentieth century, homes were expected to have telephone service. This would create a powerful network engine to drive a new information infrastructure linking wired and wireless technologies and to empower the development of fully interactive, multimedia communications. An alternative perspective, however, would simply mandate that all homes have access to at least two communication-service providers capable of delivering both traditional and new media services (including the Internet). This paradigm reinforces the traditional media producer/consumer divide that characterized mass communications throughout the twentieth century.

## THE FCC, LICENSE RENEWAL, AND REGULATORY POWER

The FCC allows stations to operate either as commercial or noncommercial-educational (public) broadcasters for up to eight years, after which the station must renew its license. This is the case for both radio and television broadcasters licensed to transmit their signals via terrestrial frequencies.

At the time of license renewal, a station must meet five basic requirements demonstrating that it has served in the public interest and met all legal requirements. A station must also accept and respond to viewer or listener complaints. Audience members, journalists, or anyone else may also review the station's "public inspection file," which contains a variety of information about the station.

Federal law regulates or prohibits various station activities. The FCC is authorized to levy a fine or even revoke a station's license for violations. Among the programming concerns for which the FCC may impose fines or withdraw licenses are the airing of obscene or indecent language and nudity when children are likely to be viewing. Generally, only the stations themselves are responsible for selecting their material, including coverage of local issues, news, public affairs, religion, sports events, and other subjects.

Among the prohibited activities for stations are knowingly broadcasting a hoax, including false information regarding a crime or catastrophe (defined as a disaster), especially when such a broadcast might cause public harm. This rule resulted largely from the 1938 *War of the Worlds* radio broadcast.

Today's FCC regulates broadcasting and sets Internet policy, including Network neutrality.

## SPECTRUM AUCTION

Since 1994, the FCC has held auctions for available electromagnetic spectrum. The auctions are open to any individual or company that makes an upfront payment and that the FCC deems a qualified bidder. Many countries auction spectrum, which can generate large revenues for governments. Some critics claim that the spectrum tends to be leased too cheaply as essentially a corporate giveaway, considering the profits accrued from the spectrum acquired.

A 2008 auction in the United States drew special attention, thanks in part to disagreements and lawsuits among bidders, including Google and several major telecommunications companies. Google requested that the auctioned spectrum be open, meaning that the winning bidder would have to keep the spectrum available to anyone to develop applications and communication tools that could be used by anyone else, along the lines of open-source business models. Google claimed this would give consumers more choices and spur greater innovation in mobile-communication devices.

Open communications like this directly threaten the established business models of telecommunication companies, and Verizon filed a lawsuit against the FCC to prevent the open requirement. In the end, Google was granted two of its four requests, creating a partially open system, and the auction generated close to $20 billion for the government.

## Regulating Commercial and Political Speech

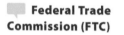

**Federal Trade Commission (FTC)**

The principal commerce regulatory body, established in 1914, at the federal level in the United States.

Free-speech issues include censorship, national security, and obscenity, although a range of other types of speech that do not fall into these categories may still have government oversight. Examples include commercial speech, political speech, and issues of privacy. The **Federal Trade Commission (FTC)** enforces antitrust and consumer protection laws, including cases of deceptive advertising in print, electronic media, and the Internet. As the Food and Drug Administration (FDA) is responsible for deceptive advertising claims for food and drugs, confusion can sometimes arise regarding which agency enforces regulations about deceptive advertising. The FTC is also responsible for enforcing the 1998 Children's Online Privacy Protection Act (COPPA), which gives parents control over what kinds of information can be collected about their children online.

Although the FTC does not regulate the Internet to the extent that the FCC does with broadcast, cable, wireless, and satellite radio, a mandate to protect consumers against deceptive advertising and business practices confers broad power. With dishonest practices that include spam, phishing, trademark infringement, breaches of consumer privacy, and false advertising claims, to name a few, the Internet has enabled people to create whole new ways to trick and cheat people while also making many traditional scams cheaper and easier to execute.

One problem for the FTC is its ability to enforce regulations and laws, especially with companies based overseas. Not only may other countries have different laws regarding the legality of spammers or phishing operations, but many such companies frequently relocate their operations and are consequently hard to catch even if the FTC or host country had the resources to do so.

The advent of camera-equipped commercial drones has brought the Federal Aviation Administration (FAA) into relevance in journalism and the media. The FAA now requires commercial drone operators to register their drones, obtain a piloting license, and operate within certain restrictions of place and manner of flight.

## COMMERCIAL SPEECH

Commercial speech, including advertising, has generally been afforded less First Amendment protection than other forms of speech, especially political speech and the news. In a landmark decision, the U.S. Supreme Court ruled in 1942 in *Valentine v. Chrestensen* that "purely commercial advertising" was unprotected by the First Amendment. Chrestensen was a businessman who dispersed leaflets advertising tours for a World War I–era submarine he had on display at a pier in New York City. The police commissioner forbade him from distributing the leaflets, which were becoming litter. Chrestensen claimed violation of his First Amendment rights, but the Supreme Court disagreed.

In the 1970s, the broad powers granted to government regarding commercial speech were restricted somewhat by cases that allowed some First Amendment protection, although not on par with other forms of speech. In 1976, the Court ruled in *Virginia State Board of Pharmacy v. Virginia Citizens Consumer Council, Inc.* that speech that does "no more than propose a commercial transaction" is entitled to at least some First Amendment protection. This was in response to a case brought by some citizens' groups in Virginia that wanted to see pharmacies advertise prices of drugs, which the state legislature had prohibited.

In some cases, however, commercial speech has been afforded more protection than one might expect. An interesting example involves a former New York City mayor. In 1997, Rudolph Giuliani was lampooned on the city buses of New York in an advertising campaign by *New York* magazine, which claimed its magazine was "possibly the only good thing in New York that Rudy hasn't taken credit for." Giuliani, who had boasted he was responsible for everything from drops in the crime rate to a booming economy, found the ads offensive and demanded their removal. In this instance, commercial speech won. Consider the conclusion of United States District Judge Shira Scheindlin, who quipped, "Who would have dreamed that the mayor would object to more publicity?" She ruled that Giuliani's administration violated the First Amendment when it ordered city buses to remove paid ads.

Advertisements for alcohol are allowed on television and radio, although ads for tobacco are not. **CRITICAL THINKING QUESTION**: If electronic media ads are not permitted for tobacco, should they be allowed for marijuana in states where its use is legal?

## Tobacco, Alcohol, and Marijuana Advertising

Most goods can be legally advertised on electronic media under the jurisdiction of the FCC, with the general exception of one product: tobacco. Advertising cigarettes, small cigars, smokeless tobacco, or chewing tobacco is prohibited on radio, television, and any other electronic medium regulated by the FCC, such as telephony. It is permissible, though, to advertise smoking accessories, cigars, pipes, pipe tobacco, or cigarette-making machines. No federal laws or FCC regulations prohibit the advertising of alcoholic beverages, such as beer, wine, and liquor, on television and radio.

A growing number of states have recently legalized recreational marijuana and even more have approved its medical sale.[16] This grassroots movement remains presently at odds, however, with federal laws that categorize marijuana as illegal and prohibit advertising the sale of illegal drugs—bans that Facebook, Yahoo, Google, and Twitter strictly enforce to avoid costly fines for such violations. Significantly, the Treasury Department now allows U.S. financial institutions to have marijuana businesses as clients. As cultural acceptance, legal support, and economic revenues for marijuana continue to grow, it will be interesting to see how the FCC responds to pressure from different advocacy groups.

## Unclear Regulatory Boundaries

Offensive advertising and subliminal programming are not clearly regulated by any single agency. Presumably, the advertiser would decide either not to run an offensive ad, or if it does and receives negative publicity, it would pull the ad to avoid further damaging its brand. In many cases, companies have abandoned ads in the face of public criticism. For example, in April 2017, skin cream maker Nivea discontinued an ad after critics charged it was racist. The controversial slogan, "White is purity," might carry a subtle message at a conscious or even subconscious level that any skin color other than white is impure. According to the FCC, subliminal advertising, messages directed to our subconscious perception, is "inconsistent with a station's obligation to serve the public interest." Still, it does not officially prohibit subliminal programming. Research has not provided conclusive evidence that subliminal messages are even understood or have an influence on behavior, and no advertisers have admitted using them.

## POLITICAL SPEECH

Historically, the heart of freedom of expression is in political speech, or speech that deals with the political process, government, elected officials, or elections. Some go so far as to contend that the only speech the founders intended when they wrote the First Amendment was political speech. Political speech is also one area where federal regulations have been most extensive.

**DISCUSSION QUESTIONS:** What types of speech would you characterize as political? List different examples, and explain your criteria. Identify some nonverbal or visual examples of political expression. Should these be afforded the same First Amendment protection as verbal communication? Why or why not?

## Equal-Time Rule

Under the **equal-time rule** from the 1934 Communications Act, if a station permits a qualified candidate for public office to use its facilities, including commentaries or paid commercials, the station must "afford equal opportunities to all other such candidates for that office." Two circumstances are exempted from the equal-time provision: when the candidate appears in a newscast, interview, or documentary and when the candidate appears during on-the-scene coverage of a news event. Candidate debates, ruled as "on-the-spot" news coverage, are thus exempt from equal-time-rule provisions. In 1981, the U.S. Supreme Court ruled in support of the equal-time rule, supporting the rights of viewers and listeners, adding that "as defined by the FCC and applied here, [it] does not violate the First Amendment rights of broadcasters by unduly circumscribing their editorial discretion, but instead properly balances the First Amendment rights of federal candidates, the public, and broadcasters."

## Fairness Doctrine

Although often confused with it, the equal-time rule is not the same as the **Fairness Doctrine**. The former deals only with giving political candidates equal time, with the exceptions noted previously. The Fairness Doctrine, adopted by the FCC in 1949, was much broader in scope, requiring broadcasters to seek out and present all sides of a controversial issue. This gave people a chance to respond on air to personal attacks, and it offered candidates airtime to respond to a station's endorsement of another candidate.

In 1969, in *Red Lion Broadcasting Co. v. FCC*, which required Red Lion Broadcasting to provide equal airtime for a politician's response to an attack, the Court held that because of the scarcity of broadcasting frequencies, the government might require a broadcast licensee to share the frequency with others who might not otherwise have a chance to broadcast their views. The Court thus gave the public a right of access "to social, political, esthetic, moral, and other ideas and experiences."

Largely discarded in 1987, the last vestiges of the Fairness Doctrine were suspended by the FCC in 2000, and a federal court overturned it entirely, ruling that the FCC had not demonstrated the value to the public of the doctrine, given the limitation it places on broadcasters' First Amendment rights. Legislative attempts to resuscitate the Fairness Doctrine in 2005 and 2008 failed. The FCC has refrained from supporting such efforts, claiming that the doctrine never really produced more diversity in programming and that channel proliferation has generated more diversity than could have been hoped for when three major commercial networks dominated television.

# Children's Programming Protections

Parents, elected officials, and others have long sought to protect children from unwanted or offensive speech and to create a media system that actively nourishes them. Considerable regulation exists to both protect and promote children's welfare in a media environment, especially the electronic media. A ratings system, similar

**equal-time rule**

The requirement that broadcasters make available equal airtime, in terms of commentaries and commercials, to opposing candidates running for election. It does not apply to candidates appearing in newscasts, documentaries, or news-event coverage.

**Fairness Doctrine**

Adopted by the FCC in 1949, it required broadcasters to seek out and present all sides of a controversial issue they were covering. It was discarded by the FCC in 1987.

Censors in Malaysia objected to a scene in Disney's remake of *Beauty and the Beast*, claiming that it promotes homosexuality, to which they are opposed. Disney refused to cut the scene, and the government of Malaysia eventually backed down from its opposition, allowing the blockbuster to be shown in the Muslim country.

The prevalence of conservative commentators such as Ann Coulter has led liberals to try to reinstate the Fairness Doctrine.

to that used for movies, gives parents a guide to program suitability for children of certain ages. Among the most important pieces of regulation designed to protect children is the Children's Television Act.

## THE CHILDREN'S TELEVISION ACT

**Children's Television Act (CTA)**

Created in 1990, it limits the amount of commercial content that programming can carry, forces stations to carry certain amounts of educational programming for children sixteen and under, and includes other provisions to protect children.

The **Children's Television Act (CTA)** took effect in 1990. It limits the amount of commercial content in children's TV programming (including broadcast, satellite, and cable) and mandates that each television station provide programming of educational and informational value for children age sixteen and younger. Programming must meet four FCC criteria:

1. Programming will be designed primarily to address children's educational and informational needs (i.e., it can't be primarily entertainment, such as a cartoon, and have as a by-product some educational value).

2. Broadcasts will air between 6 a.m. and 10 p.m., hours when children are likely to be viewing.

3. Shows will be scheduled regularly each week.

4. Each show will run at least a half hour.

In addition, commercial stations are required to identify their educational programs for children as such at the beginning of those programs; they must also identify them to publishers of program guides. Moreover, all programs aimed at children twelve and younger may not contain more than 10.5 minutes of advertising per hour on weekends and 12 minutes on weekdays. The FCC also established that at least three hours of core children's programming a week would fulfill station obligations under the CTA, "core" being defined primarily in terms of item number 1 in the list of criteria.

## VIOLENT AND SEXUAL PROGRAMMING: THE V-CHIP

Children's programming has been an area of FCC regulatory focus, which determines even the maximum number of commercial minutes for programs.

**V-chip**

A computer device that enables parents or any other viewer to program a TV set to block access to programs containing violent or sexual content based on the program rating.

Violent and sexual programming receives special attention from the FCC because of its potential implications for young viewers. With the Telecommunications Act of 1996, the federal government began regulating televised violent content in addition to sexual content. Seeking to increase parental control over their children's viewing of violent and sexual programming, the act begins by summarizing research that demonstrates the negative impact of television violence on children. It notes, "Parents express grave concern over violent and sexual video programming and strongly support technology that would give them greater control to block video programming in the home that they consider harmful to their children."

To that end, the government mandated that as of January 2000, all television sets thirteen inches or larger would come equipped with a **V-chip**, or "violence chip." The V-chip is a computer device that enables parents or any other viewer to program a TV set to prevent access to programs containing violent or sexual content based on the program rating, also called "TV Parental Guidelines." At the request of the government, the television industry agreed to broadcast signals with its own voluntary ratings system, one the V-chip can detect. These ratings appear on the TV screen for the first fifteen seconds of rated programming, permitting viewers to use the V-chip to block those programs from their sets.

On the basis of the First Amendment, all news programming is exempted from the V-chip.

In the digital age, the V-chip is no longer the only tool that restricts television viewing. All digital-media systems, including digital cable and satellite television, contain software controls that can block individual programs, entire channels, or classes of programs based on their ratings.

> **DISCUSSION QUESTIONS:** When you were younger, did you ever see movies that you were not supposed to watch because of the rating? Did your parents have parental controls on your television or computer? If so, did you get around the controls, and how did you do so? Do you believe the shows you saw were harmful to you or your friends in any way? Defend your responses.

## Intellectual Property Rights

Of significant and growing concern to those in mass communication is the protection of their **intellectual property (IP)**. IP refers to ideas that have commercial value, such as literary or artistic works, patents, software programs, business methods, and industrial processes, particularly in the form of copyright protection. A **copyright** ("copyright" refers to the legal right to make a copy of a work) is one form of intellectual property rights protection that deals with specific expressions of ideas. The other two main areas of intellectual property law are patents and trademarks.

**Patents** are intended to protect a specific form of intellectual property known as inventions. Once granted, a patent prohibits anyone from copying the invention, pattern, or design. Anyone can apply for a patent, as long as the idea is new. **Trademarks** refer to images, designs, logos, or even words or phrases. In March 2004, for instance, Donald Trump, host of *The Apprentice* reality TV show, attempted to trademark his phrase "You're Fired!" so that it could be sold on clothing and other items. The U.S. Patent and Trademark Office turned down his request because it was too similar to "You're Hired!," an educational board game whose phrase had been trademarked in 1997.

A German company that markets the liqueur Jägermeister has filed a formal legal notice opposing the logo of the Milwaukee Bucks professional basketball team. For nearly a century, Jägermeister has employed an image of a twelve-pointed buck as central to its logo. The Bucks introduced a new logo in 2015, also featuring an image of a twelve-pointed buck. Jägermeister also sponsors an international soccer team and claims that the Buck's logo is apt to cause confusion between the two brands.

A copyright exists from the moment a work is created in its fixed form—for example, written down or recorded—so simply claiming an idea does not give you a copyright to it. Inserting a © symbol (or a symbol with a P in a circle for a musical recording, ℗), along with a date and the name of the copyright owner, helps indicate that you are copyrighting a work. This is not necessary, however, nor is registration with the U.S. Copyright office, unless at some future point you wish to sue for infringement of a work (in which case, prior registration and public documentation would likely have been prudent).

**intellectual property (IP)**

Ideas that have commercial value, such as literary or artistic works, patents, trademarks, business methods, and industrial processes.

**copyright**

A form of intellectual property law that protects the right to use, publish, reproduce, perform, display, or distribute a literary or artistic work, such as a piece of writing, music, film, or video.

**patent**

A form of intellectual property law that protects the right to produce and sell an invention.

**trademark**

A form of intellectual property law that protects the right to use a particular sign, logo, or name.

The NFL has trademarked the term "Super Bowl," forbidding local restaurants, bars, and other advertisers—even in the host city—from using the term without permission. **CRITICAL THINKING QUESTIONS:** Do you agree with the NFL's claim that the words "Super Bowl" will lose their importance if used too widely? Why or why not?

A copyright is in effect for the lifetime of the author, plus 70 years, although it may be up to 125 years with a work for hire, typically owned by the employer. The rationale of a copyright is to protect not only the intellectual product but also the author/owner's financial interests. In 1989, the United States joined the Berne Convention for the Protection of Literary and Artistic Works, extending copyright protection globally.

Copyright law applies to a wide range of expression, primarily the creations of authors or artists. A copyright, not a patent, protects a nonfiction book or article as well as literary works (including newspapers, books, and magazines); musical works; dramatic works; pantomimes and choreographic works; pictorial, graphic, and sculpture works; motion pictures and other audiovisual works; sound recordings; and architectural works. The **Digital Millennium Copyright Act** extends to digital works, including those on the Internet or other online media, because if something exists on a hard drive, it is considered a fixed form.

### Digital Millennium Copyright Act

A 1998 act of Congress that reformed copyright law comprehensively to update it for the digital age. Key provisions addressed the circumvention of copyright-protection systems, fair use in a digital environment, and Internet service providers' liability for content sent through their lines.

### fair use

Allowable use of someone else's copyrighted work that does not require payment of royalties, with a number of factors that determine if something falls under fair use or violates copyright.

> **DISCUSSION QUESTIONS:** If you were a young novelist or struggling musician trying to make a living writing stories or making music, would you oppose or support greater government or corporate control of copyright if it prevented unauthorized copies of your work from being circulated? Why or why not?

## FAIR USE

Holding a copyright to a work provides the owner with an exclusive right to reproduce, distribute (over any media), perform, display, or license that work. Copyright law recognizes limited exceptions, including primarily for **fair use** of an expression, such as in a movie or book review where the reviewer might include an excerpt, or in criticism or commentary. In general, four factors determine whether the use of another's copyrighted work is legal under the "fair use" provision of the act:

1. Purpose and nature of the use (i.e., it is purely commercial, educational, or for the news, the latter two of which are generally more likely to qualify)

2. Character of the copyrighted work (some works are inherently more protected; this is a subjective matter determined by the courts)

3. Amount and extent of the excerpt in proportion to the copyrighted work in its entirety (this is determined more qualitatively than quantitatively, however; and there are no exact rules on the permissible number of words one may borrow from a text or the amount of video, audio, or image one may excerpt because even a small clip may represent the most significant creative aspect of the work)

4. Effect of the use on the copyrighted work's market potential (i.e., in dollar terms), especially when the copyrighted work is the basis for a derivative work (e.g., a movie based on a book)

The issue of fair use has become a flashpoint for digital media, especially in relation to content aggregators such as Google News or video search engines. In several recent court cases, copyright holders have sued content aggregators for copyright infringement. If, however, the content aggregator has been able to prove that it has transformed the content sufficiently—for example, by making low-resolution thumbnails of images or video clips—and to show that it is not profiting directly from doing so, it has generally won the case. Other aggregators have arrived at licensing agreements with media companies for displaying or collecting their content. Google, for instance, struck a deal with Associated Press to aggregate its news stories and keep them on Google News for a limited time.

## Privacy

We discussed the role of privacy with social media in Chapter 7, but traditional media have a rich history of raising challenging privacy issues. For entertainment media, all members of the public appearing on shows, such as reality shows, game shows, and talk shows, must sign a waiver granting permission to use their image. These people are generally not paid for such appearances, and they are essentially giving away all rights, so broad are the waivers. This protects the show's producers from lawsuits if people dislike how they were depicted. Live sporting events do not require these waivers, in part because they take place in public spaces, where people cannot expect the same right to privacy. This is why spectators' faces are not blurred out when shown at sporting events.

Issues of privacy become more complex in journalism. Journalists often find themselves trying to get information that others wish to keep private. Obtaining records or private information without breaking trespass, eavesdropping, or privacy laws can be difficult. Even secretly recording a conversation can create legal trouble for a journalist, depending on the state. State laws vary as to whether only one party or both must consent to the recording of a conversation. Even more dilemmas arise when journalists acquire private records that someone else has stolen, such as when a whistle-blower provides confidential and damaging company documents.

At the heart of the matter is what is commonly called our "right to privacy." Although this right is not explicitly articulated in the Constitution, different Amendments mention privacy. Over time, the Supreme Court has used especially the Fourteenth Amendment, which addresses equal protection under the law, to develop a concept of privacy a citizen should expect.

The right to privacy differs between private citizens and celebrities or public figures, however. People not normally in the public limelight generally have greater privacy protections than celebrities or political officials. Greater privacy also applies to people who become celebrities through unanticipated circumstances such as rescuing a child from a burning building because they did not seek public attention.

## Legal Issues in the Digital World

The courts and legal system have not kept up with the many changes to mass communication that the Internet and digital media have brought. As a result, cases decided by the courts from the mid-1990s through today can have dramatic effects because they establish precedent, becoming the basis for subsequent court decisions and legislation.

One example of just how far the legal system has had to come occurred in a 2000 ruling against Eric Corley (pen name: Emmanuel Goldstein), publisher of

*2600: The Hacker Quarterly*. He included links in the online version of the magazine to a site with the code to DeCSS, a computer program that opened encrypted DVDs and allowed them to be copied freely. Corley argued that being forced to remove the hyperlinks was an infringement of his First Amendment rights. The court disagreed, claiming that a hyperlink was not an example of free speech because it acted as a kind of "mechanism" providing access to the site. Posting the URL of a site without a hyperlink, however, would still be considered free speech. An appellate court agreed with this decision in May 2001, and Corley decided not to take the case to the Supreme Court.

Media organizations and writers, artists, and musicians—anyone creating copyrighted media content for a living—want to be fairly compensated for their work. There would be no incentive, the reasoning goes, to create something only to have it rapidly copied and distributed without financial reward for the artist. Several lawsuits currently working their way through the court system could increase control for copyright holders—which are usually media organizations and not individuals. **Open access** to information consequently could be reduced.

**open access**

A system that makes information accessible to all to discourage power imbalances that may arise from unequal access.

## DIGITAL RIGHTS MANAGEMENT

File-sharing and royalty issues related to music, and increasingly video, continue to be one of the main areas of contention in the digital space. Record labels have tried various measures to deter free file sharing, including suing customers and

---

### ETHICS IN MEDIA
## Does the Punishment Fit the Crime?

A key court ruling in 2016 placed new privacy restrictions on media. In the *Gawker* ruling, a federal court ruled that even a public figure plaintiff can win a defamation lawsuit regardless of the truthfulness of what was reported, if a jury concludes the plaintiff's privacy was violated. In this case, the jury ruled that the online gossip site Gawker had violated the privacy of Terry Bollea, better known by his professional wrestling moniker Hulk Hogan, by posting snippets of a secretly recorded video of Bollea's extramarital affair, despite the fact that Bollea had previously bragged about his affair on Howard Stern's shock-jock radio show.[17]

Court ruling chills freedom of expression. **CRITICAL THINKING QUESTIONS:** Do you think truthfulness should be a defense in a libel trial involving a public figure? Do you feel that the plaintiff in this case, Terry Bollea, bears at least some responsibility for his actions? Do you think the punishment for Gawker's infringement of Bollea's privacy is too harsh, or does it accurately reflect the damage that can occur in revealing information about the personal behaviors of a public figure?

having universities hold seminars for incoming students on the matter, but with no decrease in free downloading.

**Digital rights management (DRM)** is the use of technology to rein in copyright infringement of digital content. Encryption has had some success, although, as the DeCSS example demonstrates, it is not foolproof. A **digital watermark** is computer code (usually invisible but sometimes visible) inserted into any digital content—images, graphics, audio, video, or even text documents—that authenticates the source of that content. Watermarks can protect media assets and intellectual property from theft—or at least make illegal activities easier to track.

For instance, if a media company sends digital video over the Internet, which someone tries to copy and distribute without obtaining permission, the original copyright holder, an end user, or even an intelligent software agent can examine the content for an embedded digital watermark. If the watermark is present and is that of the original copyright holder, then it can easily be demonstrated that the redistributor is in violation of copyright law. In essence, digital watermarking is analogous to cattle branding to deter or catch rustlers.

DRM has faced resistance from some groups, such as the Electronic Frontier Foundation, which claim that media companies want to limit the capabilities of new technologies simply to increase their revenues and force digital media to behave like their analog counterparts. These restrictions anger many consumers and raise serious questions about what exactly a person is "buying" when purchasing a CD and what rights the purchaser has to that content.

Whenever a new secure system is proposed, a method to break the system is not far behind. Rather than deal with this fundamental issue, media organizations have lobbied to change laws to favor copyright holders, and they have taken people to court for merely publicizing the existence of security weaknesses in encrypted or watermark systems, arguably infringing on free speech.

## PRIVACY

Privacy issues have become increasingly important with the Internet and digital media. Not only can websites track users in ways impossible with analog media, but they can insert code, called a "cookie," onto computers and track users even after they have left that particular website. Not all cookies track relentlessly, however; and in fact, cookies, as discussed in previous chapters, can also make the web a more user-friendly environment.

Still, their overuse can be a problem. Just as a website will add a cookie to your computer, so will a website's advertisers. These **third-party cookies** also track your web usage and send information directly to the advertisers, who can determine how long you've stayed on a page and where you went afterward.

Spyware can be secretly loaded onto computers from websites and can do everything from tracking browsing behavior to recording keystrokes, a technique that can lead to the surreptitious monitoring and recording of a password or other private information by an unseen person on another computer.

In 2013, Edward Snowden, a National Security Agency (NSA) employee, revealed that the NSA had been reviewing the phone records of all U.S. citizens and the digital communications of those in other countries to find potential terrorist activities. The case reminded the public of how easily the government can work with telecommunications companies and Internet media giants to gather information about people.

---

**digital rights management (DRM)**

Technologies that let copyright owners control the level of access or use allowed for a copyrighted work, such as limiting the number of times a song can be copied.

**digital watermark**

Computer code (usually invisible but sometimes visible) inserted into any digital content—images, graphics, audio, video, or even text documents—that authenticates the source of that content.

**third-party cookies**

Cookies put on a computer by those other than the website being visited, such as advertisers.

Other legal issues involve the status of messages sent by private citizens. Is a posting to a discussion board considered "publishing," and could a poster be sued for libel? What if a person writes something libelous in a private email to a friend and that friend includes the email in a discussion-board topic? Who could be sued for libel? These and many other similar legal issues have yet to be resolved. In other words, the public, as it gains access to a worldwide distribution network, will have to start considering issues of privacy, libel, defamation, and attendant lawsuits—all issues traditional media companies must consider every day.

In April 2017, President Trump signed into law a new provision essentially ending or at least seriously undermining citizen privacy online by allowing companies such as ISPs and mobile service providers to sell consumer communication and related Internet activity to third parties without the user's knowledge or consent. This allows companies to sell consumer data in order to customize advertising, but also virtually eliminates privacy online or on mobile devices.

## CONTENT RIGHTS AND RESPONSIBILITIES

Another new area that media companies have had to contend with is the status of user-generated content (UGC). It is virtually impossible for a company to police all the content uploaded to the Internet. The question of who is responsible for the content on a site arises when someone is defamed in a user comment, as opposed to something the company itself wrote.

In general, the courts have made a "safe haven" provision for content providers, protecting them to some extent from libel lawsuits as long as they remove the offending content promptly and make good faith efforts to prevent similar transgressions. Similarly, Internet service providers (ISPs) have been considered largely immune from responsibility for what is sent over their networks, although the threat of a lawsuit can sometimes be sufficient incentive to remove offending content or to ban users, especially those accused by record labels of rampant free file sharing.

## MEDIA CAREERS

Legal considerations frame and shape all media careers. Increasingly, anyone pursuing a career in journalism or media must consider the legal and regulatory context for their work on multiple levels. The First and Fourth Amendments are particularly vital concerns. Freedom of speech and privacy are defining legal underpinnings for work in journalism and the media. Yet other laws, once deemed beyond the framework of journalism and the media, are also becoming important. For instance, media professionals now need to be familiar with laws of agencies such as the Federal Aviation Administration, evolving regulations that pertain to new technologies such as drones. Further, journalists and other media professionals must be aware of international laws, including copyright and intellectual property considerations that pertain globally where their content may appear online.

As the work of the great Anthony Lewis exemplifies, journalism reporting on legal issues in the media is a profoundly significant career pathway. Legal journalism in the twenty-first century means much more than covering U.S. laws. Successfully negotiating a global village requires advanced knowledge of the broader legal framework that applies across borders: geographic, political, and cultural.

## LOOKING BACK AND MOVING FORWARD

Many legal and regulatory issues complicate Internet media for users and producers, and the legal system generally lags far behind in dealing with these. The global nature of the Internet also raises questions about whose laws should be followed when offensive or illegal content originating in one country can be viewed online in another. The question of whether a hyperlink is protected by the First Amendment can generate heated discussions about the complex nature of digital media. Similarly, the seemingly simple question "Where does publishing occur?" can stir complicated legal debate.

With traditional media, the answer was obvious—publishing occurred in the country where the printing press was located. A book might be legally printed in one country but banned in another; thus, if a copy was smuggled into the country where it was banned, the person caught with book would be penalized, not the printer.

But on the Internet, where something is published is not at all clear. A person may create banned content in his country for his website, which is on a web server in another country where the content is not banned. Someone else may come across the content in a third country where the material is considered harmful, sacrilegious, or defamatory. In this scenario, many questions arise, such as which country's laws will be in effect in a lawsuit and what constitutes libel because it differs from country to country.

A pertinent, highly controversial case was brought forward in 2002. *Dow Jones and Co. Inc. v. Gutnick* involved an article in *Barron's* (published by Dow Jones) in October 2000 that mentioned Melbourne businessman Joseph Gutnick several times, noting he was an associate of a convicted tax evader. Although the number of print copies of *Barron's* sent to Australia was minuscule, the online readership of the magazine was over half a million, and Gutnick claimed that many more Australians would see the article than just those who subscribed to the print version. He argued his libel lawsuit should be heard in Australia, where he was defamed. Dow Jones countered that the article was actually published in the United States, where its web servers were located, and thus the case should be heard in the United States (where libel charges are harder to win than in Australia). The Australian High Court agreed with Gutnick, however, and Dow Jones eventually settled with him in 2004.

The case was of serious concern to Internet watchers and media companies because of its potential implications for publishers on the web. The ruling could mean that people could sue a media company or website according to their own country's laws, which may more severely restrict acceptable content than regulations where the material was published. On the other hand, it is arguably not fair to impose another country's views of acceptable free speech on foreign content simply because it was published on the Internet. The question remains open and will likely come up again in the future.

## MEDIA MATTERS    LEGAL LIMITS

Test your legal knowledge as it relates to the First Amendment, media regulations, and copyright.

1. "Libel" refers to defaming someone in print or broadcast, whereas "slander" is defamation that occurs through the spoken word. How do you think defamation should be classified if it appears in a YouTube video?

2. Do you think a hyperlink that takes a user to an illegal site is protected as free speech by the First Amendment? Why or why not?

3. National security issues are one of the few cases in which the government can possibly stop publication or broadcast of information. Should the government be able to use the "national security" rationale to censor videos in a situation such as

occurred following the Boston Marathon bombing in 2013 when the public pored over video footage and made inaccurate claims about identifying the suspected bombers?

4. If I tell my friend my idea for a novel and he then writes a novel based on my idea, can I sue him for copyright infringement? Why or why not?

5. (T/F) Camera-equipped drones have emerged as a potential battleground pitting First Amendment rights against concerns over national security and privacy, or Fourth Amendment rights.

**ANSWERS: 1.** Even though defamation appears on video or television as spoken words, it is still considered libel. **2.** First Amendment protection does not apply to a link, deemed by the courts to act like a mechanism that takes a person to a specific place. **4.** Copyright covers only works that are recorded in some form, so simply talking about an idea does not protect it as copyrighted. **5.** True.

## FURTHER READING

*Digital Media Law*, 2nd ed. Ashley Packard (2012) Wiley-Blackwell.

*Major Principles of Media Law: 2015 Edition.* Genelle Belmas, Wayne Overbeck (2014) Cengage Learning.

*Freedom for the Thought That We Hate: A Biography of the First Amendment.* Anthony Lewis (2008) Basic Books.

*Perilous Times: Free Speech in Wartime: From the Sedition Act of 1798 to the War on Terror.* Geoffrey R. Stone (2005) W. W. Norton.

*Born Secret: The H-Bomb, the Progressive Case, and National Security.* Gerald Marsh, Alexander De-Volpi, George Stanford, Ted Postol (2011) Kindle edition.

*Make No Law: The Sullivan Case and the First Amendment.* Anthony Lewis (1992) Vintage.

*The Associated Press Style Book and Briefing on Media Law.* Associated Press (2013) Basic Books.

*We're All Journalists Now: The Transformation of the Press and Reshaping of the Law in the Internet Age.* Scott Gant (2007) Free Press.

*Insult to Injury: Libel, Slander and Invasions of Privacy.* William Jones (2003) University Press of Colorado.

*Rethinking Global Security: Media, Popular Culture, and "The War on Terror."* Andrew Martin, Patrice Petro (eds.) (2006) Rutgers University Press.

*Who Controls the Internet? Illusions of a Borderless World.* Jack Goldsmith, Tim Wu (2006) Oxford University Press.

*Intellectual Property Law and Interactive Media: Free for a Fee*. Edward Lee Lamoureux, Steven Baron, Claire Stewart (2009) Peter Lang.

*Intellectual Property and Open Source: A Practical Guide to Protecting Code*. Van Lindberg (2008) O'Reilly Media.

*Censored 2014: Dispatches from the Media Revolution; The Top Censored Stories and Media Analysis of 2012–13*. Mickey Huff (ed.) and Project Censored (contributor) (2013) Triangle Square.

# Media Theory and Research

Just hours after the worst mass shooting in U.S. history at an Orlando, Florida, nightclub, video game publisher Electronic Arts (EA) hosted a press conference in downtown Los Angeles to promote its latest video game, Titanfall 2.[1] The sci-fi action game features animated humans battling giant machines, slaughtering each other using highly realistic, high-capacity guns.

In addition to those in attendance at the press conference, another four hundred thousand were tuned in online. First-person shooter games have long been among the most popular in the industry, and EA has been in the forefront with games such as Battlefield 1, a depiction of WWI battles that resulted in 17 million deaths.

Whether and to what extent playing video games influences real-world violence or perceptions of it is a topic of ongoing debate and research concern. In this chapter, we examine what research tells us about video game violence and other media processes. Results from a neurological study reported in 2017 further confirmed that the desensitization hypothesis is not confirmed among players of violent video games. The study found that any such effects are short-lived if apparent at all.[2]

The video game industry has long confronted charges from across the political spectrum that violent games increase violence among children and teens, concerns that have only intensified with the rise in popularity of video games and advanced technology creating hyperrealistic graphics. And the fact remains that the incidence rate of gun-related deaths in the United States is higher than that of any other industrialized country.

Yet the results from numerous studies on gaming and violence are inconclusive as to whether violent video games or TV programs increase the likelihood of aggressive or violent behavior in real life. Some studies demonstrate a correlation while others do not. And even correlation cannot prove causation. Determining causation requires a research design that measures users over time or in a controlled experimental setting, such as in the neurological study cited earlier. Furthermore, Americans play violent video games at the same rate as people in countries with little gun violence, such as South Korea and the Netherlands.[3]

## LEARNING OBJECTIVES

>> Explain the role of theory and research for media professionals.

>> Describe various types of media research.

>> Critically examine the strengths and weaknesses of various media-research approaches.

>> Discuss how digital media and the Internet are being researched in terms of new and old media theories.

>> Examine the differences between quantitative and qualitative research.

Nevertheless, people looking for explanations for inexplicably brutal acts continue to blame the simulated brutality of video games. On June 17, 2015, self-avowed racist and white supremacist Dylann Roof committed mass murder. After entering the historic Charleston Emanuel AME Church and sitting quietly through services, Roof pulled out his loaded assault rifle and shot dozens of black churchgoers, killing nine persons and wounding several others.  Roof was convicted in December 2016 of the murders and thirty-three federal crimes including hate crimes. Although we may never know exactly what motivated Roof, some have pointed to his excessive playing of violent video games as a possible agent of influence.

Research findings on media and violence can have a tremendous impact on media industries in the form of government censorship or regulations and sales of media products such as games, movies, and books, especially when the audience involved is children or youth. Media effects have been an area of keen interest since the dawn of the mass-communication era. Theories about media and communication attempt to explain the underlying processes of media, how we interact with media, and how media affect our cultures, societies, attitudes, and lives. This research takes on special importance given how much time we spend with media, demonstrated by the following findings from years of research:

> Americans spend an average of just over ten hours a day staring at a screen, and about half of that is watching television or some form of video entertainment.[4]

> By age 75, the average American will have spent nine years of his or her life watching television.[5]

> By age eighteen, a child has seen on TV two hundred thousand acts of violence, including forty thousand acts of murder.[6]

> Half (47 percent) of violent actions include no depiction of pain.[7]

> Fifty-four percent of children in the mid-1990s had a television set in their own bedroom and often watched with a friend, unsupervised.[8]

Media research is the systematic and scientific investigation of communication processes and effects that often bases its explorations on theories of media and communication. Some types of media research, such as that conducted by market research firms, are more oriented to answering practical questions, such as whether audience members remember a particular advertisement, their impressions of a product or brand, or their media use and consumption habits.

Media-research methodology, or how research is carried out, takes many forms. It can entail social scientific research using quantitative tools and statistical analysis of data, such as surveys and experiments; or it can involve critical studies using qualitative methods, such as ethnography or focus groups.

## Role of Theory and Research

For media professionals, research may seem more important than theory. Someone planning to work in journalism or advertising may see practical inquiry as more significant than academic theory. Yet media theories have had a number of profound effects. They play a foundational role, providing cognitive constructs that help us organize and make sense of the world. They also play a key role in research agendas, which then affect the questions asked during the course of investigation, the findings or discoveries, and the funding for such projects.

Research findings in turn shape public policies on the media and media industries, decisions about what and how items should be regulated, such as ratings systems for movies, music, and video games. This of course has important implications for the organization and operation of media companies, which affects everything from content development to job creation.

Media research carried out specifically for business purposes helps determine audience numbers for particular shows or networks (thus determining advertising rates and kinds of shows produced). It also helps identify which media campaigns have been more effective and which messages more persuasive, and consequently, which areas are of most interest to businesses, not-for-profit organizations, and politicians.

In short, media theories help media professionals not only to better predict or explain various phenomena, but also to better understand the world and the forces at work in it. As we will see, questions about the fundamental nature of communication and media are not new.

## MASS SOCIETY, MASS COMMUNICATION

A number of larger social, political, cultural, and scientific factors throughout the course of history have greatly influenced the study of mass communication and media theories. Here, we will explore some of these historical and sociopolitical forces.

The dramatic societal and political changes that took place in Europe and the United States during the nineteenth and twentieth centuries, thanks largely to industrialization, provide the backdrop for early theorizing on mass communication. The new demands of factory work and mass migrations to the quickly growing cities changed traditional ways of life that had remained largely the same for generations. Harsh working and living conditions produced clashes between workers and authorities, leading to various social and political movements that called for greater democracy and workers' rights.

Elites threatened by these developments found various rationales for why they should lead and most should simply follow, such as the notion of "the masses": people were largely uneducated, lacking in culture, and not intelligent enough to rule themselves. Others opposed elitism, claiming that more participation, better education, and greater distribution of wealth were necessary to create a more democratic and just society.

During these debates, which still echo today, film was starting to be recognized as an important medium of mass communication. Literacy was not needed to understand the stories in silent films, and moving images were regarded as powerful influencers, especially for the uneducated, passive masses, or other supposedly vulnerable groups such as women and children. Messages in various media could help educate, persuade, or control the masses; the question then became how best to accomplish these goals.

# Theories of Communication

Over the centuries, great thinkers have tried to define communication and understand it as a process. They have proposed a variety of theories in their attempts to explain it. One of the earliest communication theorists was the

## FIGURE 13-1 The Rhetorical Triangle

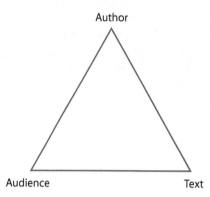

philosopher Aristotle, who in 300 BCE called the study of communication "rhetoric" and identified three primary elements within the process: the speaker, the subject, and the person addressed. This can also be defined as the rhetorical triangle (see Figure 13-1), which consists of author, audience, and text. The term "text" in this case refers to any media or objects, not only printed works. Aristotle also identified three basic rhetorical appeals to persuade an audience: pathos, an appeal that excites emotions; ethos, an appeal that establishes the speaker's credibility; and logos, an appeal that relies on logic and reasoning. Aristotle's principal ideas laid an enduring foundation for communication research even today.

The need to enrich our understanding of communication from a theoretical perspective arose with the importance that mass communication began to have in people's lives, especially as electronic communication such as radio and television became so dominant.

## TRANSMISSION MODELS

In 1949, scientists Claude E. Shannon and Warren Weaver formulated an influential model of communication.[9] Known as a transmission model of communication, it is closely related to communication theorist Harold Lasswell's famous question about media effects, which he posed in 1948: "Who says what in which channel to whom with what effect?" This model has allowed for many general applications in mass communication.

The Shannon and Weaver mathematical theory of communication is based on a linear system of electronic communication. The original formulation of the model included five main elements (see Figure 13-2). An information source formulates a message. A transmitter encodes the message into signals. The signals are delivered via a channel. A receiver decodes the signals, "reconstructing" the original message, which reaches its destination. The communication flow in this model is decidedly one-directional, from the sender to the receiver. The system has a limited capacity to provide feedback from the receiver to the information source: to acknowledge receipt of the message, to indicate whether the message

## FIGURE 13-2 Shannon and Weaver Mathematical Theory

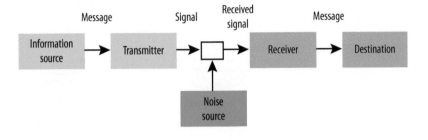

has been understood, and to communicate the receiver's reaction. The communication process can be adversely affected by noise, or interference, from the environment, possibly by way of competing or distracting messages or even electrical interference.

The model clearly explains how a telephone works. The information source speaks (encoding a message); the phone (transmitter) transforms the sound waves into electrical impulses (the signal), which are sent over the channel (the tiny box in the center of Figure 13-2); and those electrical impulses are turned back into sound waves by the phone (receiver) at the other end of the line where they are heard and (one hopes) understood (decoded) by another person (destination). Noise is any interference anywhere along the way.

The Shannon and Weaver model is especially technological in its orientation and therefore limited in its utility for understanding traditional mass communication because it does not fully reflect the role of humans in the process—specifically, how meaning is created. Moreover, the advent of digital, networked communication media is greatly expanding the interactive nature of communication, making the limited feedback capacity of the model more problematic even by its own standards.

Adapting the Shannon and Weaver model and integrating concepts from Aristotle, pioneering communication scholar Wilbur Schramm in 1954 developed a **simplified communications model** in the book *The Process and Effects of Mass Communication*, as summarized in Figure 13-3.[10]

Significantly, Schramm envisioned understanding as an integral part of human communication. He also realized that another important aspect of the traditional communication model needed correcting: In human communication, mediated or not, communication is not a one-way process. Schramm wrote, "In fact, it is misleading to think of the communication process as starting somewhere and ending somewhere. It is really endless. We are little switchboard centers handling and re-routing the great endless current of information." As a result, Schramm and Charles Osgood developed a circular model of communication. The participants exchange roles of source/encoder and receiver/decoder.

However, even this model, based on certain concepts derived from the transmission model, has its limitations for some scholars. Conceiving of people as switchboards of information processing does not adequately explain how an advertisement may tug at our heartstrings and evoke deep-ranging yet differing emotions in people or how people may see the same message very differently. For that we have to look at other theoretical traditions.

**simplified communications model**

Developed by Wilbur Schramm in 1954 and based on the mathematical theory of communication. It includes a source who encodes a message, or signal, which is transmitted (via the media or directly via interpersonal communication) to a destination where the receiver decodes it.

FIGURE 13-3 Schramm–Osgood Model

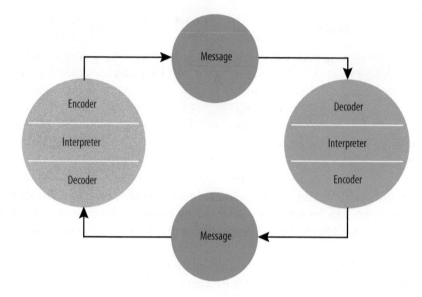

**DISCUSSION QUESTIONS:** Imagine a small classified ad on Craigslist that simply says "Baby shoes for sale. Never used." Explain the ad in terms of the transmission model, and then consider how these six words may evoke thoughts or feelings with you. Does the transmission model of communication adequately describe your feelings as well? Explain why or why not.

## CRITICAL THEORY AND CULTURAL STUDIES

A typical critique of transmission models of communication (made by others outside the critical-theory tradition as well as within) is that they treat communication as some kind of separate phenomenon independent of the people who are engaging in communication. Its technological orientation may explain an electronic signal well, but it falls far short when trying to explain the deeper meaning behind someone reading a morning paper. Defining humans as a type of switchboard center, as Schramm does, does not explain how media economics may influence what paper we are able to read or if we even have an Internet connection—nor does it help us better understand the ways in which power, identity, and a host of other factors affect how we make and share meaning through communication.

In contrast, **critical theory** is broadly influenced by Marxist notions of ideology, exploitation, capitalism, and the economy in understanding and eventually transforming society. There are many branches of critical theory, not all of which focus on media and mass communication, and they often disagree with each other on fundamental points. We will explore **cultural studies**, which tend to focus more on mass communication.

To understand a cultural-studies approach to the subject of communication, it is important first to see its intellectual heritage through the lens of critical theory and to know how it differs from traditional, or positivist, social science. Critical theorists criticize positivist researchers for applying physical science research methods inappropriately to human behavior. They do not agree that certain

**critical theory**

A theoretical approach broadly influenced by Marxist notions of the role of ideology, exploitation, capitalism, and the economy in understanding and eventually transforming society.

**cultural studies**

An interdisciplinary framework for studying communication that rejects the scientific approach while investigating the role of culture in creating and maintaining social relations and systems of power.

statistical techniques, and enough research, can uncover various "natural laws" of society and behavior.

Critical theorists not only claim that the process of scientific creation of "fact" is a social and variable process like any other (consider how Pluto has gone from being viewed as a planet to now being planetary object 134340), but they also refute that natural laws can be discovered to explain human behavior. They see the drive to predict and better control society as one more form of oppression. In short, critical theorists would say positivists ask uninspiring questions and get uninteresting—if not misleading—answers that largely describe the societal and cultural status quo as unproblematic.

Cultural-studies researchers join critical theorists in rejecting the positivist scientific approach. By utilizing a host of disciplines ranging from anthropology and sociology to political science and literary theory, they examine the symbolic environment created by mass media and study their role in culture and society. For these researchers, a television commercial can be a rich source of cultural codes and representations that tell us in subtle and not-so-subtle ways how we as members of society should act and think.

Communications scholar **James Carey**, a leading cultural-studies theorist, developed what he called a ritual view of communication: "Communication is a symbolic process whereby reality is produced, maintained, repaired, and transformed."[11] From this view, the act of reading a newspaper has less to do with receiving information than with participating in a shared cultural experience that portrays and confirms the world in a certain way. By reading the paper, we are actually participating in a ritual that produces and reproduces certain sociocultural norms played out through our actions and interactions with others.[12] The same dynamic can be said to take place with online media, such as posting photos on Flickr or texting a friend—you are not simply transmitting information but are sharing ways of doing things and ways of thinking that actually create the society we live in through our repeated actions.

James Carey was one of the most influential media and communications scholars of the twentieth century.

💬 **James Carey**

Communications scholar and historian who shaped a cultural-studies approach to communication theory.

## Media-Effects Research

The obvious way to study media influence was to identify effects of media exposure. The notion that media could harm people was already well established, dating back to the ancient Greeks. With new and powerful communication technologies that could reach millions at once, such as film, radio, and, later, television, it was not hard to imagine the power that mass communication could have over people.

Media effects have been a dominant concern in the history of media research and continue to be important today. Findings from these studies have influenced the creation of the movie-rating system, dictated regulations for the television industry, and determined what types of advertisements we view. Although earlier assumptions of direct and powerful media effects have been scaled back as newer, more complex theories developed, the idea that media affect us directly (usually negatively) is still prevalent. The history of effects research reveals the interesting roles of communication technologies in relation to social issues and norms deemed important.

### PROPAGANDA AND THE MAGIC BULLET

Some of the earliest media-effects research was conducted to better understand how mass communication persuaded people. During World War I, both the United States and Germany employed film and other media (including posters) as instruments of propaganda to generate public support for their positions in the war.

Propaganda posters during World War I led researchers to hypothesize how persuasion worked on the public.

## propaganda

The regular dissemination of a belief, doctrine, cause, or information, with the intent to mold public opinion.

## hypodermic-needle model

A model of media effects, also called the "magic bullet," that claims media messages have a profound, direct, and uniform impact on the public.

Attempts to influence an audience through mass communication, **propaganda** usually involves total control of the transmission of information, often without the audience knowing who is controlling the message. Although perhaps hard to imagine today, many people through much of the twentieth century had extremely limited sources of information—perhaps only a government radio station or a single government television station broadcasting a few hours a day.

Political scientist Harold Lasswell, during his analysis of World War I propaganda efforts, used the term "hypodermic needle" to describe the concept that media can act like a drug being injected into a passive audience. The **hypodermic-needle model** assumes that messages have a profound, direct, and uniform impact on individuals. This model has also been called the "magic bullet" model of communication and derives largely from learning theory and simple stimulus–response models in behavioral psychology.

As film became more popular and began to share space with radio as a form of mass communication in the 1920s, research about both mediums looked beyond specific political or propaganda uses and examined effects on the general public, especially children.

> **DISCUSSION QUESTIONS:** Do you think propaganda is more or less likely to happen today with social media? Why or why not?

## PAYNE FUND

Between 1928 and 1933, some of the most prominent psychologists, sociologists, and educators of the day conducted the Payne Fund studies. Published in 1933, they included a twelve-volume report on the impact of film viewing on children.[13] The studies provided a detailed examination of the effects of film in wide-ranging areas, including sleep patterns, attitudes about violence, delinquent behavior, and knowledge about foreign cultures.

The Payne Fund studies in the 1920s examined the effects of violence and sex in movies on young people.

The Payne Fund studies concluded that the same film would influence children differently depending on their backgrounds and characteristics, including age, sex, life experience, predispositions, social environment, and parental influence. One study of movies, delinquency, and crime, for instance, found that the impact of film on criminal behavior may vary with the range of themes presented as well as the social context, attitudes, and interests of the viewer. Contrary to the original assumption about largely negative effects, the Payne Fund research also revealed that children could learn some positive lessons from film and that information retention was a function of grade in school.[14]

The Payne Fund studies also created a "school of the air" that would use radio to educate children on a variety of subjects.[15] This led to the formation of the National Committee on Education by Radio (NCER) as well as the allocation of some $300,000 in the early 1930s to support U.S. broadcasting reform, which at that time meant radio.

## RADIO'S WIDER IMPACT

Radio's social effects reached far beyond children, as dramatically illustrated by events that unfolded on October 30, 1938, when Orson Welles broadcast a radio program created to sound like a news event. At 8 p.m., the Columbia Broadcasting System's *Mercury Theater of the Air* began its radio broadcast from a New York City studio. Regular listeners and others who heard the introduction understood perfectly well what was about to follow, a radio adaptation of the famous 1897 novel *War of the Worlds* by science fiction writer H. G. Wells.

Those who missed the introduction tuned in to a supposedly live orchestra, a performance whose calm ambiance was abruptly interrupted by breaking news—an announcement that Martians had landed at a farm near Grovers Mill, New Jersey. The frequent and increasingly disturbing news flashes sounded very much like reports by Walter Winchell, the radio standard of the day. As the invasion ensued, so did the panic. When it became apparent that the Martians had vastly superior weaponry, numerous residents of the eastern seaboard, especially in the New York and New Jersey area, opted to hide in their basements or even flee their homes.

A study by a psychologist showed that one in six listeners—1 million people—believed the broadcast and the Martian invasion to be real, although not all 1 million panicked and fled. Studies of the *War of the Worlds* broadcast and other radio programming demonstrated that media effects could be dramatic but were not uniform. Certain factors, including individual personalities, demographics, and psychological variables such as good critical-thinking ability, could mediate responses to media exposure.

This event focused American attention on the power of mass communication and triggered one of the first major investigations of a media program on the subject of social panic and mass hysteria as well as a debate about the government's control over the radio industry. As spectacular and strange as these incidents may be, by far the major concerns of researchers have been depictions of sex and violence, particularly since the advent of television.

Orson Welles and his *War of the Worlds* radio broadcast had many listeners believing that Martians were actually invading the East Coast.

## TELEVISION AND VIOLENCE

Much television programming is educational and entertaining, and much is peppered with violence, sex, and profanity. Consequently, many adult viewers and policymakers have pondered the effects of extended television viewing on the next generation. Are children learning to be overly aggressive, imitating what they see on the television screen? Are they learning more about the Three Stooges than the three branches of government?

Hundreds of studies have been conducted and millions of dollars spent to investigate how TV violence affects children. Among the first was a study that claimed television had become the new Pied Piper, providing a model (often not a good model) for children to imitate. Yet few early analyses could provide conclusive evidence that exposure to TV violence would have negative consequences in the real world.

Laboratory research in the 1950s by psychologist Albert Bandura and others demonstrated that children exposed to TV violence were more likely to repeat the behavior they had witnessed (e.g., beating a "Bobo doll") as well as become more aggressive—while they were still in the laboratory. Although these studies suggested that children learned by watching others, effects were documented in a laboratory setting only. Researchers who conducted the **Bobo doll studies** could not confirm that the children remained more aggressive once they left the laboratory.

Social unrest and violence in public, much of it politically motivated, rose dramatically in the 1960s. Concerned about a broad range of violence and its social causes, President Lyndon B. Johnson convened the National Commission on the Causes and Prevention of Violence in 1968. *Violence and the Media*, a report by the commission's media task force, focused not only on the quantity of violence on entertainment television but also on its quality. How did the media portray violence? Who used which weapons to kill whom? What motivated these acts? What were the consequences? Were aggressors rewarded or punished?

Professor George Gerbner of the Annenberg School for Communication at the University of Pennsylvania, who oversaw this content analysis and follow-up research, defined violence as "the overt expression of force intended to hurt or kill." Overall, Gerbner and his colleagues found the consequences of television violence unrealistic. There was rarely much pain or blood. Good guys, often as violent as bad guys, did not suffer negative consequences for their actions. And bad guys were usually punished by cops rather than courts. Whites were often the victims, while young black males and other people of color, as well as immigrants, were typically the perpetrators.

Research on TV violence continued in the 1980s and 1990s. In 1992, the American Psychological Association issued its TV violence report, *Big World, Small Screen: The Role of Television in American Society*: "The accumulated research clearly demonstrates a correlation between viewing violence and aggressive behavior. Children and adults who watch a large number of aggressive programs also tend to hold attitudes and values that favor the use of violence." Correlation is not causation, however: A relationship between television-violence viewing and aggressive behavior does not mean one necessarily causes the other.

A team of researchers at UCLA led by Jeffrey Cole conducted one of the most important studies of TV violence in the 1990s, research that indicated American network television series had become somewhat less violent while the number of "shockumentary" reality-based specials had increased dramatically. Funded by the networks themselves, the *UCLA Television Violence Report* found that overall violence decreased on ABC, CBS, Fox, and NBC during the 1994–1995 season. But reality-based programs, most

**Bobo doll studies**

Media-effects experiments in the 1950s that showed children who watched TV episodes that rewarded a violent person were more likely to punch a Bobo doll than children who saw episodes that punished a violent person.

Depictions of violence on television continue to be a concern among many groups.

commonly encountered on Fox, were especially violent, featuring real and re-created footage of police shootouts, car chases, and crashes, and animals attacking people, in some cases killing them on-air.

Research reported in 2014 by the American Academy of Child and Adolescent Psychiatry has confirmed that the levels of violence continue to be high in American television programming. Violence is common across a swath of program genres including those aimed at children, who are the most likely to be influenced by the depictions they see.

## LIMITED EFFECTS

Conducted by Wilbur Schramm, Jack Lyle, and Edwin Parker, *Television in the Lives of Our Children*, a 1960 landmark investigation of the impact of television on children in North America, concluded that some children under some conditions were likely to exhibit some negative consequences of exposure to television violence. But there was no magic bullet of media effects. From these results and similar findings developed various kinds of limited-effects models.

In this view, media are a component in a much larger and more fundamental system of influences to which we are all subject. Institutions such as the family, school, and religion are much more influential forces that shape individual tastes, attitudes, and behaviors. Media exposure contributes to and often reinforces the individual's worldview but is clearly secondary.

CONVERGENCE CULTURE
## How Free Is Academic Freedom?

The open and free-wheeling nature of social media would seem a natural forum for academics to exchange a variety of ideas grounded in their research, assertions that challenge our perceptions and enrich our dialog about society and culture. In recent years, however, a number of incidents on social media involving politically insensitive tweets, inappropriate comments about students or colleagues, and hoaxes have raised questions about academic freedom and have even cost some professors their jobs.

Early in 2015, the Marquette administration began the process of terminating political science professor John McAdams's tenure after he criticized a philosophy teaching assistant on his blog for her handling of student comments she considered homophobic. McAdams has spent some forty years in academe, most of them at Marquette. His case raises issues of academic free speech and shines a spotlight on a university's apparent inclination to strip faculty of tenure, a power that would have a chilling effect on open debates.

In 2017 a new website called the Professor Watchlist began inviting students to identify and describe professors who "discriminate against conservative students, promote

anti-American values and advance leftist propaganda in the classroom." The Professor Watchlist is a project of Turning Point USA, whose mission is to "identify, educate, train and organize students to promote the principles of fiscal responsibility, free markets and limited government."[16] A hidden agenda may be to intimidate freedom of speech on college campuses.

## Cultivation Analysis

George Gerbner's research on the long-term impact of television watching generated the theory of **cultivation analysis**, which argues that television cultivates in audiences a view of reality similar to the world portrayed in TV programs. Rather than emphasizing the impact of individual programs on individual viewers, cultivation analysis stresses cumulative effects. Coined by Gerbner, **mean-world syndrome** can result from viewing countless acts of media violence that make viewers perceive the world as more dangerous than it actually is. Designed as mainstream entertainment that is easy to understand, TV programs are powerful instruments of socialization, especially for children.

According to research by Gerbner and others, not only are those who watch more television more likely to consider the real world a more dangerous place, they are also more likely to support a more powerful system of law enforcement. Senior citizens who watch more television are more inclined to stay at home, fearful of perceived dangers. Cultivation effects are not uniform, however.

## Spiral of Silence

German communication scholar Elisabeth Noelle-Neumann developed the **spiral of silence** as a theoretical construct to explain why people may be unwilling to publicly express minority opinions. Derived from her observations of Germans during the Nazi regime in the 1930s and 1940s, the spiral of silence has been tested widely and shown to be valid in a variety of circumstances. It is based on three premises:

1. People have a natural fear of isolation.

2. Out of fear of isolation, people are reluctant to publicly express views that they feel are in the minority.

3. A "quasi-statistical organ," a sort of sixth sense, allows people to gauge the prevailing climate of opinion and determine majority views on matters of public importance.

### cultivation analysis

A theory of media effects that claims television cultivates in audiences a view of reality similar to the world portrayed in television programs.

### mean-world syndrome

A syndrome in which people perceive the world as more dangerous than it actually is, the result of viewing countless acts of media violence.

### spiral of silence

A theoretical construct that explains why people may be unwilling to publicly express opinions they feel are in the minority.

Watching too much television over years, especially news shows, can lead viewers to believe the world is more dangerous than it actually is. **CRITICAL THINKING QUESTIONS:** Do you feel more fearful in public places after viewing news like that on the Boston Marathon bombing? Is your fear greater if the violent event seems to be everywhere in the news?

A number of factors affect how people assess public opinion, particularly the media as well as their experiences and interactions with others. If a person feels a point of view matches the prevailing one, then that person will feel more comfortable expressing it publicly. If, on the other hand, a person feels out of step with public opinion, then that person will be less likely to express that opinion, thus producing a spiral of silence. In some instances, even a majority opinion, if perceived to be a minority position (possibly through biased media reporting), may not be expressed publicly.

### Third-Person Effect

Among the most interesting of media effects is the **third-person effect** of communication, the tendency for people to underestimate the effect of a persuasive message on themselves while overestimating its effect on others. This tendency sometimes encourages one group to shield another from messages it thinks will harm them.

Although many researchers have demonstrated the widespread and varied impact of the third-person effect, W. Phillips Davison first identified this communication phenomenon when examining World War II records. The Japanese had dropped propaganda leaflets to black servicemen who were going to take part in the invasion of Iwo Jima (at that time whites and blacks were segregated in the military). Stating that the Japanese were fighting white imperialists and had no ill will toward blacks, the leaflets encouraged them to surrender or desert—to no effect, however, according to records. The campaign did persuade white officers of these black troops, though, to transfer them from the combat area to avoid any potential loss of morale.

> **third-person effect**
>
> The tendency for people to underestimate the effect of a persuasive message on themselves while overestimating its effect on others.

## CRITICISMS OF MEDIA-EFFECTS RESEARCH

Although subsequent research quickly discredited the direct-effects assumptions and hypodermic-needle model of media power, many members of the public and policymakers continue to believe in these effects. When tragedies occur such as the shootings at Columbine High School in 1999; Virginia Tech in 2007; Sandy Hook Elementary School in Newtown, Connecticut, in 2012; or the DC Navy Yard in 2013, the killer's media use is always discussed. Experts may not blame comic books and radio anymore, but television, movies, the Internet, and video games are all fair game when trying to explain violent or antisocial actions. At the same time, early research such as that of Prot and colleagues (2014) suggests that playing certain video games can have positive neurological effects on the human brain or can facilitate learning with others.[17]

Much media-effects research is flawed by the belief that the audience has no will of its own. The assumption that audience members are passive dupes easily manipulated by media messages derives directly from the belief that the masses are incapable of governing themselves. Although researchers today do not believe that people can be programmed by media messages to behave a certain way, even some of the limited-effects models perceive audiences as more passive than active.

A further complication in media-effects research is how to measure media exposure. Self-reporting, a common research technique, has been unreliable because people either intentionally or unintentionally under- or overreport media exposure. Furthermore, simply measuring exposure does not really capture how we interact with media and how it may influence us.

Media-effects researchers may use new ways of assessing audience interactions. Tracking Facebook Likes, tweets, or retweets, for example, helps quantitatively measure audience engagement in different situations. New developments in social-media listening software are helping researchers measure media consumption and interaction, although concepts like sentiment and engagement are still often open to interpretation.

Even if we accept the premise of media influence, separating intertwined social, cultural, psychological, and other factors and identifying clear cause-and-effect explanations remain difficult. That certain programs, songs, or video games produce predictable and widespread behaviors or attitudes has largely been disproven, given all the other influences in our lives and the different circumstances in which each of us interacts with media.

Examining the wrong dimension of the communications process is another arguable fault in media-effects research. Some scholars claim that we have to understand the processes and economics of media products to understand the role of media in our lives. Others, such as audience-focused researchers, focus less on what media may or may not do to us and more on what we may or may not do with media.

> **DISCUSSION QUESTIONS:** Do you think that a highly interactive medium like video games could have greater effects on media users than a more passive medium such as television? Why or why not?

Teaching children media and computer literacy will help them succeed in the twenty-first century.

# Understanding the Audience

To a certain extent, mass-communications research has always been about trying to understand the audience. For advertising and public relations, knowing how the audience thinks and how to persuade it can make or break a campaign or new brand. For political communication, the audience, broadly conceived, is essentially the public and public opinion. For media companies, knowing what shows, books, music, and films audiences will like is a vital element. In scholarly communications research, the trend in audience studies in recent years has been toward seeing the audience as increasingly active in how it makes sense of the world and uses media.

## AUDIENCES CREATING MEANING

The idea that audiences create new meaning from the media content they consume may seem odd. Yet scholars who use new audience-studies approaches question the assumption that a media product comes with a predetermined and unchangeable meaning that audiences simply ingest like fast food. Earlier discussion in this book about semiotics indicated that a given meaning of a sign or symbol, once learned, tends to be taken for granted. In the following section, however, we focus on active participation in the creation of new meaning around the media we encounter and among an audience. Some approaches look at psychology, others focus on the social aspects of creating meaning, and still others examine broader cultural issues and power relations.

## Uses and Gratifications

**Uses-and-gratifications research** looks at *why* people use particular media. It examines what people do with media rather than what media do to people. Popular in the 1970s and 1980s, uses-and-gratifications research posits that people have certain needs, especially psychological needs, which they seek to satisfy through media usage. This research makes three basic claims:

1. People use the media actively for their own purposes.
2. People know what those purposes are and can articulate them.
3. Despite individual differences in media use, basic common patterns exist among people.

Modeled on an audience more active than passive, whose members hope to satisfy certain needs through the media they seek out, uses-and-gratifications research may lend itself to research on the Internet and interactive media.

Uses-and-gratifications research has its detractors, however. It has been criticized for being hard to test empirically and for circular reasoning. In other words, it's hard to know which came first—the social/psychological need or the media use. Other criticisms include its focus on psychological needs while ignoring social forces and the assumption that audiences always do know (and can articulate) why they are using media.

## Encoding/Decoding

The **encoding/decoding** model, developed by Stuart Hall in the 1970s, launched what is known as the active-audience approach. A response to dissatisfaction with previous media-effects research, it tries to examine audiences within larger sociocultural contexts. The model is complex but essentially states that media producers encode media products with meanings, which are then decoded in various ways by various audiences.

There is no guarantee the producer's preferred meaning will be accepted. Audience members have three basic options when decoding. They can choose the dominant, or hegemonic, reading, the one that the media producer likely intended and the one most people would recognize as commonsense or natural. They can select an oppositional reading in which they recognize the codes being used but reject them for their own meanings. They can also choose a negotiated reading, largely accepting the dominant meaning but adding certain variations. Decoding skills and tendencies will vary with background, education, identity, and other social factors.

## Reception Analysis

Reception analysis was a major break in audience research in a number of respects. First, it assumed that audience members actively make meaning from the media they consume. Second, researchers looked at popular entertainment such as soap operas, travel or fashion magazines, and fiction books rather than the traditional news or other "serious" programming studied in earlier years. Third, the areas of study allowed feminist and other scholars to study women in media and women as active consumers of media.

> **uses-and-gratifications research**
>
> A branch of research on media effects that examines why people use media, what they do with media rather than what media do to them.

> **encoding/decoding**
>
> A theoretical model that states media producers encode media products with meanings, which are then decoded in various ways by various audiences.

Studying pop culture can often reflect aspects of a society that other forms of media, such as news, cannot explain adequately.

The 1980s findings challenged long-held assumptions about why women read romance novels or watch a soap opera such as *Dallas*, or how teen girls perceived Madonna. Contrary to some prevailing feminist arguments that maintained these forms of popular culture demeaned women, encouraging them to see themselves from a patriarchal viewpoint as sex objects, scholars found that women actively and freely chose a variety of meanings for such content.

Reception analysis attempts to fill the holes in previous theorizing and research by looking at cultural and social patterns of media production and power relations between different groups. Some critics object, however, to the active nature it ascribes to audiences, claims that make media seem almost powerless.

> **DISCUSSION QUESTIONS:** Identify your three favorite television shows or films in recent years, along with a brief sentence on why you like(d) each one. Compare lists with classmates, and discuss your choices. What do the similarities and differences tell you about each other?

## FRAMING

**framing**

The presentation and communication of a message in a particular way that influences our perception of it.

We discussed **framing** briefly in Chapter 2, noting that the presentation of a message colors perceptions of it. The concept of framing appears widely in media studies and in other social sciences, such as sociology and psychology, sometimes in conjunction with media-studies research.

We use frames—a set of filters that help us categorize and understand our social reality—to make sense of the world in which we live. Frames emerge through our daily interactions with media and are shaped by our culture and social norms. Often our exposure to certain issues and people is solely through media in various forms (news, entertainment, advertising, etc.), framing our perceptions even more.

Message framing can have a profound effect on behavior, depending on whether a message is framed as a gain or a loss. In 1984, psychologists Daniel Kahneman and Amos Tversky presented two different scenarios to different groups of participants who were asked to make a choice regarding a hypothetical disease outbreak expected to kill six hundred people. The "gain-framed" scenario emphasized saving lives: Option A would save two hundred people, whereas option B specified a one-third probability of saving everyone but a two-thirds probability of saving no one. Overwhelmingly, participants chose option A, which seemed the less risky choice.

Other participants were given "loss-framed" choices that emphasized lives lost: Option A would kill four hundred people, while option B had a one-third probability of killing no one but a two-thirds probability of killing everyone. A large majority of participants chose option B, the risky option. This difference in selection can be explained only by how the messages were framed because identical scenarios were presented to both groups.

The aspects of framing messages are more numerous and complex than one experiment can suggest. Still, Kahneman and Tversky's research has special implications for social marketing campaigns and strategic communications. When messages are framed in terms of potential gain, people choose what seems to be the safer option to pursue a guaranteed gain. When framed in terms of losses, however, people choose the riskier option to avoid a guaranteed loss.

Consider framing's role in a social marketing campaign for reducing a sexually transmitted disease like AIDS. If the message is framed in terms of potential loss rather than potential gain, people may actually opt for the riskier behavior (un-protected sex) than what sounds like a safer option. For example, a campaign that discusses the chances of dying from AIDS contracted during sex without a condom may actually encourage unprotected sex, whereas a campaign that focuses on the benefits of condom use could promote that behavior. Of course, many more factors are involved in social marketing that targets public behavior, but a poorly chosen frame could doom a campaign from the start.

Another strand of research on mass communications, cultural studies, looks at media through broad cultural and social frameworks and media production.

# Cultural Studies

The focus on culture and broader societal issues in relation to media, seen in reception-analysis research and the encoding/decoding model of Stuart Hall, falls within a category of scholarly research developed in the 1970s called **cultural studies**. Difficult to define concisely because of its wide range of research interests, this field has seen tremendous growth from the 1990s into the early part of the twenty-first century. More and more universities have created cultural-studies departments in recent years.

Cultural-studies approaches largely reject the media-effects research tradition and examine how meaning is produced not only among audiences but also among media producers. By looking at popular culture in its many facets and with a critical eye toward issues of power, dominance, and subordination, researchers hope to better understand the role of media in perpetuating these social relations.

European versions of cultural studies tend to be Marxist and highly critical of existing politics and culture, whereas North American versions are inclined to be less critical, even celebratory, of consumer culture and media. Despite these differences, cultural-studies research is typically more normative than descriptive. In other words, it seeks to improve society rather than simply describe it.

## IDEOLOGY AND THE CULTURE INDUSTRY

The normative focus of cultural studies stems from its origins in **critical theory** and the Frankfurt School scholars who created critical theory in the 1930s and 1940s in Germany at the Institute for Social Research based in Frankfurt. Theodor Adorno, Max Horkheimer, Herbert Marcuse, and Walter Benjamin were German Marxist scholars with research interests ranging from music theory and philosophy to sociology.

The Frankfurt School coined the term **culture industry** to refer to how media businesses created mass-produced "cultural products" that were then consumed by the masses. They distinguished between "high art" (opera, classical music, etc.) and "popular art" (jazz, film, etc.), which they deemed crass, partly because of its commercial nature.

Although their particular views on art may be considered artistic snobbery, they advanced a larger political argument in that the culture industry propagates an **ideology** that helps maintain the status quo. In other words, it makes existing power relations and inequality seem natural while discouraging critical reflection among people—which they believed high art, on the other hand, encourages. In this view, media production is not simply a by-product or reflection of popular tastes and desires; it actively creates those desires and suppresses freedom.

**cultural studies**

An interdisciplinary framework for studying communication that rejects the scientific approach while investigating the role of culture in creating and maintaining social relations and systems of power.

**critical theory**

A theoretical approach broadly influenced by Marxist notions of the role of ideology, exploitation, capitalism, and the economy in understanding and eventually transforming society.

**culture industry**

A term coined by the Frankfurt School to describe how media companies produce or "make" culture in the same way that other companies produce products.

**ideology**

A comprehensive and normative body of ideas and standards held by an individual or a group.

Max Horkheimer was a prominent member of the Frankfurt School and one of the founders of critical theory.

The Frankfurt School scholars were not simply talking about authoritarian governments such as Nazi Germany, although their theory applied to these kinds of governments. They claimed that even supposedly "free market" democratic systems of government were not free at all because the media of mass communications promoted capitalist ideology while ignoring or downplaying the negative consequences of capitalist economies.

## CRITICISMS OF CULTURAL STUDIES

Cultural studies, despite its popularity in academia, still has its detractors and faults. One common complaint is the often impenetrable, jargon-laden writing of many researchers, a style that excludes almost everyone but academics. This is at odds with their broad goal of transforming society by enlightening the public about its oppression and the part the media play in that oppression.

The writing style is also criticized for hiding muddled thinking and masking mundane ideas behind grandiose jargon. In 1996, a physicist at New York University, Alan Sokal, published an article in the postmodern journal *Social Text* titled "Transgressing the Boundaries: Toward a Transformative Hermeneutics of Quantum Gravity." (Cultural studies is often situated under the larger rubric of postmodernism, a sprawling movement defined later in the chapter.) The title and prose were typical of many journal articles penned from a postmodern perspective, but Sokal's article was a hoax purposely composed to be nonsensical, suggesting the dangers of adopting merely fashionable or trendy schools of thought in general, and applying less-than-scientific perspectives to the physical sciences in particular.

In the same vein, other critics of cultural studies say that because it largely rejects scientific tenets such as the use of reason in finding truth, it cannot actually be called a science. And without any shared and consensual basis for measuring

 MEDIA PIONEERS
# Nonny de la Peña

Nonny de la Peña is a pioneering journalist who has specialized in immersive forms of storytelling such as virtual reality (VR). Called by some the "godmother" of VR, de la Peña has been among the most influential leaders in the use of 360-degree cameras in news reporting. She has produced a series of acclaimed VR news reports, including some that have appeared in *The New York Times*. Her "Project Syria" provided news users an early experience in immersive storytelling about the civil war in that Middle Eastern country. De la Peña describes VR as an empathy-building engine because it can effectively bring the user into the perspective or point of view of the story's subject in a way other media cannot. The multisensory envelopment of VR facilitates this empathy capacity.

De la Peña has been a model for others to emulate and a source of inspiration. Among others, VR developer Palmer Luckey was her student intern. A former journalism school student, Lucky went on to found the Oculus Rift virtual reality platform later bought by Facebook for some $2 billion.

the validity of viewpoints, the cultural-studies perspective cannot actually prove or refute ideas in the same way and with the same authority of traditional scientific methods.

# Sociohistorical Frameworks

Other theories draw on a variety of schools of thought, especially Marxism or critical theory, as well as a number of disciplines, such as sociology, anthropology, psychology, and even economics. These tend not to emphasize audiences as much as previous frameworks but examine instead the entire media system within larger social, political, and historical contexts. Some researchers claim that a primary focus on audiences neglects many of the most fundamental questions and answers regarding media and their effects on our world today.

## INFORMATION SOCIETY

Social scientists continue to debate the meaning and nature of the **information society**, sometimes also labeled the network, knowledge, or postindustrial society. Information-society theories posit that the prominence of communications and media has ushered in a new era that breaks drastically from the industrial society. Networks become hugely important as they bring the world closer together; and economic value lies not so much in the old manufacturing centers, as it once did, but in knowledge centers. Education and training are key for workers, valued not for manual labor but for ideas, knowledge, and creativity that enable them to make sense of and create information.

The often-utopian picture painted by information-society theorists has elicited much criticism. Some scholars, especially those influenced by Marxism or critical theory, claim that the information society actually strengthens established relations of dominance as global media corporations control more media channels, including those on the Internet. They point to earlier media types such as radio that also initially promised to be emancipatory and chronicle the relentless governmental and corporate control that rendered new media claims to increased freedom and democracy largely hollow. One example of the enduring domination of elite interests is when companies barred WikiLeaks from receiving online donations after it released secret U.S. government diplomatic cables.

A criticism of information-society theories is that they extrapolate from a small segment of the world's population. One does not have to look far to see that much of the world lives in conditions where people rarely have access to clean water, let alone the Internet or even electricity. This generates discussions regarding the **digital divide**, one of the most important Internet-audience issues today, which we return to from a global perspective in Chapter 15.

Research indicates that from the early days of public Internet, access tended to be much higher among society's economically advantaged—those with a higher education and with a legacy of higher overall print-media use. Economically disadvantaged groups, especially minority groups and the rural poor, enjoyed less Internet access and

> **information society**
>
> A society where information production has supplanted industrial production, dramatically transforming cultural, economic, and political activity.

> **digital divide**
>
> The gap between regions and demographics that have access to modern, digital-communications technology and those that have limited or no access.

According to the Pew Research Center's "Fact Tank: News in the Numbers," 87 percent of U.S. adults use the Internet, yet more than a quarter, or 27 percent of households, lack broadband Internet access from home.[18]

usage. With certain groups, this gap has closed dramatically if not disappeared. Women, for example, now make up the majority of Internet users in the United States—across economic lines. Problems of equity of access to online media will not be eliminated soon, however, especially among the economically disadvantaged and those in the developing world.

## POLITICAL ECONOMY

**political economy**

An area of study inspired by Marxism that examines the relationship between politics and economics with media ownership and the influences they all have on society and perpetuating the status quo.

Another area of media research inspired by Marxism and influenced by critical theory is **political economy**. Communication scholars in this area of study examine the production and ownership of media that determine our media environment and its effects on our social and political systems.

Robert McChesney, for example, studies the history and current status of media ownership, regulations, and laws, especially how ownership conglomeration has affected types of media. Challenging claims of increased democracy and freedom, he argues that since the 1990s, corporate interests that influence government regulations and policy decisions have controlled the Internet at the expense of public interests.

According to political-economy scholars, examining media production—who owns what media companies, how their business decisions determine types of media, how media are delivered, to whom, and in what way—reveals the underlying forces that inform power relations and dominance. Unlike other forms of audience-studies research, a political-economic viewpoint can explore areas where an audience does not actually yet exist. For example, an audience-studies researcher would not be able to study Spanish-language newspaper readership in an area that is without a Spanish-language newspaper. But the question "Why isn't there a Spanish-language newspaper in this market when 20 percent of the population is Hispanic?" would be a legitimate area of study for a political economist, as would exploring the content likely to be found in such a newspaper.

## MEDIA ECOLOGY

**media ecology**

The study of media environments and their effects on people and society.

**Media ecology**, as its name suggests, is the study of media environments and their effects on people and society. Just as an ecological system in nature is complex and can be studied from a number of perspectives or specialties (a chemist studying soil samples will see an ecosystem very differently from a biologist studying bear habitats), so too can media ecology. Media ecology examines how our media environment influences our thinking and how specific types of media affect our perceptions (medium theory).

Perhaps the most famous proponent of medium theory was Canadian scholar Marshall McLuhan, who coined the phrase "The medium is the message," arguing that the medium itself was more critical to our perception of the message than its content or its manner of production. His claims that electronic media had transformed the world into a "global village," free of the hierarchical and rigid power relations created by the culture of print media, echo what we hear about the Internet, even though he was speaking only of radio and television.

**technological determinism**

The belief that technology causes certain human behaviors.

He has been faulted for espousing a form of **technological determinism**, the belief that technology causes certain human behaviors—a charge that some forms of media ecology must still address. Others also argue that by celebrating technology, he ignored (and thereby left unchallenged) the relations of power and dominance that technological communication creates and perpetuates.

## INTERNATIONAL PERSPECTIVES
# Theories Old, Theories New, Theories Borrowed . . .

Tracing the intellectual history of currently popular media research can be a fascinating exercise that improves our understanding of how theories may influence our thinking. Some widely believed theories in the past have since been proven false or flawed, but some older theories that never caught on have also been revived when it is later discovered they have a lot to offer current research.

One example concerns early sociologists who tried to study social behavior in relational, rather than objective, terms. For decades, much of this research was ignored, but now several sociological theories rely on relational or network-oriented ways of looking at the world. The terms early sociologists used may differ from those in current research, but many of the concepts can be surprisingly similar.

Most of the theoretical frameworks in media research derive from European schools of thought in the humanities or social sciences. An American-made school of philosophical thought, pragmatism, was largely superseded

Noted French sociologist Pierre Bourdieu wrote widely for the mainstream media in France.

by European schools of thought after the early part of the twentieth century, although some social theories still feature important aspects of pragmatism.

Many ostensibly "new" theories actually have deep roots in combinations of much older theories or are combinations of different theoretical schools, with unique insights introduced for greater relevance. Some of Europe's most interesting thinkers draw from a wide variety of sources—including philosophy, literary theory, history, economics, political theory, social theory, and cognitive science—to tackle social issues and the role of media in society.

Scholars in some European countries are much more visible than their American counterparts. In France, for example, social theorists Michel Foucault and Pierre Bourdieu were virtually media celebrities in their own right, appearing on television to discuss theoretical issues and writing regularly on political and social topics for popular newspapers.

---

Despite these and other arguable weaknesses in his theories, McLuhan offered important and novel insights into how modern media affect our lives, particularly our sense of time and space. Some of his claims become even more important when considering digital media. Although technology may not be the most important component of media theory, the consequences of mass media's capacity to immediately send mass audiences the same messages are considerable.

## AGENDA SETTING

**Agenda setting** does not take as broad a view as the frameworks just mentioned, although this concept does relate directly to media messages and industries. In 1948, Paul F. Lazarsfeld and Robert K. Merton proposed that conferring status is one of the primary functions of the media. Singling someone out from the masses bestows prestige and authority on the person so identified: "The audiences of mass

**agenda setting**

Media's role in deciding which topics to cover and consequently which topics the public deems important and worthy of discussion.

Television news shapes people's sense of which of the day's issues and events matter most, setting the agenda for public debate. In June 2015, a video of a police officer detaining a young girl at a pool party in McKinney, Texas, sparked allegations of racism and fueled national conversation about police tactics.

media apparently subscribe to the circular belief that if you matter, you will be at the focus of mass attention and, if you are at the focus of mass attention, then surely you must really matter."[19]

This assertion rings truer than ever today due to our growing mix of social and mass media. As agenda setters, the media can determine which issues are perceived as important and to what degree, depending on how prominently they present them. Political scientist Bernard Cohen clearly articulated the agenda-setting model: "The press may not be successful much of the time in telling people what to think, but it is stunningly successful in telling its readers what to think about."[20]

In the 1970s, Max McCombs and Donald Shaw demonstrated that the media are especially effective at influencing public views on the importance of various issues. Moreover, McCombs and Shaw's research showed that different media play different roles in the agenda-setting process. Newspapers in particular have historically set the general agenda of public issues—such as taxes, education, crime, or health care—determining which topics the public is likely to see as important. Meanwhile, while newspapers establish which issues are on the agenda, the electronic media of television and radio are especially effective at shaping the public's views on which of these issues are most important, that is, their relative ranking.

## New Directions in Media Research

As digital and social media become fully integrated in our lives, new strands of research in the social sciences emerge in business communication, organization science, and library science, among many other fields.

Scholarship on digital media is often complicated by the fact that technologies may change rapidly, transforming user behavior or making certain topics of study less relevant or obsolete. For instance, research on user behavior on Usenet may not have much to offer researchers examining identity formation and interactions through social media today. Research can become dated during the long lead time for publication in most peer-reviewed academic journals, typically twelve to eighteen months between submission and publication.

While scholars continue to study traditional media companies, more and more are researching aspects of digital and social media. Although classifying these diverse research areas is difficult, we can briefly survey some of the broad topics of current study.

Since the origin of the Internet, researchers have studied the impact of time spent online on both children and adults. Launched in 1999, the World Internet Project, the most comprehensive and longest-running study of its kind, examines the social, cultural, and commercial impact of the Internet. Funded by a consortium of major companies interested in online communication—such as Microsoft, America Online, Disney, and Sony—the study is headed by Jeffrey Cole, current director of the Center for the Digital Future at the USC Annenberg School for Communication and Journalism and former director of the UCLA Center for Communication Policy.

These researchers are following a group of subjects over twenty years to explore various questions such as how Internet use influences family time, political leanings, and social life. This **longitudinal study** also examines online banking, credit-card purchases, buying habits, and other

Recent research has focused on the role of social media in activism and democracy. **CRITICAL THINKING QUESTIONS:** Have social media prompted you to participate in activist discussions or action? Would you record a protest event as it unfolds to post later on social media? In what circumstances might this make you feel vulnerable?

**longitudinal study**

A study that gathers data on subjects over a long period of time.

---

## ETHICS IN MEDIA
# Advertising's Effects on the Sexes

Advertising is designed to persuade people in various ways to do various things. Usually, it encourages us to buy some product or service, but it can also aspire to change attitudes and beliefs about everything from practices such as smoking to the suitability of political candidates.

A large body of academic research examines the effects of advertising, both the positive and negative influences, including its many unintended consequences. The beauty industry is particularly notorious for its almost exclusive use of ultra-thin models and other images airbrushed to perfection, unattainable ideals that make many women feel inadequate. Many studies have documented how these unrealistic body image portrayals can adversely affect perceptions of the ideal body type, both for females and males.

In recent years, a growing number of advertising campaigns have focused on building healthy images of beauty. Among the best examples is Dove, an international company that has designed and launched a series of media campaigns designed to promote what might be called "natural" beauty. Among the company's campaigns are the Dove Self-Esteem project, Dove Real Beauty Sketches, and #BeautyBias. These campaigns advocate a vision of women that is not defined

by an ultra-thin, often digitally altered image of the models depicted. Moreover, the campaigns engage audiences through multiple media channels, including print, television, and social media platforms. #BeautyBias, for example, invites users to watch films about the concept of beauty and how bias enters into cultural beliefs of what constitutes beauty. Then, individuals are invited to share their views online.

issues related to ecommerce. International representatives have been added to the initial panel including two thousand people selected from a national sample.[21]

The Pew Research Center also frequently publishes insightful research on the Internet and social media in America, typically in the form of a **cross-sectional study** on attitudes and patterns of behavior with various technologies. In April 2015, for instance, they published reports on the use of smartphones and teen use of social media. Pew conducts certain surveys repeatedly over the years, providing interesting data about how behavior and attitudes have changed over time.

The evolving role of the audience in an interactive communication environment has also spurred research. The prevalence of user-generated content challenges the traditional relationship between the audience and media producers. This movement from viewer to user or produser affects media organizations and the presentation and prevalence of different kinds of news and entertainment.

Scholars interested in politics have found a rich source of new material to study online. Early optimism about the democratizing potential of the Internet has been tempered by more realistic views, notably the recognition that the Internet also aids governments and corporations in surveillance of citizens and consumers. In 2013, game-changing documents leaked by former NSA analyst Edward Snowden made the extent of this surveillance shockingly clear. Further revelations in the media involved Internet and telecommunications giants like Google and AT&T secretly sharing consumer data with the government.

Research on social media in social movements has become popular, thanks in part to the Arab Spring, the Occupy Wall Street and Black Lives Matter protests, and popular protests in Turkey and Brazil in recent years. Activists draw inspiration from other parts of the world, sharing information and encouragement while promoting solidarity and common goals. Still, the initial enthusiasm for the empowering aspects of social media has waned in recent years, as many social movements failed to achieve their stated goals in the face of various forms of government oppression.

Recent media research has examined issues surrounding social-networking sites. Areas of study include identity formation and presentation: issues related to privacy, anonymity, and the use of fake names or usernames. Some research relates to perceptions of the self, including the idea of the "networked self" in which we see ourselves as part of communities connected by networks of communication rather than as individuals largely unaffected by our communication and social interactions.

Researchers are studying how the increasing popularity of video games may reinforce gender or racial stereotypes, how they may affect our sense of identity, whether we can learn better through game playing than traditional means, and other facets of the gaming world. The effect of violent video games on children has been studied less, though, than the impact of violent television programming.

All these areas of research draw from a broad swath of humanities and social science disciplines, including literary theory, history, ethics, political communication, psychology, sociology, anthropology, and economics. Because media research crosses multiple disciplines, media scholars today must become familiar with a broad range of knowledge, a trend likely to continue.

---

**cross-sectional study**

A study that gathers data on subjects at a specific point in time.

**DISCUSSION QUESTIONS:** In which online communities do you experience a networked self connected to other members through social communication? Do you think a requirement to use real names enhances a sense of genuine connection among members? What do you think constitutes a real or authentic identity online? Defend your views.

## Media Research: What Type of Science Is It?

Asking what type of science media research provides may seem odd, but this question raises several important issues about media studies. At the heart of the matter is whether the social sciences, such as psychology, sociology, and anthropology, can (and should) be conducted according to the rules of the natural or physical sciences.

For most of their histories as individual disciplines, the social sciences have tried to emulate the rules and methods of hard sciences, but whether this can be done properly or at all remains debatable. Is it possible to discover the same kind of natural laws for communication and media that we see in the natural sciences, such as a law of gravity? More importantly, in trying to copy scientific models that may be inappropriate for the social sciences, are we missing the point and asking the wrong questions about our social world?

The confusion about where to locate media-studies research as a form of inquiry is also reflected in the range of schools and departments where it can be found. Sometimes media studies reside within a school of journalism; other universities may locate it in a school of communications or even in an English department. To further complicate matters, scholars trained in sociology and psychology or other fields such as literary theory are responsible for much important research and theorizing on mass media and communication. Mathematicians actually developed the hugely influential transmission model of communication (discussed in Chapter 1) to help solve an engineering problem.

Broadly speaking, the debate on the type of science that media research should entail can be divided into two main camps, each with a different way of understanding the world, a distinct **epistemology**. **Positivism**, the dominant epistemology throughout the twentieth century, assumes an objective reality that can be observed, measured, and explained by a neutral observer. Rigorous testing and experimentation following the scientific method can prove or disprove hypotheses based on observations. Related theorizing may improve our understanding of the world and our ability to predict behaviors or alter phenomena with predictable results.

Several other epistemologies reject positivism in varying degrees. **Postpositivism** largely agrees with most positivist claims but also recognizes knowledge that cannot be understood through scientific means, such as religious faith.

**Social constructionism** argues that all meaning and truth are derived from social interactions, especially those involving symbols and signs, whose meanings are relativistic and change with context. Language is not simply a transparent medium that describes the world; it creates the world as we know it.

**Postmodernism**, although it has many variants, largely eschews grand theorizing and what it calls "metanarratives," overarching narratives that try to explain the world, because any such metanarrative essentially favors one worldview over

**epistemology**

A study or theory of the limitations and validity of knowledge; more simply, a way of, or framework for, understanding the world.

**positivism**

A view, common among scientists in the physical or natural sciences and many social sciences, that affirms an objective reality to be discovered and explained through rigorous scientific research.

**postpositivism**

A view that agrees largely with positivism but also recognizes knowledge that may not be revealed through scientific inquiry.

**social constructionism**

A view that claims much or all of what we know and understand about the world, including scientific knowledge, is constructed through social interactions and language.

**postmodernism**

A broad category of viewpoints that rejects grand narratives attempting to explain the world and absolute truths because truth is relative and unknowable.

others. It, like social constructionism, questions the formation of knowledge and challenges the assumption of positivist science that it is a better (or the only) way to find and establish truth.

Some of the basic elements of constructionist and postmodern thought are not entirely new or simply a reaction to the dominance of positivist science in the twentieth century. Their histories can be traced back to early philosophical traditions and later influential schools of thought in the nineteenth and early twentieth centuries, like **pragmatism**, which affirms truth in actions that work and rejects overarching or purely objective notions of truth. In some ways, such thinking is a return to the roots of theorizing about the role of media and communication.

The debate about what type of science media-studies research falls under can also be roughly mapped to the two main types of current research methodologies: **quantitative research** and **qualitative research**.

## QUANTITATIVE RESEARCH

Researchers relying heavily on quantitative techniques tend to have a positivist perspective. They assume that their research will better predict behavior, find causal effects for certain phenomena, and support or weaken certain media theories.

Quantitative studies include the familiar methods of experiments, surveys, and statistical analyses. The exact method depends on several factors, especially the goals or purposes of the research. If a study intends to suggest causality, such as whether watching violent TV programming increases violence among children, then experimental or quasi-experimental methods could be appropriate. If a study means to document the amount of violence on television, then a content analysis should be conducted. If an investigation is designed to determine how much televised violence children can recall, then a survey may be in order.

In any case, research methods are never perfect indicators, and the design of the study as well as the particular method can affect results. For example, conducting a laboratory experiment with children on the effects of television violence not only raises important ethical questions, it also creates an unrealistic media environment that makes accurate measurements problematic. The laboratory, no matter the extent to which it is altered to look and feel like a home, still cannot capture the range of environmental factors in a normal viewing experience.

Analyzing data using statistics raises its own set of problems, including incomplete or missing data that may skew results, **sampling error** that does not accurately reflect the entire population, and faulty study design that yields misleading findings. Consider a simple example of sampling error. Let's say you want to learn what students at your school think about a certain issue. You stand in the quad during the day, stopping every fifth person to ask your questions. This may seem like a **random sample**, in which every person has an equally probable chance of being selected, but in fact you have not accurately captured a sample that represents the entire student body. What about students who do not pass by the quad to get to their classes, such as those in other campus locations, or those who take only night classes?

---

### pragmatism

A school of thought affirming truths found in actions that work and rejecting the possibility of overarching or purely objective notions of truth.

### quantitative research

A method of inquiry favored in the physical sciences that focuses on numerical data and statistical measures to describe phenomena. Researchers often attempt to prove or disprove a hypothesis through the empirical method, particularly controlled experimentation.

### qualitative research

A method of inquiry favored in the social sciences that explores typically unstructured phenomena through interviews, focus groups, and participant observation among other techniques that produce descriptive rather than predictive results.

### sampling error

Error in a statistical analysis that results from selecting a sample that does not represent the entire population.

### random sample

A sample in which every person has an equally probable chance of being selected, intended to represent the entire population of study.

These and other methodological difficulties with quantitative research have encouraged the growth and acceptance of qualitative research methods.

## QUALITATIVE RESEARCH

Qualitative researchers may reject the assumptions behind quantitative research, or they may simply appreciate the limitations of such research and prefer other means to explore their areas of interest. They are generally not trying to make predictions but are focusing on description to gain a better understanding of the world as the participants see it. Qualitative research can include in-depth interviews, focus groups, and ethnography, among other techniques.

**Ethnography** involves a technique developed in anthropology in which researchers immerse themselves in a culture to observe it directly in its natural state while disrupting it as little as possible. An ethnographer studying media behaviors might enter a household, a newsroom, or an advertising agency and spend hours, days, weeks, or even months directly observing media behaviors of those involved, documenting these in note and transcript form and likely video and audio recordings. A detailed analysis would follow. The results might be used in isolation or in combination with other methods, such as interviews or even quantitative techniques such as content analysis of conversations or written memos.

A variation of ethnography is **participant-observation**. In this technique, researchers join the group they are studying, such as a fan club or an online multiplayer video game. The researchers' status as participants not only helps them better understand the world that they are observing but also encourages participants to disclose more than they might otherwise to outsiders.

**Focus groups** are widely employed by media researchers. Often, how such participants interact and discuss what is being studied provides important

**ethnography**

A variety of qualitative research techniques that involve immersion of a researcher in a particular culture to allow interaction with participants through observation, participation, interviews, or a combination of methods.

**participant-observation**

A qualitative research technique in which researchers participate as members of the group they are observing.

**focus group**

A small group of people assembled by researchers to discuss a topic. Their interactions are closely observed, recorded, and analyzed to determine people's opinions.

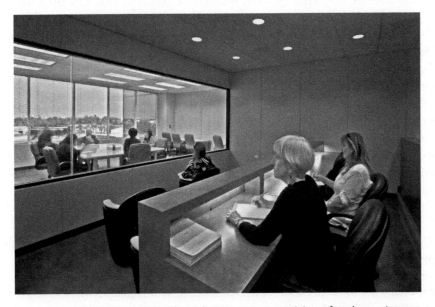

Focus-group research can provide rich insights into consumer opinions of products or issues.

insights that the researcher would not glean from individual interviews or surveys. Marketers testing consumer reactions to their brand or products favor focus groups.

Qualitative research raises its own ethical concerns and is not without weaknesses. One question is whether participants should be informed of the researcher's true role. Many would consider posing as a genuine member of a group to gain the trust of others and generate research material unethical behavior. Transparency is especially important when researching groups online where the researcher's identity may not be obvious. Another ethical issue arises when researchers see participants engaging in risky or dangerous behavior. Do they try to intervene, thus altering research findings, or simply continue to observe?

Qualitative research makes no claims, of course, to being generalizable to the larger population or being reliable in the sense of getting the same results if conducted by another researcher or with another group, even under similar circumstances. Researchers need to identify the limitations of their qualitative research and avoid, for example, representing data from a particular set of interviews like that from a quantitative random sample.

## QUALITATIVE AND QUANTITATIVE RESEARCH WORKING TOGETHER

Each methodology has its place in media research, and each methodology has its strengths and weaknesses. Ignoring one methodology over another because of a philosophical disagreement can create a blind spot for a researcher seeking comprehensive knowledge. A screwdriver can pound a nail, but a hammer works much better. Selecting the right tool from the methodological toolbox is the first step to research success.

Qualitative techniques often provide greater depth or texture to quantitative studies. In designing a survey, for example, you may not really know what issues your research subjects find important or even how they talk about certain things. Common themes may emerge from qualitative research that can then help you design a better survey. Simple observation of certain media behaviors often yields fertile insights that generate even more interesting research questions. Noting, for example, who controls the remote control in the living room may reveal something more significant about television viewing habits than specific program preferences.

Qualitative research, if conducted properly, helps you see the world creatively from other perspectives in ways foreign to quantitative research. Quantitative research, on the other hand, with its statistical techniques and its claims to represent a much larger population than that studied, is extremely powerful. People can often be persuaded of the veracity of results by simply viewing data presented in a seemingly authoritative chart or graph.

**DISCUSSION QUESTIONS:** Have you ever been involved in a study involving media or some other field such as psychology? Identify whether this was qualitative or quantitative inquiry and, more specifically, what type: a survey, a focus group, or an experiment, for example. Describe your experience and why you decided to participate.

## MEDIA CAREERS

Those interested in media research can choose from two main paths: corporate or academic. Teams of researchers work with various clients at large advertising and PR agencies, and media research underlies many important organizational decisions when determining everything from what shows to produce to which ads were most effective. In corporate research, various quantitative and qualitative methods are used to achieve fairly specific goals. In other words, you are generally trying to find answers to specific questions such as which campaign generated higher sales or better product recall.

Academic research also has goals, of course, but these can be more open-ended and exploratory, allowing the pursuit of knowledge for the sake of simply learning and sharing new insights within the scholarly community. Most academic media researchers have doctorate degrees and also teach at the schools where they conduct research. A PhD is helpful in corporate research but not necessary. For students interested in media research, even the academic track, some professional communications experience can prove invaluable, fostering a general understanding of media industries while generating particular questions of interest and relevance to media research.

Opportunities to utilize innovative new research methods, such as online surveys or digital ethnographies, are enabling novel approaches to emerging research questions both in the United States and internationally.

## LOOKING BACK AND MOVING FORWARD

As may be expected of a relatively new medium, large gaps remain in research and theory about digital media and the Internet. Early euphoria about the positive transformative effects of the Internet for society and democracy has given way to more measured, cautious statements that also recognize dangers or weak spots. The concerns about exposure to television and movie violence could be amplified when considering the amount of fictionalized and actual violent acts on the Internet.

Some scholars claim that nothing has fundamentally changed with the rise of the Internet and digital media; from a theoretical perspective, existing conceptual frameworks remain perfectly adequate for researching and explaining new media. Although true in some cases, this position creates large blind spots in a research agenda that should attempt to address the evolving nature of mass communication.

Researchers who focus on digital media tend to draw heavily from research traditions in media studies, sociology, information science, and communication studies, among other disciplines. These research frameworks correspond more or less to those applied to traditional media, ranging from the broad sociocultural perspectives to the more narrow use-and-effects research. Researchers also study how characteristics of the medium itself, such as interactivity, may affect our relation with content.

Curiously, some pre-Internet scholars could experience a revival of interest in certain lines of their work. Marshall McLuhan, for example, may have much to offer digital-media scholars, particularly his examination of the ways electronic media implode space and time and affect social relations. Uses-and-gratifications principles may prove especially fruitful in an interactive medium where users largely control what content they can get and how they get it. Political economy raises even more important questions about how powerful media companies can actually increase their control over public media systems, even as popular ideology claims that we have more freedom than ever.

---

**MEDIA MATTERS**   THEORY AND PRACTICE

1. What does the term "information society" mean to you?

2. Do you think advertising affects your decisions? Why or why not? Do you think it affects other people? If so, who is most affected, and why?

3. Do you feel that media can influence us? Why or why not? Which types of media are most influential, and why?

4. Do you believe there is an objective reality "out there" that we can describe and all agree on, or do you believe that each of us creates our own reality? Explain your response.

5. How and to what extent did your parents or guardians supervise your television viewing? Your time on the computer?

---

## FURTHER READING

*Critical Media Studies: An Introduction,* 2nd ed. Brian Ott, Robert Mack (2014) Wiley-Blackwell.

*Media Studies: Theories and Approaches.* Dan Laughey (2010) Oldcastle Books.

*Media Effects Research: A Basic Overview,* 4th ed. Glenn G. Sparks (2012) Cengage Learning.

*Media Effects: Advances in Theory and Research,* 3rd ed. Jennings Bryant, Mary Beth Oliver (eds.) (2008) Routledge.

*Quantitative Research Methods for Communication: A Hands-On Approach.* Jason Wrench, Candice Thomas-Maddox, Virginia Peck Richmond, James McCroskey (2008) Oxford University Press.

*Understanding Media Theory.* Kevin Williams (2003) Hodder Arnold.

*Understanding Media Cultures: Social Theory and Mass Communication.* Nicholas Stevenson (2002) Sage.

*Anthropology and Mass Communication: Media and Myth in the New Millennium.* Mark Allen Peterson (2003) Berghahn Books.

*Orality and Literacy.* Walter J. Ong (2002) Routledge.

*Manufacturing Consent: The Political Economy of the Mass Media.* Edward S. Herman, Noam Chomsky (2002) Pantheon Books.

*Media and Cultural Studies: Keyworks,* 2nd ed. Meenakshi Gigi Durham, Douglas Kellner (eds.) (2012) Wiley-Blackwell.

*Critical Theories of Mass Media: Then and Now.* Paul Taylor, Jan Harris (2007) Open University Press.

*More Than Meets the Eye: Watching Television Watching Us.* John J. Pungente, Martin O'Malley (1999) McClelland & Stewart.

*Understanding Media: The Extensions of Man*. Marshall McLuhan (1994) MIT Press.

*Communication, Media, and American Society: A Critical Introduction*. Daniel W. Rossides (2002) Rowman & Littlefield.

*Theories of the Information Society*, 2nd ed. Frank Webster (2002) Routledge.

*A Networked Self: Identity, Community, and Culture on Social Network Sites*. Zizi Papacharissi (ed.) (2010) Routledge.

*An Invitation to Social Construction*, 2nd ed. Kenneth Gergen (2009) Sage.

*E-Crit: Digital Media, Critical Theory, and the Humanities*. Marcel O'Gorman (2007) University of Toronto Press.

*Ethnography: A Way of Seeing*. Harry F. Wolcott (1999) Rowman & Littlefield.

*Netnography: Doing Ethnographic Research Online*. Robert V. Kozinets (2010) Sage.

*Dark Fiber: Tracking Critical Internet Culture*. Geert Lovink (2003) MIT Press.

# Mass Communication and Politics in the Digital Age

onald Trump's candidacy and election as forty-fifth president of the United States has been a challenging time for journalists and the media, in a number of ways.

For a good part of the Republican primary, when a crowded field of established Republican politicians were vying for the party's nomination, Trump was treated mostly as a joke by the media. Nevertheless, through his experience as a reality TV personality and long years of being in the public eye, he clearly knew how to best manipulate the news cycle, ensuring that he got maximum coverage.

Outrageous statements Trump made in person and over Twitter about individuals and whole groups of people helped feed the frenzied media coverage about him. These ranged from his comment about former Fox anchor Megyn Kelly that she had "blood coming out of her wherever," to his fight with the Gold Star family the Khans to his claim that Mexicans are rapists and that Muslims should be banned from entering the country. For almost anybody else running for office, any one of these would have been career-ending incidents. However, not even his taped "grab them by the p***y" remark seriously hurt his poll numbers before the election.

Almost every pundit was also proved wrong when they gave Trump almost no chance of winning. Among celebrities, only documentary filmmaker Michael Moore predicted early that Trump would win the election. Even though he lost the popular vote, he did win the electoral college and thus the presidency.

As president, Trump has continued his Twitter rampages and has continued to say and do things that media pundits keep saying is beyond too far. At the same time, the hints of a potential large-scale scandal involving Trump's campaign and Russian influence on the election keeps simmering. Trump has even undermined his own aides as they create excuses for his actions, tweets, or statements in news shows or interviews that contradict their earlier stories.

## LEARNING OBJECTIVES

>> Describe the evolving role of the media in political elections, especially pertaining to sound bites, election coverage, and opinion polls.

>> Discuss the increasing importance of political advertising in campaigns, its nature and its impact.

>> Understand how entertainment functions in political campaigns.

>> Examine the expanded part played by the Internet and social media in political campaigns.

>> Explain how social media help increase civic engagement and aid social movements.

>> Identify a correlation between political ideology and certain media habits.

Although television news especially loves the increased viewership and ratings, and newspapers such as *The New York Times* and *The Washington Post* have seen their subscriptions rise after Trump was elected, it is a double-edged sword given Trump's love-hate relationship with the media. On the one hand they rely on his antics to attract viewers and readers, but on the other hand they worry that by covering distractions they may be missing larger, more important stories.

And then there is Trump's constant complaining about the "fake news" media (whenever there is coverage he does not like), and his calling journalists "the enemy of the people"—a phrase used during Stalin's time to single out enemies of the state. Given that the American public's trust in mass media has dropped to historically low levels, some worry that such statements could leave journalists susceptible to violence.

💬 **partisan press**

A press, such as colonial newspapers, typically aligned with a particular political party and presenting information to help its cause, with no sense of objectivity or balance in news coverage.

Since the earliest days of the republic, the media have been intimately involved in our political process. The colonial newspapers were a **partisan press**, typically aligned with a particular political party and presenting information that helped its cause, with no sense of objectivity or balance in news coverage. Media also aided the Revolutionary cause. Fiery pamphlets such as Thomas Paine's *Common Sense* helped persuade colonists that they were fighting for a just and noble cause.

Yet more than journalism drives the engine of media and politics. Political advertising, particularly on television, is how most candidates, particularly presidential candidates, reach the majority of voters most often. Negative political advertising, a mainstay of politics in the United States, has been extensively researched. Political advertising also provides substantial income for media organizations and has made it necessary for political candidates to raise large sums of money from donations.

Entertainment has played an increasingly important role in helping political candidates create a more down-to-earth image. Appearances on late-night talk shows and even comedy shows like *Saturday Night Live* are now becoming the norm; and "fake news" shows, such as *The Daily Show* and *This Week Tonight*, often provide political news, particularly for young people.

The Internet and social media have also transformed politics and political elections. Some candidates have used these effectively to fundraise and communicate their messages directly to the public rather than through the media. Social media and the Internet are not only important sources of information, they are also a means by which members of the public can organize quickly and effectively regarding causes or candidates.

## Journalism and Political Coverage

Journalism has long considered itself the main conduit of political information for the public and therefore key to democratic processes. Journalism claims to be the mechanism for obtaining public unbiased and impartial information about candidates for office, sitting elected officials, the agencies they represent and operate, and relevant contemporary political issues—in other words, journalism aspires to be an engine of democracy.

Consider the words of Joseph Pulitzer, the former publisher of the *New York World* and the founder of the Pulitzer Prize, the highest award for journalistic

Jimmy Fallon was largely criticized for his softball questions to then-candidate Donald Trump, and *Late Night* ultimately fell to second place in the late night TV ratings behind Stephen Colbert's *The Late Show*. Colbert has been more politically critical and hard-hitting (although he too hosted Trump, along with other candidates).

excellence. In his proposal for founding a school of journalism, Pulitzer summarized his credo: "Our Republic and its press will rise or fall together. An able, disinterested, public-spirited press, with trained intelligence to know the right and courage to do it, can preserve that public virtue without which popular government is a sham and a mockery. A cynical, mercenary, demagogic press will produce in time a people as base as itself. The power to mold the future of the Republic will be in the hands of the journalists of future generations."[1]

Although most journalists aim to report the news fairly and in a balanced way, media critics contend the media are anything but unbiased. They claim that media companies can hardly be considered disinterested, given they, like most for-profit companies, have vested self-interests in pro-business government regulations and policies.

Like other industries, the media industry lobbies politicians to vote in favor of laws or regulations that favor the industry or key players. During the debates about the Stop Online Piracy Act (SOPA) and Protect Intellectual Property Act (PIPA) of 2012, many of the biggest media and telecom companies—such as Comcast, Disney, and News Corp., which own networks NBC, ABC, and Fox, respectively—spent tens of thousands of dollars on lobbyists.

In another example, dozens of news organizations, including *The Washington Post,* Politico, Fox News, NBC News, ABC News, and *USA Today*, vigorously lobbied the FCC to prevent greater transparency regarding political spending on advertisements. In April 2012, the FCC approved greater access to databases of such information, but with several restrictions. The rule would apply only to the big four television networks (NBC, ABC, CBS, and Fox) in the top fifty media markets and would expire after two years.

Given that news organizations frequently call for more transparency from the government and organizations they cover, critics find it hypocritical that these same organizations do not want the same level of scrutiny regarding advertising revenues they receive from political campaigns. Their stated reasons for opposing the measure ranged from difficulties and added costs of compiling and posting the information to creating an atmosphere that might hurt their deals with other advertisers.

Critics also see **media bias** in political news coverage and in the types and the coverage of news stories in general. The critics say that complex topics often do not get the airtime or depth of treatment required to truly inform the public. Instead, the media focus more on simpler topics, features on political personalities, or exposés of scandals. Existing coverage of policy issues and other important matters often lacks context and historical information that aid public understanding.

Budget cuts have also affected news coverage of politics, with many big-city newspapers closing their Washington bureaus and relying for their political news on wire services. Unfortunately, the more general wire-service coverage can miss important specific points that a Washington-based local reporter might otherwise be able to report on. Even for small-town newspapers, cuts in staff may mean less or even no coverage of politics at the state or even local level, leaving the public less informed on state or local issues that often affect them most directly.

**media bias**

A real or perceived viewpoint held by journalists and news organizations that slants news coverage unfairly, contrary to professional journalism's stated goals of balanced coverage and objectivity.

**DISCUSSION QUESTIONS:** Do you agree with Joseph Pulitzer's statement on the importance of the press in preserving American democracy? Why or why not? What trends and events, both historical and current, support your views?

## POLITICIANS USING THE NEWS

Public figures such as politicians are media savvy and use the news media to their advantage. If possible, many officials will not, for example, announce bad news until late Friday afternoon, the end of a workweek when most people do not follow the news as closely and when other news over the weekend makes it likely different stories will lead by the following Monday. Media organizations will also have more trouble contacting sources for interviews and accessing information over the weekend to follow up on the story. Of course, this strategy does not always work. Sometimes stories have enough weight to carry through the weekend and become even bigger if more information is uncovered.

A public figure may use a **news leak** for many purposes. Giving a journalist exclusive and secret information helps build the relationship between a journalist and the official as a good source of information. More importantly, it can strategically damage opponents or even halt certain programs or projects. Providing news leaks is a dangerous game, however, for giving someone confidential or classified information often entails breaking the law. If the person giving the information is discovered, he or she can be sentenced to prison, depending on the severity of the case.

Politicians often use journalists and their need for scoops to test proposals or to hurt opponents.

Similar to news leaks, politicians may use a **trial balloon** to test **public opinion** on proposals they are considering. A politician may announce plans for a new industrial park, even though no plans have been finalized. The subsequent media coverage and public discussion may reveal who might oppose the plan and whether it would be politically damaging to move forward with it.

Journalists are not naive about these techniques, of course. A journalist may fully realize why a politician is providing an exclusive scoop on a new budget proposal, but publishing the story also helps the news organization beat its competition, and the story itself may be newsworthy.

The symbiotic relationship between politicians and journalists is especially evident during elections, with both parties in the public eye. Television has changed political campaign coverage in important ways, as have polls.

### news leak

Secret information deliberately given to journalists with the hope that they will publish the item.

### trial balloon

Leaking information to the press about a proposed plan or idea to see how the public will respond.

### public opinion

The notion that the public, as a group, can form shared views or ideas about topics and that these ideas guide the public's actions.

### sound bite

The length of time a news subject is allowed to speak without editing. It also has come to refer to short, catchy utterances designed to capture media attention.

## SOUND BITES AND HORSE RACES

With the rise of electronic media in the past half-century, especially television, political communication and debate in the media have become increasingly superficial. More often than not, the horse-race aspect of the campaign—chronicling who's ahead, who's behind, and what their latest campaign tactic might be to move ahead in the polls—becomes the whole story, at the expense of coverage of issues. Critics claim news coverage of campaigns essentially disenfranchises voters, making them jaded about politics and less willing to participate politically. Emphasizing campaign strategies and depicting politicians as those who will do and say anything just to get elected increase public cynicism and apathy.

Another highly criticized aspect of campaign coverage has to do with the nature of television. In 1968, Kiku Adatto of Harvard University did a study on political **sound bites**—specifically, how long a source in a television news story was allowed to speak without editing. In 1968, the average sound bite was 42.3 seconds. Nearly a quarter of all political sound bites were at least a minute in length, providing considerable room for context. Twenty years later, in 1988, the average TV sound bite of a political candidate had shrunk by some 80 percent to just 9.8 seconds, and virtually none were a minute or longer—in fact, entire stories were often not a minute long.[2] This greatly reduces the context news can provide, let alone adequate facts about complex political issues.

## THE CHANGING TONE OF TELEVISION POLITICAL COVERAGE

The overall tone of television political coverage has also changed. Consider the research findings of Syracuse University political scientist Thomas Patterson, author of *Out of Order*. He found that in the 1960 presidential election, 75 percent of the news reports about leading candidates John F. Kennedy and Richard M. Nixon were positive in tone; only 25 percent were negative. Thirty-two years later, in the 1992 presidential election, news reports had become predominantly negative. More than half (60 percent) of the reports about then-candidate Bill Clinton and then-president George H. W. Bush were negative, and 40 percent were positive.

A study by Harvard's Shorenstein Center on Media, Politics and Public Policy released in May 2017 found that Trump's coverage was 80 percent negative in tone during his first one hundred days in office, compared to 41 percent for Obama, 57 percent for Bush, and 60 percent for Clinton. Some news outlets, like CNN and NBC, had 93 percent negative coverage for Trump. Even conservative network Fox News had 52 percent negative coverage, although the study's authors said it was hard to make a true comparison because Fox at times did not cover the same stories as other major news outlets.[3]

Many of the better online news operations, such as CBS News online, typically augment stories adapted from on-air coverage, turning the text of a sixty-second video clip (less than two hundred words perhaps) into a five-hundred-word or longer report with greater depth. More quotes may be added, or quotes repeated from the broadcast text may be extended. Much of the additional reporting is drawn from wire-service copy (e.g., Reuters, the Associated Press) pulled off the Internet or sometimes from original interviews conducted via telephone or email. Increasingly, graphics such as maps are integrated as well.

## OPINION POLLS

Increasingly, **opinion polls** drive campaign coverage. Patterson's research indicates that news becomes more favorable as poll support rises markedly or a candidate's lead widens. Conversely, media coverage becomes more negative if the candidate trails significantly or his or her poll standing drops.

Media organizations usually use one of several professional polling organizations, such as Gallup, to conduct polls. These organizations try to take random samples of the public to assess what the population as a whole is feeling about a candidate or an issue. Lower telephone response rates in recent years, as people screen calls to avoid telemarketers, have made conducting telephone polls more expensive. In contrast to the more random telephone sample, online polls represent only users who have visited the website and choose to answer the poll. And, although not considered scientifically valid, they appear increasingly on news

**opinion poll**

Usually conducted by a professional polling organization, a list of questions asking members of the public their opinions on issues or political candidates.

"TheUpshot," from the *New York Times*, used a statistical model, including poll data, to correctly predict Republicans would win a majority in the Senate in the 2014 midterm elections. **CRITICAL THINKING QUESTIONS:** Do you think polls influence election results? Are you less likely to vote if polling data indicate your candidate is unlikely to win?

### 💬 push poll

A type of political advertising that appears to be a telephone poll but is actually a telemarketing campaign to sway voters by making a favored candidate look good or by misrepresenting the opposition.

websites, and their results may be mistakenly assumed to accurately represent the point of view of the general populace.

Although the profile of the average Internet user is evolving as demographic diversity increases, a higher percentage of Internet users are likely to be white, male, and more affluent than average. Moreover, an online poll taken by a politically conservative entity, such as Fox News, will usually show vastly different results than the same poll taken by a politically liberal entity, such as MSNBC. Some polling organizations, such as Harris Interactive, conduct online polls, efforts that other organizations and the American Association for Public Opinion Research (AAPOR) typically deride as nonscientific.

Sometimes telephone "polls," called **push polls**, are actually political advertising. Push polls try to sway voters by giving them false or misleading information about opposing candidates under the guise of conducting a poll, or they try to make a candidate look good by asking leading questions. Push polls ask deliberately misleading questions such as "Would you support the policies of a candidate who will curtail some of our freedoms and raise taxes?" Few would answer "yes" to such a question, but the respondent may not realize that the pollster was referring to a certain candidate when asking it. Nevertheless, the publicized poll results would indicate that "90 percent of the people polled say they do not support Candidate Y."

> **DISCUSSION QUESTIONS:** Look at the some of the stories on the data journalism site FiveThirtyEight.com and notice how they discuss various good and bad polls. How much did polling results on similar issues differ? What were their criticisms of certain polls?

## Political Advertising

Candidates have historically employed a wide variety of techniques to reach as many people as possible directly, from whistle-stop speeches to political rallies. Partly due to the shrinking sound bite; the poll-driven, horse race, media coverage of campaigns; and a growing desire to control their own messages, candidates have turned increasingly to paid advertising. Campaigning has become increasingly expensive in the United States, as campaigns and technology become more complex and candidates attempt to reach voters through the media.[4]

The 2012 presidential election was the second in which the candidates raised more than $1 billion (the first was 2008), although the 2012 figure also includes contributions from super PACs, not immediately connected to the campaigns. In 2016, Hillary Clinton raised over $1 billion, about $500 million more than Donald Trump (see Figure 14-1). In the primaries, Trump said he would fund his own election campaign, but in fact he ended up taking $269 million from outside donors.

The funds needed to run for national, or even state, office are so great partly because of political advertising costs. Although many criticize the way campaigning has changed in U.S. elections, with huge costs being one major complaint, many media companies benefit greatly from political advertising. They are unlikely to lobby to change a system that helps their bottom line, especially when advertising revenues in general have been down.

**FIGURE 14-1** 2016 Presidential Campaign Expenditures

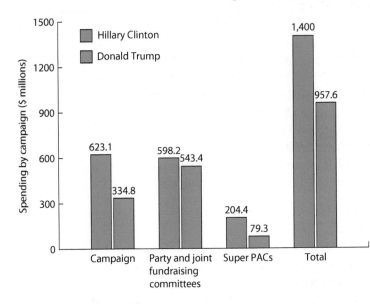

## IMPACT OF NEGATIVE ADVERTISING

Some claim that political advertising is no different from other product advertising, except that a political campaign precedes a one-day sale—the election. This mentality drives the industry, and many candidates gravitate toward negative advertising. Based on an examination of more than eleven hundred political commercials, political-communications scholar Larry Sabato concluded the following:

> Even when television is used to communicate political truth (at least from one candidate's perspective), the truth can be negatively packaged—attacking the opponent's character and record rather than supporting one's own. If there is a single trend obvious to most American consultants, it is the increasing proportion of negative political advertising. . . . At least a third of all spot commercials in recent campaigns have been negative, and in a minority of campaigns half or more of the spots are negative in tone or substance.[5]

Although some paid political spots on television simply provide information about the candidate and her or his position on the issues, most criticism and research have addressed ads that attack the opposing candidate. The rise of negative political advertising has also led news media to focus more of their coverage on the candidates' advertising.

Negative political advertising has been problematic for a number of reasons. One of the biggest concerns, Kathleen Hall Jamieson points out, is that many ads promote falsehoods or encourage the audience to make false inferences.[6] Hillary Clinton had no qualms about running negative advertising against Republican candidate Donald Trump in the 2016 election. Negative summer ads, which had children watching television in which Trump made some of his more controversial statements, failed to move the needle of public opinion about Trump in a highly polarized political climate.

## EFFECTIVENESS OF NEGATIVE ADVERTISING

Researchers Richard Lau, Lee Sigelman, and Ivy Brown Rovner tested three hypotheses regarding negative political advertisements: (1) that they work (i.e., they get voters to endorse the attacking candidate), (2) that voters dislike negative ads, and (3) that negative ads have an unintended side effect of disenfranchising the electorate.[7]

Regarding the first hypothesis, Lau and colleagues found in a study of voters in 1997 that negative ads did not work and actually decreased the favorability of voters' attitudes toward the candidate whose campaign ran the negative ad. Conversely, voters' attitudes toward the target of the ads became more favorable. A study of multiple campaigns similarly revealed that candidates who initiated negative ads lost eighteen out of twenty-five elections. They also found no strong

---

### ETHICS IN MEDIA
## Can Imagery Lead to Action?

In late May 2017, a photo of comedian Kathy Griffin holding a bloody mask of Donald Trump's head created a media stir and drew widespread condemnation from people on the left and right. She later apologized for the stunt, but, even so, many wondered how badly it may have hurt her career.

Although most people believe the photo went too far, and was at least in extremely poor taste, Griffin pointed out that President Obama had received equally bad or worse treatment from conservative rocker Ted Nugent when in 2012 he said "We need to ride into that battlefield and chop their [the Obama administration's] heads off." Nugent said that he was speaking only metaphorically and that it was not the same as what Griffin did.

Whether the imagery that arises from pictures or from words is equally as powerful and potentially damaging relates to an earlier incidence of violence against a politician in 2011, when U.S. Representative Gabrielle Giffords (D-AZ), who was holding a "Congress on Your Corner" meeting in front of a Safeway in Tucson, Arizona, was shot by Jared Loughner, who also fired randomly at the crowd with his semiautomatic pistol, wounding thirteen people and killing six, including a federal judge and Christina Taylor-Green, nine, who had been born on September 11, 2001.

Soon after the shooting, the media began to question Sarah Palin's use of gun crosshairs and terms like "targeted" and other inflammatory language on her website "TakeBack-the20," dedicated to winning back seats from Democrats. Critics of the vitriol expressed by both parties in the 2010 congressional elections wondered if such imagery and rhetoric helped spur someone like Loughner to violent action.

Loughner pleaded guilty to nineteen counts of murder or attempted murder, but whether the violent imagery and

language deployed by conservatives against politicians like Giffords influenced his actions will likely never be known. Nevertheless, the tragic incident did serve as a powerful reminder to politicians and the public that hateful partisanship and "politics as usual" rhetoric can be lethal for democracy. It also helped motivate Giffords and her husband, Mark Kelly, a retired NASA astronaut, to organize their own efforts for gun control. In 2014, they published a book, *Enough: Our Fight to Keep America Safe from Gun Violence*, and organized Americans for Responsible Solutions, a super PAC opposing gun violence. In 2016, the group raised nearly $13.5 million.[8]

preponderance of evidence indicating that negative political ads were more memorable than positive ads.

With respect to the second hypothesis, that voters dislike negative ads, their results found that six of the nine studies showed negative political ads being rated less ethical, less fair, and otherwise less liked than positive political ads, with two studies reaching the opposite conclusion and one showing no significant statistical difference.

For the third hypothesis, that negative ads contribute to voter apathy or disenfranchisement, their findings were mixed, with ten out of twenty reporting no significance differences, two showing positive outcomes, and, and eight showing significant negative outcomes. Some research indicates that alienating young viewers from the political process is one of the most significant effects of negative political advertising, which increases cynicism and decreases interest among young viewers.

Negative political advertising is controversial: Some research indicates that it turns off voters and actually hurts the politician making the negative ad.

**DISCUSSION QUESTIONS:** What type of political advertisements do you consider negative? Do your reactions vary depending on your prior views of the candidate? Can you find any examples in these ads of factual information framed in unjustly negative ways? Do ads that attack a candidate's platform affect you in the same way as ads that attack a politician's character? Why or why not?

# Politics and Entertainment

"Politics is showbiz for ugly people" is a popular saying that succinctly captures the dynamics of the campaign trail where politicians have long utilized elements of show business and entertainment to attract voters.

## POLITICAL CAMPAIGNS AND ENTERTAINMENT

Throughout the nineteenth century, election campaigns and elections themselves were very public spectacles, with parades, speeches from local leaders, music, and a generally festive atmosphere. Until well into the nineteenth century, voting occurred publicly, making it easy to see who voted for whom. The political parties created well-organized groups of supporters who persuaded others to vote for their candidates, often with promises of plum government jobs if their candidate was elected.

Songs and pithy catchphrases have long played a part in political campaigns, going back to Andrew Jackson's campaigns in 1824 and 1828. In the 1840 presidential campaign, the song and phrase "Tippecanoe and Tyler Too" became popular and helped get William Henry Harrison elected president. The use of campaign songs continued into the twentieth and twenty-first centuries, although in the past thirty years or so, candidates generally adopt pop hits rather than creating original campaign songs. One exception is will.i.am's "Yes We Can," a collaboration of various  artists that features lyrics consisting entirely of select clips of Barack Obama speeches during the 2008 presidential primaries.

Political campaigns in the nineteenth century often used entertainment such as bands and popular music to attract the public to campaign events.

There have also been ironic and humorous uses of songs that have caused some politicians mild embarrassment. Republicans and Democrats alike have used Bruce Springsteen songs at campaign events, until the Boss specifically forbade the use of his songs at Republican events. In the 2012 election, Republican vice presidential candidate Paul Ryan raised eyebrows when he said one of his favorite bands was Rage Against the Machine—a band whose angry lyrics attack much of what conservative Republicans stand for. Adele explicitly refused permission for Trump's 2016 campaign to use her songs.

Catchy slogans and symbols have also been widely used in political campaigns. Although an eye-catching logo would likely not be the main consideration for electing a president, a bad one could hurt a candidate's image in subtle but powerful ways, especially for undecided voters who may not keep up with political issues and rely more heavily on peripheral cues when deciding whom to vote for, such as how the candidate looks.

## POLITICAL DEBATES

Although not intended to be entertainment, political debates today have many of the trappings of show business, including the backdrops, the positioning of candidates, and the careful selection of live audience members. Carefully choreographed aspects aside, the actual debate remains one of the most important areas of political communication. Debates have been a proving ground for candidates to test their mettle against an opponent and to reveal their character and platform to the public.

Early debates were quite different from today's televised debates. For instance, a debate between Abraham Lincoln and Stephen A. Douglas during the 1858 Senate race lasted more than five hours, with each candidate offering detailed commentary of an hour or more on a single issue, such as abolition, their first debate topic. Further, because television and radio did not yet exist, these exchanges went unheard by anyone other than those present for the live event, although the public could read about them in newspapers. Today, a five-hour televised debate between political candidates is hard to imagine.

Arguably the most important debate between U.S. presidential candidates in the twentieth century occurred in 1960, when for the first time presidential candidates debated live on broadcast television and radio. Research conducted at the time showed that viewers of the televised debate rated John F. Kennedy, who was handsome and well groomed, as clearly superior. Nixon, whose dark stubble and "shifty" eyes gave him a more sinister look (the debate was scheduled for the evening, and Nixon had not shaved since the morning), was deemed to have lost.

Meanwhile, on radio, with listeners only able to hear what the candidates said, Nixon was judged the clear winner for his more convincing arguments. Kennedy ultimately won the presidential contest in an extremely close election, and it is not clear whether the debate was the deciding factor. But it has been the touchstone for televised campaigning ever since. Today, it is a given that one's television persona is essential for winning an election, a factor that some experts

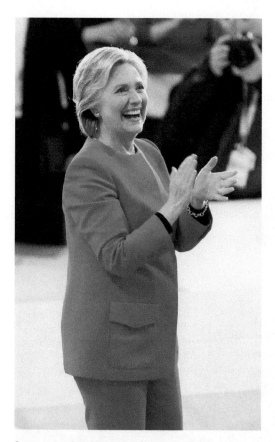

Some research indicates that focus on a female politician's appearance, even in ways that stress her physical attractiveness, damages her overall appeal to voters. **CRITICAL THINKING QUESTIONS:** Why do you think compliments about a female politician's appearance might hurt her chances of being elected? Do you think this may be true for male politicians too?

The 1960 Kennedy–Nixon presidential debate showed how powerfully television could influence public perceptions of candidates.

believe greatly helped Trump, who had much more experience in television during his years on *The Apprentice* than the more seasoned politician Hillary Clinton, despite her many years in the public eye.

## Social Media and Political Campaigns

Electronic media have been increasingly significant in political elections ever since the first use of radio in political campaigning in 1924, but the Internet and social media have created even greater changes in recent years.

In the early years of radio, Democrats employed radio effectively in the elections of both 1936 and 1940. The majority of newspapers throughout the United States openly endorsed Republican candidates for office, but the Democrats did better in the elections. Democratic president Franklin Roosevelt was masterful in his use of radio to reach the masses, providing his regular "Fireside Chats" during the 1930s and 1940s. This ushered in an era in which radio, and later, television, had the personal qualities of candidates, rather than their political-policy stances, take center stage in the campaign process.

The Internet further transformed the political communication landscape, especially regarding elections. Voters can go to a candidate's website to obtain information about a candidate's stance on an issue, make a campaign contribution, or volunteer to help the candidate's party.

Although a candidate website may have been considered groundbreaking in 1998, by 2016, it was only a part of much more robust communication strategies that included YouTube, Facebook, and Twitter. Social media allowed candidates to communicate with voters in more informal ways than they could via other media channels; and social media can also generate more attention from traditional media, particularly if an item **goes viral**. In the 2012 election, President Obama famously tweeted a response the day after Clint Eastwood's bizarre performance at the Republican National Convention in which he spoke to an invisible President Obama in an empty chair. The tweet—a simple picture of the back of President Obama's chair (with him in it) saying, "This seat's taken"—perfectly fit the terse and snarky mode so characteristic of Twitter. Eastwood's comical exchange also inspired one of the most famous **memes** from the election and even spawned its own verb "Eastwooding," the act of speaking to an empty chair.

**going viral**

The phenomenon in which a media item spreads rapidly from person to person via the Internet.

**meme**

A media item of cultural interest that spreads through repetition and replication via the Internet.

Twitter is often a medium for pithy, snarky comments from the public and politicians.

Of course with President Trump's frequent tweets, the role of Twitter has reached unprecedented levels in the public and media conversation. Shortly after the stabbing of dozens of people in London in June 2017, rather than offering sympathy to the victims, Trump used the opportunity to further promote his calls to ban people from certain Muslim-majority countries from coming to the United States. Despite his aides and lawyers telling him not to tweet, he continues to do so and creates dramas both major and minor almost every week for the administration.

Every social media user is a potential media producer, or "produser," of text and images that may be created and distributed with equal ease, two social media trends that can conspire by accident or by design to derail or even ruin a political career. Congressman Anthony Weiner became the poster boy for sexting scandals in 2011, and again in 2013, as a NYC mayor hopeful. He also played an unintentional role in the FBI reopening the email server investigation of Hillary Clinton when it was discovered that his then-wife, a key Clinton aide, had sent some emails to his laptop that may have contained classified information. In December 2014, Elizabeth Lauten, a congressman's aide, was also the digital architect of her own demise after a snarky post to her Facebook page about Malia and Sasha Obama went viral and public backlash prompted her resignation. A 2006 clip from the campaign trail of Virginia senator George Allen recorded him publicly calling an opponent's campaign worker of Indian descent "macaca," a European racial slur for African immigrants. The video

## CONVERGENCE CULTURE
# Super PACs and Media

Although a new kind of political action committee (PAC) came into existence in July 2010, it wasn't until the 2012 presidential and congressional election that people really started talking about so-called super PACs and their potentially harmful effects on the election process.

Technically called an independent expenditure-only committee, a super PAC differs from a regular PAC in that it can accept unlimited donations from individuals, corporations, unions, and associations. Traditional PACs can accept only limited funds from individuals and nothing from the other groups. Also, unlike a traditional PAC, a super PAC cannot contribute directly to a politician's campaign. Consequently, it can spend the money any way it sees fit to advocate for a favored candidate.

Even though Super PACs cannot give directly to candidates and are supposed to operate independently from the candidate or staff, many are run by former staff members or aides who have other close ties to the candidates they support. On *The Colbert Report*, Stephen Colbert famously mocked these relationships—and some of the legal loopholes that super PACs enjoy—as he "transferred" his super PAC power to Jon Stewart (the episode won a Peabody Award). Colbert actually did create a super PAC called Americans for a Better Tomorrow, Tomorrow, which had raised $1.2 million by election day, even though he spent only a fraction of the money.[9]

But other super PACs did spend, for a total of $1.3 billion during the presidential and congressional elections in 2012.

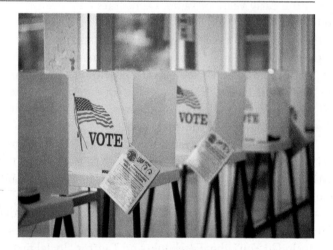

Despite two-thirds of super PAC funds supporting Republican candidates in various races, the results proved disappointing for many of those so invested. Karl Rove's super PAC, American Crossroads, endorsed eight Republican Senate candidates to the tune of $104.7 million; only two won their races. The National Rifle Association spent $11 million; none of their candidates prevailed.[10]

In the 2016 presidential election, super PACs had received more than $1.8 billion and spent about $1.1 billion, according to the Center for Responsive Politics.[11]

A video of Virginia senator George Allen repeatedly using the racial slur "macaca" at a campaign stop in 2006 was widely circulated on the Internet and credited in part with his defeat.

circulated widely on the Internet and left indelible impressions that no amount of subsequent press-release apologies could successfully whitewash or counter.

But digital media can, of course, disseminate more significant items than witty retorts or embarrassing videos. Obama's social media team proved masterful at fundraising and increasing voter registration and turnout in both the 2008 and 2012 elections. So successful was Obama's 2008 campaign at getting small donations from many people that he was the first presidential candidate to refuse taxpayer funding (and, not coincidentally, the spending restrictions that went with that). Some even claim that President Obama owed his first election win to the Internet. Joe Trippi, Howard Dean's presidential campaign manager in 2004, said that the extent and kind of Obama's Internet activity would have required "an army of volunteers and paid organizers on the ground."[12]

In 2012, Obama once again tapped this network, even though the media often commented as the race tightened in the fall that Obama supporters lacked the enthusiasm of 2008. Nevertheless, in election postmortems, many commentators observed that part of the credit for Obama's win went to his well-organized campaigns, especially in swing states, with organizing facilitated by social media and online communication between campaign managers and volunteers.

Trump's 2016 campaign also demonstrated excellent social media savvy, although it was to suppress, rather than encourage, voters. In the final weeks of the campaign, Trump's social media team spent $150 million in Facebook ads that targeted African American voters with negative messages about Hillary Clinton. The campaign team realized they could not win over voters but reasoned that suppressing voter turnout for Clinton could help them win. Further, they had a sophisticated database of voter information that they used to energize their own base of supporters with highly targeted messages.[13]

## CHANGES WITH SOCIAL MEDIA

Social media came into its own regarding elections in the changed media landscape of 2012. An October 2012 study by the Pew Internet & American Life Project found that 39 percent of Americans used social media to discuss politics. In 2016, Pew found that over half of the public got their news on the 2016 presidential election over social media sites, with Facebook far and away the most popular platform for online adults, accounting for 78 percent.

Leading up to the 2008 election, YouTube proved key in promoting Obama, according to Arianna Huffington, founder of the *Huffington Post*. It purposely positioned itself to play a potentially important role in the elections by launching the YouTube You Choose '08 campaign, which gave presidential candidates their own YouTube channels. In posted videos that the public could watch when they wanted, without commercials, candidates could speak at greater length than the sound-bite culture that dominates the mainstream news allows. YouTube also allowed people to repeatedly watch and share these videos with friends.

The transformations produced by social media are even more remarkable when we consider that neither YouTube nor Twitter even existed during the 2004 election. Yet within eight years, they had become integral components of the electoral process, and remained so in the 2016 election. Scholars and political consultants continue to study and analyze the implications for future campaigns of this evolution in mass communications, one that has recast expectations and interactions of American voters with their political candidates.

## CHANGING RULES FOR POLITICIANS

The changes in political campaigns produced by YouTube, Facebook, and other social media technologies are still not fully understood and will likely continue to develop as technologies continue to evolve. Certain fundamental shifts, however, can already be identified from the last three presidential campaigns.

Candidates seem not to have yet learned that there is no such thing anymore as an "off the record" event. In another era, journalists attending fundraisers or other gatherings that were off the record respected that whatever the candidate said there could not be reported. But today's citizen-journalists and bloggers often ignore these unwritten rules. When damaging material can be readily redirected to the public sphere via the Internet, the assumption that those present constitute a partisan audience wholly sympathetic to one's cause or sensitive to a remark's context is a dangerous supposition.

At a private fundraiser for wealthy donors in May 2012, Romney infamously characterized 47 percent of Americans as government freeloaders who paid no taxes and who considered themselves victims. A bartender catering the event, who explicitly invoked his Boston blue-collar roots when explaining his actions to ABC News, surreptitiously taped and subsequently released the "47 percent video" to the media months later as the election campaigns were heating up. It further reinforced negative perceptions of Romney as elitist, someone who if elected would be more concerned about the rich rather than the middle class.

Campaign gaffes also generate a life of their own on social media, as they are viewed again and again. Libertarian presidential candidate Gary Johnson not only could not name Aleppo, the city in Syria where many people have been killed during its long war, but days later could not name a single foreign leader when asked on MSNBC at a town hall. Although Johnson was never a major presidential contender, the gaffes nevertheless erode his credibility in the eyes of many.

Presidents are of course not immune to Internet memes. During Trump's first overseas visit as president, memes were quickly generated that showed him, King Salman of Saudi Arabia, and Egyptian president Abdel Fattah el-Sisi with their hands on a glowing orb as they opened a new anti-extremist center in Riyadh—along with Sauron from *Lord of the Rings*. To add to the humor, the creator posted

Shahak Shapira ✔
@ShahakShapira

 Follow

I PHOTOSHOPPED SARUMAN INTO TRUMP'S ORB PICTURE AND IT'S NOT EVEN WEIRD

2:22 PM - 22 May 2017

↩  ♻ 106,540   ♥ 194,200

Many memes were created and shared when Donald Trump, King Salman, and President Abdel Fatah el-Sisi placed their hands on a glowing orb at the opening of a new anti-extremist center in Riyadh.

that he had Photoshopped Sauron into the picture, commenting "and it is not even weird." Also on the trip were several animated memes of Melania Trump apparently slapping Trump's hand away as he tried to hold her hand.

A more prominent Internet presence in campaigns has made the electoral landscape more attractive to young people, a demographic that has recently proven a powerful force in helping to organize and volunteer. This bucks a trend, going back at least thirty years, of steadily declining youth participation in elections. Realizing much of his voter base was young people, Obama campaigned on college campuses days before the election in battleground states such as Ohio and Virginia. Often he appeared with Bruce Springsteen, who gave free concerts to support Obama.

Not only do the Internet and social media help politicians communicate better and organize more efficiently, they also provide the public with media and informational tools to organize their efforts more effectively and improve their communication with the government. Growing use of sophisticated databases to target voters with messages on social media will only increase in the years ahead, and will be used to not only energize voters but also send negative or dispiriting messages to opponents' voters.

## INTERNATIONAL PERSPECTIVES
# Crowdsourcing Election Monitoring

Some historical election practices in the nineteenth century in the United States look downright fraudulent to us today—political parties offering voters free transportation to polling places, providing free turkeys to families, and ballot stuffing (putting false names in ballot boxes or people voting in more than one district under different names). In the past, however, they were not considered so. Over time, more stringent rules and laws helped ensure fair elections and reduce voter fraud, incidents of which are now rare in U.S. elections. In certain foreign countries, charges of election fraud are frequent and include not only vote buying but also intimidation and actual physical violence against voters.

Election monitoring can be time-consuming and difficult, for accusations must be investigated and evidence gathered at each polling site. Social media and crowdsourcing, using raw data gathered from the public, make this process a little easier. The Venezuelan presidential election of April 2013 saw a close result between the incumbent, President Nicolás Maduro, who took over after Hugo Chávez's death, and the challenger, Henrique Capriles Radonski. Venezuela's Citizen Election Network challenged President Maduro's victory, using Twitter to document charges of election fraud in various polling stations. Follow-up investigation of the tweets confirmed dozens and in some cases hundreds of instances of election fraud and misconduct.

In Kenya's 2013 election, a company that had previously created an interactive mapping tool to track election violence reworked it to allow for crowdsourcing of the country's election. Posting updates to Uchaguzi via Twitter, SMS, mobile phones, email, and the web, citizens documented forty-five hundred cases of both good and bad acts during voting, and nearly 60 percent of the cases were investigated.[14]

In 2014, Indonesia's electoral commission (KPU) took steps to ensure extensive crowdsourcing of elections by putting large volumes of voting data online, such as scanned images of every polling station's final report. Citizens can access the data, compare it to their own experience with local polling places, and report any irregularities or potential fraud.

# Social Media and Civic Engagement

The Internet has opened a direct line of direct communication between candidates and the public. The public can see online databases that indicate how much their neighbors have contributed to which candidates. They can look at fact-checking sites, sometimes in real time, via social media to see whether candidates are telling the truth during political debates. In the 2016 election, several media organizations had post-debate fact-checking stories that analyzed various claims and their degree of truthfulness.

Email initially seemed to promise a faster, more efficient way for constituents to communicate directly with their members of Congress. A study released in 2004 by the Congress Management Foundation as part of the Communicating with Congress series of reports revealed this to be the case, although not without some pitfalls. In 2004, the House received 10.4 million communications by post and over 99 million over the Internet, while the Senate received 7.9 million communications by post and 83 million over the Internet. Overall that year, Congress received four times as many communications from citizens than in 1995, all due to the Internet. Staff, however, had not increased in the interim, meaning offices of the same size now had more work.

According to the report, almost 80 percent of congressional staffers believe that the Internet has made it easier for people to become involved in public policy, and over half believe it has increased public understanding of what takes place in Washington. A plurality of nearly half also believes that it enables politicians to be more responsive to the public.

Mass email petitions and form letters created by sites like Change.org do have their weaknesses, however. Politicians said that original, individual communications hold more weight for them. In general, a personal written letter or telephone call is given more priority than a prewritten form email in which a constituent simply clicked a button to forward to her representative. That is why online petition sites encourage people to write about the issue in their own words, even if they can provide a form letter.

## DATABASES AND GOVERNMENT TRANSPARENCY

Online databases and sites that provide direct information about political donations, voting records, and other political activities have become especially useful tools for journalists and citizens. Visitors to such sites can customize information on demand about any community in the United States or any person who may have contributed to a candidate, using data from the Federal Election Commission. The user simply enters a zip code and immediately obtains a list of everyone in that geographic area who has contributed to federal campaign committees. Alternatively, entering the first three or more letters of a last name will produce a detailed inventory of that person's contributions during any election cycle dating back to 1990.

OpenSecrets.org maintains the database and offers online a wide range of other political information, such as details on the activities of political action committees (PACs), the spending of lobbyists (which can reveal a great deal about organizations' or industries' efforts to shape the nation's political agenda), and the fundraising and spending on various political races. Not everyone agrees these public records should be widely available on the Internet.

The Sunlight Foundation offers a number of social media tools to make government more transparent and accountable.

Government transparency has become increasingly important in the digital age, as citizens want to see how their elected leaders and government operate. The Sunlight Foundation is one of the leaders in the movement to make government more open and accountable. This not-for-profit, nonpartisan organization has created a range of apps and online tools to enable citizens to do everything from search for deleted tweets by U.S. politicians (Politwoops), to track influence of political donations at the federal and state levels (Influence Explorer), to search for organizations buying ads or using other forms of political communication (Follow the Unlimited Money). One of Sunlight Foundation's projects includes Churnalism U.S., a web tool and browser add-on that highlights articles whose similarities to press releases or other material suggest plagiarized content.

> **DISCUSSION QUESTIONS:** Use one of the tools on the Sunlight Foundation's website to learn something about a bill or your local politician that you have not seen in the news. Discuss what you learned and whether it has altered your view of how the news business does its job.

## SMART MOBS

Digital media can also facilitate physical gatherings, dubbed **smart mobs** by author Howard Rheingold. Some political activists use cell phones and wireless networks to organize groups and communicate rapidly with each other. Smart mobs contributed to the 1998 overthrow of President Suharto in Indonesia and to the 2001 ousting of Philippine President Joseph Estrada, orchestrating protests via text messages. With wireless technology, mass demonstrations in various parts of a city can be roughly coordinated in real time, affording protestors a communication network almost as effective as that of police or the military. In 2011, social media tools helped the Occupy Wall Street protestors masterfully coordinate protests and attract many participants.

Handheld video- and audio-recording equipment has also aided activism. Protestors at the Republican National Convention in New York City in 2004 were encouraged to record what was happening around them, especially as police started

**smart mob**

A term coined by author Howard Rheingold to define a group of people communicating with each other via text messaging or wireless networks to coordinate their activities.

arresting people. Hundreds of protestors were arrested; and in some of the subsequent trials, video footage that directly contradicted authorities' testimony about activists' behavior was presented in their defense.

> **DISCUSSION QUESTIONS:** What are your perceptions of social movements that protest at national conventions or at international meetings like those of the World Trade Organization (WTO)? What influenced these perceptions?

## Political Polarization and Media Habits

Those unfettered by concerns about evidence or logic can simply rely on their gut response to a politician's claims, what Stephen Colbert on *The Colbert Report* often invoked as the "truthiness" of a matter. For others, tools, such as the aptly named PolitiFact, can help determine the veracity of political assertions. Another group may not follow their instincts alone yet feel little need to seek out independent fact checkers when they have trusted news sources they consider credible.

Not surprisingly, where people look for truth, which news sources they trust, may be influenced by their political ideology, especially for those at both the far right and the far left of the spectrum, about 20 percent of the overall public. According to an October 2014 Pew report titled "Political Polarization and Media Habits," nearly half of consistent conservatives identify Fox News as their main news source (see Figure 14-2). No other outlet comes close, although conservative talking heads Sean Hannity, Rush Limbaugh, and Glenn Beck also ranked high on the dimension of trust. Consistent liberals tend to gather news from a broader array of sources, trusting more media to provide information on politics and the government. Their main news sources are CNN, NPR, MSNBC, and *The New York Times*; yet a majority also trust PBS, BBC, and the national networks NBC, ABC, and CBS.

### FIGURE 14-2 Political Polarization and Media Habits

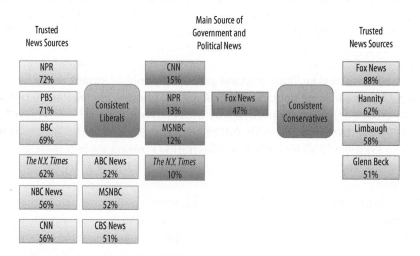

Source: Pew Research Center (October 21, 2014)

## MEDIA PIONEERS
# Bill Adair

In this multimedia, multisource world, it is increasingly difficult to sort through the competing claims of politicians, government officials, and advocacy groups. Journalist fact-checking helps people evaluate these claims and, ideally, encourages those making claims to be more careful in their public pronouncements.

PolitiFact arose from an assessment by Bill Adair, Washington correspondent for the *Tampa Bay Times* (formerly the *St. Petersburg Times*), that too little had been done to address distortions perpetrated in the 2004 presidential election.[15] Adair gathered a team of reporters to fact-check statements

by public figures and groups and report their truthfulness on the PolitiFact website. By 2008, PolitiFact was operational, and it was soon awarded the Pulitzer Prize for distinguished reporting on national affairs.[16] Adair's creative efforts to popularize such reporting include the Truth-O-Meter, a six-category scheme that assesses a claim's accuracy, ranging from "True" to "Pants on Fire" (false). PolitiFact also features a Flip-O-Meter and an evaluation of whether presidential promises have been kept.[17] This journalistic form is growing. PolitiFact now has affiliates in eighteen states and a global news project.[18]

In 2014, the Truth-O-Meter shed valuable light on the contentious matter of the Common Core curriculum transforming American schools. The Truth-O-Meter revealed that the following claim by U.S. senator Kay Hagan (D-North Carolina) was "mostly true": "The Common Core was not put together by the Department of Education in Washington. It was put together by governors and by states." In sharp contrast, Wisconsin state senator Joe Leibham (R) asserted that Common Core is a federal mandate, a claim the Truth-O-Meter determined to be false.

Working in various journalistic endeavors while majoring in political science at Arizona State University, Adair naturally gravitated toward political journalism. Covering the Washington beat for the *Times*, he was a 1997 recipient of the Everett Dirksen Award for Distinguished Coverage of Congress, among numerous other awards. In April 2013, Duke University appointed him their Knight Professor of Computational Journalism, where his goal at the Reporters' Lab in the Sanford School of Public Policy is to develop new tools and forms of journalism to address public policy and political arenas.[19]

Adair notes, "This is a time of great promise in journalism, when we can reinvent how we tell stories and how we hold government accountable." He advises students in the digital age "to learn not only journalism but also how to code—to build websites and mobile apps."[20] Bill Adair's career demonstrates the potential reward for developing the skill set to work in today's convergent media environment.

## MEDIA CAREERS

Media jobs in the political field as traditionally conceived are increasingly rare. Pursuing a career in journalism and politics requires more today than a questioning mind and advanced knowledge of politics and political processes, although these are still essential. Increasingly critical is an understanding of data and of algorithms that can analyze the data. Political and electoral processes are increasingly defined by so-called big data, massive data sets often based on social media and voter information, and the analytics used in their interpretation.

News organizations such as *The New York Times*, Politico, and the *Huffington Post* now have extensive staff led by data scientists devoted to quantitative, or numerical, inquiry, particularly political analysis. Digital companies such as Google, Facebook, and Twitter similarly employ social media and data analytics and analysts, especially during political campaigns. The emergence of computational journalism in both academy and industry underscores the increasing importance of data and its digital analysis in the toolkit of political journalists and other media professionals.

For those who may not have a penchant for data, another career possibility lies at the intersection of media and politics—satire. As the tragic terrorist attack on *Charlie Hebdo* in 2015 reveals, this pathway is not without its risks.[21] But, for those who want to provide humorous observations about institutions and public figures such as elected officials, writing satire for TV shows or other media, online or off, is an option to consider.

## LOOKING BACK AND MOVING FORWARD

As we have seen, political communication is not simply about elections and political campaigns. Media companies employ lobbyists just like other industries to influence political and regulatory decisions that may harm their business yet protect the public.

Citizens should be knowledgeable about how the media work within our political system and how they may affect basic rights such as privacy or determine the kinds of stories we see. The role of mass communication in democracies will likely be even more important in the future as the focus moves from a perceived need to inform the public to that of engaging the public in dialog. To that end, social media will also play an important part, facilitating conversations between members of the public and between the public and its elected officials.

Fostering more dialog may be one of the biggest shifts in political campaigns and elections. Encouraging participation may engage more people than ever before in these democratic processes. Something as simple as tweeting about what took place at a school board meeting or blogging for a local news organization could affect the way leaders govern as they observe citizens becoming more responsive to policy issues. Maintaining our rights to privacy while keeping governance as transparent as possible will be ongoing efforts. Many government leaders may see the greater transparency that social media in part represent as a threat to standard ways of conducting political business.

Transparency will also be vital in the international arena, where the policy decisions of a growing number of international organizations, such as the World Bank and the International Monetary Fund (IMF), can affect entire nations and the global economy. Whereas leaders within democratic nations may face increased pressure to be more transparent, the heads of these international groups, who may arguably have more power to affect national policies than elected officials do, will not be beholden to any specific public and have little incentive to make their decision-making processes transparent.

Activist groups call for closer monitoring of the increased powers of certain organizations such as the World Trade Organization (WTO). To raise public awareness about the WTO's policy decisions on global business and trade, they routinely stage demonstrations that sometimes turn violent. These social movements adopt organizing and protest tactics similar to those of antinuclear and environmental groups in the 1970s and 1980s while exploiting the power of new social media to communicate with each other and to attract media attention for their causes.

## FURTHER READING

*The Myth of Digital Democracy*. Matthew Hindman (2008) Princeton University Press.

*Mosh the Polls: Youth Voters, Popular Culture and Democratic Engagement*. Tony Kelso, Brian Cogan (eds.) (2008) Lexington Books.

*Into the Buzzsaw: Leading Journalists Expose the Myth of a Free Press*. Kristina Borjesson (ed.) (2002) Prometheus Books.

*Media Spectacle and the Crisis of Democracy: Terrorism, War, and Election Battles*. Douglas Kellner (2005) Paradigm.

*Media Politics: A Citizen's Guide*, 2nd ed. Shanto Iyengar (2011) W. W. Norton.

*unSpun: Finding Facts in a World of Disinformation*. Brooks Jackson, Kathleen Hall Jamieson (2007) Random House Trade Paperbacks.

*Tuned Out: Why Americans Under 40 Don't Follow the News*. David Mindich (2005) Oxford University Press.

*The Press Effect: Politicians, Journalists, and the Stories That Shape the World*. Kathleen Hall Jamieson (2004) Oxford University Press.

*The Obama Victory: How Media, Money, and Message Shaped the 2008 Election*. Kathleen Hall Jamieson, Kate Kenski, Bruce Hardy (2010) Oxford University Press.

*The Nightly News Nightmare: Network Television's Coverage of U.S. Presidential Elections, 1988–2000*. Stephen J. Farnsworth, S. Robert Lichter (2002) Rowman & Littlefield.

*Mass Media and American Politics*, 9th ed. Doris A. Graber (2014) CQ Press.

*Bloggers on the Bus: How the Internet Changes Politics and the Press*. Eric Boehlert (2009) Free Press.

*Entertaining Politics: Satiric Television and Political Engagement*, 2nd ed. Jeffrey Jones (2009) Rowman & Littlefield.

*Cyberprotest: New Media, Citizens, and Social Movements*. W. Van De Donk (ed.) (2004) Routledge.

*Blowing the Roof Off the Twenty-First Century: Media, Politics, and the Struggle for Post-Capitalist Democracy*. Robert W. McChesney (2014) Monthly Review Press.

*Lies, Incorporated: The World of Post-Truth Politics*. Ari Ravin-Havt, Media Matters for America (2016) Anchor.

*Deciding What's True: The Rise of Political Fact-Checking in American Journalism*. Lucas Graves (2016) Columbia University Press.

# Global Media in the Digital Age

The gruesome images and graphic stories in the global media about the Islamic State, or Islamic State of Iraq and Syria (ISIS)—beheadings of Western hostages, mass executions, and other human rights violations in territory they control—certainly have not painted an appealing picture of ISIS.

Yet despite regular news reports of their atrocities, a small but steady stream of Westerners—thirty-four hundred, including about two hundred Americans, according to counterterrorism officials—have traveled abroad to join ISIS. Many have responded to recruitment efforts that involve encrypted communications on what officials call the "dark space" of the web, an apt location for campaigns to expand an Islamist state of the darkest nature.[1]

Counterterrorism officials and media experts, while decrying these media campaigns as ISIS propaganda, admit these media-savvy efforts have been remarkably effective. Advanced marketing techniques commonly used by cutting-edge advertising and PR agencies have supplemented their social media campaign with professionally produced online magazines and high-quality videos depicting life in the Islamic State.

ISIS is just the latest, yet perhaps the most successful, example of terrorists utilizing the Internet. In the early 2000s, the FBI reported that groups such as Al Qaeda were communicating online to organize and coordinate activity within and between cells. The suspects in the lethal Boston Marathon attack allegedly learned about bomb making from Al Qaeda material available on the web.[2] Swaying disaffected people within Western countries, encouraging and guiding them to commit terrorist acts at home in the name of ISIS, is a greater concern for law enforcement and counterterrorism officials than a mass exodus to ISIS-controlled territory.

Despite Western experts' grudging acknowledgment of extremists' strategic success employing media, terrorism, like other human enterprises, is fallible. A colossal error occurred in mid-2015 when a militant posted a selfie on social media, a photo of him at a command and control center inside ISIS territory, with boastful comments about their military capabilities. This item quickly became intelligence information for the U.S. Air Force, unwittingly supplied by the enemy himself, whose building was identified and destroyed with a missile airstrike—a mission accomplished within twenty-four hours of the original post.

Global media, interconnected either technologically or economically and often in real time or near real time, developed in the mid-nineteenth century. Since the mid- to late 1800s, most countries have had printed media, such as newspapers and books; and since the early to mid-1900s, many have had systems of electronic broadcasting and motion picture production, albeit generally on a smaller scale than in the United States.

Carrier pigeons provided state-of-the-art international news delivering in the 1840s for Baron de Reuter, until surpassed by the electric telegraph.

Before the rise of mass electronic communication in the twentieth century, print journalism was a primary driver of media globalization. In the 1840s, Paul Julius Freiherr von Reuter (Baron de Reuter), founder of the Reuters News Agency in the French city of Aachen, used carrier pigeons to deliver news to Brussels. This gave him a competitive edge over other international news agencies, which used trains, slower than pigeons, to transport the news across borders. By 1851, the carrier pigeon was superseded by the newly invented electric telegraph, which could spread the news from country to country at the speed of light.

The convergence of television and the communications satellite with the launch of the Telstar satellite in 1962 enabled delivery of television programming in real time between Europe and the United States. The growth of the Internet, broadband communications, and mobile digital devices has only expanded interconnection among the world's media. Government regulations around the world have increasingly favored media globalization. Ownership of media on a global scale has grown dramatically since the 1970s as technology enabled broadcasters and publishers to extend their reach worldwide. At the same time, however, it appears that some executives of publicly owned global media conglomerates have become more concerned with company revenue and stock value than with the quality of the media products themselves.

Yet even in an era of increasing globalization, media operations around the world are diverse. Variations in local regulations and culture shape media practice and content, whether in the form of news or entertainment. In this chapter, we examine the global media system and the issues it raises for an increasingly interconnected world. We begin with an examination of four enduring theories about the nature and function of international mass communication.

**DISCUSSION QUESTIONS:** Why do you think ISIS media strategies have been so successful? How can Western countries counter ISIS media campaigns to recruit young men and women?

# Four Theories of International Mass Communication

In 1956, social scientists Fred S. Siebert, Wilbur Schramm, and Theodore Peterson presented four theories of international mass communication.[3] These theories explain how the press operates in different political, historical, and cultural environments around the world. Although the authors referred specifically to "the press," we can apply their four theories to all mass communication, including television, radio, and the Internet:

1. Authoritarian theory
2. Libertarian theory
3. Social responsibility theory
4. Soviet theory

## AUTHORITARIAN THEORY

**Authoritarian theory** describes the oldest system of mass communication whose roots extend to sixteenth- and seventeenth-century England. This system exists in authoritarian states whose governments exert direct control over the mass media. Countries governed by a small ruling class are especially likely to have an authoritarian media system.

Media in authoritarian systems are not permitted to print, broadcast, or webcast anything the government feels might undermine its authority. Content that threatens or challenges the existing political system and its values is prohibited. Anyone who violates the rules is subject to harsh punishment, including imprisonment, expulsion, or even death.

Government uses the media not only to inform the public of important events but also to shape public opinion in support of its policies. Although ownership of media can be private or public, media professionals lack editorial independence within their organizations. Foreign media are also subordinate to governmental authority. Countries where the authoritarian theory most accurately describes current systems of mass communication include China, Cuba, North Korea, Saudi Arabia, and to slightly lesser extents Singapore and Russia.

## LIBERTARIAN THEORY

**Libertarian theory**, also called free press theory, rests on the belief that the individual should be free to publish whatever she or he likes. Its roots lie in the work of seventeenth-century philosopher and writer John Milton, who argued in *Areopagitica* (1644): "And though all the winds of doctrine were let loose to play upon the earth, so Truth be in the field, we do injuriously by licensing and prohibiting to misdoubt her strength. Let her and Falsehood grapple; who ever knew Truth put to the worse, in a free and open encounter?"

💬 **authoritarian theory**

A theory of international mass communication that contends authoritarian governments exert direct control over the media.

Watchdog group Reporters Without Borders ranked Singapore 154 out of 180 countries in its World Press Freedom Index, the lowest ranking the country has ever received. Pictured here is the cover of *The Straits Times*, a newspaper closely monitored by the Singaporean government. **CRITICAL THINKING QUESTIONS:** Do you approve of authoritarian governmental control of the media as long as a country's citizens are safe and happy? What kind of penalties should these governments be able to impose for media transgressions?

💬 **libertarian theory**

A theory of international mass communication that supports the individual's right to publish whatever she or he wants, even material critical of the government or of government officials.

In libertarian theory, criticism of the government and its policies is accepted and even encouraged, and the import and export of media messages across national borders are not restricted. Media professionals have full autonomy within their organizations. Although the libertarian model is an ideal that does not realistically apply in full anywhere, elements of the theory are clearly in practice in the media of many countries.

## SOCIAL RESPONSIBILITY THEORY

**social responsibility theory**

A theory of international mass communication that perhaps best describes the media's role in democratic societies. It asserts that the media should be free from most governmental constraints to provide the most reliable and impartial information to the public.

**Social responsibility theory** best describes the systems of mass communication in most democratic societies. It holds that to provide the most reliable and impartial information to the public, the media in a democracy should be free from most governmental constraints. To operate effectively in this environment, however, the media must act responsibly. In 1947, the Commission on Freedom of the Press (known as the Hutchins Commission) articulated the media's obligations to society, which included truth, objectivity, balance, and diversity. The commission argued that a responsible media system must do more than simply report the facts. It must place them in context. This means the media must provide analysis, explanation, and interpretation.

Although social responsibility theory may best describe the system of mass communication in democracies such as the United States, Canada, France, and the United Kingdom, prioritizing public good over corporate profit both at home and abroad is a challenge in the age of global media expansion. Siebert, Peterson, and Schramm cautioned, "The power and near monopoly position of the media impose on them an obligation to be socially responsible, to see that all sides are fairly

---

### ETHICS IN MEDIA
# Humor and Ethics: The Role of Satire and Religion

The world responded in horror when terrorists attacked the editorial offices of *Charlie Hebdo* in Paris, France, on January 14, 2015, killing seventeen people in total over a three-day period that involved other sites around the City of Lights. The attackers were angered by a cartoon in the magazine satirically depicting Muhammad, the Prophet of Islam. While many viewed the attack as an attack on freedom of speech, some viewed the cartoon itself as irresponsible and unethical.

The truth is complicated and became arguably even more so when in early 2016 *Charlie Hebdo* continued its satirical commentary on Islam. The magazine published a controversial cartoon about the Syrian toddler Alan Kurdi, a refugee who died on a Turkish beach in 2015 and whose photograph was circulated widely at the time as an iconic image of the plight of the world's refugees. The cartoon not only depicted the dead boy but also two men chasing women. The headline read, "What would little Alan have grown up to be? Ass groper in Germany."

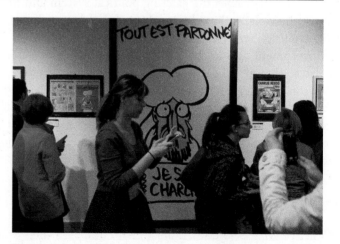

French satirical publication *Charlie Hebdo* has published controversial cartoons on a spectrum of topics. Its depictions of Islam have been particularly controversial, and some have incited violent reactions.

presented and that the public has enough information to decide; and that if the media do not take on themselves such responsibility it may be necessary for some other agency of the public to enforce it."

They added, "Freedom of expression under the social responsibility theory is not an absolute right, as under pure libertarian theory. . . . One's right to free expression must be balanced against the private rights of others and against vital social interests." A socially responsible news organization would exercise extreme care in reports about terrorist activities, for example, especially ones that might detail how bioterrorism is conducted or specify a city's disaster plans, information terrorists might use to plan future attacks.

## SOVIET THEORY

The **Soviet theory** of the press is based on a specific ideology: the communist system of government practiced in the former Soviet Union. Siebert traced the roots of this theory to the 1917 Russian Revolution and the views of Karl Marx and Friedrich Engels. According to the Soviet theory, media should serve the interests of the working class and should be publicly, not privately, owned.

Despite certain similarities between the Soviet and authoritarian systems—notably, the media being subordinate to the government—there are also important differences. In particular, the Soviet theory asserts that the media should recognize their responsibility to the people and self-regulate their content. Government censorship is not the norm. With the demise of the Soviet Union in the 1980s, this theory is now most useful as a historical reference point. One can see some elements of its philosophy, however, in the media-reform movement that argues for-profit media have been harming democracy and claims some news organizations should be publicly funded.

> **Soviet theory**
>
> A theory of international mass communication that states that the media should be publicly owned and used to further the needs of the working class.

The now-defunct Soviet Union's main newspaper was *Pravda*, meaning "truth."

**DISCUSSION QUESTIONS:** Visit a non-U.S. media company website, such as Canada's *Globe and Mail* (www.theglobeandmail.com), the British Broadcasting Corporation (www.bbc.com/news), or *the Times of India* (http://timesofindia.indiatimes.com/international-home). What value, if any, do you see in visiting internationally produced news websites and in the content they present?

Since Siebert, Schramm, and Peterson proposed their four theories of media, others have suggested a series of other media theories to help explain new developments. Among the other theories are revolutionary (for countries such as Cuba, where revolutionary change is afoot), developmental (for countries such as India, where economic development is key), and democratic socialist (for countries such as those in Scandinavia, where Marxist and libertarian approaches have merged).

# The Public, the Public Sphere, and Public Opinion

"The public" and "public opinion" are surprisingly complex concepts whose definitions are still debated by scholars today. In some ways, the public can be considered an audience for governments or politicians, but this description would be an oversimplification that fails to consider exactly how the public has evolved throughout history, how it differs today from the public in the Middle Ages, for example.

Most scholars agree that the notion of the public did not come about until the late sixteenth or early seventeenth century, when Europe was beginning to enter the modern era and governments were changing from monarchies to more representative forms of government. A new middle class arose, the **bourgeoisie**, which began to recognize the differing economic and political interests of business, government, and citizens. More importantly, the bourgeoisie recognized themselves as a separate group, apart but also a part of government and economics. Through media of the day, primarily newspapers, pamphlets, journals, and other periodicals, the bourgeoisie were able to communicate with each other about common interests and challenge government policies that did not suit them.

The forums in which the bourgeoisie debated matters of public interest included popular coffeehouses in England and salons in France, where material disseminated in print publications inspired conversation and where a sense of conventional wisdom developed through discussion among peers. The **public sphere**, as first described by German social theorist and philosopher Jürgen Habermas, was an arena for rational-critical debate, where the best argument won the day and where rank or privilege took a backseat to the quest for knowledge and truth. This ideal was not realized, of course, for a number of reasons. Women, for example, played an integral role in French salons but were excluded from discussion in bourgeoisie English coffeehouses.

Despite its many flaws in practice, the public sphere remains a rich concept in theory, a popular subject in media and mass-communication research today. Many scholars take a critical view, some arguing that commercial media have taken over the public forum and imposed new forms of (often hidden) control over what is discussed and how it is discussed. Hope still exists, though, for the Internet to rejuvenate the public sphere as a forum where users discuss subjects of mutual concern civilly and openly without fear of government censure or commercial manipulation. Nevertheless, a coherent public sphere in which all participants abide by shared rules of rational argument and civic-mindedness, the Habermasian gold standard, has proven elusive, particularly given the diversity of people online and their various, often conflicting, interests and perspectives.

**bourgeoisie**

A class of society that translates approximately to "middle class," distinguished from the aristocracy above and the proletariat (or workers) below.

**public sphere**

An idealized conversational forum in which people discuss and debate mutual interests and societal issues.

Coffeehouses and salons in the eighteenth century were important locations for development of the public sphere. **CRITICAL THINKING QUESTION:** How might gender have affected the substance and style of discussions in the coffeehouse compared to the salon?

The public sphere is key to the formation of **public opinion**, itself a contested concept, which can nevertheless be broadly defined as "what the public thinks." Public opinion pertains directly to efforts to define who exactly "the public" is and how a commonly shared opinion is formed and advanced. Is public opinion simply the aggregate of individual beliefs, writ large, or does it become something greater than the sum of its parts? If so, how does it change? And what are the effects of such changes?

The public is more complex than a mere mass of people, to which the enduring debates over proper definitions attest. Many contemporary scholars question the premise of a sole and united public, positing instead a multiplicity of publics and spheres whose interests, agendas, and access to mainstream media vary. The more recent theoretical concept of **counterpublics** recognizes a public forum of resistance for those who "perceive themselves to be excluded from or marginalized within mainstream or dominant publics and communicate about that marginality or exclusion."[4]

Public opinion, however it may be defined, is a foundational concern of democracies, and consequently so too are the media that create, shape, and spread ideas that inform and influence public opinion. Few major policy decisions are made without first testing the public waters to gauge their reaction. This is not to suggest, however, that the government is controlled by what French political historian Alexis de Tocqueville referred to in *Democracy of America* (1835) as the **tyranny of the majority**. Various groups can manipulate public opinion for their own ends, and an entire media industry—public relations—exists for the primary purpose of swaying public opinion with campaigns that cast their clients and their policies in the most attractive light possible.

PR professionals are not the only ones who can influence the masses. Just as the bourgeoisie in eighteenth-century coffeehouses found themselves with powerful new tools of mass communication, the range of media platforms people enjoy today has expanded, the result of advanced digital technology. We can start online petitions on any topic we choose, create sites that complain about products or parody politicians, post news scoops on blogs or videos of embarrassing moments in the lives of public and private figures, and act as citizen-journalists reporting injustices that other media may choose to ignore. Examples of this include the 2011 revolutions in several Arab countries. During the Arab Spring, people posted powerful images that the government-controlled media in those countries would not publish, for fear—proven correct—that they would sway public opinion.

Clearly, democratic countries are not the only nations that use social media to advance political and humanitarian causes. When a major earthquake hit China's Sichuan province on April 20, 2013, killing twenty thousand people, China's social-networking communities instantly went into action. One microblogger, Zuoyeben, who had some 5.6 million followers, posted a call for help for victims. Followers retweeted his post, prompting a wave of volunteerism and donations. A similar appeal from Li Chengpeng, a Chinese sportscaster with 7 million followers on Sina Weibo (a Chinese site similar to Twitter), yielded five hundred tents and more than twelve hundred blankets, all within two days of the quake.

Social media have also provided a forum to expose local corruption in China, even leading to the prosecution of some public officials. The government allows citizens a voice, however, only when it aligns with governmental interests, such as President Xi Jinping's anti-corruption campaign. In March 2015, for example, a documentary appeared on YouTube titled *Under the Dome* about the severe air pollution in many Chinese cities that forces schoolchildren to play "outside" under

**public opinion**

The notion that the public, as a group, can form shared views or ideas about topics and that these ideas guide the public's actions.

**counterpublics**

Public forums of resistance created by those who consider themselves to be excluded from or marginalized within dominant media and communication.

**tyranny of the majority**

A situation in which governmental laws and policies benefit the majority without concern for the welfare or rights of other groups or individuals.

plastic domes. The video struck a nerve with the Chinese public and quickly went viral. The Chinese government, despite initially approving the content, subsequently decided the topic could undermine its authority and removed the video from websites, effectively sending a clear message that the subject was not to be discussed publicly.

## Political and Socioeconomic Issues with Global Media

Radio and television are frequently used to reach remote agricultural regions in developing countries with information on health issues, agricultural techniques, and government policies. Broadcast stations are often among the first places taken in a coup because those in power—or those wishing to gain power—recognize the importance of controlling the distribution of information. Print media often foster business development in a region, although their effectiveness is limited in countries with low literacy rates or many different languages. In the networked, digital age, authoritarian governments increasingly monitor media, censoring or shutting down digital and mobile communications seen as threats to the existing regime or social order.

Foreign governments tend to control the content of their mass-communication organizations, especially television and radio, as well as online and mobile communications, far more than in the United States. In some cases, broadcasting stations are entirely government owned or run, and access can be limited by licensing restrictions for television sets or media devices such as satellite dishes.

### MEDIA IN DEVELOPING COUNTRIES

The media and companion communication technologies are instruments of economic development throughout the world. Western companies hoping to take advantage of cheap labor costs in other nations look for developed infrastructure, including transportation routes and communication networks—in addition, of course, to stable governments and corporate-friendly policies, such as low taxes.

Countries like India have become sources of relatively cheap software and computer-programming workers as well as home to database and information-processing centers. India's generally well-educated, English-speaking workforce is well positioned to profit from meeting low-end information-economy needs such as scanning documents, transcribing documents, and providing technical support for computer makers and software companies. It has also become a major producer of content, especially recorded music, motion pictures, and news media.

Some countries in Africa have been making similar moves toward fulfilling the information-processing needs of industrial countries. A data-processing company in Ghana, for example, inputs minor violations that occur in New York City, ranging from parking tickets to jaywalking. For Ghanaian workers, the pay and the working conditions are better than many other industries can offer, although hours are long and breaks short by Western standards.

Critics argue that moving information-processing work overseas is no different from sending factories there to obtain cheaper labor and avoid pollution problems and employee-benefits costs. Others who support this trend, however, respond that the information technology (IT) industry is not like industrial-era factories: It is generally nonpolluting. It can be created using existing buildings. And employees

### CONVERGENCE CULTURE
# Breaking News on a Global Scale

Breaking news has become a global media phenomenon with worldwide repercussions. U.K.-based news organization *The Guardian* has established itself as a leader in investigative journalism around the world. Since breaking the story of widespread digital surveillance activities of the U.S. National Security Agency (NSA) in 2013, *The Guardian* has continued to dig for stories, many of which have stirred considerable controversy, sometimes spurring accusations of being "fake news."

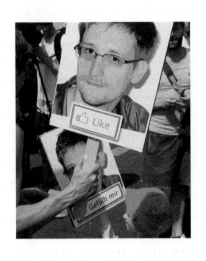

Undaunted, *The Guardian* has persisted. In July 2016, *Guardian* reporter Lucia Graves broke the story of an alleged sexual groping by Donald Trump. Graves interviewed Jill Harth, who accused Trump of having groped her in 1993 at his Mar-a-Lago resort in 1993. The story gained little traction at the time but later was further reported in other news media, including *The New York Times*.

*The Guardian* has a long history of breaking controversial news. Among its notable original reports was the news that former NSA contractor Edward Snowden had provided top-secret documents detailing the massive digital surveillance program,[5] prompting swift reaction around the world. Some applauded Snowden for blowing the whistle on the top-secret program perceived as an egregious intrusion into citizens' privacy. Others called for his arrest along with those who had published the story, alleging they were coconspirators, spies, and traitors who had violated federal law.

Media around the world subsequently tracked the whereabouts of Snowden, who fled the United States to seek asylum abroad. Relegated to five weeks of limbo in a Russian airport, Snowden was finally allowed to remain in Russia, a decision that caused a rift in U.S./Russia relations.[6] Snowden has since been granted three-year residency there, with the possibility to apply for citizenship after five years.

The media question whether privacy can exist in an age of ubiquitous digital communications and whether it should in an age of international terrorism. Years later, journalists and academics continue to examine this epic leak of top-secret documents, particularly its impact on international relations and future governmental surveillance and counterterrorism efforts.

---

receive training and education on the job that qualifies them for other jobs within information societies. The hope is that developing countries can avoid the worst effects of the industrial age as they move directly into the information age, although this remains to be seen.

Some factors hinder the growth of IT in these countries. Excessive government regulation often impedes the creation of telecommunication infrastructure that could better reach all citizens within a country. A lack of other infrastructure, such as regular electrical power, political instability, and policy changes—all these can hurt the development of telecommunication technologies.

To attract Western businesses, Singapore, Malaysia, and other Southeast Asian nations have been promoting themselves as high-speed Internet ecommerce zones. They promise a broadband

Outsourcing IT services to developing countries has provided new job opportunities for workers in those countries.

infrastructure enabling the production and distribution of video and other media content, especially to mobile users. Yet from a cultural or political perspective, rather than a technical one, the free flow of information raises important concerns. Singapore strictly controls most forms of media, even banning certain Western newspapers critical of the government; and it attempts to control citizens' access to the Internet, restrictions that Western companies, especially media organizations, may not abide.

## SEARCHING FOR TRUTH: SELF-CENSORSHIP IN CHINA

China has also become increasingly attractive to Western media as growing numbers of this massive market go online. Similar to Singapore, however, China sets restrictions on the press and Internet access remains at odds with Western practices and policies. China blocks a wide range of websites, those that publish pornography or that criticize the government, mentioning, for example, the 1989 protests and deaths in Tiananmen Square or the banned group Falun Gong.

Reporters Without Borders publishes an annual index highlighting obstacles to and violations of press freedom of information around the world. Scores on the World Press Freedom Index are based on a weighted scheme of seven different indicators: pluralism, media independence, environment and self-censorship, legislative framework, transparency, infrastructure, and abuses. (See Figure 15-1.) In 2015, it reported a decline on all fronts.

The 2017 World Press Freedom Index ranks China 176 out of 180 countries, continuing to identify it as one of the worst violators of press freedom. Earlier, Reporters Without Borders noted that since Xi Jinping took office, "the authorities have arrested more journalists and bloggers, cracked down harder on cyberdissidents, reinforced online content control and censorship and stepped up restrictions on the foreign media."[7] Vietnam, ranked in 2017 only one rung above China, introduced a law in 2013 that banned sharing news developments on blogs and social media. Reporters Without Borders describes this law, Decree 72, as part of "an all-out offensive against the new-generation Internet, which [Vietnam] sees as a dangerous counterweight to the domesticated traditional media."[8]

In 2006, Google was roundly criticized when the company chose to censor itself to enter the Chinese search engine market. Many observers noted the irony in Google's "Don't Be Evil" mantra regarding its business philosophy and wondered how the search engine giant could rationalize its decision not to include full access to sites on the Internet. Google responded that providing some access, with the hope that it might help China open its media system more, was better than offering nothing at all. Despite compromises made to enter the Internet market in China, Google still remains less popular there than homegrown search engine company Baidu.

Yahoo faced heavy criticism from the press a year earlier when the company provided user information requested by the Chinese government that helped put a Chinese journalist in jail for ten years. As long as the Communist government in China maintains strict controls over media access and the types of content allowed, Western media companies will have some difficult ethical choices to make if they do business in China.

**DISCUSSION QUESTIONS:** Find the most recent World Press Freedom Index on the website for Reporters Without Borders. Guess the ranking for your country before looking closely at the index, and then discuss why it might be ranked higher or lower than where you expected. Do you agree with the reasons cited by the index? Explain your reasoning.

**FIGURE 15-1** 2017 World Press Freedom Index

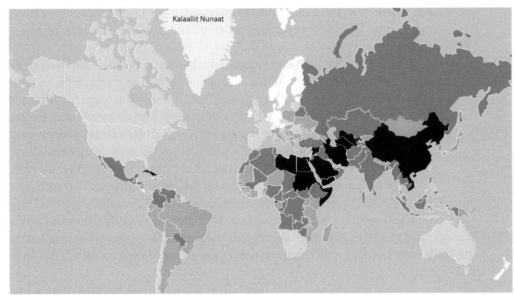

Scores range from 0 to 100, with 0 representing the highest degree of press freedom and 100 the lowest. The world map divides 180 nations into five categories:

**White**: good situation, from 0 to 15 points (21 countries)

**Yellow**: satisfactory situation, from 15.01 to 25 points (31 countries)

**Orange**: noticeable problems, from 25.01 to 35 points (62 countries)

**Red**: difficult situation, from 35.01 to 55 points (46 countries)

**Black**: very serious situation, from 55.01 to 100 (20 countries)

Source: Reporters Sans Frontières, http://index.rsf.org/#!/

| Rank | Country | Country Score |
|------|---------|---------------|
| 1 | Norway | 7.6 |
| 2 | Sweden | 8.27 |
| 3 | Finland | 8.92 |
| 40 | United Kingdom | 22.26 |
| 43 | United States | 23.88 |
| 48 | Botswana | 24.93 |
| 50 | Argentina | 25.07 |
| 52 | Italy | 26.26 |
| 91 | Israel | 31.01 |
| 120 | Afghanistan | 39.36 |
| 136 | India | 42.94 |
| 148 | Russian Federation | 49.45 |
| 168 | Saudi Arabia | 66.02 |
| 176 | China | 77.66 |
| 179 | Eritrea | 84.24 |

## THE DIGITAL DIVIDE

Nearly 80 percent of people in developed nations have Internet access. For some countries, such as Iceland, Sweden, and Norway, the number is over 90 percent. As more people get online, however, the gap widens between those who have access to the Internet and those who don't. Existing within and between nations, the **digital divide** is particularly acute for broadband, high-speed, wireless, and mobile Internet access. Because Internet access generally has a cost attached—in equipment and establishing a network connection—this gap reflects larger socioeconomic trends that already separate citizens. Some experts and policy makers worry that, if ignored, the digital divide could have increasingly serious negative consequences for society.

In the United States, early Internet users tended to be wealthier and better educated than later users. Given the importance of the information economy, some observers fear that the poor or less educated could fall even further behind given the distinct advantages of being connected, increasing the capacity to get important information, make decisions, and improve social and

**digital divide**

The gap between regions and demographics that have access to modern, digital-communications technology and those that have limited or no access.

Baidu is the homegrown search engine rival of Google in China.

economic status. Internationally, Internet usage has grown, particularly among consumers of mobile media. Yet the digital divide persists, for those with low incomes are hard pressed to afford even the least expensive smartphone, tablet computer, or wireless service.

The digital divide is apparent when looking at the different rates of Internet penetration across global regions and countries, as seen in Figure 15-2. Although as of 2017, the world average for Internet penetration is 49.6 percent, rates vary significantly from region to region. Consider, for example, North America's 88 percent and Africa's 22 percent. But such percentages tell only part of the story. Another perspective on Internet access addresses the actual number of people who are using the web in different countries. There are now more users in Asia than Europe, North America, and Latin America combined, despite having an Internet penetration of only 34.8 percent, slightly below the world average. This suggests that Asian users will truly dominate Internet access across the globe once users in Asia reach the percentages now shown for North America and Europe.

These figures are always increasing, although at different rates. Africa has shown remarkable growth in Internet penetration since 2000, growing nearly 7,000 percent. Expansion in the Middle East has also been considerable, more than 3,300 percent since 2000. Asia has grown more than 1,100 percent in Internet penetration during the same period, and even developed countries have increased their Internet penetration rates since 2000 by between 450 percent (Europe) and 187 percent (the United States). Yet even with this pervasive growth, many people still lack Internet access.

Access to the Internet is one component, but access to high-quality information is also important. Lowbrow entertainment does little to inform or educate the public. Mere access, therefore, will not bridge the digital divide if users lack the critical-thinking skills to discern high-quality information and employ it for helpful purposes, or if access is limited to a barrage of reality or game shows that do little to further public knowledge of important issues and events in the world.

Thus, the digital divide issue has two major components. The first factor is technological: providing communications technologies and access to the Internet. Computers, software, and other tools need to be purchased, and a relatively small Internet subscription fee for someone in the West may constitute an entire month's wages for someone in a developing country. The second factor is educational: teaching people how best to benefit from the online communication tools available to them. Entertainment will always be an attractive category of online media, but it is not the sole genre available to the more affluent, nor should it be for the less privileged.

Providing affordable technology to access the Internet is only part of bridging the digital divide; the other part involves teaching users how to be critical consumers of information.

Complex political and socioeconomic issues such as the digital divide and the role of the Internet in society require long-term commitments to widespread dialog. Such discussions must also consider larger quality-of-life issues such as basic health care, clean water, and education. Corporate concerns may ultimately prevail over public interests, particularly if companies feel such discussions threaten profits. Media will help (or hamper) this inquiry, although their role may not always be apparent.

**FIGURE 15-2** World Internet Users and Penetration Rates

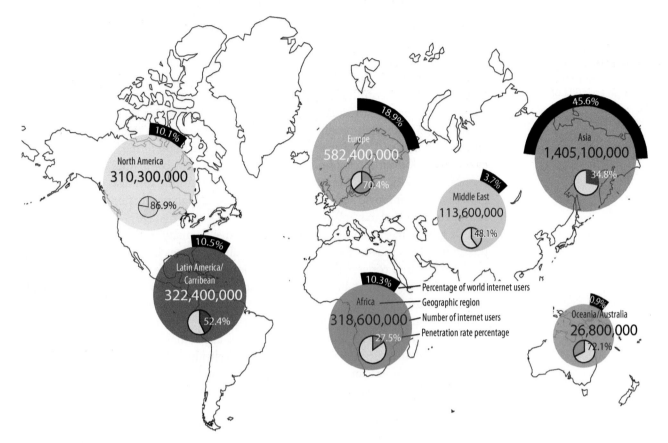

Source: Internet World Stats; www.internetworldstats.com/stats.htm

## Global Media, Local Values

Media content that exposes audiences to different lifestyles and cultures provides access to new worlds and new ways of thinking. The web has further expanded the possibilities for exploration, especially with video-sharing sites such as YouTube and a proliferation of other social media. But given the impact of concentrated media ownership on the production of media content, questions arise regarding the actual diversity of voices heard. Yes, there are more cable channels than ever, but how fundamentally diverse are many of the police crime shows or reality TV programs, and how many DIY (do-it-yourself) channels, such as HGTV, do viewers need?

**DISCUSSION QUESTIONS:** Most media organizations rely increasingly on digital paywalls for revenue, but is it fair to expect the economically disadvantaged to pay for news and entertainment content? What might be done to address the problem of the global digital divide?

## NEW WORLDS—OR CULTURAL IMPERIALISM?

**cultural imperialism**

A condition that occurs when a powerful foreign country dominates a domestic media market through an influx of its products.

The global reach of media giants and their ability to promote their programming in foreign markets raises the issue of **cultural imperialism**: when a foreign country dominates a domestic media market through an influx of its products. The large viewership for current and past shows imported from the United States, such as *NCIS*, *House*, *Grey's Anatomy*, and *The Simpsons*, suggests that this programming meets some need unfulfilled by domestic television fare.

This may be true to some extent because many countries that cannot afford to create shows with high production values air local programs that appear relatively amateurish in visual quality. Precisely because of the flood of media imports, however, many domestic television and movie production companies may not get a chance to develop fully. Countries with small populations can also discourage the growth of robust movie and television industries, as high production costs cannot be recouped in limited markets, especially when the local language is not widespread.

Of great concern from an ethical perspective to many in these countries is the possibility that citizens are absorbing alien cultural values in conflict with domestic ones. People in a conservative Muslim nation, for instance, may object to the frequently explicit content in many American television shows or movies. Although such exposure can encourage viewers to question governmental positions on freedom and democracy, shows such as *Grey's Anatomy* do not necessarily deal with political topics in any meaningful way. Still, critics argue that appreciation of and pride in traditional culture may be undermined with a slickly produced, idealized version of what it is to be American. People may lose touch with native traditions and values as they adopt distorted values based on skewed, unrealistic images of the United States.

**media hegemony**

A condition that occurs when dominant groups in society control the mass media, largely through ownership.

Hegemony is the claim that the ideas of the ruling class translate into the ideas that rule the masses in society. **Media hegemony**, as explained by scholars such as Italian Antonio Gramsci, is a concept that asserts the dominant class in society controls the mass media, largely through ownership. A Marxist economic concept, hegemony is rooted in the belief that the content of the mass media in the United States is designed to cater to the interests of the capitalist ruling elite and maintain the status quo, keeping those with wealth and in power wealthy and powerful. Hegemony suggests that a U.S.-driven global media system will turn the world into a giant commercial marketplace, and there is some evidence to support this view.

A contradictory body of research exists regarding the hegemonic nature of media content. The work of professional journalists, socialized according to certain widely held guidelines and routines, is increasingly being complemented and often contested by that of citizen reporters, freelancers, and public service journalists with diverse methods, procedures, and perspectives. And although some news stories may resonate around the world, reports vary, with different accounts that are not perceived as equally credible. For instance, during the early days of the most recent war in Iraq, most mainstream U.S. news media supported the position that the distinct possibility of weapons of mass destruction in Iraq justified military action. Yet at the same time, media beyond American borders challenged this claim, which proved ultimately to be false.

There is also little evidence that most journalists around the world tend to present pro-American positions and negative coverage of other countries. Since the early 2000s, independent international reporting has grown, and sources such as the British Broadcasting Corporation (BBC), Japan's *Asahi Shimbun*, and Argentina's *Clarin* have featured voices emanating from diverse perspectives free of American influence.

Moreover, global media production and viewership in the entertainment and sports realms have grown dramatically in the digital age as production costs have fallen and distribution possibilities have increased. Consider the success of India's

Bollywood, the Hindi-language movie industry based in Mumbai. While the name evokes America's Hollywood, Bollywood movies have their own distinct character and style that have proven to be hugely popular with both Indian and non-Indian audiences around the world. The 2014 film *PK*, the top-grossing film of all time in India, has made over $110 million worldwide in box office receipts, only half of which were generated domestically in India. Of course, Bollywood, like Hollywood, is a highly commercial system of motion picture entertainment, although its stories may differ.

Still, scholars such as Robert McChesney maintain that American hegemony shapes global digital media.[9] Google and Facebook are Internet corporate giants. Apple also plays a leading role on the world stage, with iTunes and its hugely popular mobile devices. Yet there are countervailing trends and forces. In 2014, for example, South Korea's Samsung sold more smartphones than Apple.[10] In 2012, not coincidentally the year that London hosted the Summer Olympics, Great Britain topped *Monocle* magazine's list of the most culturally influential nations, beating the United States for the first time.[11]

Brazil is known for world-famous cultural products such as Carnaval, samba and feijoada, the 2016 Rio Summer Olympics, and cachaça. **CRITICAL THINKING QUESTIONS:** When do cultural exports become a form of cultural imperialism? How would your media consumption be affected if you were to limit it to American products only?
Source: https://en.wikipedia.org/wiki/Culture_of_Brazil

> **DISCUSSION QUESTIONS:** How powerful a force is American hegemony in global digital media? What specific cultural products, trends, and events, both historical and current, support your view?

## CONVERGENCE AND ITS DISCONTENTS

In *Civilization and Its Discontents*, Sigmund Freud, the famous Viennese founder of psychoanalysis, articulated what he saw as the basic tension between the individual and civilization.[12] This tension, according to Freud, stems from the instinctive desire of the individual for freedom that conflicts with civilization's inherent need for order and stability achieved through the imposition of standard norms of behavior, or social conformity.

Similar tensions arise between global media and local culture. At its best, local culture provides a rich tapestry of diverse ideas, customs, and behaviors that can be presented on the world stage. Because of its global reach and impact, media convergence can provide unprecedented access to this richness but also generate conflict among diverse values. Ultimately, media convergence may also encourage increased cultural homogeneity, particularly given the common ownership of various media types (horizontal integration), such as book publishers, newspaper chains, and TV station groups.

On the other hand, digital technology can also disempower companies that have traditionally controlled media production and distribution. Authors, for example, can self-publish and sell their works on sites such as Amazon, bypassing traditional publishers and bookstores. Digital technology also offers the potential for new players (such as Apple and Google) to enter the field of media production and distribution. It is important to consider who benefits financially from these transformations and what cultural consequences may ensue.

Digital music distribution is another domain where media convergence may create cultural conflict. For example, within months of Apple's 2003 launch of the iTunes Store, music distribution to its iPod helped Apple achieve dominance in the music market through downloads, subscriptions, and other services. By 2005, Apple's iTunes store branched out into the delivery of video; and by 2013, iTunes had begun delivering other forms of media content including books, newspapers, and magazines. The cultural consequences of a dominant horizontally integrated digital media distribution system could be profound. Such a system could increasingly

## MEDIA PIONEERS
# Steve Chen, Chad Hurley, and Jawed Karim

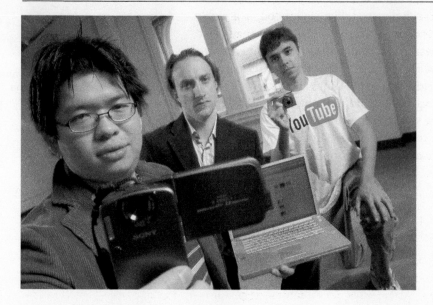

Only since 2005 have we been able to see events global and local, past and present, historic and mundane, whenever we choose. Whether it be the coronation of Queen Elizabeth II, a Beyoncé concert, an interview with Russian president Vladimir Putin, or just "Me at the zoo" (the first YouTube video uploaded), YouTube has forever changed our capacity to observe the activities of others and to display our own. In any month this year, more than 1 billion individuals will view a YouTube video, and more than a hundred hours of video will be uploaded in less time than it takes you to read this box.[13]

In 2013, YouTube became "the leading source of Internet traffic in the entire world."[14] That some 60 percent of YouTube views come from outside a creator's country is apt, given its

international founders.[15] Chad Hurley was born and raised in Pennsylvania. Steve Chen, born in Taiwan, immigrated to the United States when he was fifteen. Jawed Karim was born in Germany, the son of a Bangladeshi father and a German mother, who immigrated to America in 1992.

Like so many digital innovations, YouTube was a collaborative effort of young people: Its founders were in their late twenties when it launched. Chen and Karim studied computer science at the University of Illinois, leaving there to join PayPal, a new venture in California. Hurley, a graduate of Indiana University of Pennsylvania, became a designer at PayPal. After profiting from eBay's $1.5 billion purchase of PayPal in 2002,[16] they sought out new projects. The universal difficulty in sharing video online was their inspiration for YouTube, and the rest is global history.

In less than two years after its inception, YouTube was sold to Google for $1.65 billion in stock.[17] After YouTube, Chen and Hurley founded AVOS. Chen then left to join Google Ventures as an entrepreneur in residence, while Hurley focused AVOS efforts on developing video-sharing service MixBit.[18] Karim left shortly after the sale, earning a master's degree in computer science at Stanford University. Subsequently, he founded Y Ventures, which seeks to "help talented teams with innovative products to take the next step."[19]

foster a consumer culture worldwide as it shapes global tastes. The fundamental question remains: Does media convergence foster greater cultural uniformity, or does it advance cultural variety by enabling diverse groups to produce and consume cultural products (such as a book, a movie, or a website) of their choice?

## GLOBALIZATION OF MEDIA PRODUCTION

Media production has increasingly become an international phenomenon. One of the principal forms this takes is the international coproduction of movies and television shows, which has become much more common since the early 1990s. For example, the blockbuster film *Iron Man 3* was coproduced in China by the Walt Disney Company and China's DMG Entertainment Group. Coproductions allow companies with differing strengths and capabilities to combine creative, financial, and technological resources across countries. They also offer international locations for storytelling.

Typically, such coproductions involve international treaties and regulations, with host countries often providing tax incentives to the companies involved. Companies also often receive public funding that can enhance production budgets. As a result, movies and television shows coproduced internationally have significant economic benefits for both American and foreign media companies. Coproductions were once conceived as a means to increase collaboration between countries with large and small production industries.[20] Ideally, coproductions feature material intended for and generated by local markets whose lone funding is inadequate to support the high production values seen in American movies and television shows that typically dominate the market. In the case of *Iron Man 3*, four minutes of extra footage of Chinese actors with whom local viewers could identify were added to the Chinese version of the film.

Rather than creating culturally relevant or authentic programming, however, coproductions often recreate common Hollywood media derived from popular genres. These include reality series, adventure shows, situation comedies, science fiction, and the like. In the end, economics drives global media program production and distribution. Increasingly, Hollywood executives make movies with a global market in mind, shaping both the selection of subject matter and the manner in which stories are told. Local, authentic culture tends to take a backseat. Kathleen Kennedy, president of Lucasfilm, identifies the globalization of audiences and the industry as one of the greatest challenges currently confronting Hollywood. As countries increasingly and rightly want to create their own content and tell their own stories, "it puts the pressure on the creative community to acknowledge and recognize that it's a bigger world and you need to tell many, many different kinds of stories."[21]

## GLOBAL MEDIA FLOW

In the mid-1970s and 1980s, the United Nations Education, Scientific and Cultural Organization (UNESCO) led a global examination of the flow of news and media entertainment around the world, dubbed the New World Information and Communication Order (NWICO). The UNESCO-sponsored discussion and debate identified a number of important issues, such as long-standing concerns about the dominant influence of media from the developed world and media coverage of the developing world. Another matter was the role of new technologies with important military and commercial uses, including satellite and computer technologies.

Advances in digital technology since the 1970s have altered the debate about intercultural communication, regional coexistence, and the relative dominance of the developed world. Mass-media content, including movies and television shows, has tended to move from the developed world, particularly the United States, to less-developed countries. Moreover, the launch of satellite and cable systems around the world has facilitated a multichannel viewing environment in many places, enabling international viewing on an extraordinary level.

Research also indicates that Western news agencies have historically produced as much as 80 percent of the news distributed globally. Some observers fear that this reporting often reflects the priorities of news agencies based in New York, London, or Paris and focuses on topics such as natural disasters and military coups rather than the basic realities of poverty, pollution, and unemployment. This situation has improved more recently, however, with the growth of social media, citizen reporting, and regional news agencies such as Al Arabiya in the Middle East.

Advertising agencies and marketers of goods and services in the developed world also tend to dominate the world's global media system, with commercial messages from the West often featuring significantly in many international markets. Since the 1980s, most companies, recognizing the cultural diversity and sensitivities in various

Western backlash forced IKEA to apologize for having digitally removed images of women from its catalog produced for and distributed in Saudi Arabia.

markets, adapt their messages to the local market. But the process is not seamless. In 2012, IKEA apologized for digitally removing women from its product catalog for distribution in Saudi Arabia.[22] The global company believed it had been appropriately adapting its commercial message for local Islamic sensibilities regarding the representation of women in photographs. Once the newspaper *Metro* in IKEA's native Sweden reported these alterations, though, the story stirred such controversy in the West that the company backtracked, stating it regretted this editorial decision not in keeping with its corporate values.

## PROTECTING LOCAL VOICES

Many media critics argue that Western media, typically profit-driven and privately owned and operated, not only dominate the global flow of news and entertainment media but also carry a commercial or corporate bias. To counterbalance the influx of foreign commercial media, many countries around the world have sought to develop internally more authentic, culturally relevant media programming and content for their citizens. Although these initiatives to promote national media content often involve government funding and other incentives to buy or, as the case may be, broadcast locally, these media efforts may also succeed in attracting a more global audience.

### Some Developing Nations

Many alternative sources of local media content now exist in developing countries to help redress the historical dominance of Western information and entertainment, especially from American media companies. In Asia, examples include India's Bollywood, films that tend to reflect indigenous culture and traditions. In Africa, GhanaWeb reports local and national news and information.

In Australia or Brazil, for example, indigenous peoples, who often live in rural areas, promote a message of environmental stewardship and respect for the earth. Yet people of indigenous heritage often suffer disproportionately from poverty and other social ills, their marginalized voices drowned out by dominant world media. "Consider that indigenous peoples make up just 5 percent of the world's population," explained Kanavo F. Nwanze, president of the International Fund for Agricultural Development (IFAD). "But they are 15 percent of those living in poverty."[23]

IFAD financed the 2012 launch of the first community radio station in Malaysia. Bario Radio enables indigenous Malaysians to make vital contributions to the local and global dialog on environmental sustainability and poverty with stories about the environmental impact of development on Central Borneo, for example, and the disastrous consequences of global warming. Bario Radio also confronts stereotypes and affirms indigenous peoples' rights and identities.

Indigenous, noncommercial media complement the dominant, for-profit media channels from the West. They tell seldom-heard stories of those frequently marginalized by the economically powerful institutions that sponsor and control most commercial media. Known globally for rich oral traditions, indigenous voices are especially well suited to the use

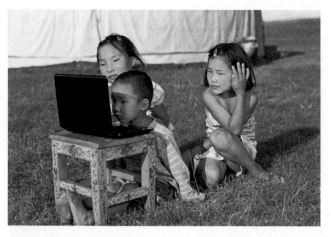

Genghis Khan's empire took over much of Asia at the speed of his mounted armies, but today the world can reach even remote areas in Mongolia at the speed of light.

of community radio, online video, and social media. These tools have allowed them to inform and educate local audiences while reaching global ones.

## A Neighbo(u)ring Nation

Many governments fund the internal production of music and other media arts as well as news and information sources. Although the United States provides limited funding for such endeavors through the National Endowment for the Arts (NEA) and the Corporation for Public Broadcasting (CPB), its neighbor to the north has extensive programs. In 1957, Canada created the Council for the Arts to "foster and promote the study and enjoyment of, and the production of works in, the arts."[24] Production grants are awarded in a variety of artistic fields, including media arts, writing, and publishing. Such initiatives help offset commercial influences in imported mainstream media while promoting artistic innovation and expression at home.

In 1968, a broadcasting act was also passed that ensured Canadian voices and stories access to Canadian airwaves. Radio and television broadcasts must feature a high percentage of "CanCon"—Canadian content created primarily by Canadian talent. At least 35 percent of the popular music broadcast on commercial radio stations between 6:00 a.m. and 6:00 p.m. Monday to Friday must be Canadian. On CBC (Canadian Broadcasting Corporation), the national public radio and television broadcaster, 50 percent Canadian popular music content is required.[25]

The digital distribution of media content, though, is circumventing these and similar long-standing regulations intended to strengthen Canada culturally, socially, and economically. American provider Netflix proved an attractive option for Canadians once it crossed the border, although the content Canadians may choose to stream is more limited. Canadians engage more with video than Americans, however, spending 5.1 more hours per month watching videos online.[26] "The competition in digital is, more or less, borderless," says Neil McEneaney, interim executive vice-president of CBC's English Services, "and many of those competitors have access to vast content resources and deep pockets."[27]

## PROMOTING GLOBAL VOICES

Farther abroad, similar initiatives have also been implemented. The Doha Film Institute in the Middle East, for example, receives arts funding from the government, with financial support from the Qatar Foundation. Also based in Qatar is the Al Jazeera Network, a pan-Arab news service and media company launched in 1996 with $137 million in funding from the emir of Qatar. Al Jazeera was the only international news organization with correspondents in Iraq during Operation Desert Fox in 1998, a U.S. military operation.[28] By 1999, Al Jazeera had begun broadcasting twenty-four hours daily, and it became increasingly well known for its coverage of the wars in Iraq and Afghanistan.

In January 2013, it acquired former vice president and Nobel Laureate Al Gore's Current TV. Paying an estimated $500 million for the cable channel, Al Jazeera almost instantly gained a significant foothold in the American television market. Al Jazeera English, which debuted in 2006, reached only 4.7 million U.S. households. Launched in 2013, Al Jazeera America (AJAM), their new English-language twenty-four-hour cable and satellite news channel, was available in over 64 million U.S. households. Headquartered in New York City, the new AJAM hired some two hundred journalists with several news bureaus around the country to build news programming content. Unfortunately for those journalists, AJAM closed in 2016, shutting down all of its U.S. operations and releasing those who worked there. AJAM never achieved a large audience, and revenues never developed to a significant degree.

With the 2016 closing of Doha, Qatar-based Al Jazeera America, U.S. audiences lost a bit of diversity in its daily news diet. **CRITICAL THINKING QUESTION:** What concerns, if any, do you have about the loss of Al Jazeera programming in the United States, and why?

The closing of AJAM notwithstanding, Al Jazeera has developed a reputation for quality journalism, specifically, according to the Index on Censorship, for combating censorship and contributing to the free and open exchange of news and information in the Arab world. Al Jazeera has also won numerous American awards for news coverage, such as the Peabody Award, the Columbia University Journalism Award, and the People's Choice Award.

Internationally, the Al Jazeera Network operates multiple sports channels, a children's channel, and a documentary channel. Other international Al Jazeera channels include Al Jazeera Balkans (a Bosnian/Croatian/Serbian-languages channel that debuted in 2011) and Al Jazeera Turk. Al Jazeera English is known for *The Stream*, a TV and online program based on social media, especially Twitter. Competition for regional news coverage in the Arab world has grown, however, since the Arab Spring of 2011. For example, Al Arabiya, founded in 2003 by a group of Saudi investors, has captured a significant share of the region's audience.

**DISCUSSION QUESTIONS:** Compare and contrast treatment of a global issue or recent big news event as reported by BBC America and another news site such as CNN or Fox News. What are some of the key differences in how the story is presented and told?

## CYBERSECURITY AND MEDIA

Media convergence—technological, economic, and cultural—continues to bring countries and peoples closer together and in so doing produces new challenges, not only for local cultural identity but also for global national security. Backlash against American foreign policy sometimes takes the form of cybercrime. Hackers from various countries have attempted to break into Western computer networks, often with considerable success. In 2016, cybercriminals hacked the systems of several digital-media companies. *The New York Times* reports that Russian hackers broke into *The Times*'s Moscow bureau computers. Chinese hackers have gained access to a variety of other American digital media operations, including Apple, Facebook, and even Google, according to the FBI. The same or a related group also attacked news organizations, including *The Washington Post* and *The New York Times*.[29] In late 2014, North Korea hacked Sony Pictures, and the ensuing scandal rocked Hollywood. Some claimed the hacking was in retaliation for a Sony motion picture called *The Interview*, whose comedic plot revolved around a secret plot to assassinate the country's controversial dictator. In mid-2015, a hacking group based in China accessed the private information of 4 million U.S. federal employees.

In St. Petersburg, Russia, a group called the Internet Research Agency has been known to coordinate complex disinformation campaigns using social media, fake websites, doctored news footage, and multiple Twitter accounts that target influential Twitter users to maximize the spread of their messages. These techniques promote pro-Kremlin messages but also to try to provoke panic by claiming (and ostensibly showing) supposed terrorist acts, such as a bombing of a chemical plant in Louisiana on the anniversary of 9/11, an incident that did not in fact occur.[30]

As the nature of online cybercrime has evolved to include cyberterrorism, the United States has made cybersecurity a top national defense priority. The Commerce Department is working with both technology and media companies to develop rules and protocols for sharing online-threat information with the government as well as strategies for cyberdefense. President Obama defended the PRISM surveillance program as vital in the war against terrorism, while others praised NSA whistle-blower Edward Snowden as a champion of the individual's rights to civil liberty and privacy.

For the media and for society, the truth likely lies somewhere in between. United States Supreme Court Justice Hugo Black argued that constitutional protection was necessary to empower a free press that should hold the government publicly accountable for secrets and deceptions.[31] Yet, without the tools to combat terrorist threats, the government cannot protect its citizens. A sustainable balance must be struck between the competing interests of freedom, security, and public accountability.

Since the election of President Trump, notions of fake news and what constitutes a fact have become hotly contested. When confronted with oftentimes critical news coverage, President Trump has responded by labeling mainstream news outlets as "fake news." Tensions between mainstream news media and the Trump administration have often reached a fever pitch with testy exchanges between the White House press secretary and the White House press seemingly the new normal.

## MEDIA CAREERS

As the fields of journalism, advertising, PR, and entertainment media are practiced all over the world, opportunities abound for people with foreign-language skills. Fluent professionals can successfully navigate the local media in the region's native language while working in English-language media abroad or operate exclusively in the local language. Entrepreneurial opportunities for international media initiatives are increasingly available for those seeking international media careers.

The United Nations (UN) and a variety of nongovernmental organizations (NGOs) need people with good professional communication skills in the field of development communication, an enterprise intended to improve the lives of locals. These campaigns focus on health communication, education, and environmental or wildlife conservation, among other areas. Communication students who major or minor in political science, international relations, foreign languages, sociology, anthropology, education, or one of the life sciences could be well positioned for NGO jobs in foreign countries.

Typical PR functions also exist in this field, such as media relations, publicity and promotion, and donor and volunteer recruitment. These jobs could be located in developing nations but are just as likely to be based at an NGO's main office in a developed country. With field offices throughout the world and many large regional offices in big cities, besides its New York headquarters, the UN strongly encourages employees to request postings in various locations every few years to expand their range of knowledge and skills.

In addition to the obvious interest in foreign cultures, a successful development-communication professional must be able to readily adapt to local customs. This career is ideally suited to people who love to travel and experience foreign cultures in depth but who are also willing to accept hardships, sometimes dangerous living conditions, and often a lower standard of living (e.g., everything from regular electricity to flush toilets may be considered a luxury, depending on the country).

## LOOKING BACK AND MOVING FORWARD

Globalization is transforming media as digital and networking technologies enable media empire building. These conglomerates can overwhelm local media enterprises and stifle indigenous voices. While government funding for international coproductions may help support authentic, local media, it does little to improve access for the masses who lack the means to buy an iPad, iPhone, Android, or Windows mobile device or subscribe to broadband telecommunications service.

The consequences of this problem, especially acute in developing nations, include reduced access not only to entertainment but also to ecommerce, public affairs news, and educational content. Although nearly half of the world's population has Internet access, the digital divide is widening between those with access and those without. As media have become more digital and networked, costly broadband or high-speed Internet service has become near ubiquitous in developed nations, exacerbating this disparity. Moreover, a growing number of digital-media enterprises on the global stage are implementing digital paywalls, an additional financial obstacle to media access.

The forms and functions of mass communication are evolving in the digital age. Siebert, Schramm, and Peterson's four theories of the press are still relevant but are best seen as ideal types and not exact models for twenty-first-century media. Traditional media are converging with social media and global ownership, and international coproduction and digital distribution are increasingly common.

Media play a critical role in political and social-cultural systems around the world. Western media have tended to dominate the worldwide flow of news and entertainment, generating pressures and tensions resulting from hegemony. Yet at the same time, digital and networked technologies have dramatically lowered the cost and other barriers to media production and distribution, enabling more global and widespread movie, television, and news production. Alternative voices are being heard more frequently on the global stage, including those of indigenous peoples and local producers. Social media and mobile technology are also enabling citizen reporters around the world to cover breaking news, from Tahrir Square to Timbuktu, through photos, video, and tweets.

Global terrorism has expanded from the physical to the virtual realm, with cyberterrorism a growing threat. While the digital landscape holds great promise for global communication, it also presents many hazards and dangers. Cybercitizens will need to be vigilant to ensure that the benefits of globally networked digital media continue to outweigh the risks.

---

**MEDIA MATTERS**  GLOBAL MEDIA

1. Identify a country that follows the authoritarian theory of communication. If offered some kind of media position there, would you consider it?

2. Which theory of communication do you think is best equipped to most effectively utilize digital and social media? Why do you think so?

3. Define the concept of the public sphere. Where online do you feel this ideal has the greatest possibility of being realized?

4. Which form of mass communication—print, radio, or television—is most effective in reaching a broad cross section of the population in a developing country? Why do you think so?

5. What role have social media played in the aftermath of disasters like the 2013 Ya'an earthquake in China or the 2015 Yangtze River ship sinking?

6. Which do you think are more susceptible to cyberattacks, established multinational media corporations or media companies in developing countries that have recently been using the Internet to reach the global stage?

---

**FURTHER READING**

*The Myth of Digital Democracy.* Matthew Hindman (2008) Princeton University Press.

*Into the Buzzsaw: Leading Journalists Expose the Myth of a Free Press.* Kristina Borjesson (ed.) (2002) Prometheus Books.

*Media Spectacle and the Crisis of Democracy: Terrorism, War, and Election Battles.* Douglas Kellner (2005) Paradigm.

*(Un)Civil War of Words: Media and Politics in the Arab World.* Mamoun Fandy (2007) Praeger.

*Cyberprotest: New Media, Citizens, and Social Movements.* W. van de Donk (ed.) (2004) Routledge.

*Religious Broadcasting in the Middle East.* Khaled Hroub (ed.). (2012) Hurst.

*Arab Media: Globalization and Emerging Media Industries.* Noha Mellor, Muhammad Ayish, Nabil Dajani, Khalil Rinnawi (2011) Policy Press.

*Real-Time Diplomacy: Politics and Power in the Social Media Era.* Philip Seib (2012) Palgrave Macmillan.

*Global Media, Culture, and Identity: Theory, Cases and Approaches.* Rohit Chapra and Radhika Gajjala (2011) Routledge.

*Detecting Bull: How to Identify Bias and Junk Journalism in Print, Broadcast and on the Wild Web,* 2nd ed. J. H. McManus (2012) Unvarnished Press.

*The Ethics of Reality TV: A Philosophical Examination.* W. N. Wyatt, K. Bunton (2012) Continuum.

*After Broadcast News: Media Regimes, Democracy, and the New Information Environment.* Bruce A. Williams, Michael X. Delli Carpini (2011) Cambridge University Press.

*American Indians and the Mass Media.* Meta G. Carstarphen, John P. Sanchez (eds.) (2012) University of Oklahoma Press.

*Communication for Development and Social Change,* 2nd ed. Jan Servaes (ed.) (2008) Sage.

*The Handbook of Development Communication and Social Change.* Karin Gwinn Wilkins, Thomas Tufte, Rafael Obregon (eds.) (2014) Wiley-Blackwell.

*The International Television News Agencies: The World from London.* Chris Paterson (2011) Peter Lang "Media and Communication" Series.

*Public Relations in Global Cultural Contexts: Multi-Paradigmatic Perspectives.* Nilanjana Bardhan, C. Kay Weaver (eds.) (2011) Routledge.

# Glossary

**actualities** Edited audio clips from interviews with people.

**ad-agency commission** A percentage amount of the cost of an advertisement taken by the advertising agency that helped create and sell the ad.

**advertising** An ancient form of human communication designed to inform or persuade members of the public with regard to some product or service.

**advertorial** Display advertisement created to look like an article within the publication, although most publications have the words "advertisement" or "paid advertisement" in tiny print somewhere nearby.

**agenda setting** Media's role in deciding which topics to cover and consequently which topics the public deems important and worthy of discussion.

**Alien and Sedition Acts** A series of four acts passed by the U.S. Congress in 1798 that, among other things, prohibited sedition, or spoken or written criticism of the U.S. government, and imposed penalties of a fine or imprisonment on conviction. Although they expired in 1801, other sedition acts have been passed periodically, especially during times of war.

**amplitude modulation (AM)** Radio carrier signal modified by variations in wave amplitude.

**Associated Press (AP)** Founded in 1848 as a not-for-profit members' cooperative by a group of six New York newspaper publishers to share the costs of gathering news by telegraph. Today, some 1,500 newspapers and 5,000 television and radio stations are members.

**astroturfing** Creating a movement controlled by a large organization or group designed to look like a citizen-founded, grassroots campaign.

**astroturfing campaign** A movement or campaign that looks as though it was created by concerned citizens as a grassroots movement when in fact it was actually created or controlled by an organization with a vested interest in the outcome.

**asynchronous media** Media that do not require the audience to assemble at a given time, such as printed materials and recorded audio or video.

**augmented reality** Digital overlays of information on a screen that correspond to what is being looked at in the real world through the screen.

**auteur** Director as storyteller.

**authoritarian theory** A theory of international mass communication that contends authoritarian governments exert direct control over the media.

**balance** Presenting sides equally and reporting on a broad range of news events.

**bandwidth** The carrying capacity and speed of telecommunication networks that determine how much information can be sent and how fast it can travel over the networks.

**banner ad** Original form of advertising on the Web, it appears across the top of a website.

**beat** Reporter's specialized area of coverage based on geography or subject. Common beats in large- or medium-sized newspapers include education, crime, and state politics.

**behavioral targeting** Advertisers tracking individuals' Web-browsing behavior to provide ads that closely match the topics of sites visited or searches made.

**Benjamin Day** Publisher of the *New York Sun* who originated the penny press in 1833 by offering his paper on the streets for a penny.

**big data** A collection of data sets too large for traditional analytic techniques to sort, analyze, and visualize.

**binge-watching** Watching a television series, usually on a streaming service such as Netflix, over several hours at a time.

**blog** Short for weblog, a type of website in which a person posts regular journal or diary entries, with the posts arranged chronologically.

**Bobo doll studies** Media-effects experiments in the 1950s that showed children who watched TV episodes that rewarded a violent person were more likely to punch a Bobo doll than children who saw episodes that punished a violent person.

**bourgeoisie** A class of society that translates approximately to "middle class," distinguished from the aristocracy above and the proletariat (or workers) below.

**branding** Process of creating in the consumer's mind a clear identity for a particular company's product, logo, or trademark.

**broadband** A network connection that enables a large amount of bandwidth to be transmitted, which allows for more information to be sent in a shorter period of time.

**broadcast** Originally a reference to casting seeds widely in a field that was subsequently applied to the fledgling electronic medium of radio and later television.

**camera obscura** A dark box or room with a small hole that allows an inverted image of an outside scene to be shown on the opposite inner wall.

**categorical imperative** In ethical thought, Kant's concept of an unconditional moral obligation that does not depend on an individual's personal inclinations or goals.

**catfish** Someone who fakes an online profile, usually to encourage another to fall in love with the false persona.

**cathode-ray tube (CRT)** Device in older televisions and computers using electron beams to transmit images to the screen.

**censorship** The act of prohibiting certain expression or content. Censors usually do not target the whole publication, program, or website but seek to prohibit some part of the content.

**Children's Television Act (CTA)** Created in 1990, it limits the amount of commercial content that programming can carry, forces

**431**

stations to carry certain amounts of educational programming for children sixteen and under, and includes other provisions to protect children.

**chilling effect** The phenomenon that occurs when journalists or other media producers decide not to publish stories on a topic after a journalist has been punished or jailed for such a story.

**circulation** Number of newspaper copies sold or distributed.

**citizen journalism** The gathering and sharing of news and information by public citizens, particularly via mobile and social media, sometimes via traditional media.

**classified advertising** Advertising traditionally found in print media, especially newspapers but also in some magazines and now increasingly online, that consists of messages posted by individuals and organizations to sell specific goods or services.

**clear and present danger** A restriction on speech when it meets both of the following conditions: (1) It is intended to incite or produce dangerous activity (as with falsely shouting "Fire!" in a crowded theater), and (2) it is likely to succeed in achieving the purported result.

**clickbait** Articles and headlines written in an exciting or dramatic way in order to get users to click to read the article, when in fact the article may not deliver on the promise of the headline.

**click-through rate (CTR)** Rate at which people click on an online advertisement to access more information.

**codex** Manuscript book of individually bound pages.

**community antenna television (CATV)** Cable television developed in 1948 so communities in hilly or remote terrain could still access television broadcasts.

**consolidation** A process whereby traditional media companies have grown fewer and much larger in the past fifty years through mergers and acquisitions.

**convergence** The coming together of computing, telecommunications, and media in a digital environment.

**cookies** Information that a website puts on a user's local hard drive so that it can recognize when that computer accesses the website again. Cookies also allow for conveniences like password recognition and personalization.

**copyright** a form of intellectual property law that protects the right to use, publish, reproduce, perform, display, or distribute a literary or artistic work, such as a piece of writing, music, film, or video.

**cord-cutters** Those who have switched from cable or other connections to Internet-delivered TV.

**cord-nevers** Those who have known only mobile or wireless Internet-delivered TV.

**correlation** Media interpretation ascribing meaning to issues and events that helps individuals understand their roles within the larger society and culture.

**cost per thousand (CPM)** Standard unit for measuring advertising rates for publications based on circulation.

**counterpublics** Public forums of resistance created by those who consider themselves to be excluded from or marginalized within dominant media and communication.

**critical theory** A theoretical approach broadly influenced by Marxist notions of the role of ideology, exploitation, capitalism, and the economy in understanding and eventually transforming society.

**cross-sectional study** A study that gathers data on subjects at a specific point in time.

**crowdsourcing** Using raw data gathered from the public and citizen-journalists to help create a news report.

**cultivation analysis** A theory of media effects that claims television cultivates in audiences a view of reality similar to the world portrayed in television programs.

**cultural imperialism** A condition that occurs when a powerful foreign country dominates a domestic media market through an influx of its products.

**cultural studies** An interdisciplinary framework for studying communication that rejects the scientific approach while investigating the role of culture in creating and maintaining social relations and systems of power.

**cultural transmission** The process of passing on culturally relevant knowledge, skills, attitudes, and values from person to person or group to group.

**culture industry** A term coined by the Frankfurt School to describe how media companies produce or "make" culture in the same way that other companies produce products.

**daguerreotype** Photograph created by exposing a positive image on a metal plate.

**David Sarnoff** Head of RCA, he promoted the development of television as a mass medium yet blocked the development of FM radio for years because RCA produced and sold AM radio receivers.

**daypart** A segment of time radio and television program planners use to determine their primary audience during that time of day or night.

**digital divide** The gap between regions and demographics that have access to modern, digital-communications technology and those that have limited or no access.

**digital immigrant** An individual who grew up in the analog media era and who generally has more trouble adapting to new digital technologies, despite perhaps a desire to use and understand them.

**Digital Millennium Copyright Act** A 1998 act of Congress that reformed copyright law comprehensively to update it for the digital age. Key provisions addressed the circumvention of copyright-protection systems, fair use in a digital environment, and Internet service providers' liability for content sent through their lines.

**digital native** A term coined in 2001 by author Marc Prensky for a member of a younger generation who has grown up with and is consequently very comfortable using digital media and adapting to rapid technological changes.

**digital rights management (DRM)** Technologies that let copyright owners control the level of access or use allowed for a copyrighted work, such as limiting the number of times a song can be copied.

**digital television (DTV)** Television system in which all information broadcast by cable or through the air is in digital, or computer-readable, form.

digital watermark Computer code (usually invisible but sometimes visible) inserted into any digital content—images, graphics, audio, video, or even text documents—that authenticates the source of that content.

digitization The process that makes media computer readable.

dime novel First paperback form whose cost of ten cents made it accessible even to the poor.

direct effects model Model of mass communication that claims media have direct and measurable effects on audiences, such as encouraging them to buy products or to become violent.

display advertising Advertising in print media that usually consists of illustrations or images and text that can occupy a small section of a page, a full page, or multiple pages.

distributed computing Individual, autonomous computers that work together toward a common goal, typically a large, complex project that requires more computing power than that of any individual computer.

earned media Favorable publicity prompted by a public relations source rather than advertising, such as a news conference, an event, or a press release; the opposite of paid media, such as advertising or product placements.

echo effect A phenomenon that occurs when people surround themselves with online voices that echo their own, reinforcing their views and the belief that those opinions are in the majority when in fact they may not be.

Edward R. Murrow A radio and, later, television journalist and announcer who set the standard for journalistic excellence during TV's golden age.

Edwin Howard Armstrong Columbia University engineering professor who invented FM radio transmission.

elaboration likelihood model (ELM) A theory of persuasion that says we process persuasive messages either through a central route or a peripheral route, depending on a range of factors.

electronic news-gathering (ENG) equipment Tools such as video cameras and satellite dishes that allow journalists to gather and broadcast news much more quickly.

encoding/decoding A theoretical model that states media producers encode media products with meanings, decoded in various ways by various audiences.

entertainment Providing or being provided with amusement or enjoyment.

epistemology A study or theory of the limitations and validity of knowledge; more simply, a way of, or framework for, understanding the world.

equal-time rule The requirement that broadcasters make available equal airtime, in terms of commentaries and commercials, to opposing candidates running for election. It does not apply to candidates appearing in newscasts, documentaries, or news-event coverage.

ethical consumerism A kind of activism in which consumers buy only products that they believe are produced ethically.

ethnography A variety of qualitative research techniques that involve immersion of a researcher in a particular culture to allow interaction with participants through observation, participation, interviews, or a combination of methods.

fair use Allowable use of someone else's copyrighted work that does not require payment of royalties, with a number of factors that determine if something falls under fair use or violates copyright.

fairness News reporting on all relevant sides of an issue that allows representatives of those various sides the same coverage.

Fairness Doctrine Adopted by the FCC in 1949, it required broadcasters to seek out and present all sides of a controversial issue they were covering. It was discarded by the FCC in 1987.

fear appeal Advertising technique that attempts to persuade the audience by scaring them, such as antismoking ads that show disfigured former smokers.

Federal Communications Commission (FCC) Established in 1934, the principal communications regulatory body at the federal level in the United States.

Federal Radio Commission (FRC) Formed by the Radio Act of 1927, the commission, the precursor to the FCC, created a policy that favored fewer high-power radio broadcasting stations rather than more numerous low-power stations.

Federal Trade Commission (FTC) The principal commerce regulatory body, established in 1914, at the federal level in the United States.

First Amendment Guarantees that Congress shall make no law restricting freedom of speech, press, or religion.

focus group A small group of people assembled by researchers to discuss a topic. Their interactions are closely observed, recorded, and analyzed to determine people's opinions.

folksonomies Collection of tags created by users that provide metadata (data about data) regarding information.

FOMO Fear of missing out, or the feeling when we look at Facebook posts of friends that they are doing more exciting things than we are doing and that we are missing important group interactions.

fourth estate Another term for the press, or journalism, which acts as a fourth branch of government, one that watches the other branches (executive, legislative, and judicial).

frame Structure or angle given a news story that influences reader understanding covering the event.

framing The presentation and communication of a message in a particular way that influences our perception of it.

free and open-source software movement (FOSS) A movement that wants software to be freely available and the source code open to anyone to make modifications and improvements.

freemium Subscriptions that provide some content for free but require a monthly subscription to take advantage of all the site has to offer.

frequency modulation (FM) Radio carrier signal modified by variations in wave length/frequency.

gamification The use of game-like mechanics in nongame settings, such as earning points, badges, or rewards for performing certain actions.

genres  Topical categories.

going viral  The phenomenon in which a media item spreads rapidly from person to person via the Internet.

gramophone  Developed by inventor Emile Berliner, it used a flat disc rather than a cylinder to record sound.

Granville T. Woods  Inventor of railway telegraphy in 1887, a type of wireless communication that allowed moving trains to communicate with each other and with stations, greatly reducing the number of railway collisions.

graphical user interface (GUI) Computer interface that shows graphical representations of file structures, files, and applications in the form of folders, icons, and windows.

graphophone  An improvement on Thomas Edison's phonograph in recording audio, it used beeswax to record sound rather than tinfoil. Developed by Alexander Graham Bell and inventor Charles Tainter.

greenwashing  The practice of companies making themselves or their products appear to be organic, environmentally friendly, or supportive of free trade when in fact they are not.

Guglielmo Marconi  Italian inventor and creator of radio telegraphy, or wireless transmission, in 1899.

Gutenberg Bible  Bible printed by Johannes Gutenberg in Europe in 1455, considered one of the first mechanically printed works.

Hays Code  A code established in 1930 by the movie industry to censor itself regarding showing nudity or glorifying antisocial acts. Officials for the Hays Office had to approve each film distributed to a mass audience.

Heinrich Hertz  Demonstrated the existence of radio waves in 1885, setting the stage for the development of modern wireless communications. The measurement unit of electromagnetic frequencies was named for Hertz.

high-definition television (HDTV) Modern television technology that produces a much higher-resolution image, sharper color, a wider aspect ratio, and superior audio. Ultra-high definition is next-generation TV with even higher resolution video. 4K TVs can display video at 4,000 lines of resolution, compared to the 420 lines of standard definition TV.

human–computer interaction  Any interaction between humans and computers, either through devices such as keyboards, mice, and touch screens or through voice recognition.

hyperlink  Clickable pointer to other online content.

hypertext  Text online linked by HTML coding to another Web page or website or to a different part of the same web page.

Hypertext Markup Language (HTML) A coding format that describes how information should look on the Web.

Hypertext Transfer Protocol (HTTP) A protocol that enables the standardized transfer of text, audio, and video files, as well as email, from one address to another.

hypodermic-needle model  A model of media effects, also called the "magic bullet," that claims media messages have a profound, direct, and uniform impact on the public.

ideology  A comprehensive and normative body of ideas and standards held by an individual or a group.

indecent speech  Language or material that, in context, depicts or describes, in terms patently offensive as measured by contemporary community standards for the broadcast medium, sexual or excretory organs or activities.

independent films  Films made by production companies separate from the main Hollywood studios.

independent labels  Small companies that produce and distribute records. Not part of the three major-label corporations, they include those producing only one or two albums a year as well as larger independents such as Disney.

infomercial  Also called "paid programming," a thirty- or sixty-minute television show that seeks to sell a product and that usually involves a celebrity spokesperson and customer testimonials.

information overload  The difficulties associated with managing and making sense of the vast amounts of information available to us.

information society  A society where information production has supplanted industrial production, dramatically transforming cultural, economic, and political activity.

instant messaging  Often abbreviated IM, a form of real-time communication through text typed over a computer network.

integrated communications  All channels of communication about a company or brand working together to create a cohesive message.

intellectual property (IP) Ideas that have commercial value, such as literary or artistic works, patents, trademarks, business methods, and industrial processes.

interactivity  For digital-media purposes, it consists of three main elements: (1) a dialog that occurs between a human and a computer program, (2) a dialog that occurs simultaneously or nearly so, and (3) the audience has some measure of control over what media content it sees and in what order.

interpersonal communication  Communication between two or more individuals, often in a small group, although it can involve communication between a live speaker and an audience.

interpretive reporting  Reporting that places the facts of a story in a broader context by relying on the reporter's knowledge and experience.

interstitial ad  Online advertisement that opens in a new window from the one the user was in.

James Carey  Communications scholar and historian who has shaped a cultural-studies approach to communication theory.

James Gordon Bennett  Founder of the *New York Herald* in 1835. He initiated features found in modern newspapers including a financial page, editorial commentary, and public-affairs reporting.

Johannes Gutenberg  German printer credited with creating the first mechanical printing press in 1455.

joint operating arrangement (JOA) Legal agreement permitting newspapers in the same market or city to merge their business operations for economic reasons while maintaining independent editorial operations.

Joseph Pulitzer  American newspaper magnate whose publications competed vigorously with those of Hearst. After 1900, Pulitzer retreated from sensational journalism, favoring instead more socially conscious reporting and muckraking. He founded the Pulitzer Prizes, annual awards for outstanding journalism.

**laugh track** A television sitcom device that generates prerecorded laughter timed to coincide with punch lines of jokes.

**Lee de Forest** Considered the father of radio broadcasting because of his invention that permitted reliable voice transmissions for both point-to-point communication and broadcasting.

**libertarian theory** A theory of international mass communication that supports the individual's right to publish whatever she or he wants, even material critical of the government or of government officials.

**listservs** Automated mailing-list administrators that allow for easy subscription, cancellation, and delivery of emails to subscribers.

**long tail** The principle that selling a few of many types of items can be as or more profitable than selling many copies of a few items, a practice that works especially well for online sellers such as Amazon and Netflix.

**longitudinal study** A study that gathers data on subjects over a long period of time.

**Louis Daguerre** Inventor of the daguerreotype, an early type of photography.

**lurking** Only reading what others write in online discussion boards but not contributing to the discussions.

**machinima** A combination of machine and cinema that uses 3-D animation techniques and characters from popular video games to make movies.

**major labels** Universal Music Group, Sony Music, and Warner Music Group—the three biggest recording-arts companies, which control much of the music industry partly through their powerful distribution channels and ability to market music to mass audiences.

**mass communication** Communication to a large group or groups of people that remain largely unknown to the sender of the message.

**mass-market paperback** Inexpensive, softcover books small enough for a back pocket and sold in bookstores, supermarkets, drugstores, and other public places.

**Mathew B. Brady** Nineteenth-century photographer acclaimed for his Civil War images and portraits of famous people.

**mean-world syndrome** A syndrome in which people perceive the world as more dangerous than it actually is, the result of viewing countless acts of media violence.

**media bias** A real or perceived viewpoint held by journalists and news organizations that slants news coverage unfairly, contrary to professional journalism's stated goals of balanced coverage and objectivity.

**media ecology** The study of media environments and their effects on people and society.

**media grammar** The underlying rules, structures, and patterns by which a medium presents itself and is used and understood by the audience.

**media hegemony** A condition that occurs when dominant groups in society control the mass media, largely through ownership.

**media literacy** The process of interacting with and critically analyzing media content by considering its particular presentation, its underlying political or social messages, and its ownership or regulation issues that may affect what is presented and in what form.

**media oligopoly** A marketplace in which media ownership and diversity are severely limited and the actions of any single media group affect its competitors substantially, including determining the content and price of media products for both consumers and advertisers.

**medium** A communication channel, such as talking on the telephone, instant messaging, or writing back and forth in a chat room.

**meme** A media item of cultural interest that spreads through repetition and replication via the Internet.

**mobile media** Handheld or wearable digital communication platforms that are Internet-connected such as smartphones and tablets.

**mods** Short for "modifications," user-created code changes that alter how video games are played or look.

**muckrakers** Journalists, particularly magazine journalists, who conduct investigative reporting on major corporations and government; they were dubbed muckrakers in the early twentieth century for the "muck" they uncovered.

**multicast** Simultaneous transmission of multiple channels of compressed content or the same content but at different times.

**multitasking** In a computer environment, doing several activities at once with a variety of programs, such as simultaneous word processing, spreadsheet, and database work while conducting real-time chat through an instant-messenger service.

**Network neutrality** The principle that broadband networks should be free of restrictions on content, platforms, or equipment and that certain types of content, platforms, or equipment should not get preferential treatment on the network.

**news hole** Amount of total space available after advertisement space has been blocked out, typically in newspapers.

**news leak** Secret information deliberately given to journalists with the hope that they will publish the item.

**Newspaper Preservation Act of 1970** Created to preserve a diversity of editorial opinion in communities where only two competing, or independently owned, daily newspapers exist.

**objectivity** Journalistic principle that says reporting should be impartial and free of bias. Because of the difficulties involved in complete objectivity, this principle has largely been replaced by the concepts of fairness and balance.

**obscenity** One of the forms of speech not protected by the First Amendment and thus subject to censorship. Although an exact definition of the term has been difficult to achieve in various court cases, generally a three-part standard is applied for media content: It must appeal to prurient interests as defined by community standards, it must show sexual conduct in an offensive manner, and it must on the whole lack serious artistic, literary, political, or scientific value.

**oligopoly** An economic structure in which a few very large, very powerful, and very rich owners control an industry or collection of related industries.

**open access** A system that makes information accessible to all to discourage power imbalances that may arise from unequal access.

opinion poll  Usually conducted by a professional polling organization, a poll asking members of the public their opinions on issues or political candidates.

opt in  When consumers choose to receive mailings or marketing material, usually by checking a box on a website when registering for the site.

outdoor advertising  Billboards and other forms of public advertising, such as on buses or taxis.

participant-observation  A qualitative research technique in which researchers participate as members of the group they are observing.

partisan press  A press, such as colonial newspapers, typically aligned with a particular political party and presenting information to help its cause, with no sense of objectivity or balance in news coverage.

patent  A form of intellectual property law that protects the right to produce and sell an invention.

payola  Cash or gifts given to radio disc jockeys by record labels in exchange for greater airplay of the label's artists or most recent songs. After several scandals in the 1950s, the practice is now illegal.

peer-to-peer (P2P)  The basis of file-sharing services, a computer communications model and network whose computers are considered equal peers who can send, store, and receive information equally well.

penny press  Newspapers that sold for a penny, making them accessible to everyone. Supported by advertising rather than subscriptions, they tried to attract as large an audience as possible.

performance-based advertising  Any form of online ad buying in which an advertiser pays for results rather than paying for the size of the publisher's audience or the CPM.

phonograph  First patented by Thomas Edison in 1877 as a "talking machine," it used a tinfoil cylinder to record voices from telephone conversations.

pitch  Request to review a client's new product or do a story about the client or the product.

place shift  Viewing TV from anywhere using the Internet to access video originally delivered digitally to the home (or another location).

political economy  An area of study inspired by Marxism that examines the relationship between politics and economics with media ownership and the influences they all have on society and perpetuating the status quo.

positivism  A view, common among scientists in the physical or natural sciences and many social sciences, that affirms an objective reality to be discovered and explained through rigorous scientific research.

postmodernism  A broad category of viewpoints that rejects grand narratives attempting to explain the world and absolute truths because truth is relative and unknowable.

postpositivism  A view that agrees largely with positivism but also recognizes knowledge that may not be revealed through scientific inquiry.

pragmatism  A school of thought affirming truths found in actions that work and rejecting the possibility of overarching or purely objective notions of truth.

preferred-position balancing theory  A legal theory that says that a balance must be struck between speech and other rights, although speech has a preferred position.

press agentry  Getting media attention for a client, often by creating outrageous stunts to attract journalists.

print-on-demand (POD)  Publication of single books or tiny print runs based on customer demand using largely automated, non-traditional book-printing methods such as the color laser printer.

prior restraint  When the government prevents or blocks the publication, broadcasting, showing, or distribution of media content, whether in print, over the air, in movie theaters, or online.

product placement  A form of advertising in which brand-name goods or services are placed prominently within programming or movie content that is otherwise devoid of advertising, demonstrating the convergence of programming with advertising content.

produsers  Audiences who no longer are simply consumers but also produce content.

propaganda  The regular dissemination of a belief, doctrine, cause, or information, with the intent to mold public opinion.

pseudo-events  Events staged specifically to attract media attention, particularly the news.

public information campaign  Media program funded by the government and designed to achieve some social goal.

public opinion  The notion that the public, as a group, can form shared views or ideas about topics and that these ideas guide the public's actions.

public service announcement (PSA)  Advertising-like message from an organization with a worthy purpose that ostensibly benefits the public and for which the media donate time or space.

public sphere  An idealized conversational forum in which people discuss and debate mutual interests and societal issues.

puffery  A type of advertising language that makes extravagant and unrealistic claims about a product without saying anything concrete.

push poll  A type of political advertising that appears to be a telephone poll but is actually a telemarketing campaign to sway voters by making a favored candidate look good or by misrepresenting the opposition.

qualitative research  A method of inquiry favored in the social sciences that explores typically unstructured phenomena through interviews, focus groups, and participant observation among other techniques that produce descriptive rather than predictive results.

quantitative research  A method of inquiry favored in the physical sciences that focuses on numerical data and statistical measures to describe phenomena. Researchers often attempt to prove or disprove a hypothesis through the empirical method, particularly controlled experimentation.

Radio Act of 1912  The act assigned frequencies and three- and four-letter codes to radio stations and limited broadcasting to the 360-meter wavelength.

Radio Act of 1927  An act of Congress that created the Federal Radio Commission, intended to regulate the largely chaotic airwaves and based on the principle that companies had a civic duty to use airwaves, a limited public good, responsibly.

random sample A sample in which every person has an equally probable chance of being selected, intended to represent the entire population of study.

rate card List of advertising rates by size, placement, and other characteristics, such as whether ads are black and white or full color. Frequency discounts are also usually offered, and the listed rates are usually negotiable, especially for large advertisers.

rating Used in broadcast media to explain the number of households that watched a particular show.

readership Number or percentage of newspaper readers.

rhetoric One of the ancient arts of discourse that focuses on the art of persuasion.

sampling error Error in a statistical analysis that results from selecting a sample that does not represent the entire population.

scrolling Simply repeating the same message in a chat room, which quickly draws the ire of other participants.

search-engine marketing Paying for certain keywords to show up high in rankings in a search engine, such as Google or Bing.

sedition Speech or action that encourages overthrow of a government or that subverts a nation's constitution or laws.

semiotics The study of signs and symbols.

sensational journalism News that exaggerates or features lurid details and depictions of events to increase its audience.

serious games Games created to be fun and educational that use game dynamics to instruct players on topics.

shield law A law intended to protect journalists from legal challenges to their freedom to report the news.

simplified communications model Developed by Wilbur Schramm in 1954 and based on the mathematical theory of communication. It includes a source who encodes a message, or signal, which is transmitted (via the media or directly via interpersonal communication) to a destination where the receiver decodes it.

six degrees of separation Notion that everyone in the world is separated from all other individuals by at most six additional nodes in a social network.

slander A type of defamation that is spoken, as opposed to written (libel), and that damages a person's reputation or otherwise causes harm.

Slashdot effect When a smaller news site's Web server crashes because of increased traffic after its mention on popular websites, named for a frequent occurrence on the very popular technology news site Slashdot.org.

small world Tight-knit social network with many strong ties.

smart mob A term coined by author Howard Rheingold to define a group of people communicating with each other via text messaging or wireless networks to coordinate their activities.

social constructionism A view that claims much or all of what we know and understand about the world, including scientific knowledge, is constructed through social interactions and language.

social games Online or mobile games that are played in real time with others or that encourage simultaneous group playing.

social marketing Advertising and marketing techniques that persuade people to change bad or destructive behaviors or adopt good behaviors.

social responsibility theory A theory of international mass communication that perhaps best describes the media's role in democratic societies. It asserts that the media should be free from most governmental constraints to provide the most reliable and impartial information to the public.

soft news day A day in which not much has happened that is newsworthy, entailing the addition of features with less real news value, such as human-interest stories.

sound bite The length of time a news subject is allowed to speak without editing. It also has come to refer to short, catchy utterances designed to capture media attention.

Soviet theory A theory of international mass communication that states that the media should be publicly owned and used to further the needs of the working class.

spam Unwanted mass emailing from advertisers.

spiral of silence A theoretical construct that explains why people may be unwilling to publicly express opinions they feel are in the minority.

subliminal advertising Persuasive messages that have supposedly unconscious effects on the audience, such as an image or word flashed almost imperceptibly on a screen.

superstation A local TV station that reaches a national audience by beaming its programming nationwide via satellite to local cable systems.

superstitial ad Online advertisement that covers part of the existing screen or moves over part of it without opening a new window.

surveillance Primarily the journalism function of mass communication, which provides information about processes, issues, events, and other developments in society.

swarming The process used by some P2P systems in which multiple downloads of the same file are temporarily coordinated to accelerate the downloading process.

synchronous media Media that take place in real time and require the audience to be present during the broadcast or performance, such as live television or radio.

tagging Using searchable keywords to define a piece of information, file, image, or other type of digital media in a nonhierarchical system.

technological determinism The belief that technology causes certain human behaviors.

Telecommunications Act of 1996 The first major regulatory overhaul of telecommunications since 1934, designed to open the industry to greater competition by deregulating many aspects of it.

theory of cognitive dissonance Theory of persuasion that states we act first and then rationalize our behavior afterward to make our actions consistent with self-perceived notions of who we are.

third-party cookies Cookies put on a computer by those other than the website being visited, such as advertisers.

third-person effect  The tendency for people to underestimate the effect of a persuasive message on themselves while overestimating its effect on others.

Thomas Alva Edison  His inventions included the electric light, the phonograph, and the Kinetoscope. Edison's lab in Menlo Park, New Jersey, had over sixty scientists and produced as many as four hundred patent applications a year.

time shift  Recording of an audio or video event for later listening or viewing.

trademark  A form of intellectual property law that protects the right to use a particular sign, logo, or name.

Transmission Control Protocol (TCP)  A part of the main protocol for the Internet that allows computers to easily communicate with each other over a network.

trial balloon  Leaking information to the press about a proposed plan or idea to see how the public will respond.

trolling  Posting deliberately obnoxious or disruptive messages to discussion groups or other online forums simply to get a reaction from the participants.

two-way symmetric model  Model of public relations that emphasizes the profession as a system of managing relationships among organizations, individuals, and their many publics.

tyranny of the majority  A situation in which governmental laws and policies benefit the majority without concern for the welfare or rights of other groups or individuals.

Usenet  One of the earliest discussion forums in use today in which participants discuss topics in categories called newsgroups.

user-generated content (UGC)  Content created by the general public for distribution by digital media.

user interface (UI)  Junction between a medium and the people who use it.

uses-and-gratifications research  A branch of research on media effects that examines why people use media, what they do with media rather than what media do to them.

V-chip  A computer device that enables parents or any other viewer to program a TV set to block access to programs containing violent or sexual content based on the program rating.

viral marketing  Promoting a product, service, or brand online through word of mouth, usually via online discussion groups, chats, and emails.

virtual reality  The replacement of the real world with a digitized, virtual one, a mainstay of science fiction stories hyped in the late twentieth century.

voice-over  An unseen announcer or narrator talking while other activity takes place, either on radio or during a television scene.

wearable media  head- or body-worn digital communication devices that are Internet-connected such as virtual reality headsets.

wiki  Website that lets anyone add, edit, or delete pages and content.

William Randolph Hearst  American newspaper magnate during the late nineteenth and early twentieth centuries whose newspapers across the United States were noted for sensational journalism and political influence.

word-of-mouth marketing  Marketing that takes place among customers through discussions with one another.

yellow journalism  Style practiced notably by publishers Pulitzer and Hearst during the late 1890s in which stories were sensationalized and often partly or wholly fabricated for dramatic purposes.

# Notes

## CHAPTER 1

1. "Nokia Sues Apple for Infringing Patents, Industry Back on War Footing," Reuters, December 22, 2016, accessed March 2, 2017, http://www.reuters.com/article/us-nokia-corp-apple-patent-idUSKBN14A228.

2. Irving Fang, *A History of Mass Communication: Six Information Revolutions* (Boston: Focal Press, 1997).

3. Lance Liebl, "The Interview Becomes Sony's #1 Online Film of All Time," *Gamezone,* January 8, 2015, accessed January 8, 2015, http://www.gamezone.com/news/the-interview-becomes-sony-s-1-online-film-of-all-time-2231-jrrl.

4. Jon Krakauer, *Into Thin Air* (New York: Anchor Books, 1999).

5. "Social TV and Second-Screen Viewing: The Stats in 2012," *Guardian*, October 29, 2012, accessed February 19, 2013, http://www.theguardian. co.uk/technology/appsblog/2012/oct/29/social-tv-second-screen-research.

6. "Speedtest Market Report: United States," August 3, 2016, accessed March 16, 2017, http://www.speedtest. net/reports/united-states/.

7. "2016 Broadband Progress Report," January 29, 2016, accessed March 16, 2017, https://www.fcc.gov/reports-research/reports/broadband-progress-reports/2016-broadband-progress-report.

8. Harold D. Lasswell, "The Structure and Function of Communication in Society," in *The Communication of Ideas*, ed. Lyman Bryson (New York: Institute for Religious and Social Studies, Jewish Theological Seminary of America, 1948), 37.

9. "Wired, Zapped, and Beamed, 1960's Through 1980's," FCC, accessed October 20, 2011, http://transition.fcc.gov/omd/history/tv/1960–1989.html.

10. Gary Gumpert and Robert Cathcart, eds., *Inter/Media: Interpersonal Communication in a Media World*, 3rd ed. (Oxford: Oxford University Press, 1986).

11. World Internet Project, accessed February 19, 2013, http://www.worldinternetproject.net/.

## CHAPTER 2

1. Adrienne LaFrance, "How the Fake News Crisis of 1896 Explains Trump," *Atlantic*, January 19, 2017, accessed June 20, 2017, https://www.theatlantic.com/technology/archive/2017/01/the-fake-news-crisis-120-years-ago/513710/.

2. Javier Hernández, "China's Response to Reports of Torture: 'Fake News,'" *New York Times*, March 3, 2017, accessed June 15, 2017, https://www.nytimes.com/2017/03/03/world/asia/china-fake-news-xie.html?smprod=nytcore-iphone&smid=nytcore-iphone-share&_r=0.

3. Marina Fang, "Kellyanne Conway Compares 'Alternative Facts' to That Best Picture Oscar Mix-Up," *Huffington Post*, March 5, 2017, accessed June 10, 2017, http://www.huffingtonpost.com/entry/kellyanne-conway-alternative-facts-oscars_us_58bc4fafe4b0d2821b4ed00e.

4. Breitbart News, "Trump: Press Lying About Inauguration Crowd Size," *Breitbart*, January 21, 2017, accessed April 15, 2017, http://www.breitbart.com/big-journalism/2017/01/21/trump-press-lying-about-inauguration-crowd-size/.

5. W. James Potter, *Media Literacy*, 2nd ed. (Thousand Oaks, CA: Sage Publications, 2001), 4–7.

6. Tom Gormley, "'Ruination Once Again': Cases in the Study of Media Effects," theory.org.uk, 1998, accessed November 4, 2002, http://www.theory.org.uk/effec-tg.htm.

7. Terence Gordon, "Marshall Who?," Marshall McLuhan, July 2002, accessed December 20, 2014, http://www.marshallmcluhan.com/biography.

8. Lisa Rein and Michael Horowitz, "Timothy Leary and Marshall McLuhan, Turned On and Tuned In," Boingboing, accessed January 24, 2015, http://boingboing.net/2014/06/03/timothy-leary-and-marshall-mcl.html.

9. "Essay: The Playboy Interview: Marshall McLuhan," Next Nature, March 1969, accessed December 15, 2014, http://www.nextnature.net/2009/12/the-playboy-interview-marshall-mcluhan/.

10. David McKnight, "Rupert Murdoch and His Influence on Political Life," *Guardian*, August 7, 2013, accessed January 10, 2015, http://www.theguardian.com/commentisfree/2013/aug/07/rupert-murdoch-australian-election-2013.

11. Christopher Mims, "31% of Kenya's GDP Is Spent Through Mobile Phones," *Quartz*, February 27, 2013, accessed May 18, 2013, http://qz.com/57504/31-of-kenyas-gdp-is-spent-through-mobile-phones/.

12. Nmachi Jidenma, "How Africa's Mobile Revolution Is Disrupting the Continent," CNN.com, January 24, 2014, accessed February 9, 2015, http://edition.cnn.com/2014/01/24/business/davos-africa-mobile-explosion/.

13. W. Lance Bennett, *News: The Politics of Illusion*, 9th ed. (Boston: Longman, 2012).

14. Naomi LaChance, "Media Continues to Refer to Brock Turner as a 'Stanford Swimmer' Rather than a Rapist," *Intercept*, September 2, 2016, accessed January 1, 2017, https://theintercept.com/2016/09/02/media-continues-to-refer-to-brock-turner-as-a-stanford-swimmer-rather-than-a-rapist/.

15. Ken Wheaton, "Children Mystified by Racial Outcry over Cheerios Ad," AdAge.com, July 17, 2013, accessed

July 18, 2013, http://adage.com/article/the-big-tent/children-mystified-racial-outcry-cheerios-ad/243136/.

16. "Ongoing Cyber Attack Hits Twitter, Amazon, Other Top Websites," Phys.org, June 27, 2017, accessed January 1, 2017, https://phys.org/news/2016-10-twitter-spotify-websites-ddos.html#jCp.

17. Walter Quattrociocchi, Antonio Scala, and Cass Sunstein, "Echo Chambers on Facebook," June 13, 2016, https://papers.ssrn.com/sol3/papers.cfm?abstract_id=2795110; and Christine Emba, "Confirmed: Echo Chambers Exist on Social Media. So What Do We Do About Them?," *Washington Post*, July 14, 2016, accessed January 20, 2017, https://www.washingtonpost.com/news/in-theory/wp/2016/07/14/confirmed-echo-chambers-exist-on-social-media-but-what-can-we-do-about-them/?utm_term=.4443a3c1f6d3.

## CHAPTER 3

1. Neil Hughes, "Apple Agrees to Pay $450 Million to Settle Ebook Price Fixing Lawsuit," Appleinsider.com, July 16, 2014, accessed April 11, 2017, http://appleinsider.com/articles/14/07/16/apple-settles-ebook-price-fixing-complaint-with-states-consumers-could-pay-450m.

2. Polly Mosendz, "Amazon Has Basically No Competition Among Online Booksellers," The Wire, May 30, 2014, accessed May 4, 2015, http://www.thewire.com/business/2014/05/amazon-has-basically-no-competition-among-online-booksellers/371917/.

3. Drew DeSilver, "Overall Book Readership Stable, but E-books Becoming More Popular," Pew Research Center, January 21, 2014, accessed April 10, 2015, http://www.pewresearch.org/fact-tank/2014/01/21/overall-book-readership-stable-but-e-books-becoming-more-popular/.

4. Andrew Perrin, "Book Reading 2016," Pew Research Center, September 1, 2016, accessed April 11, 2017, http://www.pewinternet.org/2016/09/01/book-reading-2016/.

5. Kimiko de Freytas-Tamura, "Danish Man Who Burned Quran Is Prosecuted for Blasphemy," *New York Times*, February 23, 2017, accessed April 11, 2017, https://www.nytimes.com/2017/02/23/world/europe/denmark-quran-burning.html?_r=0.

6. Marshall McLuhan, *The Gutenberg Galaxy: The Making of Typographic Man* (Toronto, Canada: University of Toronto Press, 1962), 293.

7. DBW, "Self-Publishing Maturing, Up 17% Last Year in the U.S.," Digital Book World, October 8, 2014, accessed April 10, 2015, http://www.digitalbookworld.com/2014/self-publishing-maturing-up-17-last-year-in-the-u-s/.

8. "Ebooks Are Slowly Gaining Market Share in Europe as Print Books Decline," Klaava, February 2016, accessed April 11, 2017, http://klaava.com/books/ebooks-are-slowly-gaining-market-share-in-europe-as-print-books-decline/.

9. "Entertainment and Media," PwC, accessed June 22, 2013, http://www.pwc.com/gx/en/entertainment-media/index.jhtml.

10. "eBook Trends Worldwide," Statista, accessed April 11, 2017, https://www.statista.com/outlook/213/100/ebook/worldwide#.

11. Jonathan Segura, "Print Book Sales Rose Again in 2016," *Publishers Weekly*, January 6, 2017, accessed April 11, 2017, http://www.publishersweekly.com/pw/by-topic/industry-news/bookselling/article/72450-print-book-sales-rose-again-in-2016.html.

12. "Book Market," Statista, 2017, accessed April 11, 2017, https://www.statista.com/topics/1177/book-market/.

13. "US Publishing Industry Annual Survey Reports $27 Billion in Net Revenue, 2.6 Billion Units for 2013," Association of American Publishers, June 26, 2014, accessed April 11, 2015, http://publishers.org/news/us-publishing-industry-annual-survey-reports-27-billion-net-revenue-26-billion-units-2013.

14. "The World's 56 Largest Book Publishers, 2014," *Publisher's Weekly*, accessed May 5, 2015, http://www.publishersweekly.com/pw/by-topic/industry-news/financial-reporting/article/63004-the-world-s-56-largest-book-publishers-2014.html.

15. "Revenue of the Largest Book Publishers Worldwide," Statista, 2017, accessed April 11, 2017, https://www.statista.com/statistics/234628/revenue-of-the-largest-book-publishers-worldwide/.

16. Laura Hazard Owen, "Department of Justice Clears Random House-Penguin Merger," February 14, 2013, accessed June 22, 2013, http://paidcontent.org/2013/02/14/department-of-justice-clears-random-house-penguin-merger-in-the-u-s/.

17. "Book Publishing Industry Performance," IBISWorld, 2015, accessed April 27, 2015, http://clients1.ibisworld.com/reports/us/industry/currentperformance.aspx?entid=4579.

18. Lauren Indvik, "Ebook Sales Surpass Hardcover for First Time in U.S.," June 17, 2012, Mashable, accessed April 27, 2015, http://mashable.com/2012/06/17/ebook-hardcover-sales/.

19. Lauren Indvik, "EBook Sales Expected to Reach $9.7 Billion by 2016 [Study]," December 1, 2011, Mashable, accessed June 22, 2013, http://mashable.com/2011/12/01/ebook-sales-10-billion-2016/.

20. Jennifer Maloney, "The Fastest-Growing Format in Publishing: Audiobooks," *Wall Street Journal*, July 21, 2016, accessed April 11, 2017, https://www.wsj.com/articles/the-fastest-growing-format-in-publishing-audiobooks-1469139910.

21. "The Audiobook Industry Continues to Grow," Audio Publishers Association, October 2014, accessed May 6, 2015, http://www.audiopub.org/October_APA_2013_Survey_Press_Release.pdf.

22. Alison Flood, "Printed Book Sales' Decline Slowed in 2012," *Guardian*, January 9, 2013, accessed June 22, 2013, http://www.guardian.co.uk/books/2013/jan/09/printed-book-sales-2012; Angie Han, "J.K. Rowling's

'The Casual Vacancy' Being Adapted for the BBC," Slash-Film, December 3, 2012, accessed June 22, 2013, http://www.slashfilm.com/j-k-rowlings-the-casual-vacancy-being-adapted-for-the-bbc/.

23. Ken Doctor, "Behind the Times' Surge to 2.5 Million Subscribers," Politico, December 5, 2016, accessed April 11, 2017, http://www.politico.com/media/story/2016/12/behind-the-times-surge-to-25-million-subscribers-004876.

24. Elizabeth Balboa, "The 'Failing' New York Times Now Has More Than 3 Million Subscribers, Still Has Long-Term Concerns," Benzinga.top, February 2, 2017, accessed April 10, 2017, https://www.benzinga.com/news/earnings/17/02/8986502/the-failing-new-york-times-now-has-more-than-3-million-subscribers-still.

25. "Newspaper Fact Sheet," Pew Research Center, June 15, 2016, accessed April 11, 2017, http://www.journalism.org/2016/06/15/newspapers-fact-sheet/.

26. "About Metro," accessed April 12, 2012, http://www.metro.lu/about.

27. "Ruben Salazar Project," directed by Phillip Rodriguez, accessed January 30, 2015, http://rubensalazarproject.com/.

28. *Ruben Salazar: Man in the Middle*, PBS, April 29, 2014, directed by Phillip Rodriguez.

29. Steve Mariotti, Debra DeSalvo, and Tony Towle, *The Young Entrepreneur's Guide to Starting and Running a Business* (New York: Three Rivers Press, 2000).

30. *MPA Magazine Media Factbook 2014*, MPA: The Association of Magazine Media, accessed April 22, 2015, http://www.magazine.org/sites/default/files/MPA%20Magazine%20Media%20Factbook-%202014.pdf.

31. "eCirc for Consumer Magazines," June 30, 2016, Alliance for Audited Media, accessed April 11, 2017, http://abcas3.auditedmedia.com/ecirc/magtitlesearch.asp.

32. Randall Stross, "A Shopper's Companion, Still Going Strong," *New York Times*, December 11, 2011, accessed June 23, 2013, http://www.nytimes.com/2011/12/11/business/media/consumer-reports-going-strong-at-75-digital-domain.html?_r=0.

## CHAPTER 4

1. Steve Knopper, "Taylor Swift Abruptly Pulls Entire Catalog from Spotify," November 3, 2014, *Rolling Stone*, accessed February 9, 2015, http://www.rollingstone.com/music/news/taylor-swift-abruptly-pulls-entire-catalog-from-spotify-20141103.

2. Rebecca Davison, "Taylor Swift Is Surprised with IFPI Award After Being Named World's Most Successful Artist of 2014," February 23, 2015, *Daily Mail*, accessed March 1, 2015, http://www.dailymail.co.uk/tvshowbiz/article-2965721/Taylor-Swift-surprised-IFPI-award.html.

3. Christine Hansen and Ranald D. Hansen, "Music and Music Videos," in *Media Entertainment: The Psychology of Its Appeal*, eds. Peter Vorderer and Dolf Zillmann (Mahwah, NJ: Lawrence Erlbaum Associates, 2000), 179–181.

4. Jon Ronson, "Amanda Palmer: Visionary or Egoist?," *Guardian*, June 22, 2013, accessed January 30, 2015, http://www.theguardian.com/music/2013/jun/22/amanda-palmer-visionary-egotist-interview.

5. Amanda Palmer, "The Art of Asking," filmed March 2013, TED video, accessed February 4, 2015, https://www.ted.com/talks/amanda_palmer_the_art_of_asking/transcript?language=en.

6. Stuart Dredge, "Amanda Palmer Is Crowdfunding Again, but This Time on Patreon," *Guardian*, March 4, 2015, accessed April 18, 2017, https://www.theguardian.com/technology/2015/mar/03/amanda-palmer-crowdfunding-patreon-kickstarter-fans.

7. "IFPI Global Music Report 2016," April 12, 2016, accessed April 18, 2017, http://www.ifpi.org/news/IFPI-GLOBAL-MUSIC-REPORT-2016.

8. Ed Christman and Glenn Peoples, "Album Sales Hit a New Low," *Billboard*, August 28, 2014, accessed February 9, 2015, http://www.billboard.com/articles/business/6236365/album-sales-hit-a-new-low-2014.

9. Tyler Hayes, "Digital Music Prices: Is Cheaper Better?," Hypebot, June 4, 2012, accessed February 9, 2015, http://www.hypebot.com/hypebot/2012/06/digital-music-prices.html.

10. Adrian Covert, "A Decade of iTunes Singles Killed the Music Industry," CNN.com, April 13, 2013, accessed February 9, 2015, http://money.cnn.com/2013/04/25/technology/itunes-music-decline/.

11. Jill Serjeant and Marguerita Choy, "Streaming Overtakes U.S. Digital Music Sales for First Time: Nielsen," Reuters, January 5, 2017, Retrieved April 18, 2017 accessed http://www.reuters.com/article/us-music-streaming-idUSKBN14P1YH.

12. Ed Christman, "SoundScan's Third Quarter Numbers in One Word: Bleak," *Billboard*, October 10, 2014, accessed February 9, 2015, http://www.billboard.com/biz/articles/news/retail/6281506/soundscans-third-quarter-numbers-in-one-word-bleak.

13. Craig Smith, "57 Amazing Spotify Statistics and Facts," DMR, March 18, 2017, accessed April 18, 2017, http://expandedramblings.com/index.php/spotify-statistics/.

14. Eriq Gardner, "Robin Thicke Admits Drug Abuse, Lying to Media in Wild 'Blurred Lines' Deposition," *Hollywood Reporter*, September 15, 2014, accessed February 9, 2015, http://www.hollywoodreporter.com/thr-esq/robin-thicke-admits-drug-abuse-732783.

15. Alan Duke, "Marvin Gaye Heirs Sue 'Blurred Lines' Artists," CNN.com, November 1, 2013, accessed February 9, 2015, http://www.cnn.com/2013/10/31/showbiz/blurred-lines-lawsuit/.

16. Gaius Chamberlain, "Granville Woods," The Black Inventor Online Museum, May 23, 2013, accessed August 3, 2009, http://www.blackinventor.com/pages/granvillewoods.html.

17. Bob Lochte, "The Life and Legend of Nathan B. Stubblefield: A Chronology," accessed May 17, 2002,

http://campus.murraystate.edu/academic/faculty/bob.lochte/NBSDates.htm.

18. "NPR Stations and Public Media," NPR, accessed February 9, 2015, http://www.npr.org/about-npr/178640 915/npr-stations-and-public-media.

19. "PRI Fact Sheet," Public Radio International, accessed June 28, 2013, http://www.pri.org/pri-facts.html.

20. Charles Warner, "CBS Radio-Entercom Merger Is Great News for Radio," *Forbes*, February 6, 2017, accessed June 20, 2017, https://www.forbes.com/sites/charleswarner/2017/02/05/cbs-radio-entercom-merger-good-for-radio/#5473ff1e682b.

21. "Radio Industry Revenue in the United States from 2011 to 2020 (in Billion U.S. Dollars)," accessed April 18, 2017, https://www.statista.com/statistics/259981/radio-industry-revenue-in-the-us.

22. Albert N. Greco, "The Structure of the Radio Industry," in *The Media and Entertainment Industries*, ed. Albert N. Greco (Boston: Allyn & Bacon, 2000).

23. David Carr, "'Serial,' Podcasting's First Breakout Hit, Sets Stage for More," *New York Times*, November 23, 2014, accessed February 9, 2015, http://www.nytimes.com/2014/11/24/business/media/serial-podcastings-first-breakout-hit-sets-stage-for-more.html?_r=0.

24. "Serial Podcast," WBEZ Chicago, 2014, accessed February 9, 2015, http://serialpodcast.org.

25. Matt Petronzio, "The Enduring Power of Radio in the Digital Age," Mashable, February 13, 2013, accessed February 9, 2015, http://mashable.com/2013/02/13/radio-in-the-digital-age/; "World Radio Day 2015, 13 February, 2015," UNESCO, accessed February 9, 2015, http://www.unesco.org/new/en/world-radio-day.

26. "The Infinite Dial," Edison Research and Triton Digital, 2014, accessed March 1, 2015, http://www.edisonresearch.com/wp-content/uploads/2014/03/The-Infinite-Dial-2014-from-Edison-Research-and-Triton-Digital.pdf.

## CHAPTER 5

1. "70 Percent of U.S. Consumers Binge Watch TV, Averaging Five Episodes per Sitting," Deloitte, March 23, 2016, accessed April 23, 2017, https://www2.deloitte.com/us/en/pages/about-deloitte/articles/press-releases/digital-democracy-survey-tenth-edition.html.

2. Robert Leggat, "The Beginnings of Photography," A History of Photography, accessed May 15, 2002, http://www.rleggat.com/photohistory/.

3. Ibid.

4. "Sprocket Holes: The Lumière Brothers," accessed June 3, 2002, http://www.presscard.com/sprocket-holes2.html; Gerald Beals, "The Biography of Thomas Alva Edison," accessed August 3, 2009, http://www.thomasedison.com/biography.html.

5. Erik Barnouw, *Documentary: A History of the Non-Fiction Film*, 2nd rev. ed. (New York: Oxford University Press, 1993).

6. "Raw Coverage from the Streets of Ferguson," November 24, 2014, accessed February 10, 2015, https://news.vice.com/article/raw-coverage-from-the-streets-of-ferguson.

7. Stephen J. A. Ward, "Trauma and Journalists," Center for Journalism Ethics, School of Journalism & Mass Communication, University of Wisconsin–Madison, n.d., accessed July 9, 2013, http://ethics.journalism.wisc.edu/resources/global-media-ethics/trauma-and-journalists/.

8. "Number of Netflix Streaming Subscribers Worldwide from 3rd Quarter 2011 to 1st Quarter 2017 (in Millions)," Statista, n.d., accessed April 30, 2017, https://www.statista.com/statistics/250934/quarterly-number-of-netflix-streaming-subscribers-worldwide/.

9. Ryan Faughdner, "Home Video Sales Shrank Again in 2016 as Americans Switched to Streaming," *Los Angeles Times*, January 6, 2017, accessed May 1, 2017, http://www.latimes.com/business/hollywood/la-fi-ct-home-video-decline-20170106-story.html.

10. Rebecca Ford, "CinemaCon: Kathleen Kennedy Honored with Pioneer of the Year Award," *Hollywood Reporter*, April 17, 2013, accessed August 4, 2013, http://www.hollywoodreporter.com/news/cinemacon-kathleen-kennedy-honored-pioneer-441625.

11. "Our Team: Kathleen Kennedy: President," Lucasfilm Ltd., accessed February 8, 2015, https://lucasfilm.com/our-team/kathleen-kennedy.

12. Kathleen Kennedy, email message to Mary Ann McHugh, August 7, 2013.

13. Barry R. Litman, *The Motion Picture Mega-Industry* (Boston: Allyn & Bacon, 1998), 74–88.

14. "Box Office Revenue in North America from 1980 to 2014 (in Billion U.S. Dollars)," January 1, 2015, accessed February 10, 2015, http://www.statista.com/statistics/187069/north-american-box-office-gross-revenue-since-1980/.

15. "Yearly Box Office," Box Office Mojo, accessed May 1, 2017, http://boxofficemojo.com/yearly/?view2=domestic&view=releasedate&p=.htm.

16. Stephen Zeitchik, "Popularity of 3-D Is Affecting How Screenplays Are Written," *Los Angeles Times*, April 25, 2010, accessed May 16, 2012, http://articles.latimes.com/2010/apr/25/entertainment/la-ca-3ddirector-20100425.

17. "Curtains Rise Halfway on Digital Cinema," *Business 2.0* (May 29, 2001): 32–33.

18. Megan Geuss, "Celluloid No More: Distribution of Film by Celluloid to Cease by 2013 in the US," *Ars Technica*, June 9, 2012, accessed February 13, 2013, http://arstechnica.com/gadgets/2012/06/the-silver-screen-no-more-distribution-of-film-to-cease-by-2013-in-the-us/.

19. "Cinema Technologies," National Association of Theatre Owners, n.d., accessed May 1, 2017 from http://www.natoonline.org/initiatives/cinema-technologies/.

20. Les Brown, *Les Brown's Encyclopedia of Television*, 3rd ed. (Detroit, MI: Gale Research, 1992), 528.

21. Kenneth Olmstead, Mark Jurkowitz, Amy Mitchell, and Jodi Enda, "How Americans Get TV News at Home,"

October 11, 2013, accessed February 10, 2015, http://www.journalism.org/2013/10/11/how-americans-get-tv-news-at-home/.

## CHAPTER 6

1. Sheizaf Rafaeli, "Networked Interactivity," *Journal of Computer Mediated Communication*, accessed August 3, 2009, http://jcmc.indiana.edu/vol2/issue4/rafaeli.sudweeks.html#Interactivity.

2. Elaine Mcmillion and Alissa Quart, *Hollow: The Story of a Dying County in West Virginia*, June 2013, accessed January 19, 2015, http://hollowdocumentary.com/.

3. David Dufresne, *Fort McMoney: An Interactive Game Based on an Oil Boomtown*, November 2014, accessed January 19, 2015, http://www.fortmcmoney.com/#/fortmcmoney.

4. Romain Jeanticou and Charles-Henry Groult, *Le Mystere de Grimouville: A Mystery in a French Community* (requires French), May 19, 2014, accessed January 19, 2015, http://grimouville.francebleu.fr/#/.

5. Nadine Pequeneza, *Inside Disaster Haiti*, InsideDisaster, 2011, accessed January 19, 2015, http://insidedisaster.com/haiti/.

6. Lydia Emmanouilidou, "For Rare Languages, Social Media Provide New Hope," NPR, July 26, 2014, accessed May 20, 2017, http://www.npr.org/sections/alltechconsidered/2014/07/26/333732206/for-rare-languages-social-media-provide-new-hope.

7. John Carey, *Winky Dink to Stargazer: Five Decades of Interactive Television* (Dobbs Ferry, NY: Greystone Communications, 1998).

8. Lisa Napoli, "A Gadget That Taught a Nation to Surf: The TV Remote Control," *New York Times*, February 11, 1999, accessed January 10, 2002, http://www.nytimes.com/library/tech/99/02/circuits/articles/11howw.html.

9. "Control Data Corporation Historical Timeline," Charles Babbage Institute Collections, accessed August 3, 2009, http://www.cbi.umn.edu/collections/cdc/histtimeline.html.

10. Judith Newman, "Ray Tomlinson: Inventor of E-Mail, a New Discourse," *Intelligent Systems* 9, no. 2 (July 2002), accessed August 3, 2009, http://www.chenaultsystems.com/articles/Intell33.htm.

11. Robert Hobbes' Zakon, "Hobbes' Internet Timeline," version 5.6, Zakon, accessed July 24, 2013, http://www.zakon.org/robert/internet/timeline.

12. Robert Hobbes' Zakon, "Hobbes' Internet Timeline," version 12, Zakon, accessed February 17, 2015, http://www.zakon.org/robert/internet/timeline.

13. Steven J. Vaughn-Nichols, "Chrome Is the Most Popular Web Browser of All," ZDNet, January 11, 2017, accessed May 17, 2017, http://www.zdnet.com/article/chrome-is-the-most-popular-web-browser-of-all/.

14. P. William Bane and Stephen P. Bradley, "The Light at the End of the Pipe," *Scientific American* (October 1999): 110–115.

15. "Microvision," Wikipedia, s.v., accessed July 28, 2013, http://en.wikipedia.org/wiki/Microvision.

16. "Video Game Timeline (1967–present)," Education Database Online, accessed June 20, 2013, http://www.onlineeducation.net/videogame_timeline.

17. Ibid.

18. Jimmy Thang, "The Sims 3 Set for Global Launch in 2009," *IGN*, March 19, 2008, accessed July 28, 2013, http://www.ign.com/articles/2008/03/19/the-sims-3-set-for-global-launch-in-2009.

19. "Video Game History Timeline," National Museum of Play website, n.d., accessed June 20, 2013, http://www.icheg.org/icheg-game-history/timeline/.

20. Josh Wolford, "Halo 4 Breaks Records, Sees $220 Million in Sales in First 24 Hours," *WebProNews*, November 12, 2012, accessed July 25, 2013, http://www.webpronews.com/halo-4-breaks-records-sees-220-million-in-sales-in-first-24-hours-2012-11.

21. Angela Moscaritolo, "Angry Birds Space Hits 10M Downloads in Three Days," *PCMag*, March 26, 2012, accessed July 28, 2013, http://www.pcmag.com/article2/0,2817,2402092,00.asp.

22. James Mielke, "Q&A: 'Final Fantasy' Creator Hironobu Sakaguchi on Remakes 'VX,' and Making Nice with Square Enix," Glixel, November 30, 2016, accessed May 22, 2017, http://www.glixel.com/interviews/final-fantasy-creator-sakaguchi-on-remakes-xv-and-square-w452889.

23. Joost van Dreunen, "Welcome to the New Era: Games as Media," gamesindustry.biz, October 31, 2016, accessed May 26, 2017 http://www.gamesindustry.biz/articles/2016-10-24-welcome-to-the-new-era-games-as-media.

24. Taylor Clark, "How Palmer Luckey Created Oculus Rift," Smithsonian, November 2014, accessed January 19, 2015, http://www.smithsonianmag.com/innovation/how-palmer-luckey-created-oculus-rift-180953049/?no-ist.

25. Eddie Makuch, "Minecraft Console Sales Pass PC, Series Nears 54 Million Copies Sold," *Gamespot*, June 25, 2014, accessed February 9, 2015, http://www.gamespot.com/articles/minecraft-console-sales-pass-pc-series-nears-54-million-copies-sold/1100-6420724/.

26. Amy Kraft, "Video Game Play Sharpens Elderly Minds," *Scientific American*, May 3, 2013, accessed June 20, 2013, http://www.scientificamerican.com/podcast/episode.cfm?id=video-game-play-sharpens-elderly-mi-13-05-03.

27. Janko Roettgers, "Virtual Reality Projected to Become a $7 Billion Industry This Year," *Variety*, April 11, 2017 accessed May 28, 2017, http://variety.com/2017/digital/news/virtual-reality-industry-revenue-2017-1202027920/.

28. Ian Williams, "Chinese Gamer Dies After 15-Day Session," V3, March 1, 2007, accessed May 14, 2012, http://www.v3.co.uk/v3-uk/news/1998377/chinese-gamer-dies-day-session.

29. Mike Futter, "Video Gaming Changes Adolescent Brains, May Cause Addiction," GameInformer, June 23, 2014,

accessed January 19, 2015, http://www.gameinformer.com/b/news/archive/2014/06/23/video-gaming-changes-adolescent-brains-may-cause-addiction.aspx.

30. Kimberly Stern, "Colorado State University Study Examines Potential Positive Effects of Video Games," Colorado State University News & Information, April 4, 2011, accessed May 14, 2012, http://www.news.colostate.edu/Release/5653.

31. Emma McDonald, "The Global Games Market Will Reach $108.9 Billion with Mobile Taking 42%," Newzoo, April 20, 2017, accessed May 29, 2014, https://newzoo.com/insights/articles/the-global-games-market-will-reach-108-9-billion-in-2017-with-mobile-taking-42/.

## CHAPTER 7

1. Jon Ronson, "How One Stupid Tweet Blew Up Justine Sacco's Life," *New York Times Magazine*, February 12, 2015, accessed April 10, 2015, http://www.nytimes.com/2015/02/15/magazine/how-one-stupid-tweet-ruined-justine-saccos-life.html?_r=2.

2. Emanuella Grinberg, "Chicago Torture: Facebook Live Video Leads to 4 Arrests," CNN, January 5, 2017, accessed June 20, 2017, http://edition.cnn.com/2017/01/04/us/chicago-facebook-live-beating/.

3. Katie Kindelan, "Boy Behind Viral Birthday Plea Gets 'GMA' Surprise Party," ABC News, March 7, 2014, accessed April 10, 2015, http://abcnews.go.com/blogs/headlines/2014/03/boy-behind-viral-birthday-plea-gets-gma-surprise-party/.

4. John Jantsch, "The Definition of Social Media," *Duct Tape Marketing* (blog), September 25, 2008, accessed February 20, 2009, http://www.ducttapemarketing.com/blog/2008/09/25/the-definition-of-social-media/.

5. Brian Solis, "Defining Social Media," June 28, 2007, accessed August 19, 2015, http://www.briansolis.com/2007/06/defining-social-media/.

6. "SEM Glossary of Terms," n.d., Anvil Media, accessed February 20, 2009, http://www.anvilmediainc.com/search-engine-marketing-glossary.html.

7. Clay Shirky, *Here Comes Everybody: How Change Happens When People Come Together* (New York: Penguin Group, 2009).

8. Jessica Clark and Patricia Aufderheide, "Public Media 2.0: Dynamic, Engaged Publics," February 2009, accessed March 17, 2009, http://www.cmsimpact.org/future-public-media/documents/articles/public-media-20-dynamic-engaged-publics.

9. Kathleen Chaykowski, "Why Bernie Sanders's Social Media Followers Are More Engaged than Donald Trump's," May 25, 2016, accessed April 24, 2017, https://www.forbes.com/sites/kathleenchaykowski/2016/03/25/why-bernie-sanderss-social-media-followers-are-more-engaged-than-donald-trumps/#22ea435a103d.

10. Benny Evangelista, "Social Media Sites Become No. 1 Online Activity," SFGate.com, August 3, 2010, accessed July 14, 2011, http://articles.sfgate.com/2010-08-03/business/22010227_1_online-activity-zynga-game-network-mafia-wars.

11. Sarah Frier, "Snapchat User 'Stories' Fuel 10 Billion Daily Video Views," April 28, 2016, accessed April 24, 2017, https://www.bloomberg.com/news/articles/2016-04-28/snapchat-user-content-fuels-jump-to-10-billion-daily-video-views.

12. "About [Twitter]," 2015, accessed May 15, 2015, https://about.twitter.com/company.

13. Erin Kutz, "Just a Few on Twitter Do All the Tweeting: Study," Reuters, June 5, 2009, accessed June 5, 2009, http://tech.yahoo.com/news/nm/20090605/wr_nm/us_twitter_study_3.

14. "About Tumblr," accessed May 15, 2015, http://www.tumblr.com/about.

15. Abby Liu, "Is WeChat the Next Sina Weibo in China?," Global Voices Online, July 12, 2013, accessed July 20, 2013, http://globalvoicesonline.org/2013/07/12/is-wechat-the-next-sina-weibo-in-china/.

16. "Number of Monthly Active WeChat Users from 2nd Quarter 2010 to 4th Quarter 2016 (in Millions)," Statista, accessed April 24, 2017, https://www.statista.com/statistics/255778/number-of-active-wechat-messenger-accounts/.

17. Steven Levy, "The Many Sides of Jack Dorsey," *Wired*, June 22, 2012, accessed July 15, 2013, http://www.wired.com/business/2012/06/ff_dorsey/all/.

18. Seth Stevenson, "Simplicity and Order for All," *Wall Street Journal*, October 26, 2012, written in conjunction with WSJ's Innovator of the Year Award 2012 (in technology), accessed July 15, 2013, http://www.wsj.com/articles/SB10001424052970204425904578072640691246804.

19. Gina Chon, "Square CEO Jack Dorsey Picks Up San Francisco Trash on Fridays," *Quartz*, July 5, 2013, accessed July 15, 2013, http://qz.com/100997/payments-company-square-jack-dorsey-clean-up-trash/.

20. danah m. boyd and Nicole B. Ellison, "Social Network Sites: Definition, History, and Scholarship," *Journal of Computer-Mediated Communication* 13, no. 1 (2007): article 11, accessed April 4, 2009, http://jcmc.indiana.edu/vol13/issue1/boyd.ellison.html.

21. Stan Schroeder, "Study: More Teens Are Fleeing from Facebook," Mashable, December 19, 2014, accessed May 17, 2015, http://mashable.com/2014/12/19/study-teens-fleeing-facebook/?utm_campaign=Feed%3A+Mashable+%28Mashable%29&utm_cid=Mash-Prod-RSS-Feedburner-All-Partial&utm_medium=feed&utm_source=feedburner.

22. Joshua Barrie, "Nobody Is Using Google+," Business Insider, January 20, 2015, accessed May 17, 2015, http://www.businessinsider.com/google-active-users-2015-1.

23. Axel Bruns, *Blogs, Wikipedia, Second Life, and Beyond: From Production to Produsage* (New York: Peter Lang, 2008).

24. Amanda Holman and Alan Sillars, "Talk About 'Hooking Up': The Influence of College Social Networks on Nonrelationship Sex," *Health Communications* 27, no. 2 (2012): 205–216.

25. Shayne Hughes, "I Banned All Internal Emails at My Company for a Week," *Forbes*, October 25, 2012, accessed July 21, 2013, http://www.forbes.com/sites/forbes leadershipforum/2012/10/25/i-banned-all-internal-e-mails-at-my-company-for-a-week/.

26. Sameer Hinduja, "Cyberbullying on Instagram," Cyber Bullying Research Center, May 21, 2013, accessed June 18, 2013, http://cyberbullying.us/cyberbullying-on-instagram.

## CHAPTER 8

1. Süddeutsche Zeitung, "Panama Papers: The Secrets of Dirty Money," n.d., accessed May 28, 2017, http://panamapapers.sueddeutsche.de/articles/56febff0a1bb8d3c3495adf4/.

2. Michael Hudson, "Panama Papers Wins Pulitzer Prize," ICIJ, April 10, 2017, accessed May 28, 2017, https://panamapapers.icij.org/20170410-pulitzer-prize.html.

3. "Tracing the Story of Journalism in the United States," Write Site Newsroom, accessed October 20, 2011, http://www.writesite.org/html/tracing.html.

4. "About Us," Associated Press, 2017, accessed May 28, 2017, https://www.ap.org/about/our-story/.

5. "AP's History," Associated Press, 2017, accessed May 28, 2017, https://www.ap.org/about/our-story/.

6. "AP News Values & Principles," Associated Press, 2013, accessed July 26, 2013, http://www.ap.org/company/news-values.

7. Michael G. Robinson, American Culture Studies course "1890s," Bowling Green University, spring 1996, accessed October 20, 2011, http://www.bgsu.edu/departments/acs/1890s/yellowkid/yellow1.html.

8. Joseph Pulitzer, "The College of Journalism," *North American Review* (May 1904): 641–680.

9. George Seldes, "Farewell: Lord of San Simeon," in *Lords of the Press* (New York: Julian Messner, 1938), 227–239.

10. Anna Bahr, "Latinos Onscreen, Conspicuously Few," *New York Times*, June 18, 2014, accessed February 23, 2015, http://www.nytimes.com/2014/06/19/upshot/latinos-onscreen-conspicuously-absent.html?_r=1&abt=0002&abg=0.

11. Andrew Tyndall, *Who Speaks for America? Sex, Age and Race on the Network News* (Washington, DC: 10th Annual Women, Men, and Media Study, conducted by ADT Research in conjunction with the Freedom Forum, October 20, 1998).

12. The PEW Research Center's Project for Excellence in Journalism, "Key Findings," *The State of the News Media 2013: An Annual Report on American Journalism*, March 18, 2013, accessed July 28, 2013, http://stateofthemedia.org/2013/overview-5/key-findings/.

13. Sheri Fink, "The Deadly Choices at Memorial," Pulitzer Prizes, accessed May 16, 2012, http://www.pulitzer.org/works/2010-Investigative-Reporting-Group2. Originally published in the *New York Times Magazine*, August 30, 2009.

14. "The 2012 Pulitzer Prize Winners: National Reporting," Pulitzer Prizes, accessed April 17, 2012, http://www.pulitzer.org/citation/2012-National-Reporting.

15. David Wood, "Beyond the Battlefield: From a Decade of War, an Endless Struggle for the Severely Wounded," *Huffington Post*, October 10, 2011, accessed May 16, 2012, http://www.huffingtonpost.com/2011/10/10/beyond-the-battlefield-part-1-tyler-southern_n_999329.html?ncid=edlinkusaolp00000003.

16. Jeremy W. Peters and Verne G. Kopytoff, "Betting on News, AOL Is Buying the Huffington Post," *New York Times*, February 7, 2011, accessed July 26, 2013, http://www.nytimes.com/2011/02/07/business/media/07aol.html.

17. "Hugo Chavez Dead: Venezuela's President Dies at 58," *Huffington Post*, March 5, 2013, accessed June 30, 2013, http://www.huffingtonpost.com/2013/03/05/hugo-chavez-dead_n_2296423.html.

18. The Pew Research Center's Project for Excellence in Journalism, "Overview," *The State of the News Media 2013: An Annual Report on American Journalism*, March 18, 2013, accessed July 28, 2013, http://stateofthemedia.org/2013/overview-5/.

19. Nick Porter, "Top Op-Ed Pages Offer Choice of Elites: On Reigning Issues, Convergent Perspectives," April 1, 2012, FAIR: Fairness & Accuracy in Reporting, accessed July 26, 2013, http://fair.org/extra-online-articles/top-op-ed-pages-offer-choice-of-elites/.

## CHAPTER 9

1. Louis Bien, "A Complete Timeline of the Ray Rice Assault Case," SB Nation, November, 28, 2014, accessed April 11, 2015, http://www.sbnation.com/nfl/2014/5/23/5744964/ray-rice-arrest-assault-statement-apology-ravens.

2. Alexia Elejalde-Ruiz, "Cover Girl, 'Game Face' Ad Becomes Part of NFL Scandal," *Chicago Tribune*, September 16, 2014, http://www.chicagotribune.com/business/breaking/chi-game-face-cover-girl-ad-black-eye-viral-20140916-story.html.

3. Stephen Millies, "The Ludlow Massacre and the Birth of Company Unions," *Workers World*, January 26, 1995, accessed October 31, 2002, http://www.hartford-hwp.com/archives/45b/030.html.

4. Anne Bernays, "Doris Fleischman: 1891–1980," *Jewish Women's Archive: Encyclopedia*, accessed June 12, 2015, http://jwa.org/encyclopedia/article/fleischman-doris.

5. Kim Krisberg, "Anti-Smoking Campaign Lowers Youth Smoking Rates with 'Truth' Funding Threatened," *Medscape* (2005), accessed March 10, 2013, http://www.medscape.com/viewarticle/502009.

6. Jeff Niederdeppe, Matthew C. Farrelly, and M. Lyndon Haviland, "Confirming 'Truth': More Evidence of a

Successful Tobacco Countermarketing Campaign in Florida," *American Journal of Public Health* 94, no. 2 (February 2004): 255–257, accessed September 25, 2013, http://www.ncbi.nlm.nih.gov/pmc/articles/PMC1448237/.

7. Daniel J. Boorstin, "From News-Gathering to News-Making: A Flood of Pseudo Events," in *The Modern World: The Image* (New York: Vintage, 1961), 7–44.

8. "Agency Family Trees," *Ad Age*, accessed June 12, 2015, http://adage.coverleaf.com/advertisingage/20150504?pg=71#pg72.

9. David Streitfeld, "In a Race to Out-Rave, 5-Star Web Reviews Go for $5," *New York Times*, August 19, 2011, accessed May 14, 2012, http://www.nytimes.com/2011/08/20/technology/finding-fake-reviews-online.html.

10. Myle Ott, Yejin Choi, Claire Cardie, and Jeffrey T. Hancock, "Finding Deceptive Opinion Spam by Any Stretch of the Imagination," in *Proceedings of the 49th Annual Meeting of the Association for Computational Linguistics*, Portland, Oregon, June 19–24 (Association for Computational Linguistics, 2011), 309–319, accessed May 14, 2012, http://aclweb.org/anthology/P/P11/P11-1032.pdf.

## CHAPTER 10

1. Liam Stack, "20th Century Fox Used Fake News to Promote 'A Cure for Wellness,'" *New York Times*, February 25, 2017. Accessed June 1, 2017, https://www.nytimes.com/2017/02/15/arts/fake-news-a-cure-for-wellness-movie.html?_r=0.

2. Box Office Mojo, "A Cure for Wellness," Box Office Mojo, n.d., accessed June 1, 2017, http://www.boxofficemojo.com/movies/?id=acureforwellness.htm.

3. Sandra L. Calvert, "Children as Consumers: Advertising and Marketing," *Future of Children* 18, no. 1 (Spring 2008), accessed August 9, 2013, http:// futureofchildren.org/publications/journals/article/index.xml?journalid=32&articleid=62&sectionid=306.

4. Karen Abbott, "Madame Restell: The Abortionist of Fifth Avenue," Smithsonian.com, November 27, 2012, accessed June 1, 2017, http://www.smithsonianmag.com/history/madame-restell-the-abortionist-of-fifth-avenue-145109198/.

5. Kathleen Hall Jamieson, *Dirty Politics* (New York: Oxford University Press, 1992), 54–55.

6. "Mark Ritson on Branding: Norse Fire Smokes Out Bland Brands," *Marketing Magazine*, November 1, 2006, accessed September 25, 2013, http://www.marketingmagazine.co.uk/news/534969/Mark-Ritson-branding-Norse-fire-smokes-bland-brands/?DCMP=ILC-SEARCH.

7. "What Is Content Marketing?" Content Marketing Institute, n.d., accessed June 1, 2017, http://contentmarketinginstitute.com/what-is-content-marketing/.

8. Julia McCoy, "The Content Creator's Guide to Content Marketing Ethics: 9 Simple Rules," Express Writers, September 7, 2016, accessed June 1, 2017, https://expresswriters.com/guide-to-content-marketing-ethics/.

9. Richard Shears for Mail Online, "British Man Who Put His Life Up for Sale on eBay Finally Sells the Lot for £193,000," *Daily Mail*, June 30, 2008, accessed August 9, 2013, http://www.dailymail.co.uk/news/article-1030391/British-man-life-sale-eBay-finally-sells-lot-193-000.html.

10. Steve Lohr, "Algorithms Get a Human Hand in Steering Web," *New York Times*, March 10, 2013, accessed March 10, 2013, http://www.nytimes.com/2013/03/11/technology/computer-algorithms-rely-increasingly-on-human-helpers.html?_r=0.

11. Matt Krantz, "Has Facebook Figured It Out?," *USA Today*, July 25, 2013, accessed August 9, 2013, http://www.usatoday.com/story/money/markets/2013/07/25/facebook-mobile-revolution-winner/2587117/.

12. Robin Wauters, "Study: In-Game Video Advertising Trumps TV Advertising in Effectiveness," TechCrunch, March 24, 2009, accessed March 10, 2013, http://techcrunch.com/2009/03/24/study-in-game-video-advertising-trumps-tv-advertising-in-effectiveness/.

13. Patrick Walsh, Matthew H. Zimmerman, Galen Clavio, and Antonio S. Williams, "Comparing Brand Awareness Levels of In-Game Advertising in Sport Video Games Featuring Visual and Verbal Communication Cues," *Communication & Sport* (May 8, 2013).

14. William Usher, "Gamers Hate Ads That Interrupt Gameplay, According to New Market Report," Cinemablend, 2014, accessed September 4, 2017, http://www.cinemablend.com/games/Gamers-Hate-Ads-Interrupt-Gameplay-According-Market-Report-66372.html.

15. "Worldwide Ad Spending: The eMarketer Forecast for 2017," eMarketer Report, accessed June 2, 2017, https://www.emarketer.com/Report/Worldwide-Ad-Spending-eMarketer-Forecast-2017/2002019.

## CHAPTER 11

1. Margaret Hartmann, "Everything We Know About the UVA Rape Case [Updated]," *New York Magazine*, June 30, 2105 accessed April 15, 2015, http://nymag.com/daily/intelligencer/2014/12/everything-we-know-uva-rape-case.html.

2. Sheila Coronel, Steve Coll, and Derek Kravitz, "Rolling Stone and UVA: The Columbia University Graduate School of Journalism Report," *Rolling Stone*, April 5, 2015, accessed April 15, 2015, http://www.rollingstone.com/culture/features/a-rape-on-campus-what-went-wrong-20150405.

3. T. Rees Shapiro, "U-Va. Dean Sues Rolling Stone for 'False' Portrayal in Retracted Rape Story, *Washington Post*, May 5, 2015, accessed August 2, 2017, https://www.washingtonpost.com/local/education/u-va-dean-sues-rolling-stone-for-false-portrayal-in-retracted-rape-story/2015/05/12/2128a84a-f862-11e4-a13c-193b1241d51a_story.html?utm_term=.eb2a38df5595.

4. William W. Neher and Paul J. Sandin, *Communicating Ethically: Character, Duties, Consequences, and Relationships* (Boston: Pearson, 2007); Clifford G. Christians, Mark

Fackler, Kathy Brittain Richardson, Peggy J. Kreshel, and Robert H. Woods Jr., *Media Ethics: Cases and Moral Reasoning*, 8th ed. (Boston: Allyn & Bacon, 2008), 1–34.

5. H. W. Brands, *The First American: The Life and Times of Benjamin Franklin* (New York: Doubleday, 2000).

6. William A. Henry III, "Where NBC Went Wrong," *TIME*, February 22, 1993, accessed August 16, 2011, http://www.time.com/time/magazine/article/0,9171,977814,00.html.

7. Carma Hassan, "Teen Who Was Relentlessly Bullied Kills Herself in Front of Family," CNN.com, December 1, 2016, accessed August 15, 2017, http://www.cnn.com/2016/12/01/health/teen-suicide-cyberbullying-trnd/index.html.

8. Joe Nocera, "How to Monetize Plagiarism," *New York Times*, June 7, 2013, accessed June 24, 2013, http://www.nytimes.com/2013/06/08/opinion/nocera-how-to-monetize-plagiarism.html.

9. "Dole Cans Banana Label After Oxfam Claims," 3News/NZN, May 28, 2013, accessed June 24, 2013, http://www.3news.co.nz/Dole-cans-banana-label-after-Oxfam-claims/tabid/421/articleID/299462/Default.aspx.

10. Jeff Sommer, "The War Against Too Much of Everything," *New York Times*, December 22, 2012, accessed June 1, 2015, http://www.nytimes.com/2012/12/23/business/adbusters-war-against-too-much-of-everything.html?pagewanted=all&_r=1.

11. Siobhan McGuirk, "The Aesthetics of Activism," Adbusters, October 27, 2010, accessed June 1, 2015, https://www.adbusters.org/blogs/adbusters-blog/aesthetics-of-activism.html.

12. Viviane Rutabingwa and James Kassaga Arinaitwe, "Taylor Swift Is Dreaming of a Very White Africa," NPR, September 1, 2015, accessed August 15, 2017, http://www.npr.org/sections/goatsandsoda/2015/09/01/436653602/taylor-swift-is-dreaming-of-a-very-white-africa.

13. Michael Lipka, "Muslims and Islam: Key Findings in the U.S. and Around the World," Pew Research Center, August 9, 2017, accessed August 15, 2017, http://www.pewresearch.org/fact-tank/2017/08/09/muslims-and-islam-key-findings-in-the-u-s-and-around-the-world/.

## CHAPTER 12

1. Dwight L. Teeter Jr. and Don R. Le Duc, *Law of Mass Communications: Freedom and Control of Print and Broadcast Media* (Westbury, NY: Foundation Press, 1992).

2. M. K. Mallonee and Pamela Brown, "Facebook Threats Case Heard at Supreme Court," CNN, December 1, 2014, accessed January 19, 2015, http://www.cnn.com/2014/12/01/politics/supreme-court-elonis-vs-u-s-free-speech/.

3. "Shield Laws and Protection of Sources by State," Reporters Committee for Freedom of the Press, accessed August 19, 2015, https://www.rcfp.org/browse-media-law-resources/guides/reporters-privilege/shield-laws.

4. Chairman Reed E. Hundt, Federal Communications Commission, "Not So Fast" (speech, Museum of Television and Radio, New York, New York, June 3, 1997), accessed November 8, 2002, http://www.fcc.gov/Speeches/Hundt/spreh729.txt.

5. Adam Liptak, "Anthony Lewis, Supreme Court Reporter Who Brought Law to Life, Dies at 85," *New York Times*, March 25, 2013, accessed May 26, 2013, http://www.nytimes.com/2013/03/26/us/anthony-lewis-pulitzer-prize-winning-columnist-dies-at-85.html?pagewanted=all&_r=0.

6. Doug Gross, "Under Pressure, Facebook Targets Sexist Hate Speech," CNN, May 30, 2013, accessed August 5, 2013, http://www.cnn.com/2013/05/29/tech/social-media/facebook-hate-speech-women.

7. Linda Greenhouse, "'Virtual' Child Pornography Ban Overturned," *New York Times*, April 17, 2002, accessed August 19, 2015, http://www.nytimes.com/2002/04/17/us/virtual-child-pornography-ban-overturned.html.

8. Mark Goodman, "The Radio Act of 1927 as a Product of Progressivism," *Media History Monographs* 2, no. 2 (1998–1999), accessed November 8, 2002, http://www.scripps.ohiou.edu/mediahistory/mhmjour2-2.htm.

9. Erik Barnouw, *A Tower of Babel: A History of Broadcasting in the United States*, vol. 1, *A History of Broadcasting in the United States to 1933* (New York: Oxford University Press, 1966).

10. Mark Goodman, "The Radio Act of 1927 as a Product of Progressivism," *Media History Monographs* 2, no. 2 (1998–1999), accessed November 8, 2002, http://www.scripps.ohiou.edu/mediahistory/mhmjour2-2.htm.

11. M. S. Mander, "The Public Debate About Broadcasting in the Twenties: An Interpretive History," *Journal of Broadcasting* 28, no. 2 (1984): 167–185.

12. Alan B. Albarran and Gregory G. Pitts, *The Radio Broadcasting Industry* (Boston: Allyn & Bacon, 2001), 27–29.

13. Eli Noam and Robert Freeman, "Global Competition," *Television Quarterly* 29, no. 1 (1998): 18–23.

14. Contributor, "Combating the Dangers of Journalism," *Rusty Bee*, March 21, 2011, accessed August 19, 2015, http://rustybee.com/combating-the-dangers-of-journalism/.

15. David Filipov, "Here Are 10 Critics of Vladimir Putin Who Died Violently or in Suspicious Ways," *Washington Post*, April 7, 2017, accessed August 15, 2017, https://www.washingtonpost.com/news/worldviews/wp/2017/03/23/here-are-ten-critics-of-vladimir-putin-who-died-violently-or-in-suspicious-ways/.

16. Cheryl Lee, "Will FCC Bend Rules for Marijuana Internet Advertising?" WordPress, January 7, 2015, accessed February 17, 2015, https://wjlta.wordpress.com/2015/01/07/will-fcc-bend-rules-for-marijuana-internet-advertising/.

17. Eriq Gardner, "Hulk Hogan Grilled About Sex-Filled TMZ, Howard Stern Interviews at Gawker Trial," *Hollywood Reporter*, March 8, 2016, accessed August 15, 2017, http://www.hollywoodreporter.com/thr-esq/hulk-hogan-grilled-sex-filled-873435.

**CHAPTER 13**

1. Chris Plante and T.C. Sottek, "How Do You Sell Violent Video Games After a Tragedy? Pretend Like It Didn't Happen," *The Verge*, June 12, 2016, accessed August 15, 2017, https://www.theverge.com/2016/6/12/11914658/electronic-arts-e3-press-conference-gun-violence.

2. Jonathan O'Callaghan, "Study Finds No Long-Term Effects of Violent Video Games on Empathy," *IFLScience*, August 3, 2017, accessed August 15, 2017, http://www.iflscience.com/brain/study-finds-no-long-term-effects-of-violent-video-games-on-empathy/.

3. Erik Kain, "The Truth About Video Games and Gun Violence," *Mother Jones*, June 11, 2013, accessed June 22, 2013, http://www.motherjones.com/politics/2013/06/video-games-violence-guns-explainer.

4. Jacqueline Howard, "Americans Devote More Than 10 Hours a Day to Screen Time, and Growing," CNN, July 29, 2016, accessed May 1, 2017, http://edition.cnn.com/2016/06/30/health/americans-screen-time-nielsen/.

5. "Statistic Brain: Television Watching Statistics," BLS American Time Use Survey, A.C. Nielsen Co., March 27, 2015, accessed May 24, 2015, http://www.statisticbrain.com/television-watching-statistics/.

6. Rolf Wigand Lichter, "Communication and Violent Behavior," *ICA Newsletter* 2, no. 5 (July 1999): 5.

7. "Facts About Media Violence and Effects on the American Family," National Television Violence Study, issued by Mediascope Inc., February 1996.

8. Statistics compiled by TV-Free America, Washington, DC, 1996.

9. Claude E. Shannon and Warren Weaver, *The Mathematical Theory of Communication* (Urbana: University of Illinois Press, 1971), 7.

10. Wilbur Schramm, "How Communication Works," in *The Process and Effects of Mass Communication*, ed. Wilbur Schramm (Urbana: University of Illinois Press, 1961), 5–6.

11. J. W. Carey, "A Cultural Approach to Communications," *Communication* 2 (1975): 1–22.

12. Werner J. Severin and James W. Tankard Jr., "Introduction to Mass Communications Theory," in *Communication Theories: Origins, Methods, and Uses in the Mass Media*, 5th ed. (New York: Addison Wesley Longman, 2001), 16.

13. Garth S. Jowett, Ian C. Jarvie, and Kathryn H. Fuller, eds., *Children and the Movies: Media Influence and the Payne Fund Controversy* (Cambridge, UK: Cambridge University Press, 1996).

14. P. W. Holaday and G. D. Stoddard, *Getting Ideas from the Movies* (New York: Macmillan, 1933).

15. Garth Jowett et al., "Payne Fund Radio Broadcasting Research, 1928–1935," in *Children and the Movies: Media Influence and the Payne Fund Controversy* (Cambridge, UK: Cambridge University Press, 1996).

16. Colleen Flaherty, "Being Watched: New Website Seeks to Register Professors Accused of Liberal Bias and 'anti-American values,'" Inside Higher Ed., November 22, 2016, accessed June 1, 2017, https://www.insidehighered.com/news/2016/11/22/new-website-seeks-register-professors-accused-liberal-bias-and-anti-american-values.

17. Hannah Nichols, "How Video Game Affect the Brain," *Medical News Today*, July 10, 2017, accessed August 15, 2017, https://www.medicalnewstoday.com/articles/318345.php.

18. Monica Anderson, "Technology Device Ownership: 2015," Pew Research, October 29, 2015, accessed May 1, 2017, http://www.pewinternet.org/2015/10/29/technology-device-ownership-2015/.

19. Paul F. Lazarsfeld and Robert K. Merton, "Mass Communication, Popular Taste and Organized Social Action," in *The Communication of Ideas*, ed. Lyman Bryson (New York: Institute for Religious and Social Studies, Jewish Theological Seminary of America, 1948), 95–118.

20. Bernard Cohen, *The Press and Foreign Policy* (Princeton, NJ: Princeton University Press, 1963), 13.

21. Jeffrey Cole, "Surveying the Digital Future: A Longitudinal International Study of the Individual and Social Effects of PC/Internet Technology," n.d., accessed November 5, 2002, http://www.digitalcenter.org/wp-content/uploads/2014/12/2014-Digital-Future-Report.pdf.

**CHAPTER 14**

1. Joseph Pulitzer, "The College of Journalism," *North American Review* 178, no. 570 (May 1904).

2. Daniel C. Hallin, "Sound Bite News: Television Coverage of Elections 1968–1988," *Journal of Communication* 42, no. 2 (June 1992): 5–24.

3. Thomas Patterson, "News Coverage of Donald Trump's First 100 Days," shorenstein.org, May 17, 2017, accessed June 5, 2017 https://shorensteincenter.org/news-coverage-donald-trumps-first-100-days/.

4. Herbert E. Alexander, "Financing Presidential Elections Campaigns," *Issues of Democracy, Electronic Journals of the U.S. Information Agency* 1, no. 13 (September 1996), accessed November 7, 2002, http://usinfo.state.gov/journals/itdhr/0996/ijde/alex.htm.

5. Larry Sabato, *The Rise of Political Consultants: New Way of Winning Elections* (New York: Basic Books, 1981), 165–166.

6. Kathleen Hall Jamieson, *Dirty Politics* (New York: Oxford University Press, 1992), 19–20.

7. Richard Lau, Lee Sigelman, and Ivy Brown Rovner, "The Effects of Negative Political Campaign: A Meta-Analytic Re-Assessment," *Journal of Politics* 69, no. 4 (November 2007): 1176–1209.

8. Americans for Responsible Solutions page, n.d., Opensecrets.org, retrieved September 4, 2017 https://www.opensecrets.org/pacs/lookup2.php?strID=C00540443.

9. "Super PACS," OpenSecrets.org, accessed May 8, 2012, http://www.opensecrets.org/pacs/superpacs.php.

10. Michael Isikoff, "Karl Rove's Election Debacle: Super PAC's Spending Was Nearly for Naught," accessed

on November 8, 2012, http://openchannel.nbcnews.com/_news/2012/11/08/15007504-karl-roves-election-debacle-super-pacs-spending-was-nearly-for-naught?lite.

11. "2016 Outside Spending, by Super PAC," opensecrets.org, accessed June 6, 2017, https://www.opensecrets.org/outsidespending/summ.php?chrt=V&type=S

12. Claire Cain Miller, "How Obama's Internet Campaign Changed Politics," *New York Times*, November 7, 2008.

13. Joel Winston, "How the Trump Campaign Built an Identity Database and Used Facebook Ads to Win the Election," startupgrind.com, November 18, 2016, accessed June 6, 2017, https://medium.com/startup-grind/how-the-trump-campaign-built-an-identity-database-and-used-facebook-ads-to-win-the-election-4ff7d24269ac.

14. Tom Pepinsky, "Crowdsourcing Election Monitoring," *Cornell University*, July 14, 2014, accessed January 19, 2014, http://tompepinsky.com/2014/07/14/crowdsourcing-election-monitoring/.

15. Andrew Phelps, "Inside the Star Chamber: How PolitiFact Tries to Find Truth in a World of Make-Believe," Nieman Journalism Lab, August 21, 2012, http://www.niemanlab.org/2012/08/inside-the-star-chamber-how-politifact-forges-truth-in-the-world-of-make-believe/.

16. The Pulitzer Prizes, http://www.pulitzer.org/citation/2009-National-Reporting.

17. "About PolitiFact," *Tampa Bay Times*, http://www.politifact.com/about/.

18. Brendan Nyhan, "Bill Adair, Setting Pants Ablaze No More," *Columbia Journalism Review,* April 8, 2013, http://www.cjr.org/united_states_project/bill_adair_setting_pants_ablaze_no_more.php.

19. Politifact website, n.d., retrieved September 4, 2017, http://www.politifact.com/.

20. Interview with Mary Ann McHugh and George Watson, July 24, 2013.

21. Editorial Board, "Wrong Responses to Charlie Hebdo," *New York Times*, January 16, 2015, accessed January 19, 2015, http://www.nytimes.com/2015/01/16/opinion/after-paris-attacks-wrong-responses-to-charlie-hebdo.html?

## CHAPTER 15

1. Ray Sanchez, "ISIS Exploits Social Media to Make Inroads in U.S.," CNN.com, June 5, 2015, accessed June 7, 2015, http://www.cnn.com/2015/06/04/us/isis-social-media-recruits/.

2. Cristina Corbin, Mike Levine, and the Associated Press, "Boston Bombing Suspects Built Explosives with Help of Online Al Qaeda Magazine, Official Says," Fox News, April 23, 2013, accessed July 16, 2013, http://www.foxnews.com/us/2013/04/23/marathon-attack-suspect-communicating-by-writing-sources-say-with-faith-seen-as/.

3. Fred S. Siebert, Wilbur Schramm, and Theodore Peterson, *Four Theories of the Press: The Authoritarian, Libertarian, Social Responsibility, and Soviet Communist Concepts of What the Press Should Be and Do* (Champaign: University of Illinois Press, 1956), 5.

4. Daniel C. Brouwer, "Communication as Counterpublic," in *Communication as Counterpublic: Perspectives on Theory*, eds. G. J. Shepherd, J. St. John, and T. Striphas (Thousand Oaks, CA: Sage, 2006), 195–208.

5. Glenn Greenwald and Ewen MacAskill, "NSA Prism Program Taps in to User Data of Apple, Google and Others," *Guardian*, June 6, 2013, accessed July 16, 2013, www.guardian.co.uk/world/2013/jun/06/us-tech-giants-nsa-data.

6. Steven Lee Meyers and Andrew E. Kramer, "Defiant Russia Grants Snowden Year's Asylum," *New York Times*, August 2, 2013, A1.

7. "World Press Freedom Index 2014," Reporters Without Borders, http://rsf.org/index2014/en-asia.php.

8. Ibid.

9. Robert W. McChesney, *Digital Disconnect: How Capitalism Is Turning the Internet Against Democracy* (New York: New Press, 2013).

10. "Gartner Says Smartphone Sales Surpassed One Billion Units in 2014," Gartner, March 3, 2015, accessed June 13, 2015, http://www.gartner.com/newsroom/id/2996817.

11. Tom Kelly, "Britain Ousts the U.S. as World's Most Influential Nation: Country Tops Rankings for 'Soft Power,'" *Daily Mail*, November 18, 2012, accessed July 15, 2013, http://www.dailymail.co.uk/news/article-2234726/Britain-tops-global-soft-power-list.html.

12. Sigmund Freud, *Civilization and Its Discontents*, reprint ed. (New York: W. W. Norton & Company, 2012).

13. "Statistics," YouTube, accessed August 13, 2013, http://www.youtube.com/yt/press/statistics.html.

14. Sandvine, "Global Internet Phenomena Report," 2013, Accessed August 15, 2017, http://www.sandvine.com/downloads/documents/Phenomena_1H_2013/Sandvine_Global_Internet_Phenomena_Report_1H_2013.pdf.

15. "Statistics," YouTube, accessed June 13, 2015, http://www.youtube.com/yt/press/statistics.html.

16. Miguel Helft, "It Pays to Have Pals in Silicon Valley," *New York Times*, October 17, 2006, accessed August 13, 2013, http://www.nytimes.com/2006/10/17/technology/17paypal.html?pagewanted=all.

17. Miguel Helft, "YouTube's Payoff: Hundreds of Millions for the Founders," *New York Times*, February 7, 2007.

18. Nitasha Tiku, "YouTube Cofounders Break Up the Band After Second Act Flops," *ValleyWag* (blog), June 6, 2014, http://valleywag.gawker.com/youtube-cofounders-break-up-the-band-after-second-act-f-1587208160.

19. Y Ventures, accessed August 13, 2013, http://www.youniversityventures.com/.

20. Paul W. Taylor, "Co-productions—Content and Change: International Television in the Americas," *Canadian Journal of Communication* 20, no. 3 (1995): 411–416.

21. Marco R. della Cava, "Lucasfilm's Kathleen Kennedy Has Produced Quite a Career," *USA Today*, June 6, 2013,

accessed August 5, 2013, http://www.usatoday.com/story/life/movies/2013/06/05/kathleen-kennedy-innovators-and-icons-lucasfilm/2164285/.

22. Ben Quinn, "Ikea Apologises Over Removal of Women from Saudi Arabia Catalogue," *Guardian*, October 1, 2012, accessed July 16, 2013, http://www.theguardian.co.uk/world/2012/oct/02/ikea-apologises-removing-women-saudi-arabia-catalogue.

23. International Fund for Agricultural Development, "Indigenous Media Amplify the Voices of Marginalized Rural Communities," July 31, 2012, accessed July 16, 2013, http://www.ruralpovertyportal.org/topic/voice/tags/indigenous_peoples/ipday.

24. Canada Council for the Arts, accessed August 13, 2013, http://www.canadacouncil.ca/.

25. "Canadian Content Requirements for Music on Radio," Canadian Radio-Television and Telecommunications Commission, accessed August 5, 2013, http://www.crtc.gc.ca/eng/cancon/r_cdn.htm.

26. "2015 Canada Digital Future in Focus," comScore, March 27, 2015, accessed June 13, 2015, http://www.comscore.com/Insights/Presentations-and-Whitepapers/2015/2015-Canada-Digital-Future-in-Focus.

27. Dan Fricker, "How Digital Distribution Is Transforming the Canadian Television Industry," *Huffington Post*, July 26, 2013, accessed August 5, 2013, http://www.huffingtonpost.ca/dan-fricker/how-netflix-changed-everything_b_3654983.html.

28. Department of Defense, "Desert Fox," accessed August 13, 2013, http://www.defense.gov/specials/desert_fox/.

29. Haley Tsukayama, "Apple Confirms Attack by Same Hackers Who Hit Facebook," *Daily Times News*, February 20, 2013, accessed July 16, 2013, http://www.delcotimes.com/general-news/20130220/apple-confirms-attack-by-same-hackers-who-hit-facebook.

30. Adrien Chen, "The Agency," *New York Times Magazine*, June 2, 2015, accessed June 7, 2015, http://www.nytimes.com/2015/06/07/magazine/the-agency.html?emc=edit_th_20150607&nl=todaysheadlines&nlid=69673382.

31. *New York Times Co. v. United States*, 403 U.S. 713 (1971).

# Credits

## CHAPTER 9

Page 250 Andrew Burton/Getty Images; 252 ©iStock/Yuri_Arcurs; 257 Stuart Wilson/Getty Images; 2559 Bettmann/Getty Images; 259 Bettmann/Getty Images; 261 Dennis Van Tine/STAR MAX/Ipx; 262 Blend Images/Alamy Stock Photo

## CHAPTER 10

Page 268 TM and Copyright © 20th Century Fox Film Corp. All rights reserved./Courtesy Everett Collection; 270 ©iStock/PhotoTodos; 270 Everett Collection/Shutterstock.com; 270 Anthony Behar/Sipa Press; 273 A'Leila Bundles/Madam Walker Family Archives; 275 ©iStock/ luchschen; 277 Photo by Emma McIntyre/Getty Images for Coachella; 279 ©iStock/GAnay Mutlu; 280 Sean Sprague/Alamy Stock Photo; 281 ©Netflix/Courtesy Everett Collection; 282 Bill Aron/PHOTOEDIT; 284 ©iStock/andresr; 285 Marcos Mesa Sam Wordley/Shutterstock.com

## CHAPTER 11

Page 292 AP Photo/The Daily Progress, Ryan M. Kelly; 297 DeAgostini/Getty Images; 298 Jeff Gilbert/Alamy Stock Photo; 301 Richard Ellis/Alamy Stock Photo; 301 Barbara Alper/Getty Images; 305 © Everett Collection Inc./Alamy; 306 ZUMA Press, Inc./Alamy Stock Photo; 309 Brad Barket/Invision/AP, File; 311 WENN Ltd/Alamy Stock Photo; 313 Zoonar GmbH/Alamy Stock Photo; 315 Michael Stewart/FilmMagic; 315 BSIP SA/Alamy Stock Photo; 316 Kevin Bolk

## CHAPTER 12

Page 320 William Volcov/Brazil Photo Press/LatinContent/Getty Images; 323 Stock Montage/Stock Montage/Getty Images; 324 PF-(usna)/Alamy Stock Photo; 325 The Progressive Magazine; 326 Everett Collection Historical/ Alamy Stock Photo; 328 Matthew Peyton/Getty Images; 329 Mangostar/Shutterstock.com; 329 © Ted Streshinsky/CORBIS/Corbis via Getty Images; 330 Silver Screen Collection/Getty Images; 331 Kevin Statham/Redferns/Getty Images; 331 Drew Angerer/Getty Images; 332 Fierce Baby Prods./Detective Agency/20th Century Fox/Kobal/REX/Shutterstock; 336 Oleg Golovnev/ Shutterstock.com; 338 Mark Van Scyoc/Shutterstock.com; 341 Laurie Sparham /© Walt Disney Pictures /courtesy Everett Collection; 341 Christopher Halloran/Shutterstock.com; 342 A Linscott / Alamy Stock Photo; 346 John Pendygraft-Pool/Getty Images

## CHAPTER 13

Page 352 GABRIEL BOUYS/AFP/Getty Images; 359 The Poynter Institute; 359 Archive Images/Alamy Stock Photo; 360 First National/Warner Brothers/Kobal/REX/Shutterstock; 361 CBS/Kobal/REX/Shutterstock; 362 George Kraychyk / ©Hulu / Courtesy: Everett Collection; 363 marekuliasz/Shutterstock.om; 366 wavebreakmedia/ Shutterstock.com; 367 Ali Goldstein/© Comedy Central/Courtesy: Everett Collection; 370 Fred Stein/picture-alliance/dpa/AP Images; 370 Jonathan Leibson/Getty Images; 371 Kheng Guan Toh/Shutterstock.com; 373 Louis MONIER/Gamma-Rapho via Getty Images; 375 Stacy Walsh Rosenstock/Alamy Stock Photo; 375 Mark Von Holden/Getty Images for Dove; 379 Marmaduke St. John/Alamy Stock Photo

## CHAPTER 14

Page 384 JOE RAEDLE/AFP/Getty Images; 386 NBC/Photofest; 388 Netflix/Kobal/REX/Shutterstock; 390 ©iStock/flySnow; 392 Frederick M. Brown/Getty Images; 393 Andrew Lichtenstein/Corbis via Getty Images; 393 Fotosearch/Getty Images; 394 LOGAN CYRUS/AFP/Getty Images; 395 Ed Clark/The LIFE Picture Collection/Getty Images; 396 ©iStock/hermosawave; 397 Alex Wong/Getty Images; 403 ©Duke Photography, Used with permission of Bill Adair.

## CHAPTER 15

Page 406 Zurijeta/Shutterstock.com; 408 blickwinkel/Alamy Stock Photo; 410 Alfonso Di Vincenzo/Pacific Press/LightRocket via Getty Images; 411 STF/AFP/Getty Images; 412 Mary Evans Picture Library; 415 JOHN MACDOUGALL/AFP/Getty Images; 415 © Atul Loke/panos pictures; 417 With permission from Reporters Without Borders; 418 M4OS Photos/Alamy Stock Photo; 418 wavebreakmedia/Shutterstock.com; 421 ©iStock/rmnunes; 422 ZUMA Press, Inc./Alamy Stock Photo; 424 HENRIK MONTGOMERY/AFP/GettyImages; 424 ©iStock/hadynyah; 426 Matilde Gattoni/Getty Images

# Index

## A

*A Cure for Wellness*, 269
ABC network, 46, 48, 112, 336, 362
academic freedom, 363
accessibility
  Internet, 143
  open access, 346
action
  consequence-based ethics in, 300
  dialogical ethics in, 300
  duty-based ethics in, 296
  virtue ethics in, 296
Activision Blizzard, 175, 176
activism, 210, 214, 313. *See also* civic
  engagement; social movements
  anti-consumerist, 313
  Internet, 401–402
  social media and, 375
actors, 42, 207, 315
actualities, 41
ad-agency commission, 273
Adair, Bill, 403
Adbusters, 313
addiction, 216
  cell phone, 216
  video game, 182
Advance Publications Inc., 77
advertising, 37, 42, 45, 52, 56, 271.
  *See also* communication law and
  regulation; *specific advertising and
  marketing structures; specific products*
  account manager salaries, 289
  agencies, 272–274, 286–287, 311,
    318, 379
  algorithm-driven, 209
  branding, *37*, 276–277
  business of, 286
  careers, 290
  changing trends in, 289–290
  civil rights movement and, 305–06
  content marketing, 278
  digital media and, 282
  direct mail, 281–282
  electronic media, 280–281
  email marketing, 282–283
  ethics in, 293–94, 296–97, 299–300,
    302, 306, 310–11
  formats or channels, 280–284
  historical development, 272
  Internet, 56, 75, 276

journalism and, 84
magazine, 84–85, 87
mobile, 284
movie, 52
negative effects on sexes, 375
negative political, 386, 391, 392
newspaper, 41, 45
outdoor, 281
political, 83, 390
print media, 60, 71–2, 280
product placement, 281
radio, 111
regulations, 311
revenues, 60, 288
search engine, 284
selling products and ideas, 102, 107, 311
social media and, *317*
strategic communications and, 368
subliminal, 340
television, 274, 339
tobacco, alcohol and marijuana, 297,
  311, 339, 340
toy, *311*
in video games, 102, 284–285
world's largest companies, 288
advertorials, 281
advocacy journalism, 283
African mobile phone users, 47, 117
agenda setting, 190, 200, 223, 374
alcohol advertising, 339
Alexanderson, Ernst, 108
Alien and Sedition Acts, 324
Allen, George, 397
*All in the Family*, 144, 189
ALS Ice Bucket Challenge, 285
Alterman, Eric, 51
Alternative facts, 33
alternative journalism, 236–237
Altice, 150
AM. *See* amplitude modulation
Amazon, 53, 59, 66–7 69–70, 75 102–03,
  118, 210. *See also* Kindle ebook reader,
Echo, 118
*American Idol*, 147
American Society of News Editors (ASNE),
  246, 247
American Telephone and Telegraph
  Company (AT&T), 110–11, 335
America Online (AOL), 48, 375
amplitude modulation (AM) radio, 106,
  108, 109t, 110
analog media, 106, 347

animation, 189, 353
AOL. *See* America Online
AP. *See* Associated Press
Apple, 56, 59, 66f, 102, 104, 323, 421,
  427. *See also specific products*
  antitrust suit against, 59
Arab Spring, 210, 376, 413, 426
arcade games, 171
Aristotle, 36, 254, 296, 356–57
Armstrong, Edwin Howard, 110–11
*The Artist* (2011), 128
ASNE. *See* American Society of News
  Editors
Associated Press (AP), 51f, 71, 78, 224,
  327, 345, 350
astroturf campaigns, 314
astroturfing, 212, 314
asynchronous media, 199
Atari, 170, 171, 172
*The Atavist*, 54
AT&T. *See* American Telephone and
  Telegraph Company
attitude changes, 363, 375
auction sites, online, 275–76
audience, 35–36, 40
  changes, 8, 18
  creating meaning, 366
  distribution and, 18
  fragmentation of, 209
  Internet, 371
  participation increase, 355,
    366, 407
  participation in journalism,
    248, 249
  as produsers, 187, 208–210, 376
  research and theory, 377, 381
  television, 94, 193, 208
audio media, 93. *See also* music; radio;
  recording industry
augmented reality, 180
auteur, director as, 132
authoritarian theory, 409
*Avengers* parody poster, 316

## B

backpack journalism,
Bacon, Kevin, 207
Bagdikian, Ben H., 48–49, 57
Baidu, 416
Baird, John Logie, 142